MERIWETHER LEWIS

WILLIAM CLARK

LEWIS and  CLARK: Pioneering Naturalists

by Paul Russell Cutright

INTRODUCTION TO THE BISON BOOKS EDITION BY
Paul A. Johnsgard

University of Nebraska Press
Lincoln and London

Introduction © 2003 by the University of Nebraska Press
Copyright © 1969 by the Board of Trustees of the University of Illinois
All rights reserved
Manufactured in the United States of America

∞

First Nebraska paperback printing: 1989

Library of Congress Cataloging-in-Publication Data
Cutright, Paul Russell, 1897–
Lewis and Clark: pioneering naturalists / by Russell Cutright; introduction to the
Bison Books edition by Paul A. Johnsgard.
p.   cm.
Includes bibliographical references (p.   ).
ISBN 0-8032-6434-8 (pbk.: alk. paper)
1. Lewis and Clark Expedition (1804–1806)   2. Natural history—West (U.S.)
3. Natural history—Great Plains.   4. Natural history—Northwest, Pacific.   5. Lewis,
Meriwether, 1774–1809.   6. Clark, William, 1770–1838.   7. West (U.S.)—Description
and travel.   I. Title.
F592.7.C87   2003
917.804′2—dc21   2002034967

Reprinted by arrangement with the University of Illinois Press.

Frontispiece:
The painting of Meriwether Lewis was done by John Wesley Jarvis, apparently while
Lewis was Jefferson's secretary. Courtesy of the Spokane Public Library.

The painting of William Clark was done by an unknown artist and is reproduced by
courtesy of William Clark Adreon, a great-great-grandson of Clark and the present
owner of the original.

Contents

Contents

INTRODUCTION

Paul A. Johnsgard

On the two-hundredth anniversary of the Lewis and Clark expedition of exploration of the Louisiana Territory, it is appropriate to review the available reference
materials on the many discoveries that resulted from it, which include diverse
ethnological, geographic, botanical, and zoological components. And, in order
to understand the many contributions of Paul R. Cutright, a survey of the major
Lewis and Clark literature is essential.

The first person to undertake a complete summary of the biological aspects of
the Lewis and Clark expedition was Elliott Coues, the premier American ornithologist of his time and one of the founders of the American Ornithologists'
Union. Initially a surgeon in the U.S. Army, Coues traveled widely in the American West where he gained the experience and geographic knowledge he needed
to interpret the Lewis and Clark journals. Coues's work on the Lewis and Clark
papers provided a critical foundation for later syntheses by biologists. His first
rather brief report on bibliographic aspects of the expedition in 1874 was followed in 1893 by a four-volume comprehensive treatise, still one of the primary
references needed for any serious student of Lewis and Clark.

Coues began work on his Lewis and Clark project in 1891 at the request of
Francis Harper, a New York publisher. Coues's version was initially largely based
on examining the published journals of the expedition as edited by Nicholas
Biddle. Biddle's original manuscript had been proofed and published by Paul
Allen, another New York publisher. Biddle, no biologist, was a Philadelphia law-

yer who was destined to later become president of the Bank of the United States. Coues, a highly critical scientist and grammarian, was greatly dissatisfied with the Biddle version and made substantial changes in its spellings, punctuation, capitalizations, and so forth. By a stroke of good fortune Coues had discovered the original Lewis and Clark papers in the archives of the American Philosophical Society in 1892, where they had been deposited by Biddle in 1816 and evidently completely forgotten. They amounted to some thirty codices, representing about two thousand pages of material in total. Coues managed to borrow the entire group of papers, initially paginating all of the separate volumes and indexing them. Not only was he thus able to restore portions of the manuscript that had been deleted from the Biddle version, but his own version, published as four volumes in 1893, was especially valuable in identifying the animals mentioned and described by Lewis and Clark in varying degrees of completeness.

The Coues version of the Lewis and Clark papers was also the first to provide a detailed index, an invaluable aspect of such a large and disjointed text having multiple authors. Coues provided an extended bibliographic introduction, a chapter specifically devoted to biology (based on Lewis's diary written during the expedition's time at Fort Clatsop), and a collection of memoirs. Although Coues credited Lewis and Clark with the initial discoveries of many new species of mammals, birds, and reptiles, he did not provide a single comprehensive tally of the exact number. More recently, Donald Jackson tallied a list of 25 mammal and 17 bird species apparently new to science, based on the work of Coues, in *Letters of the Lewis and Clark Expedition and Related Documents* (1962).

The plant specimens collected during the expedition were not known to Elliott Coues at the time he undertook the task of reviewing the original Lewis and Clark materials, probably because these specimens had secretly been taken to England by Frederick Pursh, to whom Lewis had entrusted them for illustrating and preparing as herbarium specimens. Pursh was working on a major monograph on the flora of northern North America (*Flora Americae Septentrionalis*, 1814), and neglected to return them to the United States. The more than two hundred specimens were not returned until Edward Tuckerman brought them back to Philadelphia's Academy of Natural Sciences in the late 1890s. Coues thus necessarily relied on Frank H. Knowlton of the Smithsonian Institution to help him identify the plants that had been mentioned in the original documents. Although not a botanist himself, Coues was sufficiently self-confident to comment critically and sometimes caustically on an 1898 paper by Thomas Meechan that dealt with the identities and collection locations of the expedition's plant specimens (written after the specimens finally had been returned and systematically studied by Meechan).

In spite of Coues's Herculean work on summarizing the Lewis and Clark papers, he was not chosen by Francis Harper to edit and publish the entire array of Lewis and Clark materials. Instead, Reuben Gold Thwaites was chosen for the task, which was published as eight volumes in 1904 and 1905. Until Gary Moulton's recent thirteen-volume publication, the Thwaites work was the primary source generally accessed by most Lewis and Clark historians.

A little-known reference on Lewis and Clark that is of surprising value to biologists is Elijah H. Criswell's *Lewis and Clark: Linguistic Pioneers* (1940). Criswell provided a wealth of information using zoological and botanical indexes, giving both Latin and vernacular names for the plants and animals the expedition encountered, as well as a list of nearly two hundred botanical terms used by Lewis, proving Lewis's substantial botanical knowledge.

The next important summary of the biological aspects of the expedition came in 1961, when Raymond Darwin Burroughs of the Michigan Department of Conservation assumed the task of extracting the information on the vertebrates encountered during the expedition. Burroughs had already published a general account of the expedition (*Exploration Unlimited: The Story of the Lewis and Clark Expedition*, 1953). His 1961 book, *The Natural History of the Lewis and Clark Expedition*, provided the first convenient way of locating the expedition's natural history observations on some 102 species of birds, 48 mammals, 14 fish, 7 reptiles, and 2 amphibians. Although no separate list of animal discoveries was provided, Burroughs concluded that Lewis and Clark may be credited with providing the first detailed descriptions of the grizzly bear, the pronghorn and mule deer, the kit (now swift) fox, the bobcat, mountain beaver, black-tailed prairie dog, Columbian ground squirrel, bushy-tailed woodrat, eastern woodrat, white-tailed jackrabbit, and Douglas squirrel (now chickaree). The Columbian race of the white-tailed deer and the Columbian black-tailed deer (now considered a race of the mule deer) were also newly discovered mammals, as was the Oregon race of the bobcat. Burroughs credits Lewis and Clark with discovering the western grebe, the whistling swan, the greater white-fronted goose, the ring-necked duck, mountain quail, greater sage-grouse, least tern, great gray owl, Lewis's woodpecker, common poor-will, Steller's jay, Clark's nutcracker, western tanager, and western meadowlark. Some of these apparent discoveries, such as the white-fronted goose and great gray owl, were actually already known from Europe, and the whistling swan of North America is also now considered to be part of the much more widespread species of tundra swan. Other animals described by Lewis and Clark that are now considered as subspecies of already known species include one or more small ("lesser") races of the Canada goose, the Franklin's race of spruce grouse, the Oregon race of the ruffed grouse, the Columbian and Great Plains races of sharp-tailed grouse, the North American race of the black-billed magpie, the white-rumped race of the loggerhead shrike, and the Pacific race of the varied thrush. At least 5 species of fish (3 salmon, 2 trout) and at least 2 species of reptiles (the prairie rattlesnake and the pygmy or short-horned lizard) were also regarded by Burroughs as being new to science, although the specific identities of some of the other fish and reptiles that Lewis and Clark described to varying degrees are still uncertain. Burroughs also included a useful numerical appendix of supplies and equipment taken on the expedition, some relevant correspondence, and a tally of animals killed.

In 1969, only eight years after Burroughs's book appeared, Professor Paul Russell Cutright produced a similar but more expansive one. Over the course of six western trips Cutright had traveled more than fifteen thousand miles to research the book. His primary goal was to prove that Lewis and Clark were "naturalists of outstanding competence." Unlike Burroughs's purely taxonomic approach, Cutright organized his book in a chronological manner. It includes a detailed account of the entire journey, with summaries of the zoological, botanical, anthropological, and geographic discoveries attached to each chapter, as well as each field being separately summarized in tabular fashion within several appendices. The book is notable in that it provides specific dates and locations for each animal sighting and each botanical collection site. Cutright's summary of the botany is especially valuable. He identified 63 type specimens of newly discovered plant species, together with their dates and locations of collection, and provided literature citations of their initial descriptions. A total of 178 plant species were tallied as being described or collected, most of which proved to be new to science. Cutright also similarly tabulated the documentation of 51 birds, 44 mammals, and 12 fishes, plus 15 reptiles or amphibians, all judged by him to represent new species or subspecies, at least as of known taxonomy in 1960. Some of these subspecies are no longer recognized, and the identifications of others might seem questionable. Nevertheless, at least 15 of the mammals and 16 of the birds represent new species as recognized by taxonomists today. Mammal species first described, or at least described carefully for the first time, include the mountain goat, the pronghorn, mule deer, grizzly bear, gray wolf, coyote, swift fox, black-tailed prairie dog, white-tailed jackrabbit, bushy-tailed and eastern woodrats, Columbian and thirteen-lined ground squirrels, chickaree, and mountain beaver. The new bird species identified by Lewis and Clark with a fair degree of certainty include the western grebe, the whistling (now tundra) swan, the ring-necked duck, greater sage-grouse, mountain quail, common poor-will, Lewis's woodpecker, broad-tailed hummingbird, Clark's nutcracker, black-headed (now Steller's) jay, pinyon jay, northwestern crow, western tanager, Brewer's blackbird, western meadowlark, and McCown's longspur. Likewise, at least 7 of the fish Lewis and Clark described are now recognized as representing new species, and at least 7 new reptiles and amphibians are apparently among those they initially described.

Thus, at least forty-five species of vertebrates were probably first observed and at least minimally described by Lewis and Clark within a period of less than three years, during an expedition in which finding a practical water route to the Pacific Ocean was a primary overarching goal. The task of giving scientific names to the group's discoveries was left to others, and thus many of the species first mentioned by Lewis and Clark were later credited to other scientists, such as George Ord for most of the mammals and Alexander Wilson for some of the birds. However, Lewis and Clark each had a new species of birds named in his honor (Lewis's woodpecker and Clark's nutcracker). Each also had a genus of plants (*Lewisia*, *Clarkia*) named in his honor by Frederick Pursh; Pursh named two species of plants in Lewis's honor.

Four decades later John J. Audubon followed Lewis and Clark up the Missouri River with the primary purpose of studying the region's birds and mammals. He rediscovered the western meadowlark that had first been recognized by Lewis and Clark as distinct, and credited the two with discovering and describing such typical Great Plains species as the grizzly bear and swift fox. Audubon himself described and either named or participated in the naming of some 34 North American birds and 28 mammals over his lifetime, although most of these names are now relegated to subspecies or discarded. At least 2 species discovered by Lewis and Clark but given formal names by Audubon have survived as valid: the common poorwill and the western meadowlark. One mammal species, the Audubon's cottontail, and 10 subspecies of birds were also named in honor of Audubon. By comparison, in the course of his long association with the U.S. National Museum, Elliott Coues named 8 species and 20 subspecies of birds, as well as 2 species and 12 subspecies of mammals, insofar as these taxonomic categories are now generally recognized. Coues also had 2 bird subspecies and 3 mammalian subspecies named after him. Most of Coues's discoveries were, however, based on museum studies of specimens brought to him rather than ones discovered as a result of his own field observations.

Paul Cutright was born in 1897 in West Virginia. He received bachelor's and master's degrees from Davis and Elkins College and the University of West Virginia, and obtained a Ph.D. in zoology from the University of Pittsburgh. Later he performed research at the Carnegie Foundation Marine Laboratory in the Dry Tortugas and at the Smithsonian Institution's Barro Colorado Island Tropical Laboratory in the Canal Zone. For forty years Cutright taught at the University of Pittsburgh, at Geneva College in Beaver Falls, Pennsylvania, and at Beaver College in Glenside, Pennsylvania. He also wrote *The Great Naturalists Explore South America* (Macmillan, 1940) and *Theodore Roosevelt, The Making of a Conservationist* (Harper & Bros., 1956). More relevant to the expedition of Lewis and Clark, in 1968 he published *Meriwether Lewis: Naturalist* (Oregon Historical Society), and *A History of the Lewis and Clark Journals* (Univ. of Oklahoma Press, 1976). His final book, written with M. J. Brodhead, was *Elliott Coues, Naturalist and Frontier Historian* (University of Illinois Press, 1981). Much of the Elliott Coues book revolves around Coues's involvement with the Lewis and Clark project, and Cutright's history of the Lewis and Clark journals provides additional insight into Coues as a seminal figure in American natural history and the Lewis and Clark story. This latter book reviews the hundreds of books, magazine articles, journal papers, and related Lewis and Clark materials, even reviewing the works of the artists and illustrators who have taken upon themselves the challenge of converting written history into visual images.

In 1962 Professor Cutright was awarded the Christian R. and Mary F. Lindback Award for Distinguished Teaching, and Beaver College additionally granted him an honorary Doctor of Letters degree. He was named Professor Emeritus of Beaver College in 1982. In 1984 he received an Honorary Degree of Pedagogy from Davis and Elkins College in Elkins, West Virginia. He continued to write into his late eighties, publishing a very useful history of Lewis's woodpecker and Clark's nutcracker in 1984 in *We Proceeded On*, the journal of the Lewis and Clark Trail Foundation. He died on 10 March 1988.

With the celebration of the bicentennial of the Corps of Discovery expedition, a new generation of Americans, weaned on tales of lunar exploration, are learning that Lewis and Clark entered a wilderness far less known to Americans than was then known about the face of the moon. As it turns out, the land acquired by the Louisiana Purchase (at the rate of less than three cents per acre) has proved to be rich beyond Thomas Jefferson's wildest dreams. It has been suggested that the forty million or so bison then roaming the Great Plains were themselves worth far more than the total approximate fifteen-million-dollar cost of the Louisiana Territory. Paul Cutright has captured the entire biological richness of Lewis and Clark's historic expedition, from the bison, grizzly bears, and other large plains mammals they saw to the least conspicuous of the plants that they described and collected. Professor Cutright has also erected a sturdy biological framework for this story of heroism and hardship, of perseverance and great good fortune. It is a story that should justifiably stir pride among all Americans.

Whenever asked by friends which of the many Lewis and Clark sources should be read first to get the best biological overview of the expedition, I always recommend beginning with Cutright's splendid book. To obtain the expedition's full details and flavor, however, the serious history buff should consider immersing himself or herself in Gary Moulton's masterful and comprehensive documentation of the Corps of Discovery's expedition, *The Journals of the Lewis and Clark Expedition.*

WORKS CITED

Burroughs, R. D. *Exploration Unlimited: The Story of the Lewis and Clark Expedition.* Detroit: Wayne State University Press, 1953.

———. *The Natural History of the Lewis and Clark Expedition.* East Lansing: Michigan State University Press, 1961.

Coues, Elliott. "An Account of the Various Publications Relating to the Travels of Lewis and Clarke (*sic*), with a Commentary on the Zoological Results of the Expedition." Washington DC: U.S. Geographical and Geological Survey of the Territories, Bulletin no. 1, 1874.

———, ed. *History of the Expedition under the Command of Lewis and Clark.* 4 vols. New York: Francis P. Harper, 1893.

Criswell, E. H. *Lewis and Clark: Linguistic Pioneers.* Columbia MO: University of Missouri Studies 15.2, 1940.

Cutright, P. R. *The Great Naturalists Explore South America.* New York: Macmillan, 1940.

———. *A History of the Lewis and Clark Journals.* Norman: University of Oklahoma Press, 1976.

———. *Meriwether Lewis: Naturalist.* Portland: Oregon Historical Society, 1968.

———. *Theodore Roosevelt: The Making of a Conservationist.* New York: Harper & Bros., 1956.

Cutright, P. R., and M. J. Brodhead. *Elliott Coues, Naturalist and Frontier Historian.* Urbana: University of Illinois Press, 1981.

Jackson, D. *Letters of the Lewis and Clark Expedition and Related Documents.* Urbana: University of Illinois Press, 1962.

Moulton, G. E., ed. *The Journals of the Lewis and Clark Expedition.* 13 vols. Lincoln: University of Nebraska Press, 1983–2001.

Pursh, F. T. *Flora Americae Septentrionalis.* 2 vols. London: White, Cochrane, 1813 ("1814," published December 1813).

Thwaites, R. G., ed. *Original Journals of the Lewis and Clark Expedition, 1805–1806.* 8 vols. New York: Dodd & Mead, 1904–1905.

To
my grandchildren
JUDY and BROOKS

and to the
memory of my brother
CLIFFORD R. CUTRIGHT

Preface

Bernard DeVoto once called attention to the fact that many technical aspects of the Lewis and Clark Expedition had been neglected and needed further comprehensive study.[1] This slighting of the scientific phases of the Expedition had its inception almost immediately after Lewis and Clark concluded their historic journey. Thomas Jefferson, early in 1807, appointed Meriwether Lewis to the post of governor of the Territory of Louisiana instead of allowing him to sit down forthwith and devote all his energies and talents to writing the narrative, including scientific discoveries, of the Expedition. He had made the appointment, jubilant at the success of the venture and desirous of honoring its young leader. It was an illusory reward and a consequential error, as Jefferson would soon learn.

Lewis, of course, had every intention of writing a full account of the discoveries and accomplishments of the Expedition. On his final visit to Philadelphia in April, 1807, he released a prospectus announcing that the history would be published in three octavo volumes, with the third "confined exclusively to scientific research, and principally to the natural history of those hitherto unknown regions."[2] Further statements indicated that he expected the volumes to appear in the near future.

A few months later Lewis arrived in St. Louis and at once assumed

[1] Bernard DeVoto, *The Course of Empire* (Boston, 1953), 621–622.
[2] Donald Jackson, ed., *Letters of the Lewis and Clark Expedition with Related Documents 1783–1854* (Urbana, Ill., 1962), 394–397. Hereinafter cited as "Jackson, *Letters.*"

his duties as governor of the newly acquired territory of Louisiana. Here, immediately beset by innumerable frustrating administrative problems, he found the political climate extremely uncongenial to literary endeavor and the enforced sedentary existence inimical to health. In ensuing months he made only minimal progress in writing the history of the Expedition, and plans for an early publication were abandoned. Then, with Lewis's sudden, unexpected death on October 11, 1809, there ensued further inevitable delay.

The two men on whom responsibility for publication now devolved, namely, Jefferson and Clark, faced the difficult task of finding a person willing and qualified to pick up the editorial reins where Lewis had laid them down. From this unhappy predicament, they soon partially extricated themselves. They prevailed upon a talented young Philadelphia lawyer, Nicholas Biddle, to assume the task of editing the narrative and persuaded Dr. Benjamin Smith Barton, physician, naturalist, and lecturer at the University of Pennsylvania, to prepare the scientific text. But the technical contribution soon suffered another setback. Due to failing health, Dr. Barton found it impossible to live up to his commitment, and Biddle, with no scientific background at his command, was left alone to determine the fate and content of the history. In 1814 (eight years after Lewis and Clark had completed their western tour) when *The Journals of the Expedition under the Command of Captains Lewis and Clark* finally appeared, it had been divested of the most significant botanical and zoological material and much of the ethnological. One has only to compare this account with *Original Journals of the Lewis and Clark Expedition* (published 1904–5) to become immediately aware of the great scientific lacunae present in Biddle's brilliant paraphrase, voids that Lewis presumably would not have allowed to occur if he had not been weighed down with, to him, the overwhelming responsibility of piloting affairs of state in Louisiana.

The Biddle account accurately stamped Lewis and Clark as master explorers, superb woodsmen, and exemplary military leaders. However, because it excluded the great bulk of scientific detail, it failed to portray the two leaders as important forerunners in such fields as botany, zoology, geography, cartography, meteorology, and ethnology. In particular, it failed altogether to establish the true measure of Meriwether Lewis as a naturalist.

Except for a brief flurry of technical activity following their return to civilization, climaxed by the publication of Frederick Pursh's *Flora*

Americae Septentrionalis (London, 1814), Lewis and Clark received scant recognition for their scientific accomplishments until 1893. In that year Elliott Coues (pronounced Cows), a foremost naturalist and extraordinary annotator, edited a reissue of the Biddle narrative. Aided by his personal experience of extensive travel in the West, his broad knowledge of biology and geography, his close association with scientists in the National Museum who helped him at every turn, and his timely rediscovery of the original manuscript journals of Lewis and Clark in the American Philosophical Society, Philadelphia, Coues produced an edition so copiously and importantly footnoted that every serious student of Lewis and Clark since has regarded it as an indispensable reference. In his annotations Coues stressed particularly the roles played by the captains as the discoverers of plants and animals previously unknown, their multiple contributions to geography, and their firsthand, reliable descriptions of Indians encountered along their route.

But even Coues' earnest attempt to add another dimension to the images of Lewis and Clark failed to a large extent; the damage had already been done. Men continued to think of them as explorers, woodsmen, and military leaders and only rarely as pioneering naturalists. Since 1893 other technical contributions have appeared, such as "Birds and Mammals Observed by Lewis and Clark in North Dakota" by Russell Reid and C. G. Gannon (1927); Elijah H. Criswell's *Lewis and Clark: Linguistic Pioneers* (1940); "Cartographic and Geographic Activities of the Lewis and Clark Expedition" by Herman R. Friis (1954); "The Contributions of Lewis and Clark to Ethnography" by Verne F. Ray and Nancy O. Lurie (1954); "Botanical Contributions of the Lewis and Clark Expedition" by Velva E. Rudd (1954); *The Natural History of the Lewis and Clark Expedition* by Raymond Darwin Burroughs (1961); and *Letters of the Lewis and Clark Expedition with Related Documents 1783–1854* by Donald Jackson (1962).

As a result of these publications (and that of the original journals), we find evidence that the clouds which in the past obscured Lewis and Clark as naturalists have gradually begun to disappear, but a substantial overcast still persists. For instance, a scientist recently, in assessing the contributions of the Expedition to zoology, declared that, "It must be borne in mind that both Lewis and Clark were engineers,"[3] and thus, by implication, in no sense naturalists.

[3] Henry W. Setzer, "Zoological Contributions of the Lewis and Clark Expedition," *Jour. Wash. Acad. Scis.*, 44, no. 11 (Nov., 1954), 357.

I have directed my efforts in this study to two primary objectives: (1) to provide greater emphasis and depth to the more neglected technical aspects of the Expedition (especially botanical, zoological, and medical) and (2) to bring Meriwether Lewis and William Clark fully onto the stage of American history as important pioneering naturalists—particularly Lewis. Of course, more remains to be done in all technical fields, notably geography and ethnology, fields in which I lay no claims to specialization. However, even here I hope that I have supplied groundwork for a fuller understanding and appreciation of Lewis and Clark's contributions.

In the preparation of this book I have spent several years and travelled more than 15,000 miles. My research included every nugget in library, museum, and learned society that I thought would illuminate any aspect of the Expedition which I have presented in this study. My correspondence with scientists and recognized Lewis and Clark scholars has clarified many obscure points in the original journals. In six western trips I have followed the Lewis and Clark trail from the mouth of the Wood River in Illinois to Cape Disappointment on the Pacific; I have travelled up and down the Yellowstone and have knelt to sip water from that "most distant fountain" of the Missouri close by the Continental Divide; I have experienced the ruggedness and wild magnificence of the Bitterroot Mountains on the Lolo Trail and have viewed from the summit of Sherman Peak the extensive praireland to the southwest and west; I have ascended the tranquil valley of Alice Creek to the top of Lewis and Clark Pass and have visited the site on Two Medicine River where Lewis and his party tangled with Blackfeet Indians; and I have floated down the Missouri through the enchantingly beautiful "White Rocks" region between the Marias and Judith Rivers.

I hope the reader will find the book imbued, at least partially, with the enthusiasm which prompted the detailed research I have dedicated to it.

I owe much to many people and to the organizations and institutions they represent. I would like to express my thanks to *American Heritage, Missouri Historical Society Bulletin, Oregon Historical Quarterly, Frontiers Magazine,* and *Montana, the Magazine of Western History* for permission to reprint portions of articles that appeared in their pages. Below I list names of librarians, archivists, scientists, and others who have rendered significant assistance in many ways:

ACADEMY OF NATURAL SCIENCES OF PHILADELPHIA
    Ruth E. Brown, head librarian
    Lillian C. Jones, assistant librarian
    Venia Phillips, former head librarian
    Maurice E. Phillips, editor of *Proceedings* of Academy, 1944–57
    Alfred E. Schuyler, curator of botany

AMERICAN PHILOSOPHICAL SOCIETY, Philadelphia
    Gertrude D. Hess, assistant librarian
    Murphy Smith, manuscripts librarian

BEAVER COLLEGE, Glenside, Pennsylvania
    Elizabeth Hammond, former head librarian
    Josephine Charles, assistant librarian

COLLEGE OF PHYSICIANS OF PHILADELPHIA
    Ellen N. Wade, curator

FILSON CLUB, Louisville, Kentucky
    Dorothy Thomas Cullen, curator and librarian

FISH AND WILDLIFE SERVICE, Washington, D.C.
    Arthur M. Greenhall, chief, mammal section, bird and mammal
    laboratories

LIBRARY COMPANY OF PHILADELPHIA
    Edwin Wolf, II, librarian

LUNA HOUSE HISTORICAL SOCIETY, Lewiston, Idaho
    Marcus J. Ware, president

MERCANTILE LIBRARY, St. Louis, Missouri
    Mary E. Mewes, reference librarian

MISSOURI HISTORICAL SOCIETY, St. Louis
    George R. Brooks, director
    Mrs. John G. Dotzman, archivist
    Mrs. Dana O. Jensen, editor of *Bulletin*
    Mrs. Fred C. Harrington, librarian

MUSEUM OF COMPARATIVE ZOOLOGY, Cambridge, Massachusetts
    James C. Greenway, curator of birds
    William C. Jolly, assistant

NATIONAL PARK SERVICE, Washington, D.C.
    Roy E. Appleman, historian

NORTH DAKOTA STATE UNIVERSITY, Fargo
    O. A. Stevens, professor of botany

OREGON HISTORICAL SOCIETY, Portland
    Allan Gibbons, curator of collections

PEABODY MUSEUM OF ETHNOLOGY AND ARCHAEOLOGY, Cambridge, Massachusetts
    Katherine B. Edsall

SMITHSONIAN INSTITUTION, Washington, D.C.
    John C. Ewers, director of history and technology
    Charles C. Handley, Jr., curator in charge of division of mammals
    David H. Johnson, curator, division of mammals
    S. H. Riesenberg, acting head curator, department of anthropology
    Velva E. Rudd, associate curator, department of botany
    T. D. Stewart, head curator, department of anthropology
    William C. Sturtevant, division of cultural anthropology
    William R. Taylor, associate curator, division of fishes
    George E. Watson, acting curator, division of birds
    Richard L. Zuse, acting curator, division of birds

STATE HISTORICAL SOCIETY OF NORTH DAKOTA, Bismarck
    Norman Paulson, museum assistant

THOMAS JEFFERSON MEMORIAL FOUNDATION (MONTICELLO), Charlottesville, Virginia
    James A. Bear, curator
    Mildred Monahan

TULANE UNIVERSITY, New Orleans, Louisiana
    Joseph Ewan, professor of botany

UNIVERSITY OF MONTANA, Missoula
    Robert S. Hoffman, professor of zoology
    Sherman J. Preece, professor of botany

UNIVERSITY OF WASHINGTON, Seattle
    Verne F. Ray, professor of anthropology

UNIVERSITY MUSEUM, UNIVERSITY OF PENNSYLVANIA, Philadelphia
    Frances Eyman, keeper of American collections

WASHINGTON STATE UNIVERSITY, Pullman
    Irven O. Buss, professor of zoology

WINTERTHUR MUSEUM, Winterthur, Delaware
    M. James

YALE UNIVERSITY LIBRARY, New Haven, Connecticut
    Archibald Hanna, librarian, Library of Western Americana

I owe expressions of gratitude, also to:

William Clark Adreon
John Bakeless
Burnby M. Bell
Raymond Darwin Burroughs
Emil DonTigny
Richard E. Dillon
Paul A. Ewald
Curtis B. Mateer

Nelson Heath Meriwether
Duncan Merriwether
Francis Mitchell
Ernest Staples Osgood
Dawson Phelps
Edwin A. Poole
Emory and Ruth Strong

I wish to thank particularly those individuals who have read critically portions of my manuscript and helped in other ways: Dr. Roy M. Chatters, head of radioisotopes and radiations laboratory, Washington State University; Larry Gill, advertising sales manager, Northwest Farm Paper Unit, Spokane, Washington; Dr. William W. Hassler, President, Indiana State University, Indiana, Pennsylvania; C. A. Peairs, Jr., attorney, Westboro, Massachusetts; Ralph S. Space, forest supervisor (1954–63), Clearwater National Forest, Orofino, Idaho; Helen B. West, archives assistant, Museum of the Plains Indians, Browning, Montana; and Dr. R. G. Williams, Joseph Leidy professor of anatomy, University of Pennsylvania School of Medicine, Philadelphia.

No words are sufficient to express my gratitude to my late brother, Dr. Clifford R. Cutright, emeritus professor of entomology, Ohio Agricultural Experiment Station, Wooster, Ohio, who was my constant companion on trips west in the wake of Lewis and Clark; and to my wife, Gladys Pennington Cutright, professor of Romance languages, who typed my manuscript and is responsible, far more than any other person, for detecting mistakes in construction and for suggesting the felicitous word or phrase.

And now, I wish to express my especial appreciation to Dr. Donald Jackson, whose stimulating cooperation and perceptive guide lines have been extremely valuable in the final revision of my manuscript. I should like further to express my gratitude to Dr. Jackson for publishing and making available *Letters of the Lewis and Clark Expedition with Related Documents 1783–1854* (Urbana, 1962), with its wealth of annotations. The extent to which I have used this work is evident in the innumerable references listed in my notes.

Prologue
to Discovery

CHAPTER ONE

As Captains Meriwether Lewis and William Clark began their historic march to the Western Ocean, they carried with them an extraordinary document, a copy of President Thomas Jefferson's instructions to them. This document had been long in the making, having its inception no later than 1793 when Jefferson, acting for the American Philosophical Society, had prepared directives for an earlier expedition that failed to materialize. Now that a new attempt would be made to probe the secrets of the West, with much better prospects of success, Jefferson fashioned a more elaborate, a more carefully worded set of instructions. Not wishing to be solely responsible for its content, he asked members of his cabinet and various scientific friends, including Meriwether Lewis, to read it and make suggestions. They found little to add or subtract, so that the document remained much as Jefferson had originally written it.

From this collective effort emerged a final paper, unique, distinguished. It was a blueprint for discovery, the product of a powerfully original and disciplined mind. No exploring party before or since has been provided with instructions so inclusive, so technically knowledgeable, so electric with ideas, so charged with foresight. From first to last, Lewis and Clark gave it the attention a cleric gives Holy Writ.

"Nature," Jefferson once said, "intended me for the tranquil pursuits of science, by rendering them my supreme delight."[1] These pursuits of which he spoke embraced all natural objects and agencies from

[1] Edwin T. Martin, *Thomas Jefferson: Scientist* (New York, 1952), 3–4.

1

the grandest to the most common: wind currents and temperature fluctuations, the advent of the first spring flowers, minerals and medicinal springs, mountains, lakes and interlocking streams, the aboriginal American and his customs, migrating birds, petrified bones of extinct animals.

Without this wide-ranging technical background, Jefferson would have been completely incapable of writing the set of instructions that went to Lewis and Clark. Indeed, without it, we may question whether there would ever have been a Lewis and Clark Expedition, a scientific venture from beginning to end.

For such reasons it is desirable, therefore, that we initially summarize Jefferson's knowledge and command of the sciences, especially biology, geography, meteorology, and ethnology, and explore these fields in some depth. We will then be in a far better position to follow and appraise the day-by-day progression of the Expedition as it conquered rivers and mountain heights on its grand tour of discovery.

[2]

In his instructions to Lewis and Clark, Jefferson wrote: observe *"climate as characterized by the thermometer, by the proportion of rainy, cloudy & clear days, by lightening, hail, snow, ice, by the access & recess of frost, by the winds prevailing at different seasons, the dates at which particular plants put forth or lose their flowers, or leaf, times of appearance of particular birds, reptiles or insects"* (VII, 249).*

In his time Thomas Jefferson was probably the best-informed meteorologist in the United States, an ardent, dedicated pioneer. He kept systematic weather records continuously for more than 50 years, jotting down data wherever he happened to be: in Williamsburg as governor of his state, in Paris as Minister Plenipotentiary to France, in Washington as President, even on the high seas as a relaxed itinerant.

Jefferson's first published weather records appeared in *Notes on the State of Virginia,* a small volume he wrote in 1780–81. This work established him as a scientist, highly regarded by his fellows-in-learning both at home and abroad. The weather records reported herein, the

---

* The great majority of quotations in this work are from *Original Journals of the Lewis and Clark Expedition 1804–1806,* 8 vols., edited by Reuben Gold Thwaites (New York, 1904–5). Here and hereafter citations from this source will appear at the end of quotations abbreviated as above.

product of observations made mainly at Williamsburg and Monticello from 1772 to 1777, emphasized rainfall, temperatures, and wind direction. We learn, for instance, that rainfall over these years averaged 47 inches.

We know, thanks to Jefferson's habitual thermometer-watching, that the weather in Philadelphia on that most celebrated of days in American history, the Fourth of July, 1776, was most pleasant. With a Fahrenheit thermometer, he determined that the temperature at 6 A.M. was 68, at 9 A.M. 72½, at 1 P.M. 76, and at 9 P.M. 73½.[2]

Jefferson not only made observations on the weather himself, but he also urged others to do the same. Writing to his daughter, Maria, from Philadelphia on March 9, 1791, while Secretary of State to Washington, he said: "I hope you have, and will continue to note every appearance, animal and vegetable, which indicates the approach of spring, and will communicate them to me. By these means we shall be able to compare the climates of Philadelphia and Monticello."[3] In this request Jefferson reveals his addiction to phenology, that science which attempts to correlate weather data with periodic biological occurrences such as the migration and nesting of birds and the flowering and fruiting of plants.

[3]

"The object of your mission is to explore the Missouri river, & such principal streams of it, as, by it's course & communication with the waters of the Pacific Ocean, may offer the most direct & practicable water communication across this continent, for the purposes of commerce. . . . Beginning at the mouth of the Missouri, you will take observations of latitude & longitude, at all remarkable points on the river" (VII, 248).

For a man who in his whole life had never travelled farther west than Harper's Ferry, Jefferson possessed a surprising knowledge of the physical features of the nation. His *Notes on Virginia*, for instance, provide a vast amount of information on rivers, both east and west, their navigability, their bars and shoals, rapids and waterfalls, islands and wildlife. The "Tanissee" was "navigable for loaded boats of any

[2] Edwin Morris Betts, ed., *Thomas Jefferson's Garden Book* (Philadelphia, 1944), 69.
[3] Betts, *Jefferson's Garden Book*, 160.

burden to the Muscle shoals,"[4] and the Mississippi yielded "turtle of a peculiar kind, perch, trout, gar, mullets, herrings, carps, spatula-fish of 50 lb. weight, cat-fish of 100 lb. weight, buffalo fish and sturgeon."[5]

One has to be impressed with Jefferson's thoughts on further opening navigation between east and west, as an ever increasing number of hardy pioneers surmounted the Alleghenies and spilled down onto the rich bottom lands of the Ohio and its tributaries. In the near future, as he saw it, easy communication by short portages would be established between interlocking branches of such streams as the Great Kanawha and James, the Tennessee and Mobile, and the Potomac and one or another affluent of the Ohio.

It should come as no surprise that Jefferson possessed a substantial knowledge of surveying and navigation and an ability to use such instruments as the quadrant, sextant, and theodolite. At Monticello in 1778 he wrote: "Placing the Theodolite on the top of the house, the Eastern spur of the High mountain intersects the Horizon 19° Westward of Willis's mountain."[6] According to Edwin M. Betts, editor of Jefferson's *Garden Book,* Jefferson used Willis Mountain, isolated and plainly visible from Monticello on clear days, as the "focal point in calculating the latitude and longitude of various surrounding places."[7] It is probable that Jefferson gave Meriwether Lewis preliminary instruction in the use of navigational instruments. Writing to Robert Patterson, Philadelphia scientist, in March, 1803, he said: "He has been for some time qualifying himself for taking observations of longitude & latitude to fix the geographical points of the line he will pass over."[8]

It is well known that Jefferson possessed an intense interest in maps and map-making and was familiar with such maps of the western world as then existed, those of d'Anville, Arrowsmith, Delisle, Cook, and Vancouver, for instance. He came by this interest legitimately, for his father, Peter Jefferson, and Joshua Fry, professor of mathematics at William and Mary College, had made (in 1751) the first map of Virginia, and it was a revision of this map that later appeared in Jefferson's *Notes on Virginia.*[9]

[4] Thomas Jefferson, *Notes on the State of Virginia* (Boston, 1832), 9. Hereinafter cited as "Jefferson, *Notes.*"

[5] Jefferson, *Notes,* 6.

[6] Betts, *Jefferson's Garden Book,* 80.

[7] Betts, *Jefferson's Garden Book,* 84–85.

[8] Jackson, *Letters,* 21.

[9] William Peden, ed., *Notes on the State of Virginia,* by Thomas Jefferson (Chapel Hill, 1955), xviii, 261.

[4]

Observe, wrote Jefferson, *"the animals of the country generally, &*
especially those not known in the U.S. the remains and accounts of any
which may [be] deemed rare or extinct" (VII, 249).

Jefferson's writings abound with references to animals. As a
farmer, he evidenced a natural concern about the damage to wheat by
the recently introduced Hessian fly and was influential in, if not primarily responsible for, the American Philosophical Society's move to set
up a committee to study its life history. Like any good amateur ornithologist, he kept track of the arrival of birds in the spring. In Philadelphia in 1791 he wrote his daughter of seeing blackbirds and robins for
the first time on February 27.[10] To James Madison in early April, 1794,
he wrote: "The lilac is in bloom, and the first whip-poor-will heard last
night."[11]

Jefferson was relatively unknown as a biologist until he tangled
with George Louis Leclerc, Comte de Buffon, one of the leading naturalists of his day and author of *Histoire Naturelle,* a compendious work
begun in 1749 and not completed until 1804. Buffon wielded great
influence, even Jefferson deferring to him on most points.

In one of the earlier volumes of Buffon's *chef d'oeuvre,* Jefferson
discovered statements which disturbed him. For example, the French
savant had written that animals common both to the Old and New
World are smaller in the latter, and that those peculiar to the New are
generally small.[12] Motivated by his distaste for allegations unsupported
by facts, his inherent passion for truth, and his great love of country,
Jefferson not only vigorously denied these statements, but also sent to
Buffon a giant moose (this animal being much larger than any native
to Europe) and soon followed this with information about the "great
incognitum" (the mastodon), bones of which, recently unearthed, attested to a creature "of five or six times the cubit volume of the
elephant."[13] Though these two animals alone were more than enough
to rescue the United States from the imputation that its fauna was
inferior, Jefferson's subsequent discovery of the giant ground sloth,
Megalonyx, further established the American position.

[10] Betts, *Jefferson's Garden Book,* 160.
[11] Betts, *Jefferson's Garden Book,* 216.
[12] Jefferson, *Notes,* 45.
[13] Jefferson, *Notes,* 42.

It is well known, of course, that Jefferson was a pioneering paleontologist and assembled a large collection of fossils in the East Room of
the White House. Among the most prized bones exhibited here were
those of *Megalonyx,* originally brought to light in Greenbrier County,
Virginia (now West Virginia). When Jefferson came to Philadelphia
in 1797 to be sworn in as Vice President of the United States, he carried
with him his treasured *Megalonyx* bones and a paper about them
which, on March 10, he read to members of the American Philosophical Society. It was his belief, he said, that the bones belonged to an
unusually large lion-like creature and that he had given it the name
Megalonyx (literally "Great Claw") because of the extreme size of its
talons.[14] Subsequently, Dr. Caspar Wistar, Philadelphia physician and
leading authority on fossils in the United States at the time, correctly
identified and described the animal as a ground sloth (not a carnivore) and gave it the binomial it bears today, *Megalonyx jeffersoni.*

[5]

". . . *make yourself acquainted, as far as a diligent pursuit of your
journey shall admit, with the names of the nations & and their numbers; their relations with other tribes or nations; their language, tradi-
tions, monuments; their ordinary occupations in agriculture, fishing,
hunting, war, arts, & the implements for these; their food, clothing and
domestic accommodations; the diseases prevalent among them & the
remedies they use*" (VII, 248) .

Jefferson's acquaintance with American Indians began when he
was quite young. He was accustomed to seeing parties of them on their
way to their burying grounds, and he retained vivid recollections of a
Cherokee chief whom his father had entertained at Shadwell. Not
generally known is the fact that the future president, while a young
man, actually excavated an Indian mound, one of several dotting the
Rivanna River valley, and later reported in full his findings.[15] Thus,
according to one modern archaeologist, he "not only has the distinction
of being among the early writers on the mounds, but has established
himself as one of the very earliest real explorers of them."[16]

[14] Thomas Jefferson, "A Memoir of the Discovery of Certain Bones of a
Quadruped of the Clawed Kind in the Western Parts of Virginia," *Trans. Amer.
Phil. Soc.,* IV (1799) , 246ff.
[15] Jefferson, *Notes,* 100–101.
[16] Henry Clyde Shetrone, *The Mound-builders* (New York, 1931) , 14.

Jefferson seems to have been far ahead of most of his contemporaries in his conviction that actual proof of Indian origin and tribal relationships would ultimately rest on language. "It is to be lamented, then, very much to be lamented," he wrote, "that we have suffered so many of the Indian tribes already to extinguish, without our having previously collected and deposited in the records of literature, the general rudiments at least of the languages they spoke. Were vocabularies formed of all the languages spoken in North and South America . . . it would furnish opportunities to those skilled in the languages of the old world to compare them with these, now, or at any future time, and hence to construct the best evidence of the derivation of this part of the human race."[17]

Jefferson did more than talk about Indian "vocabularies"; he collected them. Writing in 1809 to a friend with mutual ethnological interests, he said: "I have now been thirty years availing myself of every possible opportunity of procuring Indian vocabularies to the same set of words; my opportunities were probably better than will ever occur again to any person having the same desire."[18]

"The savage," wrote Buffon about the American Indian, "is feeble, and has small organs of generation; he has neither hair nor beard, and no ardour whatever for his female . . . he is also less sensitive, and yet more timid and cowardly; he has no vivacity of mind."[19]

Jefferson's reply to Buffon delighted his fellow countrymen. "An afflicting picture indeed, which, for the honor of human nature, I am glad to believe has no original." The American Indian "is neither more defective in ardor, nor more impotent with his female, than the white reduced to the same diet and exercise . . . he is brave, when an enterprise depends on bravery . . . he will defend himself against a host of enemies, always chusing to be killed, rather than to surrender."[20] Thus Jefferson, the amateur scientist, gave Monsieur Buffon, the professional, a badly needed lesson in the scientific method.

[6]

Observe, wrote Jefferson, *"the face of the country, it's growth & vegetable productions; especially those not of the U.S."* (VII, 239) .

17 Jefferson, *Notes,* 104.
18 Jackson, *Letters,* 465.
19 Peden, *Notes on the State of Virginia,* 58.
20 Peden, *Notes on the State of Virginia,* 63–64.

Year in and year out, Jefferson devoted more hours and more industry to plants than to any of the other productions of nature. "There is not a sprig of grass that shoots uninteresting to me," he once declared.[21] When only twenty-three, he began jotting down botanical and phenological observations in what he called his *Garden Book*. His initial entry, made in the spring of 1766, reads as follows:

"Mar. 30. Purple hyacinth begins to bloom.
Apr.   6. Narcissus and Puckoon [bloodroot, *Sanguinaria canadensis*] open.
    13. Puckoon flowers fallen.
    16. a bluish colored, funnel formed flower [possibly bluebell, *Mertensia virginica*] in lowlands in bloom.
    30. purple flag [*Iris* sp.] blooms. Hyacinth & Narcissus gone."[22]

As the years went by, Jefferson's knowledge of local herbs, shrubs, and trees advanced rapidly. In *Notes on Virginia* he listed 130 plants common to his state (from an "infinitude" of others), dividing them into four groups: medicinal, esculent, ornamental, and "useful for fabrication." In each instance he included the scientific name with the vernacular, "as the latter might not convey precise information to a foreigner."[23] Thus we have the best evidence possible that Jefferson as a young man often visited the woods and fields adjacent to his home collecting and identifying local plants, familiarizing himself with leaf and blossom and that, meantime, he had measured the worth of Linnaeus' method of classification and had fastened upon it with instant enthusiasm. Well versed in Latin, he took to binomials like a poet to iambic pentameter and was one of the first Americans to recognize the merits of this universal language devised by the great Swedish naturalist.

In no man of his time was the desire to promote the general good of mankind through an interchange of plants more highly developed than in the Master of Monticello. Noting the importance of certain European plants in the economy of that continent, he took firm steps to introduce them into the United States. He centered his efforts on dry (upland) rice and the olive, though not ignoring others, such as cork oak and a species of grass (*Sulla*). Though unsuccessful with rice and the olive, Jefferson's failures take nothing away from his standing as

21 Betts, *Jefferson's Garden Book*, 155.
22 Betts, *Jefferson's Garden Book*, 1.
23 Jefferson, *Notes*, 35.

the first American to engage seriously in efforts to introduce beneficial plants into the United States.

[7]

Jefferson instructed Lewis and Clark to make observations, these *"to be taken with great pains & accuracy, to be entered distinctly, & intelligibly for others as well as yourself . . . several copies of these, as well as your other notes, should be made at leisure times & put into the care of the most trustworthy of your attendants"* (VII, 248).

From youth to old age, Jefferson set a shining example in the commendable art of observation and note-taking, to which predilection his *Garden Book* and *Farm Book* attest most eloquently. To him, observation was the substantive key opening doors to the riches of discovery. Recordings insured permanence. It is "truly unfortunate," he once remarked, that so few public figures take notes, without which "history becomes fable instead of fact."[24]

The instructions Jefferson put into the hands of Lewis and Clark clearly reflected his appetites, his thinking, and his persistent preoccupation with scientific matters. They carried with them the prestige of the President of the United States. That Lewis and Clark regarded them as law and made observations on temperature and rainfall, mountains and interlocking streams, animals, plants, and stone-age Indians, which they then committed to writing, is now a matter of record.

In a letter to Lewis written by Clark just prior to the start of the Expedition, Clark referred to President Jefferson as "that great Chaructor the Main Spring of the action."[25] He stated a simple truth perhaps not fully recognized by many Americans even today. Jefferson was the fountainhead of the Expedition. He conceived it, nurtured it through an unsettled infancy, and followed its further development with accelerating enthusiasm and unremitting care. His planning and organizational genius, supported by his broad base of technical knowledge, which we have delineated briefly, augured almost certain success. Without taking anything away from the glory and fame attaching to the names of Lewis and Clark, the Expedition might with equal justice have been called the "Jefferson Expedition."

[24] Martin, *Thomas Jefferson: Scientist*, 19.
[25] Jackson, *Letters*, 111.

[8]

In these days of advanced geography, it is difficult to realize that when Thomas Jefferson was a small boy, just becoming conscious of the world around him, the greater portion of what is now the United States —the territorial immensity lying between the Mississippi River and the Pacific Ocean—was then almost as much a *terra incognita* to Americans as the back side of the moon is today. The Spaniards had occupied and explored a thin selvedge of it to the southwest, but the balance remained unknown and uncharted.

As Jefferson grew toward manhood, he heard much talk about this vast terrain, some of it fact, most of it hearsay, conjecture, and wildest fancy. Of whatever nature, it was more than enough to sharpen his imagination and to excite an inherent, active curiosity. This inquisitive disposition, as might be expected from what we already know about Jefferson, extended at first primarily to plants, animals, and Indians. In time, as he learned that the British and other nations had designs on this land, he became thoughtful as well as curious.

Jefferson's first public manifestation of interest in the West occurred in 1783, at the age of forty, when he was elected to Congress and helped draft basic reports on the organization of our lands between the Ohio and Mississippi. By then he envisioned that country, whatever its capacious interior might hold in the way of grassland, desert, and forest, as playing an inevitable role in the future expansion of the United States. Had not the restless American frontiersman already overrun much of the country between the Alleghenies and the remote, hurrying Mississippi? He felt strongly, too, that the United States should be in a position to divert some of the fur traffic away from the British, whose traders had already invaded distant Indian villages above the Great Bend of the Upper Missouri. From such thoughts and convictions evolved Jefferson's idea of sending an expedition to explore the West.

In December of 1783 Congressman Jefferson wrote General George Rogers Clark, hero of Vincennes and older brother of William Clark: "I find they have subscribed a very large sum of money in England for exploring the country from the Mississippi to California. they pretend it is only to promote knolege. I am afraid they have thoughts of colonizing into that quarter. Some of us have been talking in a feeble way of making the attempt to search that country. . . . How would you like to lead such a party?" (VII, 193) . Nothing came of this, Clark replying that although such a tour appealed to him, he could not undertake it because of personal financial problems besetting him at the moment.

Three years later, while in France as Minister Plenipotentiary, Jefferson met John Ledyard, a fellow countryman from Groton, Connecticut. Ledyard's chief claim to fame thus far in life had been to serve as petty officer under Captain John Cook on the latter's third voyage around the world. When Cook put in at Nootka Sound in 1778 (on the west side of Vancouver Island, British Columbia) , he and his crew made a discovery that quickly and dramatically altered the history of our Northwest. They learned that sea otter pelts, purchased from the Indians for trifles, brought fabulous prices on the Chinese markets.

Ledyard returned home confident that with proper backing he could make a fortune harvesting sea otter skins. Having failed in his attempts to obtain the assistance he sought, first in the United States and more recently in Europe, he was "now panting for some new enterprize" and alert to a proposal Jefferson made to him.[26] Why not cross Siberia to Kamchatka, sign on with a Russian fur-trader bound for Nootka Sound or thereabout, and once there, break through the Rockies to the Missouri and St. Louis? Ledyard seized upon this suggestion with enthusiasm and actually succeeded in arriving within some 200 miles of Kamchatka before a Russian officer dispatched by Empress Catherine caught up with him and obliged him to return. So Jefferson's second attempt to have the West explored, this one by the back door, came to naught.

Six years passed and by then Jefferson was in Philadelphia serving under George Washington as the latter's Secretary of State. At that time in our history, Philadelphia was not only the capital of the United States but also its largest city and its scientific center. It had achieved the latter pre-eminence after Franklin had founded the American Philosophical Society. Jefferson had been a member of this prestigious organization since 1780 and recently had been elected vice president. (From 1797 to 1814 he served as its president.) Soon after Jefferson had been elevated to the vice presidency, we find Dr. Caspar Wistar writing to Dr. Moses Marshall, a local botanist of some repute. Marshall had just returned from a 1,600-mile collecting trip to the

---

[26] Elliott Coues, ed., *History of the Expedition Under the Command of Lewis and Clark*, 4 vols. (New York, 1893) , I, xviii. Hereinafter cited as "Coues."

Altamaha River country of Georgia, where a few years earlier John Bartram had discovered *Franklinia,* one of our rarest plants. Wistar, apparently at Jefferson's instigation, wrote Marshall as follows:

Respected Friend:—By a conversation with thy uncle [Humphrey Marshall, author of *Arbustrum Americanum,* a celebrated early work on American trees], I find that thee is already acquainted with the wishes of some gentlemen here to have our continent explored in a western direction. My reason for writing at present is to inform thee of the present state of the business. Mr. Jefferson and several other gentlemen are much interested, and think they can procure a subscription sufficient to insure one thousand guineas as a compensation to any one who undertakes the journey and can bring satisfactory proof of having crossed to the South Sea. They wish the journey to be prosecuted up the Missouri, as the easiest and perhaps the most interesting track. . . . If thee has any inclination, I think it would be very proper to come to town immediately and converse with Mr. Jefferson, who seems principally interested. I am confident that no small matter will stop them if thee is disposed to engage in the business. At any rate, shall be glad to hear from thee as soon as possible.[27]

It may be concluded that Jefferson and the "several other gentlemen" referred to in this letter were all members of the American Philosophical Society, so that it was this organization, with Jefferson as its spokesman, which backed this little-known attempt to induce Moses Marshall to explore the West. But apparently not even the lure of a thousand guineas moved him to undertake the venture. At least, we find no further mention of his name in that connection.

There is mention soon, however, of André Michaux, who had been actively engaged for a number of years collecting plants in Canada and the United States. He had visited Philadelphia where he favorably impressed Jefferson and other members of the American Philosophical Society. Finding that he was agreeable to exploring in a westerly direction, the Society solicited funds to finance the enterprise. Jefferson and Alexander Hamilton each contributed $12.50, Robert Morris $20, and George Washington $25 (VII, 205) .

Michaux's exploration ended in Kentucky. Here, as Jefferson later diplomatically explained, "he was overtaken by an order from the Minister of France, then at Philadelphia, to relinquish the expedition, and to pursue elsewhere the botanical inquiries on which he was employed. . . ."[28] But such diplomatic language did not long obscure

[27] John W. Harshberger, *The Botanists of Philadelphia and Their Work* (Philadelphia, 1899) , 106.
[28] Coues, I, xx.

the truth, namely, that the French Minister, the notorious Citizen Genêt, had been attempting to organize a military expedition against the Spaniards and that Michaux was suspected of being a spy in his employ. When Jefferson learned of this development, he may have regretted a decision not to engage the services of a young man of nineteen who had earnestly sought through him the appointment given Michaux. His name was Meriwether Lewis. Thus ended, on a scratchy note, Jefferson's fourth attempt to have the West explored.

[9]

The vast tract of real estate beyond the Mississippi, named Louisiana by La Salle, belonged to France until 1762. In that year France ceded it to Spain. Forty years later Napoleon forced its return to France. By then Thomas Jefferson was President of the United States, with eyes more sharply focused on the West than ever—and with good reason. The British, ignoring treaties, continued to hold trading posts on American soil and had expanded colonizing ambitions into the Upper Missouri country. Spain refused to allow shipments of American goods to pass freely through the port of New Orleans. And now France threatened to establish a new colonial empire in the Western Hemisphere. It was high time, Jefferson reasoned, that the United States be heard from in this gigantic game of international enterprise. What action could possibly be more effective in strengthening the American position in the world and establishing a just claim to at least a portion of Louisiana (Jefferson undoubtedly had that in mind) than the successful crossing of the continent between Spanish and British holdings by American explorers, especially in light of the fact that Captain Robert Gray had recently (1797) discovered the Columbia when he successfully drove his American merchantman into the estuary of that river? Now that he was President, Jefferson could exercise the power of that office to advance his project with chances of success greatly enhanced.

Jefferson made his next move on February 23, 1801. This took the form of a letter to Meriwether Lewis, then paymaster with the rank of captain in General James Wilkinson's Army of the West. He needed a private secretary, he wrote Lewis, one who would "contribute to the mass of information which it is interesting for the administration to acquire. Your knoledge of the Western country, of the army and of all it's interests & relations has rendered it desirable for public as well as private purposes that you should be engaged in that office."[29] Strange prerequisites for a secretary, strange indeed! But the inference to be drawn seems clear. Jefferson had settled on Lewis as the man to head the next party attempting to explore the West, and desired his presence in the capital where in subsequent months he could pursue with him each preparatory step.

Lewis received Jefferson's letter in Pittsburgh, having just arrived in that frontier town from "D'Etroit." His reply, dated March 10, reads in part as follows: ". . . I most cordially acquiesce and with pleasure accept the office, nor were further motives necessary to induce my complyance, than that you Sir should conceive that in the discharge of the duties of that office, I could be serviceable to my country, or uceful to youreself; permit me here Sir to do further justice to my feelings, by expressing the lively sensibility with which I received this mark of your confidence and esteem."[30]

I think we can understand Lewis's elation and can appreciate his stilted elegance of language. He could hardly have anticipated such a stroke of good fortune. If he thought that Jefferson had him in mind to explore the West, he gave no hint of it. However, he could not have been completely blind to the two words "Western country."

Lewis set out for Washington almost at once. A lame mount and heavy spring rains delayed him, so that he did not reach his destination until April 1. Since the federal government had moved from Philadelphia to its new location on the Potomac just the preceding autumn, the President's House (so called by Abigail Adams, the first First Lady to occupy it) and the Capitol were in an unfinished state and the future Pennsylvania Avenue little more than a muddy trail bordered by bushes, briars, and stumps. When Lewis dismounted at the President's mansion (it would not be called the White House until after the British burned it in 1814 and it was painted white to cover the scars) where he would live for the next two years, he had no way of knowing that he had now embarked on a venture of such high consequence that when successfully completed, his name would forever illumine pages of American history.

Meriwether Lewis (1774–1809) now approached his twenty-seventh birthday. He had been born on August 18, 1774, seven miles to the west of Charlottesville, Albemarle County, Virginia. Not too much is known about his boyhood years, except that he early demonstrated a

[29] Jackson, *Letters*, 2.
[30] Jackson, *Letters*, 3.

fondness for adventure in the woods and fields surrounding his home and acquired, as Jefferson subsequently wrote, "a talent for observation which had led him to an accurate knowledge of the plants and animals of his own country."[31] That this knowledge was substantial is borne out by the frequency and accuracy of Lewis's later comparisons of western with eastern animals and plants. For example, on discovering the cutthroat trout (*Salmo clarkii*), he said: "These trout . . . precisely resemble our mountain or speckled trout [*Salvolinus fontinalis*] in form and the position of their fins, but the specks on these are of a deep black instead of the red or goald" (II, 150–151). And, when describing another western discovery, the dusky grouse (*Dendragapus obscurus*), he reported that it had 18 tail feathers, the same number as the eastern ruffed grouse (*Bonasa umbellus umbellus*) (II, 295).[32] Surely, not many of Lewis's contemporaries knew that the eastern ruffed grouse had exactly 18 feathers in its tail.

It should not be overlooked that Lewis's mother, Lucy Meriwether Lewis (Lucy Marks, after a second marriage), was an herb doctor. For many years she tended the sick of Albemarle County, prescribing and administering vegetable drugs (simples). Thus, because of maternal ties, Lewis learned local plants of medicinal value and their purported therapeutic properties. As we shall see, information of this kind often colored his treatment of wounds and disorders suffered by himself and other members of the Corps of Discovery.

When President Washington in 1794 issued a call for volunteers to put down an insurrection in Pittsburgh (the Whiskey Rebellion), Lewis, now twenty, joined the militia hastily formed for that purpose. At the close of the rebellion, he enlisted in the regular army and served under General "Mad Anthony" Wayne in the latter's Northwest campaign against the Indians and British. At some point in this campaign, Lewis (by then an ensign) found himself attached to the 4th Sub-Legion of Wayne's army commanded by Lieutenant William Clark. In days immediately ahead, Ensign Lewis and Lieutenant Clark, sharing the experiences of border warfare, fashioned the bonds of an enduring friendship.

Lewis was shortly advanced to the rank of captain (in 1800, at the age of twenty-six) and after Wayne's death, served under General

[31] Coues, I, xviii.

[32] The genus *Dendragapus* normally, at least, has 16 tail feathers. See Raymond Darwin Burrough's *The Natural History of the Lewis and Clark Expedition* (East Lansing, Mich., 1961), 216.

James Wilkinson, whose name would soon be linked conspiratorially with that of Aaron Burr. Given the job of regimental paymaster, he continued in that role until Jefferson's letter caught up with him at Pittsburgh.

Jefferson had watched the youthful Meriwether Lewis grow to manhood. He had followed his rapid rise in the army from private to captain and had noted approvingly his experiences with Indians and his acquisition of knowledge about the country lying west of the Alleghenies. His choice of Lewis to serve as his personal secretary would indicate that he had not forgotten the latter's ardent plea, at the age of nineteen, that he be allowed to undertake the western exploration subsequently entrusted to Michaux.

[10]

In the fall of 1802, continuing to look west, Jefferson asked the Spanish Minister in Washington if his country would "take it badly" if the United States elected to send a small party to "explore the course of the Missouri River." This, he indicated, would be purely a literary expedition and "would have no other view than the advancement of the geography." The Spanish Minister replied that a mission of that kind "could not fail to give umbrage" to his government.[33] Undaunted by the Minister's reply, Jefferson, on January 18, 1803, transmitted a secret message to Congress. He used as a pretext the circumstance that Congress would presently be considering a continuance of the act for establishing trading houses among the Indians. "An intelligent officer," he said, "with ten or twelve chosen men fit for the enterprise and willing to undertake it . . . might explore the whole line, even to the Western ocean" (VII, 208–209). This exploration, the President told Congress (as he had told the Spanish Minister), would be geographical; but it would serve additionally to pave the way for American traders to enter the Missouri valley and thus be in a position to tap the fur riches of that region presently controlled by the British. An appropriation of $2,500, he thought, would be adequate to cover the expense of such an undertaking.

"The intelligent officer" to whom Jefferson alluded in his message was, of course, Meriwether Lewis. If at the time he hired Lewis as his personal secretary, he held any doubts as to his qualifications for leading the Expedition, he no longer entertained them.

[33] Jackson, *Letters*, 4.

I had now had opportunities [he later wrote] of knowing him intimately. Of courage undaunted; possessing a firmness and perseverance of purpose which nothing but impossibilities could divert from its direction; careful as a father of those committed to his charge, yet steady in the maintenance of order and discipline; intimate with the Indian character, customs, and principles; habituated to the hunting life; guarded, by exact observation of the vegetables and animals of his country, against losing time in the description of objects already possessed; honest, disinterested, liberal, of sound understanding, and a fidelity to truth so scrupulous that whatever he should report would be as certain as if seen by ourselves—with all these qualifications, as if selected and implanted by nature in one body for this express purpose, I would have no hesitation in confiding the enterprise to him.[34]

Secrecy continued to cloak each step of the planning. It was imperative that Jefferson's actual intentions should remain unknown and unsuspected until the Expedition had "got beyond the reach of any obstacles which might be prepared . . . by those who would not like the enterprise."[35] All conferences about the impending exploration took place behind closed doors. The wording of each letter received special scrutiny. Robert Patterson perfected a cipher to be used by Lewis when sending coded messages back to Washington. When in time rumors of an upcoming western exploration leaked to the public, Jefferson quieted talk by announcing that the government planned to send a party to explore the Upper Mississippi and Lake of the Woods country (VII, 218–219).

The Expedition received additional leadership when William Clark accepted Lewis's invitation to share the exacting duties of command with him. Clark (1770–1838) was born in Caroline County, Virginia, on August 1, 1770, and was thus four years Lewis's senior. In 1785 he and the others of his family moved to Kentucky and took up residence near the Falls of the Ohio, now Louisville. Clark, then fifteen, had missed all but a minimum of schooling. His handwriting showed a lack of practice, and his spelling was picturesque. However, like many other young men of his day, he was wise in wilderness ways.

Clark gained his first military experience fighting Indians when at the age of nineteen, he joined an outfit of 200 mounted volunteers commanded by Colonel John Hardin. Later, as we know, he served under Wayne who, after a prolonged campaign, succeeded in defeating the Indians in the battle of Fallen Timbers and bringing peace once

[34] Coues, I, xxi–xxii.
[35] Jackson, *Letters*, 21.

more to what was then called "the Ohio Country." At the close of this military operation, Clark resigned from the army, one reason being that Wayne irritated him like a bee on a hound's nose. It is true that Wayne was something of a martinet. In attempting to avoid mistakes made by other leaders who had been badly defeated by Indians, he insisted on regular drill, frequent inspection of arms and accoutrement, periodic target practice, daily reconnaissance, and severe punishment for neglect of duty. Nevertheless, both Lewis and Clark profited immeasurably from their service under him. The day was not far away when they would be as demanding as Wayne had been.

On resigning from the service, Clark returned to his home where he resided quietly until July 16, 1803. On that date, he received a letter from Lewis that brought fire to his spirit unknown since his days of scrapping with Miamis, Shawnees, and Potawatomis. Would he, wrote Lewis, be interested in joining him in the fatigues, dangers, and honors of a trip to explore the trans-Mississippi West? "Believe me," he then went on, "there is no man on earth with whom I should feel equal pleasure in sharing them as with your self; I make this communication to you with the privity of the President, who expresses an anxious wish that you would consent to join me in this enterprise; he has authorized me to say that in the event of your accepting this proposition he will grant you a Captain's commission . . . your situation if joined with me in this mission will in all respects be precisely such as my own" (VII, 230).

In his letter of acceptance Clark said: "This is an immense undertaking fraited with numerous difficulties, but my friend I can assure you that no man lives with whom I would prefer to undertake and share the difficulties of such a trip than yourself" (VII, 259).

Jefferson was pleased at this turn of events. "By having Mr. Clarke with you," he wrote Lewis, "we consider the expedition double manned, & therefore the less liable to failure" (VII, 282).

Possibly Jefferson did not think of the command as joint, but that is what it became. Lewis insisted on it. Most persons today, notably army officers, shudder at the idea of joint leadership. They insist that it runs counter to all sound principles of command, is like putting two scorpions into the same bottle. As things turned out, there was no cause for concern about Lewis and Clark. In 28 months together, under conditions of almost daily hardship and tensions, they met each and every problem, seemingly without even a whisper of dissent between them. Since the two men were so unlike temperamentally and in other ways, one wonders how this could have been so. Lewis was a dreamer, intent, fine-drawn, reserved, unwavering, generally humorless. Clark was warm, companionable, a good judge of men, an easy conversationalist—but inclined to keep a portion of his counsel to himself—and highly successful in meeting the demands of actual living.

Those planning the Expedition had no cause for continued secrecy after April 30, 1803. On that date Napoleon sold Louisiana to the United States. For approximately $15,000,000 Jefferson had acquired practically all of that land mass between the Mississippi and the Rockies north of the Arkansas River. Looking at it another way, this acquisition—with others soon to follow—gave us the corn country of Iowa, Missouri, Kansas, and Nebraska, the wheat fields of the Dakotas, the gold and silver of Montana, Idaho, and California, the oil of Oklahoma and Texas, the great evergreen forests of Washington and Oregon, and the unexcelled splendors of Colorado, Utah, Wyoming, Nevada, Arizona, New Mexico, and contiguous states.

[11]

When Congress approved Jefferson's request to send an intelligent officer with ten or twelve chosen men to explore the trans-Mississippi West, he directed Lewis to leave for Philadelphia at once. His mission to that city was two-fold: to assemble necessary supplies and equipment for the Expedition and to call upon important scientists who would provide him with "a greater familiarity with the technical language of the natural sciences, and a readiness in the astronomical observations necessary for the geography of his route."[36]

Preceding Lewis's departure, Jefferson wrote nearly identical letters to Andrew Ellicott, Lancaster, Pennsylvania, and Robert Patterson, Dr. Benjamin Rush, Dr. Benjamin Smith Barton, and Dr. Caspar Wistar, all of Philadelphia and members, with Jefferson, of the American Philosophical Society. Since the recent deaths of Benjamin Franklin and David Rittenhouse, these men provided the leadership of that organization and constituted the acknowledged aristocracy of science in the United States. Jefferson's letter to Dr. Rush read as follows:

I wish to mention to you in confidence that I have obtained authority from Congress to undertake the long desired object of exploring the Missouri & whatever river, heading with that, leads to the western ocean. About 10 chosen woodsmen headed by Capt. Lewis my secretary will set out on it

[36] Coues, I, xxii.

immediately & probably accomplish it in two seasons. Capt. Lewis is brave, prudent, habituated to the woods, & familiar with the Indian manners and character. He is not regularly educated, but he possesses a great mass of accurate information on all the subjects of nature which present themselves here, & will therefore readily select those only in his new route which shall be new. He has qualified himself for those observations of longitude and latitude necessary to fix the points of line he will go over. It would be very useful to state for him those objects on which it is most desirable he should bring us information. For this purpose I ask the favor of you to prepare some notes of such particulars as may occur in his journey & which you think should draw his attention & enquiry. He will be in Philadelphia about 2 or 3 weeks hence & will wait on you (VII, 211).

Lewis left Washington for Philadelphia on March 14, travelling by way of Harper's Ferry and Lancaster. It was important that he visit the United States arsenal at Harper's Ferry to place orders for equipment and to superintend the construction of an iron boat frame which the skilled craftsmen of the arsenal would make for him. Lewis carried a letter to the superintendent of the arsenal from Henry Dearborn, Secretary of War, which ordered the former to provide Lewis with such arms and iron work as he might request. This letter points up the fact, not always understood, that the Lewis and Clark Expedition was a military one, a unit of the United States Army, as well as a scientific expedition.

The iron boat frame seems to have been a product of Lewis's inventive mind and to oversee each step of its construction, he stayed on in Harper's Ferry a full month instead of the week originally intended. Because of this delay, Lewis did not arrive in Lancaster until April 19. He went at once to the home of Andrew Ellicott (1754–1820), astronomer and mathematician, who is best remembered as the man engaged to make the original survey, under Jefferson's and Washington's supervision, of that significant moiety of real estate ceded by Maryland and Virginia which became the District of Columbia.

As Jefferson's letter to Dr. Rush attests, Lewis had already received preliminary instruction in how to use those instruments necessary for establishing latitude and longitude. Ellicott now extended this instruction. He had earlier written Jefferson: "Mr. Lewis's first object must be to acquire a facility, and dexterity, in making the observations; which can only be obtained by practise."[37] On April 20 Lewis wrote Jefferson: "I arrived at this place yesterday, called on Mr. Ellicott, and have this day commenced, under his direction, my observations &c., to per-

---

[37] Jackson, *Letters*, 23.

fect myself in the use and application of the instruments. Mr. Ellicott is extremely friendly and attentive, and I am confident is disposed to render me every aid in his power: he thinks it will be necessary I should remain here ten or twelve days."[38]

Lewis's schooling under Ellicott ran on for almost three weeks. It was May 7 when the latter addressed a letter to Robert Patterson which said that it would be handed to him by Lewis on his arrival in Philadelphia. Presumably Lewis departed on that day or the one following.

Once in Philadelphia, Lewis apparently went directly to Patterson, who, at Jefferson's request, was to continue still further Lewis's education in the use of the sextant and chronometer. A few days later he wrote Jefferson that both Patterson and Ellicott disapproved of the delicate theodolite because it would be difficult to transport and to keep in working order. They recommended instead as indispensably necessary "two Sextants . . . an artificial horizon or two; a good Arnold's watch or chronometer, a Surveyor's compass with a ball and socket and two pole chain, and a set of plotting instruments" (VII, 221).

In Lewis's next letter to Jefferson, he said that Irish-born Robert Patterson (1743–1823), a gifted mathematician who had come to Philadelphia in 1776, had been "extremely obliging" to him since his arrival and had recommended that he stay with him a few days longer to receive further instruction. It would seem that Patterson had discovered lacunae in Lewis's training that needed filling.

Lewis never did completely master the necessary aptitudes for determining latitude and longitude, in particular the latter. This failure cannot be attributed to any lack of reference books. As he left for the West, he carried with him such standard contemporary works as Patrick Kelley's *A Practical Introduction to Spherics and Nautical Astronomy* (London, 1796); *The Nautical Almanac and Astronomical Ephemeris* (London, 1781–1804); and Nevil Maskelyn's *Tables Requisite to be Used with the Nautical Ephemeris for Finding the Latitude and Longitude at Sea* (London, 1781).[39]

Presumably these volumes had been recommended by Ellicott and Patterson, although one should never overlook the hand of Jefferson in any phase of the planning of the Expedition, particularly any that had to do with books. Acknowledged to be the most eminent bibliophile of

[38] Jackson, *Letters,* 40.
[39] Donald Jackson, "Some Books Carried by Lewis and Clark," *Bull. Missouri Hist. Soc.,* XVI, no. 1 (Oct., 1959), 4–5.

his day, he actually built three personal libraries during his lifetime. His first was destroyed by fire in 1770. His second, given to Congress in 1815 when he was seventy-one, formed the nucleus of our Library of Congress, today the largest in the world. He built the third, some 1,000 volumes, during the remaining eleven years of his life.[40]

Before leaving Philadelphia, Lewis bought those navigational instruments recommended by Ellicott and Patterson. He obtained a chronometer from Thomas Parker, a clock and watchmaker, paying him $250 for it, by far the largest sum expended for any single item carried by the Expedition. After purchasing it, he sent it to Ellicott to be regulated. "She is wound up," he wrote, "and the works are stoped by inscerting a hog's bristle which you will discover by examination. She has been cleaned by Mr. Voit, and her rate of going ascertained by observation to be 14″ too slow in 24 h."[41]

[12]

Jefferson at no time seems to have considered engaging the services of a physician to accompany the explorers, being content to let Lewis and Clark handle whatever ills and miseries might befall the party. People of that day did not inquire too closely into the qualifications of doctors, many of whom had no regular training. Even John Bartram, we are told, "had an inclination to the study of physic and surgery and did much toward relieving the ailments of his poor neighbors."[42]

Jefferson's decision not to send a doctor was no doubt prompted by his familiarity with Lewis's knowledge of herb therapy and by his own lack of confidence in the physicians of his day. He had strong personal reasons for this distrust. Before he had attained the age of forty-two, he had lost his father and mother, his closest friend (Dabney Carr), his favorite sister (Jane), three children, and his wife (Martha). He lived in the days of the depleting remedies—purges, vomits, sweats, blisters— and of the blood-letting lancet, by far the most used instrument in the armamentarium of the physician. Patients recovered, if at all, in spite of medical attention received. The low state of medicine then could hardly have been otherwise. Pathogens, such as bacteria and viruses, had yet to be recognized for what they are. Almost three-quarters of a

[40] Arthur E. Bestor, David C. Mearns, and Jonathan Daniels, *Three Presidents and Their Books* (Urbana, Ill., 1963), 3.
[41] Jackson, *Letters,* 51.
[42] W. J. Youmans, *Pioneers of Science in America* (New York, 1896), 25.

century would elapse before the world would accept Pasteur's exposition of the germ theory of disease, and an even longer period of time before benefitting from use of the clinical thermometer and routines of urinalyses and blood examinations.

Though Jefferson inveighed against the doctors of his day, he did not hesitate to ask Dr. Benjamin Rush (1745–1813), the most eminent of American physicians, to advise Lewis on medical matters pertinent to the Expedition. That Dr. Rush obliged is proved by a letter Lewis wrote Jefferson soon after his arrival in Philadelphia. "Dr. Rush has favored me with some abstract queries under the several heads of *Physical History, medicine, morals* and *religion* of the Indians, which I have no doubt will be serviceable in directing my inquiries among that people" (VII, 224).

A sampling of Dr. Rush's "abstract queries," to some of which Lewis and Clark later obtained answers, follows: "What is the state of the pulse in both Sexes, Children, grown persons and in old age, by feeling the Pulse Morning, Noon & Night &c? What are their *acute* diseases? Is rheumatism, Pluricy or bilious fevers known among them? & does the latter ever terminate in a vomiting of *black matter?* What are their chronic diseases—are palsy, apoplexy, Epilepsy, Madness, the goiture (or swelled Neck) and the Venereal disease known among them? What is the mode of treating the *Small pox* particularly? What are their remidies for their different diseases?" (VII, 283).

After Lewis left Philadelphia for Washington, Dr. Rush had an afterthought. On June 11, he wrote Jefferson that he was sending a few short directions for the preservation of Lewis's health, "as well as the health of the persons under his command."[43] The directions, a few of which follow, present an interesting lesson in personal hygiene as it obtained at the beginning of the last century:

When you feel the least indisposition, do not attempt to overcome it by labor or marching. Rest in a horizontal position.

Unusual costiveness [constipation] is often a sign of approaching disease. When you feel it take one or more of the purging pills.

In difficult & laborious enterprises & marches, *eating sparingly* will enable you to bear them with less fatigue & less danger to your health.

Molasses or sugar & water with a few drops of the acid of vitriol [sulphuric acid] will make a pleasant & wholesome drink with your meals.

After having had your feet much chilled, it will be useful to wash them with a little spirit.

[43] L. H. Butterfield, ed., *Letters of Benjamin Rush,* 2 vols. (Philadelphia, 1951), II, 868.

Washing the feet every morning in *cold* water, will conduce very much to fortify them against the action of cold.

After long marches, or much fatigue from any cause, you will be more refreshed by *lying down* in a horizontal position for two hours, than by resting a much longer time in any other position of the body.[44]

Dr. Rush would have been pained to learn how many of these health rules Lewis and Clark disregarded. They ignored his injunctions to rest for two whole hours in a horizontal position with each indisposition and to wash their feet in cold water every morning. The idea of fasting to make walking less fatiguing held no appeal for them whatsoever, nor did using good liquor for washing cold feet. Also, we find no mention in any of the journals about that "pleasant and wholesome" drink compounded of sweetened water and sulphuric acid.[45]

During his stay in Philadelphia, Lewis spent $90.69 for drugs, lancets, forceps, syringes, and other medical supplies. He had prepared a list in advance and the length of it and inclusion of certain items, notably 50 dozen "Bilious Pills to Order of B. Rush," lead us to believe that Dr. Rush helped him to prepare it. He obtained some 30 different kinds of drugs all together. Those used most often on the journey were Peruvian bark, jalap, Glauber's salt, niter (potassium nitrate or saltpeter), tartar emetic, laudanum, calomel, mercurial ointment, and Rush's pills.

Thus equipped, the medical team of Lewis and Clark seemed prepared for almost any clinical contingency. Though Clark did not possess Lewis's knowledge of herb therapy, he did carry in his head (as did Lewis) the usual frontiersman's storehouse of medical information: how to set a broken limb or remove an imbedded bullet, how to cope with dysentery, croup, and a wide range of other ailments. Being often closer to disease and disaster than to doctors, he found it imperative to know about such things.

[13]

Jefferson took particular pleasure in sending Lewis to Dr. Benjamin Smith Barton (1766–1815), professor of botany at the University of Pennsylvania. Some ten years earlier at a meeting of the American Philosophical Society, Barton had read a paper in which he initially

[44] Jackson, *Letters*, 54–55.
[45] Paul Russell Cutright, "I gave him barks and saltpeter," *American Heritage*, XV, no. 1 (Dec., 1963), 60.

mentioned a plant until then known as *Podophyllum diphyllum*. "As I have not found it described by any authors, except Linnaeus and John Clayton, neither of whom had seen the flowers," Barton said, "and as it is, certainly, a new family genus, I take the liberty of making it known to the botanist by the name JEFFERSONIA, in honor of Thomas Jefferson, Esq., Secretary of State to the United States."[46] After retiring from public office, Jefferson took pains to see that *Jeffersonia diphylla* (twinleaf, in the vernacular) grew in his flower beds at Monticello.

Dr. Barton is today best known among biologists as the author of *Elements of Botany: or Outlines of the Natural History of Vegetables* (Philadelphia, 1803), the first textbook of botany written in the United States. This was one of the reference works Lewis took west with him, but it was not a gift from the author. In a memorandum still extant, we find that while in Philadelphia he purchased "1 Copy Bartons Bottony" and paid $6 for it.[47] But Lewis did leave Dr. Barton's home with a book under his arm, *The History of Louisiana* by Antoine Le Page du Pratz. Lewis carried this book with him to the Pacific and, back in Philadelphia again, returned it to its owner. That Barton had loaned it to Lewis is attested by an eye-catching inscription on the flyleaf written by Lewis. It reads: "D͏ͬ Benjamin Smith Barton was so obliging as to lend me this copy of Mons͏ͬ Du Pratz's history of Louisiana in June 1803. it has been since conveyed by me to the Pacific Ocean through the interior of North America on my late tour thither and is now returned to it's proprietor by his Friend and Ob͏ͭ Serv͏ͭ Meriwether Lewis. Philadelphia, May 9, 1807." This book is still in existence, as I recently reported.[48]

Lewis and Clark carried other natural history reference works: Richard Kirwan's *Elements of Mineralogy* (London, 1784); John Miller's *An Illustration of the Sexual System of Linnaeus,* Volume I (London, 1779), and *An Illustration of the Termini Botanici of Linnaeus,* Volume II (London, 1789); and a four volume dictionary which was probably *A New and Complete Dictionary of Arts and Science* commonly called, after the publisher, *Owen's Dictionary.*

Excepting the contribution of Du Pratz's *History* and a promise to supply "abstract queries" (VII, 224), it can only be conjectured as to other help Dr. Barton gave Lewis. As a teacher of natural history and

[46] Betts, *Jefferson's Garden Book,* 172.
[47] Jackson, *Letters,* 96.
[48] Paul Russell Cutright, "Lewis and Clark and DuPratz," *Bull. Missouri Hist. Soc.,* XXI, no. 1 (Oct. 1964), 31–35.

ardent collector of "botanicals," he was probably as well informed as anyone of his day on how best to preserve plant and animal specimens and may very well have instructed Lewis in current methods. It is possible that he attempted to provide him with "a greater familiarity with the technical language of the natural sciences," but the time for that, as we shall see, was short. Also, he could have shown Lewis how to prepare a bird-skin, but once again, so could Jefferson, who left a description of his method: "Make a small incision between the legs of the bird: take out the entrails & eyes, wipe the inside & with a quill force a passage through the throat into the body that the ingredients may find a way into the stomach & so pass off through the mouth. fill the bird with a composition of ⅔ common salt & ⅓ nitre pounded in a mortar with two tablespoonfuls of black or Indian pepper to a pound, hang it up by it's legs 8 or 10 weeks, & if the bird be small it will be sufficiently preserved in that time. if it be large, the process is the same, but greater attention will be necessary."[49]

A man of many talents, Barton spread them thinly, delving into a great many projects and completing few. Illness and premature death prevented his attaining certain important goals, a most regrettable case in point being his inability to edit and publish the scientific portions of the Lewis and Clark journals, a task which, as we shall see, he agreed late in life to undertake.

[14]

During his two years at the White House, with Jefferson as his mentor, Lewis served an important paleontological apprenticeship. When he called on Dr. Caspar Wistar (1761–1818) at the latter's home in Philadelphia, it is natural to suppose that the conversation quickly turned to fossils. Since Lewis was shortly to explore hitherto unknown parts of the continent, Wistar surely urged him to scan the Missouri River bluffs for exposed fossiliferous strata and, agreeing with Jefferson that live *Megalonyx* and mastodon might still inhabit western landscapes, to be constantly alert for any sign of these or related beasts. Reports reached Philadelphia about this time of the discovery by a Dr. William Goforth of a huge deposit of petrified bones and teeth of the mammoth at Big Bone Lick, near Cincinnati. It was probably at the prompting of Wistar that Lewis stopped at this site later in the year.

About the busiest man in Philadelphia during Lewis's stay there

[49] Betts, *Jefferson's Garden Book,* 95.

was Israel Whelan, whom John Adams had recently appointed Purveyor of Public Supplies. Even before Lewis arrived, Whelan had received a directive from the War Department to assist him in every possible way and with it, an accompanying draft for $1,000 with which to buy supplies for the Expedition. From early May well into June, Whelan worked overtime visiting retail and wholesale establishments where he purchased, from a list supplied by Lewis, a total of more than 200 different articles. Among them were 193 pounds of portable soup, three corn mills, 130 rolls of pigtail tobacco, 30 gallons of "Strong Spt. Wine," a wide assortment of Indian presents, 52 lead canisters for powder, medical and surgical supplies, mosquito netting, and oil-skin bags.[50]

When finally assembled, Lewis's supplies and equipment resembled a small mountain. He estimated the weight at 2,300 pounds. It would be a formidable job getting them to Pittsburgh by wagon where they would be loaded on a boat for the descent of the Ohio. A civilian army official, William Linnard, provided a driver for a team of five horses. When he arrived in Harper's Ferry to pick up Lewis's supplies there, he found more than he could carry so that another wagon had to be obtained.[51] From this point the conveyances made the long haul to Pittsburgh, travelling by way of Charlestown, Frankfort (now Ft. Ashby, West Virginia, just south of Cumberland, Maryland), Uniontown, and "Redstone old fort" (now Brownsville, Pennsylvania) (VII, 256).

I have been unable to determine the exact length of Lewis's stay in Philadelphia. He arrived there about May 8 and, three weeks later, wrote Jefferson that he expected to leave for Washington about June 6 or 7, so that he was there at least a full month, possibly a few days longer. We know that he was in Washington on June 19, the date on which he had written Clark inviting him to share command of the Expedition with him.

I have also been unable to find proof that Lewis while in Philadelphia visited the Philadelphia Museum, most often referred to as Peale's Museum, after its genial founder and proprietor (and celebrated artist), though there can be little doubt that he did. In 1802, the year before Lewis came to Philadelphia, Peale had moved his museum from Philosophical Hall (home of the American Philosophical Society) to the more spacious Independence Hall. Here it occupied the assembly room on the first floor, all of the second floor, and the tower rooms

[50] Jackson, *Letters*, 69–99.
[51] Jackson, *Letters*, 106.

above. By that time Peale and his son Rembrandt were able to exhibit some "200 stuffed animals, a thousand specimens of birds, 4000 specimens of insects, a collection of minerals, cabinets of serpents, fishes, etc. . . . The greatest curiosities were the famous Ulster County, N.Y. mastodon skeletons, dug from a marl-pit by Mr. Peale and joined together with infinite labor."[52]

Peale would figure prominently in the significant sequel to the Expedition, as would William Hamilton and Bernard McMahon. Hamilton was a well-known gardener of the time and owner of the estate, "Woodlands," and McMahon a prominent seed merchant. There is nothing to indicate that Lewis met either Hamilton or McMahon on his initial visit to Philadelphia.

[15]

Subsequent events suggest strongly that Lewis while in Philadelphia accomplished most of his primary objectives. In so far as his needs could then be foreseen, he outfitted the Expedition. Later, when the complement of men burgeoned from Jefferson's early estimate of 10 or 12 to 45, he added other supplies at Forts Massac and Kaskaskia and at St. Louis. It was no small task to anticipate all that he would need in the way of arms, food, clothing, camping paraphernalia, scientific instruments, and Indian presents for a party of still undetermined size that for an indefinite period of time would be out of touch with normal supply sources. This was true, even though he was experienced in military matters, had begun making lists months in advance, and had benefitted from "the most ample and hearty support that the government can give in every possible shape."[53]

Lewis's purchase of certain articles, such as portable soup, lead powder canisters, mosquito netting, oil-skin bags, and sheets of oiled linen, reflect remarkable foresight. The soup dispelled hunger when game failed. The lead canisters kept powder dry. Mosquito netting created effective barriers between men and hordes of blood-sucking, sleep-dispelling insects. Oil-skin bags excluded damaging moisture from valuable books and instruments. Large multipurpose sheets of oiled linen served as tents by night and boat covers or sails by day.

Lewis chafed under the problem of how much to purchase. For

[52] J. Thomas Scharf and Thompson Westcott, *History of Philadelphia*, 3 vols. (Philadelphia, 1884), I, 514.

[53] Jackson, *Letters*, 57.

example, was he obtaining sufficient powder? Would six papers of inkpowder be sufficient, or 500 rifle flints? He made mistakes. The three Fahrenheit thermometers he bought were all broken before he had crossed the Rockies and tobacco (except for a small cache at Shoshoni Cove) was exhausted before the party left Fort Clatsop. Lewis's most serious error, one that later gave him grave concern, was his failure to procure an adequate number of blue beads, in spite of the fact that he knew that they answered "all the purposes of money" and that the Indians coveted beads of this color above all others (VII, 237).

Additionally, in Philadelphia Lewis increased his facility in the use of navigational instruments and received advice calculated to draw his attention to "those objects only on which information is most deficient & desirable."[54] He received counsel on what instruments, reference books, and medical supplies would best serve his needs. He probably obtained instruction on current methods of preserving specimens. Above and beyond this, he lived daily in the company of the most distinguished scientists of the day: Patterson, Rush, Barton, and Wistar. As a result, Lewis must have left Philadelphia with quickened pulse, bounding enthusiasm, and heightened determination. Within a fortnight he would set out for uncharted parts of the continent where he would need a full measure of such attributes.

[54] Jackson, *Letters*, 18.

Potomac
to
Wood River

CHAPTER TWO

Meriwether Lewis served as Thomas Jefferson's private secretary for more than two years, from April, 1801, to July, 1803. I cannot find that previous writers have stressed the importance of this period to Lewis in extending his background knowledge of plants and animals and providing useful lessons in objective thinking and careful reporting. Jefferson would surely have seen to such matters, for he was a methodical man as well as the perennial student. He may actually have outlined a specific course of study for his protégé. If so, it becomes easier to comprehend the technical quality of Lewis's later descriptions of western plants and animals. As to Jefferson's competence to serve as Lewis's instructor, we have Dr. Barton's words for it that: "in the various departments of . . . botany and zoology, the information of this gentleman is equalled by that of few persons in the United States."[1]

Even if Lewis pursued no prescribed course of study, it was inescapable that much of the President's previously described enthusiasm for plants and animals rubbed off on him. Since he lived in the White House, he must have become almost a personal partner with Jefferson in the latter's deep-rooted attention to petrified bones, espousal of Linnaean nomenclature, addiction to note-taking on natural history and other themes, active participation in plant introductions, and untiring efforts to correlate seasonal data with periodic biological phenomena.

Lewis, too, while resident in the White House, had available to him at all times Jefferson's huge personal library, a veritable bonanza

[1] Betts, *Jefferson's Garden Book*, 172.

of scientific riches. Here he would have found volumes important to the explorer, such as Mark Catesby's and John Bartram's travels to the Carolinas, Georgia, and Florida, John Clayton's *Flora Virginica,* Alexander Mackenzie's account of his journey to the Pacific, and Linnaeus' taxonomic tomes. There is much to indicate that Jefferson recommended the last-mentioned to the close attention of his youthful amanuensis. As we have earlier reported, he carried west with him two Linnaean volumes on botany, and it seems most likely he also had one of the Swedish naturalist's books on zoology. As Donald Jackson has said, Lewis's later descriptions of western animals "are Linnaean; he mentions Linnaean class, genus and species names; he discusses his specimens with a proficiency that could only come from ready access to a work in zoology. If he does not have with him the portion of Linnaeus's *Systema Naturae* dealing with zoology, he must have one or more derived from it."[2] Above all, we must not lose sight of the fact that Jefferson had brought Lewis to Washington where he might supervise his preparation for leading the first government-sponsored scientific expedition to the West.

[2]

Lewis began his journey to the land of high plains and prairie dog towns on July 5, 1803. His leavetaking from the nation's capital was quiet; no crowds gathered to see him off. On the eve of his departure he wrote reassuringly to his mother: ". . . my absence will probably be equal to fifteen or eighteen months; the nature of this expedition is by no means dangerous. . . . I go with the most perfect preconviction in my own mind of returning safe and hope therefore that you will not suffer yourself to indulge in any anxiety for my safety."[3]

Lewis arrived at the burgeoning frontier town of Pittsburgh on July 15 and, one week later, advised Jefferson that the wagons from Harper's Ferry carrying his outfit had caught up with him. Soon afterwards he received Clark's letter of acceptance. Before leaving the White House, Lewis had conferred with Jefferson about a possible alternate in case Clark might be unable to share the leadership. They tentatively agreed on Lieutenant Moses Hooke, Assistant Military Agent in Pittsburgh. Now, with Clark's affirmative reply at hand, there was no further thought of what might otherwise have been the Lewis and Hooke Expedition.

[2] Jackson, "Some Books Carried by Lewis and Clark," 6.
[3] Jackson, *Letters,* 100.

Not all the news at the confluence of the Allegheny and Monongahela was so good. At an earlier date, Lewis had contracted with workmen there to construct a keelboat in which he would descend the Ohio
and, later, climb the Missouri. He had hoped to find the boat almost
ready for him. However, as he wrote Clark, the workmen were "most
incorrigible drunkards"[4] and had barely started construction. As things
turned out, the men continued to imbibe "Monongahela rye" and did
not complete the boat until the end of August. Creating further anxiety for Lewis, Pittsburgh was then in the middle of a prolonged drouth,
and it was a question whether the Ohio contained enough water to
float a large barge once it had been built. The statement that Sergeant
Gass supervised construction of this boat at the mouth of the Wood
River is false.

On August 30 Lewis wrote: "Left Pittsburg this day at 11^{ock} with a
party of 11 hands 7 of which are soldiers, a pilot and three young men
on trial they having proposed to go with me throughout the voyage."[5]
Since water in the Ohio was at a near record low, they made slow
progress. Time and again in days ahead, Lewis had to engage farmers
with their horses or oxen to snake the heavily laden boat over riffles. He
had hoped to be well up the Missouri when winter set in, but already
the leaves of buckeye, gum, and sassafras showed touches of red and
yellow, and local farmers had begun "to top ther corn and collect ther
fodder."[6] By taking the Ohio River from Pittsburgh to the Mississippi,
Lewis established the classic route soon to be followed by such other
naturalists as Thomas Say, Thomas Nuttall, and Maximilian.

Below the town of Wheeling, Lewis reported a great number of
passenger pigeons (*Ectopistes migratorius*) flying overhead following a
southeasterly course. He announced this event as casually as today's
observer might mention the passage of a flock of crows or blackbirds.
Farther along, near Marietta, Ohio (on September 11), he wrote:
". . . observed a number of squirrels swimming the Ohio and universally passing from the W. to the East shore they appear to be making to
the south; perhaps it may be mast or food which they are in serch of
but I should reather suppose that it is climate which is their object as I
find no difference in the quantity of mast on both sides of this river it

[4] Jackson, *Letters,* 125.
[5] Milo M. Quaife, ed., *The Journals of Captain Meriwether Lewis and Sergeant
John Ordway* (Madison, Wis., 1916), 31. Hereinafter referred to as "Ordway." As
Jackson (*Letters,* 125n) suggests, one of the young men may have been John Colter
and another George Shannon.
[6] Ordway, 40.

being abundant on both except the beach nut which appears extreemly scarce this season. the walnuts and Hickery nuts the usual food of the squirrell appears in great abundance on either side of the river . . . the squirrels swim very light on the water and make pretty good speed."[7]

In those days, before hunting radically reduced their numbers, gray squirrels (*Sciurus carolinensis*) were much more abundant than now and mass migrations a rather common occurrence. They continued up to about a hundred years ago, and the one Lewis witnessed may be regarded as typical. Lewis said that his dog, by jumping into the water from the boat and catching squirrels in his mouth, brought several to him. This dog, whose name appears to have been Scannon (or Scamon), journeyed to the Pacific and back and proved to be a popular as well as valuable member of the Expedition. "Of the new-foundland breed," Lewis had paid $20 for him and prized him highly for his gentleness and other commendable qualities.[8]

Lewis's companions on this trip down the Ohio undoubtedly saw squirrels swimming the river, but it is highly unlikely that any of them noted that they followed a course from west to east, swam "light on the water," and made good speed. Here we have the first recorded evidence of his competence as an observer.

Lewis and his party arrived at Cincinnati on September 28. Here he made the acquaintance of Dr. William Goforth, local physician and amateur paleontologist previously alluded to, who had recently returned from excavating the deposit of fossil remains at nearby Big Bone Lick. Dr. Goforth allowed Lewis to examine specimens recently unearthed, these including "mammoth" bones and several "grinders of the anamal supposed to be an Elephant from their affinity to the teeth of that anamal." When Lewis expressed a desire to visit Big Bone Lick, Dr. Goforth acceded to his request and even went so far as to tell him he was welcome to whatever bones he might find there. We know that his visit was successful, for on his return, he boxed up a collection of specimens and shipped them to Jefferson.

Before leaving Cincinnati, Lewis wrote Jefferson. The big question in his mind was whether certain flat, scythe-shaped tusks found at the site with "acknowledged tusks of the mammoth," belonged to that animal or another. He had discovered many specimens of both and was thus in a position to make comparisons. Before he expressed his own views about their "homogeniallogy," however, he told the President he

[7] Ordway, 42.
[8] Ordway, 42, 48, 198, 202.

wanted to describe the two forms "in order, Sir, that you may from thence draw your own inferences, and make your own deductions."[9] He then proceeded with his descriptions, lengthily and technically detailed, after which he gave it as his conviction that the flat, scythe-shaped tusks belonged to the mammoth and not to an elephant. He arrived at this verdict, of course, long before scientists had knowledge of at least four different species of elephant—mammoth, mastodon, imperial, and Columbian—that once ranged far and wide over American landscapes.

To anyone who reads this letter—perhaps the longest Lewis ever wrote in his life—it is evident that he had assimilated a sizable body of information about fossils from the combined teachings of Jefferson and Wistar. Two years earlier, for instance, he would have known nothing at all about "homogeniallogy." Unfortunately, the bones consigned to Jefferson from Big Bone Lick failed to reach their destination.[10]

The assembling of men who would constitute the Corps of Discovery—the name Lewis and Clark often applied to the party of the explorers—had its inception at Pittsburgh with the acceptance of the "three young men on trial." At Cincinnati Lewis wrote Clark that he had selected provisionally two men (presumably two of the three just mentioned) who would, he thought, "answer tolerably well."[11] Meanwhile Clark had been rounding up some of "the best woodsmen and hunters" in his part of Kentucky. He threw himself wholeheartedly into this endeavor, for it was his first opportunity to make a contribution to the progress of the Expedition. "A judicious choice of our party is of the greatest importance to the success of this vast enterprise," he commented to Lewis when writing him.[12] The men Clark chose would in time become known as "the nine young men from Kentucky." First and last they made quite a dent in American history.[13]

The other men chosen to complete the composition of the Corps came from South West Point, an army post on the Clinch River near Knoxville, Tennessee; from Fort Massac, on the Illinois side of the Ohio about eight miles below Paducah, Kentucky; from Fort Kaskaskia, on the eastern bank of the Mississippi some 50 miles downriver from St. Louis; and from St. Louis and environs. The Secretary of War had already instructed commanding officers of the army posts just

[9] Jackson, *Letters,* 126–132.
[10] Jackson, *Letters,* 132n.
[11] Jackson, *Letters,* 125.
[12] Jackson, *Letters,* 118.
[13] Jackson, *Letters,* 425.

mentioned to detach any noncommissioned officers or privates in their outfits "disposed to join Capt. Lewis, whose characters for sobriety, integrity and other necessary qualifications render them suitable for such service."[14] Long before now, it is apparent, Jefferson's estimate of "ten or twelve chosen men" as adequate for the enterprise had been abandoned.

Clark and his recruits from Kentucky joined Lewis at Louisville, and the party then moved downstream to Fort Massac, reached on November 11. After taking on more recruits here, they proceeded to the mouth of the Ohio and then up the Mississippi to Fort Kaskaskia. At this place, Lewis advised Jefferson, he had selected enough men to complete his party.[15] Obviously, he did not know then that he would add more at St. Louis.

It was December 12 when the Corps arrived at the mouth of the Dubois (Wood) River, Illinois, 18 river miles above St. Louis and directly across the Mississippi from the entrance of the Missouri. Here they soon established winter quarters. The location was "as comfortable as could be expected in the woods, & on the frontier," Clark wrote. A well-timbered bottom fringed the river, and back of it was a countryside "butifull beyond discription."[16] The passage of some 160 years has brought almost unbelievable changes to the geography of this particular site. According to a reliable informant: "The mouth of the Missouri has moved south $4\frac{1}{2}$ miles, the mouth of the Wood River has veered north .6 of a mile, and the channel of the Mississippi has shifted eastward about .6 of a mile."[17]

[3]

"Fixed on a place to build huts," wrote Clark on December 13. "Set the Men to Clearing land & Cutting Logs—a hard wind all day—flying clouds."[18] In this manner the Corps of Discovery began its stay of five months at Camp Dubois, as the Wood River cantonment is sometimes called. During these months Lewis spent most of his time in St. Louis, then a 40-year-old town of some 1,000 inhabitants, largely French. He

[14] Jackson, *Letters*, 103.
[15] Jackson, *Letters*, 145.
[16] Jackson, *Letters*, 164.
[17] Roy E. Appleman, "Lewis and Clark: The Route 160 Years After," *Pacific Northwest Quarterly*, 57, no. 1 (Jan., 1966), 8.
[18] Ernest Staples Osgood, ed., *The Field Notes of Captain William Clark 1803–1805* (New Haven and London, 1964), 3. Hereinafter cited as "Osgood."

busied himself purchasing supplies, selecting additional personnel (mostly French *engagés* to man the boats up the Missouri), and making the acquaintance of men who could supplement the meager amount of information he had been able to obtain thus far about the country beyond the Mississippi. He soon met and held discussions with some of the best-informed and most influential residents of St. Louis and environs, men like the Chouteau brothers, Auguste and Pierre, fur traders and merchants; Charles Gratiot, Swiss-born trader and brother-in-law of the Chouteaus; Carlos Dehault Delassus, Governor of Upper Louisiana; Antoine Soulard, Surveyor General; Captain Amos Stoddard, who had been designated commissioner by Jefferson to receive the newly acquired territory on its transfer to the United States; John Hay, postmaster of Cahokia; and Manuel Lisa, fur trader who would soon build the first trading post on the Yellowstone River.

In due course, Lewis met men who had personal experience of the land to the west, who had traded with Indians on the Osage River and had trapped along the Nemaha and Platte. A few of these, including two or more who joined the Corps, had wintered with tribes above the Platte. These men provided Lewis with first-hand knowledge of what he could expect to find when he himself ascended the Missouri.

At Jefferson's request, Lewis performed other duties while in St. Louis. He obtained and forwarded information about the population, agriculture, minerals, and plants and animals of Louisiana. He arranged for Pierre Chouteau to conduct a delegation of Indian chiefs to Washington. And on March 10, 1804, he witnessed the transfer of Louisiana to the United States and with others signed the official papers of cession.

Though Clark initially played no role in the high-reaching drama now assuming form, he made up for lost time at Camp Dubois. In addition to supervising construction of winter quarters, he took charge of drilling, seasoning, and disciplining his recruits and of laying in provisions for present and future use. He schooled himself—after introductory training by Lewis—in the use of those instruments necessary for taking celestial observations and calculating position. He wound the chronometer each day at noon and regularly took the altitude of the sun's lower limb with quadrant or sextant. He assumed the role of chief meteorologist, making temperature readings four or five times daily from a thermometer hung "on the N. side of a large tree in the woods" (VI, 165ff.). He recorded, too, amounts of rain and snowfall, directions of prevailing winds, and thickness of floating or stationary ice in the rivers. In attention to these matters, Jefferson himself could not have been more conscientious.

Throughout his stay on the Wood River, Clark kept a record of daily events. The existence of this record, now referred to as the "Dubois Journal," was unknown until its discovery in a St. Paul, Minnesota, attic in 1853. An extremely important find, it has since been capably edited by Ernest Staples Osgood and published by Yale University Press. Except for a few random notes and letters, it contains the only information available on what took place at Camp Dubois during the winter preceding Lewis and Clark's ascent of the Missouri. Without this journal, for example, we would have no knowledge of Clark's serious attempts to gauge how far the Expedition had to travel to reach the Mandan villages, the Rockies, and the Pacific. It was pure guess work beyond the Mandans, of course, and Clark greatly underestimated the distances. For instance, he calculated 900 miles from the Mandans to the Rockies (Continental Divide), whereas the party actually travelled nearer 1,500; and his figure for the distance from the Mississippi to the Pacific was short by almost 1,000 miles. His notes prove, too, that he believed the Corps, once under way the following spring, could reach the eastern slopes of the Rockies before winter compelled them to halt, and that the next year they could complete the journey to the coast and return to St. Louis. That he was wrong detracts not at all from his persistent efforts to look ahead and to collect all possible data so that, as he said, "we may make just Calculations, before we set out."[19]

In his diary for January 7, 1803, Clark wrote, "I drew a Map for the purpose of Correcting from the information which I may get out of the Countrey to the N.W."[20] Was this Clark's initial attempt at mapmaking? Possibly so, since we have no report of an earlier one. In 1961 Donald Jackson discovered a new map which may be a copy; in any event, it is the earliest known cartographic product of the Lewis and Clark Expedition.[21]

I have been unable to find any evidence to substantiate claims that Clark possibly had previous experience and tutoring in the art of cartography. Yet, before many months elapsed, he produced a large final map of the great land area between the Mississippi and the Pacific that today is recognized as "a major contribution to the geographic

[19] Jackson, *Letters*, 164.
[20] Osgood, 16.
[21] Donald Jackson, "A New Lewis and Clark Map," *Bull. Missouri Hist. Soc.*, XVII, no. 2 (Jan., 1961), 117–132.

knowledge of Western North America,"[22] and he himself is acclaimed a near cartographic genius. Clark's talents in this direction did not reveal themselves until he sat down in mid-winter at Camp Dubois and with paper and pen made a map of the country of open sky stretching endlessly to the west. From then on, he produced many more, the majority of which have found sanctuary in the Beinecke Library, Yale University. Collectively, they pay high tribute to his perseverance, skill, and execution of detail. His cartographical talent, it would appear, had thus far been dozing behind an unopened door of his subconscious, marking time until the proper stimulus brought it wide awake. Its emergence and subsequent development provide one of the many significant and unexpected highlights of the Expedition.

From the beginning, Jefferson and Lewis had sought all cartographic and geographic information available about the trans-Mississippi West. The success of the Expedition might hinge on it. As early as March, 1803, Albert Gallatin, Secretary of the Treasury, wrote Jefferson as follows:

I have requested Mr. King [cartographer Nicholas King] to project a blank map . . . which will give us the whole course of the Mississippi and the whole coast of the Pacific ocean within the same latitudes together with a sufficient space to the North to include all the head waters of the Port Nelson River. In this I intend to insert the course of the Mississippi·as high up as the Ohio from Ellicott's [map], the coast of the Pacific from Cook & Vancouver, the north bend of the Missouri & such other of its waters as are there delineated from the three maps of Arrowsmith & from that of Mackenzie, and the Rio Norte and other parts of the Missoury from Danville & Delisle.[23]

The idea of this map may have originated with Lewis. While still in Philadelphia he wrote Jefferson as follows: "You will receive herewith inclosed some sketches taken from Vancouver's survey of the Western Coast of North America; they were taken in a haisty manner, but I believe they will be found sufficiently accurate as to be of service in composing the map, *which Mr. Gallatin was so good as to promise he would have projected and compleated for me* will you be so obliging Sir, as to mention to Mr. Gallatin, that I have not been able to procure Danvill's map. The maps attached to Vancouver's voyage cannot be procured separately from that work, which is both too costly,

---

[22] Herman R. Friis, "Cartographic and Geographic Activities of the Lewis and Clark Expedition," *Jour. Wash. Acad. of Sciences,* 44, no. 11 (Nov., 1954), 351.

[23] Jackson, *Letters,* 27–28.

and too weighty, for me either to purchase or carry" (VII, 225; italics mine).

Whether King and Gallatin completed this map or not is conjectural. If so, Lewis may have started west with a remarkable composite combining salient features from maps of the most eminent cartographers and travellers of that time: two Americans, Nicholas King and Andrew Ellicott; two Frenchmen, Jean Baptiste d'Anville and Guillaume Delisle; and four Englishmen, Aaron Arrowsmith, Alexander Mackenzie, James Cook, and George Vancouver. In any case, his journals provide ample proof that he did carry maps of Arrowsmith, Mackenzie, Cook, and Vancouver, if no others, and that he had familiarized himself with topographic and toponymic details of each.

In November, 1803, William Henry Harrison wrote Jefferson that he was sending him "a Copy of the manuscript map of Mr. Evans who ascended the Missouri River by order of the Spanish Government much further than any other person."[24] One month later Lewis reported to Jefferson that he had obtained three maps from Antoine Soulard: one of the Osage River, one of Upper Louisiana, and a third of the Missouri from its mouth to the Mandan nation.[25] Soon afterwards Jefferson sent Lewis a map of "the Missouri as far as the Mandans . . . said to be very accurate, having been done by a Mr. Evans by order of the Spanish Government."[26]

It now appears that the map originating with Harrison, the third Soulard map, and the one sent by Jefferson to Lewis are one and the same. Though credited to Mr. Evans, it was actually the handiwork of James Mackay, Scottish trader and explorer, who probably possessed a greater fund of information about the Upper Missouri than anyone else then living.[27]

He had visited the Mandans as early as 1787, coming down from the Qu'Appelle River of Canada and in 1795, as head of a party of 30 men outfitted by the Missouri Company of St. Louis, had set out (with Spanish blessings) "to open commerce with those distant and Unknown Nations in the upper parts of the Missouri and to discover all the unknown parts of his Catholic Majesty's Dominions through the continent as far as the Pacific Ocean."[28] Mackay spent the winter

[24] Jackson, *Letters*, 140.
[25] Jackson, *Letters*, 155.
[26] Jackson, *Letters*, 163.
[27] The relationship of the Mackay map to the Harrison map was first discovered by Donald Jackson (see *Letters*, 135–136).
[28] A. P. Nasatir, ed., *Before Lewis and Clark*, 2 vols. (St. Louis, 1952), I, 97.

among the Omaha Indians whose celebrated chief, Blackbird, thwarted his farther progress. The following year, however, he did succeed in sending his lieutenant, John Evans, a Welshman who had come to the United States in search of the Welsh Indians, on up the river to the Mandans with whom he spent the winter of 1796–97. From the geographic information Evans brought back, Mackay produced a map of the Missouri (the one previously referred to) which he turned over to Spanish authorities. Copies circulated, with the result that almost simultaneously three of them reached Lewis and Clark on the Wood River.

We cannot be certain as to just what maps Clark had available on January 7 when he sketched the country to the west in his original effort. Since he had no personal knowledge of the Missouri, he needed all the help he could get. Just three days later he was the recipient of a surprise windfall. Who should show up at Camp Dubois but James Mackay, "just returned from Surveying of some lands up the Missouras."[29] Regrettably, Clark reported nothing of what went on at this meeting, surely a most important one. One result may have been a revision of Clark's map then in preparation. In any event, Lewis and Clark made the greater part of their journey through terrain for which no maps were available, in particular the immensity of land between Fort Mandan and Columbia tidewater. Clark would shortly remedy that situation.

[4]

Jefferson had promised Clark a captain's commission. It was almost time for the Expedition to start up the Missouri when Lewis received a letter from the Secretary of War, who reported that circumstances prevented him from commissioning Clark as a captain in the Corps of Engineers. The best he could do, he said, was a lieutenancy in the Corps of Artillerists.[30] Lewis, then in St. Louis, forwarded Dearborn's letter to Clark with this note: "I send you herewith enclosed your commission accompanyed by the Secretary of War's letter; it is not such as I wished, or had reason to expect; but so it is—a further explanation when I join you. I think it will be best to let none of our party or any other persons know anything about the grade, you will observe that the

[29] Osgood, 16.
[30] Jackson, *Letters,* 172.

grade has no effect upon your commission, which by G—d, shall be equal to my own."[31]

Thus began a deception that—at least to many persons—has lasted to this day, namely, that Clark held a captain's commission. The privates and noncoms under him invariably addressed him as Captain Clark, and when the story of the Expedition finally appeared in 1814, it was titled *History of the Expedition Under the Command of Captains Lewis and Clark.* We know nothing of Clark's immediate reaction to the lieutenancy. Several years later, however, he told Nicholas Biddle: "I did not think myself very well treated as I did not get the appointment which was promised me."[32]

At about this same time Lewis received more felicitous news. "I enclose you a letter [Jefferson wrote] which I believe is from some one on the part of the Philosophical society. They have made you a member."[33] Not then, or later, did this prestigious organization so honor William Clark.

[5]

As time drew near for the explorers to test their strength against that of the mud-laden flow of the Missouri, Lewis and Clark made last-minute preparations. They bought "artecles which may be wanting," these including five barrels of pork, five barrels of flour, 25½ bushels of lyed corn (hominy), and several gallons of "Woodsfords whiskey 1 Dol. pr. Gal."[34] They built lockers and benches for the keelboat. They parched large quantities of corn to be converted into meal. They melted 200 pounds of tallow with 50 pounds of hog's lard which, after cooling, they stored in small whiskey kegs. All comestibles—pork, lard, beans, dried apples, coffee, sugar—were packaged and then stowed away in designated places on one or another of the boats. Space was at a premium.

Lewis sent two boxes of specimens to Jefferson, the first in March and the other in May. These contained minerals, a horned toad (*Phrynosoma cornutum*) and slips of "the *great* Osages *Plums* [*Prunus* sp.] and *Apples* [Osage orange, *Maclura aurantiaca*]." They constituted the first shipment of natural history specimens by Lewis to Jefferson from west of the Mississippi. In an accompanying letter, he contrib-

[31] Jackson, *Letters,* 179.
[32] Jackson, *Letters,* 571.
[33] Jackson, *Letters,* 166.
[34] Jackson, *Letters,* 175–176.

uted a short description of the Osage orange. The slips (cuttings),
he said, came from trees owned by Pierre Chouteau, who had introduced them from an Osage Indian village 300 miles to the west.
The tree itself was much like that of the common black haw, though
less branched, and growing to a larger size, as much as 30 feet. Thorns
covered the smaller branches. The fruit, of an "exquisite odour" when
mature, was "the size of the largest orange, of a globular form, and a
fine orange colour. . . . So much do the savages esteem the wood of this
tree for the purpose of making their bows, that they travel many
hundred miles in quest of it."[35] This apparently was Lewis's initial
description of a plant then new to science.

The Corps of Discovery as assembled at Camp Dubois numbered
45 men.[36] There were actually two contingents: one, a group of temporary hands, and the other, the main body. The former consisted of 16
men (a corporal, six soldiers and nine professional rivermen or *engagés*) hired to perform much of the strenuous manual labor of working
the boats upstream, to return the keelboat the following spring and, if
need be, to help repel Indian attack. The latter, the permanent hard
core of the Expedition, consisted of 29 men: the two captains, an
interpreter, two French rivermen, Clark's Negro servant, York (who
would become the first of his race to cross the United States to the
Pacific), the nine young men from Kentucky, and 14 regular army
soldiers. The outfit as a whole was unique in one important respect. It
was, as previously mentioned, the first scientific exploring expedition to
the West sponsored by the United States government. Others would
soon follow.

In choosing men for the Corps, Lewis and Clark had insisted on
unmarried men who were accustomed to the woods, good hunters and
stout of body. Even before Lewis left Pittsburgh, he received a letter
from Clark which said: "Several young men (Gentlemens sons) have
applyed to accompany us, as they are not accustomed to labour and as
that is a verry essential part of the services required of the party, I am
causious in giveing them any encouragement."[37] Private Alexander

[35] Jackson, *Letters*, 170–171.
[36] The count of 45 is that of Nicholas Biddle, also of Coues. Sergeant Floyd
(VII, 4) wrote, "Serguntes and 38 working hands." Whitehouse's count (VII, 30)
is the same as Floyd's. Gass says, "43, including Captain Lewis and Captain Clarke"
in Patrick Gass, *A Journal of the Voyages and Travels of a Corps of Discovery,
under the Command of Capt. Lewis and Capt. Clarke of the Army of the United
States,* ed. David McKeehan (Ross and Haines, Minneapolis, 1958), 12. Hereinafter cited as "Gass."
[37] Jackson, *Letters*, 113.

Willard apparently was no "gentleman's son." In his old age he allegedly enjoyed telling how "his fine physique enabled him to pass the
inspection for enlistment in the expedition" at the same time that more
than one hundred others failed it.[38]

Time would prove that the commanding officers had chosen their
men wisely. In their interpreter, a half-breed named George Drouillard
(consistently referred to in the journals as "Drewyer"), they had a man
of unusual worth because of his facility with sign language and his
acknowledged skill as hunter and all-around woodsman; next to Lewis
and Clark, he was unquestionably the most valuable member of the
party. They had found him at Fort Massac, where he signed on at $25 a
month. In their sergeants, Charles Floyd, Nathaniel Pryor, John Ordway, and Patrick Gass, they had officers who could be counted on to
handle assignments diligently and efficiently. It was Ordway who assumed command on those rare occasions when both Lewis and Clark
were absent from the rest of the party. Gass, a skilled carpenter, could
build anything from a dugout canoe to a stockade. The worth of
Private John Shields to the Expedition may be gauged from Lewis's
description of him as "an artist in repairing guns, accoutrements, &c."
(VII, 358). He was one of the nine young Kentuckians selected by
Clark, as were Privates Reuben and Joseph Field, "two of the most
active and enterprising young men" of the Corps. The Field brothers
would play important roles in many of the most "dangerous and
difficult scenes of the voyage, in which they uniformly acquitted themselves with honor" (VII, 358).[39] Peter Cruzatte, son of an Omaha
squaw, proved to be efficient in handling both boats and fiddle, each
accomplishment contributing to the success of the Expedition. Cruzatte, too, provided useful information in the early weeks of the journey
because he had previously spent two winters among Indians near the
mouth of the Platte.[40] Only two of the permanent contingent, John
Newman and Moses Reed, failed to live up to what was expected of
them and had to be cut from the party.

[38] Olin D. Wheeler, *The Trail of Lewis and Clark, 1804–1806,* 2 vols. (New
York, 1904), I, 122.

[39] The "9 young men from Kentucky" appear to have been Sergeants Charles
Floyd and Nathaniel Pryor and Privates William Bratton, John Colter, Reuben
Field, Joseph Field, George Gibson, George Shannon, and John Shields. See
Jackson, *Letters,* 118.

[40] Ordway, 100. ". . . we are told by one of our French Bowman that he was 2
years up or on this River [Platte]." This Frenchman was probably Cruzatte. See also
Osgood, 11.

[6]

In his instructions to Lewis and Clark, Jefferson, as earlier mentioned, stressed the extreme importance of daily records. "Several copies of these," he insisted, "should be made at leisure times & put into the care of the most trustworthy of your attendants, to guard by multiplying them, against the accidental losses to which they will be exposed. A further guard would be that one of these copies be written on the paper of the birch, as less liable to injury from damp than common paper" (VII, 248).

Lewis and Clark made no attempt themselves to make several copies. It was difficult enough to make one, particularly at the close of a long day when the burden of fatigue was added to enervating heat or numbing cold and, commonly, the irritating presence of mosquitoes. Instead, they enjoined their noncommissioned officers to keep diaries and apparently recommended this task to privates. Detachment orders of May 26, 1804, signed by Lewis and Clark, read as follows: "The Sergts. . . . are directed each to keep a separate journal from day to day of all passing occurrences, and such other observations on the country &c as shall appear to them worthy of notice" (I, 33).

At a later date, Lewis wrote Jefferson, "We have encouraged our men to keep journals, and seven of them do so, to whom in this respect we give every assistance in our power."[41] Since Lewis and Clark kept journals too, the total, of course, adds up to nine. It is small wonder that someone has referred to this party as "the writingest crew" on record.

Six journals are extant and have been published: the two by Lewis and Clark, three by Sergeants Floyd, Gass, and Ordway, and one by a private, Joseph Whitehouse. Presumably Sergeant Pryor kept one, since he had been ordered to do so, but to date it has not come to light. In 1806 a prospectus announced the forthcoming publication of Private Robert Frazer's journal. It did not appear, and all subsequent efforts to locate it have failed. That leaves a ninth journal completely unaccounted for. The surmise that Private George Shannon wrote it does not appear to hold up. Later, when Nicholas Biddle was editing the account of the Expedition, he referred to the journals of Sergeants Gass and Ordway, but even though Shannon assisted Biddle in that work, Biddle had nothing to say about a diary by that young man.

[41] Jackson, *Letters*, 232.

Of the six published journals, only three may be regarded as complete, those by Clark, Ordway, and Gass. There are conspicuous, unaccountable gaps in that by Lewis, Floyd's ended abruptly on August 18, 1804, just before his death on the 20th, and Whitehouse's terminated on November 6, 1805. (Just recently, however, another segment of Whitehouse's journal has been discovered which extends it from November 6 until late March, 1806.)

Needless to say, these published journals bulge with information, the fruits of close, continued attention to daily events and observations. Paraphrasing somewhat the words of Elliott Coues: "The more closely they are scrutinized, in the light of our present knowledge, the more luminous they appear. The severest tests which contemporary criticism can apply serve mainly to develop their strength and worth."[42] Theodore Roosevelt, an explorer of stature himself, was impressed with the fact that "Few explorers who saw and did so much that was absolutely new have written of their deeds with such quiet absence of boastfulness, and have drawn their descriptions with such complete freedom from exaggeration."[43]

[7]

As winter slowly gave way to spring, the eyes of the explorers turned more often in the direction of the ungoverned flood of the Missouri rushing down from the unknown mountains and high plains of the West. They speculated on what they would find and what lay in store for them when finally they escaped their winter quarters and pushed their boats up this stream. Would they encounter the Welsh Indians that had thus far eluded John Evans? Would they discover giant animals such as the mammoth and *Megalonyx*? Sergeant Gass had it on good authority that they were "to pass through a country possessed by numerous, powerful and warlike nations of savages, of gigantic stature, fierce, treacherous and cruel; and particularly hostile to white men." He assured the reader, however, that "the determined and resolute character" of the men and the confidence pervading all ranks "dispelled every emotion of fear."[44]

Like other men who begin long journeys of indeterminate length and doubtful outcome, they wrote valedictory notes to parents and

[42] Coues, I, vi.

[43] Hermann Hagedorn, ed., *Memorial Edition of the Writings of Theodore Roosevelt*, 24 vols. (New York, 1923), XII, 362.

[44] Gass, 12.

friends. At least one such letter has survived. On April 8, 1804, Sergeant Ordway wrote in part:

Honored parents: I now embrace this opportunity of writing to you some more to let you know where I am and where I am going. I am well thank God and in high spirits. I am now on an expedition to the westward, with Capt. Lewis and Capt. Clark, who are appointed by the President of the United States to go on an expedition through the interior parts of North America. We are to ascend the Missouri River with a boat as far as it is navigable and then to go by land, to the westward ocean, if nothing prevents. . . . We expect to be gone 18 months or two years. We are to Receive a great Reward for this expedition, when we Return. I am to Receive 15 dollars pr. month and at least 400 ackers of first Rate land, and if we make Great Discoveries as we expect, the United States has promised to make us Great Rewards more than we are promised. . . . I have Recd. no letters Since Betseys yet, but will write next winter if I have a chance, Yours, &c.

JOHN ORDWAY Sergt. (VII, 298)

Wood River to Kansas

CHAPTER THREE

On the morning of May 14, 1804, where the Wood River falls into the Mississippi, the temperature at sunrise stood at 42°. A gentle breeze blew in from the southwest. An overcast sky threatened rain. To the established residents of this part of the country, the farmers, blacksmiths, and shopkeepers, it was just another day. They would be at their accustomed jobs of planting crops, shoeing horses, and opening tavern doors. To the group of "robust helthy hardy young men" (I, 7) comprising the Corps of Discovery, it was a day of excitement and expectancy. They were set to abandon Camp Dubois, launch their boats, and strike out for "the mountains of rock which rise up in the West."[1]

"I determined [Clark wrote] to go as far as St. Charles a french village 7 leags. up the Missourie, and wait at that place until Capt. Lewis could finish the business in which he was obliged to attend to at St. Louis and join me by land from that place 24 miles; By this movement I calculated that if any alterations in the loading of the Vestles or other Changes necessary, that they might be made at St. Charles. I Set out at 4 oClock P.M. in the presence of many of the neighbouring inhabitants" (I, 16).

Other journalists of the Corps picked up their pens on this same date. Wrote Sergeant Floyd: "the party consisted of 3 Serguntes and 38 working hands which manned the Batteow [keelboat] and two Perogues" (VII, 4).

[1] Nasatir, *Before Lewis and Clark,* II, 377.

Sergeant Ordway, in writing of their departure, said, "One Gun shot."[2]

Private Whitehouse explained that the gun fired was a swivel and that the party "Set out in high Spirits for the western Expedition" (VII, 30).[3]

Sergeant Gass contributed a fairly obvious detail: the party crossed the Mississippi, he said, before it started up the Missouri.[4]

Thus, the Lewis and Clark Expedition began its epic of exploration and, in the ways indicated, the journalists wrote opening descriptions of daily events, each with different eyes seeing what the other had overlooked, recording what the other had slighted. And so it would continue. Therein lay a primary strength of the parallel accounts.

Unfortunately we have no day-to-day account of events by Lewis for the first months of the trip, specifically from May 14, 1804, to April 7, 1805. Historians disagree on whether he wrote one or not. Reuben Gold Thwaites, for example, said: "there appears to be no doubt that he regularly kept a diary" (I, xxxv). He and others have based their beliefs on the fact that seeming fragments of such a journal exist and that these fragments match the journals in format and other respects.[5] They assert, too, that it is inconceivable that Lewis would not have kept a journal when specifically ordered by Jefferson to do so. Other historians, taking the opposite position, are puzzled by the fact that there are two additional lengthy hiatuses in Lewis's journal, one from August 13, 1805, through December of that year, and the other from August 13, 1806, to the conclusion of the journey on September 23. They are perplexed by other related matters, too; but I will delay consideration of them until more suitable moments present themselves.

The explorers travelled in three boats, presumably the same in which they had descended the Ohio: a keelboat or batteau 55 feet long which carried one large square sail and 22 oars, and two smaller craft, pirogues, one of six and the other of seven oars. The former pirogue was painted white and the latter red. These were large dugout canoes, doubtless cottonwood.[6] One writer in describing dugouts has said,

[2] Ordway, 79.

[3] Lewis and Clark apparently carried four swivels, two on the keelboat and one on each of the pirogues. These weapons were small cannon that could be turned (swivelled) in any direction.

[4] Gass, 11.

[5] For these fragments see Thwaites, I, 17, 33–35, 150–154, 253–259.

[6] On Feb. 23, 1805, weather records of Lewis and Clark state, "got the poplar perogue out of the ice." See Thwaites, VI, 183.

"sometimes these boats were made with a square stern and were then called pirogues."[7] We find no evidence, however, that the Lewis and Clark pirogues were so constructed.

Two days of rowing and sailing brought the Expedition 21 miles up the Missouri to the small town of St. Charles, peopled then by some 450 inhabitants. On May 20 Lewis arrived, accompanied by Captain Amos Stoddard, Auguste Chouteau, and other friends. The next afternoon at three o'clock the Corps moved upstream, its future as unpredictable as the river whose current they now had to master. Four days later they passed a tiny French village, La Charette, the last white settlement on the river. It would be more than two years before most of the party would again see a civilized habitation.

On June 26, five weeks after leaving St. Charles, the explorers arrived at the mouth of the Kansas (Kaw) River, the future location of Westport Landing and Kansas City. They had travelled more than 300 long, tedious, contrary miles, averaging about 10 daily.

During this first leg of the journey, the majority of the men were fully occupied with the boats fighting the Missouri current. A few others, more experienced with the rifle, spent their time hunting and keeping an eye out for chance parties of Indians. Lewis and Clark, when not themselves hunting or helping with the boats, devoted their time to surveying, reading thermometers, establishing latitude and longitude, and noting the physical features of the land. Intermittently, Lewis botanized, took stock of indigenous animals and minerals, and assembled obtainable data on Indians known to inhabit this area. Thus the immediate tasks of the explorers fell into three broad, general categories: (1) handling the boats, (2) bolstering the Expedition's larder, and (3) collecting technical data. This pattern, early set, continued, with minor emendations, throughout most of the journey.

[2]

Lewis and Clark at once established a policy, rarely broken, that one of them would stay with the boats at all times. Navigational operations might require instant decisions. As things turned out, Clark spent more time on the water than Lewis, and this arrangement seems to have come about quite naturally without prior agreement. Lewis preferred the freedom and solitude of the river banks and was the better hunter

[7] H. M. Chittenden, *History of Early Steamboat Navigation on the Missouri,* 2 vols. (New York, 1903), I, 92.

and naturalist. Clark had more of a feel for the river, took quickly to surveying and map-making, and relished the companionship of the boatmen. Though nominally in charge of navigation, Clark left the actual routine operation largely in the capable hands of Peter Cruzatte who, having ascended the Missouri on previous occasions, had a ready knowledge of its currents, banks, and sandbars and how to cope with them.

The Missouri was a moody beast, at times docile, at others untamed. In weeks and months ahead, the explorers became familiar with every caprice. For instance, there was no predicting the velocity of the stream. One day Private Whitehouse wrote: "the water run so rappid that the men of the french [red] peirogue Could not make headway by Roeing or poleing they had to jump out and push her through the water" (VII, 37). The wind was equally capricious. Near the present town of New Frankfort, they had to lay by all day on account of its stiffness.

On June 15 Clark wrote: "Set out early and had not proceeded far e'er we wheeled on a Sawyer which was near injuring us verry much" (I, 49). The Missouri often hid entire trees in its capacious bosom, leaving their concealed branches to bob up and down with the current. Such were sawyers. Under the influence of an uncertain current, they could spring up at any time or place, completely frustrating efforts of the most alert mariner.

The instability of the Missouri banks presented the unwary traveller with his greatest hazard. Consisting of fine, powdery, alluvial soil, they crumbled when struck, and undermined by rapid, onrushing water, many acres often collapsed and were carried away in a moment. When that happened, a passing boat ran the risk of being capsized and smothered under the weight of tons of earth. John James Audubon, who ascended the Missouri in 1843, viewed these cave-ins with wonder: "The banks are falling in and taking thousands of trees, and the current is bearing them away from the place where they have stood and grown for ages. It is an awful exemplification of the course of Nature, where all is conflict between life and death."[8]

Lewis and Clark had their first experience with these friable walls quite early in the journey, just above St. Charles. "We attempted," wrote Clark, "to pass up under the Lbd. [larboard] Bank which was falling in so fast that the evident danger obliged us to cross between the Starbd. Side and a Sand bar in the middle of the river" (I, 28).

[8] Wheeler, *The Trail of Lewis and Clark,* I, 144.

In their daily battles with the Missouri, the boatmen often broke oars, setting poles, and towing ropes (cordelles). One day when Sergeant Ordway steered the barge too close to the shore, a rope from the mast caught on a sycamore limb, snapping the mast in two. Such accidents, requiring repair, caused annoying delays. They lost the better part of a morning mending the mast and two whole days making 20 new oars and 600 feet of rope. Clark was proud of his boat crew. "I can say with Confidence," he declared, "that our party is not inferior to any that was ever on the waters of the Missoppie [*sic*]."[9]

During spring freshets the Missouri flood created inland pools where mosquitoes bred in tremendous numbers. As the party neared the Kansas, Ordway announced: "Got musquetoes bears [biers] from Capt. Lewis to sleep in."[10] This bier (or bar), Lewis tells us later, was "made of duck or gauze, like a trunk to get under" (II, 256). No accessory proved to be of more value to the men.

Lewis and Clark were not the only white men hitting the Missouri whitecaps in those days. Between St. Charles and the Kansas, they met at least eight rafts or canoes, each manned by a small crew of Spanish, French, or Indian traders. They had come downstream, some from the Osage and Kansas Rivers, others from the Platte and Upper Missouri. They carried precious loads of beaver fur, buffalo hides, and buffalo grease (tallow). One outfit transported $900 worth of pelts. A St. Louis trader, Regis Loisel, down from Cedar Island above the Great Bend (South Dakota), warned Lewis and Clark that they might expect trouble with the Sioux. One of the rafts carried Pierre Dorion, a French Creole who had lived for some 20 years on the Des Moines and James Rivers with the Yankton Sioux. When Lewis and Clark learned of his familiarity with the Sioux language, they persuaded him to go "back as far as the Sioux nation with a view to get some of their chiefs to visit the Presdt. of the United S." (I, 46).

The men remained injury-free and in relatively good health during this initial run of the journey. Happily the Missouri water did not then resemble today's devil's brew of topsoil, sewage, and industrial waste. They drank it neat, even though it contained "half a Comon Wine Glass of ooze or mud to every pint."[11] The regular and frequent admission of river water to gastro-intestinal tracts undoubtedly explains the occasional cases of mild dysentery reported. The numerous ulcers and boils

[9] Osgood, 53.
[10] Ordway, 87.
[11] Osgood, 60.

mentioned by Clark as plaguing the men resulted most likely from infected wounds incurred by contact with stones and snags when they had
to leap into the sullied water, as so frequently happened, to struggle
with the boats.

[3]

Lewis and Clark knew in advance that they could not always expect to
live off the land, certainly not in the beginning. There would be lean
periods as well as fat. As a result they carried 20 barrels of flour, 42 kegs
of pork, 14 barrels of parched corn meal, and lesser quantities of such
staples as sugar, coffee, salt, preserved dried apples, and biscuit. Of
course, too, they had the 193 pounds of portable soup Lewis had
purchased in Philadelphia. Their last opportunity to buy food occurred at La Charette where they obtained milk and eggs. Soon afterwards, Lewis and Clark issued an order:

"The day after tomorrow lyed corn and grece will be issued to the
party, the next day Poark and flour, and the day following indian meal
and poark, and in conformity to that rotiene provisions will continue
to be issued to the party until further orders . . . no poark is to be
issued when we have fresh meat on hand" (I, 33–34).

Obviously, the conservation of these staples assumed high priority.
When they were exhausted, the men might have to rely entirely upon
what their rifles could provide. They could not count on the Indian to
supply their needs—at least not yet.

Lewis and Clark regularly sent their best hunters afield, not only
to obtain fresh meat but also to keep a sharp lookout for casual parties
of marauding redskins. Their hunters were the "spyes" Clark referred
to now and then in his journal. Game, scarce in the vicinity of St.
Charles, gradually increased as the Expedition moved upstream. Just
below the entrance of the Kansas, Clark mentioned seeing large herds
of deer (the Virginia whitetail, *Dama virginianus*). On that same day
Clark, Lewis, and Reuben Field each killed one and George Drouillard two. Though most of the men in the party had been brought up
with guns in their hands, it was Drouillard who promptly demonstrated his superiority over the others as a hunter. For instance, on the
day they reached the Kansas, he bagged eight deer. Anticipating large
kills and the attending problem of returning the meat to camp, the
commanding officers had brought along two horses for such purposes.

The diaries reveal that from the Mississippi to the Kansas, hunters

killed at least 70 deer, a dozen or more black bear (*Ursus americanus*),
three wild turkeys (*Meleagris gallopavo*), one rabbit (*Lepus* sp.), one
woodchuck (*Marmota monax*), and one goose (probably Canada
goose, *Branta canadensis*). The figures may be regarded as fairly reliable, for the journalists could generally be counted on to mention game
animals brought in by the hunters. With appetites sharpened by hard
work, they had a keen interest in what the cooks would serve up at each
and every meal. They even expressed themselves on the condition of
the animal. If it was fat, and the meat therefore likely to be tender and
juicy, they spoke of it as "in good condition." If the reverse, it was
"pore" or "meager."

A few deer did not go far with 45 hungry men. If allowed, they
could easily have consumed four or five in a single day. On those rare
occasions when more meat was brought in than could be used immediately, it was a constant practice to jerk it. This process entailed cutting
flesh into thin slices and hanging it on scaffolding to dry in the sun or
near fires. If thoroughly dried and kept from moisture, jerky would
keep almost indefinitely. The explorers had their fill of it in months to
come.

What with flour, corn, and pork, often supplemented by roast
venison and thick bear steaks, the men did not experience hunger.
When opportunities offered, they relished such wild fruits as service
berries, strawberries, and raspberries, these being ripe and abundant in
places along the river in late May and early June. Only the French
hirelings complained about the *plat du jour,* saying they were accustomed to eating five or six times a day. They were "roughly rebuked for
their presumption."[12]

[4]

To Lewis and Clark, Jefferson's instructions amounted to an article of
faith. The enterprise they had undertaken would have been sterile and
meaningless without the more serious aspect of purposeful investigation. To that end they devoted their full cup of time and energy. They
daily assembled all possible information tending to increase the sum of
human knowledge, particularly in the fields of geography, meteorology, mineralogy, botany, zoology, and ethnology. As they journeyed
ever farther to the west, the tempo of their investigations and transcrip-
tion of notes increased accordingly. Their initial efforts in the above-

[12] Osgood, 59.

mentioned fields, if viewed closely, reveal a plan that with minor changes persisted throughout the full period of exploration. It is desirable, therefore, that we examine in some detail the nature and scope of Lewis and Clark's investigations from the Mississippi to the Kansas.

Geography

Clark assumed responsibilities for surveying the river, taking compass bearings, and determining courses and distances. He kept a record of measurements, appending them regularly to his summary of events for each day. For example, on May 22, he recorded courses and distances as follows:

S 60° W.	3	M^s	to a p^t	Lb^d Side
S 43° W.	4	M^s	to a p^t	on Stb^d Side
West .	3½	M^s	to a p^t	on Stb^d S. ps^d *Bonom*
S. 75° W.	7½	M^s	to a p^t	in Bend to Stb^d Side at the Mo. of
	18			Osage Womans R (I, 26) .

Clark assisted Lewis in making celestial observations. They followed Jefferson's charge to determine latitude and longitude "at all remarkable points on the river," these points being natural places of a durable kind such as rapids, islands, and, more particularly, mouths of larger streams. Between St. Charles and the Kansas, they attempted to establish their position at least half a dozen times. On one occasion, at the entrance of the Osage River, their efforts entailed unaccustomed time and labor. In order to get shots of the Pole Star, they had to fell all the trees on the point, this task taking them beyond midnight.

One instrument, the chronometer, required regular attention. Lewis wrote that he had to wind it every day at noon. Even so, he experienced trouble with it. "Her rate of going as ascertained by a series of observations made by myself for that purpose," he said, "was found to be 15. Seconds and 5 tenth of a second too slow in twenty four howers on *Mean Solar time*" (VI, 232). Such deviations continued and, of course, affected the accuracy of latitude and longitude, particularly the latter.

Knowledge of how to obtain latitude from the position of the sun had long been available to navigators, but equal skill in finding longitude had eluded them until recently. For determining the latter they usually carried a chronometer, an accurate clock set at Greenwich time. Once they had established local time by the sun, the difference between that and Greenwich time provided the longitude. However, since chronometers were often unreliable, they also employed astronomical methods. One, the most accurate, was to measure the angle between the moon and the sun or a fixed star, and another to determine the time of eclipse of Jupiter's satellites. Both required difficult calculations and the use of astronomical tables.

From accumulated data provided by compass, chronometer, and other instruments, Clark made maps, one after another, delineating topographic features on a winding course. This was the beginning of a series that spanned the continent, a series not improved upon until government surveys many years later.

Most of the streams falling into the Lower Missouri already had names—but not all. Lewis and Clark's topographic nomenclatural exercises, an important and continuing feature of their explorations, began early. On June 3, Clark wrote, "passed a Creek at 3 ms. which I call *Cupbord* Creek as it mouths above a rock of that appearance" (I, 38). On the next day, coming to another stream, he named it "Nightingale Creek from a Bird of that discription which Sang for us all last night, and is the first of the Kind I ever heard" (I, 38–39).[13]

In their westward march, Lewis and Clark named scores of rivers and creeks, as well as many other geographic landmarks heretofore unknown to mapmakers. Cupboard and Nightingale Creeks were the first. These streams entered the Missouri between Moreau and Cedar Creeks at a position close to present-day Jefferson City.

Though Lewis initially may not have written a diary, he did conscientiously jot down notes. During the following winter at Fort Mandan, he incorporated many of them into a report he called, "A Summary View of the Rivers and Creeks." Herein he described with scrupulous fidelity the principal Missouri affluents as far as Fort Mandan. These descriptions included information on such topics as navigability, sources, interlocking tributaries, and character of country watered by each stream. For instance, the Gasconade River "is not navigable . . . is of no great length, heads with the Marameg & St. Francis Rivers, the country watered by this river is generally broken, thickly covered with timber and tolerably fertile" (VI, 30–31). How very similar to Jefferson's descriptions of streams in his *Virginia Notes!*

[13] The bird in question is a mystery. Obviously it was not the nightingale (*Luscinia megarhynchos*), since the range of this Old World bird does not extend to the United States. Coues (I, 14) suggests the cardinal (*Richmondena cardinalis*), since at that time it was often referred to as the "Virginia nightingale." However, the song of this bird should have been familiar to both Lewis and Clark. When describing the western tanager (Thwaites, V, 111), Lewis said its beak was like that of the Virginia nightingale.

Clark, too, wrote a paper about Missouri rivers and creeks. His differed from Lewis's in that it ran more to figures. The Grand Osage River, for example, was 397 yards wide, 133 miles from the Mississippi, and entered the Missouri three miles above Muddy River (VI, 56).

As we have said, Lewis and Clark continued their geographical studies uninterruptedly throughout the journey. They were the first real geographers of the trans-Mississippi West.

Meteorology

Lewis and Clark's weather records, instituted at Camp Dubois on January 1, 1804, were continued until the party returned to St. Louis almost three years later. They took temperature readings daily at sunrise and at 4 P.M. (until they broke their last thermometer), recorded direction of prevailing winds both morning and afternoon, and noted whether the day was clear or cloudy, rainy or snowy. In Jeffersonian manner, these weather records included much additional data coupling season with biological events. On June 11, for example, "many small birds are now setting. Some have young, the whipper Will Setting." Five days later, "The Wood Duck now have it's young, this Duck is abundant, and except one solitary Pelican and a fiew gees, these ducks were the only aquatic fowls we have yet seen" (VI, 174).[14]

Mineralogy

Jefferson had instructed Lewis and Clark to pay attention to "the mineral productions of every kind; but more particularly metals, limestone, pit coal, & saltpetre; salines and mineral waters" (VII, 249). Arrived at the Gasconade, Clark wrote: "on its banks are a number of saltpetre caves, and it is believed some mines of lead are in the vicinity."[15] The Salt River, which the party reached on June 6, had "So many Licks and Salt Springs on its banks that the water . . . is Brackish, one verry large Lick is 9 ms. up on the left Side the water of the Spring in this Lick is Strong as one bushel of the water is said to make 7 lb of good Salt" (I, 41). It was important to acquire this information because the pioneer farmer required salt for preserving meat and graining hides. If he moved to a new location, he was often prompted to settle down in the vicinity of a saline.

[14] Reflecting the undeveloped state of taxonomy in the U.S. at that time is the fact that a considerable number of well-known animals had not yet been technically described. For example, the whippoorwill did not receive a scientific name (from Alexander Wilson) until 1812.

[15] Coues, I, 10.

As Lewis and Clark moved on up the Missouri they had less and less to say about minerals. The discovery of an increasing number of new and extraordinary plants and animals and stirring experiences with Indians diverted their attention from such lackluster objects as coal, limestone, and lead ore.

Botany

During the five weeks the Expedition consumed in travelling upstream to the Kansas, the journalists said little about the lush vegetation spread to view along the banks of the Missouri. They actually referred to less than two dozen plants, mostly familiar trees such as oak, ash (the wood of which they used for oars), walnut, sycamore, and cottonwood. They did indicate that timber decreased the farther west they went, with heavy forest being supplanted gradually by open meadow and recognizable plants by unfamiliar ones. Near the entrance of the Osage, for instance, Clark reported that Lewis "went out into the woods & found many curious Plants & Srubs" (I, 37).

Proof that Lewis collected some of these curious plants is to be found in an original document he wrote now preserved by the American Philosophical Society. Herein he listed and described a number with reputed medicinal virtues. The yellowroot (*Hydrastis canadensis*), for instance, was a "Sovereign remidy for a disorder in this quarter called the soar eyes," and a species of wild ginger (*Asarum*) was "a strong stomatic stimelent" (VI, 143–144). Though not medicinal, the narrow-leaved willow (*Salix longifolia*) —"taken on the 14th of June" —benefited the explorers immediately. "The wood is white light and tough," Lewis said, "and is generally used by the watermen for *setting poles* in preference to anything else" (VI, 145–146).

After he had collected a packet of cottonwood seeds in the vicinity of La Charette, Lewis wrote: "this specimine is the seed of the Cottonwood which is so abundant in this country . . . this tree arrives at a great size, grows extreemly quick the wood is of a white colour, soft spungey and light, perogues are most usually made of these trees, the wood is not durable nor do I know any other valuable purpose which it can answer except that just mentioned" (VI, 142–143).

That statement is worth remembering. In months ahead Lewis would hold the cottonwood (*Populus deltoides occidentalis*) in higher esteem. In spite of its "soft spungey" wood, it would prove to be a determining factor in the success of the Expedition.

Unfortunately, the plant specimens collected by Lewis along the

Missouri below the entrance of the Kansas have not survived. Excepting those of Osage orange and *Prunus* sent to Jefferson from St. Louis,
they were the first collected by the Expedition.

Zoology

One reason for Jefferson's choice of Lewis to head the Expedition
was his ability to recognize whatever was new in the country through
which he would pass. The animals along the lower reaches of the
Missouri—deer, bear, turkey, and so on—were identical with those
frequenting Kentucky and Virginia woodlands. Lewis and Clark properly wasted no ink describing them. However, on May 31 just below
the mouth of the Osage River, they encountered a mammal hitherto
unknown to science. Wrote Clark: "Several *rats* of Considerable Size
was Caught in the woods today" (I, 37) . This was the eastern wood rat,
Neotoma floridana. It had, according to Lewis, "the distinguishing
trait of possessing a tail covered with hair like other parts of the body
. . . it is as large as the common European house rat or reather larger,
is of a lighter colour, the hair longer; and the female has only four tits
which are placed far back near the hinder legs" (IV, 114) . During
their journey to the Pacific and back, Lewis and Clark, of course,
discovered many animals new to science (see Appendix B) . We accord
space here to the wood rat because it was the first. If specimens of it
were preserved, they have failed to survive.

On the day the explorers first saw the Kansas, Clark wrote that
they had encountered "a great number of Parrot queets" (I, 59) .
Although more than 500 different species of typical parrots have been
described for the Western Hemisphere, only one, the Carolina paroquet, *Conuropsis carolinensis,* inhabited the eastern part of the United
States at that time. This handsome bird, bright green with yellow head,
the size of a mourning dove, ranged from Florida and Virginia to
Wisconsin and Colorado. It moved about in compact flocks often numbering hundreds. Lewis and Clark were the first to encounter this
colorful bird west of the Mississippi, and thus to extend its known
range. This event occurred long before the Carolina paroquet became
extinct and joined that spectral company which now includes such
other American avians as the great auk, the heath hen, and the passenger pigeon.

Lewis, of course, was the naturalist of the Expedition, as Clark was
its cartographer. Some observers have asserted that he was more botanist than zoologist, and another that the contributions made by the
Expedition in zoology "were remarkably slight when one considers the

scope of their geographical and ethnological contributions."[16] The journals of Lewis and Clark refute both allegations.

Ethnology

Lewis had obtained in Philadelphia, as we know, long lists of questions calculated to assist him in studies of the Indian. Even before leaving Camp Dubois and St. Louis, he and Clark, in meetings with men like Pierre Chouteau and James Mackay, had begun their inquiries. They acquired additional information from members of their own party and from Loisel and Dorion whom they met descending the river with peltries.

In their slow climb upriver to the Kansas, the explorers encountered no Indians except a small detached group of Kickapoos just above St. Charles and, a few days later, a party of six hunters whom they failed to identify. However, they discovered much evidence of the recent presence of other Indians. Knowing the tendency of the Indian to attack when least expected, Lewis and Clark regularly inspected arms, sent out flankers to reconnoitre, and at each stop day and night posted sentinels.

The Indians inhabiting the Lower Missouri basin at that time included such tribes as Grand Osage, Little Osage, Kansas, Missouri, Oto, Omaha, and Iowa. They all belonged to the great Siouan linguistic family, presumably spoke languages mutually intelligible, and shared similar customs. Until recently the Missouris had been most numerous, with their principal village situated on a broad plain just below the entrance of the Grand River. Ravages of smallpox and attacks by other tribes had so far reduced their numbers, however, that they had been compelled to flee north to the Platte River where they sought safety among the Otos. Lewis and Clark located the site of the old Missouri village on June 13. At other times and places, they found Indian mounds, rock drawings, and other abandoned village sites, all testifying to a much larger native population in this area in days gone by.

In their ethnological studies, Lewis and Clark seem to have depended initially on questions of their own rather than those supplied by Dr. Rush and others. These inquired into such matters as tribal names, total population, number of warriors, languages, trade centers, kinds of pelts supplied to traders, and principal streams on which tribes resided. Holding closely to these questions, Lewis and Clark determined, for example, that the Kansas Indians numbered about 1,300,

[16] Setzer, "Zoological Contributions of the Lewis and Clark Expedition," 357.

including some 300 warriors. Their annual return from beaver, otter, deer, buffalo, and other skins amounted to about $8,000 (at St. Louis prices). They lived up the Kansas River, were at war with all other tribes, spoke the Osage language, and cultivated corn and beans. In summation, Lewis and Clark wrote that: "their trade may be expected to increase with proper management. At present they are a dissolute, lawless banditti; frequently plunder their traders, and commit depredations on persons ascending and descending the Missouri river" (VI, 84–85).

In the months devoted to the long pull upstream to the Mandan villages, and during their subsequent stay at Fort Mandan, Lewis and Clark assembled similar data about some 50 other tribes inhabiting country through which they had passed. Clark wrote it all down, painstakingly and laboriously, on a large sheet of paper, 34½ by 27 inches, made of six smaller sheets pasted together. A remarkable document, it is now preserved in the archives of the American Philosophical Society. Lewis and Clark called it, "Estimate of the Western Indians." Published by Jefferson, it bore an awesome title: *A Statistical View of the Indian Nations Inhabiting the Territory of Louisiana and the Countries Adjacent to Its Northern and Western Boundaries.*

A Statistical View was the first published study of the Plains Indians and the first technical paper emanating from Lewis and Clark. Until it appeared, bringing the Kansas, Oto, Sioux, and other tribes squarely out upon the stage of American history, these aboriginals had been no more than names to the eminent scientists of the world.

It must be evident by now, though the Expedition is barely under way, that Lewis and Clark were much more than explorers and army officers. Inspired by a scientifically minded president, and by the fascination of a new world populated by strange animals and plants and by wild savages relatively untouched by any outside cultural influence, they were on their way to becoming keen-eyed observers, disciplined inquirers, and painstaking chroniclers.

Author's note: Because a primary goal of this work is to enumerate and emphasize the many discoveries—botanical, zoological, ethnological, and geographical—made by Lewis and Clark, I propose to summarize at the end of this and succeeding chapters those findings made during the period covered by the chapter, these to include (1) animals discovered new to science; (2) plants new to science; (3) plants collected that today comprise the Lewis and Clark Herbarium in the Academy of Natural Sciences of Philadelphia; (4) Indian tribes encountered; and (5) topographic features named and/or discovered. The plant and animal summaries will be brief since appendices, with fuller data, appear *post*.

SUMMARY OF DISCOVERIES

Animals New to Science[a]

EASTERN WOOD RAT. *Neotoma floridana* (Ord). (Thwaites, I, 37; IV, 114; Coues, I, 40n; Gass, 23). Originally described in 1818.

PLAINS HORNED TOAD. *Phrynosoma cornutum* (Harlan). (Thwaites, VII, 300). Described by Harlan in 1825. Specimens of this reptile were actually shipped by Lewis to Jefferson before the Expedition started up the Missouri.

Plants New to Science[b]

OSAGE ORANGE. *Maclura aurantiaca* Nuttall = *Toxylon pomiferum* Rafinesque. (Thwaites, VII, 295–297). Described by Rafinesque in 1817. Cuttings of this plant were sent by Lewis to Jefferson prior to the start of the Expedition.

Lewis and Clark Herbarium

OSAGE ORANGE. *Maclura aurantiaca* Nuttall. Collected by Lewis in the spring of 1804.

Indian Tribes Encountered[c]

Algonquian Linguistic Family: Kickapoo.

Topographic Features Named and/or Discovered[d]

Retragrade Bend (Thwaites, I, 28).
Cupboard Creek (Thwaites, I, 38) —— Rising Creek of today (Coues, I, 13n).
Nightingale Creek (Thwaites, I, 38).
Mast Creek (Thwaites, I, 39).
Lead Creek (Thwaites, I, 40).
Sand Creek (Thwaites, I, 40).

[a] For complete list of animals discovered by Lewis and Clark see Appendix B.
[b] For complete list of plants see Appendix A.
[c] Indian tribes encountered early in the journey were known. Later, as unknown tribes are encountered, we will so indicate.
[d] Subsequently, as with Indian tribes, we will indicate topographic features *discovered* by Lewis and Clark. Unless otherwise stated, the features named, such as Nightingale Creek, do not appear on modern maps.

Kansas to Niobrara

CHAPTER FOUR

Desiring to "recruit" the party, Lewis and Clark halted at the mouth of the Kansas for three days. In this period they sunned powder, hunted buffalo, repaired pirogues, dressed deer skins, took equal and meridional altitudes, and built a six foot high redoubt of logs and brush. Though reports had the Kansas Indians out on the plains, it was well to take precautions. Such "dissolute, lawless banditti" might show up unexpectedly, bent on a hair-lifting party.

The hunters returned to camp reporting that they had been unable to get within shooting range of buffalo they had seen. Already this magnificent animal (*Bison bison*), with its characteristic shaggy coat and high-arched shoulders, which once had roamed in great numbers as far east as the Alleghenies and occasionally beyond, had been driven back well beyond the Mississippi. Though Lewis and Clark encountered it here, they had to wait eight more weeks, until August 23, before they succeeded in killing one.

The Corps moved again on June 29, travelling north now instead of west, since the Missouri alters its course where the Kansas enters. The face of the country continued to change. More and more trees sought the river valleys, as though to escape a limitless expanse of wind-whipped grass. The cottonwood began to dominate willow, ash, and other trees. From a vantage point near present-day Leavenworth, Clark surveyed approvingly the surrounding landscape: "The plains of this countrey are covered with a Leek green Grass. . . . Groops of Shrubs covered with the most delecious froot is to be seen in every derection, and nature appears to have exerted herself to butify the senery by the variety of flours . . . which strikes & profumes the Sensation."[1]

The "Leek green Grass" he alluded to may have been the big bluestem (*Andropogon* sp.), the peer of all western grasses. An erect perennial, its flower-stalks on rich bottom lands attained heights of 7 to 12 feet. It derives its name from the bluish, wax-like bloom of the stems. This beautiful plant reaches its maximum development in August, at which time in the early days men rode horseback for interminable hours through a sea of slender, graceful stalks almost as tall as the horse itself. One of the first naturalists to visit the western plains became separated from his horse and described the extreme weariness he experienced struggling through the grass.[2]

[2]

On Wednesday, July 4, Clark announced that Joseph Field had been bitten by a snake (Thwaites, I, 66). The snake was apparently innocuous. Copperheads and rattlers, the only venomous serpents native to this region, were as well-known to members of the party as coons and catamounts and would have been quickly identified. But since Lewis was now on unfamiliar terrain where snakes might belie their appearance, he took no chances when he treated Field and applied a poultice of bark and gunpowder.

The frontiersman of that day employed many remedies for snake bite, their very multiplicity affording the best evidence possible that none was entirely effective. Readers of *Huckleberry Finn* will recall how his Negro companion, after being struck by a rattler, grabbed the whiskey jug and "begun to pour it down." This was one remedy the victims of snake bite found inviting, and great faith was placed in its powers to neutralize snake venom. Doctors as well as laymen regarded it as an antidote. This belief was not only false, but dangerous; by speeding the flow of blood, alcohol only hastens distribution and absorption of venom.

The great majority of remedies then employed for snake bite were in the form of poultices. Favorite materials included onions, radishes, and freshly chewed tobacco. Poultices of bark and gunpower such as Lewis applied were also used. Doctors of the day thought that they not

---

[1] Osgood, 69.
[2] F. A. Wislizenus, *A Journey to the Rocky Mountains* (St. Louis, 1812), 145.

only drew out poison or other cause of inflammation but also acted as painkiller, antiseptic, and counter-irritant.

Physicians, however, did not regularly use gunpowder as a therapeutic agent. Explorers, frontiersmen, and Indian fighters regarded it more highly, especially for snake bite. They were known on occasion to slash the bite, introduce gunpowder, and then set fire to it. The bark employed by Lewis on this occasion could have been that of the slippery elm *(Ulmus fulva)*, the inner part of which is mucilaginous and was much used in poultices during the last century. But Lewis and Clark had with them 15 pounds of pulverized Peruvian bark *(Cinchona)*, and when anyone used the word "bark" in those days, it almost always meant *Cinchona*. Moreover, later in the journey Lewis definitely mentions employing Peruvian bark in poultices.

The 7th of July, 1804, along that part of the Missouri just below the mouth of the Platte, must have been a day of pitiless heat. Clark wrote: "one man verry sick, Struck with the Sun. Capt. Lewis bled him & gave Niter which revived him much" (I, 69–70). The victim was Private Robert Frazer, one of those who kept a journal.

The niter here employed in treating sunstroke was potassium nitrate, better known as saltpeter. Even today its usefulness as a diuretic and diaphoretic (that is, increasing urine discharge and inducing sweat) is recognized, though other drugs are more commonly used for those purposes. Lewis and Clark had two pounds of saltpeter with them and relied on it for treating a variety of unrelated disorders.

Saltpeter may have been a relatively harmless remedy, but bloodletting was not; in fact, it possibly killed more patients than it cured. For centuries, beginning even before Hippocrates and continuing almost to the present, doctors believed that practically every malady known to man, from gout and pleurisy to jaundice and cholera, could be treated effectively by drawing off blood. The practitioners of this sanguinary art included not only the physician but also the apothecary, the bath keeper, and even the barber (hence the blood-red stripes on modern barber poles). Many used leeches and were known as leech doctors, while others insisted on the sharp-edged lancet. Some had a device known as the scarificator, a box-shaped instrument that made several incisions instead of the lancet's one. Regardless of what instrument he used, the bloodletter meant business. Disease was serious and demanded vigorous procedures. With a few, the stock apothegm was "bleed until syncope," which meant in essence, draw blood until the patient is unconscious.

[3]

It required 23 days for the party to travel the distance from the Kansas to the Platte. Along the way they passed a number of abandoned Indian villages and Clark found a horse which he thought must have escaped from an Oto, but they did not see a single Indian. If time permitted, Lewis and Clark might have been tempted to excavate an Indian mound, as Jefferson had done in his youth; there were plenty of them along this stretch of the river. Their abundance indicated to Clark that this country once had been thickly settled. As the explorers neared the Platte, their bowman (probably Peter Cruzatte), who had "wintered two winters on this river," told them that the Otos resided ten leagues up the Platte and the Pawnees fifteen (I, 87).

The two captains continued their practice of denominating nameless streams, islands, and other topographic features. Ordinarily, they had good reasons for names chosen. For instance, on the Fourth of July, on discovering two unnamed creeks, they called one Fourth of July Creek and the other Independence. Two days later they camped on the larboard side of a tributary where "a whiper will perched on the boat for a short time."[3] Clark called this stream Whipporwill Creek. After consuming the last of their butter on a hitherto undesignated island, they called it Butter Island. The prairie where Joseph Field was snakebitten promptly became Joseph Field's Snake Prairie.

Frequent encounters with animals undoubtedly eased the strenuous business of navigation for the men by diverting their attention from aching backs and feet. Immediately above the Kansas, Clark reported that deer could be seen in every direction and that their tracks were "as plenty as Hogs about a farm."[4] On June 30 they saw an unusually large wolf (*Canis lupus*) on a sand bar "near a gange of Turkeys."[5] One day the two Field brothers captured a baby wolf and brought it to camp with the idea of taming it. Three days later it managed to chew through its rope and escape. On July 3 the party encountered beaver (*Castor canadensis missouriensis*) for the first time, and two days later Clark wrote that they "came to for Dinner at a Beever house, Cap Lewis's Dog went in and drove them out."[6] On still

[3] Osgood, 71.
[4] Osgood, 64.
[5] Osgood, 64.
[6] Osgood, 71.

another day, Private Silas Goodrich "caught two verry fat Cat fish."[7] Goodrich was the Izaak Walton of the party and would continue to demonstrate his skill with rod and line.

As the fauna changed, the cooks had new dishes to serve, notably catfish, beaver, and elk. Summer grapes and other wild fruit provided variety. On July 19, near present-day Nebraska City, Sergeant Ordway wrote that they "gathered a quantity of cherries at noon time & put in to the Whiskey barrel."[8] Gass added the information that these cherries were "called by some choak-cherries."[9] And Sergeant Floyd, more helpful than the other diarists in this instance, contributed the detail that "thos cherres they Gro on Low Bushes about as High as a mans hed" (VII, 19) . By putting together these observations, the botanist of today familiar with the flora of that area concludes that the plant in question was the sand cherry (*Prunus pumila*) .[10] Thus the multiple journals proved their worth in helping to solve a taxonomic problem.

[4]

Arrived at the Platte River (on July 21) , Clark wrote: "The Current of this river comes with great velosity roleing its Sands into the Missouri, filling up its Bead & Compelling it to incroach on the S [North] Shore. we found great dificuelty in passing around the Sand at the mouth of this River. Capt. Lewis and Myself with 6 men in a perogue went up this Great river Platt about 2 [one] Miles, found the Current verry rapid roleing over Sands, passing through different Channels some of them more than five or Six feet deep" (I, 86–87) .

The Platte has aptly been described as "a thousand miles long and six inches deep."[11] Its shallow waters (from which it derives its name) forbade navigation by conventional boats, a fact which delayed its exploration and the country it drained. If Lewis and Clark had followed it using horses, they would have found it a shorter and more practicable route to the Pacific. Within just a few years, the Platte Valley, at least the greater portion of its length, became a vital segment

---

[7] Osgood, 80.

[8] Ordway, 99.

[9] Gass, 25.

[10] Coues, I, 44n. Dr. O. A. Stevens, Department of Botany, North Dakota State University, in a letter to the author, confirms Coues' determination.

[11] The Platte was so named by Peter and Paul Mallet, the first Frenchmen to travel from Illinois to Santa Fé (1739) . See *Life in the Far West* by G. F. Ruxton, (Norman, Okla., 1951) , 60n.

of the Oregon Trail along which trappers, hunters, scientists, mission-aries, and adventure-seekers of many stripes travelled the first miles of the long, tedious route to Forts Laramie and Hall and across the Blue Mountains to the Columbia and the Pacific.

During a brief halt at this important confluence, Clark wrote that though the men had been troubled with large tumors on exposed parts of their bodies and with some dysentery, these afflictions had not affected adversely the general health of the party which was "quite as good as, if not better than that of the same number of men in any other situation."[12]

One week after leaving the Platte, the Corps stopped at a place they called Council Bluffs. It is impossible to determine the precise location of this site today since flood waters have seemingly long since carried it to the sea. However, it was several miles above the present city of the same name. Here, on August 2, a party of about one dozen Oto and Missouri Indians rode into camp. With them was a French-man, who resided among these Indians and acted as interpreter on this occasion.[13] Lewis and Clark gave them meat and flour, and the natives, in turn, provided the explorers with "Water millions" (I, 97).[14]

This was an important meeting, actually the first between Plains Indians and representatives of the United States government. Lewis and Clark had prepared in advance for it. Among other things, they had written a speech. Before delivering it, they erected a pole flying a flag containing 17 stars (for the 17 states in 1804) and raised their main-sail as an awning to protect them from the sun.

Lewis did the talking, with the Frenchman interpreting. It was a long talk, but the main points were as follows: he and Clark had been sent by "the great Chief of the Seventeen great nations of America" to inform them that they were no longer subjects of France or Spain. They were to live in peace with the white men and to discontinue intertribal warfare. If they paid heed to the councils of their White Father, he would soon send goods to trade for peltries and furs. The chiefs should engage traders to take them to St. Louis where they would

[12] Coues, I, 50.

[13] Clark spelled the name of this Frenchman variously: Fairfong, Farfonge, and Faufon. Efforts to identify him have failed.

[14] Melvin Randolph Gilmore in "Uses of Plants by the Indians of the Missouri River Region" (Washington, D.C., 1919) says: "The watermelons grown by the various tribes seem to be of a variety distinct from any of the many known varieties of European introduction." However, botanists I have consulted have no knowledge of a native American species of watermelon.

be provided with horses on which they might ride with comfort and safety to the Great White Father's town.[15]

With alterations pertinent to time and place, Lewis and Clark gave this same speech again and again (through interpreters, of course) to tribe after tribe between Council Bluffs and the Pacific Ocean. At the conclusion of these talks, it was customary to present gifts, including medals[16] and a U.S. flag, and then for Lewis to shoot his air gun. The notion has gained ground that he had brought it along mainly to awe the Indians, though it may be more realistic to believe that he thought it might be serviceable in case he ever ran out of powder. In any event, he ordinarily fired it as a surprise *punto culminante* following meetings. Private Whitehouse described the general response: "Capt. Lewis Shot his air gun told them that there was medician in hir & that She would doe Great execution, they were all amazed at the curiosity, & as Soon as he had Shot a fiew times they all ran hastily to See the Ball holes in the tree they Shouted aloud at the Site of the execution She would doe" (VII, 55) .

The Oto and Missouri Indians (with the Iowas) constituted a distinct branch (Chiwere) of the Siouan family. Lewis and Clark quickly ascertained the linguistic relationship between these three tribes. While still at their Council Bluffs camp, Clark wrote, "The Ottos, Airways (Ioways) & Missouries Speake the Same language."[17]

Four days after leaving Council Bluffs, the Expedition arrived near Blackbird Hill, a prominent bluff beside the Missouri in Thurston County, Nebraska, close by the present town of Macy. Lewis and Clark stopped long enough to climb to the summit of the hill, having been informed that the renowned Omaha chief, Blackbird, just before his death had instructed his people to bury him on the top of this elevation sitting erect on his favorite horse.

Blackbird had died of smallpox during a devastating epidemic that struck the Omaha and neighboring nations in 1800. When Jefferson received intelligence of this epidemic, he conceived the idea that Lewis and Clark might be the means of staying future ravages of smallpox among western Indians. In his instructions to them he included this arresting mandate: "carry with you some matter of the kine-pox, inform those of them with whom you may be of its efficacy as

[15] Jackson, *Letters,* 203–207.
[16] For more on these medals see Paul Russell Cutright, "Lewis and Clark Indian Peace Medals," *Bull. Missouri Hist. Soc.,* XXIV, no. 2 (Jan., 1968) .
[17] Osgood, 96.

a preservative from the smallpox; and instruct them and encourage them in the use of it. This may be especially done wherever you winter" (VII, 250).

Lewis carried with him some of the "matter of the kine-pox" as he left Washington for Pittsburgh. He confirmed this on his arrival at Cincinnati when he wrote Jefferson saying: "I would thank you to forward me some of the Vaxcine matter, as I have reason to believe from several experiments made with what I have, that it has lost it's virtue" (VII, 278). Since we find no further mention of smallpox vaccine in any of the journals or letters, it may be concluded that Lewis and Clark did not receive another supply. So, through no fault of theirs they lost an opportunity to add increased luster to their names as the first men to introduce this immunizing substance to peoples beyond the Mississippi.

[5]

Tragedy struck the Corps just once—when it was only three months old. On July 31, just above the mouth of the Platte, Sergeant Floyd complained that he had been sick for some time but had recovered. Three weeks later Clark wrote: "Serjeant Floyd is taken verry bad all at once with a biliose Chorlick we attempt to relieve him without success as yet, he gets worse and we are much allarmed at his Situation, all give attention to him . . . nothing will Stay a moment on his Stomach or bowels" (I, 114).

The next day (August 20) Sergeant Floyd died, probably of a ruptured gangrenous appendix. The journals reveal nothing of measures attempted to save his life. The odds are that Lewis purged and bled him. If he did the former, it may well have hastened his death, either by rupturing the appendix or by adding to inflammatory material already in the peritoneal cavity. In any event, Lewis's efforts were to no avail; probably the best medical talent of that day could not have saved him. At that time surgery was almost entirely limited to the surface of the body. It was close to a hundred years later (1887) that Dr. John Morton of Philadelphia performed the first appendectomy in the United States.

After burying Floyd at the top of a bluff just a short distance below the present location of Sioux City, Iowa, the party resumed their journey. They soon came to a small stream entering the Missouri from the northeast. To this tributary, which today runs through the heart of

Sioux City, they gave the name of Floyd's Creek. Two days later the enlisted men of the Corps chose Patrick Gass to succeed Floyd as sergeant. Private William Bratton was runner-up.

[6]

Periodically, Clark wrote that the men were all in high spirits. The animal life, ubiquitous and increasingly novel, contributed significantly to this prevailing euphoria. For example, one day Joseph Field brought in an animal that, as Private Whitehouse put it, "never was Seen by any of the party before" (VII, 46). It was a badger (*Taxidea taxus*), as Clark's description makes clear: "this animale burrows in the ground & feeds on Bugs and flesh . . . his head Mouth &c is like a Dog with its ears cut off, his hair and tale like that of a Ground hog . . . and it has a white Streake from its nose to its Sholders."[18]

According to Sergeant Ordway, Lewis had the creature skinned and stuffed in order to send it back to St. Louis.[19] Lacking evidence to the contrary, we may surmise that this badger was the first zoological specimen preserved by Lewis and that he here put into practice for the first time his taxidermic skills. Whether he employed Jefferson's recommended preservative is conjectural. We do know that before long, after the President had received the specimen, he informed a scientific friend that it was "not before known out of Europe" (VII, 327). Apparently he knew nothing of specimens sent at an earlier date from Canada to Europe where the badger had been technically described in 1778.

Another incident, of equal interest, soon followed. While negotiating a stretch of the Missouri, the men were puzzled to find the river surface for a distance of some three miles almost completely covered by a tremendous number of white feathers (VI, 126). The mystery was solved when they arrived at a sand bar blanketed by five to six thousand white pelicans (*Pelecanus erythrorhynchus*). After Lewis shot one, the men crowded around as he examined it and attempted to determine the capacity of the great pouch which depends from the mandible of all pelicans. Sergeant Gass reported the outcome: "In the bag . . . we put five gallons of water."[20]

Excitement mounted even higher on August 23, just below present-day Vermillion, South Dakota. On that date they killed their first

[18] Osgood, 94.
[19] Ordway, 103.
[20] Gass, 31.

buffalo. Since leaving Camp Dubois, they had travelled a long distance, approximately 800 miles, before sitting down to a meal of roasted bison steaks. Sergeant Ordway wrote: "Jo Fields came to the Boat informed us that he had killed a Bull Buffalow, Capt. Lewis & myself & 10 more of the party went out Bucherd [butchered] & brought it to the Boat. . . . I saw the beds & Signs of a great many more Buffalow but this was the first I ever Saw & as great a curiosity to me."[21]

Two days later Clark wrote that numerous herds of buffalo had been seen feeding in various directions (I, 123). Quite suddenly, portals to buffalo preserves had opened, revealing in quantity one of the two most conspicuous symbols of the early American West, the other being the Plains Indian.

[7]

In their travels to and from the Pacific, Lewis and Clark met a multiplicity of Indians, of many tribes, mores, and tongues. They were newcomers to the field of ethnology and had no staffs to lean on, such as textbooks and manuals providing systems of classifications. As a result, they were practically helpless in attempts to group them in any orderly manner and, beyond noting similarities of language and custom between certain tribes, made no effort to do so. Students today experience no such problems, scientists in the meantime having classified American Indians on the basis of anatomy, language, and customs.

The Indian's generally straight, black hair, skin yellow to brown, broad face, and trace of epicanthic fold, fully reveal his Mongolian origin and justify the conclusion that he came to the Americas from Asia. Anatomy thus helps to establish the position of the Indian among the major races of the world. He probably arrived in several waves, most likely crossing the Bering Strait to Alaska, whence he spread to all parts of the Western Hemisphere.

On the basis of language, Indians of Canada and the United States have been divided into approximately 50 linguistic families, each containing a group of related tribes with their dialectic subdivisions. As they moved from the Mississippi to the estuary of the Columbia, Lewis and Clark made the acquaintance of at least seven linguistic families: Algonquian, Siouan, Caddoan, Shoshonean, Salishan, Sahaptian, and Chinookan.

Culturally, North American Indians fall into 11 groups, seven of

[21] Ordway, 115.

which exist totally or partially within the limits of the United States. Lewis and Clark came into intimate contact with three of these: Plains, Plateau, and Northwest or Northern Pacific Coast.[22]

The Plains Indians, whom Lewis and Clark first encountered, occupied an area extending from southern Canada to the Rio Grande and corresponding closely to the buffalo range. About 30 different tribes all told lived in this great expanse of grassland, though some, such as the Assiniboin, Blackfeet, Cheyenne, Comanche, Crow, and Teton-Dakota, exemplified in a higher degree the typical Plains culture. They had much in common. They were nomadic people, with no fixed abodes or established community life. They lived the year around in movable, skin-covered tipis. They grew no crops, depending on other tribes for plant foods, and they had little or no knowledge of either basketry or pottery. They transported belongings on a primitive carrier, the travois, made of two trailing poles serving as shafts for horse or dog. They depended on the buffalo for necessities—food, clothing, and shelter—and had developed weapons appropriate to the hunting of this animal. They depended, too, on the horse, which had made the Plains Indian a superior, swift-charging warrior, a relentless raider, and a practised thief. He was poor or rich, depending on the size of his "stable."[23]

The Oto and Missouri tribesmen whom Lewis and Clark had recently met were atypical. They had lately emerged from eastern woodlands still retaining old established customs such as agriculture, pottery, and basketry, and they lived in earthen lodges during the winters.

[8]

Lewis and Clark first encountered Sioux Indians on August 27 at the mouth of the James River near today's Yankton, South Dakota. No Indians have left a deeper imprint on American history. Chiefs Sitting Bull and Red Cloud were Sioux, as were most of that painted, hard-riding horde that overwhelmed Custer and his men on the Little Bighorn in 1876.[24] The explorers had heard in advance a great deal about them,

[22] The other cultural groups of the U.S. are: Northern Woodlands, Southeast or Southern Woodlands, Southwest, and California.

[23] Walter Prescott Webb, *The Great Plains* (New York, 1931), 52.

[24] We are speaking now, it should be made clear, of the Sioux proper, which is just one of several divisions of the Siouan linguistic family. Those pertinent to Lewis and Clark history are: (1) Dhegiha: Kansas, Omaha, Osage, Ponca; (2)

all of it prejudicial. They had practically closed the Upper Missouri to St. Louis traders and trappers, robbing them or levying heavy tribute.

The Sioux Lewis and Clark encountered at the James River were Yankton Sioux. Clark described them as "Stout bold looking people . . . much decorated with Paint Porcupine quils & feathers" (I, 129–130). They occupied for the moment a village consisting of about 40 handsome, cone-shaped lodges (tipis) covered with red and white painted buffalo and elk skins.

About 70 Yankton Sioux attended a council held on August 30 near the mouth of the James at a place called Calumet Bluff. Lewis addressed them (presumably delivering the same speech he had given to the Otos and Missouris), presented medals and other gifts, and smoked a pipe with the chiefs. The next morning five of these chiefs took turns replying to Lewis. They promised to follow his advice to make peace with their neighbors, to make friends with St. Louis traders, and to visit their Great White Father. It is probably too easy to conclude that Lewis and Clark put implicit faith in the promises of Indians, as some writers have implied.

This meeting at Calumet Bluff was one of consequence. The Yanktons interposed no obstacles to the upstream progress of the party, a circumstance that augured well for a cordial reception by the Teton Sioux and other tribes farther along. Also, here at Calumet Bluff, with a comparatively large group of natives assembled, Lewis and Clark had their first real opportunity to study Plains Indians and their culture. "We made," said Clark, "very minute inquiries relative to their situation, numbers, trade and manners."[25] In making these inquiries they had the benefit of two excellent interpreters, Dorion and his son (the latter having been found here with the Sioux), both of whom seem to have spoken the Sioux language fluently. Much of what they learned about these natives went into *Statistical View*. For instance, we read that the Yankton Sioux numbered about 700, that they inhabited country drained by the James, Big Sioux, and Des Moines Rivers, that they were "the best disposed Sioux who rove on the banks of the Missouri," and that they foregathered periodically on the James which was then an important trade center (VI, 96).

Sergeant Ordway supplied an important ethnozoological note. In describing the shield carried by the Yankton Sioux, he said it was "made

Chiwere: Iowa, Missouri, Oto; (3) Mandan; (4) Hidatsa; (5) Dakota-Assiniboin (Sioux proper). In *Statistical View*, Lewis and Clark divided the Sioux proper into 10 groups (Thwaites, VI, 99).

[25] Coues, I, 96.

of thickest buffalow hides dressed white   covered with thin Goat [antelope, *Antilocapra americana*] Skin dressed white & ornamented with porcupine [*Erethizon dorsatum*] quills & feathers."[26]

It was while with the Yanktons that Clark wrote: "I took a Vocabulary of the Suoux Language" (I, 132). Jefferson had earlier provided Lewis with a list of several common, everyday English words and had instructed him, as he met up with each Indian tribe, to learn the Indian equivalents. The President was convinced, as we know, that the origin of the Indian could best be solved through applications of linguistic principles. Time and again during the long crossing of the continent, Lewis and Clark wrote that they had taken vocabularies. Even before they had reached the James, they had compiled a number of these. On comparing them they observed that the Sioux language is "not peculiarly their own," that it contained many words identical to those of the Omaha, Osage, and Kansas, and that "those nations at some period not more than a century or two past are of the Same nation" (I, 132). Though the two captains took vocabularies of most if not all tribes encountered, their diligence came to naught. At least, no one knows of the whereabouts of a single one today.

As Lewis and Clark resumed their journey from Calumet Bluff, they left Old Dorion and his son behind, commissioning them to effect, if possible, better relations between the Yanktons and their enemies and to employ traders to take chiefs to Washington who might be persuaded to make the trip. They lost a good interpreter when they gave Old Dorion this assignment, and they would soon have cause to regret it. Of the many difficulties presenting themselves in months ahead, the language barrier proved to be one of the most formidable.

Three days of travel brought the Expedition to the Niobrara River, some 35 miles west of today's Yankton. They were now at the threshold of the High Plains.

SUMMARY OF DISCOVERIES

Animals New to Science

MISSOURI BEAVER. *Castor canadensis missouriensis* V. Bailey. (Thwaites, I, 65). Described, 1919.

? BLUE CATFISH. *Ictalurus furcatus* Le Sueur. (Gass, 35). 1840.

? CHANNEL CATFISH. *Ictalurus punctatus* (Rafinesque). (Thwaites, I, 90). 1818.

[26] Ordway, 118–120.

BULL SNAKE; SAY'S PINE SNAKE. *Pituophis sayi sayi* (Schlegel). (Thwaites, VI, 124). 1837.

Plants New to Science

RABBIT BRUSH. *Bigelowia douglasii* Gray = *Chrysothamnus viscidiflorus* (Hook.) Nuttall. 1840.

PINK CLEOME. *Cleome serrulata* Pursh. 1814.

BROAD-LEAVED GUM-PLANT. *Grindelia squarrosa* (Pursh) Dunal. 1814.

LARGE-FLOWERED CLAMMY-WEED. *Polanisia trachysperma* T. & G. 1840.

BUFFALOBERRY. *Shepherdia argentea* Nuttall = *Hippophae argentea* Pursh. 1814.

Lewis and Clark Herbarium

HEART-LEAVED UMBRELLAWORT. *Allionia ovata* Pursh = *A. nyctaginea* Michx. Collected Sept. 1.

CANADA ANEMONE. *Anemone pennsylvanica* L. = *A. canadense* L. August 17.

PASTURE SAGEBRUSH. *Artemisia frigida* Willdenow. Sept. 2.

RABBIT BRUSH. *Bigelowia douglasii* Gray. Sept. 2.

PINK CLEOME. *Cleome serrulata* Pursh. August 25.

FIELD HORSETAIL. *Equisetum arvense* L. August 10.

WOOD HORSETAIL. *Equisetum sylvaticum* L. August 10.

BROAD-LEAVED GUM-PLANT. *Grindelia squarrosa* (Pursh) Dunal. August 17.

VIOLET PRAIRIE-CLOVER. *Petalostemon violaceum* Michx. = *Petalostemum purpureum* (Vent.) Rydberg. Sept. 2.

LARGE-FLOWERED CLAMMY-WEED. *Polanisia trachysperma* T. & G. August 25.

BUFFALOBERRY. *Shepherdia argentea* Nuttall. Sept. 4.

Indian Tribes Encountered

Siouan Linguistic Family: Oto, Missouri, Yankton Sioux.

Topographic Features Named and/or Discovered

Bald-Pated Prairie (Thwaites, I, 81).

Biscuit Creek (Thwaites, I, 63).

Buffalo Prairie (Coues, I, 83).

Butter Island (Osgood, 62).

Council Bluffs (Ordway, 103).

Council Creek (Thwaites, VII, 23).

Detachment Islands (Osgood, 101).

Floyd's River (Thwaites, I, 114) —— on maps today as Floyd's River.

Fourth-of-July Creek (Thwaites, I, 66).

Independence Creek (Thwaites, I, 66) —— still so called.

Indian Knob Creek (Thwaites, I, 92).

Gosling Lake (Thwaites, I, 66).

Jo Fields Snake Prairie (Osgood, 67).

Ordway's Creek (Ordway, 93; Coues, I, 41) .
Pelican Islands (Coues, I, 70) .
Pike Pond (Thwaites, I, 72) .
Potts Creek (Thwaites, VII, 46) .
Roloje Creek (Thwaites, I, 117) .
Sergeant Charles Floyd's Bluff (Ordway, 112) —— locatable today.
Whiperwill Creek (Osgood, 71) .
Yellow Oaker Creek (Thwaites, I, 68) .

Niobrara River
to
the Teton

CHAPTER FIVE

When Lewis and Clark passed the entrance of the Niobrara River, they stood on ground just west of the 98th meridian, an important line. Here begins the High Plains, one of the three regions comprising the Great Plains area. Of the two, one is immediately east of the High Plains, and the other is west.

The Great Plains area of the United States is that fabulous part of our land surface, almost entirely west of the Mississippi, which is characterized by an absence of trees, a generally level surface of great extent, and a subhumid to arid climate. East of the 98th meridian only two of these characteristics obtain—level surface and treeless expanse. This area is sometimes called the Prairie region. West of the High Plains is the arid, increasingly broken part of the Great Plains area. Here, also, only two of the three characteristics present themselves— absence of trees and poverty of water. Thus only the High Plains country, that median region on the threshold of which Lewis and Clark now stood, possesses all three characteristics. Constituting the heart of the Great Plains area, it extends roughly from the 98th meridian to the uneven foothills of the Rockies and, in a north-south direction, from Canada to Mexico and the Gulf.[1]

The explorers would be a long time in crossing the High Plains, one of the largest grasslands in the world, and would actually not escape until they neared the Continental Divide. In their westward progress across it, they would encounter fewer and fewer trees, principally cottonwoods, and these limited almost entirely to narrow ribbons

[1] Webb, *The Great Plains*, 3–9.

decorating the river edges. They would find the country progressively drier, with diminishing rainfall. Immediately east of the 98th line the mean annual rainfall is 20 inches or more. West of it, the average drops rapidly to 15 and then to 10 and less. While it is true that in some years the High Plains receive ample rain, well above 20 inches, in others the amount is scarcely measurable.

When members of the party, once beyond the 98th meridian, climbed out of the Missouri valley to the prairie above, they found the land stretching interminably to the horizon, a plane, unscored surface. On September 3 Sergeant Gass wrote: "There is no timber in this part of the country; but continued prairie on both sides of the river. A person by going on one of the hills may have a view as far as the eye can reach without any obstruction, or intervening object; and enjoy the most delightful prospects."[2]

In years to follow other travellers to this land, inspired and elated by what they saw, compared it to the sea. For example, Josiah Gregg, author of *Commerce of the Prairies*, wrote of the "grand prairie ocean," and it was he who first employed the term "prairie schooner."[3] To Colonel Richard Irving Dodge, the High Plains country was "like an ocean in its vast extent, in its monotony . . . in its romance, in its opportunities for heroism, and in the fascination it exerts on all those who come fairly within its influence."[4]

Many writers commented on the clearness of the High Plains air and enchanting blue of the sky. Henry Marie Brackenridge, Pittsburgh lawyer and explorer who ascended the Missouri in 1811, reasoned that these features might be due to the openness of the country, which allowed the winds to chase away the haze, or to the "light dress of vegetation, with which these plains are clothed," for "where the vegetation is luxuriant, dense vapors arise during the night; and the noxious gases are produced, which floating into the atmosphere, lessen the brightness as well as its purity."[5]

An additional characteristic feature of the High Plains, a contrary one, demands special consideration—the high winds. Against them Lewis and Clark inveighed again and again. With nothing to impede their play, they blow relentlessly and with tremendous, often savage

---

[2]Gass, 40.

[3]Josiah Gregg, *Commerce of the Prairies* (Norman, Okla., 1954), 50.

[4]Richard I. Dodge, *The Hunting Grounds of the Great West* (London, 1877), 2.

[5]Reuben Gold Thwaites, ed., *Early Western Travels*, 32 vols. (Cleveland, 1904–6), VI, 135–136. Hereinafter cited as *Early Western Travels*.

velocity. As the party neared the Niobrara, Sergeant Gass wrote: "about twelve the wind blew so hard that we could not proceed, and we landed on the north side."[6] This was a mild foretaste.

[2]

It took Lewis and Clark 20 days, from September 4 to 24, to negotiate the distance, 263 miles according to Clark, between the Niobrara and the mouth of the Bad (Teton) River where Pierre, the capital of South Dakota, stands today. Zoologically, this period would prove to be the most important and most exciting of the entire trip. Within the short space of a fortnight, Lewis and Clark would discover several species of animals entirely new to them and the scientific world. They immediately revealed the importance they attached to these discoveries by collecting specimens, making measurements, preserving skins and bones, and by writing descriptions.

It was on September 7 in Boyd County, Nebraska, at the base of a conspicuous elevation known as the Tower, that Lewis and Clark discovered the first of these unfamiliar animals, the prairie dog, *Cynomys ludovicianus ludovicianus*. "The village of these animals," Clark wrote, "covd. about 4 acres of ground on a gradual decent of a hill and Contains great numbers of holes on top of which those little animals Set erect make a Whisteling noise and whin allarmed Step into their hole" (I, 142).[7]

Obtaining specimens proved difficult. Private John Shields killed the first one. According to Sergeant Ordway, it "was cooked for the Capts dinner."[8] Having no further luck with their guns, they resorted to digging. After going down six feet and finding that the runways seemed bottomless, they gave that up and tried flooding. This became a full-scale operation, with all members of the Corps participating except a guard left with the boats. They spent a major portion of the day carrying water from the river and pouring it into the subterranean passageways. Though they persisted until nightfall, they succeeded in

---

[6] Gass, 39.

[7] Easterners first heard of the prairie dog when they read the *Baltimore Telegraph and Daily Advertiser*, July 25, 1805. This was followed by *Statistical View* (1806), Gass's *Journal* (1807), and Pike's *Expeditions* (1810), in each of which the prairie dog came in for comment. It was not technically described until 1815 when George Ord named it *Arctomys ludoviciana*. His description is to be found in William Guthrie's *A New Geographical, Historical, and Commercial Grammar*, 2 vols. (Philadelphia, 1815).

[8] Ordway, 127.

capturing only one, flushing it out alive. Clark had better luck a few days later. "I killed 4," he reported, "with a view to have their Skins Stufed" (I, 145).

The prairie dog, as almost everyone knows, is an urbanite, living in sprawling underground cities called dog towns. In days gone by, the size of some of these staggered the imagination. A well-known scientist employed by the U.S. Biological Survey found one in Texas that covered approximately 25,000 square miles, an area the size of West Virginia, and estimated that it must have contained as many as 400 million prairie dogs.[9] Today dog towns of any size are hard to find, except in remote or protected areas.

This restless burrowing rodent belongs to the squirrel family and has nothing about it suggestive of the dog except its bark which, according to Lewis, "was much that of the little toy dogs" (V, 178). The explorers had trouble settling on a name for it. In early descriptions, Clark employed ground rat and burrowing squirrel. Lewis seems to have preferred barking squirrel, a name soon adopted by most of the journalists. However, from the beginning Sergeant Ordway used prairie dog[10] and may have been the first person to employ the name by which it is known today. Two years later while on the Arkansas River, Lt. Zebulon Pike encountered a village of prairie dogs where, he said, he was "saluted on all sides by the cry of 'wishtonwish,' from which they derive their name with the Indians."[11] In this connection there is much to be said for Josiah Gregg's comment that "It would surely have contributed to the copiousness and euphony of the language, as well as to the perspicuity in the distinction of species, had we, like the Mexicans, retained the Indian names of our indigenous animals."[12] Beyond question "wishtonwish" is preferable to prairie dog, since the latter suggests a canine relationship which does not exist.

The age-old myth that rattlesnakes live on congenial terms with prairie dogs, owls, and other animals antedated Lewis and Clark. "It is said," Clark wrote soon after discovering the "ground rat," "that a kind of Lizard also a Snake reside with those animals" (I, 142). However, soon finding a rattler with a prairie dog inside it, they concluded that the belief had no foundation in fact.

[9] Vernon Bailey, "Biological Survey of Texas," *North American Fauna*, No. 26 (1905), 155.

[10] Ordway, 127.

[11] Elliott Coues, ed., *The Expeditions of Zebulon Montgomery Pike*, 3 vols. (Philadelphia, 1895), II, 431.

[12] Gregg, *Commerce of the Prairies*, 376n.

On September 12 near Rosebud Landing, South Dakota (a place now covered by the impounded water from Randall's Dam), Clark wrote that he had seen a great number of grouse. Beyond doubt he was here referring to the prairie sharp-tailed grouse, *Pedioecetes phasianellus campestris,* for Lewis later wrote that "The Prairie fowl common to the Illinois [the prairie chicken, *Tympanachus cupido pinnatus*] are found as high up as the River Jacque [James] above which the Sharpe tailed Grows [grouse] commence" (VI, 121). Lewis made it clear, too, that he had no trouble distinguishing between these two birds (similar in many respects) when he said that the grouse of the Upper Missouri had a pointed tail with "the feathers in it's center much longer than those on the sides," while "those of the Illinois" had tails "composed of f[e]athers of equal length" (IV, 121).

Ornithologists today recognize several subspecies of the sharp-tailed grouse. Lewis and Clark discovered at least two of them, the prairie form just referred to (not described until 1884) and, later, the Columbian sharp-tailed grouse, *P. p. columbianus.*

The next animal of the High Plains discovered by the explorers was the sleek-limbed, graceful pronghorn, *Antilocapra americana americana.* Though seen below the mouth of the Niobrara, they did not kill one until September 14, near the mouth of Ball Creek, Lyman County, South Dakota. Clark, who bagged this first one, wrote about the incident as follows: "I walked on shore to find an old Vulcanoe . . . in my walk I killed a Buck Goat of this Countrey, about the height of the Grown Deer, its body Shorter the horns which is not very hard and forks ⅔ up one prong Short the other round & Sharp arched, and is immediately above its Eyes the Colour is a light gray with black behind its ears down the neck, and its face white round its neck, its Sides and its rump round its tail which is Short & white; Verry actively made, has only a pair of hoofs to each foot, his brains on the back of his head, his Norstrals large, his eyes like a Sheep he is more like the Antilope or Gazelle of Africa than any other Species of Goat" (I, 147).

"Such an anamil was never yet known in the U.S. States," declared Sergeant Ordway. "The Capt. had the Skins of the Goat Stuffed in order to Send back to the city of Washington, the bones and all."[13]

Other white men, notably such explorers as Coronado, had seen the pronghorn at an earlier date, but as the artist-naturalist, Ernest Thompson Seton, observed: "Coronado and his contemporaries, when they discovered the antelope, were too busy adding to the Spiritual

[13] Ordway, 131.

Kingdom of their Masters . . . to bestow a second thought on this wonderful wild thing. It remained for Lewis and Clark, 270 years later, to give the world detailed information about the pronghorn of the Plains."[14]

This beautiful creature is, of course, not an antelope at all, and in fact has no close relative anywhere in the world. To find a correct taxonomic niche for it, scientists had to create an entirely new family (*Antilocapridae*), which it has all to itself. It is the only mammal having a hollow horn that is branched and that is shed and renewed each year. Of all American quadrupeds it is the swiftest. For a short distance it can cover ground at a rate close to 60 miles an hour and can maintain a speed of 40 miles for several minutes. Even the young fawns, only a day or two old, have been clocked at up to 25 miles for short distances. The pronghorn's coloring is distinctive and is rendered more so by its habit of raising the white hair on its rump when alarmed.

In the early days, the pronghorn ranged from Saskatchewan to Lower California and from Nebraska to the Cascade Range. Some of the earliest observers believed that they outnumbered the buffalo. Ernest Thompson Seton estimated a total approximating 100 million. By 1908 the millions north of Mexico had dwindled to less than 20,000. Since then, following the initiation and extension of a strong conservation program, their number has increased to the point that some states now allow open seasons for hunters.

As with the prairie dog, the explorers experienced difficulty in deciding on a name for this animal with "his brains on the back of his head." They first called it a goat, but soon discontinued that name, one reason being that "None of these Goats has any Beard" (I, 158). Then they tried cabre, with other spellings such as cabrie, cabree, and cabra, the Spanish word for goat. Lewis employed the word antelope from the beginning, and his continued usage no doubt had much to do with the fact that the name has persisted. (The efforts of zoologists to gain general acceptance of the name pronghorn have been no more successful than similar efforts to educate the public to employ bison instead of buffalo.)

On the same day that Lewis and Clark obtained their first specimen of the antelope and at approximately the same place, Clark wrote that Shields had "killed a *Hare* like the mountain hare of Europe" (I, 147). The explorers had discovered the white-tailed jack rabbit, *Lepus*

---

[14] Ernest Thompson Seton, *Life Histories of Northern Animals,* 2 vols. (New York, 1909), I, 230.

townsendii campanius. It was first called jackass rabbit because of its large ears, this name being later shortened.

After Lewis became better acquainted with the jack rabbit, he described it at some length. It was a solitary creature, he wrote, never more than two or three associating together at one time. He was impressed with the flexibility of its long ears, which it moved "with great ease and quickness" and could "dilate and throw them forward, or contract and fold them back at pleasure." He found by measurement that it was capable of prodigious leaps, commonly from 18 to 20 feet. In winter it changed its coat, becoming pure white "excepting the black and reddish brown of the ears which never changed" (IV, 118–119).

Lewis and Clark were correct in calling this animal a hare instead of a rabbit. Hares have longer ears and legs and travel faster than rabbits. They never make burrows and their young are born with well-developed coats of hair and with eyes open. Rabbits, on the contrary, do construct burrows and their young are born naked and blind. The early settlers of the West, uninformed on such morphological and other distinctions, misapplied the word "rabbit" so widely and often that it is now fixed in current usage.[15]

Two days later (on September 17), Clark reported that Private John Colter had killed "a curious kind of Deer of a Dark gray Colr. more so than common, hair long & fine, the ears large & long." He went on to say that the tail had a tuft of black hair at the end (I, 152). Up to this moment, the explorers had knowledge of just one kind of deer, the Virginia white-tail (*Dama virginianus*). With specimens of this new deer at hand to examine, Lewis and Clark saw at once that it differed from the familiar white-tail in several important respects. It was fully a third larger, the male particularly so. The hair was thicker, longer, and of a much darker gray. The body was not so delicately formed, and the horns branched in a different manner. It had a white rump and remarkably large ears, those of a large buck examined later measuring 11 inches in length and 3½ in width (II, 20–21).

Lewis and Clark had discovered the mule deer, *Dama hemionus hemionus,* the restive, high-headed cervine of the High Plains, and had been the first to describe it. In time they learned much about its habits. For instance, they rarely found it, Lewis wrote, "in any except a rough

[15] When specimens of the white-tailed jack rabbit collected by Lewis and Clark reached the East, some scientists mistook it for a variety of the varying hare (*Lepus americanus* Erx.). It was not recognized and described as a distinct species until 1837, when John Bachman gave it the name of *Lepus campestris.*

country; they prefer the open grounds and are seldom found in the woodlands near the river; when they are met with in the woodlands or river bottoms and are pursued, they invariably run to the hills or open country as the Elk do. the contrary happens with the common white-tailed deer" (II, 20). This tendency of the mule deer to frequent rough country explains why the explorers in crossing the Dakotas did not kill many of them; they were more abundant than the journals indicate.

Seton wrote that it was Constantine Samuel Rafinesque, who in first describing this deer in 1817, gave it the name of mule deer. That he was in error is made evident by Lewis's own statement written in 1805, 12 years earlier. "The year and tail of this anamal when compared with those of the common deer, so well comported with those of the mule when compared with the horse, that we have by way of distinction adapted appelation of the mule deer, which I think much more appropriate [than black-tailed deer, the name the French *engagés* employed]" (II, 21).

On September 16 Lewis wrote that one of his hunters had killed "a bird of the *Corvus genus* and order of the pica & about the size of a jack-daw, with a remarkable long tale. beautifully variagated. it[s] note is not disagreeable though loud—it is twait-twait-twait twait, twait; twait, twait, twait twait . . . it's head, neck, brest & back within one inch of the tale are of a fine glossey black . . . the belly is of a beautiful white . . . the plumage of the tale consists of 12 feathers of equal length by pair[s]" (VI, 130–131).

The bird in question is one familiar today to most travellers in the West, namely, the black-billed magpie, *Pica pica hudsonia*. Though known to exist in Europe, where it was a common bird, no one until now knew that its range included the western part of North America. In weeks and months ahead Lewis and Clark encountered this strikingly colored bird on many occasions. They described its nest and eggs and went into detail about its behavior. It surprised them with its tameness, since it often came within two or three feet of them to snatch away pieces of meat while they were skinning a deer or buffalo. As a rule, animals that inhabit widely separated habitats, such as Europe and North America, differ at least specifically. The magpie is an exception, a particularly interesting one since it is found around the world in the North Temperate Zone. The black-billed magpie of the United States does differ in minor respects, however, from its European counterpart, enough to make it a different subspecies. The German naturalist, Maximilian, Prince of Wied, quickly noted one of these differences when he arrived on the Upper Missouri in 1833. Its note, "twit, twit," he wrote, was quite different from that of the European magpie.[16]

The magpie had been shot on a small stream which Lewis promptly called Corvus Creek (Crow Creek today), thus employing for the first time a Latin generic term. For some reason Lewis did not take readily to "the high sounding names made from the dead languages."[17]

Near the mouth of the Niobrara Clark had written of seeing foxes on the prairie and, again, of a prairie wolf that barked "like a large fest [feist] and is not much larger."[18] On September 18 his diary included the comment that "I walked on Shore Saw Goats, Elk, Buffalow, Black tail Deer, & the Common Deer. I killed a Prairie Wolff, about the size of a gray fox bushey tail head & ears like a Wolf, Some fur   Burrows in the ground and barks like a Small Dog. What has been taken heretofore for the Fox was those wolves, and no Foxes has been Seen" (I, 155).

Lewis and Clark had discovered another animal, this time the small, remarkably sagacious canine of the western plains, the coyote or prairie wolf, *Canis latrans latrans*. Though, as in the instance of the antelope, Spanish explorers had earlier alluded to the coyote in their writings, Lewis and Clark must be given credit for bringing it to the attention of contemporary scientists. Sergeant Ordway tells us that the bones of the one shot here by Clark "was taken apart and Saved, as well as the Skin . . . in order to send back to the States next Spring, with the other Curiosities we have or may have &.C."[19]

The eery, discordant whines, yelps, and barks of the coyote accompanied Lewis and Clark to the Pacific and back. Because these sounds so resembled those of the dog, the members of the party often insisted they were hearing that animal.

After writing the description of the coyote, Clark added: "The large Wolves are very numerous, they are of a light colr. & has long hair with Coarse fur" (I, 155). This was the western gray wolf, *Canis lupus nubilus,* a different variety from that which then inhabited eastern states. When the naturalist, Thomas Say, while on Major Long's Expedition, discovered and described this subspecies (in 1834), he may have had no knowledge that Lewis and Clark had encountered it almost 20 years earlier.

[16] *Early Western Travels,* XXIII, 215.
[17] This is Charles Willson Peale's characterization. See Jackson, *Letters,* 309.
[18] Osgood, 106.
[19] Ordway, 133.

The animals just described, with the buffalo and a few lesser forms, are those most often associated with the West. Because of their beauty, abundance, singular behavior, or other characteristics, they immediately attracted the attention and admiration of the vanguard of explorers, trappers, hunters, and others who pioneered the West in the early years of the last century. Lewis and Clark expressed excitement when they discovered them, and so have millions of other Americans since. These same animals will continue to excite as long as their chief enemy, man, allows them to exist.

The High Plains presented new plants as well as animals. On September 19, for instance, Clark wrote of a creek that passes "thro a plain in which great quantities of the Prickley Pear grows, I call this Creek Prickley Pear Creek" (I, 157). Since the journals have little more than this to say about plants typical of the eastern High Plains, one easily gets the impression that Lewis and Clark paid practically no attention to the flora encountered on this leg of the trip. But that would be erroneous. Proof of the contrary is to be found at the Academy of Natural Sciences of Philadelphia, where there are several different dried, preserved plants collected by Lewis between the Niobrara and the Bad Rivers. The prickly pear (*Opuntia* sp.) is not among them, but a species of sagebrush (*Artemisia dracunculoides*) is, as well as 15 other plants all told (see complete list *post*).

On September 16 the explorers had passed the present site of Chamberlain, South Dakota, just above which they had discovered the mule deer, coyote, and magpie. Three days later they arrived at the Big Bend of the Missouri, where the river loops some 30 miles to the north and then swings back to within 2,000 yards of where the loop began. It was just below the Bend that Clark found great quantities of prickly pear and reported that the spines of this cactus nearly ruined his feet.[20]

After circling the Big Bend, the Corps arrived at Loisel's Fort, where Regis Loisel, whom they had met on the river above St. Charles, had spent the previous winter. According to Clark, the Indians who had visited Loisel had cut down all the cottonwood trees in the area to feed their horses.[21] It is not generally known, and apparently Lewis and Clark did not know until then, that cottonwood bark provided a nourishing food for horses. If judiciously fed, they actually fattened on it, particularly in winter when snow covered the prairie grasses. At such times, it was customary to cut down the trees, even the larger ones,

[20] Osgood, 142.
[21] Osgood, 144.

after which the bark was scraped off and cut into small pieces. General George A. Custer, in his winter campaign of 1868–69 against hostile tribes south of the Arkansas River, frequently exhausted his supply of forage and had to feed his horses and mules on cottonwood bark. "In routing the Indians from their winter villages," he wrote, "we invariably discovered them located upon that point of the stream promising the greatest supply of cottonwood bark, while the stream in the vicinity of the village was completely shorn of its supply of timber, and the village itself was strewn with the white branches of the cottonwood entirely stripped of their bark."[22]

On September 23 Lewis and Clark observed a great mass of smoke rising in the southwest which they correctly interpreted as an Indian signal. That evening three Indian boys who swam the river to their camp told them of two bands of Teton Sioux above, one nearby of 80 lodges and, another, farther upstream, of 60. The next day the party anchored their boats at the mouth of a river flowing in from the west. "The tribes of the Seauex Called the Teton is Camped about 2 Miles up on the N.W. Side," wrote Clark, "and we Shall Call the River after that Nation, Teton" (I, 163).

SUMMARY OF DISCOVERIES

Animals New to Science

PRONGHORN. *Antilocapra americana americana* (Ord). (Thwaites, I, 147; VI, 129). Described, 1815.

COYOTE. *Canis latrans latrans* Say. (Thwaites, I, 185; Ordway, 133; Osgood, 140). 1823.

PLAINS GRAY WOLF. *Canis lupus nubilus* Say. (Thwaites, I, 155). 1823.

PRAIRIE DOG. *Cynomys ludovicianus ludovicianus* (Ord). (Thwaites, I, 141). 1816.

MULE DEER. *Dama hemionus hemionus* (Rafinesque). (Thwaites, I, 140, 152). 1817.

WHITE-TAILED JACK RABBIT. *Lepus townsendii campanius* Hollister. (Thwaites, I, 147). 1839.

BLACK-BILLED MAGPIE. *Pica pica hudsonia* (Sabine). [A.O.U. 475] (Thwaites, I, 151; VI, 130). 1823.

PRAIRIE SHARP-TAILED GROUSE. *Pedioecetes phasianellus campestris* Ridgway. [A.O.U. 308b] (Thwaites, I, 145). 1884.

[22] Donald Culross Peattie, *A Natural History of Western Trees* (Boston, 1953), 334.

? DESERT COTTONTAIL. *Sylvilagus audubonii baileyi* (Merriam). (Thwaites, I, 148). 1897.

Plants New to Science

CUT-LEAVED SIDERANTHUS. *Amellus spinulosus* Pursh = *Haplopappus spinulosus* (Pursh) DC. 1814.

LINEAR-LEAVED WORMWOOD. *Artemisia dracunculoides* Pursh. 1814.

AROMATIC ASTER. *Aster oblongifolius* Nuttall. 1818.

MISSOURI MILK VETCH. *Astragalus missouriensis* Nuttall. 1813.

BUSHY ATRIPLEX. *Atriplex canescens* (Pursh) James = *Calligonum canescens* Pursh. 1814.

BROOMWEED. *Gutierrezia euthamiae* T. & G. = *Solidago sarothrae* Pursh. 1814.

FEW-FLOWERED PSORALEA. *Psoralea tenuiflora* Pursh. 1814.

WOODS' ROSE. *Rosa woodsii* Lindley. 1820.

Lewis and Clark Herbarium

CUT-LEAVED SIDERANTHUS. *Amellus spinulosus* Pursh. Collected September 15, 1804.

LINEAR-LEAVED WORMWOOD. *Artemisia dracunculoides* Pursh. Sept. 15.

AROMATIC ASTER. *Aster oblongifolius* Nuttall. Sept. 21.

MISSOURI MILK VETCH. *Astragalus missouriensis* Nuttall. Sept. 18.

CANADIAN MILK VETCH. *Astragalus mortoni* Nuttall = *A. canadensis* L. Sept. 5.

BUSHY ATRIPLEX. *Atriplex canescens* (Pursh) James. Sept. 21.

PRAIRIE BUTTON-SNAKEROOT. *Liatris pycnostachya* Michaux = *Laciniaria pycnostachya* (Michx.) Kuntze. Sept. 15.

LARGE BUTTON-SNAKEROOT. *Liatris scariosa* Willd. = *Laciniaria scariosa* (L.). Sept. 12.

FEW-FLOWERED PSORALEA. *Psoralea tenuiflora* Pursh. Sept. 21.

MOSSY-CUP OAK. *Quercus macrocarpa* Michaux. Sept. 5.

WOODS' ROSE. *Rosa woodsii* Lindley. Sept. 5.

LANCE-LEAVED SAGE. *Salvia lanceolata* Brouss. Sept. 21.

HARD-LEAVED GOLDENROD. *Solidago rigida* L. Sept. 13.

BROOMWEED. *Solidago sarothrae* Pursh. Sept. 15.

WILD RICE. *Zizania aquatica* L. Sept. 8.

Indian Tribes Encountered

Siouan Linguistic Family: Teton Sioux (Oglala).

Topographic Features Named and/or Discovered

No Preserves Island (Thwaites, I, 140; Osgood, 133).

Shannon Creek (Coues, I, 115n; Ordway, 131).

Boat Island (Coues, I, 112; Ordway, 128n) —— Chicot or Big Cedar Island of later maps.

Troublesome Island (Osgood, 137; Ordway, 130).

Rabbit Island (Ordway, 131).

Corvus Creek (Coues, I, 118) —— now Crow Creek (Coues, I, 118n).

Elm Creek (Thwaites, I, 157).

Prickley Pear Creek (Thwaites, I, 157).

Night Creek (Thwaites, I, 157).

Reuben Creek (Thwaites, I, 162) —— later called East Medicine Knoll
   River (Osgood, 145).

Smoke Creek (Coues, I, 127).

Elk Creek (Coues, I, 127).

Good-humored Island (Coues, I, 131).

Teton River
to
Mandans

CHAPTER SIX

Lewis characterized the Teton (Oglala) Sioux as "the vilest miscreants of the human race" (VI, 98). The Corps spent four days among them, in which time these Indians, headed by their chief, Black Buffalo, made two determined but futile attempts to arrest their further progress. Sergeant Ordway said they numbered between two or three hundred.[1] That figure, however, exaggerated their fighting potential. Like most tribes continuously engaged in intertribal warfare, their squaws outnumbered the men by as much as two and three to one. The young, able-bodied fighting men (warriors) of the tribe probably did not exceed 60 (VII, 65).

The notion has gained credence over the years that the Lewis and Clark party narrowly escaped annihilation by the Tetons. One prominent historian, for example, has recently asserted: "So large a band of Indians—they numbered several hundred and additional ones kept coming in—could easily have massacred the party."[2]

As we assess the situation, the explorers, 43 strong and armed with the best rifles then obtainable, as well as pistols and swivels, were here pitted against a force of no more than 60 warriors who relied chiefly on bows and arrows. If the Sioux had attacked, it is inconceivable that they could "easily have massacred" the disciplined, well-armed, straight-shooting band of explorers. One searches the journals in vain for intimation that Lewis and Clark had any misgivings about

[1] Ordway, 140.
[2] Bernard DeVoto, ed., *The Journals of Lewis and Clark* (Boston, 1953), 34.

90

their ability to cope with these Indians. Arguing their unconcern, they stayed with them for four days, mingling freely at all times. They feared nothing except a surprise attack, and against that they took every precaution.

[2]

The extended stay among the Teton Sioux provided Lewis and Clark with time and opportunity to collect important ethnobotanical and ethnozoological data. At one point, for example, Clark wrote that the Teton women produced special culinary triumphs, one of which was "ground potatoe" (I, 168). This is the first reference in any of the journals to the legume, *Psoralea esculenta,* known by a variety of other common names such as white apple, pomme blanche, prairie apple, and prairie turnip. The root was an important source of food to the Plains Indians. Lewis later found the plant growing wild and wrote a lengthy description of it. To him the root was tasteless and insipid, but he had no doubt that "our epicures would admire this root very much, it would serve them in their ragouts and gravies in stead of the truffles morella" (II, 10–12). When Frederick Pursh technically described this plant (1814), he had at hand a specimen brought back by Lewis. Today it forms a part of the Lewis and Clark Herbarium in the Academy of Natural Sciences of Philadelphia.

Also of ethnobotanical interest is the statement of Lewis and Clark that the Teton "tobacco" consisted of "the inner bark of a species of red willow [*Cornus* sps.] which, being dried in the sun or over the fire, is rubbed between the hands and broken into small pieces, and used alone or mixed with tobacco."[3] The French called this *bois roulé,* though it is better known as kinnikinnik. More often than not it had other ingredients, for example, the scrapings and shavings of such other plants as smooth sumac (*Rhus glabra*), bearberry (*Arctostaphylos uva-ursi*), and red-osier dogwood (*Cornus stolonifera*). To these components the Indian would sometimes add still others, creating a particular blend that appealed to his critical palate. Catlin told of smoking with a chief who mixed shavings from a dried beaver castor (perineal gland) with his kinnikinnik and then dropped on top a *soupçon* of powdered buffalo dung. After lighting the pipe, he and Catlin then "enjoyed together for a quarter of an hour the most delightful ex-

[3] Coues, I, 139.

change of good feelings, amid clouds of smoke and pantomimic gesticulations."[4]

Ethnozoology received even more attention. Lewis and Clark mentioned at least a dozen animals used variously by these Indians. The buffalo, of course, outrivalled all others in importance. The Tetons supplied the explorers with large quantities of meat from this animal. They gave them pemmican, too, a composition of well-pounded jerked beef and buffalo tallow. In preparing this, the squaw seasoned it with a fruit such as that from a wild cherry. Packed in skin bags and sealed tightly, it would remain in good condition for as much as four or five years and was always ready for use without cooking.

Private Whitehouse observed the Sioux women "dressing buffaloe hides for to make cloathing" (VII, 64), buffalo robes in particular. These were often highly decorated and sometimes served unusual purposes. For example, when Lewis and Clark went ashore at the native village they were carried by Sioux warriors from the boat to the Teton council lodge on white dressed robes (I, 167).

The Teton tipis, about 100 of them, were arranged in a large, symmetric circle and covered with white buffalo hides.[5] The average tipi required 15 to 20 hides, so that a minimum of 1,500 had been used by the Tetons of this village in covering their homes. American Indians constructed other kinds of habitations—wickiups, wigwams, hogans, earth-lodges, and cliff-dwellings—but the tipi surpassed all others in colorful appearance and attractive design, and in capturing the fancy of the westward-bound frontiersman.

Clark wrote of Teton "soldiers" whose duty it was to maintain order in the village. "They are known generally by having their bodies blacked but their distinguishing mark are . . . 2 or 3 stuffed raven skins so fixed on the small of the back . . . that the tails stick horizontally off from the body."[6] One of these raven bustles, the earliest known, was brought back by Lewis and Clark and is today in the Peabody Museum, Harvard University. The squaw who fashioned it utilized not only raven skins but also hawk feathers, porcupine quills, and a piece of ermine.[7]

[4] Harold McCracken, *George Catlin and the Old Frontier* (New York, 1959), 96.

[5] Ordway, 140.

[6] Jackson, *Letters,* 517–518.

[7] For a fuller description see Charles C. Willoughby, "A Few Ethnological Specimens Collected by Lewis and Clark," *Amer. Anthropologist,* n.s., 7 (Oct.–Dec., 1905), 633–641.

The journalists reported that the Tetons employed deer skins in making summer moccasins, elk hide for soling winter moccasins, antelope for shifts and leggings, and polecat (skunk, *Mephitis mephitis*) for tobacco pouches. When attired for important occasions, the Teton male often tied a skunk pelt to the heel of each moccasin and allowed it to trail as he walked. Clark announced that he had seen a spoon made of "the Big Horn animal [*Ovis canadensis*]" which would hold two quarts,[8] and had watched the natives use a singular musical instrument made of deer and antelope hoofs tied together that produced "a gingling noise" (I, 168).

The Sioux Indian decorated almost everything he made. The form of esthetic endeavor in which he excelled, which set him apart from most other North American Indians, was quillwork. Lewis and Clark reported porcupine quills embellishing pipe stems, head wear, and, of course, the indispensable, omnipresent buffalo robe.

Sergeant Gass told of seeing Teton dogs harnessed to "a kind of car" on which they transported their goods from one camp to another. They could haul loads, he said, of about 70 pounds.[9] The "car," of course, was the travois. When the Plains Indian decided to move, as he did customarily six to eight times during each hunting season, it was a simple matter for the hard-working squaw to pull down her home and pack it on a travois ready to be hauled away by horse or dog. George Catlin, who happened to be present on moving day, observed that: ". . . every cur of them, who is large enough . . . is encumbered with a car or sled . . . on which he patiently drags his load."[10]

The Tetons valued their dogs for another reason. According to Ordway, "they killed Several dogs and cooked them in a decent manner to treat our people with."[11] Apparently this was the first time many members of the party ate dog meat—but it was far from the last.

In describing the Indian dog, Brackenridge said: "It is nothing more than the domesticated wolf. In wandering through the prairies, I have often mistaken wolves for Indian dogs."[12] Maximilian expressed a similar opinion: "In shape they differ very little from the wolf, and are equally large and strong. Some are of the real wolf colour, others black, white or spotted black and white, and differing only by the tail being

[8] Osgood, 150.
[9] Gass, 54–55.
[10] George Catlin, *The North American Indians*, 2 vols. (Philadelphia, 1913), I, 51.
[11] Ordway, 140.
[12] *Early Western Travels*, VI, 115.

rather turned up more. Their voice is not a proper barking, but a howl, like that of a wolf."[13] It is now generally accepted that the Sioux and other North American Indians domesticated their dogs from wolves, the prairie wolf or coyote (*Canis latrans*) and the larger gray wolf (*Canis lupus*). By the time of Maximilian (1833–34), however, there may have been an infusion of canine blood from dogs of European ancestry introduced to the Upper Missouri by Canadian traders. This would explain the black and white spots to which he alluded.

[3]

The next leg of the journey, to the Arikara villages, consumed 11 days. In that time the party travelled about 150 miles, from the vicinity of present-day Pierre, South Dakota, to an island four miles above the mouth of the Grand River. They found it difficult to free themselves from the Tetons, who followed them demanding handouts. On the second day, they encountered the Tetons of the upper village, some 400 of them, streaming down the valley to join Black Buffalo's band. Lewis and Clark refused to meet with them. Though the fear persisted that these savages would make still another attempt to bar their further progress, nothing happened.

By now it was October and winter approached. Clark reported great flocks of migrating geese, ducks, swans and brant. They named a stream White Brant Creek, though the "white brant" was probably a lesser snow goose (*Chen hyperborea hyperborea*). While out on the plains the hunters encountered many magpies and sharp-tailed grouse. One day an Indian showed up with a wild turkey slung over his back. When one of the men killed a female badger, Sergeant Ordway again proved his worth as a reporter when he wrote, "had the Bones & Skin Saved in order to Send back to the States."[14]

They passed at least five abandoned Arikara villages, the last two so recently and hastily vacated that the Indians had left behind such possessions as boats, baskets, and ripe squashes. The men helped themselves to the squashes. Lewis and Clark encountered three French traders, one of whom could speak some English. This man told them of spending the previous winter 300 leagues up the Cheyenne River where he had found a number of remarkable animals, among them the white bear, a "white-booted turkey," and a quadruped with "large

[13] *Early Western Travels,* XXIII, 310.
[14] Ordway, 148.

circular horns" (I, 176). In this manner they gained advance information about the grizzly bear (*Ursus horribilis*), sage grouse (*Centrocercus urophasianus*), and bighorn sheep (*Ovis canadensis*). By now the Corps of Discovery was 1,400 miles up the Missouri; they might expect to find almost anything.

About three miles beyond the entrance of the Grand River, on October 8, the explorers came to an island (now covered by impounded water from Oahe Dam) on which they discovered the first of three Arikara villages; the other two were situated near each other on the west bank of the Missouri some four miles farther upstream. They stopped briefly to take aboard a Frenchman and then went on until they located a suitable campsite. This Frenchman was Joseph Gravelines, an agent of Regis Loisel. Since he spoke the Arikara language with some fluency, he became of value to Lewis and Clark at once as interpreter and intermediary. When Lewis returned to the island that afternoon, taking Gravelines with him, the Arikara gave him a warm welcome.

Two days later Clark's diary included the information that Gravelines, with one Pierre-Antoine Tabeau, came to breakfast (I, 185). Lewis had apparently arranged this meeting. While still in St. Louis, he had been told Tabeau could, if located, provide him with much useful information on such topics as flora, fauna, and aboriginals (VI, 270). Though the journals refer to Tabeau a number of times and acknowledge his services to the Expedition, they fail to bring him into clear focus. Actually, he was an experienced trader, then 49 years of age, who had been born in Montreal in 1755. Coming from a prominent family of *voyageurs,* he had received "more than the customary advantages of an education," and demonstrated "early indications of a literary aptitude."[15] Apparently he was even then (when Lewis and Clark found him) putting this aptitude to work by writing an account of the geography, animals, plants, and Indians of the Missouri country.

When one compares *Statistical View* with Tabeau's narrative (later published under the title, *Tabeau's Narrative of Loisel's Expedition to the Upper Missouri*), it is evident that Tabeau had supplied Lewis and Clark with considerable significant data. For example, the classification of the Sioux is so similar in both accounts that one wonders if Tabeau had allowed Lewis to read his manuscript or the two had discussed the matter together.

[15] Annie Heloise Abel, ed., *Tabeau's Narrative of Loisel's Expedition to the Upper Missouri* (Norman, Okla., 1939), 44.

Available evidence indicates that the Arikaras (also referred to by the journalists as Ricaras, Rees, and Panias) had early roots in the Southwest, whence they migrated northeast, eventually reaching the Missouri possibly before Siouan tribes. Here they established several populous towns, time and circumstance gradually separating them along a broad front. At first they lived a comparatively peaceful existence. Then the better-armed Sioux, followed by an even deadlier enemy, smallpox, cut down most of them. The survivors had no recourse but to consolidate and move upstream. As we know, Lewis and Clark had already passed a number of their empty villages, hastily abandoned in their flight to escape the Sioux. Recently their lot had further deteriorated when a schism developed between them and the Mandans with whom they had previously been on the best of terms. They expressed delight when Lewis and Clark agreed to allow an emissary to travel with them to the Mandans in an effort to settle current difficulties.

Lewis wrote that the Arikaras were "the remains of ten large tribes of Panias [Pawnees]," and numbered some 2,000 (VI, 88–89). Several years later Albert Gallatin placed them in the Caddoan linguistic family, a family of his creation with three primary divisions: a northern one represented by the Arikaras of the Dakotas; a middle one containing the Pawnee confederacy of the Platte River of Nebraska; and a southern one including such tribes as the Caddo and Wichita of Louisiana, Arkansas, and Oklahoma.

As a result of the wide-ranging migrations of the Caddoans and their consequent fission into geographically separated units, their language, once the same, underwent sensible change. Each Arikara community, for instance, developed its own particular dialect. These linguistic differences posed no problems until after consolidation, when Arikaras from separate villages perforce had to live together. Clark noted this idiomatic problem at once. "Their language is so corrupted," he commented, "that many lodges of the Same village with difficulty . . . understand all that each other say."[16]

The explorers spent five days among the Arikaras. They visited all three villages, made the usual speeches, presented medals and other gifts, and demonstrated once again the capabilities of the air gun. The natives, in turn, provided their guests with food and in their speeches assured them that the "road was open & no one dare Shut it, & we might Departe at pleasure" (I, 186).

[16] Osgood, 159.

The Arikaras differed from Siouan tribes previously encountered in more respects than language. In particular, they lived the year round in earth-lodges, and they engaged in agriculture. If one wants to read a detailed description of the construction of an Arikara earth-lodge, he can find it in Sergeant Gass's journal.[17] In this study, we are interested in it only from the ethnobotanical standpoint. Gass said that it was built of large posts and poles of cottonwood (which formed a frame), on top of which was laid a blanket of willow branches, then grass, and finally, a thick layer of clay. The grass, according to one botanist, was forked beard-grass, *Andropogon furcatus*. It was "the most common in the meadows and prairies of the State, was ordinarily used to lay on the poles to support the earth covering of the lodges."[18]

These Arikara lodges were round (irregularly polygonal), 30 to 40 feet in diameter, and warm and compact. They were invariably of a size to accommodate a large family, a number of dogs and horses, and the usual possessions such as food, beds, weapons, and clothing. To protect their horses against theft and in winter against intense cold, it was not unusual to bring them inside at night where they were tied up near the entrance and fed cottonwood bark. The earth-lodge was definitely a dry-land domicile. In a region of heavy, frequent rain, it would soon have been dissolved and washed away. While Brackenridge was among the Arikaras, he reported great activity among the squaws one morning after a lengthy downpour, as they busied themselves replacing earth which the rain had washed off the lodges during the night.[19]

In this treeless land the Indians often found it difficult to obtain enough wood to satisfy their needs. Frederick Webb Hodge, former Smithsonian scientist, is authority for the statement that the Arikaras obtained it mainly from the river in a manner which was a full test of their agility and courage. "When the ice broke up in the spring, the Indians leaped on the cakes, attached cords to the trees that were whirling down the rapid current, and hauled them ashore. Men, women, and the older children engaged in this exciting work, and although they sometimes fell and were swept downstream, their dexterity and courage generally prevented serious accident."[20]

The Arikaras cultivated the soil, raising corn, beans, squashes,

[17] Gass, 61.
[18] Gilmore, "Uses of Plants by the Indians of the Missouri River Region," 68.
[19] *Early Western Travels*, VI, 114.
[20] Frederick Webb Hodge, *Handbook of American Indians North of Mexico*, 2 vols. (Washington, D.C., 1907), I, 85.

sunflowers, tobacco, and according to Ordway, watermelons.[21] They did not farm because of any lack of game, but because tribal custom, as old as the Missouri bluffs, dictated that they should. For preparing and cultivating the land, the squaws, on whom this labor devolved, possessed just two implements, a hoe made of the shoulder blade of a buffalo or elk ingeniously fastened to a wooden handle, and a rake constructed of reeds curved at the ends. Each family worked a plot varying in size from a half to one or two acres, such plots being separated from others by rudely built brush or pole fences. In general, the more wives an Indian had, the larger his farm. "They claim no land," Lewis wrote, "except that on which their villages stand and the fields which they cultivate" (VI, 89). All other prairie land was public domain. Due to floods, lack of rainfall, and the dessicating effects of strong, persistent winds, crops often failed. An inundation in 1803 destroyed most of the Arikara crops. All too often the Sioux, in night raids, stole what had been raised by great expenditure of labor. Knowledge of these thefts caused Lewis to characterize the Arikara women as "the gardeners of the Soues" (VI, 89).

Corn, the native cereal grass (*Zea mays*), was the staple crop. "The stalk of the Arikara corn seldom exceeds two and a half or three feet in height," wrote an early observer, "and the ears form a cluster near the surface of the ground . . . the grain is small, hard, and covered with a thicker shell than that raised in warmer climates. It does not possess the same nutritive qualities as food for animals as the larger kind, but is more agreeable to the taste of the Indians."[22] The Arikaras grew several varieties and prepared them in different ways. Even though they had cultivated this plant for generations, they never learned the sophisticated art of making corn liquor.

The Arikaras dug cellars (caches) in their lodges and in nearby fields, carefully obliterating all traces of their presence. Herein they stored their corn and other farm produce for the purposes of keeping them during winter and reducing chances of their falling into the hands of enemies. Because they raised surpluses, they were partially independent of the buffalo. As a result, as Lewis pointed out, they maintained "a partial trade with their oppressors the Tetons, to whom they barter . . . corn, beans, and a species of tobacco" (VI, 89).

Lewis paid particular attention to the Arikara tobacco (*Nicotiana*

[21] Ordway, 149.
[22] Edwin T. Denig, "Of the Arikaras," ed. by John C. Ewers, *Bull. Missouri Hist. Soc.*, VI, no. 2 (Jan., 1950), 201–202.

quadrivalvis) , recognizing it as a new species quite different from that raised on Albemarle County farms. In describing it, he referred to its manner of growth, attachment of leaves, and form and color of flower. He said that the Indians preferred dried corollas to other parts, these resembling "at first view the green *tea* and in that state it is smoked by the Indians and I found it very pleasant. it does not affect the nerves in the same manner that the tobacco cultivated in the U'S dose" (VI, 149–150) . Sergeant Gass declared that it "answered for smoking, but not for chewing."[23] Before taking leave of the Arikaras, Lewis and Clark collected specimens of corn, beans, and tobacco for subsequent shipment to Jefferson.

Apparently Lewis and Clark saw bullboats for the first time on October 6. On that date at one of the abandoned Arikara villages below the mouth of the Grand River, Private Whitehouse made an entry in his diary about "Some water-crafts made out of buffalo hides" (VII, 67) . This product of aboriginal inventiveness was a craft of simple construction which resembled nothing so much as a large, round, leather-covered tub. Clark described its manufacture as follows: "2 Sticks of 1¼ inch diameter is tied together so as to form a round hoop of the size you wish the canoe, or as large as the Skin will allow to cover, two of those hoops are made one for the top or brim and the [other] for the bottom the deabth you wish the canoe then Sticks of the same size are crossed at right angles and fastened with a throng to each hoop and also where each Stick crosses each other. then the Skin when green is drawn tight over this fraim and fastened with throngs to the brim or outer hoop so as to form a perfect bason" (V, 325–326) .

The Indians customarily obtained the green hide from a bull buffalo, hence bullboat, a name which had not been coined at the time when Lewis and Clark went west. The "sticks" ordinarily were willow branches. When this singular craft had been completed, righted, and placed on the water, it possessed a high degree of buoyancy. Clark expressed amazement one day at the seeming ease with which three Arikara squaws crossed the Missouri in one during a violent windstorm with "waves as high as I ever saw them on this river" (I, 185) .

Though generally reliable, the bullboat did occasionally turn turtle. This happened when one of the Arikara chiefs was on his way home after receiving an armload of presents from Lewis and Clark. Missouri waters carried away a medal, an American flag, a cocked hat,

[23] Gass, 61.

some paint, and a twist of tobacco. According to Sergeant Ordway, he "grieved himself considerable about his loss."[24]

We must not overlook an observation by Clark here, one of interest to both botanist and zoologist. Early scientists apparently could not make much of it, even Elliott Coues, who appended no footnote of explanation. "Those people gave us to eate," Clark wrote, "a large Been (*of*) which they rob the mice of the Prarie (*who collect & discover it*) wich is verry nurrishing" (I, 187).

This bean, I find, comes from a common plant, the hog peanut or ground bean (*Falcata comosa*), a member of the pea family. It is an odd plant in that it produces two kinds of branches and two kinds of fruit, one above ground and the other beneath. The subterranean branches develop pods containing beans much the size and shape of lima beans, while those above produce much smaller, lentil-size beans. After these underground beans mature, they are dug up by a species of meadow mouse (*Microtus pennsylvanicus insperatus*), which stores them in secluded spots in quantities of a pint or more. Because they were nutritious and tasty, the Indian women eagerly sought them. It is said, however, that they would never rob the mice without leaving some other food in its place.

[4]

Lewis and Clark parted from the Arikaras on October 12. Gravelines and one of the chiefs accompanied them. Two days later the boats slipped over the invisible line subsequently established to separate North and South Dakota. Soon afterwards Lewis made an observation of ornithological significance: "This day took a small bird alive of the order of the [blank space in Ms.] or goat suckers. it appeared to be passing into the dormant state . . . the mercury was at 30 a. o. the bird could scarcely move. I run my penknife into it's body under the wing and completely distroyed it's lungs and heart yet it lived upwards of two hours this fanominon I could not account for unless it proceeded from the want of circulation of the bl[o]od the recarees call this bird to'-na it's note is at-tah-to'-na, at-tah-to'-na, to-nah, a nocturnal bird, sings only in the night as does the whipperwill. it's weight [is] 1 oz 17 Grains Troy" (VI, 132).

This observation remained unrevealed to the eyes of scientists until the publication of the *Original Journals of the Lewis and Clark*

[24] Ordway, 151.

Expedition a century later. In the meantime Audubon, while ascending the Missouri in 1843 (and completely unaware of Lewis's earlier observations), rediscovered the bird and named it Nuttall's whippoorwill (*Caprimulgus nuttallii*). He recorded that the note of this species was "cut short of much of their compounds, for it was reduced to the syllables *Oh-will, Oh-will, Oh-will,* repeated often and as quickly as is the fashion of our common species."[25] So Audubon, rather than Lewis, received credit for discovering the poor-will (*Phalaenoptilus nuttallii nuttallii*).

Lewis's most arresting statement about the poor-will was that "it appeared to be passing into the dormant state." He did not pursue the subject, though he may have been aware of claims by earlier naturalists that some birds hibernate. The well-known English naturalist, Gilbert White, for instance, had said quite a bit about "swallows (*hirundines rusticae*) being found in a torpid state during the winter."[26] Most naturalists then and for a long time afterward, while recognizing hibernation torpidity among mammals, refused to take seriously reports of a similar phenomenon in birds. Documented proof that it did occur in at least one bird—and that the poor-will—was not forthcoming until 1946–48, almost 150 years after Lewis's observation.

At that time a western scientist, Edmund C. Jaeger, kept close watch on a poor-will he had discovered in a niche of a canyon wall in the Chuckawalla Mountains of California. Visiting the bird regularly, he ascertained its body temperature to be almost 30 degrees below normal, that it lost weight and responded only slightly to handling. Its winter sleep for 1947–48 lasted a total of 85 days.[27] Since this series of observations, other ornithologists have reported similar torpidity in certain other birds.

While on the High Plains, Lewis and Clark perforce directed their attention more often to mammals than birds. Almost daily they encountered vast herds of buffalo and other ungulates. Here in southern North Dakota, for example, they were confronted with numerous antelope, perhaps more than at any other place on their travels. Just south of present-day Bismarck, Lewis reported, "Antelope are passing to the Black mountains [Black Hills] to winter as is their custom" (VI, 177).

[25] John James Audubon, *The Birds of America,* 7 vols. (Philadelphia, 1843–44), VII, 350–351.
[26] Gilbert White, *The Natural History of Selborne* (New York, 1925), 37.
[27] Edmund C. Jaeger, "Does the Poor-will Hibernate?" *Condor* (Jan.–Feb., 1948), 45–46, and "Further Observations on the Hibernation of the Poor-will," *Condor,* 51 (1949), 105–109.

As other remarks in the journals attest, these animals were crossing the Missouri *from east to west*. Ordway described the scene at one place where the Indians, taking advantage of the situation, killed upwards of 40 of them in the water using only bows and arrows.[28]

Lewis was witnessing and describing here another instance of true migration (similar to that earlier reported for gray squirrels), an uncommon phenomenon among mammals. True migration occurs when animals make seasonal journeys between regions where they reproduce and where they spend their winters. Some biologists use the term loosely. For instance, it is said that the European lemmings (*Lemmus lemmus*) migrate, whereas they rush into the sea never to return. Other animals are said to have migrated across a Siberian-Alaskan land bridge to populate North America. This is not migration, only an extension of habitat.

Because migration of mammals is uncommon, much more so than among birds, not a great deal has been written about it. Perhaps the best-known instance is that of the barren ground caribou (*Rangifer arcticus*) between the extensive Canadian barrens and timber line. Lewis and Clark witnessed, without knowing it at the time, impressive migrations of the buffalo, these beasts often passing the winters on the prairies 200 to 400 miles south of their summer feeding (and breeding) grounds. Supporting Lewis's observation of the antelope's migration west to the "Black mountains" is Ernest Thompson Seton's statement that "in the northern parts of their range, where snows are heavy and winters severe, antelope of the plains near the Rockies go toward the foot-hills, and those on the open country about the Black Hills flock thither from all points of the compass."[29]

By now the Expedition had climbed to even higher latitudes. The journals speak of hard frosts and of falling cottonwood leaves. The country was becoming more arid, evidenced by the first mention of alkali. ". . . all the streams falling from the hills or high lands," reported Clark, "[are] so brackish that the water can't be drank without effecting the person making use of it as Globesalts [Glauber's Salt]."[30]

On October 19 the party passed an abandoned Mandan village, the first ruins of that nation they had seen. The next day Peter Cruzatte wounded a "white bear," presumably a grizzly, the footprints of

---

[28] Ordway, 154.
[29] Seton, *Life Histories of Northern Animals*, I, 217–218.
[30] Osgood, 163.

which were three times the size of those of a man. Clark observed wolves following large herds of buffalo and killing weaklings unable to keep up with the herd (I, 201). One of the hunters killed an otter (*Lutra canadensis*), seemingly the first of these shy, slender, dusky-brown fur-bearers they had encountered.

Soon they passed more empty Mandan villages. Some of the hunters reported seeing a herd of buffalo with not a single cow in it. They came upon a hunting party of Mandans which included a chief. Since this was their first meeting with these Indians, about whom they had heard so much, it was an important event.

On October 26, after passing more and more Indians, the party arrived at an encampment of Mandans where they met two more chiefs and an Irish free-trader, Hugh McCracken, who had just come from Fort Assiniboine to trade for horses and buffalo robes. He would soon carry messages from Lewis and Clark to the agent of the North West Company at Fort Assiniboine. That night the Corps camped on the west bank of the Missouri just one half mile below the first Mandan village. Men, women, and children flocked to see them, Clark wrote, and Lewis walked to the village with the chiefs. Because it would have been unwise for both captains to leave the boat until they knew the intentions of the natives, Clark did not accompany Lewis.

The Expedition had arrived at the first of five Indian villages (Mandan and Hidatsa) clustered at or near the mouth of the Knife River, in the vicinity of present-day Stanton, North Dakota, and some 60 miles above Bismarck. After 166 days of immense, sustained effort, highlighted continuously by moments of peril, excitement, and stirring discovery, they had finally succeeded in reaching the fabled Mandans, a feat never heretofore accomplished by an expedition using the Missouri.

[5]

Today's student of the Mandans has available to him several sources in addition to Lewis and Clark. The first white man to visit and describe these Indians was Vérendrye (Pierre Gaultier de Varennes, Sieur de la Vérendrye). Travelling in mid-winter on foot from a post on the Assiniboine River, in company with 26 other men, he reached the Missouri on December 3, 1738, at or near the mouth of the Heart River. Here he found the Mandans living in nine villages. After a stay of two weeks, having lost meanwhile his box of trade goods and his lone interpreter, he headed back for the Assiniboine. His brief account of the trip is important because it described a highly prosperous nation as yet untouched and unmarred by the white man's diseases and generally baneful acculturation. Four years later his two sons passed through these same villages as they journeyed farther west seeking unsuccessfully a route to the Western Sea.

After the Vérendryes had pointed the way, other white men followed in their tracks. Among them were James Mackay who in 1787, as we have earlier reported, made the difficult overland trip from above the 49th parallel, and John Evans who came up the Missouri from St. Louis in 1796. Charles McKenzie, a North West Company trader, drifted down from Canada during the winter Lewis and Clark occupied Fort Mandan, and Alexander Henry, another North Wester, arrived the following summer. Both McKenzie and Henry wrote brief accounts of their visits, as did John Bradbury and Henry Brackenridge who in 1811 made hurried trips from their base among the Arikaras.

The first broad-gauged study of the Mandans was made by George Catlin, who lived among them for several weeks early in the year 1832, sketching and writing voluminously. Catlin had gone west undisciplined by formal training in either art or ethnology. His writing is interspersed by romantic imagination and apocryphal theory. Until recently, museums rarely exhibited his paintings and historians and scientists alike tended to discount his work. Beginning early in this century, however, students began to take a closer, more sympathetic look at his canvases and descriptions of Indian manners. In time it became fashionable to display his paintings, and some ethnologists were declaring that "in matters of actual fact he seems to be as reliable as any other authority."[31]

The next and final account of the Mandans (that is, of these people as an existent nation) flowered from the observational industry of Maximilian, superbly enhanced by the educated brush of his artist companion, Karl Bodmer. Maximilian was the first trained scientist to live for an extended period among these Indians of the Upper Missouri, his stay lasting through the winter of 1833–34. His subsequently published account remains today the classic study of the Mandans and is particularly valuable because just four years later smallpox revisited

[31] George F. Will and H. J. Spinden, "The Mandans, a Study of Their Culture, Archaeology and Language," *Papers,* Peabody Museum of Archaeology and Ethnology, Harvard University, III, no. 4 (1906), 87.

the Mandans and annihilated them as a nation. Probably no more than 100 survived.[32]

SUMMARY OF DISCOVERIES

Animals New to Science

POOR-WILL. *Phalaenoptilus nuttallii nuttallii* (Audubon). [A.O.U. 418] (Thwaites, I, 197; VI, 132). Described, 1844.

Plants New to Science

HOARY SAGEBRUSH. *Artemisia cana* Pursh. 1814.

LONG-LEAVED MUGWORT. *Artemisia longifolia* Nuttall. 1818.

FETID RAYLESS GOLDENROD. *Bigelowia graveolens* Gray = *Chrysothamnus graveolens* (Nuttall) Greene. 1818.

INDIAN TOBACCO. *Nicotiana quadrivalvis* Pursh. (Thwaites, VI, 149–150). 1814.

SILVER-LEAFED PSORALEA. *Psoralea argophylla* Pursh. 1814.

POMME BLANCHE; PRAIRIE APPLE. *Psoralea esculenta* Pursh. 1814.

Lewis and Clark Herbarium

HOARY SAGEBRUSH. *Artemisia cana* Pursh. Collected Oct. 1 and 2, 1804.

PASTURE SAGEBRUSH. *Artemisia frigida* Willdenow. Oct. 3.

LONG-LEAVED MUGWORT. *Artemisia longifolia* Nuttall. Oct. 1.

FETID RAYLESS GOLDENROD. *Bigelowia graveolens* Gray. Oct. 2.

VARIOUS-LEAVED SPURGE. *Euphorbia heterophylla* L. = *Poinsettia heterophylla* (L.) Kl. & Garcke. Oct. 4.

COMMON JUNIPER. *Juniperus communis* L. Oct. 17.

WESTERN JUNIPER. *Juniperus occidentalis* Hooker. Oct. 2.

SHRUBBY RED CEDAR. *Juniperus sabina* var. *procumbens* Pursh = *J. horizontalis* Moench. Oct. 16.

INDIAN TOBACCO. *Nicotiana quadrivalvis* Pursh. Oct. 12.

SILVER-LEAFED PSORALEA. *Psoralea argophylla* Pursh. Oct. 17.

POMME BLANCHE. *Psoralea esculenta* Pursh. Date uncertain.

FRAGRANT SUMAC. *Rhus canadensis* Marshall = *Schmaltzia crenata* (Mill.) Greene. Oct. 1.

Indian Tribes Encountered

Caddoan Linguistic Family: Arikara.

Siouan Linguistic Family: Omaha; Teton Sioux (Oglala); Mandan.

[32] Recently the Northern Natural Gas Co. purchased the entire collection of water colors, sketches, notes, journals, and ledgers from the Maximilian-Bodmer Expedition of 1833–34 and placed it in the custody of Joslyn Art Museum, Omaha, Nebraska. See *Transmission*, XVI, no. 2 (1967), 12–14.

Topographic Features Named and/or Discovered

Badhumored Island (Thwaites, I, 165).

No Timber Creek (Thwaites, I, 175) —— Chanker Creek (Coues, I, 143n).

Sentinel Creek (Thwaites, I, 175) —— Fox Creek (Coues, I, 149n).

Lookout Creek (Thwaites, I, 175).

Caution Island (Thwaites, I, 177).

Good Hope Island (Thwaites, I, 179).

Teal Creek (Coues, I, 153).

White Brant Creek (Thwaites, I, 180).

White Goat Creek (Ordway, 146).

Hidden Creek (Gass, 59).

Otter Creek (Osgood, 154) —— Swan Creek (Coues, I, 155n).

Grouse Island (Thwaites, I, 182).

Goodrich Creek (Thwaites, VII, 67).

Kakawissa Creek (Thwaites, I, 183).

Slate Run (Thwaites, VII, 67).

Marappa River (Ordway, 148) —— Grand River (Ordway, 148n).

Stone Idol Creek (Thwaites, I, 190) —— Spring or Hermaphrodite Creek
    (Ordway, 152n).

Pocasse (Hay) Creek (Coues, I, 166).

Chien Creek (Thwaites, I, 195).

Soharch (Girls) Creek (Thwaites, I, 195).

Charpart (Womans) Creek (Thwaites, I, 195).

Winter
at
Fort Mandan

It was high time that Lewis and Clark located a suitable spot for winter quarters. Ice would soon run in the river, the weasel and hare would put on white coats, and Aurora, with lofty flashing columns, would soon light northern skies. Some of the men had already suffered from exposure to cold. An agreeably located site, one providing sufficient timber to build a fort, was an immediate and pressing need.

The men soon found a "Bottom of large Timber"[1] adequate to their wants. The location was on the east bank of the Missouri about seven or eight miles below the mouth of the Knife River. Large cottonwoods, up to 18 inches in diameter, mingled with ash and elm of inferior size. A visitor to this region should waste no time looking for this site; it has long since been washed away by the abrasive power of the Missouri current. When Maximilian spent the winter of 1833–34 here with the Mandans, the location was in mid-stream, and not the smallest trace of it was left.[2] In 1831 the American Fur Company built Fort Clark on the west side of the river almost opposite the site.

With Sergeant Gass in charge, the men at once began construction of the fort. They felled trees, placed logs, split puncheons, lifted beams, daubed cracks, raised a roof, and placed a thick coat of earth over all. Lewis led a detachment to the nearest Mandan village to collect chimney stones. Others dug a vault 100 yards above the fort "in order to keep the place healthy."[3] They took what water they needed from the

[1] Ordway, 162.
[2] *Early Western Travels*, XXIII, 22.
[3] Ordway, 163.

river. Maximilian assures us that it was "cold, refreshing, and very wholesome."[4]

Through necessity, not choice, they built the fort of cottonwood; it was the only timber available. Out of cottonwood, too, they built tables, shelves, beds, benches, and almost everything else requiring wood. "We find the cottonwood Timber will split Tolerable well," commented Ordway.[5] The heat from huge fires that soon blazed high day and night in the rooms of the fort depended almost entirely on this wood. It not only provided warmth but also cooked slabs of buffalo, elk, deer, and antelope meat. "Cottonwood," declared Maximilian, "burns quickly, and emits much heat."[6]

The party made such progress in constructing the fort that they were able to move into it in less than three weeks—on November 30. It consisted of "two rows of huts or sheds, forming an angle where they joined each other; each row containing four rooms, of 14 feet square and 7 feet high."[7] According to their estimate, it was 1,600 miles from the Mississippi.

The workmen put the finishing touches to the roof on the 27th—and just in time. That night seven inches of snow fell. In these crude quarters the explorers passed the winter of 1804–5, a long cold one. One night the temperature dropped to 45° F below. Inside, however, the men kept warm and secure. It was "made so strong as to be almost cannon-ball proof," one of the visitors from the North West Company reported.[8]

While waiting completion of the fort, Lewis and Clark visited the different villages, held councils, and distributed the usual gifts. On these rounds they met a French-Canadian trader whom they hired as an interpreter. This was René Jusseaume, who had lived among the Knife River Indians for several years and could speak their languages. From all reports he seems to have been something of a scoundrel, but he solved immediate problems of communication. With his help, for instance, Lewis and Clark had no trouble in effecting a peace between the Mandans and Arikaras.

[4] *Early Western Travels*, XXIII, 240.
[5] Ordway, 162.
[6] *Early Western Travels*, XXIII, 245.
[7] Coues, I, 196.
[8] Ruth Hazlitt, ed., "The Journal of Francois Antoine Larocque from the Assiniboine River to the Yellowstone—1805," reprinted from Historical Section of *The Frontier, A Magazine of the Northwest*, XIV, nos. 3 and 4, and XV, no. 1 (1934), 8.

In addition to Jusseaume, Lewis and Clark soon engaged the services of Touissant Charbonneau, a former employee of the North West Company who had lived among the Hidatsas for some time and spoke their language with moderate fluency. A few days later, Clark wrote that "two Squars of the Rock mountains, purchased from the Indians by a frenchman [Charbonneau] came down" (I, 219). One of the two squaws (both were wives of Charbonneau) would shortly achieve a place for herself in American history. This was the young Indian girl now known to every school child as the Bird Woman or Sacagawea.[9] A Shoshoni girl, she had been captured by the Hidatsas on one of their far-flung hunting trips into western Montana. When Lewis and Clark discovered that she was a full-fledged Shoshoni (Snake) Indian, they at once conceived the idea that she might be of value to the Expedition in helping them obtain horses from her people which they would later need in order to cross the Rockies. They then made the bargain with Charbonneau which resulted in a woman joining a unit of the U. S. Army.

Lewis and Clark spent almost six months among the aboriginals at the mouth of the Knife, from October 26, 1804, to April 7, 1805. The Indians here, numbering about 4,000, occupied five villages. Some 1,250 of them, the Mandans, lived in two of the towns, 2,500 Hidatsas (also called Minitari, Gros Ventres, and Big Bellies) in two others, and 200 Wattasoons in the fifth. The last-mentioned group (also called Ahnahaway, Shoe, and Soulier) is generally classified by anthropologists with the Hidatsas because of similarity in language and custom. The principal chiefs whom Lewis and Clark became acquainted with were White Buffalo Robe (Wattasoon); Black Moccasin and One Eye (Hidatsa); and Black Cat and Big White (Mandan).[10]

A comparison of languages and customs affords strong evidence

[9] Much has been written about the derivation, pronunciation, and spelling of this girl's name. As to the spelling, Wheeler, Bakeless, Jackson, and the Bureau of Ethnology used Sacagawea; Biddle, Thwaites, Coues, Osgood, Quaife, and others prefer Sacajawea; still others, particularly the State Historical Society of North Dakota, insist on Sakakawea. I could be content with any of these spellings but will endeavor to stick with Sacagawea. The derivation and pronunciation of the word I leave to others.

[10] Big White's Mandan name seems to have been Sheheke or Shahaka. He was the overlord of the lower Mandan village, Matootonha, on the west bank of the Missouri four miles below the Knife. Black Cat was the principal chief of the upper Mandan town, Rooptarhe, one mile below the Knife on the east side of the Missouri. White Buffalo Robe ruled the Wattasoon village, Maharha, at the mouth of the Knife. Black Moccasin and One Eye (Le Borgne) were head men of the two Hidatsa villages both situated a short distance up the Knife.

that the Mandans and Hidatsas sprang from Siouan stock, possibly from the same immediate stem, and that the former migrated from an eastern locale, possibly Minnesota or the Great Lakes region. Sometime following Vérendrye's visit, they had moved upstream from the Heart River. When Lewis and Clark reached the Heart, they wrote of passing nine abandoned Mandan villages where lodges were collapsing and many bones, teeth, and human skulls whitened the premises (I, 202). Later that winter, while on overnight hunting trips downriver, various members of the Corps found refuge from cold and exposure in these deserted lodges.

The Assiniboins had informed Vérendrye that he would find the Mandans to be white Indians, and he did little to negate this report when he subsequently wrote: "This tribe is of mixed blood, white and black."[11] The myth spread rapidly and soon crossed the Atlantic. There in the British Isles it hatched another, namely, that the Mandans were Welsh, descendants of the Welsh Prince, Madoc, who had allegedly discovered America in the year 1170. It was this fiction that had brought John Evans to America from Wales. According to Clark, Evans "went as high as the Mandans in 1796–7 and . . . returned with a conv[iction] that there were no Welsh Indians."[12] Some twentieth-century ethnologists have concluded that "there was a tendency toward light complexion among the Mandans,"[13] while others insist that "much of the alleged blondism can be attributed to early historic white admixture, or to the normal range of variation in skin color."[14] But the fable that they were white, and descendants of European forebears, persists.[15]

[2]

The business of providing food for the party during the winter months proved formidable. It took one full-grown buffalo, or its equivalent, to feed them on any given day. The equivalent was four deer or one elk and a deer. Hunting fell off during construction of the fort, with most

[11] Lawrence J. Burpee, ed., *Journals and Letters of Pierre Gaultier de la Vérendrye* (Toronto, 1927), 340.

[12] Jackson, *Letters,* 515.

[13] Will and Spinden, "The Mandans," 101.

[14] Letter to author, July 18, 1962, from S. H. Riesenberg, Department of Anthropology, Smithsonian Institution.

[15] Gene Jones, "The Mandan Indians, Descendants of the Vikings," *Real West,* IX, no. 47 (May, 1966), 31–32.

hands shaping timbers and raising walls. However, as that job neared completion, Clark wrote (November 14) : "We are compelled to use our Pork which we doe Spearingly for fear of some falur in procureing a Sufficiency from the woods" (I, 222). With fresh meat exhausted, Drouillard was placed in charge of a party to seek game.

Lewis and Clark were much pleased when these men returned a few days later with 32 deer, 12 elk, and one buffalo. This was a "timely supply" but, appetites being what they were, good at best for no more than three weeks. Accordingly, on December 6 the hunters picked up their rifles again. Snow covered the ground, and an icy, penetrating wind blew uninterruptedly from the north-northwest. At night the temperature dropped well below zero. In spite of great fatigue and hardship, including frostbitten ears, toes, and fingers, the men killed, in five days, 36 buffalo and one deer.

Continued hunting by both explorers and Indians drove game animals farther and farther from the fort, necessitating longer journeys. At one time Clark found himself almost 60 miles from base, near the mouth of the Heart River. On December 10 Lewis wrote: "Captain Clark, who had gone out yesterday with 18 men, to bring in the meat we had killed the day before, came in at twelve o'clock. After killing nine buffalo and preparing those already dead, he had to spend a cold, disagreeable night on the snow, with no covering but a small blanket, sheltered by the hides of the buffalo they had killed . . . the weather is still exceedingly cold and the thermometer at 10° and 11° below zero."[16]

Sergeant Gass told of three hunters at a considerable distance from the fort who killed nothing for two days but a wolf which, for lack of other food, they were obliged to eat. According to Private Whitehouse, "it eat very well" (VII, 73). On February 30 Clark wrote, "I returned last Night from a hunting party much fatigued, having walked 30 miles on the ice and through Points of wood land in which the Snow was nearly Knee Deep" (I, 259). Some of the men with thin-soled moccasins blistered their feet on the uneven frozen surface of the Missouri; others broke through thin places in the ice, their clothes then freezing on their bodies.

Other difficulties plagued the men. Many of the animals killed were "meager" and consequently unfit for human consumption. If they left others unprotected, wolves, ravens, and magpies were soon at them. On long forays from the fort, there was always the possibility of en-

[16] Coues, I, 210.

countering hostile Indians. This happened in mid-February when Drouillard and three men left the fort to bring in meat that had been left in the field. Some 25 miles downriver a party of about 100 Sioux suddenly appeared who robbed them of their knives and two of their three horses. They counted themselves lucky to have escaped so easily.

Obtaining enough food to fill their stomachs would have been much more of a problem if it had not been for the proximity of Mandans and Hidatsas and their eagerness to trade. They beat paths to the fort, carrying pemmican and jerked meat, dried pumpkins and squashes, corn and beans. Clark told of the arrival one day of Big White. "He packed about 100 lb of fine meet on his squar for us" (I, 219). Presented with trifling gifts of ribbon, beads, mirrors, fish hooks, and the like, the Indians went away happy. In time, however, Lewis and Clark awoke to the unpleasant fact that their stock of trade goods had suffered disquieting depletion.

At this point, when it seemed that they might have to discontinue trade with their neighbors, the particular skills of John Shields, William Bratton, and Alexander Willard came to the rescue. Shields, the most talented of the three, was a self-made blacksmith who, since the beginning of the trip, had been in steady demand for repairing tools, guns, and other articles. When the Indians discovered his talent, they rushed to him with a wide variety of broken utensils and weapons to be repaired. Soon Clark was writing that Shields had "proved a happy reso[r]ce to us in our present situation as I believe it would have been difficult to have devised any other method to have procured corn from the natives" (I, 255).

When repair work lagged, an imaginative brave saved the day by conceiving the idea that Shields's artistry could make an iron battle-ax for him. Shields obliged, with the result that he and his helpers soon had a rash of requests for these formidable weapons. They had a zest for their work, however, since they were rewarded by watching their stockpile of Indian corn grow larger and larger. So, due to the hardihood of the hunters and the industry of Shields, Bratton, and Willard, the explorers had plenty of food and good variety throughout a winter that was longer and colder than any of them had heretofore experienced. More than that, when time came for them to resume their journey, they had a surplus of corn to stow away in their boats, a circumstance highly pleasing to the leaders of the Expedition.

With such a variety of food, none of the party suffered from dietary diseases during the winter. Some 30 years later, when Maximilian spent a winter among the Mandans, he had little to eat except corn and dried meat. Early in March he became ill and almost died. He was saved only after a Negro at Fort Clark voiced the opinion that he suffered from scurvy, basing his diagnosis on his experience with that disorder when present at Council Bluffs in 1819 with Major Stephen Long's Expedition. At that time, some 300 of that party developed scurvy, with almost one third of them dying. The Negro recommended that Maximilian be fed the small green herbs of the prairie, in particular the wild onion. After only four days on this diet, he showed improvement and from then on as he continued this regimen, his recovery was rapid.

By now it is evident that the Mandans and Hidatsas, like the Arikaras, were agriculturists. Even though they sometimes produced bumper crops of corn and other plant staples, they nevertheless relied mainly on the buffalo for sustenance. One day a Mandan chief complained to Clark that his people suffered "very much for the article of meat, and that he had not tasted any for several days" (I, 256).

After the Missouri ice had grown hard and firm, Lewis and Clark more than once had dropped their work at the fort to watch the buffalo crossing from one bank to another in great throngs. As spring thaws developed, these animals attempted to cross as usual. Many of them, however, failed in their efforts. The ice broke beneath their weight and they were swept downstream to an almost certain death. At such times Lewis and Clark looked on fascinated as the Indians displayed feats of amazing agility. "I observed," Clark wrote, "extrodanary dexterity of the Indians jumping from one cake of ice to another, for the purpose of Catching the buffalow as they float down many of the cakes of ice which they pass over are not two feet square" (I, 278–279).

If the animal caught had been dead rather longer than yesterday, so much the better. The Mandans preferred their meat high. McKenzie reported that in the spring both sides of the Missouri were covered with putrefying carcasses and that the natives sought these eagerly even though the stench was intolerable. "So fond are the Mandans of putrid meat," he declared, "that they bury animals whole in the winter for the consumption of the spring."[17]

[3]

At Fort Mandan, in his role as physician to the Expedition, Lewis tended to the health of the men under his command and, on occasion,

[17] L. R. Masson, *Les Bourgeois de la Compagnie du Nord-Ouest*, 2 vols. (Quebec, 1889), I, 337.

to that of the Indians. Now and then he went further than mere diagnosis and treatment and demonstrated his skill as surgeon. With few exceptions, the men remained healthy. In mid-winter Clark wrote, "One man taken violently Bad with Plurisie, Bleed & apply those remedies Common to that disorder" (I, 251). Soon afterwards Drouillard fell victim to the same disorder. After he had been bled and given sage tea, he was on his feet again in a day or two.

Sub-zero weather was the explorer's most stubborn enemy during the long winter months. Many of the men had to be treated for frostbite. John Newman, for example, "had his hands and feet severely frozen with which he suffered extreme pain for some weeks."[18] Early in December, Clark reported a temperature of 12° below and "several men returned a little *frost bit* my Servants feet frosted & his P——s a little" (I, 235). About all that Lewis and Clark could do for their men under these circumstances was to instruct them to immerse frostbitten parts in cold water or rub them vigorously with snow until circulation reestablished itself.

One morning a 13-year-old Indian boy limped into the fort and reported that he had spent the night in the snow protected only by a buffalo robe. Both feet were frozen and, a few days later, Lewis found it necessary to amputate the toes on one of the boy's feet. In this operation, if Lewis followed custom, he seared the cut surfaces with a hot iron. This was done to stop hemorrhage rather than to sterilize. With frozen members, however, there was ordinarily a minimum of bleeding if the surgeon cut through the dead tissue immediately beyond the living. Lewis did not sew up the wounds as would be done today. If he had been severing the leg above the knee, for example, he might have taken two or three stitches, but not in minor surgery such as removal of toes. Wounds were never sewed tight then, because they had to be left open for drainage and to allow them to granulate from the inside out. All steps—excision, cauterization, suturing—were taken, of course, without the beneficent aid of anaesthesia. Back in the "good old days," surgery was a soul-scarring ordeal.

On February 11, 1805, Sacagawea gave birth to a son. Lewis, whose obstetrical role was a minor one, described the birth as follows: "It is worthy of remark that this was the first child which this woman had born, and as is common in such cases her labor was tedious and the pain violent; Mr. Jessome informed me that he had frequently administered a small portion of the rattlesnake, which he assured me had never failed to produce the desired effect, that of hastening the birth of

18 Jackson, *Letters,* 365.

the child; having the rattle of a snake by me I gave it to him and he administered two rings of it to the woman broken in small pieces with the fingers and added to a small quantity of water. Whether this remedy was truly the cause or not I shall not undertake to determine, but I was informed that she had not taken it more than ten minutes before she brought forth   perhaps this remedy may be worthy of future experiments, but I must confess that I want faith as to it's efficacy" (I, 257–258).

Charbonneau and Sacagawea called their son Baptiste, though the members of the Expedition appear to have nicknamed him Pomp (short for Pompey). Later, as we shall see, Clark called a prominent rock formation on the Yellowstone Pompey's Tower (now Pompey's Pillar). With his father and mother, Pomp travelled with the party to the Pacific and back. It may have been something new in the annals of military organizations to have had an unweaned infant as a member.

The explorers mentioned snow blindness just once. In mid-winter a Mandan chief showed up at the fort who suffered from this affliction. "At this season of the year," Lewis commented, "the reflection from the ice and snow is so intense as to occasion almost total blindness. This complaint is very common."[19] The cure, according to Clark, consisted of "jentilley swetting the part affected, by throwing Snow on a hot Stone" (I, 262). When Maximilian later visited this country, he found the Mandans attempting to alleviate snow blindness by bathing the eyes with a solution of gunpowder and water.[20]

The Mandan and Hidatsa men, as had the Teton Sioux and Arikara, offered the explorers their wives for the night, and unmarried damsels were willing to trade themselves for a bauble. Lewis and Clark said very little about these erotic happenings and even less about the sordid sequelae. Wrote Clark tersely on January 14, "Several men with the Venereal cought from the Mandan women" (I, 248). And, a few days later, "one man verry bad with the pox [great pox or syphilis]" (I, 250). Neither Lewis nor Clark expressed any particular concern about the men so afflicted. As we shall subsequently learn, Lewis was convinced that he knew how to treat and cure syphilis.

[4]

One night soon after Lewis and Clark arrived among the Mandans, they witnessed the fury of a prairie fire. It spread with such speed that

[19] Coues, I, 235.
[20] *Early Western Travels*, XXIII, 360.

an Indian man and woman were trapped and burned to death, and others received severe burns. With rare presence of mind, a mother saved her boy by throwing a green buffalo robe over him. In reporting the event, Clark said: "The fire did not burn under the Skin, leaveing the grass round the boy" (I, 211). Readers of James Fenimore Cooper may recall that in one of his Leatherstocking Tales, *The Prairie,* the young Pawnee chieftain, Hard Heart, saved himself from a prairie fire in the same identical manner, and it is possible that Cooper borrowed the idea from Clark's account.

Although lightning caused many prairie fires and human careless-ness others, some were intentionally set. The Plains Indians, for in-stance, according to Lewis and Clark, often started fires in the spring to burn off the old grass. During the latter part of their stay at Fort Man-dan, Clark wrote: "a cloudy morning & Smokey all day from the burn-ing of the plains, which was set on fire by the *Minnetarries* for an early crop of Grass, as an enducement for the Buffalow to feed on" (I, 269).[21]

Bradbury wrote that prairie fires were frequently started by de-feated war parties, "to prevent their enemies from tracing their steps."[22] Quite often Indians set them to transmit intelligence, to report the discovery of a herd of buffalo, for instance, or to warn their people of danger. More than once, between the Platte and Niobrara, Lewis and Clark themselves had started fires. On August 17, for example, Clark wrote, "Set the Praries on fire to bring the Mahars and Soues if any were near, this being the useal Signal" (I, 111).

Regardless of origin, after the inferno had passed, the prairie was a lifeless field of black ashes, a scene of desolation and destruction. It is understandable, therefore, that Lewis believed these frequent confla-grations explained the absence of trees on the plains. "This want of timber," he declared, "is by no means attributable to a deficiency in the soil to produce it, but owes its origin to the ravages of the fires, which the natives kindle in these plains at all seasons of the year" (VII, 311). Josiah Gregg, writing 40 years later, supported Lewis's view: "It is unquestionably the prairie conflagrations that keep down the woody growth upon most of the western uplands . . . in fact, we are now witnessing the encroachment of the timber upon the prairies, wherever the devastating conflagrations have ceased their ravages." Then, allud-

---

[21] Edwin T. Denig denied this, saying that such action to facilitate hunting would have had "the contrary effect, driving the game out of their own country." See Denig, "Indian Tribes of the Upper Missouri," *46th Annual Report,* Bur. Amer. Ethnology (Washington, D.C., 1930), 408–409.

[22] *Early Western Travels,* V, 72.

ing to reported increases in rainfall and fewer drouths, he raised an interesting question: "Then may we not hope that these sterile regions might yet be thus revived and fertilized and their surface covered one day by flourishing settlements to the Rocky Mountains?"[23]

Flourishing settlements have come to the plains, but not trees, and the farmers and ranchmen living there who strive diligently to create effective shelter belts wonder if they ever will. The absence of fires has not prepared the soils for forests. If Lewis, Gregg, and others had given the matter more thought, they might have come to the conclusion, as did Lt. Zebulon M. Pike, that the plains "never afforded moisture sufficient to support the growth of timber."[24]

[5]

During the course of the winter, Lewis and Clark directed their attention toward learning everything possible about the great silent vastness, unknown and hitherto unchallenged, that lay between them and the Rockies. They obtained their information "altogether from Indians,"[25] primarily from the Hidatsas who for countless generations had made predatory raids far to the west, even to the sources of the Missouri. Some had ventured as far as the Continental Divide and from its summit had gazed upon the multiple, pine-studded ranges of the Bitterroots which appeared to follow one another endlessly in the direction of the setting sun.

With the aid of Jusseaume and Charbonneau, Lewis and Clark questioned the Indians about that part of the Missouri yet to be explored—its course and navigability, its tributaries, rapids, and waterfalls. They watched as Hidatsas drew crude maps on the bare floors of earth lodges, on white surfaces of buffalo robes, or in the ashes of dying fires. Sometimes an informant, more adept at map-making than others, would make tiny heaps of sand to portray mountains and with his finger create furrows to indicate river courses. Big White made "a Scetch of the Countrey as far as the high Mountains" (I, 245).

Lewis and Clark inquired about the Indian tribes they might expect to encounter, the number of warriors each could throw into battle, and their reputations for friendliness or hostility. On one point they made particular inquiry. Would it be possible, when finally the

[23] Gregg, *Commerce of the Prairies*, 362.
[24] Coues, *The Expeditions of Zebulon M. Pike*, II, 524.
[25] Jackson, *Letters*, 230.

boats had to be abandoned, for them to obtain horses from Indians to transport their baggage over the mountains? Assured that they would, Lewis wrote Jefferson: "the circumstances of the Snake [Shoshoni] Indians possessing large quantities of horses is much in our favour, as by means of horses, the transportation of our baggage will be rendered easy and expeditious over land, from the Missouri, to the Columbia river" (VII, 320).

The two captains took pains to question several individuals, separately and at different times, after which they compared the information thus obtained and accepted only that upon which their informants tended to agree. They had no reason to doubt, therefore, that, as the Indians said, the first important Missouri tributary falling in from the south they would come to would be the Little Missouri and, beyond that also from the south, the Yellowstone and Musselshell. They gained preknowledge, too, of such northern affluents as the White Earth, the "river which scolds all others" (Marias of today), and the Medicine. They learned also that "the Great falls is about (*800*) miles nearly West" (I, 246), that some 200 miles farther along the "missouri divides itself into three nearly equal branches," and that the most northerly of the three "is the largest, and is navigable to [the] foot of [a] chain of high mountains, being the ridge which divides the waters of the Atlantic from those of the Pacific ocean" (VI, 55).

Big White informed them that "the river rejone [Roche Jaune or Yellowstone] recvees [receives] 6 Small rivers on the S. Side" (I, 245). From the same or other source, they elicited Indian names for these six branches and English equivalents for three, namely, Powder, Tongue, and Bighorn (VI, 123). Lewis and Clark were also apprised of the facts that the Yellowstone has no tributaries of note on the north and that the country between it and the Missouri is drained largely by the Musselshell.

After talks with the Indians, Lewis wrote that the extreme sources of the Yellowstone "are adjacent to those of the Missouri, river platte, and I think probably with some of the south branch of the Columbia river" (I, 339). One historian, disagreeing with this statement, said that Lewis "seriously misconceived" the Yellowstone headwaters.[26] However, as a map of Yellowstone National Park reveals, the terminals of the Yellowstone River in the park interlock closely, both with the Madison of the Missouri and the Snake of the Columbia. Perhaps the criticism was levelled more at the suggested approximation of the

[26] DeVoto, *The Journals of Lewis and Clark,* 88.

Yellowstone and Platte; but even here Lewis had truth on his side. As everyone familiar with Wyoming topography knows, the two most important branches of the Yellowstone, the Powder and the Bighorn, both send feeders far south which dovetail with those from the North Platte.

Not all of the information Lewis and Clark obtained from the Indians proved to be accurate. They conceived the idea that the Marias River entered the Missouri below the Musselshell and that a portage of no more than half a mile would be required to bypass the Great Falls. They seemingly were misinformed, too, about routes across the Continental Divide. On the other hand, the amount of accurate information they ferreted out of the untutored Mandans and Hidatsas was extraordinary. They even learned in advance that "no Buffaloe [exist] west of the second range of the Rocky mountains" (VI, 55). Based on the geographical data elicited, Clark made a map delineating the Missouri watershed west of Fort Mandan. Considering the fact that he had not set foot on any part of this land, but rather had travelled it only vicariously, it was surprisingly accurate.

[6]

As winter began to despair, Lewis and Clark devoted more and more time to completing reports and maps, writing letters, and packing specimens, all of which would be carried downstream in the near future to St. Louis. On April 3, Sergeant Ordway wrote, "The articles which was to be sent back to the States in the Big Barge was packed and boxed up ready to go on board."[27]

The cargo to leave Fort Mandan included Lewis's "A Summary View of Rivers and Creeks" and Clark's "A Summary Statement of Rivers, Creeks and Most Remarkable Places"; also maps and at least two of the journals, one by Clark and the other by one of the sergeants, most likely Floyd's. Writing to Jefferson on abandoning Fort Mandan, Lewis was pleased to say: "I have transmitted . . . every information relative to the geography of the country which we possess" (VII, 319).

Of the letters that descended the Missouri on the keelboat only a few have survived. Two of these throw possible light on whether Lewis did or did not write a journal on the first leg of the journey. One from Lewis to Jefferson included this statement: "You will also receive herewith inclosed a part of Capt. Clark's private journal, the other part

[27] Ordway, 189.

you will find inclosed in a separate tin box. this journal is in it's original state, and of course incorrect, but it will serve to give you the daily detales of our progress, and transactions. Capt. Clark dose not wish this journal exposed in it's present state, but has no objection, that one or more copies of it be made by some confidential person under your direction, correcting it's grammatical errors &c."[28]

No one knew Clark's problems with spelling and sentence structure better than Clark himself, and he was obviously embarrassed to have his journal sent to the President. The question promptly arises as to why Lewis did not send his own journal instead—if he had one. Such a course would have obviated any necessity in Washington for copying and correcting grammatical mistakes and at the same time would have spared his friend discomfiture. Lewis made just one reference to a journal of his own when writing to Jefferson. He said that he would send it, and one or two of the best kept by his men, once the party had reached the headwaters of the Missouri. But this statement cannot be taken as *prima facie* evidence that he had a journal in form to send to Jefferson on April 7 when the keelboat left for St. Louis.

The other letter bearing on this matter, also to Jefferson, was a rough draft only. Clark began it and then turned to Lewis for assistance. The latter edited and completed it, after which Clark made a final copy. In his editing, Lewis deleted entirely Clark's opening line which said: "<As Capt. Lewis has not Leasure to Send> <write> <a correct Coppy journal of our proceedings &c>."[29] If we look closely at this excised clause to determine its meaning, it is not too difficult to conclude that what Clark was trying to say was that Lewis, for lack of time, had not as yet completed the task of converting his field notes into a journal. That Lewis struck out the clause would seem to indicate his personal wish that, as Donald Jackson has said, "Clark's statement to Jefferson be completely noncommital."[30]

In further consideration of this question, we must not overlook still another significant piece of evidence. During the winter just ended, Clark was away from Fort Mandan almost ten days on a hunting trip. For these few days, Lewis did keep a diary, though we have no like entries of his whatever for days immediately preceding or following this period. This pinch-hitting role should not be forgotten. In days

[28] Jackson, *Letters*, 231.
[29] Jackson, *Letters*, 226.
[30] Jackson, *Letters*, 226n.

ahead, more than once, Lewis would perform an identical service when separated from Clark.

As the keelboat shoved off from Fort Mandan, it carried such additional papers as *Statistical View*, muster-rolls, public accounts, and weather records. It goes without saying that when these reached Jefferson, he read them with great interest; they represented the first such data reported from the Missouri part of Louisiana Territory.

The bulk of the shipment leaving Fort Mandan was in the form of weighty boxes, trunks, and cages. These contained objects of Indian manufacture and specimens of plants, animals, and minerals. An accompanying invoice listed, for example: "Specimens of plants numbered from 1 to 60" and a parcel of roots "highly prized by the natives as an efficatious remidy in the cure of the bite of the rattle snake, or Mad dog" (VII, 322–323). These specimens, Lewis wrote Jefferson, "are accompanyed by their rispective labels expressing the days on which obtained, places where found, and also their virtues and properties when known" (VII, 318).

Indian artifacts, packed into four boxes and three trunks, included a Mandan bow and arrows, an earthen pot "such as the Mandans manufacture and use for culinary purposes," and a number of buffalo robes. One of the robes had been painted "by a Mandan man representing a battle which was fought eight years since, by the Sioux & Ricaras, against the Mandans, Minitarras & Ahwahharways" (VII, 323).

It took 25 boxes and cages to contain the zoological material Lewis and Clark consigned to Jefferson. There were skins, bones, horns, antlers, and of particular interest, six live animals: four magpies, a prairie dog, and a prairie sharp-tailed grouse.

The keelboat with its precious cargo arrived in St. Louis on May 20, six weeks after its departure from Fort Mandan. What happened to the specimens thereafter is a story comprising many facets. It will be told in a concluding chapter.

No one can justifiably contend that the winter at Fort Mandan had not gone off well. There had been almost complete harmony between the explorers and Indians. The men had escaped dietary disease and, in general, they continued in good health. And Lewis and Clark, as the wealth of documents, maps, and specimens dispatched to Jefferson eloquently attests, had reason to be proud of personal accomplishments.

SUMMARY OF DISCOVERIES

Animals New to Science

? SHORT-TAILED SHREW. *Blarina brevicauda brevicauda* (Say). (Thwaites, VII, 323). 1823.

? NORTHERN BOBCAT. *Lynx rufus pallescens* Merriam. (Thwaites, I, 236). Described, 1899.

LONG-TAILED WEASEL. *Mustela frenata longicauda* Bonaparte. (Thwaites, I, 218; Coues, I, 191n). 1838.

Plants New to Science

None certainly identifiable. It may be, however, that the roots "highly prized by the natives as an efficatious remidy in the cure of the bite of the rattle snake" Lewis sent to Jefferson were those of the NARROW-LEAFED PURPLE CONE-FLOWER, *Echinacea angustifolia* DC. (Thwaites, I, 226; VII, 323). This plant was not technically described until 1836.

Lewis and Clark Herbarium

BEARBERRY; SACCACOMMIS. *Arctostaphylos uva-ursi* (L.) Sprengel. Collected at Fort Mandan.

Indian Tribes Encountered

Algonquian Linguistic Family: Cree (Christanoes, Knistenaux); Cheyenne. Siouan Linguistic Family: Assiniboin; Hidatsa; Wattasoon; Mandan.

Topographic Features Named and/or Discovered

None.

Fort Mandan
to
the Yellowstone

CHAPTER EIGHT

As the bitterness of winter began to wane, Lewis and Clark put Sergeant Gass in charge of a 15-man detail to construct dugout canoes. With the return of the keelboat to St. Louis, these would be necessary. Such boats required large trees, and it was a question whether they could be found. Just 10 years earlier Truteau needed a dugout to carry his goods from the Arikaras to the Mandans. Though he and his men spent a fortnight and scouted upstream 75 miles, they could not locate a single tree large enough.[1]

Sergeant Gass had better luck. In a bottom a few miles above Fort Mandan, he found a clump of large cottonwoods. Out of these, during the next three weeks, he and his men built six dugouts, each large enough to accommodate a crew, trade goods, food, and assorted paraphernalia. They were cumbersome craft with which to tackle the turbulence of the Missouri, but, as we shall see, they performed in a manner exceeding what anyone had a right to expect. Just how Lewis and Clark would have met the problem of transporting the Expedition on up the river without them is a question.

When the day of departure drew near, the men aired and dried all supplies and bundled them into eight secure packs. They released the barge and two pirogues from their prisons of ice and made a new steering oar for the barge. They took stock of emergency rations and ascertained that they still had much of the flour, pork, parched meal,

[1] Nasatir, *Before Lewis and Clark*, I, 295.

and dried apples with which they had started. The portable soup remained untouched. Though their supply of trade goods had diminished appreciably, Lewis and Clark were sanguine about increasing it from passing boats, once they had reached the Pacific. They received a request from Tabeau that he and four other traders be allowed to board the keelboat when it arrived at the Arikara villages. They were happy to accede to this request, since the extra hands would increase the strength of the returning party and provide that much additional protection against possible Indian attack.

River ice delayed departure until April 7. At precisely 4 P.M. on that date, Lewis and Clark dismissed the keelboat crew (Corporal Richard Warfington in charge) and ordered them to return without delay to St. Louis. Immediately afterwards, the Corps of Discovery climbed into the fleet of eight smaller boats (six dugouts and the two pirogues) and started upstream. This latter group numbered 32, all original party members except Charbonneau, Sacagawea, the infant Baptiste (Pomp), and a Frenchman named Baptiste Lepage discovered among the Mandans. Lepage had been taken on as a replacement for Private John Newman who had been discharged for insubordination.

Though Lewis may not have kept a journal during the first months of the journey, he did so beginning on April 7. All students of the Expedition recognize fully the intrinsic value of Lewis's written contribution. He had a distinct flair for literary composition, wrote with ease, though in an archaic style, and often discursively. His literary output exceeded that of all the other journalists combined. Furthermore, and most importantly, he added a new dimension to the record of the Expedition by reporting innumerable observations and discoveries so important to science. Compared with Clark's notes, usually terse and matter-of-fact, Lewis's were far more expansive, imaginative, and discerning. As an illustration, consider a portion of his entry for April 7: "We were now about to penetrate a country at least two thousand miles in width, on which the foot of civilized man had never trodden . . . however, as the state of mind in which we are, generally gives the colouring to events, when the imagination is suffered to wander into futurity, the picture which now presented itself to me was a most pleasing one. enterta[in]ing as I do, the most confident hope of succeeding in a voyage which had formed a da[r]ling project of mine for the last ten years, I could but esteem this moment of my departure as among the most happy of my life" (I, 284–285).

[2]

It took 2½ weeks, from April 7 to 25, for the Corps to ascend the unpredictable Missouri from Fort Mandan to the Yellowstone River, a distance of about 250 miles. The picture we get of this leg of the journey, thanks to Lewis's observant eye and active pen, is highly colored with biological happenings. As the party left the Knife River villages, they noted on every hand signs of a resurgent spring. Maple and elm had produced buds and wild cherry half-formed leaves. Great flocks of migrating birds were winging their way to northern nesting sites. Magpies, bald eagles, and Canada geese had begun construction of nests, and elk were dropping their antlers. One day Clark killed a jack rabbit that was changing its coat, with some parts of the body retaining the long, white winter fur and others assuming the shorter gray characteristic of summer (I, 300). On April 17 Lewis reported that Clark had seen a curlew. This was likely the long-billed curlew (*Numenius americanus americanus*) and, if so, a bird new to science (I, 318; VI, 188).[2]

Four days of travelling brought the explorers to the mouth of the Little Missouri River. According to Lewis, it had its rise in a broken country west of the Black Hills and then followed a winding course north through the extravagant beauty of the Dakota Bad Lands (I, 298). It remained a relatively unknown stream until Theodore Roosevelt 80 years later built a ranch-house beside it north of the town of Medora and wrote engaging, highly informative stories about the picturesque country through which it flows and the wildlife inhabiting it. By then, due to man's senseless predilection to kill wantonly, the buffalo had practically disappeared from the West.

About 35 miles above the Little Missouri, the explorers arrived at the mouth of a small stream entering from the south. They called it Charbonneau's Creek, in deference to their interpreter who had spent several weeks at one time in this vicinity on a hunting trip with the Hidatsas. This was as far up the Missouri as Charbonneau had been. Lepage said that he and another Frenchman had been a few miles farther. Here then, Clark wrote, was "the highest point on the Missouri to which a white man has been previous to this time" (I, 311).

Until recently, this statement by Clark has been accepted at face

[2] Elliott Coues (I, 276) identified this bird as the long-billed curlew, as did Russell Reid and C. G. Gannon, "Birds and Mammals Observed by Lewis and Clark in North Dakota," *N.D. Hist. Quart.* (July, 1927), 17.

value by historians. However, it is now known that a few venturesome white men had previously travelled farther west, even as far as the Yellowstone. Truteau, for instance, wrote that a Canadian by the name of Ménard had been "several times among the nation of the Crows in company with the Gros Ventres [Hidatsas]" and had assured him that the Yellowstone "was navigable with pirogues more than 150 leagues above its mouth."[3] We have knowledge, too, of two other Frenchmen, LeRaye and Pardo, who accompanied Hidatsas overland to the Yellowstone in 1802, striking that river at the mouth of the Bighorn.[4]

Though these men, and perhaps others, had preceded Lewis and Clark up the Missouri as far as the Yellowstone, their accomplishments received no recognition at the time. As a result, for all practical purposes, Lewis and Clark's farther journey—across the wide expanse of Montana, over the difficult mountain ranges of Idaho, and down the swift-flowing current of the Columbia—was through a world entirely unknown to civilized man.

As a fitting introduction to this vast *terra incognita* on whose threshold the band of explorers now stood, Lewis and Clark on April 14 encountered their first grizzly bear. Two of them, disturbed when Lewis fired at an elk, quickly climbed a bluff and disappeared from view (I, 311). They were too far away for him to distinguish color, and he and the other journalists continued to refer to them as "white bear."

The navigation of this stretch of the Missouri provided the explorers with the frustration, hard labor, misery, and near disaster to which they had been accustomed since leaving the Mississippi. Additionally, they had to contend with high winds. "There is scarcely any timber to brake the wind in this quarter," Lewis declared, "& the country on both sides being level plains, wholly destitute of timber, the wind blows with astonishing violence" (VI, 187). That Lewis had good cause for this statement is proved by the fact that, during a period of eight days (April 18 to 25), the Expedition was at a complete standstill on two of them, immobilized from 9 to 5 o'clock on a third and from 10 to 5 on a fourth. On others, they travelled only short distances. Clark deplored the enforced delays, "as we cant move when the wind is high with[out] great risque, and [if] there was no risque the winds is generally a head and often too violent to proceed" (I, 333).

The spirited winds annoyed in another manner. By picking up tiny particles of sand from the river banks and sand bars and driving them

[3] Nasatir, *Before Lewis and Clark*, II, 381.
[4] Nasatir, *Before Lewis and Clark*, I, 110.

with force into the faces of the men, they produced a large number of inflamed eyes. To alleviate these inflammations, Lewis had his own special eye-wash: "a solution of white vitriol [zinc sulphate] and the sugar of lead [lead acetate] in the proportion of 2 grs. of the former and one of the latter to each ounce of water" (II, 22). Dropped into the eyes, this collyrium brought at least temporary relief.

For most of the journey to the Pacific and back, Lewis kept what amounts to a running commentary on the plant life. That from the Knife to the Yellowstone may be regarded as typical. The country on both sides of the Missouri, he wrote, was a flat, treeless plain as far as the eye could see and "generally covered with a short grass resembling very much the blue grass" (I, 308). The timber bordering the river consisted almost altogether of cottonwood, elm, ash, willow, and "box alder" (box elder, *Acer negundo*), and the undergrowth of such plants as wild rose, honeysuckle, currant, red berry (buffalo-berry), choke cherry, arrowwood, and serviceberry. On the bluffs grew clumps of dwarf cedar and great quantities of sagebrush (I, 323, 337–338).[5] Travellers to these parts today will find the vegetation much the same as in Lewis's time.

How many of these plants Lewis preserved will never be known since his entire collection assembled between Fort Mandan and Great Falls was destroyed during the following winter at the latter place. Also, because of difficulties with identification, it is impossible to say how many were new to science. However, according to the botanist Charles Sprague Sargent, Lewis's mention of "servicebury" on April 20 was the first reference in literature to the western or Saskatoon service-berry, *Amelanchier alnifolia,* not formally described (by Thomas Nuttall) until 1818.[6]

Since Lewis was conversant with Jefferson's efforts to introduce useful Old World plants into the United States, it should come as no surprise that he was particularly attentive to trans-Mississippi herbs and shrubs that might one day be grown successfully and profitably in eastern gardens. For example, when he discovered the dwarf cedar

[5] The cottonwood, of course, was *Populus deltoides occidentalis;* the elm, probably *Ulmus americana;* the ash, *Fraxinus pennsylvanica lanceolata* according to Sargent in *Garden and Forest,* X (Jan., 1897); the willow, *Salix longifolius* (Coues, I, 282); rose, probably *Rosa woodsii;* honeysuckle, *Lonicera involucrata* (Coues, I, 282); currant (*Ribes* sp.); buffalo-berry (*Shepherdia argentea*); choke cherry, probably *Prunus virginiana;* and arrowwood, *Cornus stolonifera* (Coues, I, 267).

[6] Charles Sprague Sargent, "The First Account of Some Western Trees," *Garden and Forest,* X (Jan. 20, 1897), 28.

(*Juniperus sabina procumbens*) which here adorned Missouri bluffs, he thought it would "make very handsome edgings to the borders and walks of a garden; it is quite as hansom as box [boxwood, *Buxus sempervirens*] and would be much more easily propagated" (I, 299).

On April 14 Lewis encountered a number of plants (apparently, for the most part, different species of sagebrush, *Artemisia*). "On these hills," he wrote, "many aromatic herbs are seen; resembling in taste, smel and appearance, the sage, hysop, wormwood, southernwood, and two other herbs which are strangers to me; the one resembling the camphor in taste and smell, rising to the hight of 2 or 3 feet; the other about the same size, has a long, narrow, smo[o]th, soft leaf of an agreeable smel and flavor; of this last the A[n]telope is very fond; they feed on it, and perfume the hair of their foreheads and necks with it by rubing against it" (I, 307).

If the mark of the distinguished observer is his ability to bring into play all of his faculties simultaneously, then Lewis was near his best in describing these plants. He employed practically every one of the major special senses given to him by his Creator: touch, to determine the softness of leaf; taste and smell, to compare with his Virginia "hysop" and southernwood; and sight, to note novel propensities of the antelope.

Lewis was no less attentive to birds. In occasional sorties away from the river, he encountered thousands of Canada geese (*Branta canadensis*) deployed over the surface of the plains busily feeding on the young prairie grass. Some, preferring Dakota prairieland to more northern climes, had stopped here to raise families. One day Clark shot a Canada goose on her nest in the top of a 60-foot cottonwood and obtained a single dull-white egg. He and Lewis soon discovered other nests of this bird in trees. Lewis was surprised, because from what he knew of the habits of Canada geese in the East, they invariably nested on the ground. Subsequently, when ornithologists read these reports of Lewis and Clark, they attempted to discredit them. However, later naturalists of this same region, Elliott Coues among them, discovered these birds still nesting in trees. "Geese are wise birds which know enough to get out of the way of wolves, foxes and badgers," Coues said.[7]

Just below the entrance of the Little Missouri, Lewis wrote: "saw some large white cranes pass up the river—these are the largest bird of that genus common to the country through which the Missouri and Mississippi pass. they are perfectly white except the large feathers of

7 Coues, I, 270n.

the two first joints of the wing which are black" (I, 295). These birds were whooping cranes (*Grus americana*), perhaps the first Lewis had ever seen. In the Midwest early in the last century, they could be seen at times in tremendous flocks. For instance, in 1811 Thomas Nuttall wrote that "the clangor of their numerous legions, passing high in air, was almost deafening."[8] We learn, too, that Audubon once brought down seven whooping cranes with one shot.[9] Today this bird hovers on the fine-drawn edge of extinction. The latest reports I have seen from the U.S. Fish and Wildlife Service indicate a winter population in the Aransas National Wildlife Refuge, Texas, of between 45 and 50.

Lewis reported seeing more bald eagles (*Haliaeetus leucocephalus*) at the mouth of the Yellowstone than he had seen in any other part of the country. When a hunter shot one of these birds, Ordway "took the quills to write."[10] Thus a portion at least of Ordway's journal would appear to have been written with quills from a bald-headed eagle. Our national bird is rarely seen today, and its future is increasingly a cause of grave concern to conservation-minded Americans. Before too many years this majestic avian may no longer "draw great lines across the sky."[11]

On April 14 Lewis wrote that one of the party had killed a large "hooting owl." To him it was identical with the eastern species except it was "more hooted and more thickly clad with feathers" (I, 308). According to the ornithologist, A. C. Bent, this was the Montana horned owl, *Bubo virginianus occidentalis,* and "probably the first one of this subspecies killed by white men."[12]

Between Fort Mandan and the Yellowstone, Lewis occasionally reported seeing swans. These could have been either the trumpeter or whistling swan, or both. Only the former nested in North Dakota, but both species passed through that state during migration seasons. The trumpeter swan (*Olor buccinator*) may be distinguished from the whistling (*Olor columbianus*) by its larger size and by the black bill of the adult. At the time of Lewis and Clark, great flocks of both species migrated south along the Atlantic seaboard each year; but, like any

[8] T. Gilbert Pearson, ed., *Birds of America* (Garden City, 1944), Part I, 200.

[9] R. M. de Schauensee, "Rare and Extinct Birds in the Collections of the Academy of Natural Sciences of Philadelphia," *Procs. Acad. Nat. Scis.,* XCIII (1941), 288.

[10] Ordway, 193.

[11] Pearson, *Birds of America,* II, 80.

[12] A. C. Bent, *Life Histories of North American Birds of Prey,* U.S. Nat. Museum, Bull. 170, Part 2 (1938), 348.

number of other birds, they had not yet been formally described and named. Consequently, if Lewis had written the scientific account of the Expedition as planned and had included his descriptions of these two beautiful birds, then his name, rather than that of others, would be associated with their Latin binominals.

As things turned out, the whistling swan was technically described in 1815 by George Ord, a Philadelphia naturalist, who relied on Lewis's description written eleven years earlier. And he called it whistling swan because that was the vernacular name Lewis had given it. Its note "begins with a kind of whistleing sound," Lewis had written, "and terminates in a round full note which is reather louder than the whistleing, or former part; this note is as loud as that of the large [trumpeter] swan. from the peculiar whistleing of the note of this bird I have called it the *whistleing swan*" (IV, 148). Apparently not too many modern ornithologists are familiar with the origin of the vernacular, for I have before me at this moment a well-known book on birds in which a contributor wrote, "It is hard to see just why this bird is called the Whistling Swan."[13] As to the trumpeter swan, it was formally described by the English naturalist, John Richardson, in 1831. So, regrettably, Ord and Richardson received credit which should have gone to Lewis.

Turning now from birds to mammals, we find Lewis writing soon after leaving Fort Mandan: "I have observed in many parts of the plains and praries, the work of an anamal of which I could never obtain a view. their work resembled that of the salamander [not an amphibian but a rodent, probably *Geomys pinetis pinetis*] common to the sandhills of the states of South Carolina and Georgia, and like that anamal also it never appears above the ground. the little hillocks which are thrown up by these anamals have much the appearance of ten or twelve pounds of loose earth poured out of a vessel on the surface of the plain" (I, 289).

Scientists familiar with North Dakota animals, such as Elliott Coues and the team of Russell Reid and C. G. Gannon, agree that the burrower in question was the Dakota pocket gopher, *Thomomys talpoides,* a small subterranean rodent that often does great damage in grain and alfalfa fields by cutting roots and in irrigated country by causing ditch breaks.

During the first few days after leaving Fort Mandan, the hunters experienced difficulty in supplying fresh meat; the Indians had driven

[13] Pearson, *Birds of America,* I, 116.

the game away. Then, quite suddenly, tremendous herds of buffalo, antelope, elk, and deer surrounded them once again. Lewis thought that "two good hunters could conveniently supply a regiment with provisions." He then went on to add a statement that every conservationist and friend of wildlife will applaud: "altho' game is very abundant and gentle, we only kill as much as is necessary for food" (I, 345). So it seems evident the two captains had laid down a law, one difficult to enforce; there would be no needless slaughtering of animals, no matter how abundant. By way of contrast, just six years later Bradbury (with the Overland Astorians) wrote: "it is impossible to restrain the hunters, as they scarcely ever lose an opportunity of killing, even although not in want of food."[14]

As the explorers moved upstream, their eyes met no more melancholy sight than the battered, putrefying bodies of dead buffalo lodged in the driftwood at the river's edge, stranded on bank or sand bar or floating with the current. It was an all too common, morbid, malodorous scene. In almost every instance the grizzlies and other predators had been at the bodies, attested to by their footprints in sand or clay. From the accounts left by Lewis and Clark and other travellers on the Missouri in early days, the mortality among buffalo during spring breakups was tremendous. In the spring of 1811 while Brackenridge was far down the Missouri near the mouth of the Vermillion, he reported seeing 30 to 40 carcasses floating by every day.[15]

In places Lewis found "parsels" of buffalo hair decorating rose bushes and other thorny shrubs along the river. Bleached by the elements, the hair had turned white and resembled sheep's wool, though it was "much finer and more silkey and soft" (I, 318). Lewis saw no reason why an excellent cloth might not be made of buffalo hair. A large cow he killed, he guessed, would have furnished near five pounds of good wool. The idea was not new. Joliet and others, long before, had entertained a like notion, as did Catlin at a later date.

[3]

Lewis and Clark, as we know, first encountered beaver just above the entrance of the Kansas. Since then, Drouillard and others had shot and trapped many of them. As the party neared the Yellowstone, they found this animal not only increasingly abundant, but also bigger,

[14] *Early Western Travels*, V, 148.
[15] *Early Western Travels*, VI, 87.

fatter, better clad, and cutting down larger trees. One tree was almost three feet in diameter (I, 348) .

"The men prefer the flesh of this anamal," Lewis observed, "to that of any other which we have, or are able to procure at this moment. I eat very heartily of the beaver myself, and think it excellent, particularly the tale, and liver" (I, 318) . To him, boiled tail resembled in flavor "the fresh tongues and sounds [swim-bladders] of the codfish, and is usually sufficiently large to afford a plentiful meal for two men" (I, 360) .[16]

With beaver in continuing demand, Lewis and Clark ordered that traps be set each evening. Customarily of steel, they weighed about five pounds and cost from $10 to $15. When in use they were situated in shallow water near shore and attached by a five-foot chain to a heavy stick driven into the bottom of the stream. Once a trap was set, the trapper anchored a small twig beside it and bent the free end over the water to a position immediately above the trap. The extremity of the twig was then baited with castor (castoreum) , a highly potent lure obtained from the perineal glands of the beaver. When properly prepared, according to Lewis, this bait would attract beaver from points as much as a mile away—and Lewis knew how to prepare it (I, 318) .

The beaver Lewis and Clark encountered here did not, of course, accomplish the impossible by damming the Missouri, as they did small streams. Instead they built their homes in the banks, with entrances situated above normal water level. According to Maximilian, "their chambers are then perhaps 8 feet above the surface of the water, are spacious, and adapted to the number of animals that live in them."[17]

A few days after the explorers left the Mandan villages, they caught up with three Frenchmen who were trapping beaver. This trio represented the vanguard of thousands who would soon follow. With beaver hats mounting in popularity, the demand for beaver pelts increased accordingly. In the early days of the industry, these brought about four dollars per pound and an average-sized animal carried from one to two pounds of fur. Because of the abundance of beaver in the Upper Missouri country, the individual streams were, in the words of one writer, "as rich as if sands of gold covered the bottoms."[18] The skins

[16] According to the Century Dictionary: "Some fishes' sounds are an esteemed article of food, as that of the cod, which when fried is something like an oyster so cooked."

[17] *Early Western Travels*, XXIII, 41.

[18] Hiram Chittenden, *The American Fur Trade of the Far West*, 2 vols. (Stanford, Calif., 1954) , II, 818.

were not always the customary black or dark brown. Maximilian saw one, for instance, beautifully spotted with white and said that "yellow-ish-white and pure white beaver were not infrequently caught in the Yellowstone."[19]

The fur trapper generally skinned his beaver on the spot and retained the pelt, its tail, and perineal glands. They excised the last-mentioned for three reasons. The secretion was used by the physician of the day as a stimulant and antispasmodic, by the perfumer as a fixative, and by the trapper to scent his bait.

Lewis and Clark could have had no conception at this time of the effect their reports on the abundance of beaver in the Upper Missouri valley, once they were made public, would have on the further explora-tion of the West and the expansion of the fur industry. The prime lodestone which first drew men to the Yellowstone and Three Forks of the Missouri was not gold or other metal. It was a flat-tailed, black-coated rodent, *Castor canadensis;* and no one could have foretold how quickly the trappers would bring about its near extirpation in those regions. When Lewis and Clark were dragging their dugouts upstream through the then unmapped terrain of the Dakotas and Montana, they heard on all sides and in every stream the sharp, pistol-like sounds of beaver tails slapping the water. By the time Maximilian arrived, a scant 30 years later, he heard the sound only rarely.

[4]

With the boats immobile again on April 25 because of high wind, Lewis chose four men (Drouillard, Ordway, and the two Field broth-ers) and forged ahead of the main party. He believed that he was close to the Yellowstone and he was eager to locate it. It speaks well for his geographic acumen that he walked only eight miles before he sighted this important Missouri affluent, described in such detail to him by the Hidatsas. He and Clark had had nebulous reports of it at Camp Dubois some 1,800 miles away.

The explorers translated the French name, *Roche Jaune,* into the English "Yellowstone," the name it has borne ever since. Why the French applied that name is a complete mystery. When Lewis found no yellow stones at the mouth of the river, he sent Joseph Field upstream to look for them. The latter ascended the Yellowstone eight to ten miles and found it to be a lovely stream of many turns flowing through

[19] *Early Western Travels,* **XXIII,** 250.

a beautiful valley four to five miles wide. In this reconnaissance, he discovered not a single yellow stone. He did, however, see several bighorn sheep at a distance and brought back to camp a large horn of one he picked up along the way. Joseph Field thus became the first member of the party to set eyes on the Rocky Mountain bighorn, probably the then unknown subspecies, *Ovis canadensis auduboni*.

While waiting for Clark to arrive, Lewis walked west between the two rivers. About two and a half miles from the confluence and 400 yards from the Missouri, he found a site that he thought would be ideal for a fort or trading establishment. In years to come this area saw four different forts arise. The first was built in 1822 by William Henry Ashley and Andrew Henry and was abandoned one year later. It was followed by Fort Union (1829), Fort William (1839), and Fort Buford (1866). Far and away the most celebrated of these and of all Missouri posts was Fort Union. It stood on the north bank of the Missouri about two and three-quarter miles above the mouth of the Yellowstone and almost on the future North Dakota–Montana line. Here, according to one writer, "the agents lived in a sort of barbaric splendor with a great retinue of clerks and *engagés,* with bright-blanketed Indians coming and going, trading and carousing."[20] Fort Union had its share of distinguished visitors, among them George Catlin in 1832, Maximilian and Bodmer in 1833, and Audubon in 1843.

SUMMARY OF DISCOVERIES

Animals New to Science

MONTANA HORNED OWL. *Bubo virginianus occidentalis* Stone. [A.O.U. 375j] (Thwaites, I, 308). Described, 1896.

NORTHERN FLICKER. *Colaptes auratus luteus* Bangs. [A.O.U. 412a] (Thwaites, VI, 187; Reid and Gannon, 19). 1898.

? PRAIRIE HORNED LARK. *Eremophila alpestris leucolaema* Coues. [A.O.U. 474c] (Thwaites, VI, 187; Reid and Gannon, 19). 1874.

LONG-BILLED CURLEW. *Numenius americanus americanus* (Bechstein). [A.O.U. 264] (Thwaites, I, 318; VI, 188; Coues, I, 276; Reid and Gannon, 17). 1812.

AUDUBON'S MOUNTAIN SHEEP. *Ovis canadensis auduboni* Merriam. (Thwaites, I, 343). 1901.

? POCKET GOPHER. *Thomomys talpoides rufescens* Wied. (Thwaites, I, 289). 1839.

[20] Wheeler, *The Trail of Lewis and Clark,* I, 283.

Plants New to Science

Saskatoon serviceberry. *Amelanchier alnifolia* (Nutt.) Nuttall. (Thwaites, I, 323) . 1818.

Lewis and Clark Herbarium
None.

Indian Tribes Encountered
None.

Topographic Features Named and/or Discovered
The Little Basin (Thwaites, I, 294) .
Onion Creek (Thwaites, I, 302) —— Rising and Tide Creek (Coues, I, 269n) .
Goose Egg Lake (Thwaites, I, 302) .
Goose Egg Creek (Thwaites, I, 302) .
Charbonneau's Creek (Thwaites, I, 308) —— probably today's Indian Creek (Ordway, 196) .
Sunday Island (Coues, I, 272) .
Goat-pen Creek (Coues, I, 274) .
Grand Point (Gass, 92) .
Hall's Lake (Coues, I, 275n) .
Hall's Creek (Coues, I, 275n) .
Cut Bluff (Thwaites, I, 327) .

Yellowstone
to
Marias

CHAPTER NINE

According to Lewis and Clark's calculations, they travelled 640 long, tedious, tortuous miles in ascending the Missouri from the Yellowstone to the Marias River, where the Expedition made its next appreciable halt. Though they exaggerated the distance somewhat, it was a long stretch any way you look at it, requiring more than a month to cover.

Of all the intervening tributaries, they had gained advance knowledge from the Indians of just two: a large southern one, the Musselshell, and an enigmatic northern branch of spun-out name, *"the river that scolds at all others"* (II, 115). As they came to others, heretofore unknown, they named them. The largest and most important, in order of discovery, were: Martha's River (now the Big Muddy), named "in honor of the Selebrated M.F." (I, 354); Porcupine River (today the Poplar), so called because of "an unusual number of Porcupines" (I, 362); Milk River, because "it's water . . . precisely resembles tea with a considerable mixture of milk" (II, 14); Judith's River (now Judith), named for Judy Hancock of Fincastle, Virginia, whom Clark later married; and Maria's River (now written without the apostrophe), named after Lewis's cousin, Maria Wood.

Lewis and Clark gave names to at least 30 other water courses emptying their content, generally brackish and undrinkable, into the Missouri along this portion of the river. They obviously lost no time seeking the most appropriate names for these streams. For some they took their cues from animals—hence Blowing Fly, Grouse, and Softshell Turtle Creeks—and for others they relied on events. They stepped up an earlier practice of applying names of party members. On Clark's map of this part of the Missouri, we find laid down such tributaries as Werner, Wiser, Gibson, Bratton, Windsor, Thompson, and "Sâh-câ-gerwe-âh." It is no credit to subsequent cartographers that the names of these individuals do not appear on our maps of today. Speaking forthrightly about such unwarranted changes, Elliott Coues declared: "Hundreds of names . . . should be restored, not only in equity, but on the plainest principles of the law of priority, which geographers pretend to obey."[1]

Some of the names applied by Lewis and Clark, such as Teapot Creek, Pot Island, and Grouse Creek, found scant favor with Maximilian. "We could not help observing," he wrote, "that such names are not well chosen, especially as it would not be difficult to find better ones, even by retaining the generally harmonious Indian names."[2] He seems to have overlooked entirely Yellow Bear Defeat Creek, another Missouri branch named by the captains.

[2]

Almost at once after leaving the Yellowstone, the explorers crossed the 104th meridian and entered what is now Montana. Signs of increasing aridity multiplied. The journalists reported alkali deposits (generally "salts" to Lewis) encrusting the ground in places to a depth of two or three inches, bottoms supporting only a few impoverished cottonwoods, and tributaries whose waters had been swallowed up entirely by thirsty sands. One of these feeders was the most extraordinary Lewis had ever seen. It was "as wide as the Missouri is at this place or $\frac{1}{2}$ mile wide and not containing a single drop of running water" (II, 14).

As the party neared the Marias, they found it more and more of a problem to obtain sufficient fuel for cooking food and warming chilled bodies. Live sagebrush and prickly pear, which abundantly covered bluffs and benchlands, were no fit substitute for well-seasoned timbers of willow and cottonwood in making fires. Neither were other dry-land plants which now began to appear, including one characterized by Lewis as "extreemly troublesome" (II, 25). This was the thorny, fleshy-leaved greasewood, *Sarcobatus vermiculatus,* which grows commonly in alkaline soils of the West. Another plant new to science, Lewis called it "the pulpy-leaved thorn."

In due time the explorers voiced their opinion of this arid, sterile

[1] Coues, I, 324n.
[2] *Early Western Travels,* XXIII, 61.

land. To sergeant Gass, it was "a country which presents little to our view but scenes of barrenness and desolation."[3] Whitehouse declared that it was "too much of a desert to be inhabited, or cultivated" (VII, 89). Lewis distinguished it as "truly a desert barren country" (II, 80). And to Sergeant Ordway, even less favorably impressed than the others, it was good for nothing but game and might "with propriety be called the Deserts of North America for I do not conceive any part of it can ever be Sitled as it is deficient of or in water except this River."[4]

The fiction of the Great American Desert appears to have had its inception with Coronado, who, following his travels in 1541 through the plains from New Mexico to central Kansas, wrote Charles V: "It was the Lord's pleasure that, after having journeyed across these deserts seventy-seven days, I arrived at the province they call Quivira."[5] At first a pindling myth, it grew rapidly in stature as Lewis and Clark, Pike, Long, Maximilian, and others provided sustenance. Pike, for instance, after crossing Kansas and eastern Colorado in 1806–7 on his way to discovering the peak which now bears his name, wrote as follows: "I would not think I had done my country justice did I not give birth to what few lights my examination of these internal deserts has enabled me to acquire . . . these vast plains of the western hemisphere may become in time as celebrated as the sandy deserts of Africa."[6]

Edwin James, journalist for the Long Expedition which in 1820 travelled up the Platte and down the Arkansas, wrote even more pessimistically: "In regard to this extensive section of the country, I do not hesitate in giving the opinion, that it is almost wholly unfit for cultivation, and of course uninhabitable by a people depending upon agriculture for their subsistence."[7]

One man alone, of the early visitors to the High Plains, expressed dissent. "My own opinion," declared John Bradbury, "is that it can be cultivated; and that, in process of time, it will not only be peopled and cultivated, but that it will be one of the most beautiful countries in the world."[8] Thus it was an outlander, an Englishman, who first envisioned the western prairie lands as the future site of American homes and abundant, fast-growing crops.

The desert myth died slowly, lingering on in the public mind

---

[3] Gass, 106.
[4] Ordway, 219.
[5] Quoted from Webb, *The Great Plains,* 153.
[6] Coues, *The Expeditions of Zebulon M. Pike,* II, 524–525.
[7] *Early Western Travels,* XVII, 147–148.
[8] *Early Western Travels,* V, 266–267.

throughout the first half of the last century. For example, atlases of the period contain maps showing a wide belt east of the Rockies extending from Canada to the Gulf boldly marked: The Great American Desert.

Lewis and Clark would have regarded the High Plains as even more barren and desolate if it had not been for the presence of cotton-wood. Time and again they described camp sites on agreeably shaded islands or bottoms where clumps of these trees, with their large um-brella-like crowns of shimmering, rustling leaves, effectively screened the sun's rays or diverted the water of a prairie downpour. As Lewis observed just below the entrance of the Judith, "these appearances [of cottonwood] were quite reviving after the drairy country through which we had been passing" (II, 88).

The cottonwood has managed to survive in an arid land primarily because its roots run deeper than most, enabling it to seek out water as much as 30 to 40 feet beneath the prairie floor. From the time it takes root until its trunk, weakened by age and disease, crashes to earth, its life is a battle against adversity. There is no protection from cruel winds and extremes of heat and cold, no escape to a more congenial habitat. The search for sustaining moisture goes on endlessly. The survival of a giant cottonwood under such conditions is a marvel of adaptation.

The broad-leaved cottonwood ranges west to the base of the Rocky Mountains and grows in every conceivable size and shape from insig-nificant saplings to great lofty trees as much as 80 to 90 feet in height. While exploring the valley of the Canadian River, Capt. Randolph B. Marcy measured a big-boled cottonwood that was 19½ feet in circum-ference five feet from the ground,[9] and Balduin Möllhausen, German naturalist with the Whipple Expedition, gave a lively description of another standing solitary on a Texas plain that had a diameter of 12 feet and "was remarkable both for its gigantic growth, and for the strangely twisted and entangled boughs and branches."[10] That large cottonwoods still grow on the banks of the Missouri we will shortly have occasion to mention.

[*3*]

The party moved upstream at a rate which averaged 15 to 20 miles a day, usually getting under way at sunrise and continuing until late

[9] Capt. Randolph B. Marcy, *Exploration of the Red River of Louisiana* (Washington, 1854), 40.

[10] Balduin Möllhausen, *Diary of a Journey from the Mississippi to the Coasts of the Pacific,* 2 vols. (London, 1858), I, 195.

evening. Much of the time the boatmen labored either in bitterly cold water, often up to their armpits, or scrambled over sharp-edged rocks on the banks. As a result, Lewis wrote, "Many of them have their feet so mangled and bruised . . . that they can scarcely walk or stand; at least it is with great pain that they do either" (II, 115) . One man only, Joseph Field, became ill. He suffered with dysentery and an accompanying high fever. Lewis gave him a dose of Glauber's salt and, after his fever abated, 30 drops of laudanum (I, 368) .

Glauber's salt (prepared originally by J. R. Glauber, a German chemist) was sodium sulphate and, like Epsom salt, a well-known physic. Lewis had provided himself in Philadelphia with six pounds of it, and he prescribed it frequently. He purged because that was what the doctors of his day would have done. I find it interesting that Lewis soon determined that the omnipresent alkali tasted like Glauber's salt and had the same effect. In fact, on one occasion he referred to it as "glauber salt" (I, 299) , thus anticipating what is known today, that sodium sulphate is one of the primary ingredients of alkali. Maximilian apparently thought they were one and the same, for he wrote that "Glauber salt" had been collected for use at Fort Union, where they had a considerable store of it.[11]

The laudanum Lewis administered to Joseph Field was, of course, a tincture of opium. It was used widely in those days to deaden pain and induce sleep. Lewis's customary dose of 30 drops—about two cc. or one-half teaspoonful—would not be a big dose. Its effect would probably be similar to one-half gr. of morphine hypodermically.

Though Lewis and Clark had their problems to contend with between the Yellowstone and Marias, Indians were not one of them. In several places they found discarded native articles and recently abandoned campsites but, incredibly, not once did they see a Crow, Blackfoot, Assiniboin, or other tribesman, all of whom wandered far and wide in this particular part of the Upper Missouri. Since they regarded "those gentlemen" as vicious and illy-disposed, they were just as happy not to encounter them.

They did encounter dangerous animals, however. On April 29, Lewis and an accompanying hunter killed a grizzly bear, the first bagged by any of the party. "It was," Lewis wrote, "a male not fully grown, we estimated his weight at 300 lbs, not having the means of ascertaining it precisely. The legs of this bear are somewhat longer than those of the black, as are it's tallons and tusks incomparably

---

[11] *Early Western Travels,* XXIII, 194.

larger and longer . . . it's colour is yellowish brown, the eyes small, black, and piercing; the front of the fore legs near the feet is usually black; the fur is finer thicker and deeper than that of the black bear" (I, 350–351).

Though the grizzly had been seen previously by a few explorers, notably Alexander Mackenzie, no one until now had supplied anatomical detail about it. In days immediately ahead, Lewis and Clark came upon more of these animals. In each instance, the bear, when shot, promptly charged its attacker, even though badly wounded. Some of the men escaped only by discarding their weapons and leaping into the river. All were astonished at the number of bullets required to kill them. For example, they put 10 balls through one big one, five through its lungs, before it fell.

Lewis had tended to discount what the Mandans had earlier told him about the ferocity of this monarch. Before encountering it, he had written: "The Indians may well fear this anamal, equipped as they generally are with their bows and arrows or indifferent fusees, but in the hands of skillful riflemen they are by no means as formidable and dangerous as they have been represented" (I, 351). However, after personal experiences with it, Lewis revised his thinking. "These bear being so hard to die reather intimedates us," he admitted; "I must confess that I do not like the gentlemen and had reather fight two Indians than one bear" (II, 25).

Subsequent generations of hunters, armed with more powerful weapons, experienced less difficulty in dispatching the grizzly. The muzzle-loaders carried by Lewis and Clark probably used no more powder and lead than today's thirty-two caliber Winchesters. These had been sufficient for such game as white-tailed deer and black bear but were entirely inadequate for a beast as large and powerful as a grizzly.

Lewis and Clark reported accurately their adventures with the grizzly. That these became exaggerated when retold, and the true character of the animal misrepresented, was no fault of theirs. Before long Old Ephraim (to use one of various names applied by old-time hunters to the grizzly) had gained a reputation for strength and ferocity exceeding that of any other North American quadruped; it was a killer of unbridled passion. One writer, for example, was soon informing his readers that it "literally thirsts for human blood. So far from shunning, he seldom fails to attack; and even to hunt him."[12] When George Ord

[12] H. M. Brackenridge, *Views of Louisiana* (Chicago, 1962), 55.

formally described this beast, he settled, not surprisingly, on *Ursus horribilis* as his choice of a technical name. Thus saddled with "grizzly" and "horribilis," the animal's sinister reputation grew.

Unfortunately Lewis and Clark gained most of their information about the dispositin of the grizzly while looking down the barrels of their Kentucky rifles. They saw only the wounded animal maddened with pain and fear. At such times, modern big-game hunters agree, it is truly one of the most fearsome beasts on earth. But this same animal, undisturbed and unprovoked, when not cornered, wounded, or its young threatened, is far from being the dangerous creature often depicted. Who could write more knowingly of its true character than Ernest Thompson Seton? "The Grizzly . . . never attacks man, except when provoked. That is, he is a harmless, peaceful giant, perfectly satisfied to let you alone if you let him alone."[13]

The common name for this high-shouldered carnivore evolved slowly. Until Lewis and Clark killed one, they alluded to it always as the "white bear," apparently adopting the name employed by Tabeau and others who possessed hearsay knowledge of it. Of course the color is never white (except in rare instances of albinism), as the captains quickly determined. It varies much in individual bears from yellow to brown to black, with the hairs often having lighter, whitish tips (hence the name silver-tip). For a time, as more and more specimens came to hand, Lewis and Clark referred to the "white or grey bear," the "yellow bear," and the "brown bear." Then Clark wrote of the "Brown or Grisley bear" (I, 373) and Lewis of the "brown grizly" (II, 60).[14] Many years went by before the name "grizzly" became fixed in our language. Theodore Roosevelt, for one, opposed it, arguing that "grisly," meaning horrifying or ghastly, fit this beast better than "grizzly," which has no other meaning than grey or grizzled.

[4]

It is obviously impossible for any person now alive to comprehend the abundance of game that once populated the plains of the West. Only on the African veldt in the pioneering days of Speke, Grant, Harris, and Cumming has there been anything comparable since man began recording history. Near the mouth of the Milk River, on May 6, Lewis wrote: "It is now only amusement for Capt. C. and myself to kill as

[13] Charles Elliott, ed., *Fading Trails* (New York, 1942), 42.
[14] For a fuller account of grizzly bear nomenclature see Elijah H. Criswell, *Lewis and Clark: Linguistic Pioneers* (Columbia, Mo., 1940), cxli–cxlii.

much meat as the party can consum" (II, 4). And again, two days later: "We can send out at any time and obtain whatever species of meat the country affords in as large quantity as we wish" (II, 12). Definitely he meant buffalo, antelope, deer, and elk, and possibly bear and beaver.

"The bottoms is all trod up with Game," wrote Private White-house just above the Yellowstone, "and different paths in all directions" (VII, 79). Long before the Indian arrived, the buffalo and other animals had discovered the most practical and direct routes between points of importance to them. Through long-continued use, they became well-established, much travelled highways. The Indians, once on the scene, found that they could not improve on them. Sergeant Gass said that these roads, some as much as ten feet wide, did not necessarily follow the windings of the river, "but cut off points of land and pursued a direct course."[15] After examining some of these ancient roads, Bradbury said "that no engineer could have laid them out more judiciously."[16] Many of these trails, we do not need to add, were shortly appropriated by the white man and became main highways of the future. A ribbon of asphalt or concrete across the prairieland of Colorado, Wyoming, or Montana today often overlies the route once travelled by hordes of lumbering buffalo and wide-ranging companies of moccasined Crow, Cheyenne, or Blackfeet.

During the Yellowstone to Marias run, the journalists commented again and again on the tameness of the animals. In so doing, they added materially to evidence already at hand that wilderness creatures are not inherently afraid of man, but develop fear only after experiencing his ancient propensity to kill. "I passed several buffalo in the open plain within fifty paces," Lewis declared, "they viewed me for a moment as something novel and then very unconcernedly continued to feed" (I, 367). In places buffalo barred their progress by refusing to move. As Whitehouse said, the men had "to club them out of their way" (VII, 80).

Meriwether Lewis could have passed most tests devised to determine observational competence. He was particularly proficient in seeing the little things so often overlooked, even by the well-trained naturalist. He did this effortlessly and spontaneously. Let us consider a few typical Lewisian observations chosen at random from his journal written during the Yellowstone to Marias trip:

[15] Gass, 109.
[16] *Early Western Travels*, V, 99.

April 29—"We have frequently seen the wolves in pursuit of the Antelope in the plains; they appear to decoy a single one from a flock, and then pursue it, alturnately relieving each other until they take it" (I, 351).

May 10—"We have rarely found the mule deer in any except rough country; they prefer the open grounds and are seldom found in the woodlands near the river; when they are met with in the woodlands or river bottoms and are pursued, the[y] invariably run to the hills or open country as the Elk do. the contrary happens with the common [white-tailed] deer" (II, 20).

May 11—"The wild Hysop [sagebrush] grows here and . . . the buffaloe deer and Elk feed on this herb in winter season" (II, 25).

May 24—"The beaver appears to keep pace with the timber as it declines in quantity they also become more scarce" (II, 68).

May 23—"Just above the entrance of Teapot Creek on the stard. there is a large assembly of the burrows of the Burrowing Squirrel [prairie dog] they generally seelect a south or a south Easterly exposure for their residence, and never visit the brooks or river for water; I am astonished how this anamal exists as it dose without water, particularly in a country like this where there is scarcely any rain during ¾ of the year and more rarely any due [dew]; yet we have sometimes found their villages at a distance of five or six miles from any water, and they are never found out of the limits of the ground which their burrows occupy; in the Autumn when the hard frosts commence they close their burrows and do not venture out again untill spring" (II, 63–64).

Lewis's observation that the prairie dog existed without water demands special attention. It is now known, of course, that quite a few other arid-land rodents, such as the Egyptian gerbils and North American kangaroo rats and pocket mice, will live out their life spans in good health on a diet of nothing but dry plant food in which the water content does not exceed 5 to 10 per cent. Recently a zoologist of the U.S. Fish and Wildlife Service kept two prairie dogs for seven years in a perfect state of health without once providing drinking water. They subsisted almost entirely on grains and succulent food such as lettuce and carrots.[17]

That these desert rodents, comprising a group of unusual physiological plasticity, are able to survive on such diets is due, scientists have

[17] Stanley P. Young, "Seven Years—Without Water," *American Sportsman* (Dec., 1940), 10ff.

ascertained, to their ability to obtain necessary water from their foods and to retain most of it through emission of a highly concentrated urine, the concentration made possible by a greater resorptive activity of kidneys and urinary bladder than is true in most mammals. The economy of metabolic water thus achieved is sufficient to cover most of the animal's needs.[18]

Until these facts had been established there had been much speculation. Catlin, for instance, theorized that prairie dogs must obtain water from dew or "sink wells from their underground habitations, by which they descend low enough to get their supply."[19] So far as we can find, Lewis did not speculate on this point, but he seems to have been the first to observe and report the unique phenomenon of water conservation in North American rodents.

It was Clark, not Lewis, who first reported, "antelopes are curious and will approach any thing which appears in motion" (I, 354). While at Fort Union, Audubon put this observation to the test. Finding himself one day within two to three hundred yards of a herd of pronghorn, he lay down on his back and began to kick his well-travelled heels in the air. Much to his delight, one of the pretty creatures, intrigued more than the others, promptly detached itself from the herd and trotted to within 60 yards of him.[20]

In time the antelope learned not to be deceived by such antics. Theodore Roosevelt discovered this to be the case while resident in the Dakota Badlands in the 1880's. "Nowadays," he declared, "there are very few localities indeed in which they are sufficiently unsophisticated to make it worth while trying these time-honored tricks of the long-vanished trappers and hunters."[21]

[6]

On May 8 Lewis and Clark arrived where the Milk River discharges into the Missouri. Just above this confluence, some 135 years later, the U.S. Army Corps of Engineers completed a huge earthen barrier, the Fort Peck Dam. As the water backed up behind the dam, it created a

[18] B. Schmidt-Nielsen *et al.*, "Water Conservation in Desert Rodents," *Jour. Cell. Comp. Physiology*, 32 (1948), 331–360. See also Francois Bourlière, *The Natural History of Mammals* (New York, 1954), 258.

[19] Catlin, *North American Indians*, I, 88.

[20] John Francis McDermott, ed., *Up the Missouri with Audubon* (Norman, Okla., 1951), 150.

[21] Theodore Roosevelt *et al.*, *The Deer Family* (New York, 1902), 106.

tremendous artificial lake extending approximately half the distance to the Marias River. Beginning at the head of the reservoir and continuing upstream for about 180 miles is the region known locally today as the "Missouri Breaks." This is a spectacularly beautiful area, particularly the 45-mile stretch from Judith River to Virgelle Ferry, and it is the only sizable segment of the Missouri which remains relatively unchanged since the days of Lewis and Clark. Here on either side of the river outcroppings of a white glistening sandstone form remarkable perpendicular cliffs, in places 100 feet high, and extrusions of black igneous rock in the form of dikes and cones occasionally interrupt the continuity of white. The Corps of Discovery spent the greater part of four days passing through this land of "White Rocks," from May 29 to June 1, and it was here that Lewis penned his oft-quoted words, "seens of visionary inchantment" (II, 101).

Because the sandstone is soft and friable, the forces of wind and water, perennially active, have carved it into multitudinous forms which to the imagination resemble stately towers, bombed-out fortresses, shadowy castles, phantom sailing vessels, crumbling ruins, Gothic cathedrals, and many other fancied configurations. In time some of these achieved names.

In the summer of 1965, friends of mine in Great Falls, Larry Gill and Francis Mitchell, arranged for me to take a two-day boat trip through the "White Rocks" with Emil DonTigny, veteran river-runner of Havre, Montana. DonTigny, as a result of much study and 50 or more trips through this region, has acquired a stockpile of information about its history, geology, and biology probably unsurpassed by any man now alive. As we descended the river (from Virgelle Ferry to the Judith), DonTigny pointed out such imposing formations as Pilot Rock, LaBarge Rock, Eagle Rock, Citadel Rock (often incorrectly called Cathedral Rock), Hole-in-the-Wall, and Steamboat Rock. That these have changed but little since Lewis and Clark's and Maximilian's visits can be proved by comparing their outlines of today with Bodmer's finished drawings made in 1833.

Lewis and Clark arrived at the mouth of the Judith on May 29 and approached these formations from the opposite direction. Just above the Judith they passed Ash Rapid (now Deadman) and later in the day discovered a massive heap of dead and decomposing buffalo that Indians had driven over a precipice. Wolves were at the carcasses and so tame that Clark was able to kill one with his espontoon (a combination spear and halberd once part of an army officer's standard equipment). Just above the precipice (buffalo jump), the party came to a stream entering from the south that, with the incident of the buffalo carnage fresh in mind, they called Slaughter River (now Arrow Creek). Three miles farther along, on the north side of the river, they encamped for the night in a clump of cottonwoods.

In his journal for this date, Lewis reported having seen a "great abundance of the Argalia or Bighorned anamals in the high country" (II, 92). He was now in the very heart of bighorn country and in days immediately ahead was fascinated, as observers have been ever since, by the incredible sure-footedness displayed by these graceful mountain creatures as they bounded from ledge to ledge on the sides of high and almost perpendicular precipices. "They are verry Suple and run verry fast," commented Private Whitehouse (VII, 89).

Two days later on May 31 the Corps passed through the most spectacular part of the "White Rocks" region. Lewis described it in part as follows:

The hills and river Clifts which we passed today exhibit a most romantic appearance . . . water in the course of time . . . has trickled down the soft sand clifts and woarn it into a thousand grotesque figures, which with the help of a little imagination . . . are made to represent eligant ranges of lofty freestone buildings, having their parapets well stocked with statuary . . . a number of the small martin [cliff swallow, *Petrochelidon pyrrhonota*] which build their nests with clay in a globular form attached to the wall within those nitches, and which were seen hovering about the tops of the collumns did not the less remind us of some of those large stone buildings in the U. States. . . . As we passed on it seemed as if those seens of visionary inchantment would never have and [an] end; for here it is too that nature presents to the view of the traveler vast ranges of walls of tolerable workmanship, so perfect indeed are those walls that I should have thought that nature had attempted here to rival the human art of masonry had I not recollected that she had first began her work (II, 100–101).

During the course of the day, Lewis climbed a cliff to the home of the bighorn. Here he made a significant observation, one that emphasized the abundance of this animal and its long-time residence, as well as Lewis's well-developed olfactory sense. "The sides of the Clifts where these anamals resort much to lodg," he reported, "have the peculiar smell of the sheepfolds" (II, 103).

If Lewis and Clark revisited the "Missouri Breaks" today they would find it relatively unchanged except faunally. The white walls still glisten in the sun, sheltering clumps of cottonwood still cover their campsites, prickly pear continues to bloom abundantly each spring, and cliff swallows still build globular nests and hover above sandstone columns. The buffalo and bighorn, of course, are gone, and other quadrupeds common in 1805 are now rarely encountered; otherwise the region has retained most of the wilderness features observed by Lewis and Clark more than a century and a half ago.

The same, unfortunately, cannot be said for most other parts of the Missouri. Some have been completely buried by impounded water and others irreparably scarred and divested of pristine beauty by the blighting touch of "civilized" hands. No single incident points up present unsightliness better than that experienced in 1964 by the late Ted Yates when filming his television show, "The Journal of Lewis and Clark." Yates and his party had to ascend the Missouri nearly 2,000 miles to find a remnant of land and river attractive to the cameraman's eye; that remnant was the "Missouri Breaks" of central Montana.[22]

And now even this distant green spot is threatened. If the Army Corps of Engineers has its way, it will construct a dam just above Fort Peck Reservoir which will, as one writer put it, "wipe out the wilderness, flood out the history, and so emasculate the landscape as to deprive it of all vital appeal."[23] If the plan is defeated, it will be due largely to concerted efforts of the National Park Service which has countered with a proposal to convert this remote, unsullied 180-mile stretch of the Missouri into "The Lewis and Clark National Waterway." If approved, the grandeur of this extravagant wonderland would be preserved for all time. What a fitting monument to the memory of Lewis and Clark—particularly if, as proposed, the buffalo and bighorn are reintroduced to roam once again the banks and benchlands of the region.

On June 1 the explorers left behind them this land of silence and contrasting color and just two days later halted at the conjunction of two important rivers; but which of the two was the Missouri not one of them could say.

SUMMARY OF DISCOVERIES

Animals New to Science

WESTERN WILLET. *Catopthrophorus semipalmatus inornatus* (Brewster).
     [A.O.U. 258a] (Thwaites, II, 17; Coues, I, 303–304n). Described, 1887.

[22] Ted Yates, "Since Lewis and Clark," *The American West*, II, no. 4 (Fall, 1965), 24.

[23] Gilbert F. Stucker, "Whither the Wide Missouri?" *National Parks Magazine*, 39, no. 215 (Aug., 1965) 10.

PRAIRIE RATTLESNAKE. *Crotalus viridis viridis* Rafinesque = *C. confluentus*
Say. (Thwaites, II, 41, 160; Coues, II, 373) . 1818.
GRIZZLY BEAR. *Ursus horribilis horribilis* Ord. (Thwaites, I, 350) . 1815.

Plants New to Science
GREASEWOOD. *Sarcobatus vermiculatus* (Hook.) Torrey. (Thwaites, II,
25–26) . 1838.

Lewis and Clark Herbarium
None.

Indian Tribes Encountered
None.

Topographic Features Named and/or Discovered
From the mouth of the Yellowstone River to Columbia River tide-
water, about 100 miles from the Pacific, Lewis and Clark journeyed through
country never before seen by white men. They therefore discovered (as well
as named) many of the physical features of this region, each of which we
precede by a dagger (†) to so indicate.
† Ibex Creek (Coues, I, 287n) .
† Martha's River (Thwaitcs, I, 352) —— today's Big Muddy River.
† Porcupine River (Thwaites, I, 362) —— now Poplar River.
† 2000 Mile Creek (Thwaites, I, 363) .
† Little Dry River (Thwaites, II, 3) .
† Big Dry Creek (Thwaites, II, 3) —— Elk Prairie Creek (Coues, I, 299n) .
† Lackwater Creek (Thwaites, II, 5) .
† Milk River (Thwaites, II, 10) —— Milk River of today.
† Big Dry River (Thwaites, II, 14–15) .
† Werner's Creek (Thwaites, II, 18) .
† Pine Creek (Thwaites, II, 31) —— Crabb's Creek (Coues, I, 307) .
† Gibson's Creek (Thwaites, II, 36) .
† Yellow Bear Defeat Creek (Thwaites, II, 38) .
† Sticklodge Creek (Coues, I, 309) .
† Panther Creek (Thwaites, II, 40) .
† Bratton's Creek (Thwaites, II, 44) —— Timber Creek (Coues, I, 312n) .
† Rattlesnake Creek (Coues, I, 312) .
† Wiser's Creek (Thwaites, II, 45) —— Fourchette Creek (Thwaites, II,
45n) .
† Blowing Fly Creek (Thwaites, II, 51) —— Squaw Creek (Coues, I, 315n) .
† Sâh-câ-gerwe-âh Creek (Thwaites, II, 52) —— Crooked Creek (Thwaites,
II, 52n) .
† Musselshell River (Thwaites, II, 51) —— Musselshell River.
† Windy Island (Thwaites, II, 57) .
† Grouse Creek (Thwaites, II, 59) .

† Teapot Creek (Thwaites, II, 63) ——— Yellow Creek (Coues, I, 321).

† Teapot Island (Thwaites, II, 63).

† North Mountain Creek (Thwaites, II, 68) ——— Little Rock Creek (Coues, I, 324n).

† Little Dog Creek (Thwaites, II, 68).

† South Mountain Creek (Thwaites, II, 68) ——— Armel Creek (Ordway, 217n).

† North Mountain (Ordway, 217) ——— Little Rocky Mountains.

† South Mountains (Ordway, 217) ——— Judith Mountains.

† Turtle Creek (Thwaites, II, 79).

† Windsor Creek (Thwaites, II, 80) ——— Cow Creek (Coues, I, 327n).

† Elk Rapids (Thwaites, II, 80, 84) ——— Lone Pine Rapids (Coues, I, 329n).

† Thompson's Creek (Thwaites, II, 88) ——— Birch Creek (Coues, I, 331n).

† Bull Creek (Thwaites, II, 89) ——— Dog Creek (Coues, I, 332n).

† Judith's River (Thwaites, II, 92) ——— Judith River.

† Ash Rapids (Thwaites, II, 93) ——— Deadman Rapids.

† Slaughter River (Thwaites, II, 94) ——— Arrow Creek (Coues, I, 335).

† Stonewall Creek (Coues, I, 340n) ——— Eagle Creek (Ordway, 223).

† Maria's River (Thwaites, II, 109, 130) ——— Marias River.

Marias
to
White Bear Islands

CHAPTER TEN

When Lewis and Clark arrived at the confluence of the Marias with the Missouri, they admitted being puzzled—and not a little perturbed. Nothing the Indians had told them agreed with what they found here. The "Scolding River," so they understood, should have entered farther downstream. "An interesting question was now to be determined," Lewis wrote; "which of these rivers was the Missouri . . . to mistake the stream at this period of the season, two months of the traveling season having now elapsed, and to ascend such stream to the rocky Mountain . . . and then be obliged to return and take the other stream would not only loose us the whole of this season but would probably so dishearten the party that it might defeat the expedition altogether, to this end an investigation of both streams was the first thing to be done" (II, 112–113).

The captains at once sent Sergeant Gass with two men up the south fork and Sergeant Pryor with two others up the north one, instructing them to examine each closely and report back before nightfall. Their findings revealed that the south branch was considerably wider (372 yards), shallower, swifter, and clearer. By contrast, the northern one was only 220 yards wide, but deeper, turbid, and its waters flowing "in the same boiling and roling manner which had uniformly characterized the Missouri throughout its whole course so far" (II, 114).

With this information at hand, the entire party, except Lewis and Clark, unhesitatingly plumped for the north fork as the Missouri, influenced appreciably by Cruzatte in whose judgment the men had great confidence. As the commanding officers looked at it, however, a decision of such importance should not be made hastily. Accordingly, they determined to examine the streams themselves. The next day, Clark, with Gass, Shannon, York, and the Field brothers, began a reconnaissance of the south fork, and Lewis, with Drouillard, Shields, Windsor, Cruzatte, and LePage, undertook the north. Clark went upstream 40 miles, returning on the third day. He saw enough to convince him that he had been following the Missouri. As a bonus, he discovered an important tributary of the north fork, the Teton River (Tanzey of Lewis and Clark).

Lewis devoted five days altogether to his reconnaissance. Though impeded by much rain, a resultant slippery terrain, and an abundance of prickly pear, he nevertheless ascended the north fork a distance of some 60 miles.

This stream, Lewis soon became convinced, could not be the Missouri. It bore too far to the north, it penetrated no farther than the first range of the Rockies, and it interposed no great water falls such as the Indians at Fort Mandan had told him would bar his way. Evidencing his conviction, he promptly named this affluent Maria's River (pronounced Muh-rýe-us). He then penned this paragraph: "It is a noble river; one destined to become in my opinion an object of contention between the two great powers of America and Great Britain with rispect to the adjustment of the Northwestardly boundary of the former; and that it will become one of the most interesting branc[h]es of the Missouri in a commercial point of view, I have but little doubt, as it abounds with anamals of the fur kind, and most probably furnishes a safe and direct communication to that productive country of valuable furs exclusively enjoyed at present by the subjects of his Britanic Majesty" (II, 130–131).

These opinions explain why, from that moment, Lewis determined to revisit the Marias on his return from the Pacific, to follow it if need be to its source.

Returned to base, Lewis and Clark compared notes. They had come to the same conclusion separately—and now did so jointly. The other members of the party continued to disagree with their leaders on this point but expressed their willingness to follow wherever directed. No one doubted, however, that the present dilemma could be resolved with the discovery of the falls.

During the reconnaissance period, the men left behind had been treating their wounds, dressing skins, airing paraphernalia, and scouring adjacent country for buffalo, deer, and elk. On instructions from Lewis, they saved all elk hides, these to be used soon for covering the frame of his iron boat.

Now that the decision had been made to move up the south fork, the party delayed long enough to perform certain tasks designed to accelerate travel from here on. They cached a wide variety of goods, such as hides and horns and superfluous clothing, ammunition, implements, and foodstuffs. Sergeant Gass estimated the total weight of articles buried here at about 1,000 pounds.[1] Also, they snaked the red pirogue onto an island and covered it with brush. Its crew would now be free to help with the other boats.

[2]

On the morning of June 11 after nine days of frustration and indecision, Lewis shouldered his pack and started up the south fork. He took with him Drouillard, Joseph Field, Gibson, and Goodrich. (By now, as his journal reveals, Lewis rarely left the main party for any length of time without Drouillard at his side.) Toward noon they killed four elk, took what meat they needed, and hung the rest up in trees at the river's edge where Clark and his boatmen would find it. Soon afterwards Lewis developed a violent pain in his intestines and, that evening, an accompanying high fever. Since he had no medical supplies with him, he resolved "to try an experiment with some simples" (II, 142).

Looking about for a suitable plant, Lewis's eyes fell on the "choke cherry" (probably a variety of the eastern wild cherry, *Prunus virginiana*). He had his men gather a number of twigs from this tree and after stripping off the leaves, cut the twigs into pieces about two inches in length. These were then boiled in water "untill a strong black decoction of an astringent bitter tast was produced." At dusk Lewis drank a pint of this and about an hour later downed another. By ten o'clock he was perspiring gently, his pain had left him, and his fever had abated. That night, all symptoms which had disturbed him having disappeared, he slept soundly. The next morning at sunrise, fit and refreshed, he took another swig of the remedy and resumed his march (II, 142, 144).

That evening, after having walked 37 miles during the day, Lewis

[1] Gass, 115.

admitted that he was somewhat tired. He attributed his weariness, however, to his recent indisposition and not at all to his long walk. He said that he ate a hearty supper and afterwards amused himself by pulling several "white fish" from the river (II, 145) .[2]

The following morning Lewis and his men veered away from the river to the more level, less gullied prairie land. In time they came to a small swell where they looked upon a most beautiful plain and in the distance two elevations with sides rising perpendicularly to a great height. These landmarks are today known as Crown Butte and Square Butte. When much closer to the latter, about one month later, he gave it the name of Fort Mountain.

Toward noon, fearing that he might miss the falls, if indeed they existed hereabouts, he turned his steps in the direction of the river. He took Goodrich with him and ordered the others to look for game. "I had proceded on this course about two miles," Lewis wrote, ". . . whin my ears were saluted with the agreeable sound of a fall of water and advancing a little further I saw the spray arrise above the plain like a collumn of smoke which would frequently dis[ap]pear again in an instant caused I presumed by the wind which blew pretty hard from the S.W. I did not however loose my direction to this point which soon began to make a roaring too tremendious to be mistaken for any cause short of the great falls of the Missouri" (II, 147) .

It was high noon, Thursday, June 13, 1805. Captain Meriwether Lewis had discovered the Great Falls and at the same time had solved the mystery that had stalled the Expedition for more than a week at the mouth of the Marias. This south fork would no longer be designated as such; it was indeed the Missouri.

Lewis hurried down the face of a 200-foot bluff to a ledge of rocks where he had an uninterrupted view of what he declared to be the grandest sight he had ever beheld, the water of the Missouri here dropping over a precipice more than 80 feet high. He stood motionless for a long time, completely enchanted by the beauty of the scene. At length he took his pen and attempted to put into words his first impressions. He did hope, he said, that his description might convey to the world some faint idea of this grandiose spectacle which of its kind was "second to but one in the known world" (II, 150) . At that time, excepting Niagara, the largest waterfalls of the world remained yet to

[2] Coues (II, 362n) identified the "white fish" as a kind of pike-perch (*Stizostedion canadense*) .

be discovered: for example, Yellowstone (1807), Yosemite (1851), and Victoria (1855).

Eventually Lewis tore himself away from the scene, retiring to the shade of a cottonwood; it would be a good place to spend the night. Drouillard, Gibson, and Field soon came in with choicer parts of three buffalo cows and Goodrich caught several large trout. Their supper that night, with the nearby falls providing music, went down uncommonly well. It consisted, Lewis said, of "buffaloe's humps, tongues and marrowbones, fine trout parched meal pepper and salt, and a good appetite" (II, 151).

The next morning Lewis dispatched Joseph Field with a message to Clark advising him of recent discoveries and instructing him, as he neared the falls, to look for a place where they might begin portaging. The evening before he had walked downstream and had ascertained that the walls of the canyon rose perpendicularly on either side of the river 150 to 200 feet high. It would be incumbent on Clark to discover a break in this wall through which they could transport the canoes and contents from the river to the plains above.

Leaving Drouillard and the others, Lewis now picked up his rifle and started upstream to determine the length of the upcoming portage route and which side of the river would lend itself best to this undertaking. He had walked some seven miles when he came to a second waterfall, one about 19 feet high. He would have turned back here, he said, except for a tremendous roaring ahead of him. Crossing the point of a hill, he came within view of a third fall, "one of the most beautiful objects in nature, a cascade of about fifty feet perpendicular" (II, 153).

Lewis had scarcely finished contemplating this latest discovery when, on lifting his head, he saw, about a quarter of a mile farther upstream, a fourth fall, this one with a pitch of six feet. He now began to wonder if there was no end to these cataracts. Proceeding upstream two and one-half miles, he discovered a fifth fall, this one approximately 26 feet high. On an island in midstream just below the fall, an eagle had its nest in a cottonwood. "A more inaccessable spot I believe she could not have found," Lewis observed, "for neither man nor beast dare pass those gulphs which separate her little domain from the shores" (II, 155). Lewis was pleased to find this nest; the Hidatsas had told him he might.

The uppermost of the falls discovered by Lewis is separated from the lowest by some 10 miles. In time all five acquired names. As the river is ascended, they are:

Great Falls . . . . 87 feet, $\frac{3}{4}$ inches.
Crooked Falls . . . . 19 feet
Rainbow Falls . . . . 47 feet, 6 inches.
Colter Falls . . . . 6 feet, 7 inches.
Black Eagle Falls . . . . 26 feet, 5 inches.[3]

In their journals Lewis and Clark mentioned only Crooked Falls. Clark's charts, however, show Great Falls as "Great Falls," Rainbow Falls as "Beautiful Cascade," and Black Eagle Falls simply as "Upper Pitch." According to Larry Gill, authority on the portage route, Rainbow Falls acquired that name in 1872 from Thomas B. Roberts, a railroad engineer, and Colter Falls from Paris Gibson, founder of the city of Great Falls.[4]

These falls in 1805 and for many years afterwards were superbly beautiful; about that, Lewis's choice of adjectives leaves no doubt. As the visitor to this region today quickly discovers, the beauty has vanished. Due to hydro-electric "progress," not one of the falls remains in anything like its original natural state, and Colter Falls has been completely obliterated by backwater from a dam surmounting Rainbow Falls.

From an eminence near Black Eagle Falls, Lewis ascertained that the Missouri ran smoothly above it. He could see, too, three to four miles away, a sizable stream entering from the west. From what the Indians had told him, he was convinced that this must be the Medicine River. Forgetting the lateness of the day and his distance from camp, he hurried across the intervening plain toward the stream which today is called Sun River. En route, he almost lost his life when he was suddenly charged by a grizzly. Only a leap into the Missouri saved him. On rejoining his companions, long after nightfall, he learned that "they had formed a thousand conjectures," each "foreboding" his death (II, 159).

[3] In 1807 when Lewis returned to Philadelphia, he gave $40 to the Irish-born engraver, John James Barrelet, "for two Drawings [of] water falls in full" (Jackson, *Letters,* 462, 463n). In 1810 when Clark, after Lewis's death, came to Philadelphia, he reported: "imperfect drawings have been made of the falls of the Missouri, & Columbia" (Jackson, *Letters,* 490). Presumably these drawings were made by Barrelet. Unfortunately, they have not been found.
[4] Larry Gill, "The Great Portage," *Great Falls Tribune,* Aug. 15, 1965.

[3]

On June 10, while still at the mouth of the Marias, Lewis wrote in part: "I saw a small bird today which I do not recollect ever having seen before, it is about the size of the blue thrush or catbird . . . it appeared to be very busy in catching insects which I presume is it's usual food; I found the nest of this little bird, the female which differed but little in size or plumage from the male was seting on four eggs of a pale blue colour with small black freckles or dots" (II, 140–141).

With the full text of Lewis's description before them, ornithologists have had no difficulty in identifying this bird as the white-rumped shrike (*Lanius ludovicianus excubitorides*), not technically described until 26 years later. It is the western form of the loggerhead shrike, so well known for its singular habit of impaling insects and other food on thorns and barbed wire.

While on his Marias reconnaissance, Lewis discovered two other birds: the sage grouse (*Centrocercus urophasianus urophasianus*), the largest of gallinaceous birds excepting the wild turkey, and McCown's longspur (*Rhynchophanes mccownii*), a small relative of the sparrows and finches found east of the Rockies on the plains. At first Lewis referred to this grouse as the "mountain cock" but later, on the Columbia, as the "Prairie Cock" or "Cock of the Plains." Only rarely have modern ornithologists credited Lewis and Clark with the discovery of a bird. Of interest, therefore, are the words of Arthur Cleveland Bent, Smithsonian scientist, about the sage grouse: "It was discovered by Lewis and Clark about the headwaters of the Missouri River and on the plains of the Columbia; they named it 'cock of the plains' and gave the first account of it. The technical description and the scientific name, *urophasianus*, were supplied by [Charles Lucien] Bonaparte in 1827."[5]

The trout Lewis and his men ate for supper on June 13 at Great Falls resembled, Lewis wrote, "our mountain or speckled trout in form and in the position of their fins, but the specks on these are of a deep black instead of the red or goald colour of those common to the U'. States. these are furnished long sharp teeth on the pallet and tongue and have generally a small dash of red on each side behind the front ventral fins" (II, 151).

[5] Arthur Cleveland Bent, *Life Histories of North American Gallinaceous Birds*, Bull. 162 (Washington, D.C., 1932), 299–300.

From this description by Lewis, particularly his allusion to the red slashes behind the front ventral fins, ichthyologists conclude that this trout was the celebrated cutthroat. When the English naturalist, John Richardson, described it (in 1836) and supplied its technical name, *Salmo clarkii,* he said he had bestowed that name "as a tribute to the memory of Captain Clarke who noticed it in the narrative prepared by him of the proceedings of the Expedition to the Pacific."[6] Some 20 years later, the Philadelphia naturalist, Charles Girard, named the cutthroat (from specimens collected at Great Falls) *Salar lewisii.*[7] Though the former name is the accepted one today, it is pleasing to find in the synonomy of this fish both captains receiving recognition.

On the day Clark discovered the Teton River, he said that the valley of that stream contained many cottonwoods with leaves resembling those of a wild cherry (II, 126). A few days later Lewis wrote: "The narrow leafed cottonwood grows here in common with the other species of the same tree with a broad leaf." It differed from the broad-leafed, he went on to say, only "in the shape of it's leaf and greater thickness of it's bark" (II, 145). This was the first description of the narrow-leafed cottonwood, *Populus angustifolia.* Only Lewis's untimely death, wrote one well-known scientist, "robbed him of the honor of naming this tree [which he and Clark had discovered here] and many other new species."[8]

[4]

By the time Lewis had completed his portage survey to the Sun River, Clark and his durable, long-suffering boatmen had reached a point where the "dedly sound" of falling water struck their ears. The ascent from Camp Deposit (Ordway's name for the Marias encampment) had been difficult, often hazardous, entailing frequent struggles with an ever-accelerating current. Prairie rattlesnakes (*Crotalus viridis viridis*), which inhabited the rocky ledges of the banks (and still do today), added to the dangers. One of the hunters reaching for a bush grasped a rattler by its head. Not far away, Lewis awoke to discover a large one coiled near where he had been sleeping. He killed it and then

[6] John Richardson, *Fauna Boreali-Americana; or the Zoology of the Northern Parts of British America,* 4 vols. (London, 1836), III, 225.

[7] Charles Girard, "Notes Upon the Species of the Genus Salmo, of Authors, Observed Chiefly in Oregon and California," *Procs. Acad. Nat. Scis. of Philadelphia,* VIII (1856), 219–220.

[8] Peattie, *A Natural History of Western Trees,* 330.

recorded for posterity the information that it had "176 scuta on the abdomen and 17 half formed scuta on the tale" and that its colors, while much the same as those of rattlers common to the middle Atlantic states, differed in their "form and figures" (II, 160) .

When Lewis rejoined Clark, the latter had just completed taking the boats across an extremely difficult rapid and had discovered a creek entering from the south directly opposite a large mineral spring on the north side. Aware by now that they faced a long portage, the two captains immediately took stock of their situation. They were hemmed in between two high bluffs where the only break allowing access to the plains above was the creek. They believed that if they ascended this stream (they called it Portage Creek, though it is today Belt Creek) , they would soon locate a gradual slope up which they could drag the dugouts and lading to the prairie floor. It was a piece of good luck that the creek emptied on the south side, for from what Lewis had observed, the plain there was less gullied than on the north side. As a consequence, the portaging should be easier.

Having chosen a campsite (just below Portage Creek) and unloaded the boats, Lewis and Clark conferred on how best to transport boats and goods across the plains to a base above the falls. Because it would be next to impossible for the men to carry the six heavy dugouts, they hit on the plan of building two wagons and forthwith put Sergeant Gass in charge of a detail "to p[r]epare four sets of truck wheels with couplings, toungs and bodies" (II, 165) . For this purpose—for wheels in particular—Gass needed a tree of large diameter. In his search he could find but one; it was a cottonwood. Cross-sections, 22 inches in diameter, sawed from the trunk of this large *Populus* provided the necessary wheels. Lewis doubted there was another that size within 20 miles.

While the wagonmakers toiled, others began snaking the canoes up Portage Creek. Clark, with five men, headed upstream to survey the portage route.

The region at the mouth of Portage Creek is well worth a visit today. Roads approach on both sides of the river, though, since the land is privately owned, it is necessary to make arrangements in advance. Such arrangements were made for me in 1965 by Larry Gill. I was delighted to find that the mineral spring still discharges a steady flow of water which drops over a rock-shelf directly into the Missouri. The cascade thus formed is plainly visible from the opposite side of the river. Portage Creek, some 40 to 50 feet wide at its entrance, is a lovely stream. Just below it is the small bottom where Lewis and Clark established their lower base camp. Cottonwoods, badly gnawed by beaver, stand about, but none approaching in size the one Sergeant Gass cut for wagon wheels. A little over a mile up Portage Creek one can see the slope up which the explorers dragged the dugouts to the prairie floor above. In this general area conditions have changed but little since 1805. I find myself wishing that it could be made into a sanctuary, perhaps a state park, so that it might remain permanently inviolate.

[5]

As the men began portaging, Sacagawea lay in her tent nearer dead than alive. She had been ill when Clark left the Marias, and day by day since then her condition worsened. Clark seems to have had no idea what was wrong with her, but he was attentive to her needs and did all that he knew how to do. On the first day he bled her, and on the next when she showed no signs of improving, he bled her again. He did not say how much blood he withdrew, only that the operation "appeared to be of great service to her" (II, 143). On the fourth day he gave her a dose of salts, which appeared to be of no service at all for the next morning she was "excessively bad" and her case "somewhat dangerous" (II, 159). A little later she complained of abdominal pain, and Clark "gave her the bark," applying it "externally to her region" (II, 161).

At this stage Lewis rejoined the party. He found Sacagawea's pulse rapid, irregular, and barely perceptible and her condition "attended with strong nervous symptoms, that of the twitching of the fingers and leaders of the arm" (II, 164). Immediately assuming responsibility, he continued the "cataplasms [poultices] of bark and laudnumm" instituted by Clark and ordered a man to bring a cask of water from the mineral spring nearby. He had great faith in the efficacy of this water since it was highly impregnated with sulphur and "precisely similar to that of Bowyer's Sulpher Spring in Virginia" (II, 163). He had Sacagawea drink freely of it. By evening Lewis was gratified to find her pulse stronger and more regular, her nervous symptoms somewhat abated, and her abdominal pains less severe. He hesitated in his diagnosis but believed her trouble "originated from an obstruction of the mensis in consequence of taking cold" (II, 164).

The next morning Sacagawea was so far improved that she asked for food and was permitted to eat some broiled buffalo and some soup of the same meat. To the medicine already prescribed, Lewis now added 15 drops of vitriol and considered her well on the road to recovery. And doubtless she would have continued to improve if her husband, who had been given strict orders to watch her, had prevented her from imprudently eating a meal of white apples *(Psoralea esculenta)* and dried fish. As a result of her indulgence, her pains and fever returned. After employing army language to tell Charbonneau what he thought of him, Lewis went to work on his patient again. This time he prescribed "broken dozes of diluted nitre [saltpeter] untill it produced perspiration and at 10 P.M. 30 drops of laudnumm" (II, 172). From here on the Indian woman's recovery was rapid and uncomplicated.

Sacagawea's case seems to have been a prime example of the patient's recovering in spite of the treatment. Certainly the purging and bleeding could have had no effect upon the cure except retard it. How much blood Clark withdrew is speculative. Conservative doctors of the day removed only four to eight ounces; others were not satisfied until they had siphoned off a pint to a quart. Only a few casehardened dissidents were dead set against withdrawing any at all.

The bloodletter would open any vein he could readily get at, but by long odds the most commonly used were those at the flexor surface of the elbow, the anticubital veins. Nowadays therapeutic bleeding would be done in the same area using a large syringe and needle or a large needle and rubber tube discharging into a bottle, as blood is taken for transfusions. The phlebotomists did it differently. They excised the vein, making a hole in it about one-quarter inch long. Blood was allowed to flow over the arm and drip into a basin. They probably did not often measure the blood accurately, being content to estimate the amount withdrawn. When they had taken what they thought was enough, they applied a tight bandage to stop flow. Serious infections sometimes resulted from such wounds, and occasionally the patient died.

One harmful effect of excessive bleeding is to reduce the quantity in the blood of such important minerals as calcium, magnesium, and potassium. The muscle twitching reported by Lewis in Sacagawea may very well have been a symptom of tetany induced by a deficiency of such minerals. Bleeding, too, in conjunction with purging and fever, produces dehydration. If the considerable amount of mineral water Lewis had his patient drink benefited her at all, it was because it relieved dehydration and restored vital minerals.

Lewis's empirical use of oil of vitriol, which is sulphuric acid, cannot be justified today. However, since his patient recovered, he probably made a mental note to use it again under like circumstances if they ever presented themselves. Nitre, as previously mentioned, is an active diaphoretic, and Lewis used it successfully for that purpose. The "broken dozes" he alluded to were doses administered at intervals over a period of time. At this late date one can do no more than guess at Sacagawea's trouble. Lewis's diagnosis of amenorrhea would seem as good as any other.

Lewis and Clark expressed gratification upon the recovery of Sacagawea. They were fond of her and, as Lewis said, she was "our only dependence for a negociation with the Snake [Shoshoni] Indians on whom we depend for horses to assist us in our portage from the Missouri to the columbia river" (II, 163).

[6]

Clark devoted four days to determining and surveying the portage route. He was the first white man to see the falls from the south side of the Missouri, and he was the discoverer of the Giant Spring (on his maps he called it "Large Fountain") just above Rainbow Falls. Here a tremendous flow of water, bluish in cast, boils up from under rocks near the edge of the river and immediately drops eight feet into the swift Missouri current. I am told that one-fourth of the Missouri water immediately below this fountain has been contributed by Giant Spring. After Lewis had seen it he wrote: "I think this fountain the largest I ever beheld . . . it may well be retained on the list of prodigies of this neighborhood towards which, nature seems to have dealt with a liberal hand" (II, 195).

Near Rainbow Falls, Clark was spectator to a scene which made a deep and lasting impression on him. From a vantage point at the top of the river wall, he saw two herds of buffalo descend by a narrow pass to the river's edge. As they entered the water, they were forced ever farther by those behind into deeper and deeper water and soon swept from their feet by the force of the current. Some escaped the pull of the current to reach one bank or the other. The remainder, not so fortunate, were swept over the falls. Clark no longer had difficulty in explaining the presence just below the falls of so many buffalo skeletons and putrefying carcasses. Their presence there accounted for the many grizzlies inhabiting this region, and why they were, as Lewis put it, "so tenatious of their right of soil in this neighborhood" (II, 167).

Clark's survey led him beyond Black Eagle Falls to the mouth of Sun River and then three miles beyond that stream to a point where three small islands decorated the broad expanse of the Missouri. Here the water flowed smoothly with scarcely a ripple, contained by banks only a few feet high. No longer would the explorers be in peril from falling banks. Dangers did exist here, however; a grizzly turned on John Colter and drove him into the river. By now almost every member of the party could boast of having been chased by Old Ephraim.

For obvious reasons, Clark called these islands White Bear Islands, and he chose the adjacent southern bottom as the western terminus of the portage. The best and most direct route for by-passing the falls would, he now concluded, run from Portage Creek across the plains southwesterly to White Bear Islands, a distance of about 18 miles. (The Indians at Fort Mandan, it will be recalled, had led Lewis and Clark to believe the portage would be only about one-half mile.) With his decision made, Clark instructed his men to cut sticks with which they could mark the route; they then headed for the lower camp.

Larry Gill has informed me that the portage route as established by Clark crossed at right angles the great migration route of the buffalo as they funneled in from the south in the spring to cross the Missouri on a gravel bar just a few hundred yards below the mouth of Sun River, and then, once across the river, fanned out as they moved north toward their summer range in Blackfoot country. In the fall they used the same route in travelling south to winter ranges.

During Clark's absence the party at Portage Creek had completed the two wagons, drawn the white pirogue from the water and hidden it under a cover of brush and driftwood, and had taken the dugouts up the creek to the prairie floor. In short, by the time Clark returned practically everything was set for the beginning of the portage.

Before starting the two captains made an important decision. In his letter to Jefferson from Fort Mandan, Lewis had said: "I shall dispatch [back to St. Louis] a canoe with three, perhaps four persons, from the extreme navigable point of the Missouri, on the portage between this river, and the Columbia, as either may happen" (VII, 319). Since writing that letter, he and Clark had had second thoughts on the matter. The party was entirely too small to spare even a single individual, for, as Clark wrote, "not haveing seen the Snake Indians or knowing in fact whither to calculate on their friendship, we have . . . concluded not to dispatch a canoe with a part of our men to St. Louis" (II, 175).

Lewis and Clark would later have one reason at least for regretting this decision. If a party had been sent back from this point, it would doubtless have carried plant and animal specimens collected between Fort Mandan and Great Falls. In that event these specimens, lost here during the upcoming winter, possibly would have been saved.

Portaging around the falls consumed 11 days, from June 22 to July 2. It required four trips by wagons and men, each accomplished at the expenditure of many hours of difficult labor. Prickly pear, which formed a thick spiny blanket over the portage route, contributed immeasurably to the hardship. Unless the men watched each step, it was impossible to avoid the spines of this plant; their thin-soled moccasins offered practically no defense. Though they later reinforced soles with buffalo rawhide (parfleche), this added protection failed to prevent spines from entering sides of feet and ankles. Each evening, as the portaging progressed, the men removed moccasins and suffered through the grim, painful experience of pulling cactus spines from hurting feet. If these same men could travel the portage route today, they would find much of it covered with dry-land wheat fields.

The abundance of prickly pear encountered here by Lewis and Clark may have a logical explanation. According to reliable sources, it was a natural step in the ecology of the area due to heavy overgrazing by buffalo. The soil was so thin and devoid of organic matter that even a small change affected it adversely. Thus, when the buffalo depleted the normal cover of prairie grass, it was a simple matter for the prickly pear to establish itself. Popular opinion to the contrary, overgrazing in the West was a problem in many places long before the advent of white men.

Before abandoning the lower camp, the men hid the swivel under some rocks and filled another cache. Into it went Clark's latest map of the Missouri, Lewis's desk and such dispensable items as kegs of pork and flour, guns, and ammunition. On the Fourth of July, with the portaging completed and the entire party reunited at White Bear Islands, the men celebrated briefly by dining on "a very comfortable dinner" of boiled buffalo beef, bacon, beans, and suet dumplings topped off with the last of their ardent spirits except a small amount held in reserve for illnesses.

If the iron boat had been covered and caulked by now, the explorers could have resumed their journey at once. Difficulties in obtaining materials had resulted in exasperating delays. "I begin to be extremely impatient to be off as the season is now waisting a pace," Lewis declared (II, 200). His impatience, however, did not becloud his foresight to the need of providing food for days ahead when game might become scarce. It will be remembered he had been informed by the Mandans that as he entered the mountains, he would leave the buffalo behind. Accordingly he kept his hunters busy drying meat, large quanties of it. Shannon, for instance, in just two or three days jerked 600 pounds, and Drouillard 800. Other men "tried up" buffalo grease (that is, converted fat to tallow); Charbonneau alone produced enough to fill three kegs. "The men not other ways directed," wrote Ordway, "are dressing Skins to make themselves mockinsons as they have wore them all out in the plains one pair . . . will not last more than about 2 days."[9]

When the iron boat was finally completed, it was 36 feet long, four and one-half feet wide, and capable of carrying an estimated load of 8,000 pounds. To give it a proper integument, Lewis had employed 28 elk and four buffalo hides. Not having tar or pitch with which "to pay her seams," he improvised with a paste of charcoal, beeswax, and tallow. When launched, "she lay like a perfect cork in the water" (II, 317). A few hours later the seams opened, and it was all too obvious that Lewis's cherished experiment had come a cropper. The failure was "mortifying" to him. The iron boat was to have taken the place of the two pirogues. The party had already devoted six weeks to solving the Marias-Missouri riddle and by-passing the falls, and now they faced the necessity of further delay to construct two new dugouts. But could they find cottonwoods large enough for that purpose? In this extremity, one of the hunters recalled having seen some fair-sized ones a few miles upstream. In order to find out, Clark left early the next morning by land, taking with him Sergeant Pryor, four "choppers," and three others. Ordway and eight men followed in four loaded canoes. Lewis stayed behind with the rest of the party to dismantle the iron boat and to bury it and other articles, including the dried plant specimens he had collected between Fort Mandan and Great Falls. Always looking ahead, he even buried the wagon wheels; they might be needed on the return journey.

When Clark reached the bottom where the tall timber grew, he found two big cottonwoods—just two and no more—one of them hollow at one end and both windshaken. But they would have to do. From them the axemen shaped the requisite dugouts, one 25 feet in length and the other 33. Once again cottonwood had saved the day.

[9] Ordway, 242.

A visit to this site today (locally called Canoe Camp) is rewarding, as I found out in 1965 when friends in Great Falls showed me the
way. By far the largest cottonwoods stand here (five in particular) that
I have seen anywhere in my journeyings up and down the Missouri and
Yellowstone Rivers. All five have circumferences, four feet from the
ground, of at least 17 feet, and one giant has a girth of 20 feet 2 inches
and a diameter of six and one-half feet.[10]

[7]

During the stay at Great Falls Lewis continued to discover animals
then unknown to science. One was the thirteen-striped ground squirrel
(*Spermophilus tridecemlineatus pallidus*), which was "somewhat
larger than those of the U' States" and marked longitudinally "with a
much greater number of black or dark brown stripes" (II, 216). Another was the kit fox (*Vulpes velox velox*), the smallest of all our foxes
and, in the eyes of some observers, the prettiest. According to Lewis, it
burrowed in the ground somewhat like the small wolf and its "tallons
appear longer than any species of fox I ever saw and seem therefore
prepared more amply by nature for the purpose of burrowing" (II,
216).

A third mammal discovered here by Lewis was the bushy-tailed
woodrat, better known as the Rocky Mountain pack rat (*Neotoma
cinerea cinerea*). He caught a specimen one day while moving some of
his baggage. This is the rodent with soft gray fur, large eyes, and bushy,
squirrel-like tail which possesses all the instincts of a born collector.
Seemingly its primary goal in life is to discover, carry away, and
conceal in special hideouts all sorts of useless, bright-colored, portable
objects. For instance, Theodore Roosevelt once reported finding a pack
rat collection which included a small revolver, a hunting knife, two
books, a fork, a small bag, and a tin cup.

On June 22 Lewis wrote: "there is a kind of larke here that much
resembles the bird called the oldfield lark [meadowlark, *Sturnella
magna magna*] with a yellow breast and a black spot on the croop; tho'
this differs from ours in the form of the tail which is pointed being
formed of feathers of unequal length; the beak is somewhat longer and
more curved and the note differs considerably" (II, 180). Lewis was

[10] Larry Gill has informed me of a still larger cottonwood on the W. J. Beecher
Ranch, Cascade, Montana. This has a circumference four feet from the ground of 21
feet.

here describing the western meadowlark (*Sturnella neglecta neglecta*) , almost 40 years before Audubon rediscovered it while on the Upper Missouri and gave it the technical name it bears today. In his description Audubon included this pertinent comment: "Although the existence of this species was known to the celebrated explorers of the west, Lewis and Clark . . . no one has since taken the least notice of it."[11]

In late June at White Bear Islands Lewis wrote: "The young black-birds which are almost innumerable in these islands just begin to fly" (II, 186). Elliott Coues identified these as Brewer's blackbirds (*Euphagus cyanocephalus*). If he was correct, then Lewis was the discoverer of this bird, one of the most beautiful of the blackbird race.

Near the end of his stay at Great Falls, Lewis reported shooting a passenger pigeon. His discovery of the bird here was not nearly so surprising as the fact that not one of the journalists had mentioned seeing it at any time previously on the Missouri. At that date and for many years afterwards, this beautiful creature existed in greater numbers than any other bird on earth and ranged from the Atlantic to the Rockies. Just four years later John Bradbury, in a brief period of time near the mouth of the Platte, killed 271 before he "desisted."[12] The last passenger pigeon on earth died in the Cincinnati Zoo on September 1, 1914, at 9:32 A.M.

The brief period from June 3 to July 14 had been one of outstanding discovery and accomplishment. Geographers would soon begin filling empty spaces on maps of North America with the Marias, Teton, and Sun Rivers, and the Great Falls of the Missouri. Also in due time botanists would recognize as new to science the narrow-leafed cottonwood and zoologists the sage grouse, white-rumped shrike, McCown's longspur, western meadowlark, kit fox, thirteen-striped ground squirrel, pack rat, and cutthroat trout.

SUMMARY OF DISCOVERIES

Animals New to Science

? GOLDEYE. *Amphiodon alosoides* Raf. (Thwaites, II, 143; Coues, II, 362). Described, 1819.

SAGE GROUSE. *Centrocercus urophasianus urophasianus* (Bonaparte) . [A.O.U. 309] (Thwaites, II, 124; Coues, I, 350n) . 1827.

[11] Audubon, *The Birds of America* (1843) , VII, 339.
[12] *Early Western Travels*, V, 68.

PACIFIC NIGHTHAWK. *Chordeiles minor hesperis* Grinnell. [A.O.U. 420d] (Thwaites, II, 200; Coues, II, 398). 1905.

BREWER'S BLACKBIRD. *Euphagus cyanocephalus* (Wagler). [A.O.U. 510] (Thwaites, II, 186; VI, 190; Coues, III, 875). 1829.

WHITE-RUMPED SHRIKE. *Lanius ludovicianus excubitorides* Swainson. [A.O.U. 622a] (Thwaites, II, 140; Coues, II, 361n). 1831.

PACK RAT; BUSHY-TAILED WOODRAT. *Neotoma cinerea cinerea* (Ord). (Thwaites, II, 205; Coues, II, 400). 1815.

MCCOWN'S LONGSPUR. *Rhynchophanes mccownii* (Lawrence). [A.O.U. 539] (Thwaites, II, 120; Coues, II, 461n). 1851.

CUTTHROAT TROUT. *Salmo clarkii* Richardson. (Thwaites, II, 150; Coues, I, 367n). 1836.

THIRTEEN-STRIPED GROUND SQUIRREL. *Spermophilus tridecemlineatus pallidus* Allen. (Thwaites, II, 216; Coues, II, 391). 1877.

WESTERN GOLDFINCH. *Spinus tristis pallidus* Mearns. [A.O.U. 529a] (Thwaites, II, 130; Criswell, xcv). 1890.

WESTERN MEADOWLARK. *Sturnella neglecta neglecta* Audubon. [A.O.U. 501.1] (Thwaites, II, 180; Coues, II, 388). 1844.

KIT FOX. *Vulpes velox velox* (Say). (Thwaites, II, 213; Coues, II, 404). 1823.

WESTERN MOURNING DOVE. *Zenaidura macroura marginella* (Woodhouse). [A.O.U. 316a] (Thwaites, II, 227; Burroughs, 234). 1852.

Plants New to Science

NARROW-LEAFED COTTONWOOD. *Populus angustifolia* James. (Thwaites, II, 116, 145; Coues, II, 364). 1823.

Lewis and Clark Herbarium

None.

Indian Tribes Encountered

None.

Topographic Features Named and/or Discovered

† North Mountain (Thwaites, II, 119) —— north end of Bear's Paw Mts. (Coues, I, 347).

† Barn Mountain (Thwaites, II, 119) —— West or Belt Butte of Highwoods (Coues, I, 347n).

† Lark Creek (Thwaites, II, 123) —— Black Coulee (Coues, I, 349n).

† Tower Mountain (Thwaites, II, 123) —— Main Peak of Sweet Grass Hills (Coues, I, 349n).

† Tanzey (Tansy) River (Thwaites, II, 125) —— Teton River.

† Great Falls (Thwaites, II, 147–150) —— Great Falls.

† Crooked Falls (Thwaites, II, 153) —— Crooked Falls.

† "Beautiful Cascade" (Thwaites, II, 153) —— Rainbow Falls.

† "Cascade of about 14 feet" (Thwaites, II, 154) Colter Falls.

† "Upper Pitch" (Thwaites, II, 176) —— Black Eagle Falls.

† Medicine River (Thwaites, II, 155) —— Sun River.

† Strawberry Creek (Thwaites, VII, 101).

† Shields' Creek (Thwaites, II, 162) —— Highwood Creek.

† Portage Creek (Thwaites, II, 166) —— Belt Creek.

† Willow Run (Thwaites, II, 184) —— Box Elder Creek (Ordway, 236n).

† "Large Fountain" (Thwaites, II, 170, 176) —— Giant Spring.

† White Bear Islands (Thwaites, II, 171, 176) —— White Bear Islands.

† Flattery Run (Thwaites, II, 171; VI, 8) —— Sand Coulee Creek (Thwaites, II, 171n).

† Fort Mountain Creek (Thwaites, II, 228).

White Bear Islands
to
Lemhi River

CHAPTER ELEVEN

With the two new dugouts completed, providing a flotilla of eight, the Corps (on July 15) resumed its navigation of the Missouri. The men were physically fit and ready. Sergeant Pryor's shoulder, dislocated when hefting an oversize haunch of meat, had been put back in place. A whitlow (inflammation) on the terminal phalanx of one of Bratton's fingers had healed. Whitehouse had recovered from a touch of the sun after Lewis had bled him, employing a penknife in the absence of a lancet. York, described as "verry unwell," had responded favorably to Clark's treatment of a dose of tartar emetic. Lewis disapproved of its use in this case, one of the two or three known instances where the two commanding officers failed to agree. In his practice, he asserted, he never resorted to tartar emetic "except in cases of the intermittent fever" (II, 214).

The river route from Great Falls to Three Forks, some 300 miles, ran almost due south. As a result, when the explorers arrived at that celebrated confluence, they were only slightly farther west than when they started. Just a few miles beyond Canoe Camp, Lewis and Clark came to a stream entering from the south which they called Smith's River in honor of Robert Smith, then Secretary of the Navy. For a portion of this same day, they had a good view of the volcanic mesa-type massif, Square Butte, which rises about 700 feet above the surrounding plain.

Three days later they discovered a stream discharging from the north. Lewis and Clark called it Dearborn's River, thus paying tribute to Henry Dearborn, Secretary of War. If it had been possible for the explorers to ascend this stream, which heads close to that gap in the Rockies now called Lewis and Clark Pass and over which Lewis travelled east the following spring, they would have saved themselves much time and distance. However, as we know, ever since adding Sacagawea to the party, they had been committed to Three Forks where they counted on meeting the Shoshoni and acquiring horses. The success or failure of the Expedition, as they saw it, might hinge on the fulfillment of this plan. Certainly their dugouts could not serve as a means of conveyance for any considerable distance beyond Three Forks.

On July 18 the party arrived at the great, spectacular gorge, now known as Gates of the Mountains, which cuts through a spur of the Big Belt Mountains a few miles north of the present-day city of Helena. "This evening," Lewis wrote, "we entered much the most remarkable clifts that we have yet seen, these clifts rise from the waters edge on either side perpendicularly to the hight of (*about*) 1200 feet. every object here wears a dark and gloomy aspect. the tow[er]ing and projecting rocks in many places seem ready to tumble on us. the river appears to have forced it's way through this immence body of solid rock for the distance of 5¾ Miles and . . . to have woarn a passage just the width of it's channel or 150 yards . . . from the singular appearance of this place I called it the *gates of the rocky mountains*" (II, 248) .

The chief features of the Gates remain substantially unchanged, though the water level has been raised due to the Holter Dam and resultant reservoir. During summer months tourists in increasing numbers take advantage of boat rides provided by a private company, Gates of the Mountains, Inc. On the day my party made the trip, September 10, 1964, it was cloudy and cold, but the cliffs, spotted with pine and fir, rising perpendicularly to great heights on either side, afforded mountain scenery of superb quality.

Lewis and Clark continued their practice of naming streams after members of the party. For instance, on Clark's map we find creeks laid down such as Ordway's, Gass's, Pryor's, Whitehouse's, Potts', and Howard's. Mapmakers not in the same league with Clark have replaced these names with others. Ordway's Creek, for instance, is now Little Prickly Pear Creek and Gass's Creek is Hot Springs. Smith and Dearborn, with portfolios in Jefferson's cabinet, fared better.

Beyond the Gates, the men experienced again the difficult, exhausting labor which accompanied the use of setting poles and cordelles. Solicitous of their welfare, Lewis often pitched in to help and learned, as he said, "to push a tolerable good pole" (II, 266) . Contributing to common miseries was what Lewis called "our trio of pests," namely, gnats, mosquitoes, and prickly pear. When the journalists complained of mosquitoes as "verry troublesome," as they often did, they understated. In many places, as here, these phrenetic insects hummed about them at all hours, needling incessantly. Only on nights when the mercury plunged toward freezing did they cease even momentarily their blood-sucking activities. Without mosquito netting life would have been almost unendurable. One day Lewis went ahead of the main party to look for Indians and that evening, when setting up camp, found to his dismay that he had neglected to bring his netting with him. He experienced a sleepless night, of course, and swore that he would never again be guilty of a similar piece of negligence (II, 235).

"The prickley pear is now in full bloom," wrote Lewis on July 15, "and forms one of the beauties as well as the greatest pests of the plains" (II, 231). Garnishing the river benches like large pincushions, this spiny troublemaker seemed to increase the farther the explorers ascended the Missouri. It was impossible to avoid it entirely. Lewis made camp one night above the river's edge where this cactus grew so profusely that, as he said, he "could scarcely find room to lye" (II, 252).

Below Three Forks the men encountered another pest, this in the form of a grass with barbed seeds (probably needle and thread grass, *Stipa comata*). "These barbed seeds penetrate our mockersons and leather legings and give us great pain untill they are removed," Lewis declared. Even Lewis's dog suffered, constantly biting and scratching himself "as if in a rack of pain" (II, 272).

As though attempting to offset the bitter aspect of travel, nature here provided, in abundance and great perfection, many sweet, ripe currants and serviceberries. At least three varieties of the former grew along this stretch of the river: red, yellow, and black.[1] Clark liked best the yellow ones but Lewis the black. "This currant," he declared, "is really a charming fruit and I am confident would be preferred at our markets to any currant now cultivated in the U. States" (II, 251). Ever alert to plants that might be introduced with success into the East, he preserved seeds of these currants to take back to Jefferson.

Lewis discovered in this same area two additional plants he thought might be useful if cultivated by farmers of the Atlantic sea-

[1] Coues (II, 419) identified the red currant as *Ribes hudsonicum*, the yellow as *R. aureum*, and the black as *R. viscossissimum*. Specimens of the last two are in the Lewis and Clark Herbarium, Philadelphia.

board, a species of onion and a form of wild flax. He regarded the former (identified by Coues as *Allium cernuum*)[2] as a valuable plant because it produced "a large quantity to the squar foot and bears with ease the rigor of this climate, and withall I think it as pleasantly flavored as any species of that root I ever tasted" (II, 259). The wild flax grew in the river bottoms and resembled the common flax culti-vated in the East. "The bark of the stem," Lewis wrote, "is thick [and] strong and appears as if it would make excellent flax. the seed are not yet ripe but I hope to have an opportunity of collecting some of them after they are so" (II, 244). Lewis brought back a dried, preserved specimen of this plant (collected the following year on Sun River) which today forms a part of the Lewis and Clark Herbarium in Phila-delphia. It was new to science, and Frederick Pursh, when formally describing it, honored Lewis by naming it *Linum lewisii*. According to one botanist, the stems of this flax produce, as Lewis thought, excellent fibre "which was used by and traded by the Indians."[3]

On the day after the explorers passed through Gates of the Moun-tains, in what is now Lewis and Clark County, Montana, Lewis made a discovery that would in time further brighten his name. "I saw a black woodpecker (or crow) today," he wrote, "about the size of the lark woodpecker as black as a crow. I endevoured to get a shoot at it but could not. it is a distinct species of woodpecker; it has a long tail and flys a good deal like the jay bird" (II, 252).

Today this bird is known to all as Lewis's woodpecker (*Asyndes-mus lewis*). He described it more fully the following year after he had been able to collect specimens. Lewis's woodpecker is generally de-scribed as a handsome, greenish-black bird with a silvery-gray breast and crimson belly. However, for breast and belly we prefer Lewis's words. These parts, he said, were "a curious mixture of white and blood red which has much the appearance of having been artificially painted or stained of that colour" (V, 70). In some respects it is a very unwoodpecker-like bird. It does not possess the customary undulatory flight of its kind, tends to light crosswise on a limb rather than right-side-up on the trunk, does very little hammering so characteristic of the usual woodpecker, and seldom, if ever, digs its own nest, appropriating instead one made by some other woodpecker. As one ornithologist has said, "the bird seems to forget what he is a good deal of the time."[4]

[2] Coues, II, 432, 435.
[3] Harold St. John, *Flora of Southeastern Washington* (Escondido, Calif., 1963), 268.
[4] Pearson, *Birds of America*, II, 159.

[2]

On turning each bend of the river, the explorers now scrutinized terrain ahead for recent Indian sign. On July 20 Clark saw a huge cloud of smoke rising to the west up Pryor's Creek. He concluded that the Shoshoni had heard their rifle shots and were attempting, by setting prairie fires, to warn surrounding bands of their people that Blackfeet were on the prowl nearby. This proved to be true, as they later ascertained. It was possible, of course, that Shoshoni might be close at hand, watching their every move, so Clark left pieces of cloth, paper, and linen to prove to the Indians, if found, that the guns had been fired by white men.

As the party neared Three Forks, Lewis and Clark sought word from Sacagawea that she recognized some feature of the landscape; it had been just five years since her capture in these environs by the Hidatsas. But it was not until July 22, just three days before the discovery of Three Forks, that she assured her companions that this was the river on which her people lived and that they were close to Three Forks. At about this same time, when Lewis found pine trees stripped of their bark, Sacagawea explained that this operation had been performed by Indians to obtain the soft inner parts for food (II, 249). The tree, according to one authority, was probably ponderosa pine (*Pinus ponderosa*), as it was "the bark of this species which was most generally eaten in time of famine by Indians of the West."[5]

In the meantime Clark, with Frazer, Charbonneau, and the two Field brothers, had gone ahead of the main party in the hope of encountering Shoshoni before, alarmed by gunfire, they withdrew completely from the neighborhood. They soon found a stray horse and, although unable to get close to it, were encouraged by the incident. Then, on July 25 they were partners in a much more significant event. "A fine morning," Clark wrote, "we proceeded on a fiew miles to the three forks of the Missouri those three forks are nearly of a Size, the North fork appears to have the most water and must be Considered as the one best calculated for us to assend Middle fork is quit[e] as large about 90 yards wide. the South fork is about 70 yds, wide & falls in about 400 yards below the middle fork" (II, 271).

Clark had arrived at what Lewis called "an essential point in the

---

[5] Sargent, "The First Account of Some Western Trees," 28.

geography of this western part of the Continent" (II, 277–278). He had been the first white man to set eyes on this celebrated confluence and the first to pen words about it. It was an occasion calling for jubilation; when Lewis arrived two days later, he revealed his elation in a rush of words.

Clark seemed obsessed with the urgency of his mission, namely to find Shoshoni. After scribbling a note to Lewis about his discovery and immediate plans, he and his men struck out up the north fork. They were heartened when they found fresh horse tracks and evidence of a recent prairie fire. However, after scanning the country in all directions from a mountain top, they were unable to see Indians or signs of any. That evening Clark was sick, "with high fever & akeing" in all his bones (II, 280).

The next morning, though still running a temperature, Clark determined to reconnoitre up the middle fork. Not until he had walked eight miles, with no fresh sign of Indian anywhere, did he turn back and make his way to the mouth of the river where he found Lewis and others of the main party recently arrived. By then he was a very sick man indeed. He told Lewis that he had suffered all night with a high fever, chills, "constant aking pains in all his mustles . . . and had not had a passage for several days" (II, 279). After Lewis had diagnosed his friend's condition as best he could, he prevailed on him to bathe his feet and legs in warm water and to take five Rush's pills which, he said, he had "always found sovereign in such cases" (II, 279). The next morning, Clark felt better. Two days later, being still languid and retaining a soreness in his limbs, he acceded to Lewis's plea to "take the bark" and to "eate tolerably freely of our good venison" (II, 284). From then on he improved rapidly.

Rush's pills, a product of the genius of Dr. Benjamin Rush, were well-known in those days and alluded to, often with some feeling, as Rush's "thunderbolts." Each consisted of 10 grains of calomel and 10 of jalap and conquently was a powerful physic. Lewis and Clark had started the journey west with 50 dozen of these pills, and in treating gastro-intestinal disturbances, it seems to have been a coin-tossing proposition as to whether they used them or Glauber's salt. Jalap was a powdered drug prepared from the purgative, tuberous root of a Mexican plant (*Exogonium surga*) of the morning-glory family.

Lewis and Clark agreed that it would be a mistake to regard any of the three converging streams here as the Missouri. In their judgment, this was where the Missouri began. They therefore dug deep into their grab bag of names and pulled out three brand new ones: Jefferson, for the north fork in "honor of that illustrious personage . . . *the author of our enterprise*"; Madison for the middle fork in tribute to James Madison, Jefferson's Secretary of State; and Gallatin for the most southerly fork in honor to Albert Gallatin, then Secretary of the Treasury (II, 281).

Having clothed themselves in new deerskins—"all [the men] are leather dressers and taylors," Lewis said (II, 284)—and established their position meridionally, the explorers on the morning of July 30 reloaded their dugouts and began the ascent of the Jefferson River. Except for tumors and bruises, they were in good shape; even Clark had regained his customary strength and ebullience.

About four miles upriver, they came to the precise place where Sacagawea had been taken prisoner by the Hidatsas. She retold the story of her capture. Entirely too much has been written about her "guiding" the explorers up the Missouri and across the Rockies. One writer in particular has insisted that she "piloted them with all the sureness of a homing pigeon,"[6] and another that at Three Forks she chose "the right fork [the Jefferson] leading to the encampment of her people."[7] At the mouth of the Marias, she did not point out the south fork as the one to take, and at Three Forks she did not designate the Jefferson; Lewis and Clark's decision to follow that stream was based on information obtained from Indians at Fort Mandan (VI, 55).

On August 1 Lewis chose Gass, Drouillard, and Charbonneau and forged ahead in yet another attempt to locate Shoshoni. Beaver activity had flooded much of the bottom land, requiring the men to seek higher ground in order to make any real progress. Though Lewis had been living with beaver as a relatively common animal ever since passing the Platte, he found them here in greater abundance than at any place previously. Their dams, some of them five feet high, blocked every Jefferson tributary, and the imprisoned waters flooded every valley. Lewis wrote that the dams were formed of "willow brush mud and gravel and are so closely interwoven that they resist the water perfectly . . . the brush appear to be laid in no regular order yet acquire a strength by the irregularity with which they are placed by the beaver that it would puzzle the engenuity of man to give them" (II, 300).

As is evident, Lewis, though engrossed in looking for Shoshoni,

[6] Howard R. Driggs, *The Old West Speaks* (Englewood Cliffs, N.J., 1956), 27.
[7] Virginia Cole Trenholm and Maurine Carley, *The Shoshonis, Sentinels of the Rockies* (Norman, Okla., 1964), 43.

was not blind to the clever creative work of these remarkable flat-tailed engineers. Neither was he oblivious to new plants and animals. For example, he discovered a small species of birch, "the leaf of which is oval, finely indented, small and of a deep green colour," and the stem seldom rising higher than 10 or 12 feet (II, 303).[8] This was the first account of the western paper birch (*Betula occidentalis*), undescribed technically until 1839.

He discovered, too, Richardson's blue grouse (*Dendragapus obscurus richardsonii*), then entirely new to science. It was, Lewis said, a third larger than "our phesant or pattridge [ruffed grouse, *Bonasa umbellus*] as they are called in the Eastern States" and "booted nearly to the toes and the male has not the tufts of long black feathers on the sides of the neck which are so conspicuous in those of the Atlantic" (II, 295). Later the same day Lewis wrote: "I also saw near the top of the mountain among some scattering pine a blue bird about the size of the common robin. it's action and form is somewhat that of the jay bird and never rests long in any one position but constantly flying or hoping from sprey to sprey . . . their note is loud and frequently repeated both flying and when at rest and is char-âh', chár-âh, char-âh', as nearly as letters can express it" (II, 295). Elliott Coues had no hesitation in saying that this bird was the piñon or Maximilian's jay (*Gymnorhinus cyanocephalus*), and that Lewis's words just quoted constituted the first description of this grayish-blue, sociable bird of the western mountains.[9]

On the fourth day after leaving the main party Lewis arrived at the confluence of three streams (the Three Forks of the Jefferson) where, once again, he faced the problem of which branch to follow. Choosing the middle one, he cut a green willow pole, stuck it in the bank, and attached a note to Clark apprising him of his decision. Two days later Clark and his party arrived at this junction. In the meantime a hungry beaver had appropriated the willow pole with its affixed note. Believing the right-hand branch, because of its size, to be the main stream, Clark struggled up it nine back-breaking miles before Drouillard opportunely showed up and informed him of his mistake.

With much difficulty Clark finally got back to the mouth of this fork (today the location of Twin Bridges, Montana). Here Lewis awaited him, though neither had news to cheer the other. Before

[8] See also Sargent, "The First Account of Some Western Trees," 28.

[9] Coues, II, 454n. The piñon jay was technically described by Maximilian in 1841. For a statement by Arthur Cleveland Bent see Burroughs, *The Natural History of the Lewis and Clark Expedition*, 250.

continuing their march, they gave names to the three streams here. The middle one "was that which ought to bear the name we had given the lower portion or River Jefferson" (II, 316). The north branch they called Wisdom and the smaller southern one, Philanthropy, "in commemoration of two of those cardinal virtues which have eminently marked that deservedly selibrated character [Jefferson] through life" (II, 317). Earlier they had named a small tributary downstream, Philosophy, for a third cardinal virtue. Once again presumptuous cartographers have had their ill-considered innings. Not one of these names appears on maps of today. The Jefferson (above Twin Bridges) is the Beaverhead, the Wisdom is the Big Hole, the Philanthropy is the Ruby, and the Philosophy is Willow Creek.

Lewis now determined to take Drouillard, Shields, and McNeal and push ahead to the source of the river. If necessary, he would cross the Divide and descend Columbian waters until he found the Shoshoni. "In short," he declared, "it is my resolution to find them or some others, who have horses if it should cause me a trip of one month, for without horses we shall be obliged to leave a great part of our stores, of which, it appears to me that we have a stock already sufficiently small for the length of the voyage before us" (II, 321–322). But even if he did not find horses, as this statement makes clear, he had no intention of discontinuing the journey. Aware of the risks he faced, he took time before setting out to "accomplish some wrightings" (II, 322). He brought his journal up to date and prepared instructions for Clark to follow in case some accident befell him.

[3]

Lewis and his men followed a well-marked Indian trail which led them at times over parched, undulating hills and at others through narrow, grass-covered bottoms. On August 10 they arrived at the junction of two streams, a south branch (Red Rock Creek of today) and a west branch (Horse Prairie Creek). Lewis chose the latter, since it bore in the direction he wished to pursue. After leaving a note for Clark (on a *dry* willow pole), he travelled up Horse Prairie Creek some five miles to a lovely valley he called Shoshoni Cove where he and his companions spent the night.[10]

---

[10] The junction of the two creeks, sometimes called Twin Forks, is near Armistead, Montana. The junction, the town, and Shoshoni Cove have all been recently covered by water due to the completion of Clark Canyon Dam.

At Shoshoni Cove Lewis was about 30 or 35 miles from Lemhi Pass, where the Indian trail he followed crossed the Continental Divide and the present Montana-Idaho line. Before continuing up Horse Prairie Creek, Lewis took time to reflect: "the mountains do not appear very high in any direction tho' the tops of some of them are partially covered with snow. this convinces me that we have ascended to a great hight since we have entered the rocky Mountains, yet the ascent has been so gradual along the vallies that it was scarcely perceptable by land . . . if the Columbia furnishes us such another example, a communication across the continent by water will be practicable and safe. but this I can scarcely hope from a knowledge of its having in its comparitively short course to the ocean the same number of feet to descend which the Missouri and Mississippi have from this point to the Gulph of Mexico" (II, 326–327) .

As Lewis said, the ascent of the Missouri had been gradual, and it would continue so to the Pass. The traveller today, following up Horse Prairie Creek in the explorer's footsteps, has difficulty in believing that he has actually reached the Continental Divide at an elevation of 8,000 feet. He was right, too, in suspecting that the descent of the Columbia would be far less gradual.

After a short march the next morning, Lewis saw an Indian mounted on a horse riding toward him. He managed to approach within 100 paces, making signs of friendship as he advanced. When Drouillard and Shields unwisely moved even closer, the Indian turned his horse, applied the whip, and quickly disappeared into the willow brush bordering the creek. Incredibly, this was the first Indian the explorers had seen since leaving the Mandan-Hidatsa community in mid-April four months earlier. Lewis attempted to follow the Indian, but rain soon obliterated all footprints. He camped that night convinced that the natives had been warned by now of his proximity and had retreated farther into the mountains.

By this time the stream they followed had dwindled to a mere mountain brook. Early the next morning they arrived at a place where McNeal "stood with a foot on each side of this rivulet and thanked his god that he had lived to bestride the mighty & heretofore deemed endless Missouri" (II, 335) . And just two miles farther along, the road led Lewis "to the most distant fountain of the waters of the mighty Missouri." He had thus accomplished, he said, "one of those great objects on which my mind had been unalterably fixed for many years, judge then of the pleasure I felt in all[a]ying my thirst with this pure and ice-cold water which issues from the base of a low mountain" (II, 335).

The "most distant fountain" is a spring, beautifully situated in a clump of conifers close by the Continental Divide. Lewis and Clark enthusiasts today make long journeys to the site, as to a shrine. I visited it for the first time in August, 1957, and was pleased to find that the spring and its surroundings remain much the same as when Lewis came upon it, that ice-cold water still issues from the earth, and that I had an uninterrupted view of the mountains, spottily clothed with evergreens, extending almost endlessly toward an eastern horizon. The spring, of course, is not the most distant fountain of the Missouri. To reach the ultimate source, the traveller must climb Red Rock Creek to Upper Red Rock Lake in southern Montana just west of Yellowstone National Park.

Lewis and his men stopped only briefly at the spring. They then hastened to the summit of the Pass just a short distance away. From that vantage point, they had an unhampered view of the beautiful wilderness country of the Upper Columbia watershed, where snow-topped ranges of the Bitterroots succeeded each other until lost in the far distant western haze. Lewis gazed momentarily at this scene and then plunged down the western slope, far steeper than the eastern, soon arriving at "a handsome bold runing creek of cold Clear water," a tributary of the Lemhi River. "Here," said Lewis, "I first tasted the water of the great Columbia river" (II, 335).

Hurrying on, Lewis and his three companions continued to follow the Indian road until it brought them to the Lemhi River. Toward evening they arrived at a spring where they found enough dry willow branches for a fire. Here they camped for the night, quieting appetites with the last of their pork. The next morning they set out at daybreak, still following the same Indian trail which here paralleled the Lemhi. This took them after a few miles to a lovely valley where Lewis reported "some bushes of the white maple" (II, 337). According to Sargent, this was *"Acer glabrum,* the only Maple of the Rocky Mountains with the exception, of course, of the Box Elder [*Acer negundo*] which was well known to our travellers."[11]

Just beyond this valley, the men saw about a mile ahead two Indian women, a man, and some dogs who, as they approached, disappeared behind a hill. Convinced of the futility of trying to follow them,

[11] Sargent, "The First Account of Some Western Trees," 29. *Acer glabrum* was formally described by John Torrey, but not until 1828.

Lewis determined instead to backtrack them, hoping in that way to locate their village. The road was dusty and appeared to have been travelled recently by both men and horses. They had followed this route no more than a mile when they suddenly came upon three Indian women, one of whom immediately bolted, leaving behind an old woman and a girl of about twelve. Lewis soon quieted their fears, bestowing gifts and painting their faces with vermilion, and then with the help of Drouillard's sign language urged them to conduct him to their camp.

The women understood and unhesitatingly led the way. After walking no more than two miles, they met a party of about 60 Shoshoni warriors, each mounted on an excellent horse. Quickly determining on a course of action, Lewis left his gun with the other men and carrying only a flag, strode boldly forward to meet the Indians, following on the heels of the squaws who poured out their story of meeting the white men to the Shoshoni chief. The warriors then immediately dismounted and rushed forward to receive Lewis and his men with a display of cordiality such as they had never previously experienced.

After a pipe had gone the rounds, the chief, whose name was Cameahwait, conducted Lewis to his village a few miles away. By then it was late evening, and Lewis and his men had not taken food for 24 hours. Informed of this, the Indians provided them with dried cakes of choke cherries and serviceberries, antelope, and a piece of salmon. "This was the first salmon I had seen," Lewis remarked, "and perfectly convinced me that we were on the waters of the Pacific Ocean" (II, 343).

Lewis seems to have had little difficulty in communicating with Cameahwait because of the rare talents of Drouillard, "who understood perfectly the language of jesticulation or signs which seems to be universally understood by all the nations we have yet seen" (II, 346). For instance, in a conversation that evening with Drouillard interpreting, Lewis learned that the Lemhi soon flowed into a larger stream (the Salmon), that timber was a scarce commodity on both rivers, and that it was a physical impossibility to travel down these streams to the Columbia either by land or water. If Cameahwait told the truth, this was intelligence of the worst sort. That timber was scarce, there could be no doubt. Little grew along the banks of the Lemhi but stunted cottonwood, willow, and choke cherry, nothing whatever approaching boat size.

Events of the next few days may be summarized briefly. On August 15 Cameahwait and a large party of his tribesmen mounted horses and accompanied Lewis to Shoshoni Cove. Two days later Clark and the remainder of the Corps showed up. There then ensued the dramatic meeting between Cameahwait and Sacagawea and the revelation that they were brother and sister. The next day Clark and 11 men left for the Lemhi, taking with them as much baggage as they could carry. His mission was to determine whether it would be possible for the party to descend that stream. A number of the Shoshoni, including Cameah- wait, accompanied Clark to obtain additional horses necessary for transporting everything over Lemhi Pass.

By the time Cameahwait returned (on August 22) , Lewis and the men with him had made 20 pack saddles, aired and repacked goods, and constructed another cache. Into it went parcels of tobacco, expend- able medicines, and "specemines of plants, minerals, seeds &c, which, I have collected between this place and the falls of the Missouri" (II, 376) . Just before abandoning this camp to strike out for the Lemhi, Lewis, as a last act, ordered the men to sink their dugouts in a nearby pond. As the Expedition crossed the Pass, the question uppermost in Lewis's mind was whether they would be able to travel down the Lemhi. He was eager to rejoin Clark to find the answer.

SUMMARY OF DISCOVERIES

Animals New to Science

LEWIS'S WOODPECKER. *Asyndesmus lewis* (Gray) . [A.O.U. 408] (Thwaites, II, 252; V, 70; Coues, II, 428) . Described, 1811.

RICHARDSON'S BLUE GROUSE. *Dendragapus obscurus richardsonii* (Douglas) . [A.O.U. 297b] (Thwaites, II, 256; Coues, II, 430) . 1829.

PIÑON JAY. *Gymnorhinus cyanocephalus* Wied. [A.O.U. 492] (Thwaites, II, 295; Coues, II, 454) . 1841.

WESTERN HOG-NOSE SNAKE. *Heterodon nasicus nasicus* (Baird & Girard) . (Thwaites, II, 264; Coues, II, 434) . 1852.

YELLOW-BELLIED MARMOT. *Marmota flaviventris nosophora* Howell. (Thwaites, II, 377) . 1914.

Plants New to Science

ROCKY MOUNTAIN MAPLE. *Acer glabrum* Torrey. (Thwaites, II, 337; Coues, II, 487) . 1828.

WESTERN PAPER BIRCH. *Betula occidentalis* Hooker. (Thwaites, II, 303; Coues, II, 457) . 1839.

LEWIS'S WILD FLAX. *Linum lewisii* Pursh. (Thwaites, II, 244) . 1814.

GOLDEN CURRANT. *Ribes aureum* Pursh. (Thwaites, II, 238; Coues, II, 419) . 1814.

STICKY CURRANT. *Ribes viscossissimum* Pursh. (Thwaites, II, 238; Coues, II, 419) . 1814.

NEEDLE AND THREAD GRASS. *Stipa comata* Trin. & Rupert. (Thwaites, II, 272) . 1842.

Lewis and Clark Herbarium

GOLDEN CURRANT. *Ribes aureum* Pursh. Collected July 29, 1805.

? NEEDLE AND THREAD GRASS. *Stipa comata* Trin. & Rupert. Undated specimen.

Indian Tribes Encountered

Shoshonean Linguistic Family: † Shoshoni. From the Continental Divide to Columbia River tidewater the tribes encountered by Lewis and Clark were also *discovered* by them, and we so indicate with a dagger, as with physical features.

Topographic Features Named and/or Discovered

† Smith's River (Thwaites, II, 230 —— Smith River.

† Fort Mountain (Thwaites, II, 147, 231) —— Square Butte.

† The Tower (Thwaites, II, 235) .

† Pine Island (Thwaites, II, 240) .

† Dearborn's River (Thwaites, II, 243–244) —— Dearborn's River.

† Ordway's Creek (Thwaites, II, 244) —— Little Prickly Pear Creek (Coues, II, 422n) .

† Gates of the Rocky Mountains (Thwaites, II, 248) —— Gates of the Mountains.

† Potts Creek (Thwaites, II, 251) —— Big Prickly Pear Creek (Coues, II, 427n) .

† Pryor's Creek (Thwaites, II, 256) —— Mitchell's Creek (Coues, II, 429n) .

† Onion Island (Thwaites, II, 259) .

† White Earth Creek (Thwaites, II, 260) —— Beaver Creek.

† The Ten Islands (Thwaites, II, 263) .

† Whitehouse Creek (Thwaites, II, 263) —— Duck Creek (Coues, II, 434n) .

† Gass's Creek (Thwaites, II, 269) —— Hot or Warm Springs Creek (Coues, II, 438n) .

† Howard's Creek (Thwaites, II, 272) —— Green or Sixteen-Mile Creek (Thwaites, II, 272n) .

† Jefferson's River (Thwaites, II, 281) —— Jefferson River.

† Madison's River (Thwaites, II, 281) —— Madison River.

† Gallatin's River (Thwaites, II, 281) —— Gallatin River.

† Philosophy River (Thwaites, II, 290) —— Willow Creek.

† Field's Creek (Thwaites, II, 294) —— North Boulder Creek.

† Birth Creek (Thwaites, II, 301) .

† Panther Creek (Thwaites, II, 304) —— Pipestone Creek.
† Wisdom River (Thwaites, II, 316) —— Big Hole River.
† Philanthropy River (Thwaites, II, 317) —— Ruby River.
† Rattlesnake Cliffs (Thwaites, II, 325) —— Beaverhead.
† Shoshoni Cove (Thwaites, II, 327) .
† 1000 Mile Island (Gass, 142) .
† "Most distant fountain" (Thwaites, II, 335) .
† McNeal's Creek (Thwaites, II, 344) .
† Willard Creek (Thwaites, II, 352) .

Also discovered, but not named, were such other important physical features as Red Rock Creek, Horse Prairie Creek, Lemhi Pass, and Lemhi River.

Lemhi
to
Traveller's Rest

CHAPTER TWELVE

Once over the Pass and onto the floor of the Lemhi River valley, Clark stopped only long enough to smoke a pipe with the natives who welcomed him to their village. With an old Shoshoni guide (the men called him Toby), he and his companions saddled up and hurried on downstream. Due to the lateness of the season, it was imperative that he determine promptly whether Cameahwait had spoken the truth about the impossibility of descending this stream.

Clark soon arrived where the Lemhi entered a larger stream, the present-day Salmon River. In his journal that evening he wrote: "I shall in justice to Capt. Lewis who was the first white man ever on this fork of the Columbia Call this Louis's [Lewis's] River" (III, 10). With these few words, Clark laid the firm base for the claim that the Snake River, into which the Salmon flows, should today be called Lewis's River.

About 10 miles down the Salmon, Clark passed a small feeder coming in from the north. This was Boyle Creek,[1] which would be important to the Expedition in the near future. From that point on Clark, in characteristic thoroughgoing manner, continued his descent and examination of the Salmon for another 40 miles. By then he had seen enough to convince him that the Shoshoni had not overstated the case. It would be an act of folly for the party to attempt to reach the Pacific in this direction, either by land or by water. The Salmon River, as much as he had seen of it, was a series of mad, seething,

[1] Tower Creek of Coues (II, 533).

disorderly rapids, impossible to run in boats without grave risk of disaster. The bordering mountains, tall and precipitous, pressed so close on either side as to prohibit portage without exhausting labor and extended delay. Travel by land with horses seemed equally impractical, since it would necessitate climbing a succession of mountainous spurs through fields of shattered rock. Additionally, if his experience of the last few days could be regarded as typical, it seemed most unlikely that the party would be able to obtain food in sufficient amount to satisfy normal body requirements. He agreed with his men who, near the end of his 10-day reconnaissance, expressed fear "of Starveing in a Country [such as this] where no game of any kind except a fiew fish can be found" (III, 45). Lewis and Clark had struck the Rockies, as Coues later indicated, "at perhaps the very worst point that could have been found for their journey beyond the Divide."[2]

Having reached a decision, Clark sent a message posthaste by John Colter to Lewis who, by the time it reached him, had recrossed the Pass and encamped again on the Lemhi with the Shoshoni. In this communiqué Clark described two routes, either of which might be pursued to reach the main body of the Columbia. One, which he condemned outright, was an attempted descent of the Salmon. The other, outlined to him by Toby, would require a swing across mountains to the north by pack horses to another important branch of the Columbia. Clark strongly recommended the latter route and to that end urged Lewis to buy as many horses as possible from the Shoshoni. Extra ones, he stressed, would afford just that much additional life insurance in case they could not live off the country.

Lewis and Clark's rejection of the Salmon River route must be recognized as a decision of pivotal importance. If unmindful of caution and scorning Shoshoni admonitions, they had attempted to follow that stream, their efforts would probably have ended in disaster. The days Clark had devoted to his difficult survey of the Salmon had not been fruitless.

Clark's reconnaissance paid off in other ways. For instance, just below the mouth of the Lemhi, he reported seeing "Some fiew Pigions" (III, 44). Thus it is on record that passenger pigeons were to be found in Idaho, west of the Continental Divide in the year 1805 and that Clark was the first to report their presence there. His observation may be accepted as valid because he would not have confused that bird with any other here of somewhat similar appearance such as the mourning

[2] Coues, II, 473n.

dove (*Zenaidura macroura*), and because the area is outside the range of the band-tailed pigeon (*Columba fasciata*).[3]

Also, on August 22 near the present town of Tendoy, Idaho, Clark wrote: "I saw today a Bird of the woodpecker kind which fed on Pine burs   its Bill and tale white the wings black every other part of a light brown, and about the size of a robin" (III, 17). This was the original description, though summary and not altogether accurate, of that remarkable bird currently called Clark's nutcracker (*Nucifraga columbiana*). Today, the Lewis and Clark *aficionado* following the trail of those explorers will count himself fortunate if he sees two birds in particular, Clark's nutcracker and Lewis's woodpecker.

[2]

The Shoshoni whom Lewis and Clark here encountered on the Lemhi River belonged to the Shoshonean Linguistic Family. A large group, its members ranged from eastern Oregon, Idaho, and western Montana south to Texas, New Mexico, Arizona, and California. It included in addition to the Shoshoni such other well-known tribes as the Comanche, Bannock, Ute, Piute, and Hopi. Because of the vast terrain occupied and varied climatic and topographic features, tribal habits differed markedly. The plains Comanche, for instance, subsisted largely on buffalo, while those tribes inhabiting the Interior Basin, where game was scarce, eked out a precarious existence on small animals, roots, and seeds. The latter consequently were sometimes called Digger Indians.

The Shoshoni of Lewis and Clark lived farther north than any of the other tribes of this family and at an earlier date ranged far to the east, at least as far as the valley of the Yellowstone, where they hunted buffalo in comparative safety and freedom. Later, after the Blackfeet and other tribes had obtained guns from sources denied the Shoshoni, they had been forced to flee from the buffalo country and seek sanctuary in the plateau region to the west. Here, comparatively safe from their enemies, they spent the greater part of the year. Periodically, however, driven by hunger and desperation, they made hurried, furtive dashes onto the plains to obtain buffalo. They were thus Plateau

[3] A. W. Schorger, *The Passenger Pigeon* (Madison, Wis., 1955), 256–258. Schorger lists only one other record for Idaho. He does allude to John Townsend's report of passenger pigeons in "Oregon Territory," but the Territory at that time (1836) had vague boundaries. See Townsend's *Narrative of a Journey Across the Rocky Mountains to the Columbia River* (Philadelphia, 1839), 335.

Indians with a Plains veneer. Different theories have been expressed as to how they became saddled with the name Snake Indians. Clark supplied one: they were "remarkable for taming snakes of which they have many in their country."[4] None of the Shoshoni had apparently seen white men before Lewis and Clark entered their mountainous dominion.

While with the Shoshoni, Lewis wrote the first detailed ethnological study of consequence about any of the tribes inhabiting what was then loosely called Louisiana. It is the sort of thing we wish he had done for the Mandans with whom he lived for a much longer period. His remarks about the latter, as we know, had been limited almost entirely to statistical trade data. Now, however, in describing the Shoshoni, though residing with them just 17 days, he greatly expanded his scope of treatment by supplying scientific information in addition to purely pragmatic.[5] Of prime interest to us in this study is the material in his account dealing with ethnobotany and ethnozoology.

The picture drawn by Lewis and Clark of the Shoshoni reveals a nation thwarted and degraded by near starvation. The food they supplied to the explorers emphasized that point. When Lewis first encountered them, it will be recalled, he was provided with cakes made of choke cherries (*Prunus* sp.) and serviceberries (*Amelanchier alnifolia*). While with Clark on the Salmon River reconnaissance, Sergeant Gass wrote: "The people of these three lodges have gathered a quantity of sun-flower seed [*Helianthus* sp.] and also of the lambs-quarter [*Chenopodium* sp.], which they pound and mix with service berries, and make of the composition a kind of bread which appears capable of sustaining life for some time. On this bread and the fish they take out of the river, these people, who appear to be the most wretched of the human species, chiefly subsist."[6]

One day Lewis wrote that he had observed Indian women "collecting the root of a species of fennel which grows in the moist ground and feeding their poor starved children" (III, 41).[7] At another time he described a root relished by the Shoshoni which was hard, brittle, and about the size of a small quill. When boiled, it was bitter and "naucious" to his palate (III, 13).[8]

[4] Jackson, *Letters,* 544.

[5] According to Coues (II, 479), Lewis's description of the Shoshoni "will be forever the best."

[6] Gass, 149.

[7] This "fennel" may have been Gairdner's yampah, *Perideridia gairdneri* = *Carum gairdneri.*

[8] Coues (II, 543) identified this as bitterroot, *Lewisia rediviva.*

The Shoshoni used plant material in other ways. According to Gass, they made "willow baskets so close and to such perfection as to hold water."[9] They used willow, too, for constructing crude lodges (II, 341) and well-seasoned, soft, spongy willow or cottonwood, with a blunt arrow, in fire-making (III, 21).

Lewis mentioned Shoshoni bows of cedar and pine, and plaited cords made from two different kinds of grasses, sweet grass and silk grass.[10] The only other plant referred to by the journalists here was tobacco, and it was the same as that used by the Mandans, Hidatsas, and Arikaras. The Shoshoni did not grow it, but obtained it "from the Rocky mountain Indians and some of the bands of their own nation who lived further south" (II, 342).

Animals entered more fully into the lives of these Indians than plants; Lewis's ethnozoological notes designate at least twenty different species. Of these, the two of greatest value by far were salmon and buffalo. The season for the former lasted from mid-May to early September, in which time it provided the Shoshoni with the major part of their subsistence. To obtain this fish, they employed gigs, hooks, and weirs. Lewis described a particular weir on the Lemhi as follows:

[It] extended across four channels of the river which was here divided by three small islands. three of these channels were narrow, and were stoped by means of trees fallen across, supported by which stakes of willow were driven down sufficiently near each other to prevent the salmon from passing. about the center of each a cilindric basket of eighteen or 20 feet in length terminating in a conic shape at it's lower extremity, formed of willows, was opposed to a small apperture in the wear [weir] with it's mouth up stream to receive the fish. the main channel of the water was conducted to this basket, which was so narrow at it's lower extremity that the fish when once in could not turn itself about, and were taken out by untying the small ends of the longitudinal willows, which form the hull of the basket. the wear in the main channel was somewhat differently contrived. there were two distinct wears formed of poles and willow sticks, quite across the river, at no great distance from each other. each of these, were furnished with two baskets; the one wear to take them ascending and the other in descending. in constructing these wears, poles were first tyed together in parcels of three near the smaller extremity; these were set on end and spread in a triangular form at the base, in such manner, that two of the three poles ranged in the direction

---

[9] Gass, 153–154.

[10] Sweet grass was probably *Hierochloe odorata,* which grew abundantly on the Lemhi according to Lewis (III, 4–5). Silk grass is something of a mystery, though one possibility is Indian hemp, *Apocynum cannabinum.*

of the intended work, and the third down the stream. two ranges of horizontal poles were next lashed with willow bark and wythes to the ranging poles, and on these willow sticks were placed perpendicularly, reaching from the bottom of the river to about 3 or four feet above it's surface; and placed so near each other, as not to permit the passage of the fish, and even so thick in parts, as with the help of gravel and stone to give a direction to the water which they wished. the baskets were the same in form of the others (III, 6–7).

The buffalo, when obtainable, was the primary source of food. It provided the Shoshoni with robes, moccasins, and other garments. From buffalo horn they fashioned spoons, and from buffalo hair they made halters for their horses and mules. These halters, according to Lewis, consisted of six or seven strands of hair, each "about the size of a man's finger and remarkably strong" (III, 30). For sewing pieces of leather together, they used sinews taken from the back and loins of the buffalo.

A most important article to the Shoshoni warrior was his shield, made of buffalo hide. Ordinarily it was about two and one-half feet in diameter and frequently ornamented with various painted figures and, around the edges, with feathers. Manufacture of the shield, according to Lewis, required particular attention. He described the procedure as follows:

a hole is sunk in the ground about the same in diameter with the intended shield and about 18 inches deep. a parcel of stones are now made red hot and thrown into the hole water is next thrown in and the hot stones cause it to emit a very strong hot steem, over this they spread the green skin which must not have been suffered to dry after taken off the beast. the flesh side is laid next to the groround and as many of the workmen as can reach it take hold on it's edges and extend it in every direction. as the skin becomes heated, the hair seperates and is taken of[f] with the fingers, and the skin continues to contract untill the who[l]e is drawn within the compas designed for the shield, it is then taken off and laid on a parchment hide where they pound it with their heels when barefoot. this operation of pounding continues for several days or as long as the feast lasts when it is delivered to the propryeter and declared by the jugglers and old men to be a sufficient defence against the arrows of their enemies or even bullets . . . many of them believe implisitly that a ball cannot penitrate their shields (III, 20).

For clothing the Shoshoni relied on many other fur-bearing animals besides the buffalo. Among those listed by Lewis were antelope, bighorn, deer, elk, otter, fox, marmot, beaver, mountain goat, weasel, and wolf. From the hides of these animals they made their robes, shirts, leggings, shifts, and moccasins. They also made another piece of apparel, the tippet. To Lewis, this was the most elegant Indian garment he had ever seen. It consisted of a collar about four inches wide made of a strip of dressed otter skin and 100 to 250 little rolls of "ermine" skin, each about the size of a large quill, attached to the collar and hanging down almost to the waist. When completed, it resembled a short cloak. The source of the "ermine" was the long-tailed weasel, *Mustela frenata longicauda,* whose hair turns white in winter. About this animal, Lewis said: "they are no doubt extreemly plenty, and readily taken, from the number of these tippets which I have seen among these people and the great number of skins employed in the construction of each tippet. scarcely any of them have employed less than one hundred of these skins in their formation" (II, 376–379). Cameahwait gave one composed of 140 skins to Lewis who brought it to Philadelphia on his return,[11] where the artist, Charles de St. Mémin, sketched him attired in it. We will have more to say about this tippet in a concluding chapter.

Animals contributed significantly to ornamentation among the Shoshoni. They used porcupine quills extensively, as did the Sioux and many other tribes. The quills were dyed various colors, Lewis observing red, yellow, blue, and black (II, 373). Tusks of elk and grizzly bear were strung on cords and used as ornaments for the neck, as were fish vertebrae (III, 6). Shoshoni men sometimes wore bands of fox or otter skin around the forehead, and, said Lewis, "some of the dressey young men orniment the tops of their mockersons with the skins of polecats [striped skunk, *Mephitis mephitis*] and trale the tail of that animal on the ground at their heels as they walk" (III, 4). These Indians, too, eagerly sought "the tail of the beautiful eagle or calumet bird [golden eagle, *Aquila chrysaëtos*] with which they ornament their own hair and the tails and mains of their horses" (III, 6). In describing the tippet, Lewis said that the otterskin collar was ornamented with "shells of the perl oister" (II, 378). Elliott Coues may have been correct in assuming that these shells were "bits of abalone-shell [*Haliotis* sp.]."[12]

The Shoshoni made bows not only of cedar and pine, but also of horn from elk and bighorn. Those of elk horn were "made of a single peice and covered on the back with glue and sinues like those made of wood" (III, 20). Elk horn was also used in shaping flint arrow heads and in splitting wood. For quivers, these Indians preferred otterskin.

[11] Charles C. Sellers, *Charles Willson Peale,* 2 vols. (Philadelphia, 1947), II, 240–241.
[12] Coues, II, 565n.

Employing many folds of dressed antelope hide united with glue and sand, they made a kind of armor to cover their bodies and those of their horses. This was adequate, Lewis said, "against the effects of the arrow" (III, 20).

Lewis reported:

I have seen a few skins among these people which have almost every appearance of the common sheep. they inform me that they finde this animal on the high mountains to the West and S.W. of them. it is about the size of the common sheep, the wool is reather shorter and more intermixed with long hairs particularly on the upper part of the neck. these skins have been so much woarn that I could not form a just Idea of the animal or it's colour. the Indians however inform me that it is white and that it's horns are lunated comprest twisted and bent backward as those of the common sheep. . . . I am now perfectly convinced that the sheep as well as the Bighorn exist in these mountains. (*Capt. C. saw one at a distance to day*) " (III, 30).

This is the first reference in the journals to the Rocky Mountain goat, *Oreamnos americanus americanus,* not technically described until 1816.

Shifting now from ethnozoology to medicine, we find Lewis writing on August 19:

I was anxious to learn whether these people had the venerial, and made the enquiry through the inperpreter [Charbonneau] and his wife; the information was that they sometimes had it but I could not learn their remedy; they most usually die with it's effects. this seems a strong proof that these disorders both ganaraehah [gonorrhea] and Louis Venerae [syphilis] are native disorders of America, tho' these people have suffered much by the small pox which is known to be imported and perhaps those other disorders might have been contracted from other indian tribes who by a round of communications might have obtained from the Europeans since it was introduced into that quarter of the globe. but so much detatched on the other ha[n]d from all communication with the whites that I think it most probable that these disorders are original with them (II, 373).

As to whether venereal diseases had an Old or New World origin, there seems to be no final answer. One scientist has written that to obtain such "would require a thoroughgoing reappraisal of the specimens and other basic data, as well as new lines of research."[13] Conversely, Samuel Eliot Morison is on record with the statement: "Evi-

---

[13] Letter to author, Feb. 16, 1962, from T. D. Stewart, Head Curator, Department of Anthropology, Smithsonian Institution.

dence that syphilis existed in a mild endemic form among the American Indians before 1492 is abundant."[14]

[3]

Once the decision had been made to pursue the northern route recommended by Clark, the party resumed its march on August 30, now increased in size by the addition of 29 horses and six Indians, one of whom was the guide, Toby. Soon reaching the mouth of Boyle Creek, they travelled up that stream a few miles and then crossed Bitterroot ranges until, four days later, they struck a small creek flowing north into the Bitterroot River. Latter-day students of Lewis and Clark have never been completely successful in retracing the exact route taken by the explorers. From Boyle Creek they apparently crossed over to the North Fork of the Salmon (Fish Creek of Lewis and Clark) and then followed up that important feeder to (or close to) the gap today called Lost Trail Pass. At this point they re-entered Montana. We might be better informed about the route except for the fact that Lewis, inexplicably, seems to have discontinued his diary on August 26 and apparently did not resume it (except for brief periods when separated from Clark) until January 1 of the next year.[15]

In their approach to Lost Trail Pass, Lewis and Clark took "the worst road (if road it can be called) that was ever travelled."[16] Because of precipitous mountain slopes, the pack horses now and then lost their footing, tumbled backwards, and scattered their loads far and wide. One of these spills resulted in the breaking of their last thermometer. Commented Lewis, "the loss of my thermometer I most sincerely regret. I am confident that the climate here is much warmer than in the same parallel of Latitude on the Atlantic Ocean tho' how many degrees is now out of my power to determine" (VI, 203).

Other difficulties beset them. Snow fell at the higher elevations and food ran short. With little to eat beyond choke cherries, a few

[14] Samuel Eliot Morison, *Admiral of the Ocean Sea* (Boston, 1942), 539. Since Lewis mentions both gonorrhea and syphilis, it would be only natural to assume that he distinguished between the two disorders. Apparently that was not the case, for they were undifferentiated until the work of Philip Ricord in 1838. Of course, that does not rule out the possibility that some scientists before that date may have concluded that the two diseases were or might be different manifestations of a single disease, both contracted in the same manner.

[15] The exceptions are September 9 and 10, September 18–22, and November 29 through December 1.

[16] Gass, 156.

salmon, and an occasional deer, they were forced to eat the last of their pork. A party of more than 30 persons, with appetites sharpened by strenuous mountain climbing, consumed a prodigious amount of food. Though four of the Indians soon turned back, leaving only Toby and one of his sons as guides, this departure did little to ameliorate the gastronomic problem.

On September 4, six days after taking leave of the Shoshoni, the party crossed Lost Trail Pass (or a place near that gap). They then moved down a small stream (probably Camp Creek) and soon emerged onto a valley about one mile wide clothed with "a great quantity of sweet roots and herbs, such as sweet myrrh, angelica and several others."[17] In due time this beautiful, spacious valley would receive the name of Ross's Hole. Here Lewis and Clark encountered a band of some 400 Indians who informed them that they were Ootlashoots of the Tushepau nation. From the beginning, the journalists called them Flatheads, though for no cogent reason that we can find. These Indians no more had flat heads than the Blackfeet had black feet or the Gros Ventres uniformly had big bellies. However, the name Lewis and Clark applied to them has stuck with them ever since.

Ethnologists place the Flatheads in the Salishan Linguistic Family, a group of tribes that formerly occupied a large area of the Northwest including parts of Washington, Oregon, British Columbia, Idaho, and Montana. Lewis and Clark thus met them in the southeastern extremity of this area and were the first white men to provide information about them. According to one historian, "No tribe of Indians in the United States has received more and higher encomiums than have these Ootlashoots, Salish or Flatheads. . . . Their standards of honesty and morality were and are higher than those of most Indians."[18]

Lewis and Clark held a meeting with the Flatheads, presented medals, and said they would like to trade for horses. Talk with them seems to have been limited because it had to pass through several languages. Some years later Clark told Nicholas Biddle how it went: "Our convn. [conversation] with the Tushepaws was held thro' a boy whom we found among them. . . . I spoke in English to Labieche . . . he translated it to Chaboneau in French—he to his wife in Minnetaree —she in Shoshone to the boy—the boy in Tushepaw to that nation."[19]

[17] Gass, 157.
[18] Wheeler, *The Trail of Lewis and Clark,* II, 69.
[19] Jackson, *Letters,* 519.

Flathead wealth, like Shoshoni, resided in horses. According to Lewis, each man possessed 20 to 100 head. The explorers needed more horses, not only as insurance against starvation, but also to assist their hunters in covering a wider area in search of game. Lewis and Clark succeeded in buying 11 and in trading seven of their own with sore backs for others in better condition. This brought their total to 40, including three colts.

The Flatheads, as Clark put it, were "light complected more so than common" (III, 30). Quite naturally, because of this fairness of skin (and singularity of speech), the men once again discussed the question of origin. Private Whitehouse, for instance, declared that, "we take these Savages to be the Welsh Indians if there be any Such from the language. So Capt. Lewis took down the names of evvery thing in their language, in order that it may be found out whether they Sprang or origenated from the welsh or not" (VII, 150–151).

From Ross's Hole the Expedition moved north, following down the Bitterroot River (originally called Clark's River by Lewis). Three days later on September 9 they came to a small, clear-watered tributary entering the Bitterroot from the west. To this stream they gave the name Traveller's Rest Creek, though today it is on the maps as Lolo Creek. When informed by Toby that they would ascend this stream as they began their transit of the mountains, Lewis and Clark decided to halt here for a day to establish their position meridionally, to rest men and horses, and to allow time for exploration downstream as far as the junction of the Bitterroot with a stream from the east (the Blackfoot River). The precise location of their campsite is uncertain, though it was probably about two miles up Lolo Creek—not directly at the mouth as commonly asserted—and some ten miles south of the present city of Missoula, Montana.

While encamped here, Lewis and Clark received intelligence from the Indians that if on the previous July 18th when they had reached the mouth of the Dearborn River, they had gone up that river, crossed the Divide, and descended the Blackfoot River, they could have been on Lolo Creek in something like four days—instead of the 52 it had taken them by the circuitous route just completed. Of course, at that time it would have been impossible for them to have taken this short-cut, even if they had known about it, for they then had no horses. However, looking ahead to the return journey, this was extremely good news.

SUMMARY OF DISCOVERIES

Animals New to Science

CLARK'S NUTCRACKER. *Nucifraga columbiana* (Wilson). [A.O.U. 491]
(Thwaites, III, 17; V, 75–76; Coues, II, 530). Described, 1811.

MOUNTAIN GOAT. *Oreamnos americanus americanus* (Blainville).
(Thwaites, III, 30). 1816.

Plants New to Science

INVOLUCRED FLY-HONEYSUCKLE. *Lonicera involucrata* (Rich.) Banks. 1823.

SITKA MOUNTAIN ASH. *Pyrus sambucifolius* ? [var. *pumila* Sargent]. 1847.

Lewis and Clark Herbarium

ANGELICA [probably LYALL'S ANGELICA]. *Angelica lyallii* Wats. Collected
Sept. 3, 1805.

INVOLUCRED FLY-HONEYSUCKLE. *Lonicera involucrata* (Rich.) Banks. Sept. 2.

SITKA MOUNTAIN ASH. *Pyrus sambucifolius* ? [var. *pumila* Sargent]. Sept. 4.

Indian Tribes Encountered

Salishan Linguistic Family: † Flatheads ("Ootlashoots" and "Tushepau" of
Lewis and Clark).

Topographic Features Named and/or Discovered

† Lewis's River (Thwaites, III, 10) —— Salmon River.

† Fish Creek (Thwaites, III, 50) —— North Fork of Salmon.

† Clark's River (Thwaites, III, 54) —— Bitterroot River.

† Scattered Creek (Thwaites, III, 57) —— possibly Burnt Fork Creek
(Coues, II, 588n).

† Traveller's Rest Creek (Thwaites, III, 58) —— Lolo Creek.

Lolo Trail

CHAPTER THIRTEEN

The next stage of the journey, a stirring episode of heroic scale, would test the mettle of the discoverers at every turn. By pack horse they would follow an old Indian road across the Bitterroot Mountains that had been established many years before Lewis and Clark struggled over it, probably about 1700, after the Indians had acquired horses. After twisting up through the valley and defiles of Lolo Creek, it wandered over the divide between Bitterroot and Lochsa watersheds (south of present-day Lolo Pass) and then snaked its inquiring way through the evergreen-clothed mountains, following throughout most of its length a high ridge between the North Fork of the Clearwater River and the Lochsa River. It terminated on the Weippe (pronounced Wee-ipe) Prairie in north-central Idaho some 16 miles short of the Clearwater River. Because of numerous windings and turnings, the trail was over 100 miles long (Lewis made it 140), though considerably less in an air line. Today most of its length is within the limits of the Clearwater National Forest. After an easy beginning, it becomes, as Clark said, "a most intolerable road" (III, 63), steep, tortuous, ill-defined, seemingly endless.

Lewis and Clark knew next to nothing in advance about the mountainous terrain immediately ahead. They had no maps, no books descriptive of the region, only what scant information they had elicited from the Shoshoni. Cameahwait had told them that the "Pierced nosed Indians" used this road regularly in travelling to the Missouri for buffalo, but "the road was a very bad one as he had been informed by them and that they had suffered excessively with hunger on the rout being obliged to subsist for many days on berries alone as there was no game in that part of the mountains which were broken rockey and so thickly covered with timber that they could scarcely pass" (II, 382) .

But not even this cheerless account remotely prepared them for what they actually experienced in physical and mental distress during the journey ahead. It took them 11 interminably long, wearisome, frustrating days to make the crossing. They suffered from hunger, cold, and exhaustion and endured greater privation and hardship than at any other time or place during the entire trip. Their troubles, difficult in the beginning, worsened with each passing day. If the party had been headed by less competent leadership, the Bitterroots could easily have stopped them in their tracks. Lewis, for one, radiated assurance: "I felt perfectly satisfyed," he declared, "that if the Indians could pass these mountains . . . we could also pass them" (II, 382) .

Topographically and otherwise this region of the Bitterroots has changed but little since Lewis and Clark traversed it. In 1854 Lt. John Mullan, looking for a railroad route, followed the same Indian trail. He consumed 11 days (as had Lewis and Clark) and found the road "thoroughly and utterly impracticable for a railroad route."[1] In 1866–67 Wellington Bird and Major Sewell Truax, with a Congressional appropriation of $50,000, improved the old Indian trail, and in 1939 the U.S. Forest Service supplanted that road with a much better one, the Lolo Motorway. The latter roughly parallels the Nez Perce trail followed by Lewis and Clark. In a number of places segments of the original may still be found; in fact, according to one authority, "by careful tracking a large part of the old trail can be located."[2]

When crossing the Lolo Trail for the first time today (open because of snows only from early July to about the middle of October) , the traveller should allow himself adequate time to enjoy the wild magnificence of this primeval forest. He will want to stop long enough at higher elevations to relish the extensive, unobstructed views, to seek out bits of the old trail followed by the Corps of Discovery more than 160 years ago, to examine landmarks mentioned by journalists of the Expedition and attempt to locate Lewis and Clark campsites.

The first Lewis and Clark student to cross the Lolo Trail was Olin D. Wheeler. In 1902 he and two companions, after organizing a pack

---

[1] Gov. Isaac I. Stevens, *Reports of Explorations and Surveys from the Mississippi River to the Pacific Ocean* (Washington, D.C., 1859) , 156–157.

[2] Letter to author, Dec. 19, 1964, from Ralph Space, former Supervisor of Clearwater National Forest.

train, travelled leisurely along the trail with the express purpose of determining in so far as possible the *exact* route Lewis and Clark had taken. Armed with a rough, unpublished map of the U.S. Geological Survey and Elliott Coues' copiously annotated *History of the Expedition,* they performed their mission in a manner exceeding anticipations. Perhaps the most valuable chapter in Wheeler's book, *The Trail of Lewis and Clark,* published in 1904, was that devoted to the pack-train crossing of the Bitterroots. It described the route *in extenso* and provided a useful accompanying map. Since Wheeler's survey, the most valuable published study of the Lolo Trail has been "Lewis and Clark Through Idaho" by Ralph S. Space, former Supervisor of the Clear-water National Forest. Space has travelled the trail innumerable times and knows more about it in relation to the Lewis and Clark Expedition than any man who ever lived. My own personal knowledge of this trail has been gained from two trips over it, the first in 1963, a somewhat hurried one-day transit, and the second in 1965, a leisurely two-day crossing in company with Mr. Space.

Some recent books about the Expedition have practically ignored Lewis and Clark's 1805 crossing of the Bitterroots. One account, for instance, takes them across the innumerable ranges of this wilderness region in exactly 427 words. This trip was so replete with danger, hardship, and dramatic episode, and its successful issue a personal triumph of such magnitude for Lewis and Clark, that to slight it is like minimizing the importance of the trans-Atlantic flight of the "Spirit of St. Louis" in the life of Charles A. Lindbergh.

[2]

Lewis and Clark left their Traveller's Rest camp late in the afternoon of September 11 and proceeded up Lolo Creek seven miles. They stopped for the night on a smooth bottom beside the creek where Indians had recently encamped. The next day they followed a road through thickly timbered country. Along the way they stopped briefly to inspect an Indian-made, earth-covered sweat house and a number of pine trees that had been peeled by the natives to get at the inner bark.

Early on the 13th the party arrived at a series of hot springs (now Lolo Springs though once called Boyle's Springs) where water heated by subterranean fires issued from between huge boulders. According to Whitehouse, these springs were beautiful to see (VII, 155). Regrettably they are no longer beautiful; today they comprise yet another betrayed scenic area.

A few miles beyond the springs, the explorers crossed the divide between Bitterroot and Lochsa watersheds. Sergeant Ordway said that they "found it to be only about half a mile from the head Spring of the waters running East to the head Spring of the waters running West."[3] Descending the western slope, they soon came to a large open area, now Packer Meadow, through which ran a small stream flowing west. Lewis and Clark called it Glade Creek, though it is today Packer Creek. They camped that night at the lower end of the meadow. Here the mountains, "a vast mass of curving, winding, peak-crowned spurs,"[4] closed in on them. Eight nightmarish days would ensue before they escaped. Each is a story in itself.

Saturday, September 14—Starting early, after consuming the last of their meat, the party left Packer Creek and crossed a ridge to the junction of Crooked Fork and Brushy Creeks. Here they waded Brushy Creek, climbed four miles to the summit of another ridge, and then descended to the point where Colt-killed (now Whitesand) and Crooked Fork Creeks unite to form Lochsa River (the Kooskooskee of Lewis and Clark).

Wading the Lochsa to the north side, Lewis and Clark proceeded downriver for two miles when darkness forced them to halt for the night (on the site of present-day Powell Ranger Station). The large mountain they crossed during the day, Clark said, was "excessively bad & thickly strowed with falling timber & Pine Spruce fur Hackmatak & Tamerack" (III, 66).[5] Private Whitehouse, who often surprises the reader by noting things of interest overlooked by the other journalists, reported seeing "Some tall Strait Sipress [cypress] or white ceeder" (VII, 156).[6] He was referring to the western red cedar or arbor vitae (*Thuja plicata*) that here grows abundantly at low levels, and to a great size—as much as seven feet in diameter four and a half feet above the ground and 150 feet tall. If Lewis and Clark had followed down Crooked Fork Creek instead of crossing the mountain, they would have passed through that majestic grove of cedars (upstream about four

[3] Ordway, 285.

[4] Wheeler, *The Trail of Lewis and Clark*, II, 84.

[5] According to the botanist, C. V. Piper, the "Hackmatak & Tamerack" were varieties of larch, *Larix occidentalis* (see Thwaites, III, 66n).

[6] Western red cedar (*Thuja plicata*), though seen on the Pacific Coast in 1793 by Alexander Mackenzie and by Archibald Menzies in 1796, was not formally described (by James Donn) until 1811.

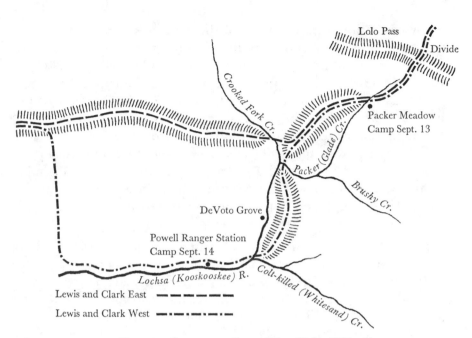

Lolo Pass
Divide
Crooked Fork Cr.
Packer (Glade) Cr.
Packer Meadow
Camp Sept. 13
Brushy Cr.
Packer (Glade) Cr.
DeVoto Grove
Powell Ranger Station
Camp Sept. 14
Lochsa (Kooskooskee) R.
Colt-killed (Whitesand) Cr.

Lewis and Clark East   ‒ ‒ ‒ ‒ ‒
Lewis and Clark West   ‒·‒·‒·‒·‒

ROUTE OF LEWIS AND CLARK SEPT. 12-14, 1805

miles from Powell Ranger Station) recently dedicated to the memory
of Bernard DeVoto, conservationist, author, and historian. He often
camped here while pursuing the trail of Lewis and Clark, and here, at
his request, his ashes were scattered.

Lewis and Clark had this day travelled through cold rain and
intermittent hail and snow, had experienced their first real taste of
Bitterroot antipathy. When they camped for the night they were hungry, miserable, and exhausted. Making matters worse, the hunters had
succeeded in killing during the day nothing except two or three grouse
on which, Gass remarked, "without a miracle it was impossible to feed
30 hungry men. . . . So Capt. Lewis gave out some portable soup,
which he had along, to be used in cases of necessity. Some of the men
did not relish this soup, and agreed to kill a colt."[7] So the 193 pounds of
portable soup that Lewis had carried all the way from Philadelphia at
last began to serve the purpose for which it had been intended. The
killing of the colt suggested the name, Colt-killed Creek, a meaningful
one with a story attached; the present Whitesand connotes nothing in
particular.

[7] Gass, 163.

By descending into the gorge of the Lochsa River, the party had veered from the main (Lolo) trail and had let themselves in for all sorts of trouble. "What the old guide meant," Wheeler remonstrated, "if he really knew what he was doing, by taking the expedition down into this cañon . . . is inconceivable, for they were simply compelled to climb out again and regain the main trail on the ridge to the north."[8] At that time a maze of Indian trails ran through these mountains, many diverging from the main one to fisheries along the streams. It would seem that Toby, an infrequent visitor to these parts, simply became confused and took the wrong one. It was a serious mistake, for it delayed the completion of the Bitterroot transit by at least a day, if not more.

Sunday, September 15—After breakfasting on colt meat, the party went on down the Lochsa about four miles to an old fishing place recognizable as such by the presence of Indian-made weirs. Private Whitehouse mentioned passing a pond on the road to this point. The pond is still there and, thanks to the initiative of Ralph Space, is today called Whitehouse Pond.

At the fishing place, aware by now of Toby's error, the explorers began the long climb out of the gorge to the ridge far above. Because of the extreme steepness of the mountain side, the trail wound back and forth as though reluctant to reach a destination. Sergeant Ordway guessed they climbed at least 10 miles before reaching the summit. Clark said that the road "was as bad as it can possibly be to pass" (III, 68). Some of the horses lost their footing and rolled down the abrupt slopes as much as 30 to 40 yards. One such tumble broke Clark's portable desk. That it was a near impossible climb may be gauged by the fact that two of the heavily laden pack animals gave out and had to be left behind.

Once they had gained the top of the ridge, they struck the main trail again, a narrow, ill-defined road which followed the elongate hog-back separating the Lochsa and North Fork of the Clearwater. The scenic grandeur of the Bitterroots was now in evidence on all sides. Clark remarked on the "high ruged [rugged] mountains winding in every direction" (III, 68). Darkness brought them to a halt on a high point of the ridge (probably about two miles east of Cayuse Junction).

[8] Wheeler, *The Trail of Lewis and Clark*, II, 91–92. The main trail from Packer Creek crossed Crooked Fork Creek about one mile above its junction with Brushy Creek, and then ran up over Rocky Point and Powell Junction. Lewis and Clark would travel this way on their return in June, 1806.

The hunters had killed nothing during the day except two grouse. Water was unobtainable. With melted snow (from an old snow bank), they prepared more portable soup and cooked the last of the horse flesh.

"Maney parts [of this country were] bare of timber," Clark observed, "they haveing burnt it down & . . . it lies on the ground in every direction" (III, 68). Clark was here suggesting that Indians had been responsible for the fires, as they may well have been. On the return trip over the Bitterroots, Lewis and Clark told about their Nez Perce guides creating a tremendous bonfire, explaining that such a conflagration would produce fair weather for the trip. However, most of the fires occurring then and now were due to natural causes. Electric storms strike these mountains, unleashing bolts of lightning which set crown fires of unbelievable magnitude and destructive force. Ralph Space has informed me that 90 per cent of the fires in the Clearwater Forest are caused by lightning, over 100 each year.

One of the most difficult problems the explorers had to contend with in crossing these mountains was the profusion of trees that had fallen across the trail. These had to be climbed over or bypassed, causing exasperating delay, and this situation persisted day after day throughout the entire transit. Another problem was finding forage and water for their horses. Except for an occasional meadow, the high country of the Bitterroots, as already mentioned, was covered by forest. When Lewis and Clark encountered grassy fields, they had no other choice but to allow the horses time to graze, even though it meant further delay. Their successful crossing depended on these animals.

Much of the virgin forest present here when Lewis and Clark struggled through it still stands, unscarred and unspoiled.[9] As a result, the traveller who crosses the Lolo Motorway today may view many of the same trees that the explorers gazed upon so many years ago. Since 1805 they have added more than 160 rings of growth to their trunks and have extended pointed tops ever higher.

The more important trees, all evergreens, constituting the Clearwater Forest then and now are, in the low country, Douglas fir (*Pseudotsuga taxifolia*), ponderosa pine (*Pinus ponderosa*), grand fir (*Abies grandis*), western larch (*Larix occidentalis*), western white pine (*Pinus monticola*), and western red cedar (*Thuja plicata*) and, at higher elevations, Engelmann's spruce (*Picea engelmannii*), lodge-

[9] Ralph Space has informed me that "from Pioneer Mine (head of Gold Creek out of Musselshell) almost to Rocky Point Lookout is virgin country."

pole pine (*Pinus contorta*), alpine fir (*Abies lasiocarpa*), and white-bark pine (*Pinus albicaulis*). (See Appendix A for those of this group discovered by Lewis and Clark.)

Monday, September 16—This was to be the bluest of blue Mondays. The men awoke to find themselves covered with a two-inch blanket of snow. It was extremely cold and windy, and the snow continued to fall. Before loading horses, the men mended moccasins and those without socks wrapped their feet in rags. Whitehouse recorded the cheerless fact that they "Set out without anything to eat" (VII, 157). They might have eased hunger pains with venison if Clark's gun had not had a loose flint. When he attempted to shoot a mule deer, his rifle failed to fire seven consecutive times, even though it had a "Steel fuzee and had never Snaped 7 times before" (III, 69).

The accumulating snow, six to eight inches by evening, almost obliterated the trail. The men kept to it only by close scrutiny of trunks and limbs of trees which bore marks put on them in previous years by Indian packs rubbing against them. Low-hanging clouds reduced the limit of visibility to less than 200 yards. Ordway's diary for that evening said, "It appeared as if we have been in the clouds all this day."[10] The road continued to follow the high ridge, a knobby one, with intervening saddles. Even on the level, it was a difficult route. Sergeant Gass declared that they "proceeded over the most terrible mountains I ever beheld."[11] Both men and horses frequently slipped and fell, and they continued the painful procedure of surmounting or skirting numerous windfalls. "I have been wet and as cold in every part as I ever was in my life," Clark wrote; "indeed I was at one time fearfull my feet would freeze in the thin Mockirsons which I wore" (III, 69).

At mid-day when the party came to a grass-covered slope, they halted to let the horses graze and to make fires to melt snow for more portable soup, the first food they had eaten since the previous evening. Wheeler placed the location of this noon camp "at or near a point known as the 'Indian postoffices,' "[12] though Ralph Space thinks it was at Spring Hill (about six miles east of the Post Offices), since the "distance checks and there is an abundance of grass."[13] The Post Offices alluded to are two piles of stone about four or five feet high that stand

[10] Ordway, 287.
[11] Gass, 164.
[12] Wheeler, *The Trail of Lewis and Clark,* II, 95.
[13] Ralph S. Space, "Lewis and Clark Through Idaho" (Lewiston, Idaho, 1964), 3.

conspicuously beside the present Lolo Motorway. Whether they were there in 1805 no one can say, for Lewis and Clark definitely made no reference to them. (They did see other similar stone piles farther west on the return trip.) It is possible, of course, that they missed them because they were snow-covered, or because the trail then ran differently. The origin of the name Post Office is unknown, though one story is that the Nez Perce Indians transmitted information by piling stones in different ways. This the Indians of today deny, claiming that the mounds are trail markers. If Lewis and Clark did make their noon stop here on September 16, they were then at the highest point on the trail at an elevation of 7,036 feet.

After completing lunch, Clark took one man and hurried ahead. Some six miles farther along, they came to a heavily timbered saddle through which ran a small stream flowing north. Here they built huge, roaring fires which proved most welcome to the remainder of the party when they straggled in later on, wet, disheartened, half-starved, and chilled to the bone. Since they had found no game whatever during the day, they killed another colt and consumed half of it. They spent the night here, though, according to Clark, the densely wooded terrain was "scurcely large enough for us to lie leavel" (III, 69) .[14]

Tuesday, September 17—When the men went to catch the horses on the morning of this day, they found that they had scattered widely. In order to allow them to move about at night to obtain what little forage the woods provided, Lewis and Clark did not hobble them. It was a gamble whether they would all remain in the immediate vicinity, but a necessary one.

Because of their distressingly late start, the party made only about 10 miles before darkness compelled them to halt for the night. Private Whitehouse wrote that they camped "at a Small branch on the mountain near a round deep Sinque hole full of water" (VII, 158) . Ralph Space thinks that the sink hole referred to "is in the first saddle east of Indian Grave Mountain."[15] Certainly there is a small pond there today that fits the description.

The hunters had another bad day and succeeded in shooting only a few grouse. One of the men chased a bear up a mountain side, but the bear outran him. That night they killed the last of their colts. "The want of provisions together with the dificul[t]y of passing those emence

---

[14] The location of this campsite is uncertain. Whitehouse said it was in a "lonesome cove" (VII, 157) . Space thinks it was on Moon Creek.

[15] Space, "Lewis and Clark Through Idaho," 4.

mountains [has] dampened the sperits of the party," Clark wrote (III, 72). The situation was even more critical than Clark's passing comment made it out to be. The successive Bitterroot ranges, tinged blue by distance, had the appearance of going on forever, and the minds of the men, weakened by privation, began to entertain the thought that they might never escape from them. To anyone who has travelled the Lolo Trail throughout its difficult length, this was a quite understandable reaction.

As a result, Lewis and Clark talked matters over and came to an important decision. Clark, with six of their best hunters, would forge ahead, starting early the next morning. He would travel as rapidly as possible with a view to escaping from the mountains and, hopefully, reaching prairie country ahead where he might expect to find game to send back to Lewis and the others who followed. With their larder bare except for portable soup and with game unobtainable on this snow-covered, elevated ridge, the two captains felt they had nothing to lose by making this move. Sergeant Ordway may have reflected something of the prevailing mood that night when he wrote, "we hear wolves howl some distance ahead."[16]

Wednesday, September 18—Clark and his party left at dawn. He seems to have had every confidence that he could find his way, since he did not take Toby with him. At a distance of about 20 miles, Clark and his men checked their horses on a high, barren part of the ridge. The day was clear, visibility excellent, and from this vantage point they could see in the distant southwest "an emence Plain and *leavel* Countrey" (III, 72). It was a moment of inexpressible joy for the seven men; their minds were now freed of the gnawing obsession that these inhospitable mountains would never end. They could only guess at the distance separating them from the level country ahead and how long it would take them to reach it, but at least it was in sight.

The elevation on which they had halted is today known as Sherman Peak, and the open Idaho country is that extending from Grangeville, about 45 miles distant, to Winchester (farther north), about 60. One of the highlights of my second crossing of the Lolo Trail was the moment when I stood with Ralph Space on the summit of Sherman Peak and could see for myself far ahead the same level plains Clark and his contingent had seen so very many years ago.

Clark covered 12 additional miles that day. Descending from Sherman Peak, he soon left the ridge and travelled almost due south until

[16] Ordway, 287.

he came to a small stream running to the Lochsa River. Here he and his men spent the night. Since they had nothing whatever to eat, they called this stream Hungry Creek. In time it became Obia Creek and so appears on older maps. At Space's instigation, its name was changed back to Hungry Creek in 1961. His success in this endeavor provides the hope that other Lewis and Clark names may be restored.

In leaving the ridge and turning south, Clark bore away from the main trail as it was in Wheeler's day and as it is today. But he appears to have followed the road as it existed then, for on the return trip with Nez Perce Indians guiding the party, they took this same route.

Back on the trail, Lewis and his companions continued to have their troubles. Some of the horses strayed again, so that they were late in getting started. Both men and animals suffered for lack of water and food. The guns of the hunters remained silent. "There is nothing here upon earth," declared Lewis ruefully, "except ourselves and a few small pheasants, small grey squirrels, and a blue bird of the vulter kind about the size of a turtle dove or jay bird" (III, 72).[17] (Note that Lewis, now separated from Clark, resumes his writing, thus providing further evidence that he had in fact laid down his pen on August 26.)

After travelling some 18 miles, they halted where they found water in a steep ravine about one-half mile from their camp. Their supper that night reveals the straits to which they had been reduced. It consisted of portable soup, a small amount of bear oil and, topping that off, 20 pounds of candles (III, 71). The explorers had strong stomachs as well as strong bodies.

Understandably, the Lewis and Clark journalists remarked not at all about the beauty of this mountainous terrain. The Lolo Trail introduces the traveller to spectacular sweeping views. It takes him through superb evergreen woods where stately pine, fir, spruce, and cedar thrust pointed crowns to the skies. It shows him pleasant valleys and deep, twisting gorges through which run silver tumbling streams seeking lower levels. Yet the explorers said nothing of this. Completely immersed in misery, they saw only the worrisome side of their existence.

Thursday, September 19—Starting early, Clark and his men moved up Hungry Creek for a distance of about six miles where they came to a small glade. Here, opportunely and unexpectedly, they encountered a stray Indian horse. Since no food had entered their stomachs in the last

---

[17] Coues (II, 600n) identified the squirrel as *Sciurus fremonti* and thought the "blue bird" was probably Maximilian's jay, *Gymnokitta cyanocephala*.

24 hours, the men were not long in reaching a decision about what to do with this animal. They promptly shot it and after filling themselves, hung the balance in a tree where Lewis could be expected to find it.

The road up Hungry Creek had been "much worse than any other part," Clark wrote, "as the hill sides are steep and at many places obliged for several yds. to pass on the sides of rocks where one false step of a horse would be certain destruction" (III, 75). Two miles beyond the glade, they left Hungry Creek on their right and struggled over two mountains before encamping on a small stream (Cedar Creek of today) in a beautiful group of huge western red cedar now fittingly called "Lewis and Clark Grove."[18]

On this morning Lewis and his party awoke to a clear, sunshiny day. According to Ordway, they ate "the verry last morcil of our provisions [whatever that may have been] except a little portable soup."[19] For once the horses had not strayed, so that they were able to make an early start. Some six miles farther along they arrived atop Sherman Peak and exulted in the view, as had Clark the day before, of the distant prairie land. Declared Sergeant Gass, "There was much joy and rejoicing among the men, as happens among passengers at sea, who have experienced a dangerous and protracted journey, when they first discover land on the long looked for coast."[20]

With invigorated step, they soon left the ridge, plunged down to Hungry Creek, and began the ascent of that stream along the part of the trail alluded to by Clark as particularly precarious. The latter had passed it without untoward incident, but Lewis was not so fortunate. One of his horses slipped from the road, tumbled nearly 100 yards down a precipitous slope, and landed on the stones of the creek below. Incredibly, twenty minutes later this animal was on the trail again, moving along with the other horses. Lewis regarded this as "the most wonderful escape" he had ever witnessed (III, 74).

They camped that night in a thicket of pine and fir on Hungry Creek and eased their hunger with more of the unappetizing portable soup. "The most of the party," Whitehouse revealed, "is weak and feeble Suffering with hunger" (VII, 159). Lewis added that "several of

---

[18] This grove was set apart and named by Ralph Space. After leaving Hungry Creek, Clark crossed the ridge west of Boundary Peak to Eldorado Creek, an eastern branch of Collins' Creek (now Lolo Creek). He then went down this stream four miles before crossing another mountain to Cedar Creek.

[19] Ordway, 288.

[20] Gass, 167.

the men [were] unwell of the disentary, breakings out, or irruptions of the Skin" (III, 74).

Friday, September 20—"I set out early," Clark wrote, "and proceeded on through a Countrey as ruged as usial passed over a low mountain into the forks of a large Creek which I kept down 2 miles and assended a high Steep mountain leaving the Creek to our left hand passed the head of several dreans on a divideing ridge, and at 12 miles decended the mountain to a leavel pine Countrey [Weippe Prairie]" (III, 77).[21]

After he had moved west across the prairie some five miles, Clark chanced upon three Indian boys who quickly tried to hide in the grass. He located two of them, tamed their fright with presents, and followed them to their village a short distance away. Here he was conducted to a lodge where a minor chief informed him, through the medium of sign language, that the head chief and all the warriors had recently departed on a punitive foray against enemies to the southwest. Indian women soon produced a small piece of buffalo meat, dried salmon, and roots of different kinds. The principal root was from the plant now called camas (*Camassia quamash*), a member of the lily family. In succeeding days and months this root would play an important role in the lives of the explorers. Clark and his men at once ate freely of it and then, trailed by some 100 native men, women, and children, moved two miles to another village where they spent the night. Lewis and Clark most often referred to these Indians as either the Chopunnish or the Pierced Noses. Today, of course, they are known to the world as the Nez Perces (pronounced "Nezz-purse" and generally spelled without a written accent).

On this same day, Lewis had trouble rounding up the horses again and started late. Ordway wrote, "we found a handful or two of Indian peas and a little bears oil which we brought with us we finished the last morcil of it and proceeded on half Starved and very weak."[22] After travelling only two miles, they discovered the horse meat Clark had happily left behind for them. Famished as they were, this find was like an interposition of Providence. We can readily believe Whitehouse's statement that they "dined sumptiously" (VII, 160). There would be

[21] As Space has reconstructed the route for this day, Clark "climbed to the top of the ridge between Cedar and Lolo Creeks. He then went down this ridge to the forks of Eldorado and Lolo Creeks; thence down Lolo Creek to the mouth of Trout Creek. From this point he climbed to Crane Meadows on Trout Creek. . . . From there he went over the shoulder of Brown's ridge and down Miles Creek to Weippe Prairie." (See Space, "Lewis and Clark Through Idaho," 6.)

[22] Ordway, 288.

no further need for portable soup. Because of the late start, Lewis made only 12 miles before darkness forced him to halt, probably on a ridge between Dollar and Sixbit Creeks. Horse meat provided an ample supper.

During the five day period when Lewis kept a journal, he contributed more faunal and floral information than all the other journalists combined during the entire Bitterroot transit. For instance, as he dropped to lower elevations on Hungry Creek he noted a pronounced warming trend and, with it, a marked change in the plant life. He mentioned "a kind of honeysuckle which bears a white bury and rises about 4 feet high not common but to the western side of the rockey mountains" (III, 77). Beyond reasonable doubt this was the shrub now called snowberry (*Symphoricarpos albus laevigatus*). He was properly impressed with red cedars (perhaps those in Lewis and Clark Grove). "I saw several sticks large enough to form eligant perogues of at least 45 feet in length" (III, 81). In time he would learn of the tremendous importance of this magnificent tree to coastal Indians. He referred also to an alder (*Alnus sinuata*), a honeysuckle (*Lonicera ciliosa*), and a huckleberry (*Vaccinium membranaceum*). All three have been identified as new to science.

On September 20 Lewis described a bird with "a blue shining colour with a very high tuft of feathers on the head a long tale, it feeds on flesh and the beak and feet black. it's note is cha-ah, cha-ah. it is about the size of a pigeon, and in shape and action resembles the blue jay" (III, 75–76). Ornithologists of today seem generally unaware that Lewis was the discoverer of this noisy bird, the black-headed jay (*Cyanocitta stelleri annectens*), a subspecies of Steller's jay, the only *blue* bird of any sort with a crest found between the Rockies and the Pacific.

On this same day, too, Lewis wrote of encountering "Three species of Phesants, a large black species, with some feathers irregularly scattered on the breast neck and belley—a smaller kind of a dark uniform colour with a red stripe above the eye, and a brown and yellow species that a gooddeel resembles the phesant common to the Atlantic States" (III, 76). A significant sentence, containing mention of three pheasants then unknown to science, though Lewis had earlier discovered the "large black species" (Richardson's blue grouse, *Dendragapus obscurus richardsonii*) on the Jefferson River. The one with a red stripe above the eye was Franklin's grouse, *Canachites canadensis franklinii*, and the third, "the brown and yellow species," was the Oregon ruffed grouse, *Bonasa umbellus sabini*.

Saturday, September 21—As his initial act of the day, Clark sent hunters out in different directions to look for game. To allay suspicion and to gain information, he himself stayed with the Indians. The chief informed him that one of their important leaders, Twisted Hair, could then be located on the Clearwater River, to the west about 15 miles, where he had gone to fish for salmon. When the hunters returned empty-handed, Clark purchased a horseload of berries, roots, and dried salmon and charged Reuben Field to deliver it to Lewis.

Late that afternoon Clark and the remaining men set out for the Clearwater, taking a road that paralleled the present Jim Ford Creek. He arrived late at night, after making the long, steep descent into the gorge of the Clearwater. Twisted Hair, whom he soon located, proved to be "a Chearfull man with apparent sincerity" (III, 82). He presented him with a medal, after which the two talked until after midnight, the conversation of necessity being limited largely to gesticulations.

Back on the trail, with the horses widely scattered still another time, Lewis was unable to move until near noon and made only 15 miles before he was compelled to halt for the night. During the day, the hunters killed a few grouse, some of the other men lifted several crayfish from a creek, and Lewis himself shot a coyote. That evening, with what remained of the horse, and with coyote, grouse, and crayfish, they made "one more hearty meal, not knowing where the next was to be found" (III, 80–81).

Sunday, September 22—Clark had made the forced march to the Clearwater primarily to have a close look at it. He found it to be a comparatively large stream, about 160 yards wide, and that ponderosa pines large enough for dugouts stood on its banks. There was no reason why, as he saw it, the Expedition could not once again take to the water. When he had made up his mind on this point, he left his men here to hunt and headed back to Weippe Prairie where he found, much to his delight, that Lewis and the remainder of the party had arrived ahead of him.

That evening Lewis wrote: "The pleasure I now felt in having tryumphed over the rockey Mountains and descending once more to a level and fertile country where there was every rational hope of finding a comfortable subsistence for myself and party can be more readily conceived than expressed, nor was the flattering prospect of the final success of the expedition less pleasing" (III, 83).

SUMMARY OF DISCOVERIES

Animals New to Science

OREGON RUFFED GROUSE. *Bonasa umbellus sabini* (Douglas) . [A.O.U. 300c] (Thwaites, III, 76; IV, 129; Coues, III, 872) . Described, 1828.

FRANKLIN'S GROUSE. *Canachites canadensis franklinii* (Douglas) . [A.O.U. 299] (Thwaites, III, 76; IV, 128–129; Coues, III, 871) . 1828.

BLACK-HEADED JAY. *Cyanocitta stelleri annectens* (Baird) . [A.O.U. 478c] (Thwaites, III, 75–76; VI, 134–135; Coues, II, 601; III, 930) . 1874.

CLARK'S NUTCRACKER. *Nucifraga columbiana* (Wilson) . [A.O.U. 491] (Thwaites, III, 17; V, 75–76; Coues, II, 530) . 1811.

MOUNTAIN GOAT. *Oreamnos americanus americanus* (Blainville) . (Thwaites, III, 30) . 1816.

Plants New to Science

GRAND FIR. *Abies grandis* Lindley. (Thwaites, III, 69; IV, 45; Coues, III, 831) . 1833.

SUBALPINE FIR. *Abies lasiocarpa* (Hook.) Nuttall. (Thwaites, II, 69; Coues, III, 831) . 1842.

SITKA ALDER. *Alnus sinuata* (Regel) Rydb. (Thwaites, III, 77; Coues, II, 605) . 1868.

CAMAS. *Camassia quamash* (Pursh) Greene. (Thwaites, III, 78; Coues, II, 603–604) . 1814.

WESTERN LARCH. *Larix occidentalis* Nuttall. (Thwaites, III, 66) . 1849.

ORANGE HONEYSUCKLE. *Lonicera ciliosa* (Pursh) DC. (Thwaites, III, 77) . 1814.

ENGELMANN'S SPRUCE. *Picea engelmannii* Parry. (Thwaites, III, 69) . 1863.

WHITEBARK PINE. *Pinus albicaulis* Engelmann. (Thwaites, III, 69) . 1857.

LODGEPOLE PINE. *Pinus contorta* Douglas. (Thwaites, III, 69) . 1838.

PONDEROSA PINE. *Pinus ponderosa* Douglas. (Thwaites, III, 66) . 1830.

COMMON SNOWBERRY. *Symphoricarpos albus laevigatus* (Fernald) Blake. (Thwaites, III, 77; Coues, III, 1041) . 1905.

PACIFIC YEW. *Taxus brevifolia* Nuttall. (Thwaites, III, 69) . 1849.

WESTERN RED CEDAR. *Thuja plicata* Donn. (Thwaites, III, 80–81) . 1811.

BLUE HUCKLEBERRY. *Vaccinium membranaceum* Douglas. (Thwaites, III, 77) . 1834.

Lewis and Clark Herbarium

None.

Indian Tribes Encountered

Sahaptian Linguistic Family: † Nez Perce (Chopunnish or Pierced Noses of Lewis and Clark) .

Topographic Features Named and/or Discovered

† Glade Creek (Thwaites, III, 64) —— Packer Creek.

† Colt-killed Creek (Thwaites, III, 66) —— Whitesand Creek.

† Kooskooskee River (Thwaites, III, 66) —— Lochsa River, and farther along, Clearwater River.

† Hungry Creek (Thwaites, III, 72) —— Hungry Creek.

† Collins' Creek (Thwaites, V, 42) —— Lolo Creek (not to be confused with Montana's Lolo Creek).

† Quawmash Flats (Thwaites, V, 119) —— Weippe Prairie.

Clearwater
to
Columbia

CHAPTER FOURTEEN

Lewis and Clark, within the short space of five weeks, had discovered three different Indian tribes then entirely unknown to the world, three that would shortly become among the most celebrated in the annals of the West: the Shoshoni, Flatheads, and Nez Perces. Geographically, these were Plateau Indians, as opposed to Plains and Pacific Coastal. Also, each belonged to a different linguistic family and spoke a language entirely different from the others. The Nez Perces constituted the principal tribe of the large Sahaptian Family, along with lesser ones such as Cayuse, Umatilla, Walula (Walla Walla), Palouse, and Klikitat. In the early 1800's the Nez Perces inhabited a considerable portion of Idaho, southeastern Washington, and northeastern Oregon. Shoshonean tribes adjoined them to the south, Salishan to the north, and Chinookan to the west.

The term Nez Perce originated with the French, who thus implied that the Indians so designated practiced the custom of piercing the nasal septum for the insertion of ornaments. In Clark's first mention of the Nez Perces he said, "They call themselves *Cho-pun-nish* or *Pierced noses*" (III, 78). He did not go on to say whether they did or did not actually pierce their noses. At a later date, however, Lewis stated that "The orniments worn by the Chopunnish are, in their nose a single shell of Wampum, the pirl & beeds are suspended from the ears" (IV, 371–372).

Within recent years, the matter of whether the Nez Perces practiced this singular custom has grown controversial and will probably remain so. For instance, I have it from one ethnologist that "The Nez

Perces certainly did pierce their noses, but only infrequently and almost never in their later years,"[1] and from another, conversant with Lewis's observation, that Lewis saw "members of other tribes among the Nez Perces."[2] No Nez Perces of his acquaintance, the latter insists, had heard anything about such a custom. Similar statements, both pro and con, could be multiplied, but to insert them here would serve no useful purpose. Of just one thing I think we can be sure, and that is that Lewis while visiting the Nez Perces did see Indians with pierced noses.

With the Nez Perces, tenure on earth was a precarious business, exacting constant toil and vigilance. Obtaining ample subsistence was a bitter, unending struggle. In summer and fall they pulled salmon from the streams and dug roots from the earth. In winter they hunted deer, elk, and antelope; in spring, to obtain buffalo, they crossed the Bitterroots to the Missouri where they often lost men and horses to the better-armed tribes of the plains. Their wealth, like that of Shoshoni and Flathead, resided in horses. With the coming of spring, Lewis and Clark would benefit from this equine plenty.

The Nez Perces raised no crops, though they took much of their aliment from the earth. Camas roots, on the word of Lewis, formed "much the greatest portion of their subsistence" (V, 124). Ranging in size from a nutmeg to a hen's egg, they were, when raw, odorless and almost tasteless. The natives began collecting them about mid-July, digging them from the soil with sticks sharpened at one end. After they had been cooked, they possessed a "sort of a sweetish taste and much the consistency of a roasted onion" (V, 127).

The Nez Perces cooked camas roots as follows. After collecting a great quantity of them, often as many as 20 to 30 bushels, they made a hole in the ground some two to three feet deep and 10 in diameter. They lined this with pieces of split dried wood and covered them with a layer of stones. They then set fire to the wood to heat the stones. After the fire had died down, they covered the stones with a thin layer of earth and, on top of that, a layer of grass. The camas roots were then piled into the pit and covered with a two to three inch layer of grass. At that point, the Indians poured water over the whole, which, on reaching the hot stones, produced a considerable volume of steam. As a final

---

[1] Letter to author, Oct. 16, 1963, from Verne F. Ray, Department of Anthropology, University of Washington.

[2] Letter to author, Aug. 31, 1965, from Deward E. Walker, Jr., Department of Anthropology, Washington State University.

step, they covered the contents with earth to a depth of about four inches and built a fire on top, which they kept alive for 10 to 12 hours. At the expiration of that time, they allowed the roots to cool two or three hours before removing them. They could be eaten at once while hot, or later, after they had been dried on scaffolds in the sun.

If the Indian woman wished to make bread of the steamed bulbs, she pounded them into a dough which she then shaped into loaves, each weighing 8 to 10 pounds. These were then returned to the pit, along with a fresh batch of uncooked roots, for a second steaming. On being removed, the loaves were fashioned into cakes of various sizes and shapes about one-half to three-quarter inch thick and then dried on sticks in the sun or over fires. If thoroughly dried, these cakes would remain in good condition for a long time. Lewis said that this bread, when plentiful, formed "an ingredient in almost every dish" the Nez Perces prepared (V, 127). To Sergeant Gass, it was palatable and nourishing and "like that sometimes made of pumpkins."[3] Even today these Indians on occasion prepare camas roots in pits as their forefathers did in Lewis and Clark's day. On a recent trip through Idaho, I saw Nez Perces in a field near Weippe Prairie digging camas roots.

The explorers experienced difficulty with the Nez Perce language. "We attempted to have Some talk with those people," Clark said, "but could not for the want of an Interpreter thro' which we could Speake, we were Compelled to converse altogether by Signs" (III, 85). What considerable information they did obtain must be credited to Drouillard's skill with sign language. For example, they learned much about the country to the west. "I got the Twisted hare to draw the river from his Camp down which he did with great Cherfulness on a white Elk skin" (III, 85).

Sign language had its inception in the remote past. It probably preceded spoken language. There are two main schools of thought as to its provenance, both agreeing that it attained its highest development on the High Plains of the West. One school maintains that it arose from a necessity for intercommunication among tribes speaking different languages. The other insists that it developed "out of the necessity for communicating over great distances," and that "it would have arisen and been widely used had all Plains Indians spoken a common language."[4] Regardless of origin, it was a language of gestures, employing hands and arms, that was perfected to the point where such com-

[3] Gass, 169.
[4] Webb, *The Great Plains,* 73.

munication was more rapid than by words. Many students of this medium of expression have commented on its similarity to the sign language of deaf-mutes. According to one prominent ethnologist, sign
language "seems never to have extended west of the mountains, excepting among the Nez Perces and other tribes accustomed to make periodic
hunting excursions into the plains."[5] So Lewis and Clark had cause to be
grateful that these Indians understood this common language. As they
moved closer to the Pacific, beyond Nez Perce dominion, they would
experience increased difficulty in communication with natives.

[2]

Lewis and Clark did not prolong their stay on Weippe Prairie with the
Nez Perces. With the days growing rapidly shorter, it was imperative
that they move along at once. Loading their horses with obtainable
food, they continued to the Clearwater where Clark had found Twisted
Hair and then five miles downstream to the mouth of the North Fork
of the Clearwater. Here, on the south side of the main stream, where
Clark located a number of large ponderosa pines, they established
Canoe Camp. At once, according to Whitehouse, "we went about
helving our axes and git in readiness to begin the canoes" (VII, 164).

The march from Weippe Prairie to the Clearwater had been a
trying one. A debilitating gastro-enteritis had suddenly struck most of
the men. On the day Clark first encountered the Nez Perces, he complained of being "verry unwell all the evening from eating the fish &
roots too freely" (III, 79), and on rejoining Lewis, had advised him
not to overeat.

The food obtained here consisted almost entirely of such Nez
Perce staples as dried salmon and camas roots, quite a change from
that to which the men had long been accustomed. Excerpts from the
journals during the next few days reveal a sorry state of affairs:

Clark (September 23) —"Several 8 or 9 men sick, Capt. Lewis sick
and complain of a *Lax* & heaviness at the stomack. . . . Capt. Lewis
scarcely able to ride on a jentle horse which was furnished by the chief,
Several men so unwell that they were Compelled to lie on the Side of
the road for Some time others obliged to be put on horses" (III,
86–87).

Gass (September 24) —"The men are generally unwell, owing to

[5] Hodge, *Handbook of American Indians*, II, 65.

the change of diet . . . the Indian provisions did not agree with us. Captain Clarke gave all the sick a dose of Rush's pills, to see what effect that would have."[6]

Clark (September 25) — "When I arrived at camp, found Capt. Lewis verry sick, Several men also verry Sick, I gave some Salts and Tarter emetic" (III, 88) .

Whitehouse (September 26) — "Several of the men Sick with the Relax, caused by a suddin change of diet and water as well as the climate" (VII, 164) .

Clark (September 26) — "Capt. Lewis Still very unwell, Several men taken Sick on the way down, I administered *Salts* Pils Galip [jalap], Tarter emetic &c. I feel unwell this evening" (III, 88–89) .

It is quite apparent that the men were in bad shape. With Lewis completely incapacitated, it was incumbent on Clark to take charge. He was an uncertain and much puzzled "doctor," but that did not deter him from prescribing Rush's pills, "to see what effect that would have," nor, as the cases multiplied, from taking seriously Hippocrates' maxim, "Desperate diseases require desperate remedies." He supplied proof of that when he administered at one time not only a dose of salts but also Rush's pills, jalap, and tartar emetic.

Though the men attributed the cause of their illness variously, it was undoubtedly a radical change in diet. The men had come down out of the mountains ravenous as wolves and had stuffed themselves with salmon and camas roots, foods altogether different from buffalo, deer, elk, and antelope to which their stomachs had become conditioned. John Townsend, young Philadelphia ornithologist with the Wyeth Expedition, recorded that when he crossed the Rockies to the Columbia watershed in 1834: "The sudden and entire change from flesh exclusively, to fish, has effected us all, more or less, with diarrhoea and pain in the abdomen; several of the men have been so extremely sick, as scarcely to be able to travel."[7] The Astorian, Gabriel Franchère, reported similarly. The salmon, he said, was "extremely fat and oily; which renders it unwholesome for those who are not accustomed to it, and who eat too great a quantity; thus several of our people were attacked with diarrhoea in a few days after we began to make this fish our ordinary sustenance."[8]

Camas roots seem to have a like effect. Elliott Coues stated that

[6] Gass, 170.
[7] Townsend, *Narrative of a Journey Across the Rocky Mountains,* 141.
[8] *Early Western Travels*, VI, 322.

they did,[9] and Lewis and Clark gradually came around to the same opinion. "This root," Lewis declared, "is pallateable but disagrees with me in every shape I have ever used it" (V, 127).

The Clearwater epidemic might have dragged on even longer if the men had not been introduced to food more agreeable to their digestive tracts. On October 9 Gass wrote, "We have some Frenchmen, who prefer dogflesh to fish; and they have got two or three dogs from the Indians."[10] Soon we find Clark writing, "Purchased all the dogs we could" (III, 123). And from then on while west of the Rockies, that is exactly what they did—purchased all the dogs they could. On October 18, for instance, they bought 40 all told, giving in return articles of such small value as beads, bells, and thimbles. Until they climbed back over the Continental Divide the following spring, back to the land of beaver tail and buffalo hump, they reduced the dog population of the Columbia River valley appreciably.

[3]

After felling five large ponderosa pines at Canoe Camp, the explorers became builders of boats again. By the first of the month, all of the men had recovered from their ailments sufficiently to be swinging axes, though many still complained of lassitude. "To save them from hard labour," Sergeant Gass wrote, "we have adopted the Indian method of burning out the canoes."[11] Heretofore, they had used altogether such implements as axe, adz, mallet, and chisel.

On the morning of October 7 with many Nez Perces looking on, the men dropped their brand new flotilla of small vessels onto the troubled surface of the swift-moving Clearwater. It consisted of one small boat and four larger ones, the former a pilot craft to be used primarily in examining the river ahead, locating rough water, and deciding on the proper channel to be taken. With these boats finally loaded, the men dipped their paddles once again and headed downstream. It would take them four days to reach the Snake River, some 60 miles away.

Before leaving Canoe Camp, Lewis and Clark had had their horses —38 of them—rounded up and branded. Twisted Hair had obligingly agreed to care for them until spring when, if all went as expected, they

[9] Coues, II, 615n.
[10] Gass, 175.
[11] Gass, 173.

would be needed for recrossing the Bitterroots. Also, the two captains had cached saddles and canisters of ammunition. The latter were buried in the dead of night "a short distance from the river at 2 feet 4 inches N. of a dead toped pine tree" (III, 98), thus keeping the place secret from the Indians. Tom Sawyer could not have done better.

If the explorers envisioned a rapid, carefree ride on the transparent bosom of the Clearwater, they were quickly disillusioned. This stream, at the bottom of a deep gorge with high hills pressing close on each side, was a series of unbridled, waspish rapids. Impelled by a sense of urgency, Lewis and Clark ran them all, not once delaying to portage. Their insistence on haste proved unwise. On the very first day one of the boats hit a rock and sprang a leak. On the next another split wide open and sank. Though they saved the boat and contents, the accident might have ended tragically since some of the men could not swim. Fortunately for them, the water here was only waist deep and the current of insufficient strength to sweep them off their feet. Lewis and Clark learned a valuable lesson from this experience. When they ran more formidable rapids farther downstream, they left this risky business to the men expert in breast and back strokes. This particular accident, which resulted in considerable delay, occurred just below the mouth of a stream falling in on the right. Lewis and Clark called it Colter Creek in honor of John Colter. Today it is Potlatch River, the principal tributary of the lower Clearwater.

During the excitement which attended the boat accident, old Toby and his son, who had faithfully guided the party over the Lolo Trail, quietly slipped away without a word to anyone. Some of the Nez Perces reported having seen them hurrying upstream. When Lewis and Clark proposed sending a man after them with their pay, Twisted Hair dissuaded them, saying that his own people in that event would surely rob them. Later it was determined that they had not departed altogether empty-handed; they had appropriated two of Lewis and Clark's horses.

On October 10 the Expedition arrived at the confluence of the Clearwater with the Snake River, called by the Indians, Kimooenim. Sergeant Gass said it was very large and "of a goslin-green color."[12] Clark, displaying geographic acumen, declared that it was the same stream they had camped on while with the Shoshoni which he had named Lewis's River.

Lewis and Clark stopped just below the junction of the Clearwater

[12] Gass, 176.

and Snake, near the present sites of Lewiston, Idaho and Clarkston, Washington. What was it like there in 1805? "No timber, barron & broken prairies on each side," declared Private Whitehouse (VII, 169).

The Snake proved to be a handsome stream except at the rapids. The party spent six days on it, each a battle to survive. They ran one seething rapid after another, their boats often carried by the currents swifter "than any horse could run" (VII, 171). At Pine Tree Rapids, on October 14, they lost bedding, copper kettles, and other articles when waves dashed over one of the dugouts stuck on a rock in midstream. This event caused Clark to assert, "We should make more portages if the season was not so advanced and time precious with us" (III, 111).

They passed many fishing camps, particularly at the rapids, though most had been abandoned with the salmon season now nearing an end. At one camp they stopped long enough to examine an underground sweat house of construction new to them. The Indians sometimes used these houses for treating diseases, attempting thereby to cure everything from the simplest ailments to more serious ones such as rheumatoid arthritis and syphilis.

Three days down the Snake, Lewis and Clark came to a northern affluent which they called Drewyer's River (in honor, of course, of George Drouillard). This is today the Palouse River, made celebrated by the spectacularly beautiful Palouse Falls, 185 feet high, situated just a few miles above the entrance of this stream. Apparently Lewis and Clark received no intelligence of this waterfall since they make no reference to it. Recently (1964), ethnologists of Washington State University, while excavating an Indian site at the junction of the Palouse with the Snake, discovered in a canoe burial a medal which may be one that Lewis and Clark presented to a native chief of this region more than 160 years ago. Though time has left its mark on this medal, the obverse shows plainly the head of Jefferson and the reverse a pair of clasped hands below a crossed peace pipe and tomahawk. (See Appendix C for the present location of other similar medals that have been discovered.)

The medals and other gifts bestowed by Lewis and Clark on Indians inhabiting banks of the Clearwater and Snake in no sense adequately compensated them for the aid they gave the explorers. They piloted them through perverse rapids, retrieved valuable property in the wake of boat accidents, and above everything else, provided them with practically every bite of food they had. During six days on the Snake, the hunters shot only a few birds. For example, on October 14 Clark wrote, "for the first time for three weeks past I had a good dinner of Blue wing Teal [*Querquedula discors*]" (III, 115). All other food—salmon, roots, and dogs—came from the Indians.

Excepting Clark, most of the men by now preferred dog meat to dried salmon. "All the party," Clark declared, "have greatly the advantage of me, in as much as they all relish the flesh of the dogs" (III, 105). Lewis, conversely, regarded it as an agreeable food and preferred it "vastly to lean Venison or Elk." He made the point, too, that while the party lived largely on dog meat, they were in good health, better than any other time since leaving buffalo country (III, 309).

By now the explorers had penetrated deep into the Interior Basin, the wide, barren, picturesque inter-mountain area between the Rockies and the Cascade Range. At Canoe Camp on the eastern fringe of the Basin Lewis and Clark found the narrow Clearwater valley and abrupt hillsides green with vegetation, including immense pines. The considerable plant life there had been due, of course, to adequate rainfall. Even before they reached the Snake, the pines and other trees had completely disappeared, and green as a dominant color had been replaced by an omnipresent tawny brown. The land on either side of the Snake, open, undulating, and destitute of any kind of timber, reminded the men of the High Plains of the Dakotas and Montana. "Not even a tree to be seen no place," Whitehouse observed (VII, 170). What little vegetation there was—hackberry (*Celtis* sp.) and willow (*Salix* sps.), for example—stuck close to the river's edge. The dominant plant of bluff and benchland was prickly pear; a new species discovered here (possibly *Opuntia polyacantha*) was even more thorny and troublesome than any they had yet encountered.

On October 16 the party left their camp on Rattlesnake Flats just above Fish-hook Rapids and in mid-afternoon arrived at the conjunction of the Snake with the Columbia. To attain this major objective, Lewis and Clark had devoted 17 long, wearisome months and had travelled, according to their estimate, 3,714 miles. They established a camp where today the state of Washington maintains Sacagawea Park. Resident Indians gave them a warm welcome. "A chief came . . . at the head of about 200 men," Clark wrote. "we gave them all Smoke, and Spoke to their chief as well as we could by signs informing them of our friendly disposition" (III, 120).

The majority of the Indians here were Wanapams, with a sprin-

kling of Yakimas (the Sokulks and Chimnapums of Lewis and Clark).
They belonged to the same linguistic family (Sahaptian) as the Nez
Perces, their languages, as Lewis quickly established by taking vocabularies, having much in common. The Wanapams, including their chief,
Cutsahnem, were friendly and orderly. The appearance and dress of
the men differed but little from that of the Clearwater natives. The
women, on the contrary, were more inclined to corpulency than any
they had yet encountered, and they flattened their heads, with the
foreheads "compressed so as to form a streight line from the nose to the
Crown of the head" (III, 125–126).

Here we find the first definite mention in any of the logs of
flattened crania. As Lewis and Clark approached the Pacific, they
observed a gradual increase in this aboriginal attempt at beautifica-
tion.

The explorers noted a surprisingly high incidence of eye troubles
among these people. "the loss of sight," Clark wrote, "I have observed
to be more common among all the nations inhabiting this river than
among any people I have ever observed. they have almost invariably
sore eyes at all stages of life. the loss of an eye is very common among
them; blindness in persons of middle age is by no means uncommon,
and it is almost invariably a concamitant of old age. I know not to
what cause to attribute this prevalent deficiency of the eye except it be
their exposure to the reflection of the sun on the water to which they
are constantly exposed in the occupation of fishing" (IV, 257–258).

Nothing quite so innocent as reflection of sun from water caused
these eye disorders. They were probably due to trachoma and venereal
disease, both maladies, it is now known, being common then among
these Indians in all stages of development and in all age groups.
Trachoma, a highly contagious form of conjunctivitis characterized by
granulations on the conjunctival surfaces, may lead to partial or complete blindness. So may gonorrheal conjunctivitis (ophthalmia neona-
torum), a well-known consequence of maternal infection at birth prevented today in civilized societies by drops of silver nitrate in the eyes
of the new-born. The organism causing this disease may invade the
blood stream from local lesions and be carried to distant parts of the
body where it can excite a variety of extragenital lesions. A special
predilection is shown for the synovial membranes of the joints where it
causes the so-called gonorrheal rheumatism. It is possible that some of
the Indians who later came to Lewis and Clark complaining of pains in
their joints suffered from this disorder. Both trachoma and gonorrhea

today yield almost completely to sulfanilamide and antibiotic therapy.

Clark noted, too, that the teeth of the Wanapam and Yakima were generally bad, with many worn down to the gum, especially in the upper jaw. This was so, he declared, in all the tribes he had visited who subsisted largely on fish and roots. He thought this decrescence might be due to the habit of these natives of eating their roots without first washing them, when they were covered with sand,[13] and to their chewing dried salmon which, as the native prepared it, was a mixture of flesh, rind, scale, bone, and grit. In this surmise he seems to have been right. The teeth of Columbia River Indians, one ethnologist has written, "are frequently worn down to the gums with eating sanded salmon."[14] By comparison, teeth of Missouri Indians, Maximilian declared were "particularly fine, strong, firm, even and as white as ivory."[15]

As we know, Lewis and Clark first encountered salmon on the Lemhi River. There, and more recently on the Clearwater and Snake, they had watched Indian men gigging these fish, had studied the structure of fish weirs, and had everywhere observed evidences of the salmon economy. At no time or place while on the above-mentioned streams, however, did they find salmon so obviously abundant as here in the Columbia. The river was spectacularly replete with them. Sergeant Ordway reported that live fish were in all places "jumping very thick."[16] Clark emphasized that the river was "crouded with salmon" (III, 122) and that the water was so clear he could see them to depths of 15 to 20 feet. Great numbers, he explained, were dead, floating on the surface and creating silvery windrows on the banks. Raven and crow banqueted on the putrescent bodies. In front of every lodge were large scaffolds of drying fish, and on the ground nearby were huge stacks of freshly caught ones which the squaws were preparing for the scaffolds.

Invited into one of the lodges, Clark watched the Indians prepare a salmon for the table. "I was furnished with a mat to set on," he wrote, "and one man set about prepareing me something to eat, first he brought in a piece of Drift log of pine and with a wedge of the elks

---

[13] About this point, Ralph Space informs me: "I believe the Indians cleaned the roots, but the process of pulverizing them with stone mortar and pestle always produced a certain amount of grit in their bread."

[14] Hubert H. Bancroft, *Native Races of the Pacific States of North America,* 5 vols. (New York, 1875–76) , I, 158.

[15] *Early Western Travels,* XXIII, 256.

[16] Ordway, 300.

horn, and a malet of stone curiously carved he Split the log into Small pieces and lay'd it open on the fire on which he put round Stones, a woman handed him a basket of water and a large Salmon about half dried, when the Stones were hot he put them into the basket of water with the fish which was soon sufficiently boiled for use   it was then taken out put on a platter of rushes neatly made, and set before me . . . after eateing the boiled fish which was delicious, I set out" (III, 124–125) .

From the scientist's viewpoint, this description is important both ethnobotanically and ethnozoologically and is a prime example of how much significant information may be crowded into a short paragraph.

"The number of dead Salmon on the Shores & floating in the river is incrediable to say," Clark asserted (III, 124) . Being totally unfamilar with the life history of this important fish, he was thoroughly puzzled by its high mortality and attempted no explanation. Today almost every school child knows that the salmon leaves the ocean and ascends coastal streams to the upper, quieter waters where eggs are laid and fertilized, after which members of both sexes customarily die. The mass migration from the sea, from saltwater to fresh, impelled by a tremendous inherent biological urge, begins most often in early spring and continues until autumn. In their upward progress the salmon conquers seemingly insurmountable barriers, being stopped only by towering waterfalls (or, as is the case today, by huge dams) . When Lewis and Clark failed to find salmon in the Bitterroot River, they reasoned correctly that a formidable barrier (Kettle Falls, for one) existed farther downstream which the salmon could not hurdle.

The explorers had reached the Columbia at a time coinciding with the final seasonal climacteric of this great anadramous fish (probably mostly king salmon, *Oncorhynchus tshawytscha*) . They had never witnessed such a piscatorial spectacle before and would never again. In fact, deplorably, no one will. Salmon runs of such magnitude no longer exist, have not for all too many years. It is an easy matter when reading the journals of Lewis and Clark to become imbued with an acute yearning for the sights and sounds of yesteryear.

SUMMARY OF DISCOVERIES

Animals New to Science
None.

Plants New to Science
OREGON WHITE-TOPPED ASTER. *Aster oregonus* Nuttall. Described, 1840.

? Netleaf hackberry. *Celtis reticulata* Torrey. (Thwaites, III, 111; Coues, II, 629) . 1828.

Many-spined opuntia. *Opuntia polyacantha* Haworth. (Thwaites, III, 120) . 1818.

? Peach-leaved willow. *Salix amygdaloides* Anderss. (Thwaites, III, 111) . 1858.

? Slender willow. *Salix exigua* Nuttall. (Thwaites, III, 111) . 1843.

Lewis and Clark Herbarium

Oregon white-topped aster. *Aster oregonus* Nuttall. Collected Oct. [?], 1805.

? Beggar-tick. *Bidens* sp. October 3.

Ponderosa pine. *Pinus ponderosa* Douglas. October 1.

Indian Tribes Encountered

Sahaptian Linguistic Family: † Wanapams ("Sokulks" of Lewis and Clark) ; † Yakimas ("Chimnapums" of Lewis and Clark) .

Topographic Features Named and/or Discovered

† Colter's Creek (Coues, II, 616n) —— Potlatch River.

† Lewis's River (Thwaites, III, 103) —— Snake River.

† Kimooenim Creek (Thwaites, III, 112) —— Tucannon River (Coues, II, 629) .

† Drewyer's River (Thwaites, III, 112) —— Palouse River.

Snake River
to
the Ocean

CHAPTER FIFTEEN

Lewis and Clark halted here—where the Snake loses itself in the Columbia—for a day and a half. Recognizing the importance of this geographic location, they established latitude and longitude and measured the width of each stream. Clark explored the Columbia north as far as the entrance of the Yakima River and through talks with Chief Cutsahnem, supplemented knowledge already obtained about the Columbia farther downstream. To insure ample food for days immediately ahead, they bought 40 dogs, and the hunters increased this amount when they succeeded in shooting several sage grouse, these largest of American grouse being common here. Lewis and Clark refused to buy salmon offered them by the Indians, suspecting that they had been "taken up on the shore dead" (III, 128).

The distance from the Snake to the Great Falls of the Columbia (Celilo Falls) was, according to Clark's yardstick, 151 miles, almost half the remaining distance to the Pacific. It took the party five days to reach this objective, each being one of prime discovery and novel episode. In this time they discovered and passed a number of important affluents, all entering from the south: the Walla Walla, John Day (Le Page's River of Lewis and Clark), and just above Celilo Falls, the Deschutes. They ran numerous rapids—Homly, Musselshell, Squally Hook, and Hellgate among the most rampant and wicked.

"About 2 oClock P.M. we Set out," wrote Private Whitehouse on October 18. "only two chiefs with us who come with us from the flat heads [viz., Nez Perces]. we proceeded on down the Columbia river, which is now verry wide from a half mile to three fourths wide and verry Smooth & pleasant . . . passd. Several Islands on which was large camps of Indians and Scaffels of abundance of Sammon" (VII, 175).

The two chiefs referred to were Twisted Hair and Tetoharsky. As the party encountered other Indians, these two proved valuable in establishing and maintaining friendly relations and, at rapids, in ferreting out the safest channels.

In late afternoon they passed the mouth of a small stream mentioned only as a "Small riverlet" (III, 131). On the return journey they identified it as the Walla Walla. Just beyond this entrance the Columbia swings hard to the west and enters the first of a series of deep gorges between this point and the western slopes of the Cascade Range. From an eminence at the top of this gorge, Clark saw a conspicuous cone-shaped mountain to the southwest. He had spotted Mt. Hood, 11,225 feet high, first sighted 13 years earlier by Lt. William Broughton of Capt. George Vancouver's Expedition and named by him for the English admiral, Samuel Hood. Well over 100 miles away, it loomed higher as the explorers neared it. Unaware until later that this was Mt. Hood, Lewis and Clark for a time called it Timm or Falls Mountain.

The party camped that night about four miles below the Walla Walla where they were visited by a group of Walula (Walla Walla) Indians headed by their chief, Yellept, a man of some local importance. Clark described him as "a bold handsom Indian, with a dignified countenance about 35 years of age" (III, 134). Chief Yellept, perhaps because he was cordially received, proved to be an important friend to Lewis and Clark when they returned the following spring. By taking a vocabulary, Lewis determined that the Walulas spoke a tongue similar to that of the Nez Perces.

That same evening Clark wrote, "We were compelled to use dri[e]d willows for fuel for the purpose of cooking" (III, 132). By now well into the heart of the Interior Basin, into its most arid and inhospitable part, Lewis and Clark found wood increasingly difficult to obtain. Of necessity, they chose camp sites strictly on the availability of fuel. Two days later Gass reported, "We could not get one single stick of wood to cook with; and had only a few small green willows."[1] And the next evening, in order to prepare a hot meal, they were "obliged to purchase wood at a high rate" (III, 142). So it had come to that—fuel was unobtainable except from the natives. That the latter demanded a high price for it is understandable, for in different villages, as Lewis

[1] Gass, 183.

and Clark observed, they were actually "drying fish & Prickley pares (to Burn in winter) " (III, 133) . With these Indians, enforced reliance on such fuel would appear to have been a measure born of desperation, pointing up the age-old struggle to exist in a barren, impoverished land.

As the Corps neared Celilo Falls, they were encouraged to believe that they might soon escape from this uninviting, treeless region. Pines began to dot higher elevations, shrubbery increased in the "hollers," and in the villages acorns and filberts appeared as items of barter. The acorns came from the Oregon white oak (*Quercus garryana*) , the only valuable timber oak of the Pacific Northwest, and the filberts from the California hazelnut (*Corylus californica*) . The Indians here, Clark reported, ate the acorns "raw & roasted and inform us they precure them of the natives who live near the falls" (III, 143) .

Nearing Celilo Falls, the explorers stopped for the night near a village of five lodges. Clark wrote that all the Indians here had pierced noses, and that the men when dressed wore "a long taper'd piece of Shell or bead put through the nose" (III, 144) . This shell, used commonly by Indians of the Northwest for nasal garnish, was a marine mollusc belonging to the genus *Dentalium,* at least one species of which inhabits the Pacific coast above and below the mouth of the Columbia. The shape resembles an elephant tusk in miniature, and for that reason it is commonly called tooth or elephant shell. Clark mentioned the length as about two inches (III, 187) .

At that particular time in history these *Dentalium* shells were much in demand by the natives, even those east of the Rockies. We have Maximilian's word for it that the Mandans would trade a horse for a handful of *Dentalium* shells.[2] Though employed for decoration, they also served as a means of exchange. Rev. Samuel Parker, an early missionary to the Northwest, wrote that he had seen Indians with two *Dentalium* shells extending through the slits in their nasal septums.[3] Whether one or two the effect, in the opinion of another witness, was to render the Indian "more hideous than the compression of his skull."[4]

On October 22, after passing the mouth of the Deschutes River, Lewis and Clark arrived at Celilo Falls. Here they encountered a great number of Indians from whom they obtained filberts, berries, a dog, some fish, and enough wood to cook their next meal. These natives were Sahaptian, though they belonged to a different tribe from those

[2] *Early Western Travels,* XXIII, 289.

[3] Rev. Samuel Parker, *Journal of an Exploring Tour Beyond the Rocky Mountains* (Ithaca, N.Y., 1840) , 140–141.

[4] Bancroft, *Native Races,* I, 228–229.

immediately upstream. Lewis and Clark called them Eneeshurs. Today they are regarded as a division of Wayampam.[5]

In Lewis and Clark's day and for many years afterward, Celilo Falls and the Narrows immediately below were most important sites to the Indians. Here was the primary mart of the Columbia, the center of the salmon economy. At the height of the season, natives converged on this location from all points of the compass. At such time the largest of the villages, of which there were several along this stretch of the river, reputedly was occupied by as many as 3,000 inhabitants. It seems to have been located at the head of the Long Narrows and may well have been the one Washington Irving made much of and identified as Wishram.

"Hither," wrote Irving, "the tribes from the mouth of the Columbia repaired with the fish of the sea-coast, the roots, berries, and especially the wappatoo, gathered in the lower parts of the river, together with goods and trinkets obtained from the ships which casually visit the coast. Hither also the tribes from the Rocky Mountains brought down horses, bear-grass, quamash, and other commodities of the interior. The merchant fishermen at the falls acted as middlemen or factors, and passed the objects of traffic, as it were, cross-handed."[6]

By the time Lewis and Clark reached the falls, the great majority of transient tribesmen had left for their homes. Neither then nor the next spring did they witness this thriving emporium at its most animated, boisterous peak. In the many baskets filled with pounded fish on the shore, however, they saw abundant evidence of the intense, sustained industry that had been in progress since early spring when the salmon began to run.

Clark described the baskets as about two feet long and one foot wide, each made of grass and rushes and lined with dried salmon skins. They had been filled with dried salmon previously pulverized between stones. When full, they were covered with fish skins, these being tied on by cords run through holes in the baskets. Each contained from 90 to 100 pounds of salmon which, if kept dry, would remain sound and sweet for several years. The custom of the Indians here was to make stacks of 12 baskets, with seven on the bottom and five on top. In passing the Short Narrows alone, Clark counted 107 baskets which, he estimated, contained close to 10,000 pounds of dried salmon.

[5] Letter to author, Oct. 16, 1963, from Verne F. Ray, Department of Anthropology, University of Washington.

[6] Washington Irving, *Astoria, or Anecdotes of an Enterprise Beyond the Rocky Mountains* (New York, 1849), 81–82.

Some of the Indians here were engaged in burying salmon for winter consumption. They dug holes of various sizes and, after lining them with fish skins, filled them with as many baskets as they would hold. Afterwards, they covered these underground pits with fish skins and a layer of earth 12 to 15 inches thick.

Lewis and Clark conjectured as to how the salmon, so abundant upstream, had been able to hurdle Celilo Falls which at that time was about 20 feet high. After they had inspected the Narrows below, they were satisfied that these fish did not necessarily have to make such prodigious leaps. At times of flood the water, unable to escape rapidly through the constricted channel of the Narrows, was forced to back up, with the result that the falls was practically obliterated. This explanation, satisfactory as far as it went, left unanswered the question as to how high salmon can leap. One of the Astorians, while descending the Snake River, claimed to have witnessed a leap of about 30 feet, "from the commencement of the foam at the foot of the fall, completely to the top."[7] When I put the question to a long-time resident of the West as to whether salmon could have hurdled the 20-foot high Celilo Falls of Lewis and Clark, he replied: "I believe 20 feet is too high. My only experience is at Selway Falls, which is 12 feet. I have seen salmon jump this falls, but it was such a block to salmon runs that the State of Idaho built a fish passage around it. From this I have come to believe that 15 feet is about the limit of a salmon's jumping ability."[8]

Convinced that the north side of the river afforded the better prospect for portaging, Lewis and Clark unloaded the boats and carried their goods to a site 1,200 yards farther downstream. The Indians helped by providing horses for transporting heavier articles. The next morning the men took the empty dugouts to the opposite side of the Columbia where they were carried around the falls and then eased into the water again. After travelling through smooth water for about one mile, they came to another pitch, one of about eight feet, down which they successfullly lowered the boats by means of elk-skin ropes. These operations consumed most of the day. According to Sergeant Gass, the appearance of this place was "terrifying, with vast rocks, and the river below the pitch, foaming through different channels."[9]

The resumption of the journey on October 24 Clark described in part as follows: "I Set out with the party and proceeded on down a

[7] Irving, *Astoria,* 276.
[8] Letter to author, May 8, 1966, from Ralph Space.
[9] Gass, 186.

rapid Stream of about 400 yards at 2½ miles the river widened into a large bason to the Stard. . . . here a tremendious rock Presented itself high and steep appearing to choke up the river . . . at this place the water of this great river is compressed into a chanel between two rocks not exceeding *forty five* yards wide and continues for a ¼ of a mile when it again widens to 200 yards wide and continues this width for about 2 miles when it is again interrupted by rocks" (III, 153).

The Expedition had arrived at the Short Narrows. Since they regarded portage here next to impossible, they elected to attempt running the canoes through the constricted channel, "notwithstanding the horrid appearance of this agitated gut swelling, boiling & whirling in every direction" (III, 154). Much to the surprise of the Indians, who had collected on the top of rocks to watch the operation, the boatmen took the dugouts through without a hitch.

Below the Short Narrows, the river widened and ran a comparatively tranquil course for a mile or more. The boats negotiated this distance without problem, and then were halted by an extremely difficult rapid where the captains issued an order to unload all of the most valuable articles and to carry them by land. The boatmen then took the canoes down, two at a time, shipping some water, but coming through unscathed otherwise. The party encamped that night at the head of the Long Narrows, the probable location of Irving's Wishram.

Lewis and Clark took a close look the next morning at what lay ahead and decided to portage their most precious possessions, as they had the day before, and attempt once again running the boats. This they did, after which the men reloaded the canoes and completed without accident the remainder of this hazardous descent through the Long Narrows.

At the conclusion of this operation, Lewis and Clark had a parting smoke with their two Nez Perce friends who now, having bought two horses, began the long ride back to their mat lodges on the Clearwater. That evening the party established their camp (Rock Fort Camp) at the mouth of Mill Creek, a small stream entering from the south, and made plans to halt here long enough to repair boats, dry goods, and allow the men a deserved interval of rest.

This site of fluvial turbulence comprising the Short and Long Narrows is called The Dalles. In the words of Olin D. Wheeler:

The region is a volcanic one, and from the monster chimneys of a subterranean furnace vast floods of lava have poured forth in all directions. The Columbia, for miles, has forced its way through these lava beds, and its escarpments and walls are lava cliffs of magnificent proportions, at places 2000 or 3000 feet high, forming scenery of the superlative sort. . . . Of all the reaches of the Columbia none is, or ever will be, more observed than that between the Great Falls and the lower extremity of the Dalles, or, as modern names go, from Celilo to Dalles City. It is a most interesting bit of scenery and historically has played an important part in the narrative of every adventurer or explorer who ever ascended or descended the river.[10]

Wheeler was a most fortunate man. He saw this imposing, unbridled stretch of the Columbia before engineers built a mighty barrier across it called the Dalles Dam. The beauty of Celilo Falls and the Narrows will be seen no more. With the completion of the dam in 1915, the impounded water covered them completely. The visitor to this region today must form his impressions of its pristine ferment and comeliness from the accounts of Lewis and Clark and those of other pioneering travellers who followed in their wake.

On October 23, just below Celilo Falls, Clark wrote: "Great numbers of *Sea Otters* in the river below the falls, I shot one in the narrow chanel to day which I could not get" (III, 150). On the following day Sergeant Gass reported: "In our way down today we saw a great many sea otters swimming in the river, and killed some, but could not get them as they sunk to the bottom."[11] Still later Clark said that in places the river was crowded with these aquatic mammals. For reasons not at all clear, students of Lewis and Clark have accepted Clark's original identification as true, completely disregarding, or unaware of, the fact that the sea otter (*Enhydra lutris*) never leaves salt water. Among these students have been men with sound zoological backgrounds, like Elliott Coues, for example, who ordinarily had no hesitation in pointing out errors in the Lewis and Clark journals when he found any. That this mistake evaded detection for so long is all the more surprising since Clark himself later corrected it. Writing at Fort Clatsop on February 23, he said: "The Sea Otter is found only on the sea coast and in salt water. Those animals which I took to be the sea otter from the Great Falls of the Columbia to the mouth, proves to be the Phosis or Seal which at a little distance has every appearance of the sea otters" (IV, 100).

The seal which had "every appearance of the sea otter" was the harbor or hair seal (*Phoca vitulina richardii*), a circumpolar species that not only invades harbors on the west coast but also ascends the

[10] Wheeler, *The Trail of Lewis and Clark*, II, 146.
[11] Gass, 186.

lower courses of rivers of that region. Lewis subsequently stated that it was found in great numbers on the coast and "as far up the Columbia river as the great falls, above which there are none" (IV, 99) .[12]

At The Dalles the journalists first referred to a fish they called "salmon trout." Lewis described it as of "a silvery white colour on the belly and sides, and a bluish light brown on the back and head . . . seldom more than two feet in length . . . narrow in proportion to their length . . . the fins are placed much like those of the salmon" (IV, 168). This fish was probably the celebrated steelhead trout (*Salmo gairdneri*) .[13]

The Dalles, it is important to understand, served as a dividing line between Northwest Coast and Plateau Indians, more particularly between the two great linguistic families, Sahaptian and Chinookan. "Those [Indians] at the *great falls* call themselves *E-nee-shur*," Clark asserted, "and are understood on the river above; Those at the Great Narrows call themselves *E-che-lute* and is understood below . . . not withstanding those people [i.e., Eneeshur and Echelute] live only 6 miles apart, [they understand] but fiew words of each others language" (III, 164) .

"This statement," Coues wrote, "well illustrates the great attention paid by Lewis and Clark to ethnology, and the discernment they showed in discriminating similar appearing Indians who were nevertheless of distinct linguistic stocks, at a time when modern scientific classification had no existence."[14]

As Lewis and Clark would discover in ensuing months, the Chinookan family included a confusion of tribes, many with names taxing their ability to spell and pronounce. They encountered first the Echelutes (or Wishram, the accepted form in present classifications), then many others such as Chilluckittequaws, Cathlapotle, Wahkiakums, Cathlamets, Clatsops, and Chinooks. In "Estimate of Western Indians," Lewis and Clark gave their number at 16,000 or more. Chinookans differed from Sahaptians in a number of significant respects. In addition to speaking a dissimilar tongue, they lived in wooden instead of mat houses, universally flattened their heads, and travelled about in

[12] C. O. Handley, Jr., Curator in charge of the Division of Mammals, Smithsonian Institution, has written me (Mar. 27, 1967) : "The animal that Lewis and Clark saw at The Dalles . . . and finally identified as a seal was undoubtedly *Phoca vitulina richardii*."

[13] Burroughs, *Natural History of the Lewis and Clark Expedition*, 263.

[14] Coues, II, 672.

beautifully constructed dugout canoes. None of them owned horses except a few at or near The Dalles.

Lewis and Clark reported a multitude of Indians inhabiting the banks of the Missouri, Clearwater, Snake, and Columbia Rivers. They thus unwittingly gave further credence to the belief, already established, that the United States supported a much larger Indian population than it actually did, and that the Pacific Northwest held a greater density than any other region. The mistake had its inception when the early explorers of this country found natives numerous along watercourses and concluded that the aboriginal population was equally heavy on plains between rivers and in forests back from lake fronts. The Indian population, of course, at all times was extremely thin. A Smithsonian scientist recently reported: "A careful study of the whole territory north of Mexico . . . indicates a total population at the time of the coming of the white men, of nearly 1,150,000, which is believed to be within ten per cent of the actual number. Of this total 846,000 were within the limits of the United States proper."[15] Because of recent increases, the Indian population of the United States today is about the same as in 1492.

Lewis and Clark quit their camp at the mouth of Mill Creek on October 28. Though they had no way of knowing it, they were still about 100 miles from the entrance of the Willamette River and 200 from the ocean. Four miles downstream they stopped at a village of eight houses occupied by natives of another Chinookan tribe. Clark rendered the name Chilluckittequaw. By taking a vocabulary, Lewis concluded that they spoke the same language as the Echelutes, though with a slight dialectic variation. Clark entered one of the houses where he watched a squaw boiling salmon in a basket. These Indians, like others along the Columbia, excelled in making baskets of bear grass and cedar bark fibers so closely interwoven that they would hold water without benefit of gum or rosin to seal interstices. Bear grass (*Xerophyllum tenax*) grows at higher elevations and is abundant along the Lolo Trail among other places. Each plant consists of a dense basal tuft of harsh slender leaves a foot or more in length. It was these leaves that the Indians used in making their baskets. Soon after snows melt, the plant sends up a magnificent flower head, a creamy-white plume, which is visible from afar, particularly when an open mountain slope is covered with them. One of the most beautiful sights I have ever seen

---

[15] Rose A. Palmer, *The North American Indians*, Smithsonian Scientific Series, No. IV (New York, 1929), 7.

was such a slope near the summit of Logan Pass in Glacier National Park. Purportedly bears have a liking for the roots of this attractive plant, hence the name bear grass.[16]

Because of a high wind, Lewis and Clark stopped with the Chilluckittequaws longer than contemplated. The delay provided their first opportunity to observe Chinookan canoes in action and the Indian's consummate skill in operating them under adverse conditions. The strong wind, Clark declared, did not "retard the motions of these people at all, as their canoes are calculated to ride the highest waves" (III, 166).

On the next day Clark wrote of mountains rising high on both sides of the river and pine and oak more in evidence than heretofore. The party had reached the eastern flanks of the Cascade Range. Soon they passed three important tributaries of the Columbia hitherto unseen by white men. They called them Cataract River, Labiche's River, and Canoe Creek. On maps of today they appear as Klickitat, Hood, and White Salmon Rivers.

Passing Wind River (Cruzatte's of Lewis and Clark), the explorers on October 30 arrived at the Cascades of the Columbia, a series of wild, impetuous rapids, the first and most dangerous of which Clark called "the great Shute" (III, 174). From the beginning to the end of these rapids, a distance of several tortuous miles, the river dropped at least 60 feet. It took the party the better part of three days to reach the calm waters below the Cascades, days devoted almost entirely to portaging and carefully lowering unloaded boats through rock-studded spume. The beauty and turbulence of the Cascades will be seen no more. Imprisoned water behind Bonneville Dam, completed in 1940, covered them entirely.

I find it odd that Lewis and Clark, while fully dedicated to denominating rivers, rapids, and islands, rarely gave thought to names for more prominent topographic features such as waterfalls, mountain ranges, and mountain passes. A particular case in point is the massive, elevated barrier here through which the Columbia has torn a gigantic gash in its rush to the sea. The closest Lewis and Clark appear to have come in naming it was an offhand reference the following spring to "the Western mountains" where they had found game scarce as they descended the river (IV, 225).

Whether the name "Cascade" for these mountains originated from

---

[16] Ralph Space informs me that he has heard the story of bears eating the roots of bear grass, but in all his years in the woods he has seen no evidence of it.

the circumstance that such rivers as the Columbia issue from the mountains in a series of cascades, or from the fact that numerous finespun waterfalls pitch from the steep sides of the gorge created by the Columbia, is indeterminable. A better case can, perhaps, be made for the latter claim, since many waterfalls do cascade in misty plumes and broken curtains down the precipitous slopes on either side of the river here. As Lewis and Clark wrote: "Down these heights frequently descend the most beautiful cascades, one of which, a large creek, throws itself over a perpendicular rock 300 feet above the water, while other smaller streams precipitate themselves from a still greater elevation."[17]

The other journalists commented similarly on the considerable number, height, and beauty of these waterfalls, many of which have long since been given names. Among the more spectacular which the traveller through the Columbia gorge may today identify and enjoy are: Horsetail, 221 feet; Latourell, 249; Wahkeena, some 400; and Multnomah, the most celebrated, 620.

The Cascade Mountains form a great climatic barrier. East of this elevated range is the timberless, nearly arid country through which the Corps had just passed. The atmosphere, having lost most of its moisture to the western slopes of the Cascades, provides a minimum of rainfall. Extremes of heat and cold are experienced, depending on latitude and season. To the west of the Cascades is a strip of land some 150 miles wide where meteorological and topographic features differ radically. Due to warm ocean currents, excessive cold is unknown. Rainfall is abundant. Noble forests clothe valleys and mountain sides, thus affording sustenance and protection to a profusion of wild creatures. The rivers run full of many kinds of fish.

As the explorers passed from the east to the west of the Cascades, it was like entering another world. The transition from the dry, sterile plains to the green, wooded coastal terrain was, the journalists wrote, "as grateful to the eye as it is useful in supplying us with fuel."[18]

Immediately below the last of the rapids, Lewis and Clark found the river flowing unruffled and with "everry appearance of being effected by the tide" (III, 180). Though the boats did now ride on tidewater, the party was still more than 100 miles from the Pacific. Just below the Cascades, too, they had their first sight of one of the most conspicuous and celebrated landmarks of the Columbia River valley. Clark described it as a perpendicular rock about 800 feet high and 400

[17] Coues, III, 937.
[18] Coues, II, 688.

yards in circumference. It is today Beacon Rock. When the party ascended the river in the spring, they spoke of this "silent sentinel" being visible at a distance of 20 miles.

With the river flowing smooth again, the explorers made better time. On November 3, they came to a sizable stream entering from the south. Because it discharged great quantities of sand, it reminded them of the Platte. Clark, in trying to wade it, found its shallow bottom a quicksand and forthwith called it Quick Sand River. It is the Sandy of today. In appraising the region here, Lewis and Clark thought it might be "a good wintering Place" (III, 191), and as we shall see, they later did seriously consider locating here for the winter instead of on the coast.

On the following day, they arrived at a village of Skilloot Indians, still another Chinookan tribe. It was these Indians who apparently introduced Lewis and Clark to another edible, highly nutritious root; at least they first identify it here. "This root," Clark wrote, "they call *Wap-pa-to* which the Chinese cultivate in great quantities called the *Sa-git-ti-folia* or common arrow head, *(we believe it to be the Same)* it has an agreeable taste and answers very well in place of bread. we purchased about 4 bushels of this root and divided it to our party" (III, 196–197).

Thus we find Clark reporting on the presence of broad-leaved arrowhead (*Sagittaria latifolia*) in the Northwest and supplying both vernacular and generic names—no doubt with an assist from Lewis. The white starchy tubers of this plant contributed as importantly to the welfare of coastal Indians as did camas bulbs to natives of the Interior Basin. Also, they helped feed the Lewis and Clark party in weeks ahead.

Just below the Skilloot village, the boats of the party followed a channel to the north of a large island. They first called it Image Canoe Island, then Wappato, though today it is Sauvies. Because it interposed its considerable length between them and the mouth of the Willamette River, they did not discover that important Columbian tributary until the following spring.

From November 5 to 8 the Corps moved rapidly toward the ocean, averaging about 30 miles a day. Only Lt. Broughton and his crew had previously seen this beautiful valley between the Cascade and Coast Range. At that time and place, as one prominent historian has said, "nature's wild magnificence was still fresh; primeval forests unpro-faned; lakes and rivers and rolling plains unswept; it was when countless villages dotted the luxuriant valley; when from the warrior's camp-fire the curling smoke never ceased to ascend."[19]

What a variety of plant communities the explorers had passed through and become familiar with since leaving Camp Dubois on the Mississippi! In the beginning they had been enveloped by a great deciduous forest composed of lofty oak, maple, ash, walnut, hickory, and sycamore. In due time they came to the High Plains, empty of all trees except for clumps of cottonwood and willow along the river courses. As they began their transit of the Rockies, they entered a green coniferous world of spruce, fir, pine, and cedar, persisting until they dropped down into the arid, treeless country of the Interior Basin. Now, finally, they had entered another green world, the most important coniferous forest in our land. Here, mighty trees, far larger than any of them had ever seen before in their lives, surrounded them on all sides: Douglas fir, Sitka spruce, mountain hemlock, western red cedar, and many others. The grandest of all, the sequoias, grew farther south, of course, so that Lewis and Clark unfortunately missed seeing them. Only a few hardwoods grew in this coastal forest penetrated by Lewis and Clark, among them the vine maple (*Acer circinatum*), broad-leaved maple (*Acer macrophyllum*), and black cottonwood (*Populus trichocarpa*). Lewis collected specimens of each and brought them back with him to Philadelphia where they may be seen today. Not one of them had at that date been technically described and named.

At this particular stage of the journey, waterfowl impressed the explorers more than trees. Again and again they speak of tremendous numbers of ducks, geese, brant, cranes, gulls, swans, cormorants, and other aquatic birds. One pinpoint of land in the Columbia quickly became Brant Island, and another Island of Fowls. Emphasizing even more the abundance of waterfowl here was Clark's comment of November 5: "I could not sleep for the noise kept [up] by the Swans, White & black brants Duck &c. . . . they were emencly numerous and their cries horrid" (III, 199).

The journalists presently reported a line of hills directly in front of them running in a northwest-southeast direction. They had caught their first glimpse of the Coast Range. As with the Cascades, they made no attempt to name this mountain range. Shortly they passed Mt. Coffin (an Indian burial place), Pillar Rock, and the mouth of the Cowlitz River. A few miles above the Cowlitz, they had missed a stream entering from the north, today's Lewis's River. Below these tributaries,

[19] Bancroft, *Native Races,* I, 154–155.

they came to a village occupied by Cathlapotle Indians and then to another by Wahkiakums. On November 7 Clark uttered those words familiar to all Lewis and Clark *aficionados:* "Ocean in view! O! the joy" (III, 207n). But Clark was still 25 to 30 miles from the Pacific, at a point where the great width of the river had caused him to make this mistake.

On the following day, after rounding a promontory, the party came to Gray's Bay, a conspicuous indentation on the north side of the Columbia estuary (Lewis and Clark called it Shallow Nitch Bay). Because of high winds and waves, they were forced to hug the shoreline for several miles and, finally, as the swells mounted, "to form an encampment on a Point scercely room sufficent for us all to lie cleare of the tide water" (III, 211). The location was almost opposite the present city of Astoria, Oregon, and just above Ellice's Point (Blustery Point of Gass).

An occasional self-styled expert maintains that well-planned expeditions preclude mishaps, that each reverse or catastrophe results from inadequate foresight. The thesis has much to recommend it, but it would have taken a mind of unparalleled omniscience to anticipate and prevent what happened to the Lewis and Clark party during the next seven days (November 9 to 15); it was a week of dispiriting misery and intolerable frustration when, pinned down to a slender selvedge of shoreline because of incessant rain and high wind, they were helpless to advance or retreat. Throughout this period, they were as wet as water could make them, with nothing to drink except rain water and little to eat except pounded salmon. Their canoes and even their lives were endangered by huge tree trunks, some as much as 200 feet long and four to seven feet in diameter, tossed by the waves against the shoreline.

On the fifth day (November 13), Colter, Willard, and Shannon struck out in a canoe and succeeded in rounding the point. Colter returned the next day and reported a good sandy beach on the opposite side of the point that would make an excellent campsite. Later that same day, Lewis, with Drouillard, Frazer, and the two Field brothers, also rounded Ellice's Point. Lewis was eager to proceed on foot from Colter's sandy beach to the coast to determine if a bay existed near the mouth of the river "as laid down by Vancouver" and if, by chance, some merchantman might even then be lying at anchor. But it was not until the afternoon of the following day (November 15) that the bulk of the party escaped from that "dismal nitich" where they had been held immobile for seven days of sustained misery. Fortunately the

Engraving of Lewis by William Strickland, done in 1816 from an original drawing by Charles de Saint-Mémin. Lewis is dressed in a "tippet" presented to him by the Shoshoni chief, Cameahwait.

The discoveries by Lewis and Clark of the Carolina parroquet (above) and the passenger pigeon west of the Mississippi represented extensions of ranges for these two species.

Bird skin of Lewis's woodpecker, probably sent to Peale's Museum by Lewis and Clark.

America Herb: Lewis & Clark

Ex Herb Pursh

Buffalo-berry, collected at the mouth of Niobrara River in the fall of 1804. Arrow shows where a part of the plant was removed, presumably by Frederick Pursh.

Bearberry, collected by Lewis at Fort Mandan.

Bitterroot (*Lewisia rediviva*). Specimens of this plant in the Lewis and Clark Herbarium were collected by Lewis on July 1, 1806, at the mouth of Lolo Creek (Traveller's Rest), Montana.

Sketch of the eulachon, done by Clark in his journal entry for Feb. 25, 1806.

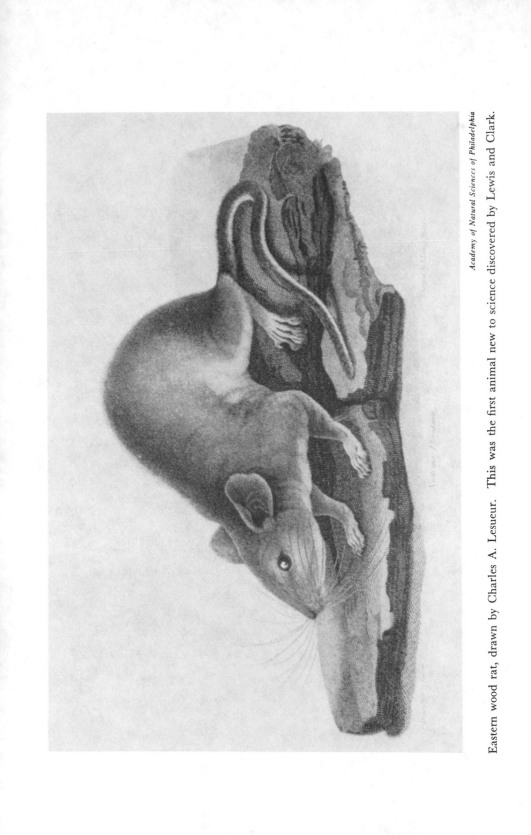

Eastern wood rat, drawn by Charles A. Lesueur. This was the first animal new to science discovered by Lewis and Clark.

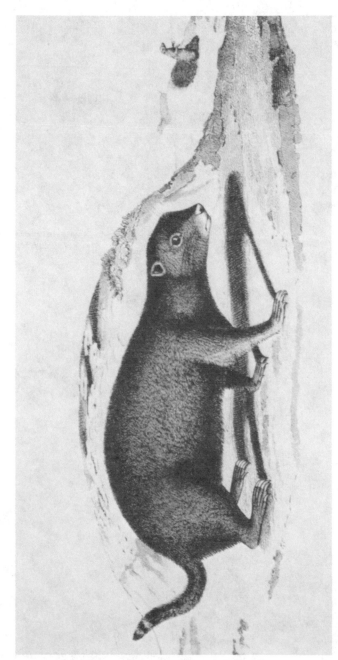

Black-tailed prairie dog, drawn by Alexander Rider in 1826.

Rice root, collected by Lewis on April 10, 1806, on the lower Columbia River.

Sagebrush. This is one of the several species taken to London by Pursh and later returned to America by Edward Tuckerman.

Clark's nutcracker (left) and Lewis's woodpecker, originally sketched by Alexander Wilson and completed by Alexander Lawson.

Western tanager (upper left), Clark's nutcracker (lower left), and Lewis's woodpecker (right), drawn by Alexander Wilson and engraved by Alexander Lawson.

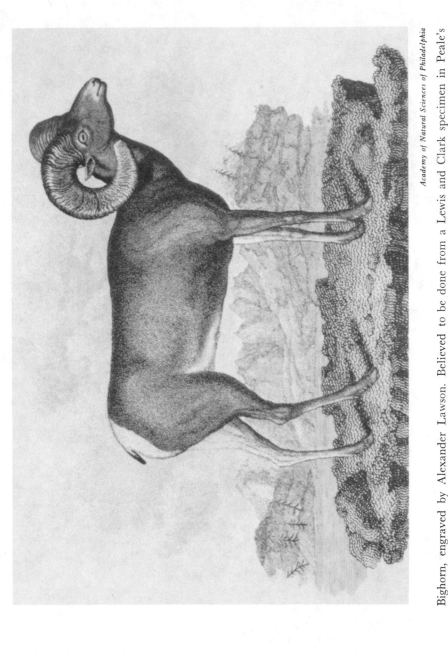

Bighorn, engraved by Alexander Lawson. Believed to be done from a Lewis and Clark specimen in Peale's Museum.

Pronghorn. This portrait was made by Lawson, probably from a specimen collected by Lewis and Clark and mounted by Charles Willson Peale.

Ragged robin (*Clarkia pulchella*). This is the first drawing of this plant, done for Pursh's *Flora Americae Septentrionalis*, 1814.

weather had remained relatively mild. Only one man had suffered any physical ill effect from the ordeal; he developed a cold.

At long last, here on the west side of Ellice's Point, the Corps of Discovery had its first view of the Pacific Ocean, with Cape Disappointment standing up boldly to the right and Point Adams, a low-lying sand-spit stretching far out into the river, visible to the left. Not one of the journalists expressed the emotion they must have felt at reaching this goal, after they had consumed precisely 18 months in so doing.

Appropriating boards from a deserted Indian village, Clark and his men quickly constructed a make-shift shelter. The location was at the upper end of Baker's Bay (Haley's Bay of Lewis and Clark). It was evident to Clark that they had gone as far as possible by water, high waves precluding the further use of canoes. The remaining miles could easily be made on foot, thus completing, pursuant to Jefferson's instructions, the "long desired object of exploring the Missouri & whatever river, heading with that, leads into the western ocean" (VII, 211).

Lewis, Drouillard, Frazer, and the Field brothers were the first of the party to visit Cape Disappointment and gaze upon the wide expanse of the Pacific. Here, 13 years earlier on May 12, 1792, Robert Gray, captain of the American merchantman, *Columbia Rediviva,* had made important history by discovering the Columbia River. After Lewis had reached the top of Cape Disappointment and observed visible landmarks from that elevation, he turned north and explored the coast for a number of miles. On November 17 he rejoined Clark, followed by several Indians of the Chinook tribe. Soon afterwards Clark set out for the coast, accompanied by ten volunteers, "all the others being well contented with what part of the Ocean & its curiosities which could be seen from the vicinity of our camp" (III, 229).

En route Reuben Field killed "a Buzzard [*Vulture*] of the large kind" (III, 232). This was the California condor (*Gymnogyps californianus*), a great bird fully as large as its more celebrated Andean relative. This particular specimen proved to be 9½ feet from wing tip to wing tip and 3 feet 10¼ inches from bill to end of tail. Apparently, its head ultimately ended up in Peale's Museum (III, 233). The present range of this great vulture is limited almost entirely to coastal mountainous regions of southern California and a portion of Lower California. Ornithologists fear that it may soon join the ranks of other extinct birds of this continent.

As Clark neared the Cape, Indians pointed out to him a small cove where, they said, trading vessels generally lay at anchor once inside the bar. Here they were protected from winds and had access to fresh water for refilling casks and excellent timber for general refitting and repair. When boats put in, trading was lively, with Indians exchanging skins, salmon, and roots for guns, beads, knives, blankets, and other articles. Unfortunately there was no trading vessel in the cove at this time.

From the inlet it was just two miles to Cape Disappointment, "an elevated, circular knob, rising with a steep ascent 150 or 160 feet above the water . . . and covered with thick timber on the inner side, but open and grassy in the exposure to the sea."[20] When he had attained the summit, Clark wrote: "The men appear much Satisfied with their trip, beholding with astonishment the high waves dashing against the rocks & this emence Ocian" (III, 234). According to Lewis and Clark's calculations, they had travelled from the mouth of the Missouri a total of 4,162 miles to reach this "land's end."

From the Cape, Clark followed the coast north, soon passing a headland he called Lewis Point (now North Head) where nearby he made a zoological discovery of consequence. "The deer of this Coast," he wrote, "differ materially from our Common deer in as much as they are darker, deeper bodied, Shoerter ledged [legged] horns equally branched from the beem the top of the tail black from the rute [root] to the end. Eyes larger and do not lope but jump" (III, 237). With these few words, Clark gave the world its first account of the Columbian black-tailed deer (*Dama hemionus columbianus*). Once accorded species rank (with various scientific names including *Cariacus lewisii*), it is today regarded by systematists as a subspecies of the mule deer.

After two full days of exploration and discovery, Clark and his party returned to base on Baker's Bay where they found a great rabble of Indians. Most of these were Chinooks, including a prominent chief called Concomly, but also several Clatsop Indians who had crossed the estuary from homes on the south side, and a few Chehalis.[21] Among the Chinooks was an "old Baud" who had brought to camp six of her daughters and nieces with the intent "of gratifying the passions of the men of our party and receiving for those indulgiences Such Small [presents] as She (the old woman) thought proper to accept of" (III, 241). Accepting the inevitable, Lewis and Clark distributed pieces of ribbon to the men "to bestow on their favorite Lasses, this plan to save the knives & more valuable articles" (III, 240). The relations of the men with these squaws later created health problems.

[20] Coues, II, 713–714.
[21] Lewis and Clark referred to these Chehalis Indians as Chiltz. Unlike the Chinook and Clatsop, who were Chinookan, the Chehalis were Salishan.

The absence of a trading vessel at the mouth of the Columbia was a major disappointment to Lewis and Clark. They had long since exhausted such staples as salt and flour, and trade goods had dwindled until the supply remaining could have been contained in a handkerchief. Replenishment of such items would have done much to ease anxiety about the future. Lewis and Clark remembered all too well their dependence on blue beads and other trinkets for obtaining food, horses, and fuel on the out journey. What would it be like on the return without trade goods?

One of Jefferson's instructions had been: "On your arrival at the coast endeavor to learn if there be any port within your reach frequented by the sea-vessels of any nation, and to send two of your trusty people back by sea, in such way as shall appear practicable, with a copy of your notes, and should you be of opinion that the return of your party by the way they went will be eminently dangerous, then ship the whole, & return by sea by way of Cape Horn or the Cape of Good Hope, as you shall be able" (VII, 251).

Since the threat of losing important records hung over their heads at all times, Lewis and Clark would have relished the opportunity of returning copies of these by sea. It would have been a satisfaction, too, if they could have shipped articles picked up along the way that took up precious space in dugouts. The thought of the entire party returning by sea seems never to have entered their minds; they had already laid plans for unfinished business en route by land.

Quickly putting aside their disappointment at not finding a vessel here, Lewis and Clark turned to immediate problems. After polling members, they arrived at two important decisions. They would spend the winter on the coast and would establish quarters on the south side of the estuary. Although some sentiment existed for wintering farther up the Columbia near the mouth of the Sandy, there were sound reasons for not considering that plan seriously. One, they still entertained hopes that a trading vessel would show up some time during the winter. Two, proximity to the ocean would enable them to obtain salt. Three, the climate near the coast, from all present indications, would be much milder than inland, an important factor considering their present state of near nakedness. And four, the Indians had assured them that elk were common on the south side of the river here, and this animal was "much larger than Deer, easier to kill, & better meat (in the winter when pore) and Skins better for the clothes of the party" (III, 249).

SUMMARY OF DISCOVERIES

Animals New to Science

COLUMBIAN BLACK-TAILED DEER. *Dama hemionus columbianus* (Rich.). (Thwaites, III, 237). Described, 1829.

COLUMBIAN SHARP-TAILED GROUSE. *Pedioecetes phasianellus columbianus* (Ord). [A.O.U. 308a] (Thwaites, IV, 121; Coues, III, 868). 1815.

HARBOR SEAL. *Phoca vitulina richardii* (Gray). (Thwaites, III, 150; IV, 99–100). 1864.

STEELHEAD TROUT. *Salmo gairdneri* Rich. (Thwaites, IV, 167; Coues, III, 893). 1836.

CALIFORNIA NEWT. *Triturus torosus torosus* (Rathke). (Thwaites, IV, 155). 1833.

GREAT-TAILED FOX. *Vulpes fulva macroura* Baird. (Thwaites, IV, 93–94; Coues, III, 848). 1852.

Plants New to Science

VINE MAPLE. *Acer circinatum* Pursh. (Thwaites, IV, 57; Coues, III, 834). 1814.

MADRONE. *Arbutus menziesii* Pursh. (Thwaites, III, 260). 1814.

DULL OREGON GRAPE. *Berberis nervosa* Pursh. (Thwaites, IV, 62). 1814.

CALIFORNIA HAZELNUT. *Corylus californica* (DC). (Thwaites, III, 148). 1864.

OREGON BOXWOOD. *Pachistima myrsinites* (Pursh) Raf. = *Ilex? myrsinites* Pursh. 1814.

OREGON WHITE OAK. *Quercus garryana* Douglas. (Thwaites, III, 143).

Lewis and Clark Herbarium

VINE MAPLE. *Acer circinatum* Pursh. Collected October 30, 1805.

? ASTER. *Aplopappus* sp. October [?], 1805.

MADRONE. *Arbutus menziesii* Pursh. November 1.

DULL OREGON GRAPE. *Berberis nervosa* Pursh. October [?].

MENZIES' ROCKWEED. *Egregia menziesii* (Turn.) Aresch. November 17.

OREGON BOXWOOD. *Pachistima myrsinites* (Pursh) Rafinesque. November 16.

Indian Tribes Encountered

Sahaptian Linguistic Family: † Walulas (Walla Wallas) ; † Pishquitpahs (probably either Umatillas or Cayuse, though Coues identified them as Pishquow, a Salishan tribe; see Coues, II, 649n) ; † Eneeshurs (a division of Wayampam).

Chinookan Linguistic Family: † Echeloots or Echelutes (Wishram) ; † Chilluckittequaws; † Skilloots; † Cathlapotles; Wahkiakums; Cathlamets; Chinooks; Clatsops. (Presumably the last four tribes had been discovered by Lt. Broughton.)

Salishan Linguistic Family: Chehalis (Chiltz of Lewis and Clark).

Topographic Features Named and/or Discovered

† Wallahwallah River (Thwaites, IV, 337) —— Wallawalla River.

† Lepage's River (Coues, II, 655) —— John Day River.

† Clark's River (Thwaites, IV, 310) —— Deschutes River ("Towornehooks" of the Indians).

† "Great Falls" (Thwaites, III, 147) —— Celilo Falls ("Timm" of Indians).

† Short Narrows (Thwaites, III, 158, map) —— Short Narrows.

† Long Narrows (Thwaites, III, 158, map) —— Long Narrows.

† Quinnette Creek (Thwaites, III, 159n; IV, 284) —— Mill Creek.

† "Range of mountains" (Thwaites, III, 159) —— Cascade Range.

† "Sepulchar" Island (Thwaites, III, 170) —— Sepulchre Island.

† Cataract River (Thwaites, III, 170) —— Klickitat River, Washington.

† "Labeasche" River (Thwaites, III, 171) —— Hood River, Oregon.

† Canoe Creek (Thwaites, III, 171) —— White Salmon River, Washington.

† "Grand Shute" (Thwaites, III, 172) —— Cascades of the Columbia.

† New Timbered River (Thwaites, III, 174) —— Wind River, Washington.

† "Beaten" Rock (Thwaites, III, 180) —— Beacon Rock.

† Strawberry Island (Thwaites, III, 180).

† Quick Sand River (Thwaites, III, 192) —— Sandy River, Oregon.

† Seal River (Thwaites, III, 192) —— Washougal River, Washington.

† Diamond Island (Thwaites, III, 193) —— Government Island.

† Image-canoe Island (Thwaites, III, 198, 201) —— Sauvies Island (Lewis and Clark called it also Wappatoo Island).

Author's note: In 1792 Lt. Broughton ascended the Columbia as far as the future location of Fort Vancouver. Presumably, therefore, he discovered the following physical features named by Lewis and Clark.

Columbia or Wappatoo Valley (Thwaites, III, 202) —— Columbian Valley, between Cascade and Coast Ranges).

"High hills" (Thwaites, III, 204) —— Coast Range.

Coweliskee River (Thwaites, III, 204) —— Cowlitz River, Washington.

Sturgeon Island (Thwaites, III, 206) —— Puget's Island.

Cape Swells (Thwaites, III, 210) —— upper boundary of Gray's Bay.

Shallow Nitch Bay (Thwaites, III, 211) —— Gray's Bay, north side of Columbia.

Haley's Bay (Thwaites, III, 224) —— Baker's Bay, north side.

Chinook River (Thwaites, III, 232) —— Wallacut River, Washington.

Clark's Point of View (Thwaites, III, 234) —— False Tillamook Head, Oregon.

Point Lewis (Thwaites, III, 236) —— North Head, Washington.

Fort Clatsop

CHAPTER SIXTEEN

The Corps abandoned their Baker's Bay camp on November 23 and moved upstream to a narrower part of the river where they might cross with safety. They billeted that night near their previous campsite of November 7. The next day, after reaching the opposite bank, they turned their canoes once more toward the coast, hugging closely the shoreline in the event they might have to land quickly if swells at any time threatened to swamp their cumbersome crafts. After passing a number of inlets, they arrived at a Cathlamet village whose inhabitants differed little in language and appearance from the Chinooks. From them they obtained fish and wappato.

The following morning they came to a remarkable finger of land, a slender, tree-clad promontory extending into the estuary. A mile and a half long and four miles around, it was only 50 yards wide where it joined the shore. Lewis named it Point William (honoring Clark), unaware that in 1792 Lt. Broughton had called it Tongue Point, the name it bears today. Rounding this attenuated cape, the party hurriedly grounded their boats when waves kicked up dangerously. Here on a pebble-covered beach which faced the site of present-day Astoria, they made camp and lived for eight days while Lewis, with five picked men (Drouillard, Reuben Field, Shannon, Colter, and Labiche) moved on downstream to seek a location suitable for winter quarters.

Clark and his contingent, awaiting Lewis's return, existed miserably. They had little to eat except dried fish, some squirrels, and a few "fat and delicious" hawks. With tents and sails in shreds, they had no means of protecting themselves from rains that fell continuously.

When Lewis returned (on December 8), he brought gratifying news; he had found "a good situation and Elk sufficient to winter on" (III, 266).

Two days later the entire party left their cheerless camp on Tongue Point, coasted round the future location of Astoria and crossed a bay to the mouth of a small stream falling in from the south. The bay, which they called Meriwether's, is now Young's, and the stream, known to the natives as Netul, is presently Lewis and Clark River. They turned their boats into this river and ascended it for about two miles to a conifer-covered point of land on the west side some 300 yards back from the river and 30 feet above high tide. This was the place Lewis had chosen on which to build a winter bastion. It was, wrote Clark, "certainly the most eligable Situation for our purpose of any in its neighborhood" (III, 270). Here, about four miles from the ocean, they erected Fort Clatsop and lodged until March 23.

[2]

Fort Clatsop had little in common with Fort Mandan. It stood at sea level, beside a tidal stream, whereas the timbers of Fort Mandan had rested on the High Plains at an elevation of some 1,800 feet. Wintry winds at Fort Clatsop regularly blew warm and gentle; those at Fort Mandan—cold and sharp—cut to the bone. Fort Mandan had been surrounded by empty, treeless prairie; Fort Clatsop was hemmed in by a dense wood of giant evergreens resembling a tropical rain forest. As a rule it was impossible to see objects more than 100 yards away. Here on the Pacific, elk displaced buffalo as the dominant quadruped. Even the Indians differed, exhibited varied skills, spoke a dissimilar tongue, and rode elegant canoes instead of spirited horses.

Lewis and Clark took stock. For a full month now, except for the briefest of periods, they had not known what it was like to be dry. Their clothes were dropping off of them. Rain continued to pelt them, and their only protection was a canopy of evergreen branches. It was a marvel that they remained generally healthy. One thing was certain: conditions would not improve until they had a roof over their heads and they had found elk whose flesh would sustain them and whose hides would provide new coats, trousers, and moccasins. They needed salt too, having been without it for several weeks.

They wasted no time. Lewis immediately sent hunters into the woods. Clark, with five men, set out to blaze a trail to the ocean which would presently be followed by salt makers. Everyone else began clearing ground for the fort. This went up rapidly, was ready for occupancy in about three weeks. The job was less difficult than anticipated, wrote Sergeant Gass, "as we have found a kind of timber in plenty which splits freely and makes the finest puncheons I have ever seen. They can be split 10 feet long and 2 broad, not more than an inch and a half thick."[1] Opinions differ as to whether the timber was Douglas fir (*Pseudotsuga taxifolia*), suggested by Coues,[2] grand fir (*Abies grandis*), the choice of Charles Sprague Sargent,[3] or Sitka spruce (*Picea sitchensis*). In describing what botanists think was Sitka spruce, Lewis said the timber of that tree "rives better than any other species which we have tryed" (IV, 41). All three trees grew commonly on the banks of the Lewis and Clark River, as did mountain hemlock (*Tsuga mertensiana*) and western white pine (*Pinus monticola*).

On the elk-skin cover of his field book, Clark drew the ground plan of Fort Clatsop.

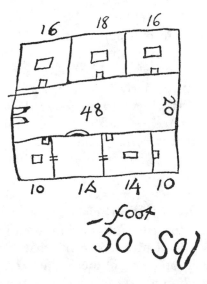

As this sketch indicates, Fort Clatsop was 50 feet square and contained two rows of huts, the two being separated from each other by

---

[1] Gass, 210–211.

[2] Coues, II, 734. Douglas fir was named for the British botanist, David Douglas, who arrived at the mouth of the Columbia 20 years after Lewis and Clark, though it was apparently discovered by Archibald Menzies in 1791 at Nootka Sound, Vancouver Island, British Columbia.

[3] Sargent, "The First Account of Some Western Trees," 29.

a parade ground 20 feet wide and 50 feet long. The three huts comprising one row were squad rooms occupied by rank and file. Of the four rooms in the other row, Charbonneau, Sacagawea, and Pomp had the one to the left, Lewis and Clark the adjoining one, and York and an orderly the third. The fourth served as a meat house. Gates opened at each end of the parade ground.

On December 24 the fort had a roof on it and the men moved in. Clark wrote that their Christmas dinner "consisted of pore Elk, so much Spoiled that we eate it thro' necessity, Some Spoiled pounded fish and a fiew roots" (III, 290–291). Sergeant Gass added that they ate their food without salt and Ordway remarked, soberly if not happily, that "we have no ardent Spirits, but all are in good health which we esteem more than all the ardent Spirits in the world."[4]

The fort, when completed, left much to be desired. For one thing, the chimneys smoked badly, and for another, the rooms swarmed with fleas. On the day after Christmas Clark wrote that these insects were so troublesome that he had slept but little for two nights, and the men had "to kill them out of their blankets every day" (III, 291). They never succeeded in eliminating fleas from Fort Clatsop. As soon as they managed to reduce the population, visiting Indians renewed it.

On December 28 Lewis and Clark sent Joseph Field, Bratton, Gibson, Willard, and Wiser to the coast to make salt. These five men chose a location about 15 miles to the southwest of Fort Clatsop just above Tillamook Head and within the limits of the present town of Seaside. They had as neighbors four lodges of Tillamook and Clatsop Indians. Employing five large kettles, they evaporated sea water at such a rate that by January 5 they were able to send a gallon of salt back to the fort. "We found it excellent, fine, strong, & white," Lewis wrote (III, 313).

Salt-making proved to be a slow, tedious operation, but by keeping kettles boiling day and night, the men managed to average three to four quarts daily. In time they accumulated a stock of about 20 gallons, 12 of which were put into iron-bound kegs and saved for the return journey. This amount, Lewis and Clark estimated, should be sufficient to last them until they opened caches on the Missouri.

In 1899 Olin Wheeler visited that part of the Oregon coast where Joseph Field and his crew had made salt. Local residents pointed out to him what they claimed was the exact spot. After he had turned up ashes and burned stones, he was convinced that this was indeed the

[4] Ordway, 318.

place.[5] Some time later Seaside citizens, with the sanction and backing of the Oregon Historical Society, built a reconstruction of the cairn here and surrounded it with an iron fence. In 1962 when I visited the reconstruction, I found it ringed with Seaside homes but still in an excellent state of preservation.

The new year (1806) began auspiciously on Lewis and Clark River. "The party Saluted our officers at day break this morning by firing at their quarters," wrote Sergeant Ordway, whose sentences did not always convey the meaning intended.[6] Far and away the most important event of the day was Lewis's resumption of journalistic efforts, his pen having been almost totally inactive—or so it would seem—since the Corps departed from the Shoshoni on the Lemhi River in late August. From here on, until near the end of the journey, Lewis and Clark, except when separated, wrote parallel accounts with the two often approaching identicality. Apparently Clark copied Lewis verbatim. If this was so—and we have no reason for thinking otherwise—the circumstance offers yet more evidence that Lewis failed to write daily accounts between late August and the end of December, 1805. Throughout that period, Clark's entries are couched in language typically Clarkian; beginning January 1, they are patently Lewisian.

[3]

Day in and day out, the job of obtaining food outrivalled all others. This was made doubly difficult by adverse weather conditions. Rain was the great recurring wretchedness—cold, penetrating, disabling, persistent. During the stay at Fort Clatsop, a period of more than four cheerless months, rain fell every day except 12 and skies remained cloudless only six.

Contributing to the difficulties of the hunters were the numerous bogs or "slashes" of this low-lying region through which they of necessity had to struggle, often immersed to midriff; the abundance of great fallen timbers over which they had to clamber with their burdens; and the fact that they often had to pass the night in the open, sometimes without even a fire to warm them or cook their food. Clark gave us an idea of what it was like when forced to spend a night in the depths of this sodden forest: "rained all the last night we covered our selves as well as we could with Elk skin, & set up the greater part of the night, all wet I lay in the wet verry cold" (III, 281).

[5] Wheeler, *The Trail of Lewis and Clark,* II, 207.
[6] Ordway, 319.

As the winter progressed, the elk, their principal dependence for subsistence, moved farther and farther away from the fort. This meant that the hunters, after killing and butchering these animals, often faced the near herculean task of carrying the meat several miles on their backs through morass and heavy undergrowth to get it back to base. They faced the certainty, too, that delay would vitiate their efforts; the warm days and night, so characteristic of the 1805–6 winter, hastened spoilage.

Sergeant Gass reported that in the period from December 1 to March 20, the hunters killed 131 elk.[7] More than any other, this animal provided the party with food and clothing during the rigors of the winter. At a much later date the well-known scientist, C. Hart Merriam, described this elk as a new species and named it *Cervus roosevelti* in honor of Theodore Roosevelt. Today it is a subspecies only, *Cervus canadensis roosevelti*.

In satisfying the appetites of the explorer, an elk did not go as far as one might surmise. For instance, on a jaunt to the shore one day, Clark and 15 companions consumed at one meal all but eight pounds of a large, full-grown buck. Certain parts of this animal appealed to the taste more than others. On one occasion Lewis stressed his enjoyment of a particularly palatable meal consisting of a marrowbone and broiled brisket. "This for Fort Clatsop," he declared, "is living in high style" (IV, 49).

With little but elk meat day after day to satisfy appetites, the men welcomed almost any departure from this diet. In late February Clark wrote:

This evening we were visited by Comowool the Clatsop Chief and 12 men women and children of his nation. . . . The Chief and his party had brought for sail a Sea Otter skin some hats, stergeon and a species of small fish which now begin to run, and are taken in great quantities in the Columbia R. about 40 miles above us by means of skimming or scooping nets. . . . I find them best when cooked in Indian stile, which is by roasting a number of them together on a wooden spit without any previous preparation whatever. they are so fat they require no additional sauce, and I think them superior to any fish I ever tasted, even more delicate and lussious than the white fish of the lakes which have heretofore formed my standart of excellence among the fishes (IV, 102–103).[8]

---

[7] Gass, 229.

[8] For a sketch of the eulachon by Clark see the frontispiece of Vol. IV of *Original Journals*.

This small fish (with a length of 10 to 12 inches) was the eulachon or candle fish, *Thaleichthys pacificus,* and "unknown to science when discovered by Lewis and Clark."[9] In the spring it ascends rivers of the Northwest in tremendous numbers, usually in advance of the salmon. These fish are extremely fat when they start upstream, so much so that "when dried and a wick drawn through the body they may be used as candles"[10]—hence the name candle fish. The well-known ichthyologist, David Starr Jordan, agreed with Clark that it was the best flavored fish in American waters.

On the occasion of Chief Comowool's visit just mentioned, the two captains bought a half bushel of candle fish (they generally referred to them as "anchovies") and a number of sturgeon, the white or Columbia River sturgeon (*Acipenser transmontanus*). The latter, the largest of fresh-water fishes, attains an enormous size. The Astorian, Gabriel Franchère, reported some taken from the Columbia 11 feet in length, one of which weighed 390 pounds after removal of eggs and intestines. It contained nine gallons of eggs.[11] David Douglas told of another 10 feet in length that weighed 400 to 500 pounds.[12] The largest on record, according to a reliable source, was taken at Astoria and weighed 1,900 pounds.[13]

It is the eggs of the sturgeon, of course, that constitute the delicacy, caviar, but not until they have been divested of their membranes and carefully mixed with Luneberg salt. This specially prepared fish roe is by far the most valuable part of the sturgeon. At current retail prices, the nine gallons of eggs Franchère reported taken from a single sturgeon would realize approximately $1,500.[14]

In early January Clatsops brought meat to the fort obtained from the body of a whale recently washed ashore just below the salt makers' camp. Lewis found it to be "verry palitable and tender" and resem-

[9] Coues, III, 895n. This fish was not technically described until 1836 when Sir John Richardson named it *Salmo pacificus,* erroneously regarding it as a species of salmon. Actually it belongs to the smelt family, *Osmeridae.*

[10] David Starr Jordan, *A Guide to the Study of Fishes,* 2 vols. (New York, 1905), II, 124.

[11] *Early Western Travels,* VI, 322.

[12] A. G. Harvey, *Douglas of the Fir: A Biography of David Douglas, Botanist* (Cambridge, Mass., 1947), 52.

[13] David Starr Jordan, B. W. Evermann and H. W. Clark, *Check List of the Fishes and Fishlike Vertebrates of North and Middle America North of the Northern Boundary of Venezuela and Colombia* (Washington, 1930), Part II, 34.

[14] This figure is based on information obtained from Reading Terminal Market, Philadelphia. Fresh caviar currently (1965) retails at about $40 a pint.

bling "the beaver or dog in flavor" (III, 312–313). With so much choice fresh meat close at hand, apparently there for the taking, Clark immediately selected 12 men to accompany him and struck out for the coast. However, he had underestimated the industry of the Indians, for when he arrived he found only a skeleton. He did not return to the fort empty-handed though. With the small amount of trade goods he carried, he was able to buy from the Clatsops some 300 pounds of whale meat and a few gallons of oil. This acquisition put Clark in a rare frame of mind. "Small as this stock is I prize it highly," he exulted, "and thank providence for directing the whale to us; and think him much more kind to us than he was to jonah, having Sent this Monster to be *Swallowed by us* in Sted of *Swallowing of us* as jonah's did" (III, 325).

This whale, Clark said, measured 105 feet in length. No doubt this was an estimate rather than an actual measurement, for the largest animal known to exist on earth today, possibly the largest ever to exist, the great blue whale (*Balaenoptera musculus*), does not exceed the length Clark mentioned.

[3]

During the winter the men experienced the usual number of accidents and disorders. Willard split a knee with a tomahawk, Pryor dislocated a shoulder, Joseph Field suffered from "Biles on his legs," and York complained of a "Cholick & gripeing."

On February 22 Lewis wrote: "we have not had as ma[n]y sick at one time since we left Wood River. the general complaint seems to be bad colds and fevers, something I believe of the influenza" (IV, 95). One of the victims was Gibson. Lewis initially gave him "broken dozes of diluted nitre . . . made him drink plentifully of sage tea, had his feet bathed in warm water and at 9 P.M. gave him 35 drops of laudanum" (IV, 73). Later, Gibson's fever continuing obstinate, he prescribed barks and a dose of Dr. Rush's pills which in many instances he had "found extreemly efficatious in fevers which are in any measure caused by the presence of boil [bile]" (IV, 78).

At about this same time Bratton (one of the salt detail) showed up at the fort ill and "much reduced." The next day Lewis wrote, "Bratton is still very weak and complains of a pain in the lower part of the back when he moves which I suppose proceeds from debility. I gave him barks" (IV, 77–78).

The journals fail to credit Private William Bratton with any unusual act of heroism or with being party to any of the more breathtaking moments of the Expedition except once being closely pursued by a grizzly. He was a skilled gunsmith, and as we know, he was runner-up to Gass in the election to choose a successor to Sergeant Floyd. We would know little else about him if he had not become the only member of the party to be ill for an extended period of time.

The "barks" (a bark poultice) administered by Lewis provided no relief to Bratton's aching back, his condition worsened, and for a time he was unable to sit up. Lewis then applied "a bandage of flannel to the part and bathed and rubed it well with some vollatile linniment which I prepared with sperits of wine, camphor, castile soap and a little laudinum" (IV, 141).

As the moment for abandoning Fort Clatsop neared, Bratton still remained very much incapacitated. On March 21, two days before starting the return journey, Lewis wrote: "Bratton is now so much reduced that I was somewhat uneasy with rispect to his recovery; the pain of which he complains most seems to be seated in the small of his back and remains obstinate. I believe that it is the rheumatism" (IV, 195). Bratton's recovery occurred suddenly, almost dramatically—but not until two months later. It will be described at the proper moment.

In mid-March Lewis wrote: "we were visited this afternoon by . . . a Chinnook Chief his wife and six women of his nation which the old baud had brought for market. this was the same party that had communicated the venerial to so many of our party in November last, and of which they have finally recovered. I therefore gave the men a particular charge with rispect to them which they promised me to observe" (IV, 170).

Though Lewis here referred to "so many" of the party having contracted venereal disease, he actually denominated only two. On January 27 he wrote that Goodrich "has recovered from the Louis Veneri [*lues veneris*] which he contracted from an amorous contact with a Chinnook damsel" (IV, 16), and four days later he "discovered that McNeal had the pox, gave him medicine" (IV, 27). The pox, of course, was the great pox, syphilis, not smallpox.

Lewis mentioned only mercury in his treatment of venereal disease, meaning either mercury ointment or calomel, or both. Mercury ointment was then commonly applied by inunction, that is, by rubbing this medication into the skin, generally that of the volar surface of the left fore-arm. However, one medical authority suspects that Lewis "followed the accepted method of the day, *e.g.*, a priming dose of calomel and jalap to 'clear the bowels' for the subsequent calomel, in pill form, which was given until sore gums appear, and then discontinued. After the soreness cleared, calomel was readministered until the primary lesion disappeared."[15]

Lewis was unable to find that the Chinookan Indians themselves employed any "simples which are sovereign specifics" in the treatment of syphilis, and he doubted that they had any means of effecting a cure. From his observations syphilis, once contracted by these natives, continued throughout life, ending either in decrepitude or premature death, "tho from the uce of certain simples together with their diet, they support this disorder with but little inconvenience for many years, and even enjoy a tolerable share of health" (IV, 16).

As is well known, syphilis manifests itself in three stages: a primary one extending from the appearance of the initial sore, a small red papule (chancre), until the onset of constitutional symptoms; a secondary stage characterized by skin eruptions (the pox); and the tertiary, which shows up much later, often many years after the original infection, in the form of general paresis, locomotor ataxia, or other equally grave manifestation.

It is highly unlikely that Lewis cured any syphilis using mercury. This drug may have been effective in clearing up the primary and secondary stages, but not the third. That Lewis believed he had cured this dread disease in his men is quite obvious from his own confident statements. For instance, writing at Fort Clatsop, he asserted that he had cured Goodrich as he had "Gibson last winter by the uce of mercury" (IV, 16). Six months later, however, we note that "Goodrich and McNeal are both very unwell with the pox which they contracted last winter with the Chinnook women" (V, 180).

It is impossible to say whether any members of the Expedition incurred gonorrhea as well as syphilis from the Indians. If either Lewis or Clark used the syringes they had at hand for urethral irrigation, they probably loaded them with sugar of lead. The effectiveness of potassium permanganate solution, so useful at a later date in the treatment of gonorrhea, was unknown to them, and they were almost a century away from the arsenical compounds and even further from penicillin.

Most of the explorers seem to have come through the rigors of the 28-month journey completely untouched by the "pox." Sergeant Gass,

[15] Dr. Drake W. Will, "The Medical and Surgical Practice of the Lewis and Clark Expedition," *Jour. of Hist. of Med. and Allied Sciences*, XIV, no. 3, 273–297.

for one, lived to be ninety-nine and to take a twenty-year-old wife when he was sixty-five who bore him six children. However, some 20 years after the party returned to St. Louis Clark listed the Expedition members and their whereabouts if living. By that time, according to this list, 15 of the party were already dead, including Gibson, Goodrich, and McNeal.[16]

[4]

Fort Clatsop was a port in a storm, a temporary abode to be evacuated at the earliest practicable moment. Lewis and Clark had no sooner entered it than they began looking ahead, preparing for the day when they would leave it. They saw to their guns. Drouillard's, for instance, needed a new lock and Pryor's a cock screw. "But for the precaution taken in bringing on these extra locks, and parts of locks, in addition to the ingenuity of John Shields," said Lewis, "most of our guns would at this moment [have] been entirely unfit for use; but fortunately for us I have it in my power here to record that they are all in good order" (IV, 193).

Lewis could boast, too, about the condition of their powder, which had been sealed from the start in lead canisters. Inspecting it here, he found it just as dry as when first encased in spite of the fact that at one time or another it had been exposed to moisture. In mid-January Lewis wrote: "This evening we exhausted the last of our candles, but fortunately had taken the precaution to bring with us moulds and wick, by means of which and some Elk's tallow in our possession we do not yet consider ourselves destitute of this necessary article" (III, 340). Other examples of Lewis's foresight have been mentioned in preceding pages. Collectively, they add cubits to his stature as a leader.

Before abandoning Fort Clatsop, Lewis and Clark looked to the repairing of canoes, saw to it that cracks were caulked and knees added. To replace two boats carried away by the tide, they purchased one from the Indians and deliberately appropriated another "in lue of the six Elk which they [the Clatsops] stole from us last winter" (IV, 177).

During the winter the men produced a large quantity of leather for clothing. Sergeant Gass said, for instance, that they made 338 pairs of moccasins, which figures out to about 10 for each person. "This stock," he emphasized, "was not provided without great labor, as the

[16] Jackson, *Letters,* 638–639.

most of them are made of the skins of elk."[17] A single elk skin, according to one reporter, was good for about 12 pairs of moccasins, that of a deer for only five or six.[18] Lewis and Clark did not describe the method they employed to convert raw skins into leather. However, it probably followed closely that of the western Indians, a method much the same everywhere north of Mexico. This entailed a number of steps such as scraping, tanning, stripping, and softening. One important prerequisite for best results, ample sunshine, was practically nonexistent at Fort Clatsop.

Clark toiled at map-making during the winter. For instance, he produced one "of the country which we have been passing from Fort Mandan to this place" (IV, 68). As this map made clear, the Expedition could save much time and distance on their return to the Missouri. Instead of following the windings of the Snake River, for example, they could reduce mileage by ascending the Walla Walla River for several miles and then striking directly across country to the mouth of the Clearwater. Also, and more importantly, they could take a route from Traveller's Rest by way of the Blackfoot and Sun Rivers to Great Falls instead of the much longer Bitterroot-Lemhi-Jefferson loop which they had travelled going west.

Even before Lewis and Clark left Fort Clatsop, they had determined on these two short-cuts. Also, they had decided to split the party at Traveller's Rest, with one group under Lewis proceeding directly to Great Falls, and the other, under Clark, setting forth for Shoshoni Cove, Three Forks, and the Yellowstone. Having arrived at these decisions, they abandoned an idea, earlier entertained, of leaving two men at the mouth of the Columbia with logs and maps, who would await the arrival of some trading vessel on which they would take passage for the long sea voyage back home. The captains did not wish to weaken the party for the return trip by even as much as two men.

[5]

While Clark made maps, Lewis wrote animal biographies, described plants, and filled notebooks with ethnobotanical and ethnozoological data. When on January 1 he again picked up his pen, his literary contributions resembled release of long-imprisoned water. At no other time during the entire trip did he display such initiative as a naturalist

[17] Gass, 227.
[18] *Early Western Travels,* XXIII, 31.

and provide such quantitative evidence of his skill as observer and reporter of the biological scene. A summary of what he had to say may best be presented under four headings: botany, zoology, ethnobotany, and ethnozoology.

Botany

Lewis referred to some three dozen plants while at Fort Clatsop, barely mentioning a few but writing at length about others. He devoted time and space to two groups in particular: (1) the great conifers of that area, such as Douglas fir, western hemlock, grand fir, western white pine, and Sitka spruce, and (2) those plants providing edible roots and fruits. He arrived on the Pacific after most leaves had fallen and departed before spring flowers began to bloom. If his stay had been extended, he unquestionably would have supplied much additional botanical data.

Lewis's comparatively brief description of the Oregon grape (*Berberis aquifolium,* the Oregon state flower) serves to illustrate something of his ability to delineate important features of a plant: "The stem . . . is from a foot to 18 inches high and as large as a goosqu[i]ll; it is simple unbranc[h]ed and erect. it's leaves are cauline, compound and spreading. the leaflets are jointed and oppositely pinnate, 3 pare & terminating in one, sessile, widest at the base and tapering to an accuminated point, an inch and a quarter the greatest width, and 3 inches & a ¼ in length, each point of their crenate margins armed with a subulate thorn or spine and are from 13 to 17 in number. they are also veined, glossy, carinated and wrinkled; their points obliquely pointed towards the extremity of the common footstalk" (IV, 61–62).

We have had the opportunity of examining the preserved specimen of this plant which Lewis collected and brought back to Philadelphia. Its leaves, as he said, are indeed cauline and compound, and each glossy, carinated leaflet bears a crenate margin armed with subulate spines.

During the 28-month journey, Lewis employed altogether, according to my count, at least 200 technical botanical terms. At Fort Clatsop alone he used some 60 of them. Assembled, they make an impressive list:

radicle	peduncle	revolute	imbricated
radix	capsule	lineal	palmate
fusiform	membranous	stellate	lobate
depressed	spheroid	radiate	sinuses

ovate	bract	affixed	repand
lamella	fructification	alternate	incisure
capillary	cauline	footstalk	subulate
caulis	crenate	acute	carinated
hispid	obtuse	serrate	ternate
procumbent	insertion	channeled	lanceolate
diffuse	decurrent	entire	decursively
flexuous	declining	acerose	pubescence
pericarp	pinnate	acuminate	annual
globular	sessile	petiolate	perennial
pellicle	multipartite	gibbous	

Only rarely did Lewis exhibit a Latin-derived taxonomic botanical word. However, when referring to "a species of bryer" (possibly *Rubus macropetalus*), he declared it to be of "the class Polyandria and order Polygynia" (IV, 256). In only one instance, so far as we have been able to find, did he use a full-fledged binomial, and that when writing about the wappato or broad-leaved arrowhead. "The Sagittaria Sagittifolia," he said, "does not grow on this river above the Columbia valley" (IV, 223). Lewis's almost total disregard of Linnaean nomenclature is unexpected. As we know, he had received instruction in Latin as a young man and, during his two years in the President's Mansion, had lived with Jefferson who displayed the scientific name quite as often as the vernacular.

Lewis's Fort Clatsop diary contains information extending the geographical range of plants heretofore unknown except in the East. For example, no one until then apparently knew that the cattail (*Typha latifolia*) and broad-leaved arrowhead both put down roots in soil of the Columbia estuary. His journal provided useful information, too, on the ecological range of certain plants (that is, the particular environment they required). The coastal arrowhead, for instance, restricted itself to the marshy grounds along the Columbia "commencing just above the Quicksand River, and extending downwards for about 70 miles" (IV, 10).

In his attention to plants native to the environs of Fort Clatsop, Lewis invariably supplied dimensions. He was, of course, much impressed with the size of the huge conifers constituting the surrounding forest. The Sitka spruce, he said, "grows to imence size . . . in several instances we have found them as much as 36 feet in the girth or 12 feet diameter perfectly solid and entire. they frequently rise to the hight of 230 feet, and one hundred and twenty or 30 of that hight without a limb" (IV, 41). At the same time that he measured maximal features, he applied tapeline to minimal. For that purpose he carried a "tape with feet & inches marked on it, confined within a circular or leathern box" (VII, 232). The needles of the Douglas fir, for instance, were one inch long and one-twentieth wide (IV, 41) and those of the grand fir one-eighth by one-sixteenth (IV, 45). The leaf of the broad-leaved maple (*Acer macrophyllum*) was eight inches long and 12 wide. Apparently Lewis brought this leaf back with him, for the one in the Academy of Natural Sciences I measured not long ago was precisely eight inches long and 12 wide.

Again and again when describing Pacific coast plants, Lewis demonstrated his familiarity with eastern counterparts. The berry of the blue elderberry (*Sambucus glauca*) was pale sky blue while that of the Atlantic states (*S. canadensis*) was a deep purple (IV, 49). The leaf and fruit of black alder (*Alnus oregana*) were exactly like those of the common eastern alder (*A. rugosa*), but the former plants "grew separately from different roots and not in clusters or clumps as those of the Atlantic States" (IV, 55). The berry of the western Solomon's seal "when grown and unripe is not specked as that of the [eastern] Solomon's Seal [*Smilacina racemosa*] berry is" (IV, 16–17). This noting of the unspecked berry may be cited as another excellent example of Lewis's ability to observe the little things so often overlooked.

Jefferson, as we know, had instructed Lewis to pay attention to "climate as characterized by . . . the dates at which particular plants put forth their flowers, or leaf" (VII, 249). Some examples of his industry in this phenological direction at Fort Clatsop were as follows. On March 22, for example, "the leaves and petals of the flowers of the green Huckleburry [*Vaccinium parvifolia* ?] have appeared. some of the leaves have already obtained ¼ of their size" (VI, 210). And on March 24, the day after the Corps had abandoned Fort Clatsop, "the brown bryery shrub with a broad pinnate leaf has begun to put fourth it's leaves. the polecat Colwort [probably western skunk cabbage, *Lysichiton kamtschatcense*] is in blume" (VI, 210).

Lewis devoted considerable space in his Fort Clatsop journal to some half dozen roots and an equal number of fruits that provided Chinookan Indians (and the explorers, too) with sustenance. Since this material is more relevant to ethnobotany, it will be considered *post*.

As a fitting conclusion to this summary account of the Fort Clatsop flora, we would stress the fact that 14 of the plants here recognized by

Lewis now reside in the Lewis and Clark Herbarium of the Academy of Natural Sciences of Philadelphia.[19]

Zoology

At Fort Clatsop Lewis alluded to some 100 animals altogether: approximately 35 mammals, 50 birds, 10 reptiles and fish, and five invertebrates. He wrote at sufficient length about most of these to make it possible for subsequent zoologists to identify them. For example:

There is a third species of brant in the neighbourhood of this place which is about the size and much the form of the pided [pied] brant. they weigh about 8½ lbs. the wings are not as long nor so pointed as those of the common pided brant [apparently American brant, *Branta bernicla hrota*] . . . a little distance around the base of the beak is white and is suddenly succeeded by a narrow line of dark brown. the ballance of the neck, head, back, wings, and tail all except the tips of the feathers are of a bluish brown of the common wild goose. the breast and belly are white with an irregular mixture of black feathers which give that part a pided appearance. from the legs back underneath the tail, and aro[u]nd the junction of the same with the body above, the feathers are white. the tail is composed of 18 feathers; the longest of which are in the center and measure 6 Inches with the barrel of the quill; those on the sides of the tail are something shorter and bend with their extremities inwards toward the center of the tail. the extremities of these feathers are white. the beak is of a light flesh colour. the legs and feet which do not differ in structure from those of the goose or brant of the other speceis, are of an orange yellow colour. the eye is small; the iris is a dark yellowish brown, and pupil black. the note of this brant is much that of the common pided brant from which in fact they are not to be distinguished at a distance, but they certainly are a distinct spe[c]i[e]s of brant (IV, 170–171).

The bird here described, ornithologists recognize, was the white-fronted goose, *Anser albifrons frontalis*, not formally described and named until 1858, 52 years later. Though Lewis used a minimum of technical words in his description, he nevertheless supplied adequate data on color, shape of wings, number and length of tail feathers, color of iris, and note.

---

[19] These 14 plants are: vine maple (*Acer circinatum*), broad-leaved maple (*Acer macrophyllum*), red alder (*Alnus rubra*), bearberry (*Arctostaphylos uva-ursi*), spinulose shield-fern (*Aspidium spinulosum*), Oregon grape (*Berberis aquifolium*), dull Oregon grape (*Berberis nervosa*), edible thistle (*Cirsium edule*), brown alga (*Egregia menziesii*), salal (*Gaultheria shallon*), deer-fern (*Lomaria spicant*), orange honeysuckle (*Lonicera ciliosa*), evergreen huckleberry (*Vaccinium ovatum*), and bear grass (*Xerophyllum tenax*).

As with plants, Lewis rarely employed the Latin-derived taxo-nomic zoological word. However, in writing of the eulachon or candle fish, he said that it was "of the Malacopterygious Order & Class Clu-pea" (IV, 102–103). While still on the Missouri, he had stated that the magpie belonged to the *"Corvus genus* and order of the pica" (VI, 130).

In his Fort Clatsop notes, Lewis occasionally came up with a sentence or simile that catches the eye. For instance, the fore legs of the western badger (*Taxidea taxus neglecta*) were "formed like [those] of the ternspit dog" (IV, 110), and the bellies of some squirrels were of a "tanners ooze colour" (III, 261). While at Great Falls, he had written that the thirteen-lined ground squirrel had spaces between stripes "marked by ranges of pure white circular spots, about the size of brister blue shot" (II, 216).

Lewis extended the known geographic range of many animals. A few, for example, heretofore known only east of the Mississippi, were the coot (*Fulica americana*), blue-winged teal (*Querquedula discors*), and canvas-back (*Nyroca valisneria*). He obtained information, too, on the ecologic range of different species. The canvas-back, he said, was never found above tidewater (IV, 148) and the harbor seal (*Phoca vitulina richardii*), only "as far up the columbia river as the great falls, above which there are none" (IV, 99).

From Lewis's Fort Clatsop writings, we learn that he paid atten-tion to food habits of animals. The sage grouse, for instance, fed almost entirely on the leaves and buds of the pulpy leafed thorn [greasewood, *Sarcobatus vermiculatus*] (IV, 124). The coot subsisted "principally on moss and other vegitable productions of the water" (IV, 152), the elk on salal (IV, 40–41), and the red-breasted merganser (*Mergus serrator*) on crayfish (IV, 149). To obtain at least some of the above information, Lewis must have examined stomach content. The gizzard of the sage grouse was "large and much less compressed and muscular than in most fowls" (IV, 124).

Lewis conscientiously measured and counted. The eulachon was 10 to 12 inches long and the fins of this fish next to the gills had 11 rays each, those of the abdomen eight, and those of the pinna-ani 22 (IV, 102). The tail of the sage grouse was "composed of 19 feathers of which that in the center is the longest, and the remaining 9 on each side deminish by pairs as they recede from the center" (IV, 124).

As he did with plants, Lewis provided zoological data correlating season and periodic biological phenomena. On March 7, for instance, he reported that elk were beginning to shed their horns (VI, 209), on March 15 "the birds were singing very agreeably . . . particularly the robin," and on March 16 the eulachon had ceased to run (VI, 210).

Lewis demonstrated his inherent ability, as he had earlier, to see minutiae. For instance, he could not recall, he said, ever seeing sage grouse except in the neighborhood of greasewood; and in the act of flying the tail of this same grouse resembled that of the passenger pigeon (IV, 124). He wrote, too, that the gait of the Columbian black-tail corresponded to that of the mule deer in "bounding with all four feet off the ground at the same time when running at full speed and not loping as the common deer or antelope do" (IV, 87).

Lewis and Clark refrained from burdening themselves with any considerable amount of zoological material for the return journey; it was much easier to transport plants than bones, hides, and horns. They did bring back skins of such mammals as mountain beaver (*Aplodontia rufa rufa*),[20] Columbian ground squirrel (*Spermophilus columbianus columbianus*), mountain goat (*Oreamnos americanus americanus*), and sea otter (*Enhydra lutris*). Among Lewis's effects found in his trunks at Grinder's Tavern on the Natchez Trace following his death was a handsomely dressed sea otter skin.[21]

But the facts about Lewis's zoological record from Fort Clatsop that impress most are not his measurements, attention to food habits, or remarks about distribution, but his tally of a hundred or more animals indigenous to the lower reaches of the Columbia, and descriptions, at greater or lesser length, of at least two dozen species and subspecies then new to science.

Before we leave this summary of Lewis's zoology, it should be pointed out that he included a number of animal biographies about species not native to the Lower Columbia, but to the Rockies and Interior Basin. For instance, he wrote about Franklin's grouse which, he said, he had not seen since leaving the mountains. These inclusions raise the question as to why they appear in the Fort Clatsop journal, if he actually kept a diary during the period he was crossing the Bitterroots and descending the Clearwater, Snake, and Columbia. Earlier, from Fort Mandan to the Lemhi, he had recorded events and observations as they occurred.

[20] This is the "sewellel" of Lewis and Clark. It is a rodent, but *not* a beaver.
[21] Jackson, *Letters*, 471.

Ethnobotany

Lewis obtained most of his Chinookan ethnobotanical (and ethnozoological) data from nearby Clatsop, Chinook, and Cathlamet Indians. Acquiring it had been difficult for lack of an interpreter. As a
result, he had had to rely on generally meaningless "signs" and to
utilize what little knowledge he had been able to gain of Chinook
jargon, that unique *lingua franca* consisting of Indian, French, and
English words by means of which the numerous Northwestern tribes
conversed with each other and with the whites.

More than half of the plants Lewis referred to in his Fort Clatsop
journal benefitted Chinookan Indians in one way or another. We will
discuss them under appropriate headings, such as food, apparel, weapons, and boats.

Foods—Lewis described several roots which played important roles in
the Indian dietary economy: "shannetahque" (edible thistle, *Cirsium
edule*), "rush" (horsetail, *Equisetum telmateia*), "fern" (western
bracken, *Pteridium aquilinum pubescens*), cattail (*Typha latifolia*),
and wappato (*Sagittaria latifolia*).

The root of the thistle, as Lewis described it, was from 9 to 15
inches in length and the width of a thumb. When first taken from the
ground it was white and almost as crisp as a carrot. After cooking, it
became black and was more sugary than any of the other native roots.
Though sometimes eaten raw, it was inferior in that condition (IV, 3).

The root of the horsetail was about one inch in length and thick as
a man's thumb. The pulp was white, brittle, and easily chewed. It was
ordinarily eaten after it had been roasted. To Lewis's palate it was
"reather insipid in point of flavour" (IV, 7).

The root of the bracken varied in size from that of a goose quill to
a finger, with the center divided into two equal parts by a ligament. On
either side was a white substance which, when roasted in embers, was
"much like wheat dough and not very unlike it in flavour, though it
has also a pungency which becomes more visible after you have chewed
it for some time; this pungency was disagreeable to me, but the natives
eat it voraciously and I have no doubt but it is a very nutricious food"
(IV, 5).

"The Indians of this neighbourhood," Lewis wrote, "eat the root
of the Cattail or Cooper's flag. it is pleasantly taisted and appears to be
very nutricious. the inner part of the root which is eaten without any
previous preparation is composed of a number of capillary white flexa-

ble strong fibers among which is a mealy or starch like substance which readily desolves in the mouth and seperate from the fibers which are then rejected. it appears to me that this substance would make excellent starch; nothing can be of a purer white than it is" (IV, 121–122).

The most valuable of all roots eaten by Chinookan natives was the wappato, though it did not grow in the vicinity of Fort Clatsop, no closer than the Cathlamet villages which were about 15 miles from the ocean. The bulb of this plant was about the size of a hen's egg and, when roasted, tasted much like a potato. It grew in swampy places and the native women, to obtain it, travelled in small canoes. Once at the chosen site, they left the canoes and slipped into the water, sometimes up to their necks, and loosened the bulbs with their feet. These then floated to the surface and were tossed by the women into the boats (IV, 217–218). Lewis said that the coastal tribesmen would dispose of their most valuable articles to obtain this root (IV, 215).

The identity of another root described by Lewis has not definitely been established. In writing about it, he said: "I observe no difference between the liquorice of this country and that common to many parts of the United States where it is also sometimes cultivated in our gardens . . . the natives roast it in the embers and pound it slightly with a small stick in order to make it seperate more readily from the strong liggament which forms the center of the root . . . this root when roasted possesses an agreeable flavour not unlike the sweet pittaitoe" (IV, 10). Coues identified this plant as the wild licorice, *Glycyrrhiza lepidota,* though specifying that the licorice of eastern gardens was the introduced European species, *G. glabra.*[22] David Douglas, on the other hand, identified it as the seashore lupine, *Lupinus littoralis* (III, 230n), and he may have been right, for this plant is sometimes called Chinook licorice. Both species grow along the Pacific coast in Oregon and Washington.

According to Lewis, Clatsop and Chinook Indians relished the fruit of a number of local plants. His journal referred more particularly to salal (*Gaultheria shallon*), evergreen huckleberry (*Vaccinium ovatum*), cranberry (*Vaccinium oxycoccus intermedium*), saccacommis or bearberry (*Arctostaphylos uva-ursi*), and Oregon crab apple (*Pyrus fusca*).

The fruit of the salal (called shallon by Lewis) was "a deep purple berry about the size of a buck short or common black cherry" (IV, 52). The natives baked it into large loaves. Apparently this was the "Shelewell" of Clark. While he was encamped on Baker's Bay an

[22] Coues, III, 824.

Indian woman gave him a kind of soup "made of bread of the *Shele-well* berries mixed with roots" (III, 274).

The evergreen huckleberry was also deep purple in color. "The natives," wrote Lewis, "either eat these berrys when ripe immediately from the bushes or dryed in the sun or by means of their sw[e]ating kilns; very frequently they pound them and bake them in large loaves of 10 or fifteen pounds; this bread keeps very well during one season and retains the moist jeucies of the fruit much better than by any other method of preservation. this bread is broken and stired in could water untill it be sufficiently thick and then eaten; in this way the natives most generally use it" (IV, 14).

The cranberry was "a light brown bury reather larger and much the shape of the black haw" (IV, 12). Lewis said it was "precisely the same common to the U' States, and is the production of marshey or boggy grounds" (IV, 19).

The fruit of the bearberry was scarlet and about the size of a small cherry (IV, 12). "The natives," wrote Lewis, "on this side of the Rocky mountains who can procure this berry invariably use it; to me it is a very tasteless and insipid fruit . . . the natives usually eat them without any preperation. the fruit ripens in september and remains on the bushes all winter . . . these berries are sometimes geathered and hung in their lodges in bags where they dry without further trouble, for in their most succulent state they appear to be almost as dry as flour" (IV, 21–22).

"There is a wild crab apple which the natives eat," Lewis said. "this growth differs but little in appearance from that of the wild crab of the Atlantic States. but the fruit consists of little oval burries which grow in clusters at the extremities of the twigs like the black haws. the fruit is of a brown colour, oval form and about double as large as the black haw . . . when the fruit has been touched by the frost [it] is not unpleasant, being an agreeable assed [acid]" (III, 261–262).

In November while still on the north bank of the estuary, Clark mentioned a berry he said the natives called "solme" and used for food. Lewis's later description stated that the plant producing this berry was much the same size and shape as the "Sollomons Seal" of the Atlantic states, though the berries were "not Specked as the Solomon's seal berry is" (IV, 16–17). Subsequently, one writer indicated that solme was the native name for the wild cranberry (III, 221n). However, Lewis's description is clearly that of false solomon's seal (*Smilacina* sp.), different species of which grow throughout Washington.[23]

[23] Coues, III, 826n.

Tobacco—Chinookans smoked the dried, crumbled leaves of bearberry —as did members of the Lewis and Clark party at Fort Clatsop— though they sometimes mixed these leaves with those of their own species of tobacco. The latter was planted and cultivated in specially prepared fields. According to David Douglas: "The Nicotiana is never sowed by the Indians near the villages lest it should be pulled and used before it comes to maturity; they select for its cultivation an open place in the wood, where they burn a dead tree or stump, and strewing ashes over the ground, plant the tobacco there."[24] During the winter Clark reported arrival at the fort of Indians from whom he bought "about 3 pipes of their tobacco in a neet little bag made of rushes. This tobacco was much like what we had Seen before with the *Sosone* or Snake Indians" (III, 300).

Apparel—Chinookan Indians covered their bodies with a minimum of clothing. Men ordinarily wore nothing whatever except a robe, and women a robe, skirt, and in cold weather, a vest. Since robes ordinarily required several skins, they had to be sewed together. For this purpose, the Indians used cords of cedar bark (*Thuja plicata*) and "silk-grass."[25] The skirt, according to Lewis, was "a tissue of white cedar bark, bruised or broken into small shreds, which are interwoven in the middle by means of several cords of the same materials . . . this tissue is sometimes formed of little twisted cords of the silk-grass knotted at their ends and interwoven as described of the bark . . . they also form them of flags [*Iris* sp.] and rushes [probably in this case bulrushes, *Juncus* or *Scirpus*] which are woarn in a similar manner" (IV, 85–86).

Occasionally the Clatsops and Chinooks wore brimless, cone-shaped hats which were held on the head by strings passing under the chin. Each of these was made of cedar bark and bear grass (*Xerophyllum tenax*), "wrought with the fingers so closely that it cast the rain most effectually" (IV, 24).

Domestic Utensils—Chinookans manufactured many bowls, platters, spoons, and baskets, all used for cooking, serving, and eating their different foods. Bowls and spoons were carved out of solid pieces of wood such as cedar or pine. Platters, on which they served fish, roots, and berries, were ordinarily plain mats made of rushes or flags. Baskets used for cooking were closely woven so as to be watertight, and usually

[24] David Douglas, "Sketch of a Journey to the Northwestern Part of the Continent During the Years 1824–1827," *Oreg. Hist. Quart.*, 5–6 (1904–5), 261.

[25] "Silk-grass" may have been any one of several plants, Indian hemp, *Apocynum cannabinum*, among them.

of cedar bark and bear grass. Baskets and bags used for purposes other than cooking were less closely woven and ordinarily made of the same materials, but sometimes of rushes, flags, silk-grass, and sedges (*Carex* sp.) .

Weapons and Fishing Tackle—Chinookan bows, flat and thin, were usually shaped from "the heart of the arbor-vita or white cedar" (III, 346) . Arrows were usually of two parts, a long feathered one made "of light white pine [*Pinus monticola* ?] rather larger than a swan's quill" (III, 347) , and a shorter, thinner part with arrowhead made of some harder wood. For fishing, these Indians employed "the common streight net, the scooping or diping net with a long handle, the gig and the hook and line" (III, 350) . Nets and lines were made of silk-grass or cedar bark.

Houses—Chinookan dwellings were customarily semi-subterranean, about 20 feet wide and 30 long, and fabricated of timber most suitable and available. Those at or near the coast, such as Clatsop, were of spruce (*Picea sitchensis*) or fir, either Douglas (*Pseudotsuga taxifolia*) or grand (*Abies grandis*) , while those in the region of The Dalles were most often of western red cedar (*Thuja plicata*) . Rafters, posts, and ridgepoles were lashed together with cedar cords. Roofs were of cedar bark or boards kept in place with cedar fibers. For splitting timbers, the Clatsop and other Indians used wedges fashioned from wood of the Oregon crab apple (*Pyrus fusca*) . When properly seasoned, this was extremely hard. The natives used these same wedges, too, for splitting firewood and hollowing out canoes. "I have seen," Lewis declared, "the natives drive the wedges of this wood into solid dry pine which it cleft without fracturing or injuring the wedg[e] in the smallest degree" (IV, 19–20) .

Boats—Chinookans constructed dugouts of many sizes and shapes, some of them up to 50 feet in length and capable of carrying 20 to 30 passengers. These were handsome craft, usually of cedar but sometimes of fir. Many were decorated at the bow with "images," these being grotesque representations of animal or man carved from the same piece of timber as the boat.

It is appropriate that we conclude this section on ethnobotany with a further word about the western red cedar, certainly one of the most majestic trees native to the Northwest. As Lewis's frequent references to it indicate, no plant was quite so important to Chinookan Indians. They used it in many ways in addition to building boats. In summary, they relied upon the wood for culinary vessels such as bowls, platters, and spoons and employed tremendous amounts in building their homes. They also used slabs of bark. Freshly taken from the tree, these often provided roofing and, in temporary dwellings, siding. Coarse fibers taken from the lining of the bark served to fabricate everything from mats, platters, and baskets to hats, cords, nets, and fish lines. Cedar fibers, too, lashed house timbers together, tied mats in place around burial canoes, and bound infants to boards in the head-flattening process. Shredded bark, almost as fine as cotton, made clothing, bedding for infants, and cranial pads for head-flattening.

Ethnozoology

In their perennial struggle to exist, Clatsop, Chinook, and Cathlamet Indians made use in some way of almost every animal, large or small, that inhabited the region of the Lower Columbia River. Lewis's abundant ethnozoological notes list those used most commonly, some for food, others for clothing, weapons, or ornamentation.

Food—In the vicinity of Fort Clatsop, Chinookan Indians found such land mammals as deer, elk, bear, and squirrel and such aquatic ones as seal, sea otter, and porpoise. Occasionally, as we know, the sea provided a whale. Among birds, ducks, geese, and swans abounded, at least seasonally. The river itself provided sturgeon, eulachon, salmon, and other fish. All of these and many others went into the flesh pot.

In the economy of the Chinookans, however, no animal was quite so important as the the salmon. The Columbia and its vast network of tributaries provided spawning grounds for five different species of salmon, all belonging to a single genus, *Oncorhynchus*. Of these, the most important by far was the Chinook or king salmon (*O. tshawytscha*). Lewis regularly referred to it as the "common salmon" (he encountered it more often than any other species) and said it was this species that "extends itself into all the rivers and little creeks on this side of the Continent, and to which the natives are so much indebted for their subsistence" (IV, 163).

The Chinook salmon is aptly called "king," being unequaled by any other fish the world over in commercial value, and of greater economic importance in the Pacific Northwest as a food fish than all other species combined. It is also considerably the largest of the five, averaging 20 or more pounds, with an occasional giant tipping the scales at near 100.

The Chinook salmon usually begins its first run (two others follow) late in March and may travel up the Columbia 1,000 miles or more. Those that enter the river earliest tend to travel farthest. In Lewis and Clark's day, before men built great dams, they journeyed to the remote, swift-flowing streams rushing down from the western walls of the Continental Divide, even to such tiny affluents as Boyle Creek of the Lemhi and Hungry Creek of the Lochsa. In their progress upstream, they averaged two to four miles a day, accelerating their speed as they neared spawning grounds.

The sockeye or blueback salmon (*O. nerka*) averages only about five pounds in weight, habitually runs in the spring, and was next in importance as a food fish to Chinookans. Lewis and Clark called it "red charr" and seemingly first encountered it in Gray's Bay on November 11, just before they rounded Ellice's Point. Wrote Clark, "We purchased of the Indians 19 red charr which we found to be excellent fish" (III, 216). Lewis's later description, by which we recognize the red charr as the sockeye, reads in part as follows: "The red Charr are reather broader in proportion to their length than the common salmon . . . the nostrum [rostrum] exceeds the lower jaw more and the teeth are neither as large nor so numerous as those of the salmon. some of them are entirely red on the belley and sides . . . and none of them are variagated with the dark spots which make the body of the other" (IV, 164).

The silver or coho salmon (*O. kisutch*), averaging five to eight pounds, runs later, from July to November, and next to Chinook and sockeye is the most important member of the genus. The journalists consistently referred to it as the "white salmon trout." When Clark first sampled the flesh of this fish (October 26 at The Dalles) fried in a little bear's oil, he declared it to be "the finest fish he had ever tasted" (III, 161). Writing at Fort Clatsop in mid-March, Lewis said: "The *white Salmon Trout* which we had previously seen only at the great falls of the Columbia has now made it's appearance in the creeks near this place . . . it is thicker in proportion to it's width than the [common] salmon. the tongue is thick and firm beset on each border with small subulate teeth in a single series" (IV, 174).

If the explorers at any time encountered the hump-backed salmon (*O. gorbusha*) or the dog salmon (*O. keta*), they failed to identify them. Parenthetically, all five species of salmon were technically described and named a few years before the Expedition reached the Pacific, so that Lewis's descriptions of them have no claim to priority.

According to Lewis, coastal natives employed the "common net" in taking salmon and trout, the scooping net for small fish, and gig and hook for "taking such fish as they can procure by their means" (III, 350).

As we know, Chinookans generally cooked fresh salmon in water-tight baskets by introducing heated stones. Others, beyond immediate needs, they preserved by drying on scaffolds in the sun. In the case of the eulachon, wrote Lewis, "the natives run a small stick through their gills and hang them in the smoke of their lodges, or kindle a small fire under them for the purpose of drying them. they need no previous guting &c and will cure in 24 hours" (IV, 131). They cooked sturgeon by means of steam. Again according to Lewis:

a brisk fire is kindled on which a parcel of stones are la[i]d. when the fire birns down and the stones are sufficiently heated, the stones are so arranged as to form a tolerable level surface, the sturgeon which had been previously cut into large fletches is now laid on the hot stones; a parsel of small boughs of bushes is next laid on and a second course of the sturgeon thus rep[e]ating alternate layers of sturgeon and boughs untill the whole is put on which they design to cook. it is next covered closely with matts and water is poured in such a manner as to run in among the hot stones and the vapor arrising being confined by the mats, cooks the fish   the whole process is performed in an hour, and the sturgeon thus cooked is much better than either boiled or roasted (IV, 131–132).

Clark had the opportunity of watching Clatsops cook whale blubber to obtain oil. This operation was performed in large wooden troughs in which they placed water and meat and then hot stones. The resultant oil was poured into the "bladders and the guts of the whale" (III, 333).

Clothing—Lewis reported Chinookan robes, the main article of apparel, made from skins of such animals as mountain beaver or "sewellel" (a rodent that looks and acts like a pocket gopher but is not a beaver), Oregon bobcat, mountain goat, elk, deer, bear, raccoon, beaver, and sea otter. "The most esteemed and valuable of these robes," Lewis declared, "are made of strips of the skins of the Sea Otter net [knit] together with the bark of the white cedar or silk-grass. these strips are first twisted and laid parallel with each other a little distance assunder, and then net or wove together in such a manner that the fur appears equally on both sides, and unites between the strands" (IV, 185). In writing about the mountain goat, Lewis said that he had seen many skins of that animal "in possession of the natives dressed with the wool on them and a[l]so seen the blankets which they manufacture of the wooll of this sheep" (IV, 96).

For ornamentation, these Indians made necklaces of bear claws, elk teeth, and shells of different kinds, especially *Dentalium*. Apparently most of the *Dentalium* shells came from the Strait of Juan de Fuca where they were abundant. One writer said that the natives took them from "the sand, at low water."[26] Chinookan Indians in The Dalles region sometimes decorated garments with porcupine quills.

Weapons and Fishing Tackle—Clatsop and Chinook customarily made bow-strings of elk sinews and covered backs of bows with the same material "laid on with a Gleue which they make from the sturgeon" (III, 346). They fashioned quivers out of skins from a young bear or wolf (III, 457).

Though most of these Indians had by now acquired guns from whites, they still used bow and arrow when hunting. Lewis wrote that many of the elk killed at Fort Clatsop contained arrow heads put there at some former date by the natives (III, 347). They employed spears or gigs to capture sea otter, beaver, and porpoise, deadfalls or snares to trap wolf, raccoon, fox, and the like, and large pits, some 20 by 30 feet, to obtain elk.

Trade—Lewis's Fort Clatsop journal contained much ethnozoological and ethnobotanical data on intertribal commerce, on casual trade between Indians and the white visitors who infrequently entered the estuary, and, of course, on traffic that persisted during the winter at the fort between the explorers and neighboring tribesmen. As previously indicated, there was continuous trade on the river, with canoes moving downstream carrying such plant and animal products as pounded salmon and bear grass and others travelling upstream laden with wappato, sturgeon, and eulachon. At the mouth of the river, in trading with the whites, the natives exchanged "dressed and undressed Elkskins, skins of the Sea Otter, common otter, beaver, common fox, spuck [young sea otter], and tiger cat" for guns, knives, kettles, blankets, tobacco, beads, and other articles (III, 328). At Fort Clatsop, Lewis and Clark traded mainly for sea otter skins and for food, particularly fish and native edible roots.

In one sense at least, Lewis's ethnological studies must be regarded as even more important than his biological. The plants and animals he described at such painstaking length are, by and large, still with us, whereas the Indians are not. Even before Lewis and Clark first sighted

[26] Elliott Coues, ed., *New Light on the Early History of the Greater Northwest: The Manuscript Journals of Alexander Henry and David Thompson*, 2 vols. (Minneapolis, 1965), II, 753.

the breakers of the Pacific, the population of coastal tribes had been appreciably reduced by smallpox. Just two decades later, a devasting epidemic of malaria struck suddenly, killing most that remained. The few who survived, as they mingled increasingly with whites, underwent rapid cultural change. In less than a generation the once flourishing Chinookan family, for all practical purposes, had ceased to exist.

SUMMARY OF DISCOVERIES

Animals New to Science

WHITE STURGEON. *Acipenser transmontanus* Rich. (Thwaites, III, 234; IV, 131–132; Coues, III, 896). Described, 1836.

WESTERN GREBE. *Aechmophorus occidentalis* Lawrence. [A.O.U. 1] (Thwaites, IV, 142; Coues, III, 882). 1858.

WHITE-FRONTED GOOSE. *Anser albifrons frontalis* Baird. [A.O.U. 171] (Thwaites, IV, 170; Coues, III, 884). 1858.

MOUNTAIN BEAVER; "SEWELLEL." *Aplodontia rufa rufa* (Raf.). (Thwaites, IV, 109; Coues, III, 861). 1817.

RING-NECKED DUCK. *Aythya collaris* (Donovan). [A.O.U. 150] (Thwaites, IV, 210; Coues, III, 889). 1809.

LESSER CANADA GOOSE. *Branta canadensis leucopareia* (Brandt). (Thwaites, IV, 145; Coues, III, 885). 1836.

ROOSEVELT'S ELK. *Cervus canadensis roosevelti* Merriam. (Thwaites, III, 263). 1898.

WESTERN COMMON CROW. *Corvus brachyrhynchos hesperis* Ridgway. [A.O.U. 488b] (Thwaites, III, 257). 1887.

NORTHWESTERN CROW. *Corvus caurinus* Baird. [A.O.U. 489] (Thwaites, IV, 129; Coues, III, 874). 1858.

WESTERN AMERICAN RAVEN. *Corvus corax sinuatus* Wagler. [A.O.U. 486] (Thwaites, IV, 129). 1829.

WESTERN PILEATED WOODPECKER. *Dryocopus pileatus picinus* (Bangs). [A.O.U. 405c] (Thwaites, IV, 132). 1910.

TOWNSEND'S CHIPMUNK. *Eutamias townsendii townsendii* (Bachman). (Thwaites, IV, 107). 1839.

PACIFIC FULMAR. *Fulmarus glacialis rodgersii* (Cassin). [A.O.U. 86.1] (Thwaites, IV, 141; Coues, III, 881). 1862.

OREGON BOBCAT. *Lynx rufus fasciatus* Raf. (Thwaites, IV, 92; Coues, III, 847). 1817.

STRIPED SKUNK. *Mephitis mephitis notata* (Howell). (Thwaites, IV, 118). 1901.

WHISTLING SWAN. *Olor columbianus* (Ord). [A.O.U. 180] (Thwaites, IV, 147; Coues, III, 885). 1815.

OREGON JAY. *Perisoreus canadensis obscurus* Ridgway. [A.O.U. 485] (Thwaites, III, 309; Coues, II, 743) . 1873.

TOWNSEND'S MOLE. *Scapanus townsendii* (Bachman) . (Thwaites, IV, 113; Coues, III, 864) . 1839.

WESTERN GRAY SQUIRREL. *Sciurus griseus griseus* Ord. (Thwaites, IV, 106; Coues, III, 854) . 1818.

DOUGLAS'S SQUIRREL; CHICKAREE. *Tamiasciurus douglasii douglasii* (Bachman) . (Thwaites, IV, 106; Coues, III, 858) . 1836.

RICHARDSON'S RED SQUIRREL. *Tamiasciurus hudsonicus hudsonicus* (Bachman) . (Thwaites, IV, 107; Coues, III, 855) . 1839.

WESTERN BADGER. *Taxidea taxus neglecta* Mearns. (Thwaites, IV, 110) . 1891.

EULACHON; CANDLE FISH. *Thaleichthys pacificus* (Richardson) . (Thwaites, IV, 102; Coues, II, 807) . 1836.

? WESTERN WINTER WREN. *Troglodytes troglodytes pacificus* Baird. [A.O.U. 722a] (Thwaites, IV, 133; Coues, III, 876) . 1864.

Plants New to Science

RED ALDER. *Alnus rubra* Bongard. (Thwaites, IV, 55; Coues, III, 833) . 1832.

EDIBLE THISTLE; "SHANATAQUE." *Cirsium edule* Nuttall. (Thwaites, IV, 3) . 1841.

SALAL. *Gaultheria shallon* Pursh. (Thwaites, IV, 52) . 1814.

SEASHORE LUPINE; "CULWHAYMA." *Lupinus littoralis* Douglas. (Thwaites, IV, 10) . 1828.

SITKA SPRUCE. *Picea sitchensis* (Bong.) . (Thwaites, IV, 41; Coues, III, 832) . 1832.

WESTERN WHITE PINE. *Pinus monticola* Douglas. (Thwaites, IV, 47) . 1837.

WESTERN BRACKEN. *Pteridium aquïlinum pubescens* Underw. (Thwaites, IV, 5) . 1900.

OREGON CRAB APPLE. *Pyrus fusca* Raf. (Thwaites, IV, 19; Coues, III, 826) . 1830.

MOUNTAIN HEMLOCK. *Tsuga mertensiana* (Bong.) Carr. (Thwaites, IV, 43; Coues, III, 830) . 1832.

EVERGREEN HUCKLEBERRY. *Vaccinium ovatum* Pursh. 1814.

Lewis and Clark Herbarium

SPINULOSE SHIELD-FERN. *Aspidium spinulosum* Sw. = *Dryopteris spinulosa* (Muell.) Kuntze. Collected January 20, 1806.

EDIBLE THISTLE. *Cirsium edule* Nuttall. March 13.

SALAL. *Gaultheria shallon* Pursh. January 20.

SQUIRREL-TAIL GRASS. *Hordeum jubatum* L. March 13.

OREGON MOSS. *Hypnum oreganum* Sull. January 20.

FERN. *Lomaria spicant* Desv. = *Blechnum boreale* Pursh. January 20.

SILVER-WEED. *Potentilla anserina* L. March 13.

Huckleberry. *Vaccinium myrtillus* L. January 20.
Evergreen huckleberry. *Vaccinium ovatum* Pursh. January 27.

Indian Tribes Encountered

Salishan Linguistic Family: † Tillamooks (Killamucks of Lewis and Clark) .

Topographic Features Named and/or Discovered

Point William (Thwaites, III, 253) —— Tongue Point.
Meriwether Bay (Thwaites, III, 270) —— Young's Bay.
† Fort River (Thwaites, III, 359) —— Lewis and Clark River (referred to often in journals as Netul River, the Indian name) .
† Clatsop River (Thwaites, III, 320) —— Necanicum River.
† Kilamox River (Thwaites, III, 325) —— possibly Wilson River of today.

Fort Clatsop
to
Camp Chopunnish

CHAPTER SEVENTEEN

"The leafing of the hucklebury reminds us of spring," reflected Lewis on March 22 (IV, 196). Early in the afternoon of the next day, when the rain halted and the sky cleared, the Corps of Discovery evacuated Fort Clatsop. Filled with delight "as in freedom won," the men stepped into their loaded canoes and dropped down the river to Young's Bay. On departing, Clark wrote: "At this place we had wintered and remained from the 7th of Decr. 1805 to this day and have lived as well as we had any right to expect, and we can say that we were never one day without 3 meals of some kind a day either pore elk meat or roots, notwithstanding the repeated fall of rain which has fallen almost constantly" (IV, 197).

Before leaving, in a ceremony untinged by regret, Lewis and Clark presented Fort Clatsop to Chief Comowool. It was an outright gift, an expression of gratitude to the Clatsop leader who had demonstrated his friendship and helpfulness in many ways. Comowool neglected the property given to him. Just six years after the party abandoned it, Gabriel Franchère, on visiting it, found only "piles of rough, unhewn logs overgrown with parasite creepers."[1] Several years later (1836) John Townsend reported: "I walked today around the beach to the foot of Young's Bay, a distance of about ten miles, to see the remains of the house in which Lewis and Clark's party resided during the winter which they spent here. The logs of which it is composed, are still perfect, but the roof of bark has disappeared, and the whole vicinity is overgrown with thorn and wild currant bushes."[2]

[1] *Early Western Travels*, VI, 259.
[2] Townsend, *Narrative of a Journey Across the Rocky Mountains*, 256.

With the further passage of time all traces of the fort disappeared. However, in 1955 on the occasion of the Lewis and Clark sesquicentennial celebration, historically minded citizens and organizations of Oregon joined forces to build a replica of Fort Clatsop on the site of the original, following closely the floor-plan and dimensions as drawn by Clark on the elk-hide cover of his field book. Three years later, by appropriate action, Congress created the Fort Clatsop National Memorial, thereby insuring the preservation of the site for all time. Visitors to the Memorial today are impressed with the replica of the fort, the inviting surroundings, and the attractive, recently constructed museum devoted to interpreting the story of Lewis and Clark.

[2]

From Young's Bay the explorers worked their way slowly upriver, averaging 15 to 18 miles a day. They kept to the south side, nosing in and out of narrow channels. With the shoreline low and swampy, it was difficult to find satisfactory campsites. Periodic storms created winds, high waves, and strong currents. Flood tides caused problems. Sergeant Ordway wrote that "the tide rose higher than common [last night] and came in under my blankets before I awoke and obleged me to move twice."[3] At times, with both wind and tide contrary, it was impossible for the party to advance until the tide changed.

They were rarely out of sight of Indians, Chinooks proffering sea otter skins, Clatsops returning home with loads of wappato and eulachon, Cathlamets trolling for sturgeon. A Cathlamet chief, pleased with a medal bestowed on him, presented Lewis and Clark with a large sturgeon. Other Indians gave them seal meat. They welcomed these gifts, for the hunters who ranged ahead each day found game scarce.

On the third day after leaving the fort, Lewis announced that their supply of tobacco had been reduced to a few carrots, and that the men accustomed to using it (all but seven) and to whom he was now obliged to deny its use, "suffer much for the want of it" (IV, 203). In this contingency the chewers substituted wild crab apple bark and the smokers filled their pipes with the inner bark of the red willow (*Cornus occidentalis* ?) and bearberry. At the same time, they looked forward to opening the caches in Shoshoni Cove where they had stored tobacco on the way out.

Almost daily, Lewis reported animals and plants observed. For

[3] Ordway, 332.

instance, on March 24 he noted "a few Cormorant, duckinmallard, butterbox, and common large geese" (IV, 198).[4] On the following day he wrote that the bottom lands supported a heavy growth of cottonwood, sevenbark, gooseberry, greenbriar, and "the large leafed thorn." The thorn was then in bloom, and Indians advised him that it bore a fruit about an inch in diameter that was good to eat (IV, 201).[5] A day or so later, he said that he had been able to obtain from the natives "a dryed fruit which resembled the raspburry and which I be[l]eive to be the fruit of the large leaved thorn . . . it is reather ascid tho' pleasantly flavored. I preserved a specimen of this fruit" (IV, 207).

Since Lewis demonstrated such an obvious interest in this plant, no doubt believing that it might profitably be introduced into the East, he thereby drew the attention of later botanists to it. At first they were uncertain as to its identity, though they now generally agree that it was the salmonberry (*Rubus spectabilis*), a shrub common to wet places in the Coastal Zone that produces, quite early in the spring, a delicate red flower and in mid-summer, a fruit like a raspberry or loganberry. The evidence most firmly supporting this identification is a preserved specimen of this plant in the Lewis and Clark Herbarium of the Academy of Natural Sciences of Philadelphia with an affixed purple tag bearing the significant statement in Lewis's handwriting: "Fruit like a raspberry. Columbia, March 27, 1806."[6]

Six days of paddling brought the Expedition beyond the Coast Range and shortly to Deer Island. Here Lewis wrote that "the upper point of this island may be esteemed the lower side or commencement of the Columbia valley" (IV, 213). This island (close to the present town of Deer Island, Oregon) was well named, since the hunters after arriving quickly killed seven white-tails from a herd of some 100 encountered. Other animals abounded. Ordway reported that a species of garter snake was "as thick as the Spears of Grass."[7] Waterfowl, too, were more numerous than at any place visited since leaving the pur-

[4] The cormorant was probably the Farallon cormorant (*Phalacrocorax auritus albociliatus*) (see Burroughs, 182). The duckinmallard was the mallard (*Anas platyrhynchos*), the butterbox the bufflehead duck (*Charitonetta albeola*), and common goose the Canada goose (*Branta canadensis*).

[5] The cottonwood was black cottonwood (*Populus trichocarpa*), sevenbark was *Physocarpus opulifolius*, gooseberry was *Ribes divaricatum*, and greenbriar was *Rubus macropetalus*. (See C. V. Piper's identification, Thwaites, IV, 201n.)

[6] The salmonberry was one of 13 Lewis and Clark plants later figured by Frederick Pursh in his *Flora Americae Septentrionalis*.

[7] Ordway, 333. The snake may have been the northwestern garter snake, *Thamnophis sirtalis concinnus*.

lieus of Fort Clatsop. Among the fowl was a duck, somewhat smaller than the mallard, which was entirely new to Lewis. Ornithologists who later read his description identified it as the ring-necked duck (*Aythya collaris*). Coues, for instance, declared, "L. and C. are again discoverers of a new species; for this duck was unknown to science in 1806."[8]

On March 29 the explorers came to the mouth of a considerable stream which they had overlooked in their descent of the Columbia. The natives called it *Cah-wah-na-hi-ooks*, though it is on maps of Washington today as Lewis's River, where it may be seen separating Cowlitz County from Clark County. Three days later, while encamped at the mouth of the Washougal River (opposite the entrance of the Sandy), Lewis and Clark received disquieting news. Natives who were travelling downstream informed them of an acute food shortage among tribes at The Dalles and the Narrows. As a result of a long, difficult winter, they had exhausted their stores of dried fish, and they could not count on the salmon running again until the full of the next moon— about the first of May. That evening Lewis wrote:

we did not doubt the veracity of those people who seemed to be on their way with their families and effects in search of subsistence which they find it easy to procure in this fertile valley. This information gave us much uneasiness with rispect to our future means of subsistence. above [the] falls or through the plains from thence to the Chopunnish there are no deer Antelope nor Elk on which we can depend for subsistence; their horses are very poor most probably at this season, and if they have no fish their dogs must be in the same situation, under these circumstances there seems to be but a gloomy prospect for subsistence on any terms; we therefore took it into serious consideration what measures we were to pursue on this occasion (IV, 228).

They promptly dismissed, for two reasons, the idea momentarily entertained of encamping here until the salmon returned. One, any extended delay might jeopardize their chances of reaching St. Louis before ice claimed the Missouri; two, they might lose their horses entrusted to the Nez Perces who had informed them, on parting, of their intention to cross the mountains to hunt buffalo as early as the season would allow.

Deeming it imperative, therefore, that they continue upstream without delay, they resolved that they would bend every effort to acquire a few of the more elegant native canoes to trade for horses owned by the Eneeshur and other Indians residing in the vicinity of the falls. With horses they could travel faster than in boats, and in case all

[8] Coues, III, 889n. See also Thwaites, IV, 210, and Burroughs, 324.

other food sources failed, they could fall back on horse meat. "For we now view the horses," Lewis declared, "as our only certain resource for food" (IV, 233).

While at this same camp, Lewis and Clark were informed by Indians that the Sandy River headed at the base of nearby Mt. Hood and ran only a short course. This intelligence came as a surprise, for they had regarded the Sandy as a large river, one that drained all of the immense inter-mountain valley to the south. "We were now convinced." Lewis wrote, "that there must be some other considerable river which flowed into the Columbia on it's southside below us which we have not yet seen . . . we indeavoured to ascertain by what stream the southern portion of the Columbian valley was watered but could obtain no satisfactory information of the natives on this head" (IV, 227).

By a piece of luck, on the very next day a number of Indians came upstream, two of whom resided, Lewis and Clark were informed, at the falls of a large river—they called it the Multnomah—which emptied into the Columbia on the south side only a few miles below their present encampment. Even though it meant delay, Clark turned back downstream at once, taking with him seven picked men and an Indian guide. If such a stream existed, it would alter appreciably the geography of this region as he had heretofore conceived it and had portrayed it on his maps.

Late that afternoon Clark and his companions found the Multnomah, the river known today as the Willamette. Three elongate islands guarding its mouth had effectively hidden it from the explorers until now. The next morning Clark travelled up it about seven miles to the vicinity of present-day Portland. He was impressed with its size and convinced that it drained all that vast tract of country between the Coast Range and Cascades as far south as "the waters of the Gulf of California, and no doubt it heads with the Rochejhone [Yellowstone] and Del Nord [Colorado] River" (IV, 339). At no other time did Clark go quite so far astray geographically. In later years he doubtless learned that practically the entire length of California intervenes between the Willamette drainage and that of the Colorado, and that effective barriers such as the Cascades and Interior Basin prevent a Willamette juxtaposition with the Yellowstone.

The party tarried three days at the mouth of the Washougal. In that time, they not only discovered the Willamette but also killed and jerked the meat of several bear, elk, and deer. As they resumed their journey, they were optimistic that with the addition of salmon, dogs, and roots they could obtain from the Indians, and with whatever else the hunters provided, they would make out until they arrived again on the Clearwater. If not, there was that "certain resource" of horse meat.

On Sunday, April 6, near Beacon Rock, Reuben Field killed and brought to Lewis a bird resembling the Virginia quail (bobwhite, *Colinus virginianus*), though differing from it markedly in its plumage. For one thing, two feathers about two and a half inches long extended upward and backward from the crown. Lewis characterized it as "a most beautiful bird," wrote a lengthy description of it (the first), and then preserved its skin (IV, 252–253). This was the bird now known as the mountain quail (*Oreortyx pictus pictus*), formally described and named by David Douglas in 1829, 23 years later. Later we will report on the fate of this skin preserved by Lewis.

[3]

Lewis and Clark spent 10 long, grueling days in passing the Cascades and Narrows and finally floated their boats on placid water above Celilo Falls. At no other time during the entire journey did they express so much concern about their relations with the Indians. At each stop the latter surrounded them, numerous, bold, often insolent, and bent on stealing any article left unguarded for a single moment. Though the explorers were continuously on the alert, they lost knives, axes, tomahawks, blankets, and other possessions. The natives even attempted to steal Lewis's dog.

Not until the party arrived near the mouth of Hood River did they again encounter horses, 10 or 12 owned by a tribe of Willacums. "The country below this place," Lewis explained, "will not permit the uce of this valuable animal except in the Columbian valley and there the present inhabitants have no uce for them as they reside immediately on the river and the country is too thickly timbered to admit them to run the game with horses if they had them" (IV, 280).

Above Hood River they found horses much more numerous, in most villages vastly outnumbering their owners; and it was here, against the background of hostility and thievery already described, that Lewis and Clark began dickering for these animals. Initially, they met with no success whatever, being greatly handicapped by the slender amount and variety of trade goods they had to offer. Trading improved, however, when the natives evinced an interest in the kettles owned by the party. For three of these, all they could spare, Lewis and

Clark acquired five horses. Clark then tried in vain to obtain others with offers of clothing, ribbon, knives, pieces of brass, yellow beads, and the like. His luck did not turn until after he had ministered to the squaw of one of the chiefs, a "sulky Bitch . . . somewhat afflicted with pains in her back" (IV, 298). When she professed profound relief from camphor and warm flannel, Clark regarded the moment propitious for talking trade with the chief who owned more horses than all the other people in the tribe combined. The moment was indeed right, for when he made an offer for two horses, the chief accepted without demur.

To transport their goods overland, Lewis and Clark needed a minimum of 12 horses. By April 21, after a solid week of feverish bartering such as this rapids-infested stretch of the river had never before experienced, they had acquired only 10—10 of literally thousands then tossing their manes on the north rim of the Columbia. Finally, at Celio Falls, forced to the opinion that these savages would part with no more horses, they decided to move on upriver, travelling partly by land and partly by water. They loaded nine of the horses with most of their goods, saving the tenth for Bratton who continued unable to walk. The rest of their belongings went into two canoes, with Colter and Potts in charge of one and Gass and Reuben Field the other.

[4]

As the Expedition again resumed its march, leaving behind forever the roar of the falls and the perpetual jabber of alien Chinookan tongues, Lewis had more than one reason for writing: "The plain is covered with a rich virdure of grass and herbs from four to nine inches high and exhibits a beautiful seen particularly pleasing after having been so long imprisoned in mountains and these almost impenetrably thick forrests of the seacoast" (IV, 290).

After they had travelled 14 miles, they encamped in an Eneeshur village of seven mat lodges, their Nez Perce guide (whom they had found at the Narrows) having informed them that the next village was too far away to be reached that night. From the Indians they bought four dogs, berries, root bread, and fuel. Twelve miles of travel the following morning brought them to the next village. Here, much to their satisfaction, they obtained six more horses, enough to allow them to discard their boats and journey entirely by land. They sold the dugouts to the natives, made additional pack saddles, and were on their way again. Three days later they encountered a party of Walla

Wallas (Walulas), including Chief Yellept, whom they had met the previous October. This local sachem, recalling the medal and other gifts presented to him on that occasion, greeted them cordially and invited them to his village situated almost directly across from the mouth of the Walla Walla River. That evening Yellept supplied important information. As Lewis reported it: "there was a good road which passed from the columbia opposite to this village to the entrance of the Kooskooskee [Clearwater] . . . there were a plenty of deer and antelope on the road, with good water and grass. we knew that a road in that direction if the country would permit it would shorten our rout at least 80 miles" (IV, 329).

Clark's map-making during the winter, as we know, had showed him the possibility of such a short-cut. Now that Yellept had assured Lewis and Clark that a road actually existed, they determined at once to follow it, highly pleased at the prospect of avoiding the sinuosities of the Snake and thereby reducing appreciably the distance to the Clearwater. The next day, with canoes provided by the Walulas, they transported their effects across the Columbia to the mouth of the Walla Walla. Since game might not be as plentiful as the Indians had indicated, they obtained 12 dogs.

The explorers covered the distance from the Columbia to the Clearwater in six days. The old Indian trail took them across present-day Walla Walla, Columbia, Garfield, and Asotin Counties of southeastern Washington and, beyond the Snake River, a small portion of Nez Perce County, Idaho. The plains, sandy and aromatic with sage brush (today given over largely to dry-land wheat farming), reminded Lewis of the Missouri plains, save for a conspicuous lack of buffalo and other prairie quadrupeds.

Yellept had provided additional horses, so that they now travelled with a total of 23. The acquisition of dogs proved to be an astute bit of foresight. What few game animals populated this semi-arid land kept their distance. During the transit, the hunters killed just one duck, one deer, two beaver, and one otter. Thus, before completing the short-cut they had consumed all available food. Even when they reached an Indian village on the Snake River, they succeeded in obtaining only two lean dogs and "a few cakes of half cured bread made of a root which resembles the sweet potatoe" (IV, 354). These additions to the larder provided a skimpy meal for more than 30 hungry robust frontiersmen.

The root here alluded to appears to have been that of a plant the

Indians called cous (with other spellings such as cows and cowish). A member of the carrot family (*Umbelliferae*), it is today technically known as *Lomatium cous*. As Lewis and Clark moved up the Clearwater River, they encountered the Nez Perces digging these roots in many places, and Lewis presently gave the world its first description:

The cows is a knobbed root of an irregularly rounded form not unlike the gensan [ginseng, *Panax quinquefolius*] in form and consistence. this root they collect, rub off a thin black rhind which covers it and pounding it expose it in cakes to the sun. these cakes are about an inch and 1/4 thick and 6 by 18 in width, when dryed they either eat this bread alone without any further preparation, or boil it and make a thick musilage; the latter is most common and much the most agreeable. the flavor of this root is not very unlike the gensang. this root they collect as early as the snows disappear in the spring and continue to collect it until the quamash [camas] supplys it's place which happens about the latter end of June" (V, 12).

Cous became an important food to the party in days ahead and on one occasion at least, after Potts had cut his leg, it was used in a poultice (V, 155).

Three miles up the west bank of the Snake, Lewis and Clark met again their old friend and guide, Chief Tetoharsky. He advised them to cross the river here and, on reaching the Clearwater—about four miles upstream—to ascend the north side of that stream. This, he said, would provide the best route to the village of Twisted Hair, with whom they had left their horses. Taking the chief's advice, they forded the Snake at once and the next morning arrived at a Nez Perce town on the Clearwater. Once again, with no blue beads or other goods to strike the fancy of the Indians, they found it next to impossible to obtain food. In this predicament, where the men faced substantial tightening of belts, they were again rescued by a lucky circumstance. While here the previous fall, Clark had treated a man who had not walked for months. His applications of volatile liniment had resulted in a complete cure, and ever since then the Indian had been loud in his praise of Clark's miraculous powers as a therapist. As a direct result, Clark now found his medical services in great demand. "My friend Capt. C. is their favorite phisician," Lewis declared, "and has already received many applications. in our present situation I think it is pardonable to continue the deseption for they will not give us any provision without compensation in merchandize and our stock is now reduced to a mere handfull" (IV, 358).

Moving farther up the swift-running Clearwater, the party encamped that night at the mouth of Potlatch (Colter's) River where they found the largest Indian lodge any of them had ever seen, one 156 feet long and 15 wide. Here Lewis and Clark succeeded in obtaining only a small quantity of cous roots and bread. Thus, when about 50 of the Indians crowded around Clark seeking medical aid, he announced that he would not minister to them unless they produced either dogs or horses in payment. As a consequence, a chief at once promised to deliver a horse if Clark would treat an abscess on his wife's back. "I examined the abscess," Clark related, "and found it was too far advanced to be cured. I told them her case was desperate. Agreeably to their request, I opened the abscess. I then introduced a tent and dressed it with bisilican; and prepared some dozes of the flour of sulpher and cream of tarter which were given with directions to be taken on each morning" (IV, 362).

In those days a tent consisted of a roll of lint or linen, unsterilized, of course. It was supposed to expedite drainage and by keeping the surface of the wound open, to insure the formation of new tissue from the inside out. If a tent was not used, the wound tended to heal at the surface, thus precluding drainage. In similar situations today, surgeons generally employ rubber tubes of various kinds, called drains, some of which are open, others filled with gauze. The basilicon here employed by Clark was a salve for external application. It consisted ordinarily of such ingredients as resin, yellow wax, and lard. Cream of tartar (potassium bitartrate) is both diuretic and cathartic. It is best known as an ingredient of baking powder. Combining it with flowers of sulphur, although an excellent fungicide and insecticide, would not have altered its effect.

Clark's calculated stratagem paid off. The chief, true to his word, produced a horse, as did a father whose daughter received treatment for rheumatism. Soon Clark was besieged by "a croud of applicants," each and every one bearing a gift of food to recompense him for eye wash, liniment, or other medication. The chief's horse, incidentally, was promptly killed and eaten, "much to the comfort of all the party" (IV, 363).

On May 7 the party crossed the Clearwater to the south side and "ascended the hills to the wright which are here mountains high" (IV, 368). Once out of the gorge, they travelled across level, grass-covered prairie spotted here and there with pines.

"We are informed," Lewis wrote, "that the natives in this quarter were much distressed for food in the course of the last winter; they were compelled to collect the moss which grows on the pine which they boiled and eat; near this camp I observed many pine trees which appear to have been cut down about that season which they inform us was done in order to collect the seed of the long-leafed pine which in those moments of distress also furnishes the article of food; the seed of this speceis of pine is about the size and much the shape of the large sunflower; they are nutricious and not unpleasant when roasted or boiled" (V, 4).

The longleafed pine referred to here was the yellow or ponderosa pine (*Pinus ponderosa*), the only pine which grows in that vicinity. On windy days at the right time of the year, if one stands beneath these trees, he may be showered with tiny bits of what seem to be brown, paper-like material. These are the seeds, dislodged from the pine cones, each of which contains hundreds of seeds all fitting neatly between the scales.

The "moss" growing on the ponderosa pines here on the Clearwater was not a moss at all, but a lichen (*Alectoria jubata*), a filamentous species occurring abundantly at all altitudes in the Bitterroots. It hangs from the branches of conifers in gray-green or black streamers, horse-tail fashion, much like Spanish moss depending from trees in southern swamplands. The trees ringing Packer Meadow, at the eastern end of the Lolo Trail, are full of it. The natives prepared this lichen in different ways, one writer stating that it was mixed with wild onions and pit-roasted.[9] In any form it was a starvation diet—as were the pine seeds also.

The principal Nez Perce chiefs, it will be recalled, had been away on a punitive foray when Lewis and Clark had arrived at Weippe Prairie the previous fall. They met one of these leaders, Cut Nose, at the village they had just left. Cut Nose was with them when on May 8 they found Twisted Hair. An altercation between the two ensued. The cause, soon determined, stemmed from intensive jealousies which had developed after Cut Nose and the other chiefs had returned with their war party to find that Twisted Hair had been a hero in a drama they had missed. As a consequence, the explorers now learned, the latter had relinquished any further attention to the horses entrusted to him and they were now scattered. Also, water had exposed their saddles, though Twisted Hair, on learning of it, had placed them in another cache where they now were (V, 6–7).

[9] Leslie Spier and Edward Sapir, "Wishram Ethnology," *Univ. of Wash. Publications in Anthropology*, 3, no. 3 (1930), 184.

Lewis and Clark had no more than straightened up from the impact of this blow than they were staggered by another. The snow still lay so deep in the Bitterroots, the Nez Perces advised them, that it would be futile to attempt a crossing before the first of June at the very earliest—and some of their informants insisted that mid-June was a more realistic date. "This," wrote Lewis, "is unwelcome intelligence to men confined to a diet of horsebeef or roots, and who are as anxious as we are to return to the fat plains of the Missouri and thence to our native homes" (IV, 369).

The next morning Twisted Hair sent two of his men in search of the missing horses and then himself accompanied Private Willard to Canoe Camp to look for the saddles. Later in the day these men returned with 21 of the horses and half of the saddles.

Another day of travel, this one through eight inches of snow, brought the party to Lawyer's Canyon Creek at a point about three and a half miles above its entrance into the Clearwater. Here they met Broken Arm (Tunnachemootoolt), the most powerful of the Nez Perce chiefs, whose lodge stood on the bank of the creek, and two lesser chiefs, Hohastillpilp and Yoomparkkartim.

If the Indians had advised Lewis and Clark correctly about the snow in the mountains, and there was no reason for thinking otherwise, then they would be detained in this general neighborhood for as much as a month or more. It was imperative, therefore, that they at once select a campsite and construct temporary quarters adequate to protect themselves from cold and rain. They chose a level bottom, thinly covered with ponderosas, on the east bank of the Clearwater River near the present town of Kamiah, Idaho County, Idaho. Lewis appeared pleased with the location for as he said, "we are in the vicinity of the best hunting grounds from Indian information, are convenient to the salmon which we expect daily and have an excellent pasture for the horses" (V, 33).

Lewis and Clark gave no name to this site. Almost a century later, Elliott Coues referred to it as Camp Chopunnish, and subsequent writers have continued the name. Excepting Forts Mandan and Clatsop, the explorers stayed here longer than at any other place on the entire trip. Occupying the site today is a sawmill and lumber yard owned and operated by Potlatch Forests, Incorporated. The adjacent canyon walls stand relatively unchanged, impressive, beautiful, and still "mountains high."

SUMMARY OF DISCOVERIES

Animals New to Science

OREGON PRONGHORN. *Antilocapra americana oregona* V. Bailey. (Thwaites, IV, 287). Described, 1932.

PACIFIC RATTLER. *Crotalus viridis oreganus* (Holbrook). (Thwaites, IV, 323). 1840.

? HARRIS'S WOODPECKER. *Dendrocopos villosus harrisi* (Audubon). [A.O.U. 393c] (Thwaites, IV, 246; Coues, III, 930). 1838.

WESTERN YELLOW-BELLIED MARMOT. *Marmota flaviventris avara* (Bangs). (Thwaites, IV, 320). 1899.

MOUNTAIN QUAIL. *Oreortyx pictus pictus* (Douglas). [A.O.U. 292a] (Thwaites, IV, 252; Coues, III, 936). 1829.

WESTERN FROG. *Rana pretiosa pretiosa* (Baird & Girard). (Thwaites, IV, 216). 1853.

? WESTERN FENCE LIZARD. *Sceloporus occidentalis* Baird & Girard. (Thwaites, IV, 155; Coues, III, 899). 1852.

? NORTHWESTERN GARTER SNAKE. *Thamnophis sirtalis concinnus* (Hallowell). (Thwaites, IV, 155; Coues, III, 900). 1833.

Plants New to Science

BIGLEAF MAPLE. *Acer macrophyllum* Pursh. (Thwaites, III, 174; IV, 57; Coues, III, 834). 1814.

SMALL-FLOWERED COLLINSIA. *Antirrhinum tenellum* Pursh. 1814.

DARK-LEAVED MUGWORT. *Artemisia ludoviciana* Nuttall. 1818.

OREGON GRAPE. *Berberis aquifolium* Pursh. (Thwaites, IV, 61–62). 1814.

WILD HYACINTH. *Brodiaea grandiflora* Pursh. (Thwaites, IV, 291). 1814.

BALSAM ROOT. *Buphthalmum sagittatum* Pursh. 1814.

SUGAR BOWLS. *Clematis hirsutissima* Pursh. 1814.

NARROW-LEAVED COLLOMIA. *Collomia linearis* Nuttall. 1818.

NUTTALL'S DOGWOOD. *Cornus nuttallii* Audubon. (Thwaites, IV, 246; Coues, III, 930). 1840.

BLACK HAWTHORN. *Crataegus douglasii* Lindley. 1810.

MENZIES' LARKSPUR. *Delphinium menziesii* DC. 1818.

SLENDER TOOTHWORT. *Dentaria tenella* Pursh. 1814.

YELLOW FAWN LILY. *Erythronium grandiflorum* Pursh. 1814.

MISSION BELLS; RICE ROOT. *Fritillaria lanceolata* Pursh. 1814.

YELLOW BELL. *Fritillaria pudica* (Pursh) Spreng. 1814.

LINEAR-LEAVED PHACELIA. *Hydrophyllum lineare* Pursh. 1814.

COUS. *Lomatium cous* (Wats.) Coult. 1814.

UROPAPPUS. *Microseris macrochaeta* (Gray) Schultze-Bip. 1838.

? "FENNEL" of Lewis and Clark. Possibly *Perideridia gairdneri* (H. & A.) Mathias. 1838.

LEWIS'S LOMATIUM; BISCUIT ROOT. *Peucedanum simplex* Nuttall. 1814.

SHOWY PHLOX. *Phlox speciosa* Pursh. 1814.

SLENDER POPCORN FLOWER. *Plagiobothrys tenellus* (Nutt.) Gray. 1851.

BLACK COTTONWOOD. *Populus trichocarpa* Torr. & Gray. (Thwaites, IV, 201). 1852.

CANYON GOOSEBERRY. *Ribes menziesii* Pursh. 1814.

RED-FLOWERED CURRANT. *Ribes sanguineum* Pursh. 1814.

THIMBLEBERRY. *Rubus nutkanus velutinus* Brew. 1818.

SALMONBERRY. *Rubus spectabilis* Pursh. 1814.

PESTLE PARSNIP. *Smyrnium nudicaule* Pursh. 1814.

LARGE-HEADED CLOVER. *Trifolium macrocephalum* (Pursh) Poiret. 1814.

WESTERN WAKE-ROBIN. *Trillium ovatum* Pursh. 1814.

Lewis and Clark Herbarium

BIGLEAF MAPLE. *Acer macrophyllum* Pursh. Collected April 10, 1806.

WILD ONION. *Allium* sp. April 30.

RED ALDER. *Alnus rubra* Bongard. March 26.

SASKATOON SERVICEBERRY. *Amelanchier alnifolia* (Nutt.) Nuttall. April 15.

SMALL-FLOWERED COLLINSIA. *Antirrhinum tenellum* Pursh. April 17.

DARK-LEAVED MUGWORT. *Artemisia ludoviciana* Nuttall. April 10.

OREGON GRAPE. *Berberis aquifolium* Pursh. April 11.

FETID RAYLESS GOLDENROD. *Bigelowia graveolens* Gray. May 6.

WILD HYACINTH. *Brodiaea grandiflora* Pursh. April 20.

BALSAM ROOT. *Buphthalmum sagittatum* Pursh. April 14.

FIELD CHICKWEED. *Cerastium arvense* L. April 22.

MINER'S LETTUCE. *Claytonia perfoliata* Donn. April 17.

SPRING BEAUTY ? *Claytonia siberica* L. April 8.

SUGAR BOWLS. *Clematis hirsutissima* Pursh. May [?], ("On waters of Columbia").

NARROW-LEAVED COLLOMIA. *Collomia linearis* Nuttall. April 17.

BLACK HAWTHORN. *Crataegus douglasii* Lindley. April 29.

MENZIES' LARKSPUR. *Delphinium menziesii* DC. April 14.

SLENDER TOOTHWORT. *Dentaria tenella* Pursh. April 1.

SHOOTING STAR. *Dodecatheon meadea* L. April 16.

YELLOW FAWN LILY. *Erythronium grandiflorum* Pursh. May 8.

MISSION BELLS. *Fritillaria lanceolata* Pursh. April 10.

YELLOW BELL. *Fritillaria pudica* (Pursh) Spreng. May 8.

LINEAR-LEAVED PHACELIA. *Hydrophyllum lineare* Pursh. April 17.

CRYPTANTHE ? *Krynitsia* sp. April 17.

COUS. *Lomatium cous* (Wats.) Coult. April 29.

UROPAPPUS. *Microseris macrochaeta* (Gray) Schultze-Bip. April 17.

"FENNEL." Possibly *Perideridia gairdneri* (H. & A.) Mathias. April 25.

PARSLEY ? *Peucedanum* sp. April 15.

LEWIS'S LOMATIUM. *Peucedanum simplex* Nuttall. May 6.

SHOWY PHLOX. *Phlox speciosa* Pursh. May 7.

SLENDER POPCORN FLOWER. *Plagiobothrys tenellus* (Nutt.) Gray. April 17.

BLACK COTTONWOOD. *Populus trichocarpa* Torrey & Gray. (Tag says, "Cottonwood of the Columbia R. June 1806." If Columbia, then March or April.)

WILD CHERRY ? *Prunus* sp. May 7.

OREGON WHITE OAK. *Quercus garryana* Douglas. March 26.

GOLDEN CURRANT. *Ribes aureum* Pursh. April 16.

CANYON GOOSEBERRY. *Ribes menziesii* Pursh. April 8.

RED-FLOWERING CURRANT. *Ribes sanguineum* Pursh. March 27.

THIMBLEBERRY. *Rubus nutkanus velutinus* Brew. April 15.

SALMONBERRY. *Rubus spectabilis* Pursh. March 27.

PESTLE PARSNIP. *Smyrnium nudicaule* Pursh. April 15.

LARGE-HEADED CLOVER. *Trifolium macrocephalum* (Pursh) Poiret. April 17.

WESTERN WAKE-ROBIN. *Trillium ovatum* Pursh. April 10.

Indian Tribes Encountered

Chinookan Linguistic Family: † Clannahmannamums (Thwaites, IV, 213) ; † Cathlahcumups (Thwaites, IV, 218) ; † Clannahquahs (Thwaites, IV, 218) ; † Multnomahs (Thwaites, IV, 219) ; † Shahalas (Four tribes: Yehus, Clahclellahs, Wahclellahs, and Neerchookios; Thwaites, IV, 223; VI, 116) ; † Cashhooks (Thwaites, IV, 233) ; † Nechacolees (Thwaites, IV, 236) ; † Elutes (possibly Echelutes, Thwaites, IV, 269) ; † Wyach-hichs (Thwaites, IV, 275) ; † Willacums (Thwaites, IV, 282) ; † Smack-shops (Thwaites, IV, 281) .

Sahaptian Linguistic Family: † Skaddatts (Thwaites, IV, 296) ; † Wahhowpums (Thwaites, IV, 317) .

Athapascan Linguistic Family: † Clackstar or Claxtar (Thwaites, IV, 218; Coues, III, 915n) .

Salishan Linguistic Family: † Skeetssomish (Thwaites, IV, 363; Coues, III, 990n) .

Topographic Features Named and/or Discovered

† Fanny's Island (Thwaites, IV, 204) —— Grim's Island.

† Fanny's Bottom (Thwaites, IV, 204) .

† Deer Island (Thwaites, IV, 207) —— Elallah Island (Coues, II, 911) .

† "Cahwahnahiooks" River (Thwaites, IV, 214) —— Lewis's River.

† Cathlahpohtle Island (Thwaites, IV, 216) .

† White Brant Island (Thwaites, IV, 224) .

† Multnomah River (Thwaites, IV, 238) —— Willamette River.

† Brant Island (Thwaites, IV, 260) .

† Youmalolum River (Thwaites, IV, 327) —— Umatilla River.

† "Bold Creek" (Thwaites, IV, 341) —— Touchet River.

† Commearp Creek (Thwaites, V, 14) —— Lawyer's Canyon Creek.

Camp Chopunnish
and
Bitterroots

CHAPTER EIGHTEEN

From May 14 to June 10, the Expedition marked time beside the Clearwater—restive and dispirited. Lewis spoke bitterly of "that icy barrier which separates us from my friends and country, from all which makes life esteemable" (V, 45). The spirits of the men waxed and waned with the rise and fall of water in the Clearwater, the river indicating from day to day the rate at which snow had melted in the mountains.

Life quickly settled into a pattern at Camp Chopunnish, with each day devoted largely to the never-ending business of obtaining food. It was not enough at this stage to provide for everyday needs; there was also the necessity of accumulating a surplus for the trip into and over the Bitterroots where, if experience repeated itself, game would be unobtainable. This dual task proved difficult. For one thing, the hunters found fewer deer and bear than anticipated. For another, the salmon never did show up, even though "the dove is cooing which is the signal as the Indians inform us of the approach of the salmon" (VI, 217). Once again, of necessity, they turned to the Indians for help.

Leading up to this, Lewis and Clark took inventory of their remaining trade goods. Divided equally, each man's share consisted of one awl, one knitting pin, one-half ounce of vermilion, two needles, a few skeins of thread, and a yard of ribbon. This was, as Lewis admitted, "a slender stock indeed with which to lay in a store of provisions for that dreary wilderness" (V, 52). Since it was obviously inadequate, they added to it by cutting brass buttons from clothing, converting chain links into awls, and concocting a salve (basilicon) out of pine resin, bear oil, and beeswax. Also, from their medicine chest they extracted empty vials and pill boxes and a few bottles of eye wash. Searching more closely through their belongings, they unearthed sundry scraps of iron and excess pieces of fish net. Eventually Lewis and Clark concluded that some of their remaining files and bullets were expendable.

In succeeding days, as opportunity allowed, the men pocketed their meager minim of needles, pins, and buttons and headed for the Indian villages where "the noise of the Indian women pounding roots sounded like a nail factory" (V, 16). It was amazing how many bushels of roots and bread they obtained for these trifles. Their acquisition, Lewis declared, was not much less pleasing to them "than the return of a good cargo to an East India Merchant" (V, 98). Finally (on June 6), he was in a position to announce that they had accumulated a quantity of roots and bread adequate for their transit of the Bitterroots.

The men of the party would have been ordered to dig native roots except for the fact, as Lewis explained, "there are several speceis of hemlock which are so much like the cows that it is difficult to discriminate them from the cows and we are affraid that they might poison themselves" (V, 52–53). The plant related to cous growing here most to be feared, I am informed, is the water hemlock, *Cicuta douglasii;* it is violently poisonous, especially the tubers, to most domesticated animals and to man.[1]

When salmon failed to show up in the Clearwater, Lewis and Clark, on hearing that they were running in the Snake River, dispatched Sergeant Ordway, Frazer, and Wiser to investigate the report. However, the distance proved much greater than expected, a three-day journey each way, so that the salmon they obtained had spoiled by the time they got them back to the Clearwater.

[2]

The local Nez Perce medicine men must have regarded Clark with green-eyed envy. Apparently it was nothing unusual for him to treat 40 to 50 patients daily. For instance, on May 12 he wrote that he had been "closely employed until 2 P.M. administering eye water to about 40 grown persons" and prescribing treatment to others with additional complaints (V, 27). They drifted in from miles around. When four

[1] Letter to author, Dec. 1, 1965, from William H. Baker, Professor of Botany, University of Idaho.

arrived one day from the Snake River, Lewis observed: "our skill as physicians and the virtue of our medicines have been spread it seems to a great distance" (V, 58).

Clark treated cases of "scrofela," rheumatism, "weaknesses in the back and loins," and "loss of use of limbs." To a squaw "whose spirets were very low and hip[p]ed [depressed]" he gave 30 drops of laudanum (V, 50). For another, who complained of "a gripeing and rheumatic effections," he prescribed a dose of cream of tartar and flowers of sulphur (V, 48). To a chief with an obscure ailment he gave "some simple cooling medicines" (V, 27). When occasion demanded, he dosed with glauber salts. Many had simple complaints, easily relieved, but others suffered with "disorders entirely out of the power of Medison" (V, 27). He wished most devoutly, Clark declared, that he possessed the means to help "these poor afflicted wretches" (V, 58).

Whether Lewis and Clark realized it or not, they ran great risks in treating these simple, untutored savages. One writer, describing his attempts to vaccinate Assiniboin children, stated: "should any accident happen to the child . . . the vaccination would be blamed for it and the good-hearted operator would find himself in a position of danger. There is also great risk in giving them medicines, for should the patient die the whites would be blamed for poisoning him."[2] Fortunately, as Clark observed, "All of these poor people thought themselves much benifited by what had been done for them" (V, 50).

Illnesses plagued the explorers—as well as the Indians—here at Camp Chopunnish. York, for example, complained of colic and Frazer, Joseph Field, and Wiser of violent pains in their heads. Lewis attributed these troubles "to their diet of roots to which they have not been accustomed" (V, 38). Then there was Bratton's chronic back ailment. Incapacitated, he had made the long trip up the Columbia and across country to the Clearwater by boat and by horse. On his arrival at Camp Chopunnish, he was still disabled. His cure came suddenly and impressively. Lewis described it in these words:

John Shields observed that he had seen men in a similar situation restored by violent sweats. Bratton requested that he might be sweated in the manner proposed by Shields to which we consented. Shields sunk a circular hole of 3 feet diamiter and four feet deep in the earth. he kindled a large fire in the hole and heated well, after which the fire was taken out a seat was placed in the center of the hole for the patient with a board at bottom for his feet to rest on; some hoops of willow poles were bent in an arch crossing each other

[2] Denig, "Indian Tribes of the Upper Missouri," 428.

over the hole, on these several blankets were thrown forming a secure and thick orning of about 3 feet high. the patient being striped naked was seated under this orning in the hole and the blankets well secured on every side. The patient was furnished with a vessell of water which he sprinkled on the bottom and sides of the hole and by that means created as much steam or vapor as he could possibly bear. in this situation he was kept about 20 minutes after which he was taken out and suddenly plunged in cold water twice and was then immediately returned to the sweat hole where he was continued three quarters of an hour longer then taken out covered up in several blankets and suffered to cool gradually, during the time of his being in the sweat hole, he drank copious draughts of a strong tea of horse mint (V, 60–61) .[3]

This treatment of alternating heat and cold was effective (it is used successfully in similar cases today) . The very next day Bratton was walking about, almost entirely free of pain. Within two weeks he had so far recovered that, as Lewis wrote, "we cannot well consider him an invalid any longer, he has had a tedious illness which he boar with much fortitude and firmness" (V, 117) .

Bratton's obscure lumbar ailment, which he endured for four long months, cannot definitely be diagnosed at this late date. Medical men have suggested sciatica, infectious arthritis, and an inflamed sacro-iliac joint. Whatever caused the ache, it undoubtedly was aggravated by the penetrating damp and cold that characterized the long winter months at Fort Clatsop. His cure was apparently permanent. He fought in the War of 1812 and, later, in the battle of Tippecanoe. In 1819 he married and in time became the father of 10 children, each of whom, no doubt, heard many times the story of the "Sweat Hole of Camp Chopunnish."

Bratton's successful treatment produced an interesting sequel. As soon as the Indians along the Clearwater heard about it, they brought to Camp Chopunnish a chief who seemed in the best of health in every respect except that for three years he had been unable to move a single limb. When friends of the chief pressed Lewis and Clark to give him the same treatment accorded Bratton, they agreed. They did even better. Over the next two to three weeks, they sweated the chief three times. At the end of that period, they were pleased to report that the Indian "was fast on the recovery, he can bear his weight on his legs, and has acquired a considerable portion of his strength" (V, 117) .

[3] The "horse mint" was tentatively identified by C. V. Piper as *Lophantus urticaefolius* (see Thwaites, V, 61n) .

The chief was most likely the victim of hysteria, since it seems unlikely that he would have malingered for three years. Medical men find the case most interesting, it being one of the earliest recorded observations dealing with psychiatric matters in Indians. Equally interesting was Lewis's remark on first meeting the chief. "I am confident," he said, "that this would be an excellent subject for electricity and much regret that I have it not in my power to supply it" (V, 63). According to one outstanding medical historian: "Electricity as a therapeutic agent was first used about 1750. Benjamin Franklin had a hand in the matter by suggesting that electricity be used in nervous diseases. Galvani discovered the electrical properties of excised tissue late in the 18th century and devised machines to deliver the current. This would have been well known to Rush, who was probably the source of Lewis's information. It would have been a good thing to use electricity on the chief. It would certainly have surprised him and, since there wasn't anything wrong with him organically, it would probably have put him on his feet sooner than the sweating did."[4]

At the same time Bratton and the chief were having their miseries sweated out of them, the infant son of Sacagawea and Charbonneau fell ill. Pomp, now 15 months old, would seem to have been an exceptionally healthy boy until May 16, 1806. On that date Lewis wrote: "Charbono's child is very ill this evening; he is cuting teeth and for several days past has had a violent lax, which having suddenly stopped he was attacked with a high fever and his neck and throat are much swolen this evening. We gave him a dose of cream of tartar and flour of sulpher and applyed a poltice of boiled onions to his neck as warm as he could well bear it" (V, 56).

The child seemed better in the morning, though the swelling in the neck remained. Lewis and Clark, therefore, continued the onion poultices. The next day (Saturday), with the neck swollen even more, they gave the boy another dose of cream of tartar and applied a fresh onion poultice. On Sunday (May 25) Lewis wrote, "The child is more unwell than yesterday. we gave it a doze of cream of tartar [the third in four days] which did not operate. we therefore gave it a clyster [enema] in the evening" (V, 63). The next morning the child's fever had left him and he was appreciably improved. The swelling in the neck had subsided somewhat, too, though Lewis thought that it might yet "terminate in an ugly imposthume a little below the ear" (V, 68).

[4] Letter to author, Feb. 19, 1962, from Dr. R. G. Williams, Joseph Leidy Professor of Anatomy, University of Pennsylvania Medical School.

A few days later (June 5), the cervical inflammation having subsided entirely, Lewis discontinued the onion poultices and applied instead a plaster of basilicon. This was, in Clark's words, "a plaster of sarve [salve] made of the rozen of the long leafed [ponderosa] pine, Beeswax and Bears oil mixed" (V, 169). The composition of this ointment proves Lewis and Clark's ability to improvise when need be and suggests that the original supply of "2 lbs. Ung. Basilic Flav." had been exhausted.

Most probably Pomp's trouble was tonsillitis complicated by an infected cervical lymph gland (Coues' diagnosis of mumps can be discounted). Lewis's statement that the infected gland might terminate in an ugly abscess below the ear indicated that he knew what he was talking about, for that is the location of the important lymph node that, in days before chemotherapy, frequently abscessed and broke through the skin. The onion poultices, except for their heat value, most likely had little effect.

[3]

During his enforced stay at Camp Chopunnish, Lewis made a number of significant zoological observations and discoveries. For instance, he had his first real opportunity here to examine closely Clark's nutcracker and Lewis's woodpecker when, as he said in referring to the latter, "we killed and preserved several of them" (V, 70).

On June 6, he wrote:

we meet with a beautiful little bird in this neighbourhood about the size and somewhat the shape of the large sparrow . . . it measures 7 inches from the extremity of the beek to that of the tail . . . the beak is reather more than half an inch in length, and is formed much like the virginia nightingale [the cardinal, *Richmondena cardinalis*] . . . the plumage is remarkably delicate; that of the neck and head is of a fine orrange yellow and red . . . the breast, the sides, the rump and some long feathers which lie between the legs and extend underneath the tail are of a fine orrange yellow. the tail, back and wings are black e[x]cept a small stripe of yellow on the outer part of the middle joint of the wing . . . (V, 111).

This was the first description—"clear and unmistakable," according to Coues[5]—of the lovely western tanager, *Piranga ludoviciana*, perhaps the most brilliantly colored of Pacific Coast songbirds.

These three birds—nutcracker, woodpecker, and tanager—all first

[5] Coues, III, 1036n.

described by Lewis and Clark, fared better than others they discovered. Specimens of each ultimately found a home in Peale's Museum. They will come in for extended comment later.

It will be recalled that Lewis, while on the Upper Missouri, had had abundant opportunity to study the grizzly bear. Since no two of these beasts appeared in identical coats, he entertained doubts as to whether all belonged to the same species. Here on the Clearwater, as the hunters brought in several carcasses, he had time and opportunity to examine their coats more closely and to compare them. Colors varied from white to jet black, from bay to light reddish-brown and "black with white hairs intermixed." "Perhaps," he reflected, "it would not be unappropriate to designate them the variagated bear" (V, 34). Not long afterwards, displaying excellent common-sense taxonomic acumen, he concluded that there was just one species of grizzly: "These bear gave me a stronger evidence of the various colored bear of this country being one speceis only, than any I have heretofore had . . . in short it is not common to find two bear here of this speceis precisely of the same colour, and if we were to attempt to distinguish them by the collours and to denominate each colour a distinct speceis we should soon find at least twenty" (V, 37–38).

Lewis had no trouble distinguishing the grizzly (*Ursus horribilis*) from the black bear (*Ursus americanus*). The former (the "hohost" of the Nez Perces) was larger, its talons longer, and its "poil" (down or fine hair) was longer, thicker, and finer. Also, it did not hibernate, never climbed trees, and was "far from being as passive as the common black bear" (V, 38). However, the Nez Perces convinced Lewis that two species of the "common kind" inhabited the Clearwater country, a "redish brown black" as well as the plain black. In time, scientists gave full recognition to the former, calling it the cinnamon bear (*Ursus cinnamomeus*), and even today, as one writer has pointed out: "Reputable zoologists still disagree about the scientific status of the cinnamon bear which has at various times during the past one hundred years been shifted from a subspecies to a distinct species: from a subspecies to a mere color phrase of the black bear: and recently again has been restored to the status of a subspecies."[6]

Lewis was far more industrious as a botanist at Camp Chopunnish and on the Lolo Trail than his journal indicates. Approximately one fourth (close to 50 all told) of the dried preserved specimens constituting the Lewis and Clark Herbarium were collected by Lewis in Idaho

[6] Burroughs, *The Natural History of the Lewis and Clark Expedition*, 56.

on the return journey. Obviously, the collecting and pressing of these plants required much time and attention, and it is surprising that Lewis said practically nothing whatever about these matters.

Of these several plants, the most celebrated today is the ragged robin, *Clarkia pulchella,* named eight years later by Frederick Pursh in honor of William Clark. A member of the evening primrose family, ragged robin, or beautiful Clarkia as it is sometimes called, derives its name from the fact that at first glance its flowers appear to have been torn to ribbons. Actually there are four deeply lobed petals of a bright pink-purplish hue. Lewis discovered it on June 1, 1806, in the valley of the Clearwater. This study would be wanting if we did not include *verbatim* at least one of Lewis's extended descriptions of plant or animal of which there are so many in his journals. For our purpose, we have chosen *Clarkia pulchella:*

I met with a singular plant today in blume of which I preserved a specemine; it grows on the steep sides of the fertile hills near this place, the radix is fibrous, not much branched, annual, woody, white and nearly smooth. the stem is simple branching ascending, [2–½ *feet high*] celindric, villose and of a pale red colour. the extremities of the branches are flexable and are bent downward near their extremities with the weight of the flowers. the leaf is sessile, scattered thinly, nearly linear tho' somewhat widest in the middle, two inches in length, absolutely entire, villose, obtusely pointed and of an ordinary green. above each leaf a small short branch protrudes, supporting a tissue of four or five smaller leaves of the same appearance with those discribed. a leaf is placed underneath ea[c]h branch, and each flower. the calyx is a one flowered spathe. the corolla superior consists of four pale perple petals which are tripartite, the central lobe largest and all terminate obtusely; they are inserted with a long and narrow claw on the top of the germ, are long, smooth & deciduous. there are two distinct sets of stamens the 1st or principal consists of four, the filaments of which are capillary, erect, inserted on the top of the germ alternately with the petals, equal, short, membranous; the anthers are also four each being elivated with it's fillament, they are linear and reather flat, erect, sessile, cohering at the base, membranous, longitudinally furrowed, twice as long as the fillament naked, and of a pale perple colour. the second set of stamens are very minute are also four and placed within and opposite to the petals, these are scarcely persceptable while the 1st are large and conspicuous; the filaments are capillary equal, very short, white and smooth. the anthers are four, oblong, beaked, erect, cohering at the base, membranous, shorter than the fillaments, white naked and appear not to form pollen, there is one pistillum; the germ of which is also one, cylindric, villous, inferior, sessile, as long as the 1st stamens & marked with 8 longitudinal furrows. the single style and stigma form a per-

fect nonpetallous corolla only with this difference, that the style which eli-
vates the stigma or limb is not a tube but solid tho' it's outer appearance is
that of the tube of a monopetallous corolla swelling as it ascends and gliding
in such manner into the limb that it cannot be said where the style ends, or
the stigma begins; jointly they are as long as the corolla, white, the limb is
four cleft, sauser shaped, and the margins of the lobes entire and rounded.
this has the appearance of a monopetallous flower growing from the center
of a four petalled corollar, which is rendered more conspicuous in consequence of the 1st being white and the latter of a pale perple. I regret very
much that the seed of this plant are not yet ripe and it is pro[ba]ble will not
be so during my residence in this neighbourhood (V, 95–97).

This description demonstrates what Lewis could do, and often did
do, with root, stem, leaves, and flowers in hand. It lacks only a Latin
binomial. If he had supplied one (such as *Clarkia pulchella,* which
Pursh provided), then botanists would be forced to recognize Lewis as
being the one who first formally described this plant.

Among other beautiful well-known plants (all new to science)
collected by Lewis here in Idaho and brought back to Philadelphia
were camas (*Camassia quamash*), yellow bell (*Fritillaria pudica*),
Lewis's syringa (*Philadelphus lewisii*), purple trillium (*Trillium
petiolatum*), and mariposa lily (*Calochortus elegans*). *Clarkia* and *Calochortus* were two of four new genera created by Pursh on the basis of
plants returned by Lewis and Clark.

[4]

Lewis and Clark eventually recovered all their horses (except for the
two Toby and his son had appropriated) and obtained still others from
the Nez Perces. By the end of May they had a respectable stable with
some 65 mares, stallions, and geldings grazing and growing fat on the
herbiage surrounding their encampment. They reasoned that the
march over the Lolo Trail would be greatly expedited if each member
of the party had two horses, one to ride and another to carry his
possessions.

Before quitting Camp Chopunnish, Lewis and Clark attempted to
anticipate any and every contingency that might arise during the
Bitterroot transit. In the matter of obtaining guides, they met with
complete failure. Twisted Hair begged off because of a sick brother,
and Tunnachemootoolt declared that the selection of young men to
accompany them would have to wait on a meeting of his nation in
council. As on previous occasions, Clark consulted the Indians about

the geography of the country, and the latter obliged by making crude maps. "It is amazing to study the Indian maps," a prominent cartographer has written, "and then go to the resulting American maps and notice the many items taken from them unchanged. Great is the debt owed to the Indians who, with sticks and stones and in the sand, made clear the way ahead and on either side to Lewis and Clark."[7]

June arrived and, with it, a growing impatience to be on the move. Though Lewis and Clark had repeatedly been warned by the Nez Perces that it would be impossible to begin a crossing of "that wretched portion of our journey" before the middle of the month, they determined to break camp in advance of that time and move to Weippe Prairie. Here they hoped to find game more abundant, thus making it possible to supplement their present stock of fresh meat. "Not any of us have yet forgotten our suffering in those mountains in September last," Lewis declared, "and I think it probable we never shall" (V, 98).

On the morning of June 10, the explorers arose early, saddled their horses, and departed. They zigzagged their way up the high north side of the Clearwater canyon to the top of the ridge, plunged off into Lolo (Collins) Creek canyon, and then scrambled out of this gorge to the broad sweep of the plains above. As planned, each man had his own horse to ride and another to carry his belongings. They camped that night on Weippe Prairie near the spot where they had first met the Nez Perces in September last. It had been a long wearisome day. Only those persons familiar with the Clearwater terrain have any idea whatever as to the depth of the Clearwater and Lolo canyons, the steepness of their walls, and the effort necessary to climb them. Bare facts, such as Kamiah having an elevation of about 1,200 feet and Weippe Prairie some 3,100 feet (a difference of 1,900), do not help much. Actually, negotiating the sharp downward-upward passage of Lolo canyon was the most difficult part of the day's journey.

Lewis and Clark approached Weippe Prairie at a most propitious moment—when the camas was in full bloom. Their campsite, some 2,000 acres of level prairie devoid of any tree or shrub, was brightened by a multitude of light-blue camas flowers, reminding Lewis of a "lake of fine clear water." He said that he was so completely deceived on first coming in sight of this display that he would have sworn he was looking at a body of water (V, 132). Others since have been similarly

[7] Carl I. Wheat, *Mapping the Transmississippi West*, 3 vols. (San Francisco, 1958), II, 43.

misled. For example, Father Nicolas Point wrote, "The flower of this plant is a beautiful blue in color and makes the plain on which it abounds look like a lake."[8] We can better sense the beauty of the scene as these men beheld it if we recall that the camas is a lily, and that the flowers individually and collectively possess the loveliness ordinarily associated with that plant.

The Corps bivouacked on Weippe Prairie for four days. In that time they jerked meat, fought mosquitoes, and all the while kept hoping that the snows would "have melted more off the mountains and the grass raised to sufficient hight for our horses to live" (V, 122).

On the morning of June 15, unable to restrain their impatience longer, they up-saddled and struck out for the mountains. On entering the dense lowland forests of larch, cedar, and ponderosa pine, they began to experience once again those difficulties which had beset them here the previous fall, namely, slippery roads and fallen trees. After crossing a mountain, from the top of which they had an extensive view of snow-covered ranges ahead, they came down to a meadow on Eldorado Creek where they camped for the night.

Lewis's diary for the day includes the information that he had "found the nest of a humming bird, it had just begun to lay its eggs" (V, 136). As to this observation Coues said: "Credit Lewis and Clark with the discovery of this species [broad-tailed hummingbird, *Selasphorus platycercus*], which was unknown to science until described . . . by [William] Swainson, 1827."[9]

The next day, as the road took the party deeper into the mountains, they found snow still lying in the valleys, in places as much as two to three feet deep. Flowers like the pretty fawn lily (*Erythronium grandiflorum*), that had bloomed earlier along the Clearwater, were here just beginning to show their yellow petals. Alpine conifers began to supplant cedars and ponderosas. "These appearances in this comparatively low region," Clark wrote, "augurs but unfavorably with respect to the practicability of passing the mountains" (V, 137). Conditions farther along that day increased his premonitions of worse yet to come. By late afternoon eight to 10 feet of snow covered much of the road. That they could make any headway at all was due to the fact that the snow was hard-packed, hard enough to bear the weight of both men and horses. The presence of so much snow, however, made it increasingly difficult for Drouillard to locate the trail. They camped that

[8] Father Nicolas Point, *Wilderness Kingdom* (New York, 1967), 166.
[9] Coues, III, 1044n.

night on Hungry Creek where, on September 10 last, Clark had killed a stray horse.

The next morning (June 17), they went down Hungry Creek about seven miles and then began to climb toward the summit of the great, elongate hogback separating the North Fork of the Clearwater from the Lochsa.

This . . . mountain we ascended about 3 miles when we found ourselves invelloped in snow from 12 to 15 feet deep . . . here was winter with all its rigors; the air was cold, my hands and feet were benumbed. we knew that it would require five days to reach the fish wears at the entrance of Colt Creek, provided we were so fortunate as to be enabled to follow the proper ridges of the mountains to lead us to that place; of this Drewyer our principal dependance as a woodman and guide was entirely doubtfull . . . if we proceeded and should get bewildered in these mountains the certainty was that we should loose all our horses and consequently our baggage inst[r]uments perhaps our papers and thus eminently wrisk the loss of the discoveries which we had already made . . . under these circumstances we conceived it madnes[s] in this stage of the expedition to proceed without a guide . . . we therefore came to the resolution to return with our horses while they were yet strong and in good order and indevour to keep them so untill we could procure an indian to conduct us over the snowey mountains (V, 140–141).

With this decision made, Lewis and Clark instructed their men to build a scaffold upon which they left food and baggage, even instruments and valuable papers, deeming them safer here than subject to the dangers of the road. After covering them as best they could, they began their "retrograde march . . . a good deal dejected" (V, 142).

The choice to turn back, to retrace their steps some 50 miles, was the most painful one Lewis and Clark were forced to make during the entire journey. It was particularly galling when they reflected that they had brought it on themselves by starting the transit without an Indian guide. They stumbled down the mountainside and camped that night again on Hungry Creek. Early in the morning the captains dispatched Drouillard and Shannon back to the Nez Perces to obtain a guide and rejoin them as soon as possible. They were to offer a rifle by way of inducement and, if that failed, to step up the offer as far as three rifles and ten horses.

Three days later the party was back on Weippe Prairie, not by choice, but because of a shortage of game along the way. Drouillard and Shannon, with three Nez Perces, rejoined them in mid-afternoon of the 23rd. For the compensation of two rifles, these Indians had agreed to lead the party through the multiple ranges of the Bitterroots. There now being no need for further delay, Lewis and Clark at once ordered the men to round up the horses and hobble them so that they might be assured of an early start the next morning. On the day before the hunters had surprised even themselves by killing eight deer and three bear, thus providing the party with a supply of fresh meat adequate for immediate needs.

[5]

The Corps had expended 11 days in making the east-west transit of the Bitterroots the previous September. This time they covered the distance in seven—June 24 to 30 inclusive. The guides knew the slopes and saddles, the twistings and short-cuts, almost as well as they knew details of home terrain along the Clearwater. On June 26 the party again reached the top of the mountain where, on the 17th, they had left most of their baggage and had begun their retreat. "The snow has subsided near four feet since the 17th inst.," Lewis wrote; "we now measured it accurately and found from a mark which we had made on a tree . . . that it was then 10 feet 10 inches . . . it is now generally 7 feet" (V, 161). There seems no question that the spring of 1806 was unusually late. According to Ralph Space, whose personal familiarity with this country goes back more than 40 years, the snow is normally gone by late June except in a few shaded places.[10]

The explorers hastily retrieved their baggage and, after crossing Sherman Peak, began the long journey on top of the dividing ridge. Late in the evening, they came to an untimbered mountain side (Bald Mountain) with southern exposure where the sun had melted the snow. Because the horses needed food and rest, and they could not expect to reach a similar grassy place farther along that day, they stopped here for the night, even though they had made only 13 miles.

They continued their march along the hogback the next morning, soon arriving at a place where Indians, at some time in the past, had "raised a conic mound of stones 6 or eight feet high and on it's summit erected a pine pole of 15 feet long" (V, 164). This was one of several cairns on the Lolo Trail similar to those at Indian Post Office, and the only one Lewis and Clark reported seeing on either of their trips

[10] Space, "Lewis and Clark Through Idaho," 15.

through these mountains. Located not far from Indian Grave, it is not to be confused with either of the two Post Offices encountered today by travellers farther east on the road, close to Lewis and Clark's campsite of September 16 of the previous year.

At this particular place Lewis wrote: "we were entirely surrounded by these mountains from which to one unacquainted with them it would have seemed impossible ever to have escaped; in short without the assistance of our guides I doubt much whether we who had once passed them could find our way to Traveller's rest in their present situation for the marked trees on which we had placed considerable reliance are much fewer and more difficult to find than we had apprehended" (V, 164–165).

The deep snow of the heights actually proved to be an asset. It was hard, almost like glacial ice, so that even the horses with their great weight did not sink into it more than two or three inches; and it covered the big rocks and large fallen timbers that had slowed their progress so much on their initial crossing. "We came further today," wrote Ordway, "than we went in 2 when we came over [before]."[11]

The horses looked "extremely gant" to the captains the next morning, but the guides gave assurance that they would reach a good feeding ground about noon. After marching about six miles they passed their campsite of September 15, and one and a half miles farther along came to the road from Colt-killed (Whitesand) Creek up which they had struggled on the outward journey. Keeping to the ridge instead of retracing steps to the depths of the Lochsa gorge, they soon arrived at the grassy spot promised by the guides. In deference to the horses, they camped here for the night.

Sunday, June 29, proved to be memorable for every member of the party. Starting early, they soon came to the end of the ridge (Rocky Point) and dropped down onto Crooked Fork, striking it about one and a half miles above the entrance of Brushy Creek. They then forded Crooked Fork and climbed a steep mountain to its summit where they hit their old trail which they followed to Packer Meadow. After a brief halt here for lunch, they crossed the divide (near present-day Lolo Pass) and soon arrived at Lolo Hot Springs. That night, for the first time in weeks, the men slept with minds and bodies relaxed. They had successfully conquered the great snow-covered barrier that had stood

[11] Ordway, 370.

up so formidably between them and home. Tomorrow's march down Lolo Creek to Traveller's Rest would be a comparatively easy one.

[6]

Lewis and Clark halted two days at Traveller's Rest, "on the south side of the creek a little above it's entrance into Clark's [Bitterroot] river" (V, 173).[12] Here they made final plans for the division of the party. Lewis, with Drouillard, Gass, Thompson, McNeal, Goodrich, Werner, Frazer, and the two Field brothers, would take the most direct route for Great Falls, and Clark, with the remainder of the party, would head for Shoshoni Cove, Three Forks, and the Yellowstone.

In making these arrangements, it may be taken for granted that Lewis and Clark had weighed carefully their chances of success or failure. By now they had obtained from the Nez Perces a general knowledge of terrain immediately ahead, including the shortest routes to Great Falls. They had the advantage of good summer weather and they had reason to believe, from past experience, that Indians, if encountered, would prove friendly. Nevertheless, when the moment of parting arrived, Lewis wrote: "I could not avoid feeling much concern, although I hoped this separation was only momentary" (V, 183).

One important incident of the stop at Traveller's Rest has been generally overlooked. On July 1, Lewis collected several specimens of a fleshy-leaved, low perennial bearing beautiful rose-colored flowers, which he then proceeded to carry some 3,000 miles by horse, boat, and stagecoach to Philadelphia where he entrusted them to Frederick Pursh. Six years later, Pursh described this plant and gave it the name of *Lewisia rediviva*. In the vernacular it is, of course, the bitterroot, and it is the most celebrated of all plants brought back by Lewis. Because of it, we have the Bitterroot Mountains and Bitterroot River. Residents of Montana have made it their state flower. From the botanists' view it is special because Pursh, in calling it *Lewisia*, created a new genus. As a final note, visitors to the Academy of Natural Sciences of Philadelphia can find there today six somewhat faded flowers of bitterroot, returned by Lewis at the time when Thomas Jefferson was President of the United States.

[12] Ralph Space places this campsite opposite the mouth of Sleeman Gulch about two miles up Lolo Creek from its entrance into the Bitterroot River.

SUMMARY OF DISCOVERIES

Animals New to Science

COLUMBIAN TOAD. *Bufo boreas boreas* (Baird & Girard). (Thwaites, V, 87; Coues, 1018). Described, 1852.

? CABANIS'S WOODPECKER. *Dendrocopos villosus hyloscopus* (Cab. & Heine). [A.O.U. 393d] (Thwaites, V, 136; Coues, III, 1044). 1863.

PACIFIC TREE FROG. *Hyla regilla* Baird & Girard. (Thwaites, V, 87; Coues, III, 1018). 1852.

WESTERN HORNED TOAD. *Phrynosoma douglasii douglasii* (Bell). (Thwaites, V, 80; Coues, III, 899). 1833.

WESTERN TANAGER. *Piranga ludoviciana* (Wilson). [A.O.U. 607] (Thwaites, V, 111; Coues, III, 1035). 1811.

BROAD-TAILED HUMMINGBIRD. *Selasphorus platycercus platycercus* (Swainson). [A.O.U. 432] (Thwaites, V, 136; Coues, III, 1044). 1827.

COLUMBIAN GROUND SQUIRREL. *Spermophilus columbianus columbianus* (Ord). (Thwaites, V, 69; Coues, III, 856). 1815.

Plants New to Science

OREGON SUNSHINE. *Actinella lanata* Pursh. 1814.

HAIR-GRASS. *Aira brevifolia* Pursh. 1814.

? TOLMIE'S ONION. *Allium tolmiei* Baker. (Thwaites, V, 88; Coues, III, 1830). 1840.

? LYALL'S ANGELICA. *Angelica lyallii* Wats. 1840.

NORTHWEST CRIMSON COLUMBINE. *Aquilegia formosa* Fischer. (Thwaites, V, 138). 1824.

? LONG-TAILED WILD GINGER. *Asarum caudatum* Lindley. (Thwaites, V, 165). 1831.

MARIPOSA LILY. *Calochortus elegans* Pursh. 1814.

SCARLET GILIA. *Cantua aggregata* Pursh. 1814.

BUCKBRUSH; CHAPARRAL. *Ceanothus sanguineus* Pursh. 1814.

STICKY LAUREL. *Ceanothus velutinus* Douglas. 1831.

RAGGED ROBIN. *Clarkia pulchella* Pursh. (Thwaites, V, 95–96). 1814.

WESTERN SPRING BEAUTY. *Claytonia lanceolata* Pursh. 1814.

LINEAR-LEAVED MONTIA. *Claytonia linearis* Douglas. 1834.

MOUNTAIN LADY'S SLIPPER. *Cypripedium montanum* Doug. (Thwaites, V, 173). 1840.

CUT-LEAVED DAISY. *Erigeron compositus* Pursh. 1814.

WESTERN WALLFLOWER. *Erysimum asperum* (Nutt.) DC. 1821.

BLUE BUNCH WHEATGRASS. *Festuca spicata* Pursh. 1814.

SHRUBBY PENTSTEMON. *Gerardia fruticosa* Pursh. 1814.

TASSELS. *Geum triflorum* Pursh. 1814.

? YELLOW-FLOWERING PEA. *Lathyrus ochroleucus* Hook. (Thwaites, V, 138). 1834.

BITTERROOT; ROCK ROSE. *Lewisia rediviva* Pursh. 1814.

SILKY LUPINE. *Lupinus sericeus* Pursh. 1814.

NORTHERN SUN-CUP. *Oenothera heterantha* Nuttall. 1840.

OWL'S CLOVER. *Orthocarpus tenuifolius* (Pursh) Benth. 1814.

SILVER OXYTROPE. *Oxytropis argentata* Pursh. 1814.

CASCADE PENTSTEMON. *Pentstemon serrulatus* Menzies. 1813.

COMMON LOMATIUM. *Peucedanum utriculatum* C. & R. 1840.

VIRGATE PHACELIA. *Phacelia heterophylla* Pursh. 1814.

AMERICAN JACOB'S LADDER. *Polemonium caeruleum* A. Gray. 1863.

WHITE MILKWORT. *Polygala alba* Nuttall. 1814.

SITKA MOUNTAIN ASH. *Pyrus sambucifolia* ? [var. *pumila* Sargent]. 1847.

CASCARA SAGRADA. *Rhamnus purshiana* DC. 1825.

? UMATILLA GOOSEBERRY. *Ribes cognatum* Greene. (Thwaites, V, 121). 1907.

? CLUSTER ROSE. *Rosa pisocarpa* A. Gray. (Thwaites, V, 121). 1872.

RAYLESS CAMOMILE. *Santolina suaveolens* Pursh. 1814.

NARROW-LEAVED SKULLCAP. *Scutellaria angustifolia* Pursh. 1814.

NARROW-PETALED STONECROP. *Sedum stenopetalum* Pursh. 1814.

OCEAN SPRAY. *Spiraea discolor* Pursh. 1814.

CLUSTERED SWERTIA. *Swertia fastigiata* Pursh. 1814.

LEWIS AND CLARK'S SYNTHYRIS. *Synthyris missurica* (Raf.) Penn. 1814.

SMALL-HEADED CLOVER. *Trifolium microcephalum* Pursh. 1814.

? WESTERN HUCKLEBERRY. *Vaccinium occidentale* A. Gray. (Thwaites, V, 168). 1876.

CALIFORNIA FALSE HELLEBORE. *Veratrum californicum* Durand. 1855.

BEAR GRASS. *Xerophyllum tenax* Pursh. 1814.

Lewis and Clark Herbarium

YARROW. *Achillea millefolium* L. Collected May 20, 1806.

OREGON SUNSHINE. *Actinella lanata* Pursh. June 6.

WINDFLOWER. *Anemone quinquefolia* L. June 15.

? LYALL'S ANGELICA. *Angelica* sp., probably *A. lyallii* Wats. June 25.

LIVERWORT. *Bazzania trilobata* (L.) S. F. Gray. July 1.

MARIPOSA LILY. *Calochortus elegans* Pursh. May 17.

CALYPSO. *Calypso borealis* Salisb. June 16.

CAMAS. *Camassia quamash* (Pursh) Greene. June 23.

SCARLET GILIA. *Cantua aggregata* Pursh. June 26.

BUCKBRUSH. *Ceanothus sanguineus* Pursh. June 27.

STICKY LAUREL. *Ceanothus velutinus* Doug. No date. Probably June 24–29 since accompanying tag says "On Rocky Mts."

SAND CHERRY. *Cerasus pumila* (L.). May 29.

RAGGED ROBIN. *Clarkia pulchella* Pursh. June 1.

WESTERN SPRING BEAUTY. *Claytonia lanceolata* Pursh. June 27.

LINEAR-LEAVED MONTIA. *Claytonia linearis* Douglas. June 27.

CUT-LEAVED DAISY. *Erigeron compositus* Pursh. No date. Probably May 14 to June 10 since tag says "On banks of Kooskooskee."

WESTERN WALLFLOWER. *Erysimum asperum* (Nutt.) DC. June 1.

YELLOW FAWN LILY. *Erythronium grandiflorum* Pursh. June 5.

SHRUBBY PENTSTEMON. *Gerardia fruticosa* Pursh. June [?]. "Rocky Mountains."

TASSELS. *Geum triflorum* Pursh. June 12.

KOELER'S GRASS. *Koeleria cristata* (L.) Pers. June 10.

BITTERROOT. *Lewisia rediviva* Pursh. July 1.

ORANGE HONEYSUCKLE. *Lonicera ciliosa* (Pursh) DC. June 5 and 16.

SILKY LUPINE. *Lupinus sericeus* Pursh. June 5.

NORTHERN SUN-CUP. *Oenothera heterantha* Nuttall. June 14.

OWL'S CLOVER. *Orthocarpus tenuifolius* (Pursh) Benth. July 1.

SILVER OXYTROPE. *Oxytropis argentata* Pursh. July [?].

OREGON BOXWOOD. *Pachistima myrsinites* (Pursh) Raf. June 16.

CASCADE PENTSTEMON. *Pentstemon serrulatus* Menzies. May 20.

COMMON LOMATIUM. *Peucedanum utriculatum* C. & R. June 10.

VIRGATE PHACELIA. *Phacelia heterophylla* Pursh. June 9.

AMERICAN JACOB'S LADDER. *Polemonium caeruleum* A. Gray. June 27.

WESTERN SNAKEWEED. *Polygonum bistortoides* Pursh. June 12.

? CHERRY. *Prunus* sp. June 27.

WILD BLACK CHERRY. *Prunus virginiana* L. May 29.

SITKA MOUNTAIN ASH. *Pyrus sambucifolia* [var. *pumila* Sargent]. June 27.

CASCARA SAGRADA. *Rhamnus purshiana* DC. May 29.

STICKY CURRANT. *Ribes viscossissimum* Pursh. June 16.

RAYLESS CAMOMILE. *Santolina suaveolens* Pursh. June 9.

NARROW-LEAVED SKULLCAP. *Scutellaria angustifolia* Pursh. June 5.

NARROW-PETALED STONECROP. *Sedum stenopetalum* Pursh. June 15, July 1.

OCEAN SPRAY. *Spiraea discolor* Pursh. May 29.

CLUSTERED SWERTIA. *Swertia fastigiata* Pursh. June 14.

LEWIS AND CLARK'S SYNTHYRIS. *Synthyris missurica* (Raf.) Pennell. June 26.

SMALL-HEADED CLOVER. *Trifolium microcephalum* Pursh. July 1.

PETIOLED WAKE-ROBIN. *Trillium petiolatum* Pursh. June 15.

CALIFORNIA FALSE HELLEBORE. *Veratrum californicum* Durand. June 25.

BEAR GRASS. *Xerophyllum tenax* Pursh. June 15.

Indian Tribes Encountered

No additional tribes.

Topographic Features Named and/or Discovered

No new features.

Lewis Explores the Marias

CHAPTER NINETEEN

On July 3 Lewis, accompanied by Nez Perce guides and his nine men, took leave of his "worthy friend and companion Capt. Clark" and headed for the Great Falls of the Missouri. After a march of about 12 miles down the Bitterroot River, they came to the confluence of that stream with Clark Fork. Just below this junction, they constructed three rafts and crossed Clark Fork to the north bank. According to Sergeant Gass, this river was then "about 150 yards wide, and very beautiful."[1] That night they camped near the present city of Missoula.

During the evening the Nez Perces informed Lewis of their intention of turning back the next day "as they were afraid of meeting with their enimies the Minnetares." They assured him, however, that the road ahead was "a well beaten track" and that he would have no trouble finding it (V, 185). This road, as they outlined it, would take him up the Blackfoot River to a pass over the Continental Divide (now Lewis and Clark Pass in Lewis and Clark County, Montana) and then down the Sun (Medicine) River to Great Falls. The Nez Perces further advised Lewis that as he neared the Divide the road would fork and that although both forks led to the Missouri, he should take the left one.[2]

Lewis and party travelled up the Blackfoot River until on July 6 they came to the forks in the road alluded to by the Indians. They took the left one, as directed, which brought them onto Lander's Fork, a northern tributary of the Blackfoot. The next day, after they had followed this affluent a few miles, they took an easterly course across

[1] Gass, 282.
[2] The right fork would have taken Lewis over Cadotte's Pass and down the Dearborn River.

309

intervening ridges to a smaller stream, Alice Creek. A short march up this creek brought them to the Pass.

Lewis and Clark Pass (6,000 feet high) is easily accessible to the public today, though infrequently visited. About halfway between Roger's Pass and the town of Lincoln on Montana State Highway 20, a dirt road turns north up Alice Creek. One reaches the Pass by following this road some 14 to 15 miles. Unless driving a jeep, it would be wise to leave the car and walk the last mile since the road is winding and steep. Arrived at the summit, the visitor will be pleased to find that the Forest Service has erected a marker there bearing the inscription: "Capt. Meriwether Lewis on his return journey crossed the Continental Divide through this Pass on July 7, 1806." The drive up Alice Creek to the Pass is through a country of clean air and satisfying stillness where beautiful stands of evergreen forest alternate with extensive open meadows. It is a rewarding drive, as are the views from the top of the Pass.

While following the ancient Indian trail up the Blackfoot toward the Divide, Lewis made a number of observations of particular interest to the biologist. On July 5, for instance, he reported "a great number of pigeons breeding in this part of the mountains" (VI, 221). What makes this observation most significant is that Lewis had discovered passenger pigeons *nesting* west of the Continental Divide, far beyond the limits of their principal nesting area, and at a date later in the year than customary. As one ornithologist has pointed out, it was an unusual time "for *many* to be nesting."[3]

Again, on July 5, Lewis wrote: "there are many wild horses on Clarkes River about the place we passed it we saw some of them at a distance" (V, 190). These were the first he had encountered, though earlier he had written that they were said to be found in many parts of the extensive plains country (IV, 74). Since the Blackfeet, Nez Perces, Flatheads, and other Indians of this region owned innumerable horses, it was inevitable that some of them would escape to form nuclei of wild herds. Not needing additional mounts and eager to reach the Missouri without delay, Lewis passed this group with little more than a glance. Within only a few years the discovery of wild horses by the western traveller elicited an outburst of excitement followed by hastily made plans to capture one or more, employing such methods as lassoing, encirclement, or creasing (that is, by shooting to stun the animal without causing permanent injury). By then the idea—false from the

[3] Schorger, *The Passenger Pigeon,* 258.

beginning—had gained credence that wild horses were somehow superior to others.

On July 7 at or near the Divide Lewis reported that Reuben Field had wounded a "moose deer" near their camp (V, 194). Apparently the explorers did not bag a single moose (*Alces alces*) during the entire trip; the only other references to this animal are one by Ordway on May 10, 1805, stating that the hunters had seen several "moose deer" on that day, and another by Lewis on June 2, 1806, asserting that moose, according to Indian information, were common on the Salmon River. However, it is possible that Lewis and Clark did bring back with them moose antlers obtained somewhere along the route, for a pair attributed to them hangs today at Monticello.[4] Parenthetically, Lewis's mention of moose on the Salmon River caused Elliott Coues to declare: "Here Lewis and Clark lead the naturalists, as usual; for the American moose as distinguished from the Old World form . . . had no scientific standing in their day."[5] As Coues knew, it was not recognized and described as a distinct subspecies until several years later.[6]

Before crossing the Divide, Lewis, as his journal attests, collected and preserved a number of plant specimens. Some of these at least comprise a part of that unique collection in the Academy of Natural Sciences of Philadelphia to which we have already alluded so many times: among them, western blue flag (*Iris missouriensis*), silvery lupine (*Lupinus argenteus*), shrubby cinquefoil (*Potentilla fruticosa*), and black twinberry (*Lonicera involucrata*).

Lewis and party completed the journey from Traveller's Rest to the Missouri in just eight days. The route was shorter by almost 600 miles than the one they had followed going west. They encountered no Indians en route, though they saw fresh horse prints and other evidence that "Minnetarees" (probably Blackfeet) had recently passed this way. Once beyond Lewis and Clark Pass, they turned northeast, crossing small streams feeding into Dearborn's River, until they came to Sun River and shortly afterwards to the high, flat plains bordering the

[4] James A. Bear, Jr., Curator of Thomas Jefferson Memorial Foundation, has written me (Sept. 27, 1966) as follows: "The [moose] antlers were at the University of Virginia for years, first in one place and then in another, and finally coming to rest in the old Biology Building. Fiske Kimball brought them to Monticello and as far as anyone here can recall they have always been associated with the Lewis and Clark Expedition."

[5] Coues, III, 1032n.

[6] It would seem that the form Lewis encountered in western Montana was still another subspecies of moose, *Alces alces shirasi*.

Missouri. Lewis exhibited more elation than for months: "the morning was fair and the plains looked beautiful . . . the air was pleasant and a vast assemblage of little birds which croud to the groves on the river sung most enchantingly. . . . I sent the hunters down Medicine river to hunt elk and proceeded with the party across the plain to the white bear Islands which I found to be 8 ms. distant . . . it is now the season at which the buffaloe begin to coppelate and the bulls keep a tremendous roaring we could hear them for many miles and there are such numbers of them that there is one continual roar" (V, 199) .

Lewis arrived at White Bear Islands almost one year to the day since leaving them the previous July. His first thought was to cross the Missouri to open the caches and determine the condition of their content. To that end he had his men shoot buffalo (for their hides) and collect branches from nearby willows. With these hides and branches they constructed two boats, one "after the mandan fassion [i.e., a bullboat] with a single skin in the form of a bason and the other . . . of two skins on a plan of our own" (V, 200) . In these hastily built craft, they crossed the river.

On opening the main cache, Lewis was dismayed to find that water from spring floods had entered it. Certain articles, such as a valuable map of the Missouri and the wagon wheels, had survived, but his collection of plant specimens had been completely destroyed, as had a number of bear skins he prized highly. The loss of the plants—the entire lot collected between Fort Mandan and Great Falls—distressed him beyond words.

Lewis had devoted much time and labor to the preservation of these specimens, far more than most people realize. The job of pressing plants was not as simple as it sounds, even under optimum conditions of warm, sunshiny weather. Plants, of course, are full of moisture, and require constant attention until fully dry, namely, exposing them to air and transferring to dry paper for many days running. Some plants, the more succulent ones, naturally demanded more time than the others. During those periods when Lewis was most active botanically—as at Camp Chopunnish, for example—he may well have had as many as 30 or 40 plants to look after daily. This meant removing them one at a time from the press, opening them to the sun, returning them to the press, and taking pains all the while to be certain that identification labels remained affixed. But this was not all by any means. Even after the plants had been dried, he had to supervise their transportation and keep an eye on them continuously to prevent their loss to rain, flash-flood, fire, mildew, capsize, and the like. Maximilian later lost a valuable collection when the boat on which he was descending the Missouri caught fire and burned. Such losses were more than minor catastrophes, resulting as they did in the defeat of prime scientific objectives and the complete vitiation of weeks and months of dedicated effort and inquiry. How many specimens Lewis lost at Great Falls will never be determined.

Lewis soon learned of another loss at White Bear Islands, his men informing him that seven of their 17 horses had disappeared, presumably stolen by Indians. This was bad news, primarily because he would now be unable to take more than three men with him on his upcoming Marias reconnaissance, instead of six as earlier planned. He chose Drouillard (a foregone conclusion) and the two Field brothers.

[2]

Lewis's determination to explore further the Marias River provides us with still another instance of his undoubted courage. Although designing Indians, for all he knew, were looking over his shoulder at that very moment, he was starting off into an unknown country with only three men at his back, and at the same time was leaving behind a party of only six, to all appearances regarding it of sufficient size to cope with grizzly bears and possible redskins and surmount all problems incident to portaging. He had no positive knowledge then that it would soon be strengthened by the arrival of Sergeant Ordway and nine other men. Before he rejoined Sergeant Gass and his contingent, he would be party to the spilling of Indian blood and would himself escape death by a mere hair's breadth.

As Lewis left the Missouri on July 16, he advised Gass that he expected to rejoin him at the mouth of the Marias not later than August 5, but that if he did not show up by September 1, then he and his men should make all possible haste to join Clark at the entrance of the Yellowstone.

After recrossing the Missouri and stopping long enough to make sketches of Rainbow and Great Falls, Lewis headed across the plains in a slightly west of north direction which would bring him soon to the Teton River and then to the Marias. The country, interminably wide and level, looked "like a well shaved bowling green, in which emence herds of buffaloe were seen feeding attended by their scarcely less numerous sheepherds the wolves" (V, 206). Antelope, thinly but widely dispersed, often followed them "at no great distance for miles, frequently halting and giving a loud whistle through their nostrils" (V, 205). Once again Lewis makes note of the congenital curiosity of the graceful, high-stepping pronghorns.

As the party arrived at the Teton, they saw where a buffalo had recently been wounded and suspected that it had been shot by an Indian. They made camp that night concerned about Blackfoot proximity. "I keep a strict lookout every night, I take my tour of watch with the men," Lewis reported (V, 208).

About noon of the next day they arrived at the Marias, striking it some six miles above the farthest point explored by Lewis a year earlier. As they began its ascent, they kept to the plains some distance from the river where the terrain was less gullied. Game decreased perceptibly, and the condition of the prairie floor deteriorated. "A great quan[ti]ty of small gravel is everywhere distributed over the surface of the earth," Lewis declared, "which renders travling extreemly painfull to our bearfoot horses. the soil is generally a white or whiteish blue clay, this where it has been trodden by the buffaloe when wet has now become as firm as a brickbat and stands in innumerable little points quite as formidable to our horses feet as the gravel" (V, 210). Small stagnant pools, strongly impregnated with mineral salts, provided the only water out on the prairie. According to Lewis, the buffalo preferred this to the less impregnated water of the streams (V, 211).

Three days of travel across this timberless tableland brought Lewis to the junction of Two Medicine River and Cut Bank Creek, the two streams that merge to form the Marias. Since, as we know, one of his main reasons for making this reconnaissance was to look for a stream flowing south into the Missouri from the Saskatchewan region that might serve to divert some of the Canadian fur trade to the United States, he accordingly went up Cut Bank Creek, the more northerly of the two conjoining streams. In doing so, he doubtless had in mind, too, the view held by Jefferson that Louisiana Territory included all that area drained by the Missouri, even portions that might conceivably extend beyond the 49th parallel.

After Lewis had followed the twistings of Cut Bank Creek for two days, he came to a beautiful valley in which stood a clump of large cottonwoods. From the top of a bluff on the north side of the creek, he could see that this stream here veered sharply to the west and soon entered the mountains. "I thought it unnecessary," Lewis then wrote, "to proceed further and therefore encamped resolving to rest ourselves and horses a couple of days at this place and take the necessary observations. . . . I now have lost all hope of the waters of this river ever extending to N. Latitude 50°" (V, 214).

In a fruitless attempt to establish longitude, Lewis stayed on four days. The period introduced both misery and frustration. The weather turned foul, with rain and a cold penetrating wind that blew with more than customary violence. A persistent cloud cover effectively obscured all heavenly bodies. Uncommonly large mosquitoes tormented them day and night. On July 23, game being unobtainable, they were forced to satisfy demands for food by eating a mush of cous roots mixed with oil rendered from tainted meat. The next day the hunters, returning to camp empty-handed, declared that "it was useless to hunt within 6 or 8 miles of this place that there was no appearance of game within that distance" (V, 217). They reported, too, that Indians had lately been in the neighborhood. At this particular point of time, made critical by lack of food, passenger pigeons suddenly appeared. From flocks that alighted in the cottonwoods, they shot enough to ease hunger pains.

Lewis did not forsake this inhospitable site until the morning of July 26. For obvious reasons he called it Camp Disappointment. He would have stayed longer, in a last effort to determine longitude, except, as he said, he now began to be apprehensive about reaching "the United States within this season" unless he exerted himself to the full. Lewis was then at the most northerly point attained at any time during the entire journey, about 12 miles northeast of present-day Browning, Montana, approximately 113° W. Longitude and 48° 40' N. Latitude.

Camp Disappointment may be reached easily today. Driving west from the town of Cut Bank along U.S. Highway 2 for 19 miles to Meriwether, one turns north there on Route 444 (locally known as Meriwether Road) for four miles and then turns west onto a small side road. Camp Disappointment is about two miles from this last turn.

From Camp Disappointment, Lewis and his three companions travelled in a southeasterly direction, crossing Willow Creek after about five miles and Two Medicine River after about 12. Soon afterwards they came to Badger Creek, where it empties into Two Medicine River. "The rose honeysuckle and redberry [buffaloberry, *Shepherdia argentea*] bushes constitute the undergrowth," Lewis commented, "there being but little willow in this quarter . . . here it is that we find three species of cottonwood which I have remarked in my voyage assembled together; that speceis common to the Columbia [*Populus trichocarpa*] I have never before seen on the waters of the Missouri, also the narrow [*P. angustifolia*] and broad leafed speceis [*P. deltoides occidentalis*" (V, 218–219).[7]

While ascending the Missouri the year before, Lewis had spoken of the Blackfeet Indians as a lawless, vicious band of wretches whom he wished to avoid at any cost. In mid-afternoon of the 26th, after fording Badger Creek and climbing to the plain above, he drew out his telescope and discovered, less than two miles away, a party of eight Indians with 30 horses. He recorded this as an unpleasant sight, particularly so since the Indians had also seen him. Determining at once to make the best of the situation and to approach them in a friendly manner, he told his men that if these savages should attack he would "resist to the last extremity preferring death to that of being deprived of my papers instruments and gun and desired that they would form the same resolution" (V, 220).

With that decided, they rode forward. On coming up with the Indians (Lewis called them "Minnetarees of Fort de Prairie," though they were actually Piegan Blackfeet),[8] they dismounted, shook hands all around, and smoked a pipe, after which Lewis presented gifts to three of them who professed to be chiefs. These formalities out of the way, the Indians agreed to Lewis's proposal that they encamp together on Two Medicine River. They then mounted and descended a very steep bluff to a small bottom—about one half mile long and some 250 yards wide—in which stood close together three solitary cottonwood trees. Here, near the river, they made their camp.

That night they smoked and conversed until a late hour, Drouillard eliciting through sign language the disquieting information that these Piegans represented a much larger band encamped just one-half day's march away. When the party sought sleep, Lewis took the first watch until eleven-thirty, by which time all the Indians seemed to be sound asleep. Lewis then woke Reuben Field, cautioning him to keep a sharp lookout and to inform him immediately if any of the Blackfeet

[7] Montana botanists to whom I have put the question of three different species of cottonwood on Two Medicine River have been unable to confirm or deny. However, C. S. Sargent suspected that Lewis mistook the common balsam poplar (*P. balsamifera*) for *P. trichocarpa*. (See Sargent, "The First Account of Some Western Trees," 40.)

[8] The Piegan Blackfeet were one of three divisions of Blackfeet, the others being Blackfeet proper and Blood.

attempted to leave camp; he feared they might try to steal their horses. He then fell asleep and slept soundly until awakened shortly after daybreak when he heard Drouillard yell, "damn you let go of my gun" (V, 224). Events immediately preceding and following Lewis's return to consciousness are best told in his own words:

This morning at daylight the indians got up and crouded around the fire. J. Fields who was on post had carelessly laid his gun down behind him near where his brother was sleeping, one of the indians . . . slipped behind him and took his gun and that of his brother unperceived by him, at the same instant two others advanced and seized the guns of Drewyer and myself, J. Fields seeing this turned about to look for his gun and saw the fellow just running off with her and his brother's he called to his brother who instantly jumped up and pursued the indian with him whom they overtook at the distance of 50 or 60 paces from the camp s[e]ized their guns and rested them from him and R. Fields as he seized his gun stabcd the indian to the heart with his knife the fellow ran about 15 steps and fell dead; of this I did not know untill afterwards, having recovered their guns they ran back instantly to the camp; Drewyer who was awake saw the indian take hold of his gun and instantly jumped up and s[e]ized her and rested her from him but the indian still retained his pouch, his jumping up and crying damn you let go of my gun awakened me. I jumped up and asked what was the matter which I quickly learned when I saw drewyer in a scuffle with the indian for his gun. I reached to seize my gun but found her gone, I then drew a pistol from my holster and terning myself about saw the indian making off with my gun I ran at him with my pistol and bid him lay down my gun which he was in the act of doing when the Fieldses returned and drew up their guns to shoot him which I forbid as he did not appear to be about to make any resistance or commit any offensive act, he droped the gun and walked slowly off, I picked her up instantly. Drewyer having about this time recovered his gun and pouch asked if he might not kill the fellow which I also forbid as the indian did not appear to wish to kill us, as soon as they found all of us in possession of our arms they ran and indeavored to drive off all the horses I now hollowed to the men and told them to fire on them if they attempted to drive off our horses, they accordingly pursued the main party who were dr[i]ving the horses up the river and I pursued the man who had taken my gun who with another was driving off a part of the horses which were to the left of the camp. I pursued them so closely that they could not take twelve of their own horses but continued to drive one of mine with some others; at the distance of three hundred paces they entered one of these steep nitches in the bluff with the horses before them being nearly out of breath I could pursue no further, I called to them as I had done several times before that I would shoot them if they did not give me my horse and raised my gun, one of them jumped behind a rock and spoke to the other who turned around and stoped at the distance of 30 steps from me and I shot him through the belly, he fell to his knees and on his wright elbow from which position he partly raised himself up and fired at me . . . being bearheaded I felt the wind of his bullet very distinctly (V, 223–225).

Since Lewis had left his shot pouch behind and consequently could not reload his gun, he hurriedly retraced his steps to camp. Finding that they had more than enough horses, with the addition of those left by the Piegans, he ordered his men to saddle up, stressing the importance of reaching the mouth of the Marias and rejoining Sergeant Gass as soon as possible—for the very good reason that the Indians might be reinforced and pursue. They tarried long enough, however, to remove amulets from the two dead Indians. These were later displayed in Peale's Museum.[9]

Astride their horses again, they soon climbed out of the gorge to the plain above—a difficult ascent because of the height and steepness of the canyon wall—and took a course to the south of east, riding rapidly. They made such good time that by 3 P.M. they had reached the Teton River, striking it about five miles above where they had passed it going out. Lewis estimated that they had already covered 63 miles. After a brief rest, they rode 17 more miles before dark. They halted again, killed a buffalo, ate their supper, and then went on—now by moonlight. They did not stop again until 2 A.M., by which time they had put behind them an additional 20 miles for a total of approximately 100 since they set out from their camp that morning. They dismounted and slept, at a point not far from today's Fort Benton.

Up at dawn (July 28), Lewis and his men, though saddle-sore and aching in every joint and muscle, remounted and went on, hoping to reach the mouth of the Marias before the day was far advanced. Some 12 miles of riding brought them close to the north bank of the Missouri where they heard rifle shots. "We quickly repared to this joyfull sound," Lewis exclaimed, "and on arriving at the bank of the river had the unspeakable satisfaction to see our canoes coming down" (V, 228).

The canoes (the white pirogue and six dugouts) carried not only Gass and his crew but also Sergeant Ordway and his contingent of nine men who had successfully completed the descent of the Missouri from Three Forks to this point (after parting from Clark). What extraordinary luck! The formalities of this reunion consumed no time at all. Lewis and his weary companions climbed into the boats, leaving their

[9] Charles Willson Peale, "Memoranda of the Philadelphia Museum." See also Jackson, *Letters*, 477.

horses to whatever destiny the Montana plains might provide. Soon afterwards they arrived at the confluence of the Marias and Missouri and hurriedly opened the main cache. Due to a cave-in, most of the articles had suffered injury, particularly some large grizzly bear skins Lewis treasured and had hoped to take back to Jefferson. The gunpowder, corn, flour, pork, and salt had survived the winter in fair shape, as had the contents of smaller caches near the point. The red pirogue had been injured beyond repair.

The entire party, now 20 strong, re-embarked and moved downstream 15 miles before making camp for the night on the south side of the river, thus putting the broad flow of the Missouri between them and any possible pursuer. Shortly after dark a violent storm, accompanied by rain, hail, thunder, and lightning, struck them and continued until near morning. "No[t] having the means of making a shelter," Lewis wrote, "I lay in the water all night" (V, 229). And in that manner ended what had been for Meriwether Lewis the most dramatic day of the entire trans-continental journey, including one of the most remarkable rides since Roland and his rider brought the good news from Ghent to Aix.

[3]

The precise locations of Camp Disappointment and Lewis's encounter with the Blackfeet long remained undetermined. That these have recently been established has been due to the joint efforts of the Museum of the Plains Indian, Browning, Montana, Mrs. Helen B. West, Archives Assistant of the Museum, and two Boy Scout officials of Cut Bank, Montana, Robert H. Anderson and Ed Mathison. What started out as a simple, routine historical marker program, limited to pinning down the site of the Lewis-Blackfeet incident, soon evolved into a much more ambitious project, namely, following Lewis every mile of the way from the forks of the Marias up Cut Bank Creek to Camp Disappointment, south to Two Medicine River, and then down that stream to the site of the July 26th encampment, a distance altogether of more than 50 miles.

It was Anderson, an experienced airplane pilot, who "conceived the idea of following Lewis's journey from the air, using aerial equipment and maps in checking the explorer's compass bearings and distances."[10] In fact, without the airplane, Mrs. West, Anderson, and Ma-

[10] Helen B. West, "Meriwether Lewis in Blackfeet Country" (Browning, Montana, 1964), Preface.

thison agree, the project could not have succeeded. Of course other factors contributed measurably to their achievement, notably a thorough knowledge of the existing terrain gained from exhaustive ground study and close attention to the original Lewis and Clark journals and pertinent collateral material. They began their work in the winter of 1962–63 and concluded it in 1964. It was a difficult task, commendably and admirably executed. Mrs. West has told the story in a recent bulletin, "Meriwether Lewis in Blackfeet Country," published by the Museum of the Plains Indian.

No longer does the Lewis and Clark student have any doubts as to the exact spot where Lewis, Drouillard, and the two Field brothers grappled with the Piegan Blackfeet on the morning of July 27, 1806. It may now be visited. My opportunity came in late June, 1965, when I received a letter from Mrs. West which read: "I would enjoy showing you the location of Lewis's encounter with the Blackfeet Indians. It is a particularly picturesque spot, and the historical and aesthetic appeal makes it a most interesting place to visit. However, it is as yet unmarked, and it is almost impossible to give directions for reaching there; you would need me or Robert H. Anderson of Cut Bank as a guide."[11]

Six weeks later (on August 3) I arrived in Cut Bank about noon, after driving that morning from Great Falls with my late brother, Dr. C. R. Cutright, research entomologist, Ohio Agricultural Experiment Station, Wooster, Ohio. Here we met Mrs. West and Mr. Anderson, two of that young, energetic, engaging trio whose discoveries had been responsible for bringing us from our homes in Pennsylvania and Ohio, and who were now ready to show us the way to the small bottom on Two Medicine River where occurred long ago the most dramatic event of Lewis and Clark's 28-month journey from the Mississippi to the Pacific and back.

The road we followed took us south through rolling, treeless, prairie lands in the eastern part of the Blackfeet Indian Reservation to the Two Medicine River. Crossing it, we turned upstream, the road in places becoming almost indiscernible, so that I could now fully understand Mrs. West's statement that it was nearly impossible to provide directions. The main topographic features of this country, we were told, had changed hardly at all since 1806. For instance, as we neared our objective, we left our road and drove through fields of virgin prairie grass.

[11] Letter to author, June 23, 1965, from Helen B. West.

Our hosts soon pointed out the eminence where Lewis had stood on July 26 when he first saw the Blackfeet, then the butte, about one and three-quarter miles to the east, where the Indians and their horses had halted, and finally the intermediate point where both groups initially met. We drove to the latter place, where we had an unobstructed view of this beautiful High Plains country and of the Two Medicine valley below us, including the bottom where Lewis and the Indians had encamped almost exactly 159 years earlier. Here we left our car and began, on foot, the descent to the valley, working our way cautiously down the steep, rocky, heavily scored canyon wall. Some twenty minutes later, close to the river, Mrs. West and Mr. Anderson pointed out to us the place where, they are convinced, Lewis and his men had bivouacked on that memorable night of July 26, 1806, underneath a clump of three large cottonwoods. And right now, more than a century and a half later, we found that we were standing, incredibly, in the shade of three narrow-leaved cottonwood trees!

This is the only conceivable place [Mrs. West has written] which could fit such a description [as Lewis's]. The descent into the canyon is precipitous but still possible to negotiate with horses. Topographical map and field examinations show this bottom to be about 250 yards wide, ½ mile long, surrounded by bluffs almost 250 feet high, with—and this is possibly the most conclusive identification—cliffs washed by the river both above and below. In addition, as described by Lewis, we find that "the bluffs are so steep that there are but few places where they could be ascended, and are broken in several places by deep nitches which extend back from the river several hundred yards, their bluffs being so steep that it is impossible to ascend them.

As an additional and scarcely believable bonus we find at the probable location of the camp, three large and venerable cottonwoods. Is it possible that they are the "three solitary trees" described by Lewis under which his party and the Indians camped? [12]

The three cottonwoods lifting their shiny-leafed crowns to the sun are indeed venerable. Close examination reveals them to be windshaken and rotten at the core, the latter condition precluding any possibility of determining their age by borings. It may be too much to conclude that these are the same identical trees that gave shelter to Lewis, though the coincidence—if it is a coincidence—is most remarkable. But everything else in this remote, picturesque valley is remarkable.

[12] West, "Meriwether Lewis in Blackfeet Country," 13.

Mrs. West and Mr. Anderson showed us the probable spot where Reuben Field sank his knife into one of the Blackfeet, and the site upstream where the main party of Indians, pursued by Drouillard and the Field brothers, attempted to escape with most of the horses. They then escorted us in the opposite direction, following Lewis's probable route as he chased two of the Piegans with other horses, including his own, to "one of those steep nitches in the bluff" some 300 paces away. It was here, after shouting to the Indians that he would shoot if they did not free his horse, and they paid no heed to his warning, that he put a bullet into one of them; whereupon the same Indian, from his knees, though mortally wounded, fired a shot that fanned the hair on Lewis's head.

Inevitable changes have come to this small area of bottomland since Lewis's brush with death. Recent floods, for instance, have altered its appearance by heaping innumerable timbers on the banks of the river. No longer can one expect to find the passenger pigeon or the buffalo, though Mr. Anderson supplied evidence that at least one of that great shaggy legion of quadrupeds had survived until comparatively recent times when he turned over a slab of stone to show us a weatherbeaten skull that he had discovered in the course of his field studies. Still other animals have disappeared from this region, or occur less abundantly, but the visitor can still find bearberry, honeysuckle, and wild rose (mentioned by Lewis) and, of course, cottonwood—perhaps three species.

It is to be hoped that this small, historic portion of the Two Medicine River valley and its immediate environs may be preserved in its present form for all time. Present and future generations of Americans should not be denied the privilege of enjoying its beauty and, at the same time, of reliving Lewis's exciting rencontre with the Piegan Blackfeet. According to the ethnologist, John C. Ewers, this meeting was significant historically for at least four reasons:

(1) It marked the first meeting of official representatives of the United States with members of the northwesternmost group of people residing in the recently purchased Louisiana—the Piegan Indians; (2) It marked the first armed conflict between official representatives of the United States and Plains Indians; (3) It marked the only armed conflict between members of the Lewis and Clark Expedition and Indians, and probably the most serious threat to the successful accomplishment of that great exploring expedition; and (4) It marked the beginning of hostilities between members of the most powerful tribe of Indians on the Northwestern Plains and the American citi-

zens. It was the first cause of Blackfeet opposition to Americans which continued for a full quarter century (until 1831), and effectively prevented the establishment of American trade in a large segment of the northwestern portion of our country as it was constituted at that time.[13]

Since my visit to Camp Disappointment and the Two Medicine River site, Mrs. West and others have importuned officials in Washington to confer National Historic Landmark status on these two historic places. As a result, Camp Disappointment has received such status. This action holds out promise that the Two Medicine site will soon gain like rank.

In his hurried reconnaissance, it should not be overlooked, Lewis not only explored the Marias but also discovered in so doing a number of important affluents, notably Two Medicine River and Cut Bank, Willow, and Badger Creeks. Of interest to the botanist is the fact that he collected and brought back with him six plants which today may be seen in the Academy of Natural Sciences of Philadelphia. These are Nuttall's atriplex (*Atriplex nuttallii*), red false mallow (*Cristaria coccinea*), scapose primrose (*Oenothera caespitosa*), violet prairie clover (*Petalostemon violaceum*), greasewood (*Sarcobatus vermiculatus*), and white-margined spurge (*Euphorbia marginata*). All were new to science except the clover. One of these, surprisingly, Lewis collected on July 28, the last day of his hell-to-leather ride from Two Medicine to the Missouri. This was the white-margined spurge.[14] In examining this plant at the Academy not long ago, I found myself wondering how many men under like circumstances, even though botanically minded, would have noticed such a modest, unpretentious specimen.

[4]

After Lewis and his party left their camp below the Marias (on the morning of July 29), they made excellent progress downstream in spite of wind and rain. They passed the mouth of the Musselshell on August 1, the Milk on August 4, and arrived at the Yellowstone three days later. Here Lewis found a note from Clark. It said that he and his party had reached this important confluence on August 3 and that they had

[13] West, "Meriwether Lewis in Blackfeet Country," 2.

[14] This specimen bears a tag on which Pursh had written, "July 28, 1806. On the Yellowstone River. M. Lewis." But Lewis, on that date, was on the Marias River nearing the Missouri.

moved on down the Missouri in an attempt to locate a place less populated with mosquitoes.

Lewis caught up with Clark just five days later, on August 12. It was a stroke of exceedingly good fortune that the reunion occurred at this particular time. Just the day before Lewis had been felled by a bullet which, according to Sergeant Ordway, struck him "in his back side."[15] As Lewis described this painful incident:

. . . opposite to the birnt hills there happened to be a herd of Elk. . . . I determined to land and kill some of them accordingly we put too and I went out with Cruzatte only. We fired on the elk I killed one and he wounded another, we reloaded our guns and took different routs through the thick willows in pursuit of the Elk; I was in the act of firing on the Elk a second time when a ball struck my left thye about an inch below my hip joint, missing the bone it passed through the left thye and out the thickness of the bullet across the hinder part of the right thye; the stroke was very severe; I instantly supposed that Cruzatte had shot me in mistake for an Elk as I was dressed in brown leather and he cannot see very well; under this impression I called out to him damn you, you have shot me, and looked toward the place from whence the ball had come, seeing nothing I called Cruzatte several times as loud as I could (V, 240).

Receiving no answer, Lewis rushed to the conclusion that he must have been shot by an Indian and not Cruzatte. He therefore, though in great pain, hobbled back to the boat where he reported to his companions what had happened and directed them to follow him and give pursuit. When his wound soon became so painful and his thigh so stiff that he could travel no farther, the rest of the party went ahead. They returned about 20 minutes later, bringing Cruzatte with them and reporting that they could find no trace of Indians. The truth now seemed obvious. Peter Cruzatte, though a skilled boatman, was unfortunately blind in one eye and myopic in the other; he had shot Lewis unintentionally and, because of embarrassment, had remained mute when Lewis called out to him.

Sergeant Gass helped Lewis dress his wounds. They introduced tents of patent lint into the ball holes and later that day applied a poultice of powdered Peruvian bark. As mentioned before, these tents kept the surface of the wound open, expedited drainage, and insured granulation from the inside out.

With all members of the Expedition together again, Clark took

[15] Ordway, 387.

over as physician to his friend. He described the injury as a very bad flesh wound. When he first dressed it, Lewis fainted dead away.[16] On joining Clark, Lewis wrote:

as wrighting in my present situation is extremely painfull to me, I shall desist untill I recover and leave to my fri[e]nd Capt C. the continuation of our journal. however I must notice a singular Cherry which is found on the Missouri in the bottom lands about the beaver bends and some little distance below the white earth river. this production is not very abundant even in the small tract of country to which it seems to be confined. the stem is compound erect and subdivided or branching without any regular order it rises to the hight of eight or ten feet seldom puting up more than one stem from the same root not growing in cops as the Choke Cherry dose. the bark is smooth and of a dark brown colour. the leaf is peteolate, oval accutely pointed at it's apex, from one and a ¼ to 1½ inches in length and from ½ to ¾ of an inch in width, finely or minutely serrate, pale green and free from pubessence. the fruit is a globular berry about the size of a buck-shot of a fine scarlet red; like the cherries cultivated in the U' States each is supported by a separate celindric flexable branch peduncle which issue from the extremities of the boughs the peduncle of this cherry swells as it approaches the fruit being largest at the point of insertion. the pulp of this fruit is of an ascid flavour and is now ripe. the style and stigma are permanent. I have never seen it in bloom (V, 243–244) .

Thus, characteristically, Lewis found strength for one last expansive botanical account. It was his final contribution to the famous journals; so far as we know, he did not pick up his pen again until he arrived in St. Louis.

But that is not the end of the story of the "singular Cherry," for in the Lewis and Clark Herbarium one can find today a specimen collected on August 10, 1806. It bears an affixed card which reads: "A Cherry found near the beaver bents on the Missouri." Since it is most unlikely that Lewis collected two different species of cherry near that unique place he alluded to as the "beaver bents," it must be assumed that this specimen (since identified as pin cherry, *Prunus pennsylvanica*) is the one he described on August 12.

SUMMARY OF DISCOVERIES

Animals New to Science

SHIRAS'S MOOSE. *Alces alces shirasi* Nelson. (Thwaites, V, 194; Coues, III, 1032) . Described, 1914.

[16] Ordway, 389.

? FORSTER'S TERN. *Sterna forsteri* Nuttall. [A.O.U. 69] (Thwaites, V, 237; Coues, III, 1133) . 1834.

Plants New to Science

NUTTALL'S ATRIPLEX. *Atriplex nuttallii* Wats. 1874.
RED FALSE MALLOW. *Cristaria coccinea* Pursh. 1814.
SILVERBERRY. *Elaeagnus argentea* Pursh. 1814.
WHITE-MARGINED SPURGE. *Euphorbia marginata* Pursh. 1814.
GREAT-FLOWERED GAILLARDIA. *Gaillardia aristata* Pursh. 1814.
WESTERN BLUE-FLAG. *Iris missouriensis* Nuttall. 1834.
INVOLUCRED FLY-HONEYSUCKLE. *Lonicera involucrata* (Rich.) Banks. 1823.
SILVERY LUPINE. *Lupinus argenteus* Pursh. 1814.
LARGE MONKEY FLOWER. *Mimulus luteus* Pursh. 1814.
SCAPOSE PRIMROSE. *Oenothera caespitosa* Nuttall. 1813.
LOUSEWORT. *Pedicularis scopulorum* Gray = *P. elata* Pursh. 1814.
ANTELOPE BRUSH. *Purshia tridentata* (Pursh) DC. 1814.
GLAUCOUS ZYGADENE. *Zygadenus elegans* Pursh. 1814.

Lewis and Clark Herbarium

NUTTALL'S ATRIPLEX. *Atriplex nuttallii* Wats. Collected July 20, 1806.
BALSAM ROOT. *Buphthalmum sagittatum* Pursh. July 7.
RED FALSE MALLOW. *Cristaria coccinea* Pursh. July 20.
SILVERBERRY. *Elaeagnus argentea* Pursh. July 6.
WHITE-MARGINED SPURGE. *Euphorbia marginata* Pursh. July 28.
GREAT-FLOWERED GAILLARDIA. *Gaillardia aristata* Pursh. July 6.
SQUIRREL-TAIL GRASS. *Hordeum jubatum* L. July 12.
WESTERN BLUE-FLAG. *Iris missouriensis* Nuttall. July 5.
JUNIPER. *Juniperus communis* L. July 7.
LEWIS'S WILD FLAX. *Linum lewisii* Pursh. July 9.
INVOLUCRED FLY-HONEYSUCKLE. *Lonicera involucrata* (Rich.) Banks. July 7.
SILVERY LUPINE. *Lupinus argenteus* Pursh. July 7.
LARGE MONKEY FLOWER. *Mimulus luteus* Pursh. July 4.
SCAPOSE PRIMROSE. *Oenothera caespitosa* Nuttall. July 17.
LONG-BEAKED PEDICULARIS. *Pedicularis groenlandica* Retz. July 6.
LOUSEWORT. *Pedicularis scopulorum* Gray. July 6.
VIOLET PRAIRIE CLOVER. *Petalostemon violaceum* Michaux. July 22.
LEWIS'S SYRINGA. *Philadelphus lewisii* Pursh. July 4.
WHITE MILKWORT. *Polygala alba* Nuttall. August 10.
SHRUBBY CINQUEFOIL. *Potentilla fruticosa* L. July 5.
PIN CHERRY. *Prunus demissa* Nuttall = *P. pennsylvanica* L. August 10.
ANTELOPE BRUSH. *Purshia tridentata* (Pursh) DC. July 6.
GREASEWOOD. *Sarcobatus vermiculatus* (Hook.) Torrey. July 20.
GLAUCOUS ZYGADENE. *Zygadenus elegans* Pursh. July 7.

Indian Tribes Encountered

Algonquian Linguistic Family: † Blackfeet (Piegan).

Topographic Features Named and/or Discovered

† "Cokahlaroosh" River (Thwaites, V, 185) —— Blackfoot River.

† Werner's Creek (Thwaites, V, 190) —— Clearwater River (Thwaites, V, 190n).

† Seaman's Creek (Thwaites, V, 191) —— Clear Creek (Coues, III, 1074n).

† "N. Fork of the Cokahlariskit" (Thwaites, V, 191) —— Salmon Trout Creek (Coues, III, 1074n).

† "Prairie of the Knobs" (Thwaites, V, 191) —— Blackfoot or Steven's Prairie (Coues, III, 1074–1075n).

† "Creek on N. Side" (Thwaites, V, 193) —— Lander's Fork of Blackfoot.

† "A small stream" (Gass, 285) —— Alice Creek.

† "Dividing ridge" (Thwaites, V, 194) —— Lewis and Clark Pass.

† Shishequaw mountain (Thwaites, V, 195) —— Heart Mountain (Coues, III, 1079n).

† Buffaloe Creek (Thwaites, V, 208) —— Antelope or Pondera Creek (Thwaites, V, 208n; Coues, III, 1088n).

† "A northern branch" (Thwaites, V, 212) —— Cut Bank Creek. The main or "southern branch" is today's Two Medicine River.

† "A small creek" (Thwaites, V, 218) —— Willow Creek (Coues, III, 1096n).

† "S. branch" (Thwaites, V, 218) —— Badger Creek (Coues, III, 1097n).

† Battle Creek (Thwaites, V, 226) —— Birch Creek (Coues, III, 1105n).

Clark Explores
the Yellowstone

CHAPTER TWENTY

On the same day that Lewis left Traveller's Rest for Great Falls, Clark set out for Shoshoni Cove, Three Forks, and the Yellowstone. Twenty men and Charbonneau's squaw and son accompanied him. They made good time ascending the Bitterroot River, having at their disposal a complement of 50 horses to facilitate travel. The valley, 10 to 15 miles wide, was "boutifully versified with small open plains covered with a great variety of Sweet cented plants, flowers & grass" (V, 245).

Near the end of the third day, they arrived at Ross's Hole where, the previous fall, they had met the Flatheads (Ootlashoots). Here Clark made an important decision. Instead of retracing his steps by way of Lost Trail Pass, North Fork of the Salmon, Lemhi River, and Lemhi Pass to Shoshoni Cove, he would attempt a short-cut. By so doing he saved himself both time and distance. The roundabout Lemhi-Salmon route was close to 130 miles long, and the explorers had been seven days negotiating it. The short-cut proved to be 73 miles, the way Clark figured it, and he completed it in just three days.

This short-cut began in the southern part of Ravalli County near the present-day town of Sula, and terminated in Beaver County near Armistead. On leaving Ross's Hole on July 6, Clark and his party veered to the left up Camp Creek[1] and soon afterwards crossed the Continental Divide at a gap now known as Gibbon's Pass. Beyond the Pass they were again on Missouri waters, specifically tributaries of the Big Hole (Wisdom) River. The road from here to the Cove followed an almost straight southeasterly course and Clark had no trouble

---

[1] Coues (III, 1122n) and Wheeler (*The Trail of Lewis and Clark,* II, 318), agree that Clark went up Camp Creek.

finding it, for as he said, the buffalo and Indians "always have the best route & here both were joined" (V, 250).

Later that day, Clark came to a plain where he observed great quantities of camas just beginning to bloom and saw evidence that Indians had recently been digging the roots of that plant. Sacagawea informed him that she had often as a child visited this plain and that the stream they were descending was a branch of the Wisdom River. Farther along she pointed to a gap which she said they would need to cross to reach Shoshoni Cove. The party camped that night not far from the site of the battle of the Big Hole, a bloody event between forces of Gen. John Gibbon and Chief Joseph that took place during the Nez Perce War of 1877.

The next day they came to and crossed the Big Hole River and later the gap Sacagawea had indicated.[2] Beyond the gap they dropped down to a beautiful valley and encamped near some hot springs which discharged their waters into Grasshopper (Willard's) Creek.

On July 8 the party went down Grasshopper Creek 11 miles and then took a course "S. 20° E" for several more miles until they came to Shoshoni Cove (V, 253). The men "scarcely gave themselves time to take off their saddles before they were off to the deposit" (V, 254) — after several months of deprivation they could chew and smoke tobacco again.

According to Clark, they found everything in the cache in good shape except for a little dampness. Into this deposit, it may be recalled, had gone not only tobacco but also expendable medicines and specimens of plants, seeds, and minerals that Lewis had collected between this place and Great Falls. That being the case, if the plant specimens did come through the winter undamaged, then we might expect to find a number of them among those in the Lewis and Clark Herbarium at Philadelphia. However, of all the pressed plants in that collection, only one, golden currant (*Ribes aureum*), was collected between Great Falls and Shoshoni Cove. Possibly others mildewed from too much moisture and had to be discarded.

The next morning Clark had the canoes raised, washed, repaired, and otherwise readied for an early departure the following day. They left as planned, with Sergeant Pryor and a few men taking the horses by land and the others manning the boats. Whereas it had taken the Corps almost three weeks the summer before to ascend the Jefferson

[2] Wheeler places this gap on Bald Mountain. See *The Trail of Lewis and Clark,* II, 321.

and Beaverhead from Three Forks to this point, Clark and his contingent made the return trip in that many days. On one day alone, they passed six of their previous campsites.

After a brief halt at Three Forks (on July 13), Sergeant Ordway and nine men (Collins, Colter, Cruzatte, Howard, Lepage, Potts, Whitehouse, Willard, and Wiser) took to the canoes and struck out for Great Falls. Six days later they arrived at their destination and joined Sergeant Gass and his five companions. In late afternoon Clark and the remaining members of the party (Pryor, Bratton, Gibson, Hall, Labiche, Shannon, Shields, Windsor, York, Charbonneau, Sacagawea, and the infant Pomp) "set out from the head of the Missouri at the 3 forks, and proceeded on nearly East 4 miles and encamped on the bank of Gallatines River which is a butifull navigable stream" (V, 259).

For a description of the exploration of the Yellowstone, we have available to us just one journal, that by Clark. Lewis had taken Gass with him, and Ordway was now descending the river. Pryor probably kept a journal since, as we know, he and the other sergeants had been ordered to do so; but if so, it has been lost.

Because of the numerous creeks feeding into the Gallatin, each dammed by beaver in one or more places, Clark had to pursue a winding, uncertain course as he made his way upriver. In time, Sacagawea directed him to a deeply worn buffalo road which, once reached, took the party to the gap today known as Bozeman Pass. According to one writer: "It was and is a low, easy, natural pass, and the Southern word *gap* used by Clark expresses its character precisely. . . . There are no rocks, the hills are rather low and the sides smooth, tufted, and at the higher parts lightly timbered . . . on the farther side . . . the waters run into the Yellowstone."[3]

Clark first hit the Upper Yellowstone near the site of present-day Livingston. At that point he was less than 50 miles from the geysers, waterfalls, and mud pots of Yellowstone National Park. Oddly enough, John Colter, who would shortly discover this wonderland, was at that moment with Sergeant Ordway in a cottonwood canoe riding Missouri waters to the White Bear Islands. Colter joined the ranks of other men who failed to receive recognition while alive for outstanding achievement. People simply did not believe his stories about geysers and hot springs and spoke derisively of "Colter's Hell"—a name for Yellowstone that has not completely disappeared from our vocabulary even today.

[3] Wheeler, *The Trail of Lewis and Clark,* II, 327.

Clark's journal for July 15 includes his first words about the Yellowstone River: "struck the Rochejhone ½ a mile below the branch we came down & 1½ Ms. below where it passes out of the Rocky Mountains. river 120 Yds. wide bold, rapid and deep" (V, 264). He went on to say that the bottoms contained cottonwood, willow, honeysuckle, and wild roses, but he could "See no timber sufficient[ly] large for a canoe which will carry more than 3 men and such a one would be too small to answer my purpose" (V, 265). Game abounded, with many beaver, buffalo, elk, deer, and antelope. One of the hunters soon shot a buffalo for a unique purpose, namely to obtain leather with which to make moccasins for their sore-footed horses. According to Clark, these improvised "horseshoes" seemed "to releve them very much in passing over the stoney plains" (V, 266).

Some of the men shortly sustained painful injuries. Charbonneau, while chasing a buffalo, was thrown from his horse when it stepped into a badger hole, stumbled, and catapulted him over its head. He escaped with multiple contusions of hip, shoulder, and face. Gibson fared worse. In attempting to mount his horse, he fell on a snag which penetrated his thigh two inches, causing such a deep, painful wound that he was unable to walk for several days. This incident occurred on a small tributary of the Yellowstone which at once received the name of Thigh Snagged Creek.

When Clark located some cottonwoods near this creek, he decided to halt for three days to build dugouts and to allow time for Gibson to recover from his injury. Since the trees were not as large as he would have liked, he determined to make two boats and lash them together. Each would be about 28 feet long, 16 to 18 inches deep and from 16 to 24 inches wide. When tied together, they made a sturdier craft and would be large enough to carry all members of the party and their baggage. Earlier Clark had considered making bullboats but abandoned the idea when he concluded that such vessels would be difficult to manage in the rapid, shallow waters of the Yellowstone.

The exact location of the boat-building site (Coues called it Camp Cottonwood) is in doubt. Wheeler was inclined to put it some six miles below the mouth of the Stillwater River and close to the present town of Columbus.[4] Wherever it was, Crow Indians discovered it. On the morning of the 21st, the party awoke to discover that 24 of their horses had disappeared during the night. There was little doubt that Indians had stolen them for the men had earlier seen smoke rising in the

[4] Wheeler, *The Trail of Lewis and Clark,* II, 342.

southeast, Charbonneau had reported a redskin on one of the cliffs above the river, and Sergeant Pryor, following the theft, found an Indian moccasion near the camp which had every appearance of recent use. While at Fort Mandan, Lewis and Clark had been informed that Crows (a Siouan tribe related to the Hidatsas) frequented territory adjacent to the Yellowstone.

On the morning of the 24th, after the two cottonwood canoes had been constructed and lashed together, Clark had them loaded and the party resumed their journey. Sergeant Pryor, with Shannon and Wiser, followed with the remaining horses. By now the explorers should have held the cottonwood in high esteem. Of all western trees it contributed more to the success of the Expedition than any other. Lewis and Clark were men of great talent and resourcefulness, masters of ingenuity and improvisation. Though we think it probable that they would have successfully crossed the continent without the cottonwood, don't ask us how!

Soon after leaving Camp Cottonwood, the party arrived at the mouth of a largish stream entering from the south which they called Clark's Fork—a name it still bears. Just below this tributary Clark put Sergeant Pryor, Shannon, Hall, Windsor, and the horses across the river to the south bank and instructed them to proceed overland without delay to the Mandan villages. On his arrival there, Pryor was to take a dozen or so horses and set out immediately for the Assiniboin establishments to find Hugh Heney and induce him if possible to lend his services in persuading Indian chiefs to travel with Lewis and Clark to Washington. If Heney agreed to the proposal, he was to be given three horses. The others were to be used for obtaining articles in short supply, such as pepper, salt, sugar, coffee, tea, tobacco, and "2 small Kegs of Sperits" (V, 287).

The Yellowstone below Clark's Fork deepened and ran more rapidly. The explorers made excellent time, as much as 80 miles in one day. On the afternoon of Friday, July 25, they arrived, Clark wrote, "at a remarkable rock situated in an extensive bottom of the Stard. Side of the river & 250 paces from it. this rock I ascended and from it's top had a most extensive view in every direction. This rock which I shall call Pompy's Tower is 200 feet high and 400 paces in secumpherance and only excessable on one Side which is from the N.E. the other parts of it being a perpendicular clift of lightish coloured gritty rock on the top there is a tolerable soil of about 5 or 6 feet thick covered with short grass" (V, 292–293).

"Pompy's Tower," now called Pompey's Pillar, is downriver 28 miles from present-day Billings, Montana. Writers have advanced various theories to explain the origin of the name. Wheeler, for example, thought that Clark had in mind the celebrated Egyptian pile at Alexandria.[5] But Clark most certainly named it after Sacagawea's infant son whom he called "my boy *Pomp*" (VII, 329) .

When I visited Pompey's Pillar during the summer of 1964, I found it privately owned and the immediate surroundings overgrown with a maze of briars and shrubbery, making it difficult to approach. The view from the top is as extensive and beautiful as ever, and the inscription, "Wm. Clark, July 25, 1806," is still legible. Since my visit, I am happy to say, Pompey's Pillar has been designated a National Historic Landmark. Dedication ceremonies were held on July 10, 1966.

Clark's inscription (perhaps the West's rarest autograph) is about half way up the trail on the eastern face of the rock and is protected by a bronze-framed shatterproof glass. This has replaced the old wrought-iron grille originally placed over the signature by the Northern Pacific Railroad.

William Clark apparently was not the discoverer of Pompey's Pillar. Ten months earlier, on September 15, 1805, Francois Antoine Larocque (on his trip west from the Mandan community previously alluded to) descended a southern tributary of the Yellowstone to its mouth, and discovered nearby "a whitish perpendicular rock on which was sketched with red soil a battle between three people on horseback and three others on foot."[6] His account makes it reasonably certain that this "perpendicular rock" was Pompey's Pillar.

The farther the party descended the Yellowstone the more abundant game became. "For me to mention or give an estimate of the different Species of wild animals on this river particularly Buffalow, Elk Antelopes & Wolves would be increditable," Clark declared. "I shall therefore be silent on the subject further" (V, 290) . Happily, he did not remain entirely silent. In places the buffalo (because it was now "running time" with them) kept up such a loud bellowing near their camps that the men, in order to sleep at all, had to drive them away with gunfire. On occasion great herds swam the river at night so close to their camps that Clark feared they would trample their boats to bits. One day the party quickly beached their twin dugout when, on round-

<hr>

[5] Wheeler, *The Trail of Lewis and Clark,* II, 352.
[6] Hazlitt, "The Journal of Francois Antoine Larocque from the Assiniboine River to the Yellowstone—1805," 22.

ing a bend, they found themselves bearing down on a tremendous herd crossing the river immediately ahead of them. Such was its size that they had to lay to for an hour before it passed. Hungry wolves crept into their camps while the men slept. One night "a wolf bit Sergt. Pryor through his hand when asleep, and this animal was so vicious as to make an attempt to seize Windsor, when Shannon fortunately Shot him" (V, 326).

In the absence of Lewis, Clark may have felt that he should assume a more active role as naturalist. Soon after coming to the Yellowstone, he described a species of fish unfamiliar to him as follows: "it was 8 inches long formed like a trout. it's mouth was placed like that of the sturgeon   a red streak passed down each side from the gills to the tail" (V, 266).[7] Just above Camp Cottonwood he wrote: "It may be proper to observe that the emence Sworms of *Grass hoppers* have distroyed every sprig of Grass for maney miles on this side of the river, and appear to be progressing upwards" (V, 276). On July 25 he reported seeing a herd of 40 bighorn and a few days later announced that he had been successful in obtaining heads, skins, and bones of a bighorn ram, a female, and a yearling ram. Elsewhere he reported great numbers of geese, passenger pigeons, doves, hawks, ravens, crows, larks, sparrows, eagles, and cliff swallows. His botanical notes, though fewer than zoological, make it clear that the hills on each side of the Yellowsone were spottily covered with evergreens, that bluffs and benchlands supported a heavy growth of prickly pear, and that the bottom vegetation was limited largely to such trees as cottonwood, willow, ash, and elm and to such shrubs as currants, roses, choke cherry (from which they obtained axe handles), sumac, and buffalo-berry. In one place he interposed an ethnobotanical note when writing of "Sweet grass [probably *Hierochloe odorata*] which the Indian plat and ware around their necks for its cent which is of a strong sent like that of the Vinella" (V, 289).

On July 26 Clark arrived at the entrance of the Big Horn River. He recognized it at once, even though the advance information he had obtained from the Indians at Fort Mandan had been sketchy. (Just one year later Manuel Lisa would build a fort here.) Clark walked up the Big Horn seven miles to the mouth of a small feeder he called Muddy Creek. If he had gone a few miles farther, he would have come to the entrance of the Little Big Horn, in the valley of which 70 years later

[7] This fish may have been the mountain sucker, *Pantosteus platyrhynchus*. Coues (III, 1138) identified it as *P. jordani*.

Chiefs Sitting Bull, Crazy Horse, Dull Knife, White Bull, and their band cut down Custer and his men of the 7th U.S. Cavalry.

In descending the Yellowstone, Clark named numerous streams, nine of them (in addition to Clark's Fork) after members of the Expedition:

July 16—Shield's River . . . . name persists.
July 18—Bratton's Creek . . . . Bridger Creek of today.
July 24—Pryor's River . . . . name persists, but as Pryor's Creek.
July 25—Shannon's River . . . . apparently Sand Creek now.
July 25—Baptiste's Creek . . . . now Pompey's Pillar Creek.
July 26—Hall's River . . . . unidentifiable today.
July 27—Labiche's River . . . . today's Sarpy River.
July 30—York's Dry River . . . . unidentifiable.
August 2—Joseph Field's Creek . . . now Charbonneau Creek.

On August 3, after 19 days on the Yellowstone, Clark and his party arrived at the Missouri. I find it difficult to agree with one writer who said that on this reconnaissance from Traveller's Rest by way of Shoshoni Cove, Three Forks and the Yellowstone to the Missouri, nothing much happened.[8] Clark was the first white man to cross Gibbon's Pass and to give an account of the country between that point and Shoshoni Cove. He was the first white man to ascend the Gallatin River and surmount Bozeman Pass. He was the first to explore the upper part of the Yellowstone, from near present-day Livingston to Pompey's Pillar. He was the first (in spite of Larocque's earlier visit) to bring the Yellowstone as an important river to the attention of the civilized world. He was the first to discover and name many important tributaries of the Yellowstone. He was the first to announce the great abundance of wild game animals, particularly beaver, native to the valley of this river.

Clark spent just one night at the mouth of the Yellowstone; he had the best of reasons for pushing on down the Missouri. Multitudinous mosquitoes made life almost unendurable, particularly to those men "who have no bears [biers] to keep them off at night, and nothing to Screen them but their blankets which are worn and have maney holes" (V, 322). At their next campsite conditions were no better, and the men experienced another sleepless night. Clark wrote that while hunting, he could not keep the mosquitoes off his rifle barrel long enough to take sight on a bighorn and thereby missed (V, 323). Consequently the

[8] DeVoto, *The Journals of Lewis and Clark*, 448.

party moved farther downstream, attempting to find an insect-free location where they could await Lewis's arrival.

Early on the morning of August 8, Clark and his men quickly came to life when two bullboats unexpectedly arrived from upstream carrying Sergeant Pryor, Shannon, Hall, and Windsor. These men had quite a story to tell. Two days after separating from Clark, they awoke to find that during the night Crow Indians had paid another visit and had stolen their horses, leaving not a single one. (Which men had stood guard, if any, the journals do not say.) Though they attempted to catch up with the Indians, tracking them for five miles, they soon concluded their efforts were bootless and headed back to the river, hitting it at Pompey's Pillar. Here they killed two buffalo and demonstrated their craftsmanship by making two bullboats, each 7 feet 3 inches in diameter and 16 inches deep. One would have been adequate, but if it capsized they might lose all their weapons. These vessels performed perfectly, passing through the worst rapids without taking a drop of water and being unaffected by the strongest winds. Pryor and his three companions rode in them for 12 days before catching up with Clark.

The theft of the horses meant that Clark had lost most of his bargaining power; he had little left with which to trade for much-needed staples. In this predicament, he foresaw only one solution and that was "to procure as many skins as possible" (V, 327). He recalled that the Mandans had shown a marked interest in obtaining hides of buffalo and other large quadrupeds.

As the party moved still farther downstream, they were surprised to meet two white men from Illinois, Joseph Dickson and Forest Hancock. From them they obtained the first news from home in more than two years. They learned, too, that the Mandans and Hidatsas were at war with the Arikaras again. Dickson and Hancock had been on a hunting and trapping trip upriver, and returned with Clark to the Mandan villages.

It was at noon on the following day (August 12) that Lewis and his men caught up with Clark. "I was alarmed on the landing of the Canoes to be informed that Capt. Lewis was wounded by an accident," Clark commented. "I found him lying in the Perogue, he informed me that his wound was slight and would be well in 20 or 30 days this information relieved me very much" (V, 330).

If mosquitoes had not annoyed Clark at the mouth of the Yellowstone, causing him to move downstream, he and Lewis would have been united five days earlier on August 7, the date Lewis and his men reached that confluence. The two leaders had been separated a total of 40 days, with the Expedition at one time or another split into five different groups. That these contingents reunited here on the Missouri without appreciable delay and without loss of life—or even serious injury—may be regarded as one of the extraordinary happenings of the entire trip. When the Crows took the horses from Sergeant Pryor and his three companions, they might easily have taken four scalps as well. And it cannot be forgotten that the Blackfoot bullet that missed Lewis came close enough to stir the hair on his head.

The timing almost exceeded credibility. Ordway reached Great Falls just three days after Lewis had left for the Marias and in time to assist Gass with the portaging. When Lewis, fleeing from the Piegans, reached the Missouri, he found coming downriver, Ordway, Gass, and their men. Finally, Lewis arrived at the Yellowstone only four days after Clark had left, and he caught up with him just five days later— even though he had a bullet hole in his thigh.

The exact site of the Lewis-Clark reunion has not been definitely established, though it seems to have been near the mouth of Char- bonneau Creek (perhaps modern Indian Creek), in Mountrail County, North Dakota, some 30 miles upstream from the entrance of the Little Missouri.

SUMMARY OF DISCOVERIES

Animals New to Science

? SOFT-SHELLED TURTLE. *Amyda spinifera spinifera* (Le Sueur). (Thwaites, V, 307; Coues, III, 1159). Described, 1827.

? MOUNTAIN SUCKER. *Pantosteus platyrhynchus* (Cope). (Thwaites, V, 266; Coues, III, 1138). 1894.

Plants New to Science
None.

Lewis and Clark Herbarium
None.

Indian Tribes Encountered
Siouan Linguistic Family: Crow.

Topographic Features Named and/or Discovered
† "West Fork" [of Bitterroot] (Thwaites, V, 247) —— Nez Perce River.

† Flour Creek (Thwaites, V, 248) —— Flower Creek of Biddle (Coues, III, 1121).

† "Dividing Mountain" (Thwaites, V, 249) —— Gibbon's Pass.

† Glade Creek (Thwaites, V, 249) —— possibly Trail Creek (Thwaites, V, 249n).

† "Large Creek from the right" (Thwaites, V, 250) —— Pioneer Creek (Thwaites, V, 250n).

† Willard's Creek (Thwaites, V, 253) —— Grasshopper Creek (Coues, III, 1126).

† "low dividing ridge" (Thwaites, V, 262) —— Bozeman Pass.

† Shields River (Thwaites, V, 264) —— Shields River.

† Stinking Cabin Creek (Thwaites, V, 268).

† Rivers Across Creeks (Thwaites, V, 269) —— Big Timber River (from north) and Boulder River (from south) (Coues, III, 1138–39n).

† Otter River (Thwaites, V, 269) —— Sweetgrass Creek (Coues, III, 1139n).

† Beaver River (Thwaites, V, 269) —— Lower Deer or Big Deer Creek (Coues, III, 1139n).

† "Thy Snag'd Creek" (Thwaites, V, 271) —— Upper Deer Creek (Thwaites, V, 271n).

† Bratton's Creek (Thwaites, V, 272) —— Bridger's Creek (Coues, II, 1139n).

† Clark's Fork (Thwaites, V, 288) —— Clark's Fork.

† "Small creek" (Thwaites, V, 289) —— Cañon Creek (Thwaites, V, 289n).

† Pryor's River (Thwaites, V, 290) —— Pryor's Creek of today.

† Horse Creek (Thwaites, V, 291).

Author's note: If Larocque struck the Yellowstone in 1805 at or near Pompey's Pillar, then the following features named by Clark were presumably discovered by Larocque.

"Pompy's Tower" (Thwaites, V, 292) —— Pompey's Pillar.

Shannon's River (Thwaites, V, 294) —— apparently modern Sand Creek (Coues, III, 1151n).

"Baptiests Creek" (Thwaites, V, 295) —— Pompey's Pillar Creek (Thwaites, V, 295n).

Hall's River (Thwaites, V, 298).

Elk Creek (Thwaites, V, 302) —— Alkali Creek (Coues, III, 1156n).

"R. Labeech" [Labiche] (Thwaites, V, 302) —— Sarpy River (Thwaites, V, 302n).

Windsor's River (Thwaites, V, 303) —— Van Horn's or Pease's River or Creek (Coues, III, 1156n).

White Creek (Thwaites, V, 304).

Little Wolf River (Thwaites, V, 304) —— Great Porcupine River
(Thwaites, V, 304n).

Table Creek (Thwaites, V, 304) —— Little Porcupine River (Coues, III,
1158n).

York's Dry River (Thwaites, V, 310).

Red Stone River (Thwaites, V, 310) —— Powder River.

Coal River (Thwaites, V, 312) —— O'Fallon Creek (Thwaites, V, 312n).

Ibex River (Thwaites, V, 316) —— Smith's Creek (Coues, III, 1166n).

"Jo: Fields Creek" (Thwaites, V, 316) —— Charbonneau Creek (Thwaites,
V, 316n).

Last Miles

CHAPTER TWENTY-ONE

With the aid of practiced muscle and accelerated paddle, the Corps of Discovery now moved rapidly downstream. They soon swept by the entrance of the Little Missouri and on August 14 found themselves once again among the friendly Mandans, Hidatsas, and Wattasoons. "We saluted them by firing our Swivvels and blunderbusses a number of times," wrote Sergeant Ordway, "and they answered us with a blunderbuss and Small arms and were verry glad to see us."[1]

The party made their camp about three to four miles above Fort Mandan, on the west side of the river opposite Black Cat's village (Upper Mandan). Clark said that he visited Black Cat, smoked a pipe, and ate some "simnins" (squashes) with him. Evidencing customary aboriginal instability, the occupants of this village had recently quarrelled and a number of them had moved across the river.

With Lewis physically incapacitated, Clark of necessity assumed additional responsibilities. An initial act was to provide the men with foods that had long been missing from their meals. "Some of these Indians," Gass said, "were very kind and obliging; furnishing us with corn, beans and squashes."[2] Clark's most important duty here, however (as he and Lewis saw it), was to persuade one or more of the local chiefs to make the trip to Washington. He called them together and using all the eloquence at his command, exhorted them to visit their Great White Father that they might listen to his counsel, receive his gifts, and hasten the delivery of "those Supplies of Marchindize which would be Sent to their Country and exchanged as before mentioned for a moderate price in Pelteries and furs &c." (V, 339–340).

The chiefs—Big White, Black Cat, White Buffalo Robe, One Eye (Le Borgne), and others—listened attentively to Clark's plea. When

[1] Ordway, 389.
[2] Gass, 304.

he had finished, they replied that such a visit would give them much pleasure, but common sense dictated otherwise. As surely as they entered the domain of perennial enemies, the Teton Sioux in particular, they would fall victim to their ruthlessness. Clark's repeated assurances of full protection seemed fruitless. Soon afterwards, however, René Jusseaume told him that Big White would make the trip if (1) he were permitted to take his wife and son with him and (2) if Jusseaume, wife, and two children were allowed to accompany him. This, stated Clark, "we were obliged to agree to do" (V, 343).

Before the Corps quit this Knife River community, John Colter requested permission to join Dickson and Hancock, who planned to leave at once for the Montana beaver country, "deturmined," as Sergeant Ordway put it, "to stay until they made a fortune."[3] Lewis and Clark granted Colter's request and provided him with ball, powder, and other supplies adequate for two years. Colter, as we know, would shortly stumble into history by discovering the natural wonders of today's Yellowstone National Park. He would be the first white man, too, to gaze upon the beauty of the Teton Mountains and of Jackson's Hole.

The Charbonneau family did not accompany the Expedition to St. Louis. Clark had a tender spot in his heart for the infant Pomp. "I offered," he said, "to take his [Charbonneau's] little son a butifull promising child who is 19 months old to which they both himself & wife wer willing provided the child had been weaned. they observed that in one year the boy would be sufficiently old to leave his mother & he would then take him to me if I would be so friendly as to raise the child for him in such a manner as I thought proper" (V, 344–345).

In time Sacagawea and Charbonneau brought their child to St. Louis, where Clark lived up to his word by taking him into his home and sending him to school. Young Pomp thus became one of the first Indians west of the Mississippi to experience the white man's education. In later years, he travelled widely as the companion of Prince Paul Wilhelm, Duke of Württemberg, who met Pomp while on a trip up the Missouri in 1824 and took him to Germany that same year. Back on American soil, some five years later, Pomp became a guide and interpreter to many white travellers in the West, including Clark's son, Jefferson Clark.[4]

[3] Ordway, 390.
[4] Russell Reid, "Sakakawea, the Bird Woman," *State Hist. Soc. North Dakota* (1950), 13–14. See also Jackson, *Letters*, 640n.

On August 17 Clark smoked a final pipe with the Indians and received assurances that they would keep the peace. Big White and Jusseaume and families took their places in the boats. Many of the Mandans, convinced they were seeing the last of Big White, cried aloud. Clark ordered a final salute, after which paddles cut the water in unison.

Three miles downstream, the party halted briefly while Clark went ashore to have a look at Fort Mandan. Since his departure in April of the previous year, all of the original huts had been burned to the ground except one. A few pickets next to the river still stood in place. When Maximilian stopped here 27 years later, he could not even find the site; the unceasing, corrosive force of the Missouri water had carried it away altogether.

Four days later the party arrived among the Arikaras. They halted just long enough to urge them to keep the peace and to invite their chiefs to visit the nation's capital. These Indians, too, expressed fear of the Teton Sioux and replied that they would await the return of their chief who had gone to Washington with Joseph Gravelines the year before. Unfortunately, they would not see him again; he died while on the journey. This death led to all sorts of trouble subsequently between Arikaras and whites.

On August 22 Clark reported: "my worthy friend Capt. Lewis is recovering fast, he walked a little today for the first time. I have discontinued the tent in the hole the ball came out" (V, 358). On the following day he said, "this hole in his thy where the ball passed out is closed and appears to be nearly well. the one where the ball entered discharges very well" (V, 358). (On August 18 Lewis had attained his 32nd birthday; Clark had celebrated his 36th on August 1.)

Four days later the Corps passed a well-remembered site, the mouth of the Bad (Teton) River, where two years earlier the Tetons had attempted to bar their progress upstream. On this occasion, there was not an Indian anywhere to be seen. The next day they rounded the Big Bend and just beyond killed a fat buck elk. This was a timely acquisition since they had exhausted their meat supply. Lewis tried out his legs again and "hurt himself very much by takeing a longer walk . . . than he had strength to undergo, which caused him to remain very unwell all night" (V, 362).

Near present-day Chamberlain, the party halted to obtain specimens of such animals as the magpie, prairie dog, pronghorn, and mule deer. They knew this would be just about their last opportunity, for they were fast approaching the Pine Ridge Escarpment, eastern limit of the High Plains. The best the hunters could do was to shoot two prairie dogs. A day or so later Joseph Field succeeded in killing three mule deer.

On August 30, above the Niobrara, some 80 to 90 Indians appeared on the north bank of the Missouri. Clark met with three of them on a sandbar in midstream to determine tribal affiliation.

They informed me that they were Tetons and their chief was *Tar-tack-kah-sab-bar* or the black buffalow this chief I knew very well to be the one we had seen with his band at Teton river which band had attempted to detain us in the fall of 1804. . . . I told those Indians that they had been deef to our councils and ill treated us as we assended this river two years past, that they had abused all the whites who had visited them since. I believed them to be bad people & should not suffer them to cross to the Side on which the party lay, and directed them to return with their band to their camp. that if any of them came near our camp we Should kill them certainly (V, 366).

That evening, to protect themselves from possible attack, they encamped on a sandbar in the middle of the river. A severe thunder storm struck them during the night, and the accompanying high winds broke cables on two of the boats and drove two others, with Wiser and Willard aboard, to the north shore. It was not until the storm had subsided—some three hours after it began—that they were able to retrieve the canoes and resume their sleep.

On September 1 the Expedition passed the Niobrara and on the 3rd met two boats carrying a party of white men commanded by James Aird, a Scotch trader licensed to trade with the Sioux. From these men they learned that Alexander Hamilton had been killed in a duel with Aaron Burr. They obtained, too, some flour and four carrots of tobacco. That evening Clark wrote, "I am very happy to find that my friend Capt. L's is so well as to walk about with ease" (V, 375).

At noon of the next day, they stopped at Floyd's Bluff. Here they found that Sergeant Floyd's grave had been opened by Indians and left half covered. After refilling it, they went on. Just 10 days had been consumed in travelling from the Mandans to this point; in going upstream two years before it had taken them 167 days to travel the same distance.

Two days later the explorers met traders in the employ of Auguste Chouteau. "We purchased a gallon of whiskey," Clark reported, "and gave to each man of the party a dram which is the first spiritious licquor which had been tasted by any of them since the 4 of July 1805 [at Great Falls]. several of the party exchanged leather for linen Shirts and beaver for corse hats. . . . We advised this trader to treat the Tetons with as much contempt as possible" (V, 378).

Hereabouts Clark commented: "the *evaporation* on this portion of the Missouri had been noticed as we assended this river, and it now appears to be greater than it was at that time. I am obliged to replenish my ink Stand every day with fresh ink at least 9/10 of which must evaporate" (V, 379). This ink carried by Lewis and Clark interests us, and we would like to know more about it. That it was of superior quality is evident, for the calligraphy of the original journals is almost as clear and fresh as though inscribed yesterday. All we know about it to date is that Lewis, while in Philadelphia, obtained from the Public Store "6 papers of Ink Powder" (VII, 240).

On September 8 the Corps, having "ply'd their orers very well," swept by Council Bluffs and soon afterward arrived at White Catfish Camp, 78 miles below their camp of the preceding day. The next morning they passed the mouth of the Platte without stopping, being "extreamly anxious to get on, and every day appears [to] produce new anxieties in them to get to their country and friends. My worthy friend Cap Lewis has entirely recovered his wounds are heeled up and he can walk and even run nearly as well as ever he could" (V, 380).

There would be no more wounds to bandage, no more ailments to treat. In assessing the competence of Lewis and Clark as medical practitioners, it is reasonable to say that if either had subsequently studied medicine, he would have distinguished himself. Lewis, from what we know of him, would have come nearer being the astute, discerning diagnostician. Clark certainly would have had much the better bedside manner. The one incontrovertible fact about the medical practice of these two men is that in 28 months, and travelling some 8,000 miles in a land of parched sands, rampaging rivers, and unpredictable savages, they had lost but one man, and the best medical brain of the day, even the eminent Dr. Rush, could probably not have saved him. Thomas Jefferson, we are convinced, made no mistake in entrusting the health and welfare of the party to these two resourceful, clearheaded scions of our American frontier. In fact, considering the low state of medicine in the world at that time, who can conscientiously insist that the Expedition would have fared better in the hands of a qualified doctor than in those of Meriwether Lewis and William Clark?

On September 10 Clark recorded that they met four Frenchmen in a small pirogue on their way to trade with the Pawnee Loups. These traders informed Lewis and Clark that Lt. Zebulon M. Pike and Lt. J. B. Wilkinson (son of Gen. James Wilkinson) had set out on an expedition up the Arkansas River (V, 381). This operation, commanded by Pike, was the second government-sponsored expedition to the West. Before long the world would have word of Pike's Peak.

Two days later the Corps met a party which included old friends, namely, Joseph Gravelines, Pierre Dorion, and Capt. Robert McClellan, the last-named having served with Lewis and Clark under General Wayne. These men had been sent by the President to notify the Arikaras that their chief who had journeyed to Washington with Gravelines had died while in that city. They had been instructed, too, Clark wrote, "to make every enquirey after Capt. Lewis my self and the party" (V, 383). By this time, Jefferson, as well as many other friends and relatives of Lewis and Clark, had begun to despair of ever seeing them again. The last word received had come from Fort Mandan in April of the previous year, some 18 months earlier.

Before leaving the High Plains, Lewis and Clark, as mentioned, had made final additions to their stockpile of zoological specimens. It should come as no surprise therefore to learn that Lewis, on this last leg of the journey, collected and preserved still more plants. How many we will never know, though at least three have survived to become a part of the Lewis and Clark Herbarium in Philadelphia. On August 27, for instance, while rounding the Great Bend below Pierre, South Dakota, he collected a specimen of false indigo (*Amorpha fruticosa*); on August 29, at or near the mouth of the White River, he collected pink cleome (*Cleome serrulata*); and on September 14, while in the vicinity of present-day Leavenworth, Kansas, he collected a specimen of simple-leaved ampelopsis (*Cissus ampelopsis*), a member of the grape family. This ampelopsis, so far as we know, was the last plant collected by Lewis on the journey to the Pacific and back.

Continuing to move rapidly downstream, the party arrived on September 15 at the mouth of the Kansas where the two captains stopped long enough to "let the men geather Pappaws or the custard apple [i.e., the oblong yellowish fruit of the papaw, *Asimina triloba*] of which this country abounds, and the men are very fond of" (V, 385). Two days later, above Grand River, they met another old friend, Capt. John McClallan, who informed them that they "had been long Since given out [up] by the people of the U.S. Generaly and almost forgotton, the President of the U. States had yet hopes of us" (V, 385).

Descending the river now "with great velocity," the Expedition passed the Osage River on September 19 and the Gasconade on the 20th, below which they saw some cows. This was a welcome sight and "caused a Shout to be raised for joy" (V, 389). Later the same day they arrived at the tiny frontier village of La Charette where the inhabitants "acknowledged themselves much astonished in seeing us . . . we were supposed to have been lost long since" (V, 390).

On September 21 Clark wrote: "at 4 P.M. we arrived in Sight of St. Charles. the party rejoiced at the Sight of this hospita[b]l[e] village . . . this day being Sunday we observed a number of Gentlemen and ladies walking on the bank. we saluted the village by three rounds from our blunderbuts and the Small arms of the party, and landed near the lower part of the town. we were met by great numbers of the inhabitants. we found them excessively polite . . . and seem to vie with each other in their politeness to us all" (V, 391–392).

Two years and four months had elapsed since Lewis and Clark, on May 21, 1804, had started upstream from St. Charles. Two days later they arrived in St. Louis. Here Clark wrote again: "we Suffered the party to fire off their pieces as a Salute to the Town. We were met by all the village and received a harty welcom from its inhabitants &c. here I found an old acquaintance Majr. W. Christy [a former Louisville neighbor] who had settled in this town in a public line as a Tavern Keeper. he furnished us with store rooms for our baggage and we accepted of the invitation of Mr. Peter Chouteau and took a room in his house" (V, 394).

Sergeants Ordway and Gass concluded their journals on the 23rd. Clark continued his for three more days, reporting that he and Lewis wrote several letters, purchased some clothes, attended dinners and a ball, and sunned skins and other articles before placing them in a storeroom. Lewis, on opening his trunk, found that all of his papers were wet and some seeds spoiled. Clark's final entry (for September 26) said only: "a fine morning we commenced wrighting &c" (V, 395).

[2]

More than 160 years have elapsed since the Corps of Discovery completed its monumental feat of crossing the continent and returning to St. Louis. What happened afterwards to each of the 32 adult individuals who constituted the party making this incredibly successful transit? Four sources provide most of the information available to us: (1)

Clark's Cash Book for 1825–28, on the front cover of which he listed members of the Expedition and appended such terse comment as "dead" or "in St. Louis"; (2) Elliott Coues' *History of the Expedition Under the Command of Lewis and Clark* (I, 253–257) ; (3) Olin D. Wheeler's *The Trail of Lewis and Clark* (I, 54–135) ; and Donald Jackson's *Letters of the Lewis and Clark Expedition with Related Documents 1783–1854* (370–372 *passim*) .

A careful reading of the material in these primary sources reveals some unexpected and extraordinary facts. Sixteen of the 32 were dead by no later than 1828. The 16 were: Privates John Collins, John Colter, Peter Cruzatte, Joseph Field, George Gibson, Silas Goodrich, Baptiste Lepage, Hugh McNeal, John Potts, John Shields, John Thompson, Peter Wiser, Interpreter George Drouillard, Sergeant John Ordway, Sacagawea, and Captain Meriwether Lewis. Of these 16 who died prematurely, there is no certain knowledge of the manner of death except in the cases of Drouillard and Potts, who were killed by Blackfeet Indians, and Colter, who purportedly died of jaundice. Arguments persist about Sacagawea's death, some historians claiming that she died of old age late in the nineteenth century. However, Clark stated (Cash Book for 1825–28) , "Se car ja we au Dead," and this assertion is supported by the trader, John Luttig, who reported on December 20, 1812: "this evening the wife of Charbonneau a Snake Squaw, died of a putrid fever . . . aged abt 25 years."[5] As is well known, circumstances surrounding the death of Lewis are still controversial. Such students of the Expedition as Elliott Coues, Olin D. Wheeler, John Bakeless, and Richard Dillon are on record as believing that he was murdered, while others like Ernest Staples Osgood, Donald Jackson, and Dawson Phelps[6] are inclined to think he died by his own hand. As to the 16 who lived beyond 1828, the majority of them, such as Privates Hall, Howard, Labiche, Werner, and Windsor, the journalists Whitehouse and Frazer, and one of "the most active and enterprising young men," Joseph Field, vanished like so many plunging stars. Finally, and incredibly, information is so wanting on the post-expeditionary lives of this gallant band of explorers that marked grave sites are known for only five: Lewis, Clark, Gass, Bratton, and Willard. Time and history forgot all too quickly many of the heroes constituting the Corps of Discovery.

[5] John C. Luttig, *Journal of a Fur-trading Expedition on the Upper Missouri 1812–1813,* ed. Stella M. Drumm (New York, 1964) , 106.

[6] Dawson A. Phelps, "The Tragic Death of Meriwether Lewis," *William and Mary Quarterly,* 3rd ser., XIII, no. 3, 1956.

SUMMARY OF DISCOVERIES

Animals New to Science

None.

Plants New to Science

PINK CLEOME. *Cleome serrulata* Pursh. Described, 1814.

Lewis and Clark Herbarium

FALSE INDIGO. *Amorpha fruticosa* L. Collected August 27, 1806.
SIMPLE-LEAVED AMPELOPSIS. *Cissus ampelopsis* Pers. September 14.
PINK CLEOME. *Cleome serrulata* Pursh. August 29. (As previously reported,
    Lewis discovered this species and collected a specimen on August 25,
    1804, two years earlier.)

Indian Tribes Encountered

No new tribes.

Topographic Features Named and/or Discovered

None.

The Fate
of the
Lewis and Clark Booty

CHAPTER TWENTY-TWO

Historians have tended to conclude their accounts of the Lewis and Clark Expedition with its arrival in St. Louis or, if they went further, with the subsequent lives of the two leaders. They have not been equally diligent in describing the fate of the numerous plant and animal specimens, Indian artifacts, and other objects collected by the explorers and brought back with them. As a consequence, present-day students of Lewis and Clark are often frustrated by incomplete, and sometimes faulty, answers to such questions as: What specimens collected on the Missouri and Columbia watersheds actually succeeded in reaching the Atlantic seaboard? Which botanical and zoological specimens were new to science? What impact did they have on American naturalists of that day? Which naturalists participated most actively in studying and technically describing the new species? Where did the specimens find temporary or permanent homes? What effect did their arrival have on the development of American museums and on further exploration of the West? What celebrated artists took notice of them? What specimens have survived to this day?

No person, now or in the future, can be expected to provide full and unqualified answers to all of the above questions. The men who could help most have long since died. However, it is possible to extend and clarify existing knowledge by supplying newly discovered facts and by bringing together in one place a mass of data, heretofore only partially assimilated, gleaned from numerous, often ancient, periodicals, monographs, diaries, broadsides, technical books, newspaper files, and manuscript letters.

The Lewis and Clark specimens constitute three groups: (1) minerals, plant cuttings, and a horned toad shipped to Jefferson from St. Louis in the spring of 1804; (2) objects assembled in the ascent of the Missouri to Fort Mandan and during the ensuing winter at the fort; (3) material collected on the journey from Fort Mandan to the Pacific, during residence at Fort Clatsop, and on the long return trip to St. Louis.

In the pages to follow, we propose to discuss the fate of the Lewis and Clark specimens under three headings: ethnological, botanical and zoological—and in that sequence. (We exclude consideration of minerals for the reason that, although several did reach Jefferson, and later Philadelphia, nothing definite is known of their whereabouts—if any are actually extant.) [1]

Ethnology

As an invoice attests, Lewis and Clark, on April 7, 1805, forwarded to Jefferson from Fort Mandan a Mandan bow and quiver of arrows, a Mandan cooking pot, and seven buffalo robes. One of the robes had been "painted by a Mandan man representing a battle fought 8 years since, by the Sioux & Ricaras, against the Mandans, Minitarras & Ahwahharways" (VII, 322–323) . The following year Lewis and Clark brought back additional objects, most of which had been collected west of the Rockies.

The majority of these objects soon found a home in Peale's Museum. Jefferson retained a few of them. Writing to Peale on September 6, 1805, after he had received the Fort Mandan consignment, Jefferson said: "There are some articles which I shall keep for an Indian Hall I am forming at Monticello, e.g. horns, dressed skins, utensils &c." [2] One year later, when he heard from Lewis that the latter had arrived safely in St. Louis and that the Mandan chief, Big White, accompanied him, the President replied: "Tell my friend of Mandane . . . that I have already opened my arms to receive him. Perhaps while in our neighbor-

---

[1] The possibility exists that some of these minerals may be rediscovered. Recently Dr. Venia Phillips, formerly Head Librarian, Academy of Natural Sciences of Philadelphia, called my attention to Dr. Adam Seybert's "Record Book of Minerals." Herein Dr. Seybert (1773–1825) , one of the earliest mineralogists associated with the Academy, listed some two dozen mineral specimens as "brot back by Captn. Lewis." Presumably these were on loan to the Academy (or to Dr. Seybert personally) from the American Philosophical Society. They may still be at the Academy, but to date my efforts to locate them there have failed.

[2] Jackson, *Letters*, 260.

hood it may be gratifying to him, & not otherwise to yourself to take a ride to Monticello and see in what manner I have arranged the tokens of friendship I have received from his country particularly as well as from other Indian friends: that I am in fact preparing a kind of Indian Hall."[3] According to one historian, Jefferson's Indian Hall was situated in the entrance hall at Monticello and was "filled with Indian relics, bones, rocks and minerals. It was to become a show place for visitors in his retirement."[4] Though some of these Indian relics originated with Lewis and Clark, they have unfortunately disappeared; not one of them is to be found at Monticello today.

Because Charles Willson Peale exhibited many of the ethnological (and zoological) specimens returned by Lewis and Clark, it is important to become better acquainted with the man and his museum. Peale has been described as "a slender man of medium build with a long, thin nose, large blue eyes and long, brown, unpowdered hair."[5] Born in Chestertown, Maryland, he studied art under John S. Copley, Boston, and Benjamin West, London. After his return to the United States from England, he quickly established a reputation as a portrait painter, one of his earliest paintings depicting George Washington in the uniform of a Virginia colonel. In 1784, after he had been commissioned to make drawings of some mastodon bones, he observed that the presence of the bones in his Philadelphia studio attracted visitors and much comment. With times hard and prices high, he determined to make a try at augmenting his income by displaying these and other natural history objects and charging a fee to see them. That was the beginning of Peale's Museum—in his own home at Third and Lombard Streets. Once friends learned of his budding project, they sent him curiosities to add to his collection. Benjamin Franklin, for instance, presented him with a dead French Angora cat, Robert Patterson contributed a paddle fish, and George Washington a brace of golden pheasants. Of necessity, he declined certain gifts—such as Washington's offer of a horse.[6]

Peale continued to exhibit in his own home until 1794 when the American Philosophical Society leased to him all but two rooms of its newly completed Philosophical Hall. A few years later, as his museum

---

[3] Jackson, *Letters*, 351.

[4] Betts, *Jefferson's Garden Book*, 331.

[5] Charles Coleman Sellers, *Charles Willson Peale*, 2 vols. (Philadelphia, 1947), I, 1.

[6] Sellers, *Charles Willson Peale*, II, 244.

expanded rapidly, he moved it, as we know, to Independence Hall. Here he occupied most of the space in that building rent free, due to the generosity of the Pennsylvania state legislature. As an adjunct to his museum, Peale maintained a menagerie of sorts in the yard behind Independence Hall. Here from time to time he kept such live animals as monkeys, parrots, eagles, and, briefly, two grizzly bears. When one of the bears broke out of its cage one night, terrifying Peale's family, he had to shoot it and its mate. These bears had been brought from the West by Lt. Pike, not by Lewis and Clark as some writers have stated.

Peale's Museum was no jumble of wonders, no hodgepodge of weird natural history specimens, such as that found in those days in other museums. On the contrary, it was "an orderly exposition of natural history, based on the Linnaean classification . . . [and] the first modern museum in that it sought not only to aid the scholar but to teach the populace."[7] And Peale was no ordinary museum proprietor. In a day when taxidermy was virtually unknown in Philadelphia, he taught himself that art (beginning with Franklin's Angora) and so far succeeded that when some of his mounted birds fell into the hands of a scientist a century later, the latter affirmed: "It is quite easy to recognize C. W. Peale's birds by their fine condition. He was a good taxidermist."[8] It was Peale, too, who originated habitat arrangement, that is, placing mounted specimens in front of backgrounds painted to create the illusion of an actual, natural environment. A full century would elapse before other museums revived this practice. "Peale has not been conceded a permanent place among the early American naturalists," one writer has commented, "although his contribution toward the awakening of popular interest in the subject, especially ornithology, has doubtless exceeded that of all his American predecessors."[9]

Peale's Museum was scientifically important for other reasons. It contained the prize haul of the Lewis and Clark Expedition, and this in itself provided increased prestige and a stimulus to Peale to improve the quality of his exhibits. Records show, too, that Peale and his sons maintained friendly and continued associations with other museums and corresponded regularly with such distinguished European scien-

[7] Charles Coleman Sellers, "Peale's Museum," *Trans. Amer. Phil. Soc.*, 43 (1953), 235ff.

[8] Charles J. Maynard to Witmer Stone, Feb. 18, 1900. Manuscript Collection, Library, Academy of Natural Sciences of Philadelphia.

[9] Frank L. Burns, "Charles W. and Titian R. Peale and the Ornithological Section of the Old Philadelphia Museum," *Wilson Bulletin*, XLIV (March, 1932), 23.

tists as Baron Cuvier, Jean Baptiste Lamarck, and Maximilian, Prince of Wied. "But the chief cause of the importance ascribed to Peale's collection," declared Harvard zoologist Walter Faxon, "lay in the use made of it by that remarkable coterie of naturalists who made Philadelphia the metropolis of natural history during the early part of the nineteenth century."[10] The group referred to by Faxon included such well-known figures of that day as Alexander Wilson, George Ord, Thomas Say, and Constantine Samuel Rafinesque, who described type specimens in Peale's Museum, including several of those collected by Lewis and Clark.

According to the early Philadelphia historian, Dr. James Mease, Peale displayed his specimens in four rooms designated by him as the Marine Room, the Quadruped Room, the Long Room, and the Back Room.

The Marine Room, situated on the third floor, exhibited numerous shells, corals, fish, lizards, turtles, and a snake skin 26 feet long.

The Quadruped Room contained approximately 200 mammals "mounted in their natural attitudes," each carrying a label with Latin, French, and English inscriptions. Among the most remarkable of these animals were the "long clawed grizly bear from the Missouri" and the "big horned sheep and the prong horned antelope, both brought by Captain Lewis from the rocky mountains."

The Long Room was Peale's pride and joy. Here he displayed in glass cases more than 1,000 mounted birds, including a bird of paradise, a flamingo, and a "hooping crane from the capes of Delaware." Above the bird cases Peale had hung, in neat gilt frames, "two rows of portraits, one hundred and fifteen in number, of distinguished personages, painted from life." Among the 115 at the time Dr. Mease wrote (1811) were portraits of both Lewis and Clark. Lewis sat for Peale in 1807 and Clark in 1810. Appropriately, both portraits found a permanent home in Independence Hall.

The Back Room housed Peale's collection of Indian objects, such as "native spears, war clubs, stone hatchets, cups, pipes, and utensils." (A number of these, of course, had been collected by Lewis and Clark.) Peale displayed in this room, too, "a figure and striking likeness in wax, of the late Captain Lewis."[11] After Peale had completed this wax likeness of Lewis, he wrote Jefferson in part as follows: "A few

[10] Walter Faxon, "Relics of Peale's Museum," *Procs. Mus. Comp. Zoology,* LIX (1915), 19ff.

[11] Dr. James Mease, *The Picture of Philadelphia* (Philadelphia, 1811), 311–314.

weeks ago I completed a wax figure of Capt. Lewis and placed it in the Museum . . . the figure being dressed in an Indian dress presented to Capt. Lewis by Comeawhait, Chief of Shoshone Nation. . . . The figure has its right hand on its breast and the left holds the Calmut [calumet pipe] which was given me by Capt. Lewis. In a tablet I give the story in a few words, and then add, 'This mantle, composed of 140 ermine skins, was put on Capt. Lewis by Comeawhait. . . .' "[12]

Peale's Museum continued to reside in Independence Hall for a quarter of a century, until 1828, one year after its founder's death. At that time it was moved to the Arcade on Chestnut Street above Sixth and in 1838 to a building at Ninth and Sansom Streets. Eight years later, following a gradual decline in revenue, many of the objects were sold at auction, though the natural history collection (including apparently the ethnological) remained intact and on display until 1850. In that year approximately one half of the remaining collection was bought by P. T. Barnum, the extraordinary showman, and the other half by Moses Kimball, proprietor of the Boston Museum. Fire consumed Barnum's half when his American Museum in New York City burned to the ground on July 13, 1865. Kimball's portion remained in the Boston Museum until about the turn of the century when a number of Peale's American Indian objects in it were acquired by the Peabody Museum of Archaeology and Ethnology, Harvard University, and several bird skins by Harvard's Museum of Comparative Zoology.

Having sketched this brief description of Peale and his museum, we may now give our full attention to the ethnological material brought back by Lewis and Clark. Of prime importance to our knowledge of this collection is an existing document preserved today by the Historical Society of Pennsylvania. This is Peale's "Memorandum of specimens and Artifacts," actually an accession book, in which he listed "Articles collected by Merriwether Lewis Esqr. and William Clark Esqr. in their voyage and Journey of Discovery, up the Missouri to its source and to the Pacific Ocean." The list mentions more than a score of items (with much duplication in such categories as tobacco pouches, pipes, arrows, moccasins, feathers, and roots), about half of which came from tribes residing west of the Rockies. We cannot regard it as a complete list, since we know that Jefferson kept some of the objects for his Indian Hall and Lewis and Clark retained others (Clark later had his own museum in St. Louis).

Of particular interest to us in this study are the ethnozoological

[12] Sellers, *Charles Willson Peale*, II, 240.

and ethnobotanical objects listed by Peale. In the former category were porcupine quills ornamenting a tobacco pouch, a piece of white buffalo skin, tail feathers of the eagle (presumably golden eagle), a dress made of crow or raven skins worn by police officers, and the dress worn by Captain Lewis. The last-mentioned may well have been (or included) the tippet of ermine skins presented by Cameahwait. Ethnobotanical items were limited to roots and bread, primarily cous (*Lomatium cous*) and camas (*Camassia quamash*).[13]

What happened to these several Indian articles? Probably some of them perished in the conflagration of 1865 that destroyed Barnum's Museum. Others may be seen today in the Peabody Museum. Attributed to Lewis and Clark (and Peale's Museum) are: a Mandan buffalo robe with painted design, a woman's hat (probably Clatsop), a woman's painted moose skin garment, a Cree woman's dress, an ornament of ravens' skins, an elbow ornament of raven skins, a Chinook fiber skirt, an otter skin tobacco pouch, and an elk antler bow.

This is a much-prized collection. The objects comprising it had travelled a vast number of miles from Sioux, Mandan, Nez Perce, and Clatsop villages before they reached sanctuary, first in Philadelphia and then in Boston and Cambridge. Some are prized more highly than others, for example, the Cree woman's dress decorated with the oldest dated piece of western beadwork and the Chinook fiber skirt, one of the few surviving pieces of Chinook culture. Regrettably, certain other Indian artifacts once in Peale's Museum, such as the amulets taken by Lewis from the bodies of the two Blackfeet on Two Medicine River and the ermine skin dress worn by Lewis, do not form a part of this Peabody collection.[14]

The only other Indian objects returned by Lewis and Clark we have been able to locate are fragments of two Mandan pots in the University of Pennsylvania Museum. With them is a handwritten note stating: "Ancient Mandan kettles. Their only culinary vessel." One pot consists of a nearly complete rim and neck and about 14 body shards, while all that remains of the other is an incomplete rim and neck and six fragments. These two vessels parallel each other in every essential detail and were probably products of a single potter. One of these may be the earthen pot "such as the Mandans manufacture, and use for

[13] Jackson, *Letters*, 476–479.
[14] For more about these objects see Peabody Museum's "List of American Indian Objects in the Peabody Museum entered in the Old Catalogue as having originated in the Peale Collection" and Willoughby's "A Few Ethnological Specimens Collected by Lewis and Clark," 633–641.

culinary purposes" consigned to Jefferson from Fort Mandan by Lewis and Clark on April 7, 1805.

Report has it that George Catlin while in St. Louis (about 1830) obtained from Clark "a number of [Indian] specimens from the Columbia River region which are now in the National Museum."[15] As to this material, John C. Ewers, Smithsonian anthropologist, has written me: "Yes, we have some Catlin materials from the Columbia River in the U.S. National Museum. But whether they were (1) collected by Catlin himself when he was in the Northwest in the 1850's, or (2) collected by Lewis and Clark, or (3) collected by Clark alone after the expedition or (4) collected by someone else and transferred to George Catlin, it would be difficult, perhaps impossible to ascertain on the basis of existing and very fragmentary records."[16]

We cannot afford to ignore additional ethnological material growing out of the Expedition which is extant today. Lewis and Clark, we recall, were responsible for three different Indian delegations which visited Jefferson in the 1805–7 period. Since these were the first trans-Mississippi aboriginals to appear in the East, they attracted much comment and attention. Among the most fascinated observers in Washington at that time was Sir Augustus J. Foster, secretary to the British Minister. Foster determined to take back to England with him portraits of these Indians and for that purpose engaged the services of artist Charles B. J. Févret de St. Mémin, a refugee from the French Revolution who had built for himself a considerable reputation in the United States by making inexpensive portraits of prominent people. How many sketches St. Mémin made for Foster is unknown.[17] On Lewis's return from the West, he learned of them and, once in Philadelphia, paid St. Mémin $83.50 "for likenesses of the Indians &c. necessary to my publication."[18] This sum may have been for portraits already completed (of Indians comprising the first and second delegations), or for portraits to be made of Big White and other chiefs making up the third delegation. Several of St. Mémin's Indian sketches, both crayon and water color, have survived. A water color, for instance, of an Osage warrior may be found at the Henry Francis du Pont Winterthur

[15] Willoughby, "A Few Ethnological Specimens Collected by Lewis and Clark," 633.

[16] John C. Ewers to author, Nov. 17, 1965.

[17] For St. Mémin's relations with Foster see Dorothy Wollon and Margaret Kinard, "Sir Augustus J. Foster and 'The Wild Natives of the Woods'," *William and Mary Quart.*, 3rd ser., IX, no. 2 (April, 1952).

[18] Jackson, *Letters*, 411n.

Museum, Winterthur, Delaware; a crayon sketch of Big White is at the American Philosophical Society, Philadelphia; and there are seven or eight crayon sketches at the New York Historical Society. Additional water colors are known to be privately owned.[19]

These possess ethnological value because they represent the earliest known portraits of Plains Indians and because St. Mémin demonstrated excellent craftsmanship in depicting such characteristic Indian features as the prominent cheek bones, bold nose, and thin lips, as well as typical hair dress, paint, and arm-bands. In short, he drew Indians who looked like Indians. St. Mémin, too, made portraits of Lewis and Clark (see Appendix C) .[20]

American ethnology suffered a great loss when the Lewis and Clark collection of Indian handicraft was broken up and partially destroyed. Only those scientists familiar with the scarcity of early nineteenth century Indian material can fully appreciate the extent of this loss.

Botany

The Lewis and Clark botanical material brought back by the Expedition consisted of cuttings, seeds, roots, and dried, preserved plants. For example, the shipment of specimens from Fort Mandan contained: "A carrot of Ricara tobacco . . . Some Seed of the Mandan tobacco . . . an ear of Mandan corn . . . a Specimen of a plant, and a parsel of its roots, highly prized by the natives as an efficatious remidy in the cure of the bite of the rattle snake, or Mad dog . . . [and] Specimens of [dried, pressed] plants numbered from 1 to 60" (VII, 322–323) .[21]

[19] Five St. Mémin water colors were sold to private parties at public auction, May 13–15, 1954, by Parke-Bernet Galleries, Inc., New York City, who "cannot disclose their names."

[20] Charles Willson Peale made profile sketches (silhouettes) of some of the Plains Indians. He sent these (or some of them) to Jefferson on Feb. 6, 1806, with this comment: "Some of these savages have interesting characters by the lines of their faces." (See John C. Ewers, *Artists of the Old West* (Garden City, N.Y., 1965) 19; also Jackson, *Letters,* 289n.) These silhouettes by Peale are today the property of the Smithsonian.

[21] Smithsonian botanist Velva E. Rudd, writing in *Jour. Wash. Acad. of Scis.,* 44 (Nov., 1954) , 354, speaks of two bundles of dried plants sent from Fort Mandan, one with numbers 1–60, the other 1–67. Doubtless she confused the latter with a shipment of earths, salts, and minerals numbered 1–67. The American Philosophical Society in acknowledging receipt of the plants numbered 1–60, mentioned additionally "wild Prairie Timothy Seeds" and "Seeds of a Species of Pine with a pod," but no other plant material.

When Jefferson received the Fort Mandan material he promptly sent it to the American Philosophical Society. The minutes of that organization for November 15, 1805, read in part as follows:

The following donations were received. . . . A box containing various specimens of plants, earths and minerals collected by Captn. Meriwether Lewis and by him presented to the Society.

These articles were forwarded by the President [Jefferson, who was then not only President of the U.S. but also of the A.P.S.] who desires that the seeds may be sent to Mr. [William] Hamilton.

Resolved that the seeds transmitted by the President be referred to Mr. Wm. Hamilton with a request that he plant them in due season and report as soon as may be to the Society the nature of the plants produced by them with such descriptions & specimens as may serve for the information of the Society or the Public, and that the Secretaries be enjoined to give him due information of this resolution.

The Hortus siccus [collection of dried botanical specimens] is referred to Dr. [Benjamin Smith] Barton who is to examine the same and report to the Society. He is at the same time requested to reserve the seeds which are to be transmitted to Dr. Hamilton.[22]

On the following day the secretary of the Society, John Vaughan, listed the dried plant specimens (1 to 60) that Lewis had presented to the Society. This list, prepared from accompanying data provided by Lewis, is still in existence and is carefully preserved in the Society's library. Vaughan prefaced it with these words: "Donations November 16, 1805 from Meriwether Lewis Dried Plants &c put into Dr. B. S. Bartons hands for examination."[23]

Lewis himself brought back the second lot of dried, preserved plants. While in Washington he received a letter from Bernard McMahon (c. 1775–1816), Philadelphia florist, gardener, seed-merchant, and author of *The American Gardener's Calendar,* a 648-page tome which almost overnight became the horticulturists' bible and continued to be the standard authority for 50 years. As we shall see, McMahon played an important role in the future history of the Lewis and Clark herbarium specimens. His letter to Lewis reads in part as follows:

I have heard that, in your tour, you had collected a number of specimens of new and curious plants, and that you intend to bring some of them

---

[22] From manuscript minutes of the American Philosophical Society for Nov. 15, 1805.

[23] Vaughan's list provides scant descriptive material other than dates of collection. In Thwaites, VI, 141–151 (from Codex R, 4–53) may be found brief to lengthy descriptions of about half of the 60 plants.

to this City for examination; if so, I would wish you to be here before the 20th inst. as there is at present a young man boarding in my house, who, in my opinion, is better acquainted with plants in general, than any man I ever conversed with on the subject; he was regularly bred to the business in Saxony, lived with Mr. [William] Hamilton esqr. two years, who, *between you and me*, did not use him well; he was employed for these last twelve months collecting, to the southward, specimens for Dr. Barton, and arranging them, for whom he is to depart, to the northward, on similar business, about the 20th inst. He is a very intelligent and practical Botanist, would be well inclined to render you any service in his power, and I am confident would defer his intended journey, to the first of May to oblige you.[24]

The man whom McMahon thus introduces anonymously was Frederick Pursh (1774–1820), an experienced German botanist who had come to the United States in 1799 at the age of twenty-five. As McMahon indicated, he had worked for William Hamilton and was presently employed by Dr. Barton as a collector. Before many years elapsed, Pursh would gain lasting fame as a botanist, and he would owe a measure of it to plants from the far-away Missouri and Columbia watersheds collected by Meriwether Lewis.

Lewis first met Pursh soon after his arrival in Philadelphia in April. On May 10 (as an entry in his Account Book attests), he gave him $30 "for assisting me in preparing drawings and arranging specemines of plants for my work," and on May 26, just before Pursh left to continue collecting for Dr. Barton, he gave him an additional $40.[25]

Before Pursh left Philadelphia, Lewis surrendered to him his entire collection of herbarium specimens. The German botanist subsequently described the transfer in these words:

A small but highly interesting collection of dried plants was put into my hands by this gentleman, in order to describe and figure those I thought new, for the purpose of inserting them in the account of his Travels, which he was then engaged in preparing for the press. . . . The collection of plants just spoken of was made during the rapid return of the expedition from the Pacific Ocean toward the United States. A much more extensive one, made on their slow ascent towards the Rocky Mountains and the chains of the Northern Andes, had unfortunately been lost, by being deposited among other things at the foot of these mountains [at Great Falls]. The loss of this first collection is the more to be regretted, when I consider that the small

[24] Jackson, *Letters,* 398.
[25] Lewis's "Account Book" is now the property of the Missouri Historical Society, St. Louis. See also Jackson, *Letters,* 463n.

collection communicated to me, consisting of about one hundred and fifty specimens, contained not above a dozen plants well known to me to be natives of North America, the rest being either entirely new or but little known.[26]

It would appear that Dr. Barton, after receiving the Fort Mandan shipment of plants in November, 1805, had thoughts of describing this collection himself; at least we have his word for it that he was preparing a catalog of the Lewis plants that would "serve as a beginning of a Flora Missourica."[27]

However, Dr. Barton's plan died aborning, perhaps because his health had begun to falter. This would explain why Lewis, on his return, turned his complete collection over to Pursh rather than to Barton.

Pursh spent the summer and early fall of 1807 collecting for Barton in New York and Vermont and returned to Philadelphia and McMahon's home on October 5. His commitments to Barton now terminated, he at once began devoting his full time to describing and sketching the plants Lewis had left with him. In the meantime, the latter had gone to St. Louis to assume his duties as the first governor of Louisiana Territory.

Several months went by. On January 17, 1809, McMahon wrote Jefferson as follows: "I am very anxious to learn when Governor Lewis may be expected here, as I have detained a man [Pursh] in my house upwards of twelve months, drawing & discribing his plants, which he left with me for that purpose. This was accomplished in May last as far as it could be done in the absence of Govr. Lewis, and he told me on leaving this City he expected to be here again in that month. This man, who is completely adequate to the task, is becoming very uneasy, and I wish him not to leave the neighbourhood till the arrival of Mr. Lewis, by whose particular instructions only, he can finish the drawings of some very important, but imperfect specimens."[28]

Lewis did not again visit Philadelphia nor did he ever again communicate with McMahon. Winter gave way to spring and Pursh, unable to prosecute his labors without further instructions from Lewis, left for New York City where he had found employment with the Elgin Botanic Gardens of Dr. David Hosack. And then, before long, news reached Philadelphia of Lewis's death on October 11, 1809, at an

[26] Pursh, *Flora Americae Septentrionalis*, I, x–xi.
[27] *Philadelphia Physical and Medical Journal*, 2 (1805), 176.
[28] Jackson, *Letters*, 446.

obscure wayside place, Grinder's Tavern, on the Natchez Trace in Tennessee. This sudden, completely unforeseen turn of events raised difficult problems for which there was no immediate or easy solution. McMahon expressed some of them in a letter to Jefferson, on December 24, soon after learning of the tragedy:

> I am extremely sorry for the death of that worthy and valuable man Govr. Lewis. . . . I have, I believe, all his collection of dried specimens of plants . . . and several kinds of *new* living plants, which I raised from the seeds of his collecting . . . the original specimens are all in my hands, but Mr. Pursh, had taken his drawings and descriptions with him, and will, no doubt, on the delivery of them expect a reasonable compensation for his trouble.
>
> As it appears to me probable that you will interrest yourself in having the discoveries of Mr. Lewis published, I think it a duty incumbent on me, to give you the preceding information, and to ask your advice as to the propriety of still keeping the living plants I have, from getting into other hands who would gladly describe them and publish them, without doing due honor to the memory and merit of the worthy discoverer.[29]

From what McMahon said about the dried specimens, it seems obvious that he had no knowledge of the fact, not generally known until much later, that Pursh had taken with him on leaving for New York not only drawings and descriptions but also several of Lewis's pressed plants. It would appear, too, that he had taken them without obtaining permission from his host or anyone else. He removed duplicates of some, and in other instances with only a single specimen available, he either detached a part or took the entire plant. On examining the Lewis and Clark plants at the Academy today, one can see clearly where parts had been severed from such specimens as vine maple (*Acer circinatum*) and buffalo-berry (*Shepherdia argentea*).

After three years in New York with Dr. Hosack, Pursh left on a collecting trip to the West Indies. On his return to the United States, he took passage almost immediately for London, carrying with him his pick of Lewis's plants as well as drawings and descriptions.

Early in January (1810) Clark came to Philadelphia. It was important that he locate materials Lewis had left there and hasten publication of the journals. Soon after arriving, he informed a friend that he had found the original plant specimens, was sending to New York for the sketches and descriptions held by Pursh, and was experiencing

[29] Jackson, *Letters*, 485–486.

"some difficulty of getting a proper scientificul Charrutor to Compile that part of the work relative to Botany, Mineralogy & Zoology."[30]

So Clark, like McMahon, believed that all of the original plant specimens he and Lewis had brought back from the West were still in Philadelphia. Presumably he paid Pursh the amount due him, and we have Pursh's word for it that he "transmitted [to] Clark all the drawings prepared for the work."[31]

Before Clark left Philadelphia, he arranged with Nathaniel Biddle, a young lawyer of that city, to collaborate with Dr. Barton in completing the history of the Expedition, with the latter developing the scientific chapters. Writing to Biddle from Virginia on February 20, 1810, Clark said: "I brought the books [journals] with me [from Philadelphia] to Copy such parts as are intended for the Botanical work which I shall send to Dr. Bartin."[32] To Henry Dearborn, two months later, Clark said that Biddle had been with him in Fincastle, Virginia, where they discussed the narrative and that the latter, on his return to Philadelphia, took with him for Dr. Barton "such parts as relate to science only" and "specimens of plants &c."[33] Clark clarified further Barton's role when he addressed him on May 22:

You will have seen Mr. N. Biddle who was with me some time at Fincastle and recved from him a Copy of such part of my journal as I had Copied from the original, which I hope with the assistance of the specimens and what information the young gentleman who will hand you this letter (Mr. George Shannon) Can give you at sundry times, may enable you to proceed in the Scientific part of my work, which I am extreemly happy to find you are willing to engage in. I have wrote to Mr. Peale requesting him to permit you to discribe all & every of the animals &c. which he has received from the late Lewis and myself. The dried specimens of plants, I requested Mr. McMahon (when in Phila.) to deliver to Mr. Conrad [John Conrad, who had agreed to publish the journals], who will place them in your hands. I have also requested Mr. McMahon to supply you with living specimins when he may have Two or more—and to give you every opportunity of inspecting them in his Garden &c. On this subject I have instructed Mr. Shannon. I have given Mr. M. [McMahon] a hint about the necessity of making the specimins sacredly private between your self & myself and Mr. Shannon &c.[34]

[30] Jackson, *Letters,* 490.
[31] Pursh, *Flora Americae Septentrionalis,* I, x. If Pursh did leave drawings with Clark, they have been lost.
[32] Jackson, *Letters,* 494.
[33] Jackson, *Letters,* 546.
[34] Jackson, *Letters,* 548.

Clark's letter authenticates the point that Dr. Barton is now firmly committed to the task of writing the scientific chapters, even though, as we have surmised, he may earlier have blown hot and cold about the undertaking. Unfortunately, as is well known, he failed to carry out the agreement because of further deterioration of health. One may wonder if he was sensible of the enviable opportunity thus eluding him, that of heightening his stature among American men of science by describing the many botanical treasures returned by Lewis and Clark.

Reverting now to Pursh, we find that he arrived in London during the winter of 1811–12. Here he at once began working under the patronage of A. B. Lambert (1761–1842), vice president of the Linnaean Society and well-to-do cabinet-naturalist; he devoted his time almost exclusively to writing *Flora Americae Septentrionalis,* which he published in 1814. This was an admirably executed, two-volume work that, in breadth of treatment, exceeded anything heretofore written about the North American flora. Herein Pursh described 124 plants collected by Lewis and Clark, identifying each with the abbreviated legend, *"v.s. in Herb. Lewis."*

In an era when botanists were not always as scrupulous as today about extending credit where credit was due, it is refreshing to note that Pursh consistently took pains to acknowledge his indebtedness. Not only that, but in the case of Lewis and Clark, he honored them, as we know, by creating the genera *Lewisia* and *Clarkia* and by naming three new species after Lewis: Lewis's wild flax (*Linum lewisii*), Lewis's monkey flower (*Mimulus lewisii*), and Lewis's syringa (*Philadelphus lewisii*). Additionally, reflecting the importance he attached to the Lewis and Clark collection, he illustrated his *Flora* with 13 plants from that herbarium—13 of a total of 27 illustrations.[35]

Such handsome recognition perhaps mitigates to a degree Pursh's seeming deviation from probity in misappropriating the plants while resident in McMahon's home. Actually, how fortunate for Lewis and Clark! If Pursh had not described and figured these plants, the odds are that in due time they would have been described by other taxonomists who, either ignorant of or indifferent to Lewis and Clark as the origi-

[35] The 13 plants of Lewis and Clark Pursh chose for illustrating his *Flora* were: *Claytonia lanceolata, Berberis aquifolium, Berberis nervosa, Lilium pudicum, Helonias (Xerophyllum) tenax, Rubus spectabilis, Clarkia pulchella, Gaultheria shallon, Tigarea (Purshia) tridentata, Gerardia fruticosa, Mimulus lewisii, Psoralea esculenta,* and *Lupinaster macrocephalus.* By comparing Pursh's drawing of *Berberis aquifolium* at the Academy, it may be seen that he copied quite faithfully the original.

nal discoverers, would have withheld the credit so generously extended by Pursh.

Pursh died in 1820, and the specimens he had obtained in the United States remained in Lambert's hands until the death of the latter in 1842. Later that same year they were sold at auction. Attending the sale, by good fortune, was a wealthy young American botanist, Edward Tuckerman, who had recently graduated from Harvard College and would later occupy a chair at Amherst College as professor of botany. Tuckerman subsequently described his successes at the auction as follows: "At Lambert's sale I acquired one half his old American Herbm. This was disposed in 2 cabinets—the first contains all Pursh's plants—and the 2nd—all the rest (Fraser, Bradbury, Lewis & Clark, Nuttall &c) this last I bought."[36]

Tuckerman soon returned to New England, bringing with him his recently acquired botanical prizes. Fourteen years later, in 1856, he presented most of them, including Lewis and Clark specimens, to the Academy of Natural Sciences of Philadelphia. In searching for accession records that would document Tuckerman's gift to the Academy, I was successful in finding (in the manuscript collection of the Academy's library) the precise evidence which I sought. This is in the form of a previously unpublished letter written by Tuckerman at Amherst College on May 3, 1856, and addressed to Dr. John L. LeConte, then corresponding secretary of the Academy. The letter follows:

I beg to inform you that I despatched one Case, and one Parcel containing the collection of plants purchased by me in London in 1842, by Harnden's Express, on Thurday last & trust they have already safely reached the Academy.

What I have sent contains all of the Lambert collection, which was in the Cabinet purchased by me, & all the Reliquae of Pursh's herbarium, which were sold separate from the main herbarium (which last went to the British Museum) excepting only the *Potamogetons* [pondweeds] which I have reserved.

The latter collection (Pursh's) would probably have also been bought for the British Museum, had the character of its content been known at the sale; but the lot was described as "American plants" and as such I bought it at a venture, at a comparatively low price.

It is very gratifying to me that these valuable specimens are now to be

[36] Joseph Ewan, "Frederick Pursh, 1774–1820, and his Botanical Associates," *Procs. Amer. Phil. Soc.*, 96, no. 5 (1952), 625. It was the diligent pursuit of Joseph Ewan, Tulane University botanist, who disclosed Tuckerman's role in this important botanical episode.

preserved in the Museum of the Academy, and I hope it will not be found that the collection has suffered any serious damage from insects during the last few years. I beg however to suggest that an early examination be made of it as to this point, as it has latterly been exposed to such injury.

I look forward with much pleasure to a prolonged visit to the crypto-gamick treasures of the Academy as soon as it shall be possible for me to leave home & I remain meanwhile, Yours very truly,

Edw. Tuckerman

So the Lewis and Clark plants that Pursh took with him as he left Philadelphia—at least most of them[37]—finally came back to that city, after an interval of almost 50 years. How many did Pursh transport across the Atlantic to the British Isles? How many of these did Tucker-man return? How many are at the Academy today? As to the first and second questions, it is highly unlikely that anyone will ever discover the precise answers. I will attempt a reply to the third in a subsequent paragraph.

The Lewis and Clark specimens left behind in Philadelphia were, as previously stated, entrusted by Clark to Dr. Barton. That was in 1810. Incredibly, we find no further mention of the whereabouts of these plants until 1896, almost a century later. As one scientist put it, they were "entirely lost to the botanical world" (VI, 152). In that year, Harvard's Charles Sprague Sargent, authority on American trees, sug-gested to Thomas Meehan, botanist at the Academy of Natural Sci-ences, that some of the Lewis and Clark plant specimens might conceiv-ably be found stored away in some forgotten recess at the American Philosophical Society. It proved to be an inspired suggestion. "After long and diligent search," Meehan wrote later, "packages of plants were found . . . in the original packages . . . with the freedom of three quarters of a century the beetles had made sad work in the bundles. In a few cases the specimens had been wholly reduced to dust, and only fragments were yet in other cases. Generally, however, they were in fair condition."[38] Pursh's and Lewis's handwriting on labels proved these specimens to be the long-missing ones of Lewis and Clark. Their discovery was, as Coues expressed it, "one of the happiest and most important that could have been made."[39] Since the Philosophical So-

[37] Joseph Ewan has assured me that Lewis and Clark plants are today in the British Museum and/or Kew Gardens. In a letter to me (Sept. 21, 1966), he referred to *Caprifolium ciliosum* as an example.

[38] Thomas Meehan, "The Plants of Lewis and Clark's Expedition Across the Continent, 1804–1806," *Procs. Acad. Nat. Scis. Phila.* (1898), 13–14.

[39] Elliott Coues, "Notes on Mr. Thomas Meehan's Paper on the Plants of Lewis and Clark's Expedition Across the Continent," *Procs. Acad. Nat. Scis. of Phila.* (1898), 292.

ciety had no facilities for taking care of herbarium specimens, they placed them on loan to the Academy, where they have been ever since.

When Meehan published a report of this discovery in 1898 (after he and two other botanists, Drs. B. L. Robinson and J. M. Greenman of Gray Herbarium, had made all possible determinations), he listed approximately 180 different species. Quite naturally his report made no attempt to include those specimens presented earlier to the Academy by Tuckerman.

Although the Lewis and Clark Herbarium has been examined by many individuals since 1898, mostly by systematists with extensive knowledge of specific plant families, not one has made public a full detailed report about it or, to my knowledge, has undertaken a comprehensive study. As the years since then have gone by and Lewis and Clark enthusiasts have multiplied, a mounting curiosity has developed as to what specimens, and how many, actually survive at the Academy.

During the summer of 1966, with the approval and cooperation of Dr. Alfred E. Schuyler, present Curator of Botany, I attempted to locate and examine all existing specimens of this extremely valuable and interesting collection. The task, not an easy one, was made more difficult by the circumstance that many of the plants were scattered throughout the large Type Collection at the Academy. At Dr. Schuyler's suggestion, I have brought together in one place all specimens we have been able to locate. Here they have been arranged alphabetically according to genera, and special folders appropriately marked have been prepared for each genus. As a result, the accredited visitor to the Academy may henceforth find the collection assembled as a unit and experience little or no difficulty in locating any particular plants he might wish to examine.

Before I proceed to give my findings, I think it would be well to report on previous estimates of the size of the collection. Pursh, it will be recalled, stated that Lewis put into his hands about 150 specimens. That this figure was low is proved by Meehan's report which listed some 180 exclusive of those Pursh took with him to England. A few years later (1904) Stewardson Brown, then Assistant Curator of Botany at the Academy, wrote that: "The collection, as preserved in the Herbarium of the Academy of Natural Sciences today, consists of one hundred and seventy-three recognizable species, mostly in fair condition" (VI, 153). Fifty years later, Velva E. Rudd, Assistant Curator of Botany, U.S. National Museum, wrote: "About 200 herbarium specimens remain as tangible evidence of botanical collections made by

Meriwether Lewis in the course of the 2-year-long, 1804–1806, Lewis and Clark Expedition."[40] In 1966 R. D. Burroughs, botanist and conservationist, wrote an article for *Natural History* in which he referred to "a total of 188 specimens" at the Academy, perhaps deriving that figure from Meehan's 1898 report.[41]

My own examination extended over a period of several weeks and was materially aided, as stated, by valuable advice and cooperation from Dr. Schuyler. A summary report follows:

(1) At last count, there are today 216 herbarium sheets comprising the Lewis and Clark collection at the Academy. Since duplication exists (four sheets of silver sage, *Artemisia cana,* for example), it naturally follows that the number of species represented is less. The collection would be more impressive, of course, if the plants Lewis collected in 1805 between Fort Mandan and Great Falls had not been destroyed.

(2) Due to indifferent, incomplete, and fragmentary specimens, one can only approximate the actual number of species. Stewardson Brown's count of 173 must be regarded as close, though it is unlikely that any two contemporary botanists would arrive at the same figure. Conservatively, 70 to 75 of them were new to science when Lewis collected them, and many others, not new, were valuable because their discovery verified an appreciable extension of range. Fortunately, each and every specimen located by Meehan at the American Philosophical Society has been accounted for.

(3) I have located 39 specimens that Pursh took with him to London and Tuckerman later returned to the United States. These (often referred to as "Lambert specimens," though actually a part of the Lewis and Clark Herbarium) are easily distinguishable because of the distinctively watermarked paper on which they had been mounted while in London and by affixed tickets bearing the handwriting of Lambert or Pursh.

(4) Of Lewis and Clark species, I count 62 that at one time or another have been filed in the Academy Type Collection, 24 of them being Lambert specimens. This considerable number emphasizes one reason why botanists attach so much importance to the Lewis and

[40] Velva E. Rudd, "Botanical Contributions of the Lewis and Clark Expedition," *Jour. Wash. Acad. Scis.,* 44, no. 11 (1954), 351.

[41] R. D. Burroughs, "The Lewis and Clark Expedition's Botanical Discoveries," *Natural History,* LXXV, no. 1 (Jan., 1966), 59.

Clark Herbarium. It should perhaps be explained that a specimen is generally regarded as a type when it is apparent that the author of the name has closely examined that specimen, has based his description on it, and has cited it with said original description. It is of great importance because it is a preserved plant which can be consulted to determine the correct or incorrect application of the name (*Lewisia rediviva*, for instance) to a group of plants (e.g., species). At the time of Lewis and Clark, naturalists did not make it a practice to designate type specimens, so that taxonomic botanists of today often find it necessary to consult early herbaria to find and designate appropriate specimens as types.

(5) Considering time lapses, difficulties related to transportation, and inevitable handling and deterioration, the specimens are in surprisingly good condition. As I appraise them, some 10 per cent are in an excellent state of preservation, 50 per cent good, 30 per cent fair, and the remainder poor (that is, fragmentary or completely missing except for identification tags). One specimen, that of mission bells (*Fritillaria lanceolata*), is in such superlative condition that it might have been collected only yesterday, and it is doubtful if a better one exists in any collection. Yet this specimen was eased from the soft earth of Brant Island in the lower reaches of the Columbia River on April 10, 1806, more than a century and a half ago.

(6) A number of the sheets attract attention because they bear (usually in the lower left-hand corner), small affixed tickets of a distinctive purplish-colored paper with data in Lewis's own handwriting. The data consists generally of a number (buffalo-berry, *Shepherdia argentea*, for instance, is No. 39) and where and when the plant had been collected. It is quite apparent that these tickets had been scissored (by unknown hands at a later date) from larger sheets of paper since their size and shape conform to the space occupied by Lewis's data. This paper is much like blotting paper and must have been the kind Lewis took west with him for pressing his plants. Supporting this view are two books of herbarium specimens in the Academy formerly the property of Dr. Barton with paper bearing a marked resemblance in thickness and bibulous quality to that of the purple tickets. Since Lewis had consulted Dr. Barton in Philadelphia in 1803, it is within the range of probability that the latter instructed him in the latest methods of preserving plants and may actually have suggested, or provided him with, this kind of paper.

Those sheets which do not bear Lewis's purple tickets are usually supplied with others in Pursh's handwriting, the latter having obviously copied Lewis's data. This attention to date and place can be traced to Jefferson, who was, of course, meticulous in such matters. As a result, with few exceptions we know precisely when and where Lewis collected each plant.

(7) Over the years prominent botanists have examined the Lewis and Clark *hortus siccus*. Many of them have identified themselves by leaving annotations on the sheets in either pen or pencil. The first, of course, were Lewis, Pursh, and Lambert, and then after a long hiatus Meehan, Robinson, and Greenman. Among those of more recent years were such plant specialists as C. V. Piper, Washington State University; Per Axel Rydberg, New York Botanical Garden; Lewis C. Wheeler, Gray Herbarium; A. S. Hitchcock, Smithsonian Institution; Stewardson Brown and F. W. Pennell, Academy of Natural Sciences.

(8) The majority of the plants came from west of the Continental Divide. Of approximately 200 dated sheets (the remainder are dateless), Lewis collected 135 on the Columbian watershed and 65 on the Missouri. Broken down another way, he obtained 60 on the journey from St. Louis to Fort Mandan, only 10 from Fort Mandan to the Pacific (due largely to the loss suffered at Great Falls and possibly at Shoshoni Cove) and 130 during the winter at Fort Clatsop and on the return to St. Louis. The earliest dated specimen is a horsetail (*Equisetum arvense*) collected on August 10, 1804, near the mouth of the Little Sioux River, Iowa, and the latest a vine of the grape family (*Cissus ampelopsis*) obtained on September 14, 1806, in the environs of present-day Leavenworth, Kansas.

About one-fourth of the entire Herbarium was collected in Idaho on the return trip, the majority at Camp Chopunnish. The stay at this camp (from May 14 to June 10) happily coincided with the appearance of a host of local spring flowers, including, it will be recalled, the beautiful ragged robin and mariposa lily.

In concluding this report, we should add that many of the plants discovered and described by Lewis are missing from the Lewis and Clark Herbarium. A number quickly come to mind, such as the western serviceberry (*Amelanchier alnifolia*), narrow-leaved cottonwood (*Populus angustifolia*), grand fir (*Abies grandis*), lodgepole pine (*Pinus contorta*), and Engelmann's spruce (*Picea engelmannii*). Thus, as Elliott Coues remarked: "There remains for some one the agreeable and useful task of reviewing Lewis and Clark's botanical *text* as distinguished from their specimens."[42]

[42] Coues, "Notes on Mr. Meehan's Paper . . . ," 292.

The seeds, roots, and cuttings collected in the West by Lewis and Clark ended up in the hands of several individuals. Jefferson kept some for himself, Peale received others, definitely roots of cous (*Lomatium cous*) and camas (*Camassia quamash*), and Lewis and Clark sent seeds to relatives and friends ("I send my sister Croghan some seed of several Kinds of Grapes," Clark wrote his brother-in-law, William Croghan, on April 2, 1805).[43] The great majority of seeds as well as roots and cuttings were given, however, to Hamilton and McMahon.

William Hamilton (1745–1813) has already been referred to in this work as the owner of the estate, "Woodlands," situated near Bartram's Gardens. A wealthy, dedicated votary of landscape gardening, he surrounded his home with extensive gardens and greenhouses which contained the largest and most elaborate collection of native and exotic plants then known to the United States. Jefferson, a frequent visitor at Woodlands, declared that: "With its collections, its taste, and its style," it is "the only rival which I have known in America to what may be seen in England."[44] Not the least of Hamilton's accomplishments was the introduction into the United States of such exotics as the camellia, Lombardy poplar, Norway maple, and ginkgo.[45] Hamilton's mansion still stands in Woodlands Cemetery near the University of Pennsylvania, and as late as 1899 one of the original ginkgos was still living. Arbophiles from distant parts of the world, when in Philadelphia, journeyed there "to see the magnificent specimen."[46]

At about the same time the American Philosophical Society passed a resolution to refer the shipment of Fort Mandan seeds to Hamilton, Jefferson wrote Hamilton in part as follows:

Mr. Madison mentioned to me your wish to receive any seeds which should be sent me by Capt. Lewis. . . . I lately forwarded to Mr. Peal for the Philosophical Society a box containing minerals & seeds from Captain Lewis, which I did not open, and I am persuaded the Society will be pleased to dispose of them so well as into your hands. Mr. Peale would readily ask this. I happen to have two papers of seeds which Capt. Lewis enclosed to me in a letter, and which I gladly consign over to you, as I shall anything else which may fall into my hands & be worthy of your acceptance. One of these

[43] Jackson, *Letters,* 230. At one time Lewis apparently sent "6 different seeds" to Henry Muhlenberg (see Jackson, *Letters,* 354n).

[44] Sarah P. Stetson, "William Hamilton and his 'Woodlands'," *Pa. Mag. Hist. and Biog.,* 73 (1949), 26–33.

[45] Scharf and Westcott, *History of Philadelphia,* II, 873. See also (for Norway maple) Harshberger, *The Botanists of Philadelphia,* 434.

[46] Harshberger, *The Botanists of Philadelphia,* 434.

is of the Mandan tobacco, a very singular species, uncommonly weak & probably suitable for segars. The other had no ticket but I believe it is a plant used by the Indians with extraordinary success for curing the bite of the rattle snake & other venomous animals.[47]

Interest in plants mounted when the electrifying news reached the East in the fall of 1806 that Lewis and Clark had successfully completed their transit of the continent and would soon arrive in Washington and Philadelphia. One of the persons impressed by this intelligence was McMahon who on December 26 wrote Jefferson: ". . . your goodness I hope will excuse my anxiety to procure some seeds of the indigenous plants of the western parts of America, if you received such from Capt. Lewis on his return. A small portion of every kind you could conveniently spare, would greatly oblige me and perhaps, render me essential service, and it would be of some importance to get them as soon as you could make it convenient to have them forwarded, that each kind might be treated according to its apparent nature, and different methods tried to effect its successful propagation with the greater degree of certainty, especially the nondescripts if any."[48]

Jefferson replied that Lewis had brought back a considerable number of seeds and that he had advised him "to confide principal shares of them to Mr. Hamilton of the Woodlands & yourself, as the persons most likely to take care of them, which he will accordingly do. He will carry them on to Philadelphia himself."[49]

It was extremely important, as Jefferson indicated, that the seeds be placed with trustworthy individuals. Others, putting desire for personal recognition above integrity, might publish descriptions and thereby deprive Lewis of that honor. That this was no idle precaution is proved by McMahon's later statement to Jefferson: "I had strong reason to believe that this opportunity was coveted by ——— which made me still more careful of the plants."[50]

In ensuing months and years McMahon, Jefferson, and Hamilton reported on their successes with the seeds, roots, and cuttings. In these reports they supplied names of seeds received and planted and plants cultivated from them. McMahon's reports (all to Jefferson) follow:

March 27, 1807—"The dwarf Cedar of the plains of Missouri, I take from the seed, to be a species of *Juniperus*; the *Shallan* of the Clatsops, a

[47] Jackson, *Letters,* 269.
[48] Jackson, *Letters,* 354–355.
[49] Jackson, *Letters,* 356.
[50] Jackson, *Letters,* 485.

Vaccinium; and the flowering Pea of the plains of Arkansas, a Lupinus."[51]

April 2, 1807—"I have fine crops already up of the Aricara Tobacco, and perennial flax. . . ."[52]

April 10, 1807—"I have several sorts growing of the seeds you were pleased to send me, among which are four varieties of Currants, and I am confidant that I shall have plants from every kind I received. . . ."[53]

June 28, 1808—". . . I have fine plants of *all* the varieties of Currants (7) and Gooseberries (2) brought by Govr. Lewis, and of about 20 other *new species* of plants, as well as five or six new *genera.*"[54]

February 28, 1812—"This morning I done myself the pleasure of sending you by Mr. Gilmer a box containing the following articles:

No. 1. Ribes odoratissimum (mihi). This is one of Captain Lewis's and an important shrub, the fruit very large, of a dark purple colour, the flowers yellow, showey and *extremely fragrant.*

No. 2. Symphoricarpos leucocarpa (mihi). This is a beautiful shrub brought by Lewis from the River Columbia, the flower is small but neat, the berries hang in large clusters and of a snow white colour and continue on the shrubs, retaining their beauty, all the winter, especially if kept in a greenhouse. The shrub is perfectly hardy; I have given it the trivial name of Snowberry-bush.

No. 3. The Yellow Currant of the River Jefferson; this is specifically different from the other, but I have not given it a specific botanical name."[55]

Jefferson's reports emanated from Monticello:

April 18, 1807—"Ricara beans very forward . . . [planted] Missouri great Salsafia . . . flowering pea of Arkansa from Capt. Lewis . . . the yellow [lily] of the Columbia."[56]

April 24, 1807—". . . put into each [flower bed] 1. or 2. seeds of the honeysuckle of Lewis's river."[57]

May 1, 1807—"planted Pani [Pawnee or Arikara] corn in the orchard."[58]

[51] Betts, *Jefferson's Garden Book,* 345. The *Juniperus* referred to may have been *J. horizontalis.* The "Shallan" was *Gaultheria shallon.* The "flowering pea of the plains" is not readily identifiable though possibly purple vetch, *Vicia americana.*

[52] Betts, *Jefferson's Garden Book,* 346. The tobacco was *Nicotiana quadrivalvis* and the flax, *Linum lewisii.*

[53] Betts, *Jefferson's Garden Book,* 347.

[54] Betts, *Jefferson's Garden Book,* 373. McMahon's allusion to new genera and species may indicate that he had consulted Pursh about these plants. His count of seven varieties of currants seems high.

[55] Betts, *Jefferson's Garden Book,* 481.

[56] Betts, *Jefferson's Garden Book,* 334–335.

[57] Betts, *Jefferson's Garden Book,* 336.

[58] Betts, *Jefferson's Garden Book,* 336.

August 11, 1807—"my Pani corn planted the same day [as Quarantine corn] was a week or fortnight later [in producing roasting ears] . . . mr. Randolph's Mandan corn planted 10 days before my Quarantine & Pani yielded rosten ears the 4th of July. it is now fit to grind. an ear of Mandan corn which I gave him, planted May 15, gave rosten ears a few days only later than that planted Apr. 20."[59]

We have been able to find only one report from Hamilton, this a letter to Jefferson dated February 5, 1810: "Mr. Lewis's seeds have not yet vegetated freely, more however may come up with this coming spring. I have nevertheless obtained plants of the yellow wood, or Osage apple, seven or eight of gooseberries & one of his kinds of Aricara tobacco, have flowered so well as to afford me an elegant drawing of it."[60]

We are now in a position to list tentatively those seeds, roots, and cuttings alluded to by McMahon, Peale, Jefferson, and Hamilton as having been brought back by Lewis and Clark (ones new to science will be preceded by an upper-case "N" and questionable determinations by an interrogation mark) :

BEAN. "Ricara bean." A form of *Phaseolus vulgaris*.

N BITTERROOT. *Lewisia rediviva*. Pursh reported roots grown by McMahon.

N CAMAS. *Camassia quamash*. Roots in Peale's Museum.

CEDAR. "Dwarf Cedar of the plains of Missouri." Probably *Juniperus horizontalis*.

? CONE-FLOWER. "Plant . . . for curing the bite of the rattle snake." Possibly *Echinacea angustifolia*.

CORN. Mandan and "Pani." Varieties of Indian corn, *Zea mays*.

N COUS. *Lomatium cous*. Roots in Peale's Museum.

N CURRANTS. McMahon's count of seven species seems high. Beyond much doubt he grew golden currant (*Ribes aureum*), red-flowered currant (*R. sanguineum*), and sticky currant (*R. viscossissimum*). Another possibility was Missouri currant (*R. odoratum*). All four species were new to science.

N FLAX. "Perennial flax." Lewis's wild flax (*Linum lewisii*).

N GOOSEBERRY. McMahon says he grew two species. These may have been the snowy gooseberry (*Ribes niveum*) and canyon gooseberry (*R. menziesii*), both new to science. Another possibility (not new) was smooth gooseberry (*R. oxyacanthoides*).

? "LILY." "Yellow lily of the Columbia." Possibly yellow bell (*Fritillaria pudica*), a species new to science.

[59] Betts, *Jefferson's Garden Book*, 336.
[60] Betts, *Jefferson's Garden Book*, 363.

N   OSAGE ORANGE. *Maclura aurantiaca.*
?   "PEA." "The flowering pea of the plains of Arkansas." Possibly purple
    vetch *(Vicia americana)* .
N   SALAL. "The Shallan of the Clatsops." *Gaultheria shallon.*
    SALSIFY. "Missouri great Salsafia." Salsify or oyster plant *(Tragopon
    sp.)* .
    SNOWBERRY BUSH. Perhaps *Symphoricarpos albus = S. racemosus.*
N   TOBACCO. Mandan and Arikara *(Nicotiana quadrivalvis)* .[61]

Some of the seeds and cuttings soon crossed the Atlantic. In the
spring of 1813, Jefferson asked McMahon if he could assemble a collection which he proposed sending to M. Thöuin, Curator of the Royal
Botanical Society in Paris.[62] Later the same year he sent cuttings of the
snowberry to his friend Madame Noailles de Tessé. He said, "Its
beauty consists in a great produce of berries of the size of currants, and
literally as white as snow, which remain on the bush through the
winter."[63]

In due time, contemporary seed catalogs began to advertise certain
of the plants introduced by Lewis and Clark. For example, McMahon's
The American Gardener's Almanac for 1815 offered for sale the Arikara kidney bean, perennial flax, Mandan corn, and *"Symphoricarpos
vulgaris."*[64] Robert Carr's *Periodical Catalogue* of 1828, listing plants
on sale from Bartram's Garden, included Osage orange valued for its
"beautiful foliage and curious fruit" and "Lewis's Missouri ornamental Currant." Kendrick's *Orchard List* (Boston, 1833) listed "Jeffer-

[61] There doubtless were others. *Clarkia* and *Berberis,* for example, were later
grown widely in the East. In this connection, one should not overlook a scrap of
paper in the Missouri Historical Society on which Clark jotted down kinds of seeds
returned by the Expedition:

A List of Seed

The flesh coloured Flower	Yellow Currant
Wild parsnip	Service Berry
Wild Plumb	Ricara Currant
Peas, common to the Columbian Plains	Red Currant
Flowers from Clarks River	Rocky Mountain Cherry
[. . .] Species of Sun Flower	[. . .] Cherry of the River Rochejhone
Shallon Cherry	Egg Plant
Honey Succle	Wild Flax
Black Currant	Large species of tobacco
Purple Currant	

[62] Jackson, *Letters,* 583–584.
[63] Betts, *Jefferson's Garden Book,* 520.
[64] The flax could have been the Old World species, *Linum perenne,* or *L.
lewisii.* Doubtless the *Symphoricarpos* was the "snowberry" so much admired by
Jefferson.

son's Missouri fragrant currant" and "Snowberry, a very hardy shrub from the Rocky Mountains."[65]

And what of these trans-Mississippi plants today; did Lewis and Clark's efforts to introduce them into the East prove fruitless? At least two or three species of currants have found wide acceptance as ornamentals, particularly the red-flowering currant (*Ribes sanguineum*), and Osage orange is still found as a hedge plant in places. Here and there, too, one finds in gardens *Lewisia, Clarkia, Berberis aquifolium,* and *Symphoricarpos.*

Zoology

Lewis and Clark's shipment of zoological specimens from Fort Mandan early in 1805 included: "1 tin box containing insects, mice &c" and a unique collection of skins, horns, and bones of such animals as pronghorn, mule deer, prairie dog, white-tailed jack rabbit, coyote, long-tailed weasel, badger, elk, and bighorn sheep. In addition, and surprisingly, the captains consigned to Jefferson six live animals: four magpies (*Pica pica hudsonia*), one sharp-tailed grouse (*Pedioecetes phasianellus campestris*), and one prairie dog (*Cynomys ludovicianus ludovicianus*).

The attempt to ship live animals from the remote Dakota plains across the intervening miles to the Executive Mansion on the Potomac doubtless originated in the enterprising mind of Lewis. It was an audacious move, a calculated risk. Certain it is that Jefferson, in his comprehensive instructions to the two leaders, had included no suggestion to this effect; he had insisted only on their paying close attention to "the animals of the country generally, & especially those not known to the U.S." (VII, 249).

The cargo left Fort Mandan aboard the keel-boat in charge of Corporal Warfington. No mention is made in any of the journals as to what person, or persons, had been assigned the responsibility of caring for the live animals—cleaning cages, supplying water and food, and the like. However, one such person at least seems to have been Antoine Tabeau, the experienced trader whom Lewis and Clark had first met, it will be recalled, at the Arikara villages the previous fall. He had provided the captains with much useful information and was even then writing an account of his many and varied experiences and observations. In this account (subsequently published) Tabeau wrote that he

[65] Rodney H. True, "Some Neglected Botanical Results of the Lewis and Clark Expedition," *Procs. Amer. Phil. Soc.,* 67 (1928), 18.

had brought downriver from the Arikara villages a prairie dog that Lewis was sending to the President of the United States and he had found through experiment that that singular animal never drank, and that "Capt. Lewis had already kept it three months without being able to make it swallow a drop of water, although it accepted very readily biscuit, corn, nuts, etc."[66]

Forty-five days after leaving Fort Mandan, the keel-boat tied up at St. Louis after a journey of approximately 1,600 miles. Here the shipment was turned over to Pierre Chouteau, one of the men who had most actively assisted Lewis and Clark the previous year in getting the Expedition underway. Chouteau at once had his hands full. It was up to him to provide quarters for the Indians (Arikara, Sioux, Omaha, Oto, and Missouri chiefs taken aboard the barge on its way downstream and comprising the second delegation that would visit Jefferson) and make all necessary arrangements for their further journey. He had responsibility, too, for the welfare of the natural history specimens and for determining the route best calculated to get them safely to the President. Proof that all six live animals had survived the voyage down the Missouri to St. Louis is to be found in an existing letter stating that one Henry K. Mullin had been paid the sum of $5 "for keeping four magpies, a prairie hen [sharp-tailed grouse] and a prairie dog."[67]

Three weeks went by. On June 12 Chouteau wrote Jefferson that he had received Lewis and Clark's trunks and the cages of live animals and had shipped them to New Orleans. "I thought that this would be the surest way to have these animals arrive safe and sound in federal city."[68] At about this same date he addressed himself to William C. C. Claiborne, Governor of Orleans: "Capn. Lewis having sent by his barge from the Missoury river two trunks, two cages or boxes with some birds and one ditto with a prairy Dog, which are to be send according to his instructions, to the President of the United States, I send them to you by Mr. Mallock according to his receipt here annexed, as the only proper authority to take them with safety to Washington city. I beg you will give me notice of theyr safe arrival at New Orleans."[69]

About three weeks later, after following the meanderings of the

[66] Abel, *Tabeau's Narrative of Loisel's Expedition to the Upper Missouri,* 83n.
[67] Pierre Chouteau Letterbook, Missouri Historical Society. See also Jackson, *Letters,* 249n. Mullin was a sergeant in Capt. Amos Stoddard's company in the Regiment of Artillerists.
[68] Pierre Chouteau Letterbook.
[69] Jackson, *Letters,* 248–249.

Mississippi some 1,000 miles, the cargo reached Claiborne, who forthwith wrote Jefferson that he had received several trunks and boxes, a cage with four birds and "a small living animal somewhat resembling our common Gray Squirrel." The little animal, he went on to say: "seems to be sick & I fear will not live. The Birds are well, and have excellent appetites; I shall be very careful of them, and propose forwarding the whole to Baltimore by the Ship Comet that will probably sail for that port in fifteen days."[70]

Two days later Claiborne wrote the President again, this time to advise him that the prairie dog was on the mend and he had hopes that it would live. As the sailing date of the *Comet* neared, he penned a note to the Collector of Baltimore: "I have taken the Liberty to address to your care one Hoggshead three Boxes and two Cases directed to the President of the United States and which were this day put on Board the Ship Comet Captain McNeal bound for Baltimore. The Hoggshead & Boxes Contain curiosities which were collected by Captain Lewis in his Voyage up the Missouri; in one case is a living animal called the wild dog of the Prairie, and in the other are four Birds, called the Missouri Magpies. I hope they may reach you safely, and I must ask the favour of you to forward them by land, to the city of Washington."[71]

Since Claiborne makes no mention in his letters of the grouse, it must be taken for granted that it had died en route to New Orleans. One can only guess at the cause of death: malnutrition, radical temperature change, confinement, neglect—each a valid possibility. Even if it had been in the hands of a person trained in the care of birds, it might still have died. The wonder is that the four magpies and the "wild dog of the Prairie" had survived.

In the days ahead the *Comet* entered the Gulf, rounded the Florida peninsula, and followed up the east coast to Chesapeake Bay. In Baltimore the collector of that port promptly placed the consignment on a vehicle bound for Washington. On August 12 the Executive Mansion's major-domo, Etienne Lemaire, wrote Jefferson (then in Monticello) saying: "I have just received by Baltimore a barrel and 4 boxes, and a kind of cage in which there is a little animal very much resembling the squirrel, and in the other a bird resembling the magpie of Europe. . . ."[72] In a subsequent letter Lemaire advised the President

[70] Jackson, *Letters*, 250.
[71] Jackson, *Letters*, 253.
[72] Jackson, *Letters*, 253–254.

that he had put the magpie and prairie dog "in the room where Monsieur receives his callers."[73]

At about this same time, perhaps in the same mail with Lemaire's letter, Jefferson received information from Henry Dearborn about the shipment in general and the condition of the live animals:

> The various articles sent by Captain Lewis by the way of New Orleans arrived yesterday at your house from Baltimore. Suspecting that vermin had made their way into the packages, I took the liberty of requesting your Steward to have the boxes opened, in which there were great numbers of vermin. I then had the cask opened in which the Buffalo Robes & other dressed articles were packed, all which were in Good order, no vermin having found their way into the cask, but as the robes & other skins appeared a little damp, I advised Le Mare to have them exposed to a dry air for twenty four hours & then after sprinkling them with snuff, to have them separately covered with linnen & put into trunks or boxes, and within three or four weeks to have them examined and aired if necessary. The undressed skins, the skeletons, horns, &c. &c., I directed to be cleaned from vermin, and after being exposed to the air for one day, to be put into boxes. The box containing, as I presumed, minerals & earths, was not opened. One magpie and the little burrowing dog or squirrel, are alive and appear healthy, the latter is undoubtedly of the family of what we call woodchucks, or ground hogs. The Buffalo robes are good skins, well dressed, and highly embellished with Indian finery. Some of the undressed skins are considerably injured, but I hope they will receive no further injury.[74]

As this letter makes grievously evident, three of the four magpies had died in transit from New Orleans to Washington. The incredible fact remains, however, that the two animals still alive had survived a journey of more than four months, in which time, on river barge and ocean-going vessel, they had travelled in excess of 4,000 miles, had experienced wide and sudden shifts in temperature, had been attended by at least half a dozen different caretakers, and had been provided with an unknown variety of foods. Only the hardiest of animals could have withstood the multiple abuses inherent in such a journey.

Damage to skins, such as Dearborn reported, occurred commonly in those days; entire shipments of great value were often completely destroyed. Much of the injury could have been avoided or at least reduced by proper cleaning and packaging, transporting at the right season of the year, and more frequent examination of packages en

[73] Jackson, *Letters,* 256.
[74] Jackson, *Letters,* 254–255.

route to trading posts. All such measures would have deterred insect activity responsible for most of the damage.

The skins shipped to Jefferson by Lewis and Clark would no doubt have fared much better if they had been transmitted during winter months instead of summer and if they had been carried overland instead of in holds of boats. It is a matter of record that the damage to furs in other shipments about this time from St. Louis to eastern cities by way of New Orleans was so great that the Superintendent of Indian Trade, Thomas McKenney, ordered all furs in future to be sent by land. "There is not room enough in a steam boat to unpack and beat the skins," he declared, "and the heat of her works would breed worms faster than they could be got out—nor will she stop long enough to perform this unpleasant and tedious operation on shore."[75]

The "worms" referred to were the larvae of insects, primarily those of clothes moths and certain Dermestid beetles, such as carpet beetles. These larvae, as almost every housewife knows, feed on organic matter of animal origin—woolens, furs, feathers, and the like. Certain other larvae, such as those of the skin beetles (*Trogidae*), subsist on dried, decomposing animal matter, and they cannot be ruled out when considering the "vermin" Dearborn mentioned. Today, napthalene, paradichlorobenzene, dieldren, chlordane, DDT, and other insecticides are widely used for controlling these moths and beetles.

What insect repellants, if any, Lewis and Clark used we have been unable to determine. Some of the traders of that period employed turpentine, others powdered tobacco (snuff). Charles Willson Peale had his own particular methods of preserving specimens, learned only after years of experimentation induced by insect damage in his museum. After finding turpentine inadequate, he "brewed a great kettle of arsenic solution in his garden, dipping the specimens therein and making himself thoroughly sick in the process. The final choice was arsenic for the skins of small birds and small animals, bichloride of mercury (corrosive sublimate) for the larger ones."[76] Here and there in his museum he displayed signs reading, "Do not touch the birds, they are covered with arsenic poison."[77]

On receipt of Lemaire's letter, Jefferson replied at once, instruct-

[75] Ora Brooks Peake, *A History of the United States Indian Factory System, 1795–1822* (Denver, 1954), 142.

[76] Sellers, *Charles Willson Peale,* I, 253.

[77] Sellers, *Charles Willson Peale,* I, 259.

ing him to open all packages of skins and furs, dry and repackage "in strong linen to keep the worm-fly out," and to take particular care "of the squirrel & pie . . . that I may see them alive at my return. Should any accident happen to the squirrel his skin & skeleton must be preserved. . . ."[78]

Some six weeks passed before Jefferson left the quiet pastoral environment of Monticello for the demanding official life of Washington. On his arrival (October 4), he had his first opportunity to examine the strange and exciting collection of objects Lewis and Clark had sent from Fort Mandan on the distant Upper Missouri. Acting upon what seems to have been a predetermined plan, he at once wrote Charles Willson Peale informing him that of the treasures received from the West, he proposed keeping certain horns, dressed skins, and Indian utensils to liven his Indian Hall at Monticello. A box of minerals, at Lewis's request, would go to the American Philosophical Society. The remainder of the items he was shipping to him for inclusion in the Peale Museum. He listed them as follows:

2 skins of the white hare
2 skeletons of do.
   A skeleton of the small or burrowing wolf of the prairie [coyote]
   A male and female Blaireau [badger] or burrowing dog of the prairies
      with the skeleton of the female
13 red fox skins
   Skins of the male & female antelope with their skeletons
2 skins of the burrowing squirrel of the prairies [prairie dog]
1 living burrowing squirrel of the prairies
1 living magpie
   A dead one preserved[79]

Acknowledging receipt of the above (October 22), Peale said in part that the prairie dog "is a handsome little Animal, smaller and much more gentle than our Monax [woodchuck] & I expect like it will not eat during the winter, for this eats but little at present. It shall be kept in a Warm Room for tryal. I am surprised to see the Magpie so correctly like that of Europe, for I have always found some difference in the Birds which has been discribed as belonging to both continents. It is interresting to get the living one in good condition, for a better comparison and also to give it a place near one I have from Great Britain handsomely mounted. I am very thankful for these additions to

[78] Jackson, *Letters*, 255.
[79] Jackson, *Letters*, 260–261.

the Museum, every thing that comes from Louisiana must be interresting to the Public."[80]

So the magpie and the prairie dog, still very much alive, had come to the end of their travels. Almost seven months after having been torn from their far-away grassland home, they had arrived in the scientific and intellectual capital of the western world and had been lodged in Independence Hall. How many of the thousands of visitors to Independence Hall today know that this most highly revered American shrine at one time housed a celebrated museum and for a brief period displayed two live animals sent from the distant Dakotas by America's foremost explorers?

No doubt business picked up appreciably at Peale's Museum as news spread throughout the city of the arrival of strange animals from "Louisiana," a name with a ring then almost as foreign as Kalihari and Katmandu today. Since scientists of the American Philosophical Society had a particular stake in the Lewis and Clark Expedition, they must have visited it often. Those figuring most prominently in the immediate future of the magpie and prairie dog were Dr. Barton, Alexander Wilson, and George Ord. Another interested visitor was Alexander Lawson (not a member), who has been called "the father of the art of engraving in this country."[81]

Dr. Barton had a good look at the prairie dog and voiced the opinion to Jefferson that it was: "Arctomys Citillus, common in the North of Asia, never known, before, to be a native of our Western cont[inent]."[82] It soon became apparent, however, that this gregarious burrowing rodent was new to science, with its range limited to the treeless plains of North America. George Ord reinforced that point when he technically described it in 1815 and gave it the name *Arctomys ludovicianus*. He based his description solely on Lewis and Clark's observations and their specimens in Peale's Museum.

Though a man of creditable attainments, George Ord (1781–1866) is today a relatively obscure figure among American scientists. Even his birthplace, whether Europe or America, is uncertain. A ships' chandler by vocation, he early became associated with that small, energetic group of more advanced naturalists who in 1812 founded the Academy of Natural Sciences of Philadelphia, and from

[80] Jackson, *Letters*, 267.
[81] Bayard H. Christy, "Alexander Lawson's Bird Engravings," *The Auk*, XLIII, no. 1 (Jan., 1926), 58.
[82] Jackson, *Letters*, 271.

1851 to 1858 he served as its president. He is best known among scientists for a biography of his close friend, Alexander Wilson, for completing Wilson's *American Ornithology* (after the latter's death in 1813), and for writing the first systematic work on the zoology of North America by an American.[83] Ord has one more claim to fame; he formally described more of the animals new to science discovered by Lewis and Clark than any other man. We are not done with him yet.

The prairie dog was still alive as late as April 5, 1806. On that date Peale informed Jefferson: "I will attemp[t] a description of the Marmot accompanied with a drawing of it, when it becomes more animated, as it must be soon, as the spring becomes warmer, at present it stirs but little."[84] This is the last report we have of the much-travelled "burrowing squirrel of the prairies." It may never have become more animated, for Peale's description and drawing have not come to light.

The magpie seems to have survived the winter. Some observers thought it identical with the European species. Jefferson had not expected this to be so. "From my observations while in Europe on the birds and quadrupeds of that quarter," he wrote Wilson, "I am of opinion there is not in our continent a single bird or quadruped which is not sufficiently unlike all the members of its family there to be considered specifically different."[85] However, ornithologists today regard the American magpie and its European congener as belonging to the same species (*Pica pica*). The two differ, however, subspecifically, as we remember Maximilian was quick to note when he arrived on the Upper Missouri in 1833.

After the magpie died, Peale mounted it. Wilson then used it as a model for his drawing that appeared in his multi-volume work on North American birds. Alexander Lawson contributed the engraving. (We will shortly return to Wilson and Lawson.)

To conclude our remarks on the live magpie and prairie dog, there remains only to add that not before or since have any other animals been privileged to reside in both the President's Mansion and Independence Hall and, in travels about the country, have passed through the solicitous hands of such a distinguished group of men as

---

[83] This first American "zoology" was published in 1815 in the "Second American Edition" of William Guthrie's *A New Geographical, Historical and Commercial Grammar; and Present State of the Kingdoms of the World,* Ord having been persuaded to make this contribution by the Philadelphia publishers, Johnson and Warner. Herein (2, 302) is his description of the prairie dog.

[84] Jackson, *Letters,* 302.

[85] Alexander Wilson, *Birds of America,* 9 vols. (Philadelphia, 1808–14) III, iii.

Captains Meriwether Lewis and William Clark; William Claiborne, Governor of Orleans; Henry Dearborn, Secretary of War; Thomas Jefferson, third President of the United States; Charles Willson Peale, eminent painter and Curator of the Philadelphia Museum; Alexander Wilson, outstanding artist-naturalist; and Alexander Lawson, foremost engraver.

[2]

As earlier stated, Lewis, after returning from the West, arrived in Philadelphia in April of 1807, bringing with him specimens collected from Fort Mandan to the Pacific and back that had not preceded him. Now a national hero, he was in much demand socially and so occupied professionally that he had little time for leisure. He did sit for a portrait by Peale[86] and attended three stated meetings of the American Philosophical Society (April 17, June 19, and July 17), some three and one-half years after his election to that organization. Lewis's main objective in Philadelphia was to arrange for the publication of his and Clark's journals. As a prospectus soon released attests, a correlative aim was "that every subject of natural history which is entirely new . . . shall be accompanied by the appropriate engraving illustrative of it."[87]

He turned at once to Alexander Wilson for bird portraits, and, as previously reported, to St. Mémin and Pursh for Indian and plant sketches. "It was the request and particular wish of Captain Lewis made to me in person," Wilson wrote following Lewis's death, "that I should make drawings of each of the feathered tribe as had been preserved, and were new."[88]

Wilson (1766–1813) had come to the United States in 1794 at the age of twenty-eight. Before leaving the British Isles, he had attended school briefly, learned the weaver's trade, written some indifferent poetry, peddled goods through the countryside, and spent a short period in prison for libel. Once in Philadelphia, he discovered friends and patrons in the persons of William Bartram (son of John Bartram), George Ord, and Alexander Lawson. Encouraged by these friends—who recognized his latent talents—Wilson undertook the task

---

[86] On Feb. 10, 1807, Peale had written Jefferson that he wished to make a portrait of Lewis for his Museum. (See Jackson, *Letters,* 373.) The portrait today is in the Independence National Historical Park Collection, along with that of Clark made by Peale in 1810.

[87] Jackson, *Letters,* 397.

[88] Wilson, *Birds of America,* III, 31–32.

of producing a comprehensive illustrated work on the birds of the United States, a most extraordinary undertaking since he then knew only a few of the commonest birds in this country and had had no formal training in drawing or technical writing. Yet, with the unremitting help of his recently acquired friends, he succeeded in completing seven of nine volumes of his *American Ornithology* (Ord, as mentioned, finished the work after Wilson's death). This was the first inclusive study of birds of the United States and is today a collector's item.

Of the birds Lewis and Clark brought back in 1806, Wilson made drawings of three. Not only that, he described and named them. One was the Louisiana (now western) tanager, *Piranga ludoviciana;* a second was Lewis's woodpecker, *Asyndesmus lewis;* and the third Clark's crow (today Clark's nutcracker), *Nucifraga columbiana.* The drawings subsequently appeared together on Plate XX in Volume III of Wilson's *American Ornithology,* this volume appearing in 1811.

Writing of the tanager, Wilson said:

This bird, and the two others that occupy the same plate, were discovered, in the remote regions of Louisiana, by an exploring party under the command of Captain George [*sic*] Merriwether Lewis and Lieutenant, now General William Clark, in their memorable expedition across the continent to the Pacific Ocean. They are entitled to a distinguished place in the pages of AMERICAN ORNITHOLOGY, both as being, till now, altogether unknown to naturalists, and as natives of what *is,* or at least *will be,* and that at no distant period, part of the territory of the United States. The frail remains of the bird now under consideration [i.e., western tanager] have been set up by Mr. Peale, in his Museum, with as much neatness as the state of the skin would permit.[89]

For more than 150 years ornithologists have been familiar with the fact that Wilson made drawings of Lewis's woodpecker and Clark's nutcracker. It has not been generally known, however, that Wilson's *original sketches* of these two birds—that is, the summary sketches he passed along to his engraver, Alexander Lawson—still exist and are prized possessions of the Academy of Natural Sciences of Philadelphia. These sketches, of course, differ perceptibly from the finished products that later appeared in Wilson's ornithological opus. I have examined them closely and find that Wilson made them on a good grade of white paper employing pen and ink primarily, though shading lightly with pencil here and there. I have used the word sketch advisedly, for

[89] Wilson, *Birds of America,* III, 27. Here we find proof that Peale mounted the tanager.

Wilson did little more than outline shape and posture and indicate claws, wings, and tail feathers. Also, he made no attempt to color or to draw to scale. For instance, he portrayed the woodpecker as eight inches long, while the actual length of the living bird is about 10½.

Wilson transmitted these rough sketches to Lawson, probably about 1810 (only a few months after Lewis's death). Since a close friendship existed between the two men, Lawson had no doubt indicated to Wilson exactly what he wanted in the way of a drawing—or all that he deemed necessary, provided Wilson stood over him to answer questions while he engraved. In fact, since Wilson had had no formal training in drawing, it is highly likely that William Bartram (who had helped illustrate Barton's *Botany*) and Lawson gave him the only lessons in drawing he ever received. M. E. Phillips, who edited *Proceedings* of the Academy of Natural Sciences, 1944–57, and is an authority on the life of Lawson, has advised me that most of Wilson's bird paintings were colored by Lawson's daughters. Lawson (1772–1845) has been generally overlooked in previous papers about the Lewis and Clark Expedition. According to one writer, his animal engravings were "incomparably superior to what was being produced elsewhere in America at that day."[90] He came to the United States from Scotland in 1792, two years before Wilson, and made Philadelphia his home. In succeeding years he became "intimately connected with American ornithology, and with the most elegant works on natural history that have been produced in this country."[91]

A comparison of Wilson's original black and white sketches of the woodpecker and nutcracker with the completed portraits in his *American Ornithology* reveal that they are identical in size and shape. Thus there can be little doubt that the former served as models for the latter.[92]

Some of us who, in classroom and elsewhere, have been bandying

[90] Christy, "Alexander Lawson's Bird Engravings," 56.
[91] Christy, "Alexander Lawson's Bird Engravings," 59.
[92] In May, 1807, Peale wrote: "The drawings for Governor Lewis's Journal I mean to draw myself to be engraved for the work." (See Jackson, *Letters,* 411.) One month later he had completed three drawings for Lewis which were "much to his [Lewis's] satisfaction" (Jackson, *Letters,* 411n). As to these drawings, Clark later wrote: "Mr. Peal has drawn three of the berds, the Braroe [badger] & Antilope, and an engraving has been made of the Big Horn and horned Lizard" (Jackson, *Letters,* 490). Extant today, at the American Philosophical Society, are Peale's drawings of Lewis's woodpecker and mountain quail (*Oreortyx pictus*). There is also a sketch of a horned toad ascribed to Peale, though Jackson (*Letters,* 277n, 411n) produces evidence that it was drawn by Pietro Ancora, a painter who came to Philadelphia in 1800. Peale's drawings of the badger and antelope have not been found.

Latin binomials like *Amoeba proteus* and *Homo sapiens* for much of our adult lives, find it difficult to accept the fact that at the time when Wilson produced generic and specific names for Lewis's woodpecker and Clark's nutcracker, there were only a few persons in the United States who endorsed the advantages afforded by the Linnaean system of classification and nomenclature, and fewer still who had won what Linnaeus called "everlasting remembrance" by technically describing and naming plants and animals. Most people were inclined to view the high-sounding Latin names with reserve if not actual disdain.

Though many plants and animals of our country had already been described, the work had been done almost entirely by European naturalists. Carolus Linnaeus, the great Swedish taxonomist who started it all, had been in the forefront, though others, like the Germans, J. F. Gmelin and P. S. Pallas, had been active. By way of evidence, if a scientist leafs through a modern check-list of animals, such as that of the American Ornithologists Union for North American birds, he will find that less than a score of the several hundred avian species and subspecies listed had been described by American naturalists prior to the return of Lewis and Clark from the Pacific. One also discovers, surprisingly, that quite a few of our birds, although well-known to naturalists, were yet unknown to science. For example, the whippoor-will (*Antrostomus vociferus*) did not acquire a Latin binomial until Gmelin provided one in 1812, and the ubiquitous crow (*Corvus brachyrhynchos*) was equally nameless until 1822.

Almost at once after Wilson described the three Lewis and Clark birds mentioned above, the taxonomic climate in the United States began to change. The example he had set was quickly followed by such other American naturalists as Ord, Rafinesque,[93] and Say,[94] and they also described animals returned by Lewis and Clark. A list follows:

Alexander Wilson

1811. Lewis's woodpecker, *Picus torquatus* Wilson = *Asyndesmus lewis* Riley.

[93] Constantine Samuel Rafinesque (1784–1842) was born in Turkey and came to Philadelphia in 1802. After a period as professor of botany at Transylvania University, Kentucky, he returned to Philadelphia where he wrote numerous books and pamphlets. A passion for creating new species and genera became a monomania with him.

[94] Thomas Say (1787–1834) was born in Philadelphia and became one of the founders of the Academy of Natural Sciences and a chief contributor to its *Journal*. He was geologist on the Long Expedition of 1819–20 and in 1825 accompanied Richard Owen to New Harmony, Indiana. His principal work is *American Entomology*, 3 vols. (Philadelphia, 1824–28).

1811. Clark's nutcracker, *Corvus columbianus* Wilson = *Nucifraga columbiana* (Wilson).

1811. Western tanager, *Tanagra ludoviciana* Wilson = *Piranga ludoviciana* (Wilson).

George Ord

1815. Columbian ground squirrel, *Arctomys columbianus* Ord = *Spermophilus columbianus columbianus* (Ord).

1815. Black-tailed prairie dog, *Arctomys ludoviciana* Ord = *Cynomys ludovicianus ludovicianus* (Ord).

1815. Bushy-tailed wood rat, *Mus cinereus* Ord = *Neotoma cinerea cinerea* (Ord).

1815. Grizzly bear, *Ursus horribilis* Ord.

1815. Mountain goat, *Ovis montanus* Ord = *Oreamnos americanus* (Blainville).

1815. Oregon ruffed grouse, *Tetrao fusca* Ord = *Bonasa umbellus sabini* (Douglas).

1815. Columbian sharp-tailed grouse, *Phasianus columbianus* Ord = *Pedioecetes phasianellus columbianus* (Ord).

1815. Pronghorn, *Antilope americana* Ord = *Antilocapra americana americana* (Ord).

1818. Western gray squirrel, *Sciurus griseus griseus* Ord.

1818. Eastern wood rat, *Mus floridana* Ord = *Neotoma floridana* (Ord).

Constantine Rafinesque

1817. Mountain beaver, *Anisonyx rufa* Rafinesque = *Aplodontia rufa rufa* (Raf.).

1817. Mule deer, *Cervus hemionus* Rafinesque = *Dama hemionus hemionus* (Raf.).

1817. Oregon bobcat, *Lynx fasciatus* Rafinesque = *Lynx rufus fasciatus* Raf.

1818. Prairie rattler, *Crotalus viridis viridis* (Rafinesque).

Thomas Say

1823. Short-tailed shrew, *Sorex brevicauda* Say = *Blarina brevicauda brevicauda* (Say).

1823. Coyote, *Canis latrans* Say.

1823. Plains gray wolf, *Canis nubilis* Say = *Canis lupus nubilis* Say.

1823. Swift fox (kit), *Canis velox* Say = *Vulpes velox velox* (Say).

It goes without saying that if Lewis had lived to write the account of the Expedition (including a volume devoted exclusively to science), then he, instead of Wilson, Ord, and the others, would today be recognized and honored as the discoverer and describer of most if not all of the above species. He would receive credit, too, for other species described at later dates, such as the sage grouse (*Centrocercus urophasianus urophasianus*) described by Charles Lucien Bonaparte in 1827; mountain quail (*Oreortyx pictus pictus*) by David Douglas in 1837; white-tailed jack rabbit (*Lepus townsendii campanius*) by John Bachman in 1837; poor-will (*Phalaenoptilus nuttallii nuttallii*) by John James Audubon in 1839; and piñon jay (*Gymnorhinus cyanocephalus*) by Maximilian in 1841.

Taxonomists then, as now, disagreed on nomenclature. There was no meeting of the minds, for example, on the proper technical name for the prairie dog. In 1815, as we know, George Ord, regarding this animal as a marmot, had christened it *Arctomys ludoviciana*. Two years later Rafinesque renamed it *Cynomys socialis*. In 1825 Richard Harlan[95] got into the act by calling it *Arctomys latrans*. The matter did not resolve itself until 1858 when S. F. Baird proposed *Cynomys ludovicianus*, the name which has stood up since.

Such resultant confusion in synonomy, as well as a developing penchant for creating new species on questionable grounds, soon brought deserved, heavy-handed censure. One contemporary naturalist, Dr. John D. Godman, acrimoniously challenged the farrago of "barbarous new names" and deplored the flood of "genera and species, founded on trivial, accidental, or imperfectly noted differences between creatures which, to all rational observers, appear the same."[96] Conversely, he praised men like Thomas Say who adhered to original nomenclature.

As taxonomic activity increased in Philadelphia, so did literature about American animals. Wilson's *American Ornithology* (1808–14) was soon followed by George Ord's "Zoology," actually a section of some 70 pages devoted to vertebrate animals in William Guthrie's *A New Geographical, Historical, and Commercial Grammar; and Present State of the Kingdoms of the World* (2nd American edition,

---

[95] Richard Harlan (1796–1843) was born in Philadelphia and practiced medicine there after graduating from the University of Pennsylvania Medical School. In 1821 he was elected professor of comparative anatomy of the Philadelphia Museum. He published *Fauna Americana* (1825) and *American Herpetology* (1827), these being the works for which he is best known.

[96] Dr. John D. Godman, *American Natural History*, 3 vols. (Philadelphia, 1826), I, xv. Godman (1794–1830) was born in Maryland, studied medicine in Baltimore, and practiced in various places, including Philadelphia. He was professor of natural history in the Franklin Institute of Pennsylvania and a member of the American Philosophical Society and Academy of Natural Sciences.

1815) ;[97] Dr. Richard Harlan's *Fauna Americana; being a Description of the Mammiferous Animals Inhabiting North America* (1825) ; Dr. John D. Godman's *American Natural History* (1826–28) ; and J. and T. Doughty's *The Cabinet of Natural History and American Rural Sports* (1830–32) .[98]

With these published works American zoology, as we think of it today, had its inception. Though about animals, they bore little resemblance to zoological texts of the twentieth century, their content being limited almost entirely to birds and mammals. The authors gave scant space to reptiles, amphibians, and fishes and practically none at all to the vast concourse of invertebrate animals; and they, of course, supplied no chapters on such subjects as physiology, embryology, ecology, and genetics which occupy so much space in modern texts. Significantly, these books were all published in Philadelphia and, for the most part, written by Philadelphians who had access to Peale's Museum and consequently to the Lewis and Clark specimens. We have little doubt that the impetus for the publication of these works arose in some measure from that collection. All four texts contain frequent references to Lewis and Clark animals, and two of them (those by Godman and the Doughtys) provided illustrations of grizzly bear, American badger, coyote, antelope, prairie dog, bighorn, "moose deer," and mountain goat. These animal portraits, by such contemporary artists as Alexander Rider[99] and Charles A. Lesueur,[100] deserve particular attention because the majority of them were of animals not previously figured. Godman's *American Natural History* was unique in that it was the first illustrated "zoology" text published in the United States, just as Wilson's book had been the first illustrated ornithology in this country.

Early references to Lewis and Clark specimens appeared in such

[97] William Guthrie (1708–70) was a schoolmaster in Aberdeen and, later, author in London. The second American edition of his "Grammar" is supposed to have been the work of John Knox.

[98] T. Doughty (1793–1856) was Thomas Doughty, a Philadelphia artist, sometimes referred to as "a pleasing landscape painter." J. Doughty was his brother.

[99] Alexander Rider, a historical and miniature painter, came to Philadelphia from Germany in 1811. He produced illustrations of the prairie dog and bighorn for Godman and antelope for the Doughtys.

[100] Charles A. Lesueur (1778–1846) was a French artist who came to the U.S. in 1816. He wrote widely on ichthyology, particularly on genus *Catostomus*, and furnished most of the plates which lent distinction to early volumes of the *Journal* of the Academy of Natural Sciences. He also made drawings of grizzly bear, badger, coyote, antelope, and mountain goat for Godman.

other printed matter of the day as *The Philadelphia Medical and Physical Journal* (founded and edited by Dr. Barton), *Transactions* of the American Philosophical Society, and the *Journal* of the Academy of Natural Sciences. George Ord, for instance, published his original description of the mountain goat in the first volume of the Academy's *Journal.* "It is to Captain Lewis," he wrote, "to whom belongs the honour of having been the first to assure his countrymen, by the exhibition of a genuine specimen that the animal does exist." Ord's calling it a sheep *(Ovis montana)*, when it is a goat, led to all sorts of nomenclatural confusion at later dates.

If Lewis and Clark had discovered living mammoths or mastodons in the West, as Jefferson and Wistar had thought possible, then that event would doubtless have transcended other zoological achievements. But they did almost as well with grizzly bear, pronghorn, mule deer, prairie dog, and magpie.

The activity, taxonomic and otherwise, generated by the arrival of these animals in the East went beyond what we have previously described. Almost at once men began to lay plans to visit the country of silence, space, and wide serenity reported by Lewis and Clark. The next few decades saw a succession of determined naturalists crossing the Mississippi and heading west along the Missouri, Platte, and Arkansas Rivers, each motivated to a degree by the accomplishments of Lewis and Clark. These men—John Bradbury, Thomas Nuttall, Titian Peale, Thomas Say, John Townsend, and John James Audubon, to mention a few—would greatly extend existing knowledge of western plants and animals. The far-reaching effects of the Lewis and Clark Expedition suffer depreciation if the achievements of these individuals are slighted.

[3]

As previously reported, several of the Lewis and Clark specimens, following the demise of Peale's Museum, went to the Boston Museum. Here they remained, unheralded and relatively unnoticed, until the turn of the century some fifty years later. On February 9, 1900, Charles J. Maynard, a New England dealer in specimens of natural history, wrote Witmer Stone, then Curator of Birds in the Academy of Natural Sciences. Maynard advised Stone that he had recently acquired "a large portion" of the birds formerly in Peale's Museum, that many of them had unquestionably been mounted by Peale, and that some, presented to Peale by George Washington, were so labelled.

A few days later Maynard wrote Stone again, saying: "Thank you for your kindness in replying to my questions about the Peale collection. I have that collection, or a greater portion of it, as far as the birds are concerned, beyond a shadow of doubt. There are few men living better able to prove this than myself. The collection itself, however, furnishes ample proof of this, first in the fact that some of the birds were marked (and one still is) as having been presented by Gen. Washington; second, that here are Alexander Wilson's birds. The labels have been changed, unfortunately, but no one can look at them without seeing their resemblance to Wilson's plates."[101]

Maynard made no attempt to keep his acquisition a secret. On April 13 of that same year he inserted a notice in the *Boston Evening Transcript* stating that he would exhibit the birds and that "Two of the most valuable birds in the collection are an English skylark, from the old Charles Willson Peale collection made [beginning] in 1784 in Philadelphia, and a Golden Pheasant presented to Mr. Peale by George Washington. These specimens have recently been discovered by C. J. Maynard of Newtonville, after having been lost for over fifty years."[102]

Apparently Maynard and Stone continued to correspond, with the former supplying additional information about the birds he had acquired; for somewhat later Stone reported: "Among them, Mr. Maynard informs me, is a specimen of Lewis's woodpecker, without much doubt the original specimen [collected by Lewis], and probably the only one of this historic collection that is still extant" (VI, 121n).

Maynard stored these specimens in his barn at Newtonville where they remained until they were obtained from him by the Boston Society of Natural History. Soon afterwards they "were wrenched from their stands and packed into tin cases, to the great detriment of their legs and plumage," and such original labels as still existed "were removed from the specimens and put into a paper envelope which was afterwards lost."[103] In 1914 this priceless collection, or what was left of it, found a home in the Museum of Comparative Zoology, Harvard University, where it is today.

Even staid Harvard scientists manifested excitement over this acquisition, with the result that Walter Faxon (incidentally Theodore Roosevelt's zoology teacher in the late 1870's) soon gave it his close personal attention "with a view to the recovery of specimens described

[101] Maynard-Stone correspondence is from Manuscript Collection, No. 450, Library of Academy of Natural Sciences.
[102] Faxon, "Relics of Peale's Museum," 126.
[103] Faxon, "Relics of Peale's Museum," 126–127.

and figured by Wilson in his 'American Ornithology'." In an engaging article entitled "Relics of Peale's Museum," he reported on a total of 53 North American birds, most of which were very probably the originals of Wilson's figures. One of them was a Lewis's woodpecker. About it Faxon wrote: "A single venerable looking specimen, probably either the type, which was No. 2020 of the Peale Museum (Lewis and Clark Expedition), or else one of the two individuals shot by T. R. Peale near the Rocky Mountains, on the Long Expedition, I presume."[104]

This bird skin is still at the Museum of Comparative Zoology, more than 50 years after Faxon wrote the above, and an even more "venerable looking specimen" now. But is it one of the specimens collected by Lewis in 1806 while at Camp Chopunnish on the Clearwater River in Idaho? Witmer Stone, for one, thought it likely. If so, then it is the only animal known to exist (as Stone surmised) of all those collected and brought back by the Expedition. The only other zoological material I have been able to locate are elk and moose antlers at Monticello and a single mountain goat horn in the Filson Club, Louisville, Kentucky. Of these, the moose antlers may be suspect, since there is no mention in any of the Lewis and Clark journals of a moose being killed during the course of the continental transit. However, that does not rule out the possibility of moose antlers having been picked up along the way.

Now is the appropriate moment, I believe, to reflect on Peale's repeated attempts to have his museum nationally endowed. As early as 1802 he enquired of Jefferson as to "whether the United States would give an encouragement and make provision for the establishment of this Museum in the city of Washington." He entertained fears, he said, "that some fatal stroke may scatter the precious deposits, the fruits of so many years of anxious care."[105] Each such effort, then and thereafter, ended in failure, though not even in his moments of greatest concern did he envision how calamitous the "fatal stroke" would actually be, how irretrievably his "precious deposits" would be scattered and lost. He made a final effort in 1818–19. When this attempt also proved fruitless—because Congress regarded Washington as too small to support a museum—he made a perceptive prediction. "The time will come," he said, "when they shall be sorry for having let it slip through their fingers."[106] O his prophetic soul!

[104] Faxon, "Relics of Peale's Museum," 136.
[105] Sellers, *Charles Willson Peale*, II, 150.
[106] Sellers, *Charles Willson Peale*, II, 322.

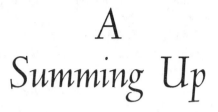

A
Summing Up

CHAPTER TWENTY-THREE

It took time for the world to comprehend the magnitude of Lewis and Clark's achievements—if, indeed, it has to this day. In pages to follow, I shall attempt to enumerate the more significant ones as they have crystallized in the course of this study, presenting them under five headings: ethnological, geographical, zoological, botanical, and general.

Ethnology

Lewis and Clark initiated the first official relations between the United States government and Indians of the Missouri Valley, Rocky Mountains, and Columbia watershed.

They were actual discoverers of such important tribes as Shoshoni, Flathead, Nez Perce, Yakima, Walula, and Wishram.

They defined, in effect, the three great cultural areas of the West, namely, Plains, Plateau, and Northwest Coast.

They instituted the first language studies of at least six different trans-Mississippi linguistic families: Siouan, Caddoan, Shoshonean, Salishan, Sahaptian, and Chinookan.

In spite of difficulties interposed by language barriers, they obtained and recorded abundant valuable ethnological data on a wide spectrum of topics, ranging from pathology, population, and physical characteristics to weapons, apparel, habitations, and seasonal round of activities.

Of some one hundred "abstract queries" submitted by Jefferson, Dr. Rush, and others, Lewis and Clark acquired answers to practically all at one point or another in their 28-month journey.

Lewis's descriptions of the Shoshoni and Lower Columbian Chinookan tribes rate as classics among early accounts of American Indians.

Lewis and Clark's comprehensive data on aspects of material culture serve time and again as departures for comparative studies.

All modern studies of prehistoric and historic trade among the Indians of the Upper Missouri perforce draw initially from Lewis and Clark's "Estimate of the Eastern Indians," perennially important as the first survey of these tribes.

Much of the data obtained by Lewis and Clark on the several Chinookan tribes have particular value today because with the virtual extinction of these Indians in the 1830's, comparable data have since been unobtainable.

Geography

Lewis and Clark succeeded in accomplishing Jefferson's basic goal, which was "to explore the Missouri river, & such principal streams of it, as it's course of communication with the waters of the Pacific Ocean, may offer the most direct & practicable water communication across the continent. . ." (VII, 248) .

They were the first to recognize and describe the broad general physiographic areas through which they travelled between the Mississippi River and the Pacific Ocean.

They ended the long, long search for an overland Northwest Passage.

They established the fact that the North American continent was wider than had been supposed.

They determined that the Columbia, until then regarded as a relatively small coastal stream, was a mighty continental river with a vast interior drainage.

They confirmed the true greatness of the Missouri and at the same time disproved the erroneous prevailing notion that it headed in the Southwest.

They discovered that two mountain systems (Rockies and Cascade Range) , instead of one, separated the headwaters of the Missouri from the Pacific Ocean.

They surveyed the entire route from the Mississippi to the Pacific and made astronomical observations at "all remarkable points" (VII, 248) .

They discovered and named hundreds of topographic features, each of which Clark laid down on a series of maps that established him as a cartographer of rare talent. (Today more towns, rivers, creeks, counties, animals, and plants bear the names of Lewis and Clark than any other figures in American history with the possible exception of such illustrious leaders as Washington, Jefferson, Franklin, and Lincoln.)

Clark's final map delineating the entire route from Wood River to Cape Disappointment is recognized by modern mapmakers as "a major contribution to the geographic knowledge of Western North America."[1]

Zoology

Meriwether Lewis contributed importantly to the development of American zoology by making the first faunal studies in the newly acquired Louisiana Territory and by heeding Jefferson's directive to observe "the animals of the country generally, & especially those not known in the U.S." (VII, 249) .

He discovered and made known to the world numerous fish, reptiles, birds, and mammals unheard of previously.

He was the first to collect bird-skins, horns, bones, hides, and other zoölogical material and to ship these—and new species of live animals —from western habitats to eastern communities.

Lewis greatly extended the ranges of animals previously not known to exist west of the Mississippi. For example, he widened the range of the passenger pigeon to include all that region between the mouth of the Missouri and its source in the Rocky Mountains.

He was the first to describe many western animals and in language sufficiently detailed and technical to make determinations of these animals an easy matter for later naturalists who read his descriptions.

By making numerous observations on the relations of western animals to their environment, Lewis initially introduced ecological methods of study to regions beyond the Mississippi. His discovery that prairie dogs never drink water is a case in point.

The Lewis and Clark journals and collections, soon made available to learned men, had the immediate effect of stimulating zoological activity in such diverse fields as taxonomy, animal portraiture, publication, and museum development.

Excited by Lewis and Clark's zoological discoveries, other naturalists soon joined succeeding government-sponsored expeditions dispatched to the West.

[1] Friis, "Cartographic and Geographic Activities of the Lewis and Clark Expedition," 351.

American zoology, as a science distinct from natural history, took firm root, in part at least, from the discoveries of Lewis and Clark.

Botany

As naturalist to the Expedition, Meriwether Lewis greatly enriched American botany by making the first studies of plants indigenous to western plains, mountains, deserts, and river valleys.

He was the first to collect and preserve specimens of herbs, shrubs, and trees in these then remote areas of our country.

He extended the range of many plants heretofore known only east of the Mississippi.

Lewis initiated phenological studies in the West by assembling information which correlated weather data with periodic biological phenomena.

Many of the plants discovered and described proved to be new species, and a few were soon recognized as constituting new genera (for example, *Lewisia* and *Clarkia*).

By describing numerous plants used by the Indians medicinally, nutritionally, and in other ways, Lewis proved himself to be a capable ethnobotanist.

Lewis and Clark were the first to introduce valuable trans-Mississippi herbs and shrubs to the Atlantic seaboard. From seeds, roots, and cuttings, eastern gardeners were soon successfully growing western plants.

The most important tangible botanical result of the Expedition was a collection of more than 200 dried, preserved specimens constituting today the Lewis and Clark Herbarium in the Academy of Natural Sciences of Philadelphia.

General

Lewis and Clark introduced new approaches to exploration and set a pattern for future similar expeditions by systematically recording abundant data on a wide range of subjects such as weather, fauna, flora, geography, and Indians.

Lewis and Clark's topographic discoveries and resultant maps became prime foundation stones on which Americans constructed their claim to "Oregon."

Their reports on the abundance of beaver and other important fur-bearing animals on Missouri and Columbian waters resulted in the development of the American fur trade in the West.

A most important consequence of the Expedition was the publication of the Lewis and Clark journals which are, of course, among the glories of American history. They have long since established themselves as classics in the vast literature of discovery and exploration. Paraphrasing Elliott Coues, "The more closely they are scanned, in light of present knowledge, the more luminous they appear."[2]

The journey stands, incomparably, as the transcendent achievement of its kind in this hemisphere, if not in the entire world. Whereas Louisiana Territory had been "an area of rumor, guess and fantasy,"[3] now that Lewis and Clark had revealed it, it was a focus of reality.

[2]

There remains the task of attempting to refute a double-barrelled criticism levelled at Jefferson and Lewis: that Jefferson was at fault in not choosing a "trained naturalist" to accompany the Expedition and that Lewis, by inference, had no valid claim to the title of naturalist. Elliott Coues, although an admirer of Lewis, seems to have been the first to cast doubt on Jefferson's judgment when (in 1893) he wrote: ". . . the most serious defect in the organization of the Expedition was the lack of some trained scientist."[4] Others have since made the same criticism, with some going so far as to disparage Lewis and Clark's botanical and zoological contributions. For instance, in evaluating the work of early American naturalists in the West, one team of writers opined that "little need be said here concerning the famous Lewis and Clark expedition of 1804, since no trained naturalist was included in the party."[5]

In this instance, Jefferson was wiser than his critics. His main problem, as Donald Jackson has aptly pointed out, "was to get a few men to the Pacific and back, encumbered no more than necessary by equipment, and intelligent enough to recognize and collect . . . the natural resources of the region."[6] But there was another reason why Jefferson did not choose a "trained naturalist," one previously unmentioned so far as I have been able to determine. Trained naturalists did not exist in America at that time—trained, that is, in the sense that they had pursued a course of study in college or university to prepare them for that specialization. Many of the naturalists of the day (or

[2] Coues, I, vi.

[3] DeVoto, *The Journals of Lewis and Clark,* iii.

[4] Coues, I, xx.

[5] Roland H. Alden and John D. Ifft, "Early Naturalists in the Far West," *Occasional Papers of Calif. Acad. Scis.,* No. XX (San Francisco, 1943), 19.

[6] Jackson, *Letters,* 218n.

natural philosophers as they were often called), men like Benjamin Smith Barton, Caspar Wistar, John Godman, Thomas Jefferson, and Henry Muhlenberg, had been formally educated not as naturalists, but as physicians, lawyers, and preachers of the gospel. Their genuine, enthusiastic preoccupation with animals, plants, and other aspects of nature was purely avocational. Others, though professional men, had experienced no academic training in any field. For example, Alexander Wilson was a weaver by trade, Thomas Nuttall a printer, C. S. Rafinesque a merchant, Thomas Say an apothecary, George Ord a ships' chandler, and John Bartram a farmer. All of these men had gained their knowledge of fauna and flora through their own efforts or from instruction provided freely by other self-taught individuals. If any of them enjoyed a biological edge on Meriwether Lewis, it came not through any formal training but from added years of field experience and a greater command of Linnaean nomenclature.

A modest man, Lewis recognized and even exaggerated his shortcomings. One day while at Fort Clatsop he sat down to describe Douglas fir, Sitka spruce, and other great evergreen trees constituting the forest surrounding him. He began by saying, "I shall describe [them] as well as my slender botanical skil will enable me" (IV, 41). But, as we should know by now, Lewis was blessed with capabilities often missing in naturalists, particularly an outstanding, inherent observational competence, an all-inclusive interest, and an objective, systematic, philosophical approach to understanding the natural world. Nothing refutes Lewis's self-appraisal, and deprecating remarks of others, more eloquently than his own abundant writing, so much of which has been presented in preceding pages.

In the context of the day, Lewis was an unusually capable naturalist, one with attitudes more consistent with scientists of the twentieth century than with those of his own.

When Thomas Jefferson wrote his own epitaph, he said he wanted to be remembered for three things: as author of the Declaration of Independence; as creator of the statute of Virginia for religious freedom; and as founder of the University of Virginia. If Jefferson had realized "how central the Lewis and Clark Expedition was to a particularly golden age in American history,"[7] and the full scope of its accomplishments, then he, motivated by the same sense of values that caused him to list the founding of the University of Virginia as one of the three rubrics in his epitaph, might well have added a fourth.

[7] Letter from Helen B. West to author, June 1, 1967.

Appendix A

Plants Discovered by Lewis and Clark

The only previously attempted catalogue of plants discovered by Lewis and Clark was Elijah H. Criswell's "The Botanical Index," which appeared in his 1940 monograph, *Lewis and Clark: Linguistic Pioneers.* Criswell characterized it as "a complete list not only of the new species discovered, but also of all the species . . . mentioned by the discoverers." A valuable catalogue, it is regrettable that the author did not separate those species actually discovered by the explorers from those previously discovered by others, and also that he failed to include many of those plants collected by Lewis which today comprise the Lewis and Clark Herbarium in the Academy of Natural Sciences of Philadelphia.

I shall not list all plants mentioned by the leaders of the Expedition, only those which had not been formally described on the dates they encountered them and were, therefore, unknown to the scientific world at large. Some had been previously collected. For example, Archibald Menzies, English botanist with Vancouver, had visited the Northwest in 1792 and collected specimens of grand fir, *Abies grandis,* the plant which heads my list; but Menzies did not describe it. Meriwether Lewis first described the grand fir (in 1806), though he failed to publish his description; that task was performed later (1833) by another English botanist, John Lindley. Thus, if Lewis had been successful in publishing his projected volume on the scientific accomplishments of the Expedition and had included his description of *Abies grandis,* then his name would today be associated with its discovery rather than that of Lindley. My basis for inclusion, therefore, as indicated, hinges on whether the plant in question encountered by Lewis and Clark had earlier been technically described.

I have listed the plants alphabetically by scientific name (instead of employing the sequence generally adopted by botanists in taxonomic works), and have arranged data in three columns. The first includes scientific and common names, requisite synonymy, publications in which original descriptions appeared, and the all-important publication dates. The second contains (1) data in the form of quotations from Lewis or Pursh, taken, unless otherwise stated, from the herbarium sheets and (2) reference sources. The third column indicates precise localities where Lewis collected and/or encountered each dated plant.

I preface those plants of the Lewis and Clark Herbarium appearing in my list with an upper-case "A" (for Academy). Those of this collection that had been carried by Pursh to England (often referred to as Lambert specimens) are prefaced with a capital "L." Those which have been designated by botanists as type specimens I have preceded with "T." Questionable determinations are preceded by interrogation marks.

For nomenclature, I have relied primarily on (1) *Illustrated Flora of the Northern States and Canada* by Britton and Brown; (2) *Vascular Plants of the Pacific Northwest* by Hitchcock, Cronquist, Ownley, and Thompson; and (3) *Illustrated Flora of the Pacific States* by Abrams and Ferris. I have been materially aided, too, by *Check List of Native and Naturalized Trees of the United States* (Agriculture Handbook No. 41) by Little; Criswell's "Botanical Index"; Elliott Coues' numerous annotations in *History of the Expedition Under the Command of Lewis and Clark;* and "The Plants of Lewis and Clark's Expedition Across the Continent, 1804–1806" by Thomas Meehan. Coues relied mainly on F. H. Knowlton of the U.S. National Museum for botanical determinations, and Thwaites on C. V. Piper, Washington State University botanist, and William Trelease, Director of the Missouri Botanical Garden, St. Louis.

BOTANICAL CATALOGUE

Abies grandis Lindley.
Penny Cyclop., 1:30. 1833.
GRAND FIR.

Thwaites, IV, 45 (identified by C. V. Piper); Coues, III, 831.

Described by Lewis, Feb. 6, 1806, at Fort Clatsop, Clatsop Co., Oregon.

Abies lasiocarpa (Hook.) Nutt.
= *Pinus lasiocarpa* Hooker.
Fl. Bor. Am., 2:163. 1842.
SUBALPINE FIR.

Thwaites, III, 69; Coues, III, 831.

Lolo Trail. Bitterroot Mountains, Idaho Co., Idaho. Sept. 15, 1805.

A.L.T. *Acer circinatum* Pursh.
Fl. Am. Sept., 1:267. 1814.
VINE MAPLE.

"On the great rapids of Columbia, Octbr. [?], 1805." Thwaites, IV, 57; Coues, III, 834.

The great rapids (Cascades) were reached on Oct. 30. Below Wind River. Skamania Co., Wash., on north, and Hood River Co., Oregon, on south.

Acer glabrum Torrey.
N.Y. Lyc. Nat. Hist. Am., 2:172. 1828.
ROCKY MOUNTAIN MAPLE.

Thwaites, II, 337; V, 137; Coues, II, 487.

First encountered, Aug. 13, 1805, on Lemhi River, Lemhi Co., Idaho.

A.L.T. *Acer macrophyllum* Pursh.
Fl. Am. Sept., 1:267. 1814.
BIGLEAF MAPLE.

"A large timber tree from the grand rapids of the Columbia. Apr. 10, 1806." Thwaites, III, 174; IV, 57; Coues, II, 679; III, 834.

Collected at Cascades below Wind River. Site now covered by water behind Bonneville Dam.

? *Actaea arguta* Nuttall
= *A. spicata* var. *arguta*
Torr.
Torr. & Gray Fl. N. Amer., 1:35. 1838.
WESTERN RED BANEBERRY.

Thwaites, II, 337; Coues, III, 488 (identified by Coues).

Encountered by Lewis, Aug. 13, 1805, on Lemhi River, Lemhi Co., Idaho.

A.L.T. *Actinella lanata* Pursh
= *Eriophyllum lanatum* (Pursh) Forbes.
Fl. Am. Sept., 2:560. 1814.
OREGON SUNSHINE.

"On the uplands on the Kooskooskee [Clearwater] River. June 6th, 1806." Thwaites, IV, 323 (det. by C. V. Piper).

Collected at Camp Chopunnish near present town of Kamiah, Idaho Co., Idaho.

A.T. *Aira brevifolia* Pursh.
Fl. Am. Sept., 1:76. 1814.
HAIR-GRASS.
Piper identified this specimen as *Poa sandbergii* Vasey, and A. S. Hitchcock as *P. Canbyi* (Scrib.) Piper.

"The most common grass through the plains of Columbia and near the Kooskooskee R. June 10th, 1806."

On this date Lewis and Clark left Camp Chopunnish for Weippe Prairie. Idaho or Clearwater Co., Idaho.

? *Allium geyeri* S. Wats.
Proc. Am. Acad., 14:227. 1879.
GEYER'S ONION.

Thwaites, II, 263; Coues, II, 435 (det. by Coues).

Described by Lewis, July 23, 1805, in central Broadwater Co., Montana, near Three Forks.

? *Allium tolmiei* Baker
= *A. douglasii* var. β.
Hook.
Fl. Bor. Amer., 2:185. 1840.
TOLMIE'S ONION.

Thwaites, V, 88; Coues, III, 1030 (det. by Coues).

Described by Lewis, May 30, 1806, Camp Chopunnish, Idaho Co., Idaho.

? *Alnus rhombifolia* Nutt.
Sylva, 1:33. 1842.
WHITE ALDER.

Thwaites, III, 205; Coues, II, 698, 724 (det. by Coues).

Encountered by Lewis and Clark, Nov. 6, 1805, mouth of Cowlitz River, Cowlitz Co., Wash.

A. *Alnus rubra* Bongard.
Acad. St. Petersb. Mem. Ser. 6, Sci. Math. Phys. Nat., 2:162. 1832.
RED ALDER.

"Black alder of the Pacific Ocean, grows to a large size. March 26th, 1806." Thwaites, IV, 55 (det. by Piper); Coues, III, 833.

Collected between Puget's Island and Cowlitz River. Cowlitz Co., Wash., on north and Columbia Co., Oregon, on south.

? *Alnus sinuata* (Regel) Rydb.
= *A. viridis sinuata* Regel.
DC Prod., 26:183. 1868.
WAVY-LEAVED OR SITKA ALDER.

Thwaites, III, 77 (det. by Piper); Coues, II, 605 (Coues suggests *Alnus incana* ?).

Observed by Lewis, Sept. 20, 1805, on Lolo Trail, Idaho Co., Idaho.

A. *Amelanchier alnifolia* (Nutt.) Nuttall.
Gen. Pl., 1:306. 1818.
SASKATOON SERVICEBERRY.

"Service berry. A small bush, the Narrows of Columbia R. Apr. 15, 1806." Thwaites, IV, 273; V, 121.

On April 15 Lewis and Clark camped at mouth of Mill Creek (Rock Fort Camp) where now is town of The Dalles, Wasco Co., Oregon.

A.T. *Amellus spinulosus* Pursh
= *Sideranthus spinulosus* (Nutt.) Sweet.
Fl. Am. Sept., 2:564. 1814.
CUT-LEAVED SIDERANTHUS.
See Britton & Brown, III, 379.

"Prairies, Sept. 15, 1804."
"On the Columbia, Octbr. [?], 1805."

On Sept. 15, Expedition passed mouth of White River, Lyman Co., S.D., just below present-day Chamberlain. Oct., 1805: 1–10, Clearwater R.; 10–16, Snake R.; 16–30, Columbia R.

A.? *Angelica lyallii* Wats.
= *A. arguta* Nuttall.
T. & G. Fl. N. Amer., 1:620. 1840.
LYALL'S ANGELICA.
See Hitchcock *et al.*, III, 514.

"Angelica within the Rocky mountains in moist places. June 25th, 1806. The flowering one taken in Septb. 3rd, 1805." Thwaites, V, 138 (det. by Piper).

On Sept. 3, 1805, Expedition on North Fork of Salmon R., Lemhi Co., Idaho. On June 25, 1806, on Hungry Creek, travelling east over Lolo Trail.

A.T. *Antirrhinum tenellum* Pursh
= *Collinsia tenella* (Pursh) Piper.
Fl. Am. Sept., 2:421. 1814.
SMALL-FLOWERED COLLINSIA.
See Britton & Brown, III, 189.

"Rockford Camp, April 17th, 1806."

Rock Fort Camp, The Dalles, Wasco Co., Oregon.

Aquilegia formosa Fischer.
DC Prod., 1:50. 1824.
NORTHWEST CRIMSON COLUMBINE.

Thwaites, V, 138 (det. by Piper).

Observed by Lewis, June 16, 1806, on Lolo Trail, Idaho.

A. *Arbutus menziesii* Pursh.
Fl. Am. Sept., 1:282. 1814.
MADRONE.

"A middle sized tree with a remarkable smooth bark, which scales off in the manner of the birch; & red berries in clusters. Co-

Cascades of the Columbia.

A.L.T. *Artemisia cana* Pursh.
Fl. Am. Sept., 2:521. 1814.
HOARY SAGEBRUSH.

lumbia, Novbr. 1st, 1805." Thwaites, III, 260.

"On the bluffs, Oct. 1, 1804. Another variety of wild sage growth of high and bottom prairies; Oct. 2, 1804. Growth of the high bluffs."

South Dakota, above mouth of Cheyenne River. Dewey Co. on west, Sully Co. on east.

A. *Artemisia dracunculoides* Pursh.
Fl. Am. Sept., 2:521. 1814.
LINEAR-LEAVED WORM-WOOD.

"Sept. 15, 1804. Growth of the open plains."

South Dakota, near mouth of White River. Lyman Co., on west and Brule Co. on east. Just below Chamberlain.

A.T. *Artemisia longifolia* Nuttall.
Gen. Pl., 2:142. 1818.
LONG-LEAVED MUGWORT.

"Wild sage on the bluffs, Oct. 1, 1804. No. 53, Oct. 3d. Flavor like the camomile, radix perennial; growth of the high bluffs."

South Dakota, above mouth of Cheyenne River.

A.L. *Artemisia ludoviciana* Nutt.
Gen. Pl., 2:143. 1818.
DARK-LEAVED MUGWORT.

"Artemisia species. Columbia River, April 10, 1806. Artemisia. Rockford Camp."

Probably April 16, since Lewis and Clark did not reach Rock Fort Camp until April 15. Wasco Co., Oregon.

? *Artemisia tridentata* Nutt.
Trans. Am. Phil. Soc.
(II), 7:398. 1841.
SAGEBRUSH.

Thwaites, IV, 304 (identified by Piper).

Observed by Lewis, April 20, 1806. Narrows of the Columbia just below Celilo Falls.

? *Asarum caudatum* Lindley.
Bot. Reg., 17. 1831.
LONG-TAILED WILD GINGER.

Thwaites, V, 165 (identified by Piper).

Noted by Lewis, June 27, 1806, on Lolo Trail, Idaho Co., Idaho.

A. *Aster oblongifolius* Nuttall.
Gen. Pl., 2:156. 1818.
AROMATIC ASTER.

"Big Bend of the Missouri, Sept. 21, 1804."

South Dakota, just above Big Bend. Lyman Co. to the south, Buffalo Co. to north.

A. *Aster oregonus* Nuttall
= ? *Seriocarpus oregonensis* Nuttall.
Trans. Am. Phil. Soc.
(II), 7:302. 1840.
OREGON WHITE-TOPPED ASTER.
See Hitchcock *et al.*, V, 91.

"On Lewis [Snake] River, Oct. [?], 1805."

Lewis and Clark were on Snake River Oct. 10 to 16, the greater part of that time in southeast Wash.

A. *Astragalus missouriensis* Nutt.
Gen. Pl., 2:99. 1818.
MISSOURI MILK VETCH.

"No. 36. 18th Sept. [1804 probably]. The growth of the high prairies."

South Dakota, just below Big Bend of Missouri.

A.T. *Atriplex canescens* (Pursh) James
= *Calligonum canescens* Pursh.
Fl. Am. Sept., 2:370. 1814.
BUSHY ATRIPLEX.
See Britton & Brown, II, 19.

"Big Bend of the Missouri, Sept. 21, 1804."

South Dakota. Big Bend as stated.

A. *Atriplex nuttallii* Wats.
Procs. Am. Acad., 9:116. 1874.
NUTTALL'S ATRIPLEX.

"A half shrub from the high plains of the Missouri. July 20, 1806."

On this date Lewis was just below forks of Marias River, probably between Pondera and Toole Cos., Montana.

A.L.T. *Berberis aquifolium* Pursh.
Fl. Am. Sept., 1:219. 1814.
OREGON GRAPE.

"Lewisia ilicifolia. Nov. genus. Mountain holly. Great rapids of Columbia. Apr. 11, 1806." Thwaites, IV, 61.

Cascades of Columbia.

A.L.T. *Berberis nervosa* Pursh.
Fl. Am. Sept., 1:219. 1814.
DULL OREGON GRAPE.

"Lewisia nervosa. New genus. Mountain holly, from the great Rapids of the Columbia. Oct. [?], 1805." Thwaites, IV, 62.

The Narrows below Celilo Falls.

? *Betula fontinalis* Sargent.
Bot. Gaz., 31:219. 1901.
SPRING BIRCH.

Thwaites, IV, 342 (identified by Piper).

Observed by Lewis, April 30, 1806, on Walla Walla R., Walla Walla Co., Wash.

Betula occidentalis Hooker
= *B. papyrifera occidentalis* (Hook.) Sargent.
Fl. Bor. Amer., 2:155. 1839.
WESTERN PAPER BIRCH.
See Abrams, I, 512.

Thwaites, II, 303; Coues, II, 457; Sargent, *Garden and Forest*, X, Jan., 1897.

Observed by Lewis, Aug. 3, 1805. Jefferson River, Madison Co., Montana.

A.L.T. *Bigelowia douglasii* Gray
= *Chrysothamnus viscidiflorus* (Hook.) Nuttall
= *Crinitaria viscidiflora* Hooker.
Fl. Bor. Am., 2:24. 1834.

"Big Bend of the Missouri, Sept. 2, 1804."

South Dakota. Big Bend as stated.

RABBIT BRUSH.
See Hitchcock *et al.*, V,
130.

A.L.T. *Bigelowia graveolens* Gray
= *Chrysocoma graveolens*
Nuttall
= *Chrysothamnus grave-
olens* (Nutt.) Greene.
Gen. Pl., 2:136. 1818.
FETID RAYLESS GOLDENROD.
See Britton & Brown, III,
376.

"A low shrub growing
in the rocky, dry hills
on the Kooskooskee,
May 6, 1806."
"No. 54. Oct 2. Grows
from 18 inches to 2½
feet. it is the growth
of the high bluffs. Oct.
2, 1804."

On May 6, 1806, above
mouth of Potlatch
(Colter) R. on Clear-
water, Nez Perce Co.,
Idaho. On Oct. 2,
1804, above entrance
of Cheyenne R. at
Little Bend of Mis-
souri, S.D.

A.L.T. *Brodiaea grandiflora*
Pursh
= *B. douglasii* Wats.
Fl. Am. Sept., 1:223. 1814.
WILD HYACINTH.

"Hyacinth of the Co-
lumbia plains, Apr. 20,
1806."

Celilo Falls, Klickitat
Co., Wash.

? *Bromus marginatus* Nees.
Steud. Syn. Pl. Glum.,
1:322. 1854.
LARGE MOUNTAIN BROME
GRASS.

Thwaites, V, 107–108
(identified by Piper).

Observed by Lewis,
June 5, 1806, at Camp
Chopunnish, Idaho
Co., Idaho.

A.T. *Buphthalmum sagittatum*
Pursh
= *Balsamorrhiza sagittata*
(Pursh) Nuttall.
Fl. Am. Sept., 2:563. 1814.
BALSAM ROOT.
See Abrams & Ferris, IV,
106.

"Rocky Mts., dry hills,
July 7, 1806."
"The stem is eaten by
natives without any
preparation. On the
Columbia, Apr. 14,
1806."

On July 7, Lewis and
Clark Pass, Lewis and
Clark Co., Montana.
On April 14, just be-
low The Dalles, Wasco
Co., Oregon.

A.T. *Calochortus elegans* Pursh.
Fl. Am. Sept., 1:240. 1814.
MARIPOSA LILY.

"A small bulb of a
pleasant flavor, eat by
the natives. On the
Kooskooskee, May 17,
1806."

Camp Chopunnish,
on Clearwater River,
Idaho Co., Idaho.

A.T. *Camassia quamash*
(Pursh) Greene
= *Phalangium quamash*
Pursh.
Fl. Am. Sept., 1:226. 1814.
CAMAS.

"Near the foot of the
Rocky Mountains on
the Quamash flats
[Weippe Prairie].
June 23, 1806."

Weippe Prairie, Clear-
water Co., Idaho.

A.T. *Cantua aggregata* Pursh
= *Gilia aggregata* (Pursh)
Spreng.
Fl. Am. Sept., 1:147. 1814.
SCARLET GILIA.

"On Hungry Creek,
June 26, 1806."

Hungry Creek as
stated. Lolo Trail,
Idaho Co., Idaho.

A.T. *Ceanothus sanguineus*
Pursh.

"Near the foot of the
Rocky Mountains on

Impossible. The party
had crossed Collins

Fl. Am. Sept., 1:167. 1814.
BUCKBRUSH; CHAPPARAL.

Collins Creek, June 27, 1806."

[Lolo] Cr. on June 24. Now 3 days' travel east on Lolo Trail, Idaho Co., Idaho.

A. *Ceanothus velutinus* Dougl. ex Hook.
Fl. Bor. Am., 1:125. 1831.
STICKY LAUREL; MOUNTAIN BALM.

"An evergreen; a shrub about 8 or 9 feet high. On the Rocky Mountains; waters of the Kooskooskee [no date]."

Probably June 24–29, 1806, in the Bitter-roots, travelling east.

? *Celtis reticulata* Torrey.
Lyc. Nat. Hist. N.Y. Ann., 2:247. 1828.
NETLEAF HACKBERRY.

Thwaites, III, 111; Coues, II, 629, identifies as *Celtis reticulata.* Piper says *C. occidentalis* L.

Observed by Lewis, Oct. 12, 1805, on Snake River near Riparia, Whitman Co., Wash.

? *Cirsium drummondii* T. & G.
= *C. foliosum* (Hook.) DC
= *Carduus foliosus* Hooker.
Fl. Bor. Amer., 1:303. 1833.
LEAFY OR DWARF THISTLE.
See Abrams & Ferris, IV, 532.

Thwaites, II, 263; Coues, II, 435 (identified by Coues as *Cnicus drummondii*).

Observed by Lewis, July 23, 1805, Broad-water Co., Montana, just north of Three Forks.

A. *Cirsium edule* Nuttall
= *Cnicus edulis* Gray.
Trans. Am. Phil. Soc. (II), 7:420. 1841.
EDIBLE THISTLE; "SHANA-TAQUE."

"Carduus or Thistle-Roots, eatable. Fort Clatsop, March 13, 1806" (Thwaites, IV, 3).

Fort Clatsop as stated. Clatsop Co., Oregon.

A.T. *Clarkia pulchella* Pursh.
Fl. Am. Sept., 1:260. 1814.
RAGGED ROBIN; BEAUTIFUL CLARKIA.

"A beautiful herbaceous plant from the Kooskooskee and Clark's [Bitterroot] River, June 1, 1806."

Camp Chopunnish, Idaho Co., Idaho.

A.T. *Claytonia lanceolata* Pursh.
Fl. Am. Sept., 1:175. 1814.
WESTERN SPRING BEAUTY.

"Headwaters of the Kooskooskee, June 27, 1806."

On this date, not on Clearwater, but on divide between N. Fork of Clearwater and Lochsa Rivers, Idaho Co., Idaho.

A. *Claytonia linearis* Dougl. ex Hook.
= *Montia linearis* (Doug.) Greene.
Fl. Bor. Am., 1:224. 1834.
LINEAR-LEAVED MONTIA.

"On the waters of the Kooskooskee within the Rocky Mountains, June 27, 1806."

On Lolo Trail, Idaho Co., Idaho.

A.T. *Clematis hirsutissima* Pursh
= *C. douglasii* Hooker.
Fl. Am. Sept., 2:385. 1814.
SUGAR BOWLS.

"On the plains of the Columbia River. May [? ?]."

No doubt May, 1806, since explorers were not on Columbia in May, 1805. Possibly on Clearwater below Camp Chopunnish.

A.L.T. *Cleome serrulata* Pursh
= *C. integrifolia* Torr. & Gray.
Fl. Am. Sept., 2:441. 1814.
PINK CLEOME.

"Specimens from White River, Aug. 29, 1806." "Aug. 25th, 1804, growth of the open prairie."

On Aug. 29, 1806, party passed mouth of White R. as stated. Lyman Co., S.D. On Aug. 25, 1804, near entrance of Vermillion R., Clay Co., S.D.

A. *Collomia linearis* Nutt.
Gen. Pl., 1:126. 1818.
NARROW-LEAVED COLLOMIA.

"Rockford Camp, April 17, 1806."

Rock Fort Camp, The Dalles, Wasco Co., Oregon.

Cornus nuttallii Audubon.
T. & G. Fl. N. Am., 1:652. 1840.
NUTTALL'S OR MOUNTAIN DOGWOOD.

Thwaites, IV, 246 (det. by Piper); Coues, III, 930.

Mouth of Sandy River, Multnomah Co., Oregon.

Corylus californica (DC) Rose
= *C. rostrata californica* DC.
Prod., 16:133. 1864.
CALIFORNIA HAZELNUT.

Thwaites, III, 148 (identified by Piper).

Reported by Lewis, Oct. 22, 1805, on Columbia near mouth of Deschutes River.

A. *Crataegus douglasii* Lind.
Edward's Bot. Reg., 21. 1810.
BLACK HAWTHORN.

"Deep purple haw, Columbia River, April 29, 1806."

Mouth of Walla Walla River, Walla Walla Co., Wash.

A.T. *Cristaria coccinea* Pursh.
Fl. Am. Sept., 2:453. 1814.
RED FALSE MALLOW.

"Plains of Missouri, July 20, 1806."

Near the forks of Marias R., probably Glacier Co., Mont., on modern-day Blackfeet Indian Reservation.

Cypripedium montanum Dougl.
Lindl. Gen. & Sp. Orchid., 528. 1840.
MOUNTAIN LADY'S SLIPPER.

Thwaites, V, 173 (identified by Piper); Coues, III, 1059.

Discovered and described by Lewis, June 30, 1806, at or near Lolo Hot Springs, Lolo Creek, Missoula Co., Montana.

A. *Delphinium menziesii* DC.
Syst. Veg., 1:355. 1818.
MENZIES' LARKSPUR.

"On the Columbia, April 14, 1806. A sort of larkspur with 3 styles."

One day's journey below The Dalles, Wasco Co., Oregon.

A.L.T. *Dentaria tenella* Pursh.
Fl. Am. Sept., 2:439. 1814.
SLENDER TOOTHWORT.

"On the banks of the Columbia near quicksands, April 1, 1806."

Near mouth of Sandy R. (Quicksand R. of Lewis and Clark). Multnomah Co., Oregon.

? *Echinacea angustifolia* DC.
Prod., 5:554. 1836.
NARROW-LEAVED PURPLE CONEFLOWER.

Thwaites, I, 281: "Specimens of a plant, and a parcel of its roots highly prized by the natives . . . in cases of the bite of the rattle Snake."

Sent by Lewis to Jefferson from Fort Mandan, McLean Co., N.D.

A.T. *Elaeagnus argentea* Pursh.
Fl. Am. Sept., 1:114. 1814.
SILVERBERRY.

"Silver tree of the Missouri, from the Prairie of the Knobs. July 6, 1806."

Blackfoot or Stevens' Prairie of today. One day's journey west of Lewis and Clark Pass.

? *Elymus condensatus* Presl.
Rel. Haenk., 1:265. 1830.
GIANT RYE-GRASS.

Thwaites, V, 107–108 (identified by Piper).

Noted by Lewis, June 5, 1806, at Camp Chopunnish, Idaho Co., Idaho.

A.L.T. *Erigeron compositus* Pursh.
Fl. Am. Sept., 2:535. 1814.
CUT-LEAVED DAISY.

"On the banks of the Kooskooskee" [no date].

Probably Camp Chopunnish, May 14 to June 10, 1806.

A. *Erysimum asperum* (Nutt.) DC.
Syst. Veg., 2:505. 1821.
WESTERN WALLFLOWER.

"On the Kooskooskee, June 1, 1806."

Camp Chopunnish, Idaho Co., Idaho.

A.T. *Erythronium grandiflorum* Pursh.
Fl. Am. Sept., 1:231. 1814.
YELLOW FAWN LILY.

"From the plains of the Columbia near Kooskooskee River, May 8, 1806. The natives reckon the root unfit for food."
"On the waters of the Kooskooskee, June 5, 1806."

On May 8, party on south side of Clearwater above Potlatch R., Nez Perce Co., Idaho. On June 5, Camp Chopunnish.

A.T. *Euphorbia marginata* Pursh.
Fl. Am. Sept., 2:607. 1814.
WHITE-MARGINED SPURGE.

"On the Yellowstone River, July 28, 1806."

More likely the Marias R., since Lewis, the botanist of the party, was descending the Marias on that date.

A.T. *Festuca spicata* Pursh.
Fl. Am. Sept., 1:81. 1814.
BLUE BUNCH WHEATGRASS.

"On the plains of the Columbia, June 10, 1806."

On this date Lewis and Clark abandoned Camp Chopunnish and journeyed to Weippe Prairie. Idaho or Clearwater Co., Idaho.

? *Fraxinus latifolia* Benth.
= *F. oregona* Nuttall.
Bot. Voy. Sulphur, 33.
1844.
OREGON ASH.
See Hitchcock *et al.*, IV,
57.

Thwaites, III, 260;
Coues, II, 724 (det. by
Coues).

Observed by Clark,
Nov. 30, 1805, on
south side of Colum-
bia near present-day
Astoria, Oregon.

A.L.T. *Fritillaria lanceolata*
Pursh.
Fl. Am. Sept., 1:230. 1814.
MISSION BELLS; RICE ROOT.

"Specimen of a lilia-
ceous plant obtained
on Brant Island, 10th
of April, 1806, the root
of this plant is a squa-
mous bulb and is eaten
by the natives."

Brant Island as stated,
just above Beacon
Rock. Skamania Co.,
Wash., on north and
Multnomah Co., Ore-
gon, on south.

A.L. *Fritillaria pudica* (Pursh)
Spreng.
Fl. Am. Sept., 1:228. 1814.
YELLOW BELL.

"Plains of Columbia
near the Kooskooskee,
May 8, 1806. The bulb
is the shape of a bis-
cuit which the natives
eat."
"On the headwaters
of the Missouri. May
[?]."

On May 8 above Pot-
latch R., Nez Perce
Co., Idaho. As to 2nd
specimen, party at no
time on headwaters of
Missouri in May.
Probably Columbia.

A.T. *Gaillardia aristata*
Pursh.
Fl. Am. Sept., 2:573. 1814.
GREAT-FLOWERED GAILLAR-
DIA.

"Rocky Mts., dry hills,
July 6, 1806."

One day's travel west
of Lewis and Clark
Pass, Lewis and Clark
Co., Montana.

A. *Gaultheria shallon* Pursh.
Fl. Am. Sept., 1:283. 1814.
SALAL.

"The shallon, sup-
posed to be a species
of *Vaccinium*. On the
coast of the Pacific
Ocean, Jan. 20, 1806"
(Thwaites, IV, 52).

Fort Clatsop, on
Lewis and Clark
River, Clatsop Co.,
Oregon.

A.L.T. *Gerardia fruticosa* Pursh
= *Pentstemon fruticosa*
(Pursh) Greene.
Fl. Am. Sept., 2:423. 1814.
SHRUBBY PENTSTEMON.

Pursh wrote: "In great
abundance in the pine
forests of the Rocky
mountains. June
[?]."

No doubt June, 1806.
Probably Lolo Trail,
Idaho Co., Idaho.

A. *Geum triflorum* Pursh.
Fl. Am. Sept., 2:736. 1814.
TASSELS.

"On open ground,
common on waters of
the Kooskooskee, June
12, 1806."

Weippe Prairie, Clear-
water Co., Idaho.

A.L. *Grindelia squarrosa*
(Pursh) Dunal
= *Donia squarrosa* Pursh.
Fl. Am. Sept., 2:559. 1814.
BROAD-LEAVED GUM-PLANT.

"No 40, taken on the
17th of August, 1804,
at our camp near the
old Maha village, and
is the growth of the
prairies."

Near old Omaha In-
dian village and
Omaha Creek, Dakota
Co., Nebraska. Just
south of present-day
Sioux City, Iowa.

A. *Hydrophyllum lineare* Pursh
= *Phacelia linearis* (Pursh) Holz.
Fl. Am. Sept., 1:134. 1814.
LINEAR-LEAVED PHACELIA.

"Rocky Camp. April 17, 1806."

Rock Fort Camp, The Dalles, Wasco Co., Oregon.

A. *Iris missouriensis* Nuttall.
Jour. Acad. Nat. Scis. Phila., 7:58. 1834.
WESTERN BLUE-FLAG.

"A pale blue species of flag, Prairie of the Knobs, July 5, 1806."

Blackfoot or Stevens' Prairie. Lewis and Clark Co., Montana.

Larix occidentalis Nuttall.
N. Amer. Sylva, 3:143. 1849.
WESTERN LARCH.

Thwaites, III, 66; V, 135 (identified by Piper).

First observed, Sept. 14, 1805, Bitterroot Mountains, Idaho.

? *Lathyrus ochroleucus* Hooker.
Fl. Bor. Am., 1:59. 1834.
YELLOW-FLOWERING PEA.

Thwaites, V, 138 (identified by Piper).

Noted by Lewis, June 16, 1806, Lolo Trail, Idaho.

A.T. *Lewisia rediviva* Pursh.
Fl. Am. Sept., 2:368. 1814.
BITTERROOT; ROCK ROSE.

"The Indians eat the root of this. Near Clark's [Bitterroot] River, July 1, 1806."

Mouth of Lolo (Traveller's Rest) Creek, Missoula Co., Montana.

A.L.T. *Linum lewisii* Pursh.
Fl. Am. Sept., 1:210. 1814.
LEWIS'S WILD FLAX.

"Perennial flax. Valleys of the Rocky Mountains, July 9, 1806."

On that date Lewis was descending the Sun River approaching Great Falls, Cascade Co., Montana.

A. *Lomatium cous* (Wats.) Coult. & Rose
= ? *Cymopterus campestris* Nuttall.
Cont. U.S. Nat. Herb., 7:214. 1900.
COUS.

"An umbelliferous plant of the root of which the Wallowallas make a kind of bread. The natives call it shappalell. April 29, 1806."

Mouth of Walla Walla River, Walla Walla Co., Wash.

A. *Lonicera ciliosa* (Pursh) DC
= *Caprifolium ciliosum* Pursh.
Fl. Am. Sept., 1:160. 1814.
ORANGE HONEYSUCKLE.

"On the Kooskooskee, June 5, 1806."
"Rocky Mountains, June 16, 1806."

On June 5, Camp Chopunnish. On June 16, Lolo Trail, Hungry Creek. Idaho Co., Idaho.

A. *Lonicera involucrata* (Rich.) Banks
= *Xylosteum involucratum* Rich.
App. Frankl. Jour., 733. 1823.
INVOLUCRED FLY-HONEY-SUCKLE.

"Shrub within the Rocky Mountains, found in moist ground near branches of rivulets. July 7, 1806."
"No. 5 found on the waters of the Columbia. Sept. 2, 1805."

On July 7, 1806, Lewis crossed Lewis and Clark Pass, Montana. On Sept. 2, 1805, the party was ascending N. Fork of Salmon River, Lemhi Co., Idaho.

A. *Lupinus argenteus* Pursh. Fl. Am. Sept., 2:468. 1814. SILVERY LUPINE.

"On the Cokahlaiskit [Blackfoot River], July 7, 1806."

On the headwaters of the Blackfoot River near Lewis and Clark Pass.

Lupinus littoralis Doug. Bot. Reg., 14:1198. 1828. CHINOOK LICORICE; SEASHORE LUPINE; "CULWHAYMA."

Thwaites, IV, 10.

Described by Lewis, Jan. 24, 1806, at Fort Clatsop.

A.T. *Lupinus sericeus* Pursh. Fl. Am. Sept., 2:468. 1814. SILKY LUPINE.

"Flowers cream colored with a small tinge of blue. On the Kooskooskee, June 5, 1806."

Camp Chopunnish, on the Clearwater River, Idaho.

A. *Maclura aurantiaca* Nutt. = *Toxylon pomiferum* Raf. Am. Month. Mag., 2:119. 1817. OSAGE ORANGE.

Thwaites, VI, 153; VII, 296.

St. Louis, Missouri. Specimens sent from that city by Lewis to Jefferson on March 26, 1804.

A. *Microseris macrochaeta* (Gray) Schultze-Bip. = *M. linearifolia* (Nutt.) Schultze-Bip. = *Calais linearifolia* DC. Prod., 7:85. 1838. UROPAPPUS. See Hitchcock *et al.*, V, 264.

"Rock Camp. April 17, 1806."

Rock Fort Camp, The Dalles, Wasco Co., Oregon.

Mimulus lewisii Pursh. Fl. Am. Sept., 2:427. 1814. LEWIS'S MONKEY FLOWER.

Pursh: "On the head springs of the Missouri, at the foot of Portage hill, Aug., *v. s. in Herb. Lewis.*"

"Portage hill" is obscure, unless Lemhi Pass. The party arrived there in Aug., 1805. No specimen known; may be in London.

A. *Mimulus luteus* Pursh = *M. guttatus* DC. Hort. Monspel., 127. 1813. LARGE MONKEY FLOWER. See Hitchcock *et al.*, IV, 343.

"On the waters of Clark's [Bitterroot] River, July 4, 1806."

On Blackfoot River above present-day Missoula, Missoula Co., Montana.

A.T. *Nicotiana quadrivalvis* Pursh. Fl. Am. Sept., 1:141. 1814. INDIAN TOBACCO.

"Specimen of the Ricara's tobacco, taken 12th of October, 1804. This is the tobacco which they cultivate."

Upper Arikara villages, about 15 miles above mouth of Grand River, Corson Co., S.D.

A.L. *Oenothera caespitosa* Nutt.

"Near the falls of the Missouri, 17th July,

On that date Lewis travelled from Great

Fras. Cat., 1813.
SCAPOSE PRIMROSE.

1806."

Falls to Teton (Tansy) River. Cascade and Teton Cos., Montana.

A. *Oenothera heterantha* Nuttall.
T. & G. Fl. N. Am., 1:507. 1840.
NORTHERN SUN-CUP.

"In moist ground on the Quamash flats [Weippe Prairie], June 14, 1806."

Weippe Prairie, Clearwater Co., Idaho.

? *Opuntia fragilis* (Nutt.) Haw.
= *Cactus fragilis* Nutt.
Gen. Pl., 1:296. 1818.
BRITTLE OPUNTIA.

Thwaites, II, 51; Coues, I, 317 (det. by Coues).

Noted by Lewis, May 20, 1805, just below mouth of Musselshell R. Garfield Co., Mont., on south and Phillips Co. on north.

Opuntia polyacantha Haworth
= *O. missouriensis* DC
= *Cactus ferox* Nutt.
Gen. Pl., 1:296. 1818.
MANY-SPINED OPUNTIA.
See Britton & Brown, II, 573.

Thwaites, III, 120 (identified by Piper).

Lewis noted, Oct. 16, 1805, on Snake River, Wash. Franklin Co. on north and Walla Walla Co. on south.

A. *Orthocarpus tenuifolius* (Pursh) Benth.
= *Bartsia tenuifolia* Pursh.
Fl. Am. Sept., 2:429. 1814.
OWL'S CLOVER.
See Hitchcock *et al.*, IV, 354.

"Valley of Clark's [Bitterroot] River, July 1, 1806."

Mouth of Lolo (Traveller's Rest) Creek, Missoula Co., Montana.

? *Oxalis oregona* Nuttall.
T. & G. Fl. N. Am., 1:211. 1818.
OREGON WOOD-SORREL.

Thwaites, VI, 210 (identified by Piper).

Noted by Lewis, March 15, 1806, at Fort Clatsop.

A.T. *Oxytropis argentata* Pursh.
Fl. Am. Sept., 2:473. 1814.
SILVER OXYTROPE.

"Near the head of Clark's [Bitterroot] River. July [?], 1806."

Possibly July 1, 1806, when party was encamped on Bitterroot R. at mouth of Lolo Creek.

A. *Pachistima myrsinites* (Pursh) Rafinesque
= *Ilex? myrsinites* Pursh.
Fl. Am. Sept., 1:119. 1814.
OREGON BOXWOOD.
See Hitchcock *et al.*, III, 410.

"Rocky Mountains, June 16, 1806."
"A small shrub about 4 feet high with a small purple berry, evergreen. Near the Pacific Ocean, November 16, 1805."

On June 16, 1806, Lolo Trail (Hungry Creek), Idaho Co., Idaho. On Nov. 16, 1805, party encamped on Baker's Bay in sight of ocean, Pacific Co., Wash.

A. *Pedicularis scopulorum*
Gray?
= *P. elata* Pursh.
Fl. Am. Sept., 2:425. 1814.
LOUSEWORT.

"On the low plains on the heath of Clark's [Bitterroot] River, July 6, 1806."

Approaching Lewis and Clark Pass, on headwaters of Blackfoot River (not Bitterroot), Montana.

A. *Pentstemon serrulatus*
Menzies
= *P. diffusus* Douglas.
Ex Smith in Rees, Cycl. 26, No. 5. 1813.
CASCADE PENTSTEMON.
See Abrams, III, 763.

"Camp on the Kooskooskee, May 20, 1806."

Camp Chopunnish on Clearwater River, Idaho Co., Idaho.

? *Perideridia gairdneri* (H. & A.) Mathias
= *Ataenia gairdneri* Hook. & Arn.
= *Carum gairdneri* Gray.
Bot. Beechey, 349. 1838.
GAIRDNER'S YAMPAH; "FENNEL."
See Abrams, III, 233.

"A species of fennel root eaten by the Indians, of an annis taste; flowers white, Columbia River, April 25, 1806."

Between Celilo Falls and mouth of Walla Walla River, Benton Co., Wash.

A. *Peucedanum simplex* Nuttall
= *Lomatium triternatum* (Pursh) Coult. & Rose
= *Sesili triternatum* Pursh.
Fl. Am. Sept., 1:197. 1814.
BISCUIT ROOT; LEWIS'S LOMATIUM.
See Abrams, III, 266.

"A root 5 or 6 inches long eaten raw or boiled by the natives. On the Kooskooskee, May 6, 1806."

Above mouth of Potlatch River (Colter's Creek) on Clearwater, Nez Perce Co., Idaho.

A. *Peucedanum utriculatum* C. & R.
= *Lomatium utriculatum* C. & R.
Fl. N. Amer., 1:628. 1840.
COMMON LOMATIUM.
See Hitchcock *et al.*, III, 568.

"A great horse medicine among the natives. On the Kooskooskee, June 10, 1806."

On this date Lewis and Clark travelled from Camp Chopunnish to Weippe Prairie, Idaho and Clearwater Cos., Idaho.

A.L.T. *Phacelia heterophylla* Pursh.
Fl. Am. Sept., 1:140. 1814.
VIRGATE PHACELIA.

"Root fibrous, plant from 3–4 feet high; dry situations. On the Kooskooskee, June 9, 1806."

Camp Chopunnish.

A.T. *Philadelphus lewisii* Pursh.
Fl. Am. Sept., 1:329. 1814.
LEWIS'S SYRINGA.

"A shrub from the Kooskooskee, May 6, 1806."
"On the waters of Clark's [Bitterroot]

On May 6, party just above Potlatch R. (Colter's Cr.) on south side of Clearwater, Idaho. On July

River, July 4, 1806." | 4 Lewis was on Blackfoot R. above present-day Missoula, Missoula Co., Montana.

A.T. *Phlox speciosa* Pursh.
Fl. Am. Sept., 1:149. 1814.
SHOWY PHLOX.

"A shrub about 4 feet high. On the plains of the Columbia. May 7, 1806."

On the south side of the Clearwater below Camp Chopunnish.

Picea engelmannii Parry
= *Abies engelmanni* Parry.
Acad. Sci. St. Louis Trans., 2:122. 1863.
ENGELMANN'S SPRUCE.

Thwaites, III, 69 (identified by Piper).

Noted by Lewis and Clark, Sept. 16, 1805, on Lolo Trail, Bitterroot Mountains, Idaho Co., Idaho.

Picea sitchensis (Bong.) Carr.
= *Pinus sitchensis* Bong.
Acad. Imp. Sci. St. Petersb. Mem. Ser. 6, Sci. Math. Phys. Nat., 2:164. 1832.
SITKA SPRUCE.

Thwaites, IV, 41 (identified by Piper); Coues, III, 832.

Described by Lewis, Feb. 4, 1806, at Fort Clatsop.

Pinus albicaulis Engelmann
= *P. cembroides* Newb.
U.S. Repts. Expl. Miss. Pacif., 6 (3):44. 1857.
WHITEBARK PINE.

Thwaites, III, 69 (identified by Piper).

Noted by Lewis and Clark, Sept. 16, 1805, on Lolo Trail.

Pinus contorta Douglas.
Arb. Frut. Brit., 4:2292. 1838.
LODGEPOLE PINE.

Thwaites, III, 69 (identified by Piper).

Noted by Lewis and Clark, Sept. 16, 1805, on Lolo Trail.

Pinus monticola Douglas.
Lamb. Pinus ed., 2,3:27. 1837.
WESTERN WHITE PINE.

Thwaites, IV, 47 (identified by Piper).

Described by Lewis, Feb. 6, 1806, at Fort Clatsop.

A. *Pinus ponderosa* Douglas.
Hort. Brit., 387. 1830.
PONDEROSA PINE.

"On the Kooskooskee. On river bottoms in rich land west of the mountains. Oct. 1, 1805."

At Canoe Camp near present-day Orofino, Lewis Co., Idaho.

A. *Plagiobothrys tenellus* (Nutt.) Gray
= *Myosotis tenella* Nutt. ex Hook.
Kew Jour. Bot., 3:295. 1851.
SLENDER POPCORN FLOWER.
See Abrams, III, 574.

"Rocky Camp, April 17, 1806."

Rock Fort Camp, The Dalles, Wasco Co., Oregon.

A. *Polanisia trachysperma* T. & G.
Fl. N. Am., 1:669. 1840.
LARGE-FLOWERED CLAMMY-WEED.

"Aug. 25th [1804?]. Growth of the open prairies."

On Aug. 25, 1804, the party was at or near mouth of Vermillion R., Clay Co., S.D.

A. *Polemonium caeruleum* A. Gray
= *P. van bruntiae* Britton.
Gray's Man. Ed., 4, App. 1863.
AMERICAN JACOB'S LADDER.
See Britton & Brown, III, 63.

"Headwaters of the Kooskooskee, June 27, 1806."

On Lolo Trail, Idaho.

A.T. *Polygala alba* Nuttall
= *P. senega* var. *tenuifolia* Pursh.
Fl. Am. Sept., 2:750. 1814.
WHITE MILKWORT.

"A kind of Seneca snake root. On the Missouri, August 10, 1806."

At or near mouth of Little Muddy R. (White Earth R. of Lewis and Clark), N.D. Williams Co. on north of Missouri, McKenzie Co. on south.

A.T. *Polygonum bistortoides* Pursh.
Fl. Am. Sept., 1:271. 1814.
WESTERN SNAKEWEED.

"In moist ground on Quamash flats [Weippe Prairie], June 12, 1806."

Weippe Prairie, Clearwater Co., Idaho.

Populus angustifolia James.
Long's Exp., 1:497. 1823.
NARROWLEAF COTTONWOOD.

Thwaites, II, 145; Coues, II, 364.

Described by Lewis, June 12, 1805, on north bank of Missouri between Marias R. and Great Falls. Chouteau Co., Montana.

Populus deltoides occidentalis Rydb.
N.Y. Bot. Gard. Mem., 1:115. 1900.
PLAINS COTTONWOOD.

Thwaites, I, 323 *et seq.*

Encountered regularly in High Plains country.

A. *Populus trichocarpa* Torr. & Gr.
Icon., Pl. 9, Pl. 878. 1852.
BLACK COTTONWOOD.

"Cotton tree of the Columbia R. June [?], 1806."

Probably collected on Clearwater, since party not on Columbia in June.

A.L.T. *Psoralea argophylla* Pursh.
Fl. Am. Sept., 2:475. 1814.
SILVER-LEAF PSORALEA.

"No. 48. No. 103. Oct. 17, 1804. A decoction of this plant used by the Indians to wash their wounds."

Southern N.D., near mouth of Cannonball R. Emmons Co. to the east and Sioux and Morton Cos. to the west.

A.L.T. *Psoralea esculenta* Pursh. Fl. Am. Sept., 2:475. 1814. POMME BLANCHE; PRAIRIE APPLE.

Pursh: "On the banks of the Missouri . . . June, July [1804?], *v. s. in Herb. Lewis.*"

If June or July, then on Lower Missouri. The party did not reach the Platte until July 21.

A.L. *Psoralea lanceolata* Pursh. Fl. Am. Sept., 2:475. 1814. LANCE-LEAVED PSORALEA.

Pursh: "On the banks of the Missouri . . . July, Aug. [1804?]."

Possibly collected somewhere between the Platte and Vermillion.

A.L. *Psoralea tenuiflora* Pursh. Fl. Am. Sept., 2:475. 1814. FEW-FLOWERED PSORALEA.

"Big Bend of Missouri, Sept. 21, 1804."

Just above Big Bend on that date. Lyman Co., S.D., on south, Hughes Co. on north.

? *Pteridium aquilinum pubescens* Underw. Nat. Ferns, ed. 6, 91. 1900. WESTERN BRACKEN.

Thwaites, IV, 5 (identified by Piper as *P. aquilina lanuginosa*).

Described by Lewis, Jan. 22, 1806, at Fort Clatsop.

A.T. *Purshia tridentata* (Pursh) DC = *Tigarea tridentata* Pursh. Fl. Am. Sept., 1:313. 1814. ANTELOPE BRUSH; BLACK SAGE.

"A shrub common to the open prairie of the knobs, July 6, 1806."

Blackfoot or Stevens' Prairie just west of Lewis and Clark Pass, Lewis and Clark Co., Montana.

Pyrus fusca Rafinesque = *P. rivularis* Doug. Med. Fl., 2:254. 1830. OREGON CRAB APPLE. See Hitchcock *et al.*, III, 164.

Thwaites, IV, 19 (identified by Piper); Coues, III, 826.

Described by Lewis, Jan. 28, 1806, at Fort Clatsop.

A. *Pyrus sambucifolia*? [var. *pumila* Sargent] = *Sorbus sitchensis* Roemer. Fam. Nat. Syn., 3:139. 1847. SITKA MOUNTAIN ASH. See Hitchcock *et al.*, III, 189.

"No. 24. Found the 4th day of Sept. 1805. A small growth only, rising to the height of 15 feet."
"On the tops of the highest peaks and mountains, June 27, 1806."

On Sept. 4, 1805, the party crossed Lost Trail Pass from N. Fork of Salmon, Lemhi Co., Idaho, to Ross's Hole, Ravalli Co., Mont. On June 27, 1806, Lolo Trail, Idaho.

A. *Quercus garryana* Douglas. Fl. Bor. Am., 2:159. 1839. OREGON WHITE OAK.

"A sort of white oak, Columbia, March 26, 1806."

Below mouth of Cowlitz R. Cowlitz Co., Wash., on north, Columbia Co., Ore., on south.

A. *Rhamnus purshiana* DC. Prod., 2:25. 1825. CASCARA SAGRADA.

"A shrub apparently a species of *Rhamnus*. About 12 feet high in clumps; fruit a 5-valved purple berry,

Camp Chopunnish on Clearwater River, Idaho.

which the natives eat and esteem highly. . . . On the waters of the Kooskooskee, May 29, 1806."

? *Rhododendron macrophyllum* G. Don. = *R. californicum* Hooker. Gen. Hist. Pl., 3:843. 1834. CALIFORNIA RHODODENDRON. See Hitchcock *et al.,* IV, 27.

Thwaites, III, 259; Coues, II, 724 (iden. as *R. californicum*).

Noted by Lewis and Clark, Nov. 30, 1805, near present-day Astoria, Oregon.

? *Rhus trilobata* Nuttall = *R. aromatica* var. *trilobata* Gray. T. & G. Fl. N. Am., 1:219. 1838. SQUAW BUSH. See Hitchcock *et al.,* III, 409.

"No. 57. Oct. 1, 1804. First discovered in the neighbourhood of the Kancez River."

Near mouth of Cheyenne R., S.D. Sully Co. on east, Dewey or Stanley Co. on west.

A.T. *Ribes aureum* Pursh. Fl. Am. Sept., 1:164. 1814. GOLDEN CURRANT.

"Yellow flowering currant. Near the narrows of the Columbia. April 16, 1806." "Yellow currant of the Missouri, July 29, 1805."

On Apr. 16, 1806, below Celilo Falls, Klickitat Co., Wash. On July 29, 1805, Three Forks, Gallatin Co., Montana.

? *Ribes cereum* Douglas. Trans. Hort. Soc. London, 7:512. 1830. WHITE SQUAW CURRANT.

Thwaites, II, 169–170 (identified by Piper).

Described by Lewis, June 18, 1805, at Great Falls, Cascade Co., Montana.

? *Ribes cognatum* Greene = *Grossularia cognata* (Greene) Cov. & Brit. Pittonia, 3:115. 1907. UMATILLA GOOSEBERRY.

Thwaites, V, 121 (identified by Piper).

Noted by Lewis, June 10, 1806, en route from Camp Chopunnish to Weippe Prairie.

? *Ribes divaricatum* Douglas. Trans. Hort. Soc. London, 7:515. 1830. STRAGGLY GOOSEBERRY.

Thwaites, IV, 201 (identified by Piper).

Noted by Lewis, March 25, 1806, on lower Columbia near Puget's Island.

A. *Ribes menziesii* Pursh = *Grossularia menziesii* (Pursh) Cov. & Britt. Fl. Am. Sept., 2:732. 1814. CANYON GOOSEBERRY.

"Deep purple gooseberry, Columbia River, Apr. 8, 1806."

Below Beacon Rock and Lower Cascades. Skamania Co., Wash., on north, and Multnomah Co., Oregon, on south.

A. *Ribes sanguineum* Pursh. Fl. Am. Sept., 1:164. 1814. RED FLOWERING CURRANT.

"Columbia, March 27, 1806."

Near mouth of Cowlitz R., Cowlitz Co., Wash.

A.T. *Ribes viscossissimum* Pursh. Fl. Am. Sept., 1:163. 1814. STICKY CURRANT.

"Fruit indifferent and gummy. The heights of the Rocky Mountains, June 16, 1806."

Hungry Creek on Lolo Trail, Idaho Co., Idaho.

? *Rosa nutkana* Presl. Epim. Bot., 203. 1851. NOOTKA ROSE.

Thwaites, V, 121 (identified by Piper); Coues, III, 1041.

Noted by Lewis, June 10, 1806, en route from Camp Chopunnish to Weippe Prairie, Idaho.

? *Rosa pisocarpa* A. Gray. Proc. Amer. Acad., 8:382. 1872. CLUSTER ROSE.

Thwaites, V, 121 (identified by Piper).

Noted by Lewis, June 10, 1806, between Camp Chopunnish and Weippe Prairie.

A. *Rosa woodsii* Lindl. Mon. Ros., 21. 1820. WOODS' ROSE.

"The small rose of the prairies, it rises from 12 to 14 inches high; does not vine. Rosa. Open prairies, Sept. 5, 1804."
"October 18, 1804, the small rose of the prairies."

On Sept. 5, above mouth of Niobrara, S.D., Bon Homme Co. on north, Knox Co., Nebr., on south. On Oct. 18, Morton Co., N.D.

A. *Rubus nutkanus velutinus* Brew. = *R. parviflorus* Nuttall. Gen. Pl., 1:308. 1818. THIMBLEBERRY. See Hitchcock *et al.*, III, 179.

"A shrub of which the natives eat the young sprouts without cooking. On the Columbia, April 15, 1806."

Rock Fort Camp, The Dalles, Wasco Co., Oregon.

A. *Rubus spectabilis* Pursh. Fl. Am. Sept., 1:348. 1814. SALMONBERRY.

"Fruit like a raspberry. Columbia, March 27, 1806."

Near mouth of Cowlitz R. Cowlitz Co., Wash., on north, Columbia Co., Oregon, on south.

? *Rubus vitifolius* Cham. & Sch. = *R. macropetalus* Douglas. Linnaea, 2:10. 1827. PACIFIC BLACKBERRY. See Abrams, II, 457.

Thwaites, IV, 201 (identified by Piper).

Noted by Lewis, March 25, 1806, two days' travel above Fort Clatsop.

? *Salix amygdaloides* Anderss. Ofv. Svensk. Vetensk.

Thwaites, III, 111 (identified by Piper).

Noted by Lewis, Oct. 12, 1805, on Snake River near present

Akad. Forh., 15:114.
1858.
PEACH-LEAVED WILLOW.

? *Salix exigua* Nuttall.
Sylva, 1:75. 1843.
SLENDER WILLOW.

Thwaites, III, 111
(identified by Piper).

Observed by Lewis,
Oct. 12, 1805, on
Snake River near
Riparia, Whitman
Co., Wash.

town of Riparia,
Whitman Co., Wash.

? *Sambucus glauca* Nuttall
= *S. cerulea* Rafinesque.
Alsogr. Amer., 48. 1838.
BLUE ELDERBERRY.

Thwaites, IV, 49
(identified by Piper);
Coues, III, 835.

Described by Lewis,
Feb. 2, 1806, at Fort
Clatsop.

A.L.T. *Santolina suaveolens*
Pursh
= *Matricaria matricari-*
oides (Less.) Porter.
Fl. Am. Sept., 2:520. 1814.
RAYLESS CAMOMILE.
See Hitchcock *et al.*, V,
266.

"An agreeable smell.
On the Kooskooskee,
June 9, 1806."

Camp Chopunnish,
on the Clearwater R.,
Idaho Co., Idaho.

A. *Sarcobatus vermiculatus*
(Hook.) Torrey
= *Batis vermiculatus*
Hooker.
Fl. Bor. Am., 2:128. 1838.
GREASEWOOD.
See Hitchcock *et al.*, II,
213.

"A small branchy
shrub from the plains
of Missouri. July 20,
1806."

Just below forks of
the Marias River, Gla-
cier Co., Montana.

A.T. *Scutellaria angustifolia*
Pursh.
Fl. Am. Sept., 2:412. 1814.
NARROW-LEAVED SKULLCAP.

"On the Kooskooskee.
June 5, 1806."

Camp Chopunnish,
Clearwater R., Idaho
Co., Idaho.

A.T. *Sedum stenopetalum*
Pursh.
Fl. Am. Sept., 1:324. 1814.
NARROW-PETALED STONE-
CROP.

"Valley of Clark's [Bit-
terroot] River, July 1,
1806."
"On the naked rocks
of the Kooskooskee,
June 15, 1806."

On July 1, at mouth
of Lolo [Traveller's
Rest] Creek, Missoula
Co., Montana. On
June 15, just east of
Weippe Prairie, Clear-
water Co., Idaho.

A.L.T. *Shepherdia argentea*
Nuttall
= *Hippophae argentea*
Pursh.
Fl. Am. Sept., 1:115. 1814.
SILVERY BUFFALO-BERRY.

"No. 39. Obtained at
the mouth of the river
Quicourre [Niobrara]
from which place up-
wards it is abundant."
No date, but Lewis
and Clark reached
Niobrara Sept. 4,
1804.

Mouth of Niobrara R.
Bon Homme Co., S.D.,
on north, Knox Co.,
Nebr., on south.

A.T. *Smyrnium nudicaule* Pursh = *Lomatium nudicaule* (Pursh) Coult. & Rose. Fl. Am. Sept., 1:196. 1814. PESTLE PARSNIP. See Abrams, III, 268.

"Supposed to be a *Smyrnium*. The natives eat the tops and sometimes boil it with their soup. On the Columbia, April 15, 1806."

Rock Fort Camp, The Dalles, Wasco Co., Oregon.

A.T. *Solidago sarothrae* Pursh = *Gutierrezia sarothrae* (Pursh) Brit. & Rusby. Fl. Am. Sept., 2:540. 1814. COMMON MATCHWEED; BROOMWEED. See Hitchcock *et al.*, V, 209.

"No. 32. Specimens of aromatic plants on which the antelope feeds; these were obtained 21st of Sept. 1805 [1804], at the upper part of the big bend of the Mo."
"No. 59. 1804, 19th September, the growth of high and bare prairies which produced little grass, generally mineral earth."

On Sept. 21, just above Big Bend, S.D., with Hughes Co. on north and Lyman Co. on south. On Sept. 19, just below Big Bend. Buffalo Co. on east and Lyman Co. on west.

A. *Spartina gracilis* Trinius. Mem. Acad. St. Petersb. (VI), 6:110. 1840. INLAND CORD-GRASS.

No ticket affixed; hence no locale or date.

A.T. *Spiraea discolor* Pursh = *Holodiscus discolor* (Pursh) Maxim. Fl. Am. Sept., 1:342. 1814. OCEAN SPRAY. See Abrams, II, 414.

"A shrub growing much in the manner of Nine Bark. On the waters of the Kooskooskee, May 29, 1806."

Camp Chopunnish, Clearwater River, Idaho Co., Idaho.

A. *Stipa comata* Trin. & Rupert. Mem. Acad. St. Petersb. (VI), 5:75. 1842. NEEDLE AND THREAD GRASS.

No ticket affixed; hence no date or locale.

A.T. *Swertia fastigiata* Pursh. Fl. Am. Sept., 1:101. 1814. CLUSTERED SWERTIA.

"In moist wet places, on the Quamash flats [Weippe Prairie], June 14, 1806."

Weippe Prairie as stated. Clearwater Co., Idaho.

? *Symphoricarpos albus laevigatus* (Fernald) Blake = *S. racemosus* var. *laevigatus* Fernald. Rhodora, 7:167. 1905.

Thwaites, III, 77 (identified by Piper); Coues, III, 1041 (det. as *S. racemosus*).

Noted by Lewis, Sept. 20, 1805, on westward transit of Lolo Trail, Idaho.

COMMON SNOWBERRY.
See Abrams & Ferris, IV,
48.

A.T. *Synthyris missurica*
(Raf.) Penn.
= *Veronica reniformis*
Pursh.
Fl. Am. Sept., 1:10. 1814.
LEWIS AND CLARK'S SYN-
THYRIS.
See Abrams, III, 798.

"On Hungry Creek,
June 26, 1806."

Hungry Creek as
stated. Lolo Trail,
Idaho Co., Idaho.

? *Tanacetum nuttallii* T. &
G.
= *Sphaeromeria argentea*
Nutt.
Tr. Am. Phil. Soc. (II),
7:402. 1841.
TANSY.
See Hitchcock *et al.*, V,
319.

Thwaites, II, 126;
VII, 96.

Noted by Clark, June
6, 1805, on Teton R.,
Chouteau Co., Mon-
tana.

Taxus brevifolia Nuttall.
N. Am. Sylva, 3:86. 1849.
PACIFIC YEW.

Thwaites, III, 69
(identified by Piper).

Likely one of "8 dif-
ferent kinds of pine"
referred to by Lewis
and Clark, Sept. 25,
1805, on Lolo Trail.

Thuja plicata Donn.
Hort. Cantab. Ed., 6:249.
1811.
WESTERN RED CEDAR; WEST-
ERN ARBOR VITAE.

Thwaites, III, 80–81;
V, 135; Coues, II, 605.

First observed, Sept.
20, 1805, on Lolo
Trail.

A.L.T. *Trifolium macrocephalum*
(Pursh) Poiret
= *Lupinaster macrocepha-
lus* Pursh.
Fl. Am. Sept., 2:479. 1814.
LARGE-HEADED CLOVER.

"A species of clover
near Rockford Camp,
on high hills, April
17, 1806."

Rock Fort Camp, The
Dalles, Wasco Co.,
Oregon.

A.L.T. *Trifolium microcephalum*
Pursh.
Fl. Am. Sept., 2:478. 1814.
SMALL-HEADED CLOVER.

"Valley of Clark's [Bit-
terroot] River, July 1,
1806."

Mouth of Lolo [Trav-
eller's Rest] Creek,
Missoula Co., Mon-
tana.

A.T. *Trillium ovatum* Pursh.
Fl. Am. Sept., 1:245. 1814.
WESTERN WAKE-ROBIN.

"Columbia River near
the rapids, Apr. 10,
1806."

Lower Cascades above
Beacon Rock. Ska-
mania Co., Wash., on
north, Multnomah
Co., Oregon, on south.

A.T. *Trillium petiolatum* Pursh.
Fl. Am. Sept., 1:244. 1814.
PETIOLED WAKE-ROBIN.

"The flowers brown with a fruit of brick-red. On the waters of the Kooskooskee, June 15, 1806."

Left Weippe Prairie on this date on abortive attempt to cross Bitterroots. Clearwater Co., Idaho.

Tsuga mertensiana (Bong.) Carr.
= *Pinus mertensiana* Bongard.
Ac. Imp. Sci. St. Pet. Mem. Ser. 6, Sci. Math. Phys. Nat., 2:163. 1832.
MOUNTAIN HEMLOCK.

Thwaites, IV, 43–44 (identified by Piper); Coues, III, 830.

Described by Lewis, Feb. 5, 1806, at Fort Clatsop.

? *Urtica lyallii* S. Wats.
Proc. Am. Acad., 10:281. 1875.
LYALL'S NETTLE.

Thwaites, VI, 210 (identified by Piper).

Noted by Lewis, March 25, 1806, two days' travel above Fort Clatsop.

Vaccinium membranaceum Dougl.
Fl. Bor. Amer., 2:32. 1834.
BLUE HUCKLEBERRY.

Thwaites, IV, 50 (identified by Piper).

Described by Lewis, Feb. 7, 1806, at Fort Clatsop.

? *Vaccinium occidentale* A. Gray.
Bot. Calif., 1:451. 1876.
WESTERN HUCKLEBERRY.

Thwaites, V, 168 (identified by Piper).

Described by Lewis, June 28, 1806, as "whortleberry." Lolo Trail.

A. *Vaccinium ovatum* Pursh.
Fl. Am. Sept., 1:29. 1814.
EVERGREEN HUCKLEBERRY.

"A shrub of 7 or 8 feet high, supposed to be a species of Vaccinium. The berries are eaten by the natives. On the Pacific Ocean. Fort Clatsop, Jan. 27, 1806."

Fort Clatsop as stated. On Lewis and Clark River, Clatsop Co., Oregon.

A. *Veratrum californicum* Durand.
Jour. Phil. Acad. (II), 3:103. 1855.
CALIFORNIA FALSE HELLEBORE.

"A plant growing in wet places with a single stem and leaves clasping round one another, no flower observed. On the Kooskooskee, June 25, 1806."

Hungry Creek, Lolo Trail, Idaho Co., Idaho.

A.T. *Xerophyllum tenax* (Pursh) Nutt.
= *Helonias tenax* Pursh.
Fl. Am. Sept., 1:243. 1814.
BEAR GRASS; WESTERN TURKEY-BEARD.

"The leaves are made use of by the natives to make baskets and other ornaments. On high land, Rocky Mountains [Bitterroots], June 15, 1806."

Just east of Weippe Prairie, Clearwater Co., Idaho.

A.T. *Zygadenus elegans* Pursh = *Anticlea elegans* (Pursh) Rydb. Fl. Am. Sept., 1:241. 1814. GLAUCOUS ZYGADENE. "On the Cokalaishkit [Blackfoot] R., July 7, 1806." On this date Lewis crossed Continental Divide at Lewis and Clark Pass, Lewis and Clark Co., Montana.

A close scrutiny of the above reveals such facts as:

Of the total of 178 plants, 140, more than two-thirds, were discovered west of the Continental Divide. A balance in favor of the east might well have resulted, of course, if the plants cached by Lewis at Great Falls had not been destroyed by flood waters during the winter of 1805–6.

Of the overall total, 55, or almost one-third, were discovered in what is now Idaho, namely, at or in the immediate environs of Camp Chopunnish, on the Weippe Prairie, or along the Lolo Trail.

Of the total, 77 were described by Frederick Pursh—almost one half.

Two-thirds, 117 in all, are to be found today in the Lewis and Clark Herbarium at the Academy of Natural Sciences of Philadelphia.

Twenty-eight of the total are "Lambert" specimens, that is, had been carried by Pursh to London and returned to the United States by Edward Tuckerman.

Appendix B

Animals Discovered by Lewis and Clark

Two lists of animals discovered by Lewis and Clark have appeared heretofore. In 1940 Elijah H. Criswell prepared a zoological index similar to his botanical one, and in 1962 Donald Jackson produced "a trial list." (See Jackson, *Letters,* 293–298.) As with the plants, Criswell made no attempt to separate described species from undescribed. Jackson included only birds and mammals.

My index of animals includes only those which had not been formally described on the dates Lewis and Clark encountered them, and is limited to vertebrates. The invertebrates mentioned in the journals—insects, crustaceans, mollusks, and the like—are few in number and generally impossible to identify with any degree of certainty. For convenience, I list the animals alphabetically by technical names and divide them into four groups: fishes, reptiles and amphibians, birds, and mammals. The data accompanying each species (or subspecies) are arranged, as with the plants, in three columns. The first includes scientific and vernacular names, requisite synonymy, publication in which original description appeared, and the all-important publication date. The second contains (1) reference sources and (2) quotations descriptive of species from Lewis, Clark, and Coues, except where otherwise stated. The third column indicates localities (and dates) where Lewis and Clark collected or found each animal. Questionable determinations are preceded by interrogation marks.

For nomenclature of fishes, I have consulted primarily *Check List of the Fishes and Fishlike Vertebrates of North and Middle America North of the Northern Boundary of Venezuela and Colombia* by Jordan, Evermann, and Clark.

For nomenclature of reptiles and amphibians, I have depended on *Check List of North American Amphibians and Reptiles* (4th ed., 1939) by Stejneger and Barbour, and *A Check List of North American Amphibians and Reptiles* (6th ed., 1953) by Karl P. Schmidt.

For birds, I have relied almost entirely on *Check-List of North American Birds* (5th ed., 1961), prepared by a committee of the American Ornithologists' Union.

For mammals, my chief sources were *The Mammals of North America* by Hall and Kelson (including their extremely useful distribution maps) and *List of North American Recent Mammals* (U.S. National Museum Bulletin 205) by Miller and Kellogg. Supplementary works of value include *Lewis and Clark: Linguistic Pioneers* by Criswell; *History of the Expedition Under the Command of Lewis and Clark,* edited by Coues; *The Natural History of the Lewis and Clark Expedition* by Burroughs; and "Birds and Mammals Observed by Lewis and Clark in North Dakota" by Reid and Gannon.

FISHES

Acipenser transmontanus Richardson.
Fauna Bor.-Amer., 3:28. 1836.
WHITE STURGEON.

Thwaites, III, 234: "saw a Dead Sturgen 10 feet long on the sand." Coues (III, 896) : "New to science in 1806 . . . another of the many uncredited discoveries of our almost inexhaustible authors."

Reported by Clark, Nov. 11, 1805, on the Pacific coast just north of Cape Disappointment, Pacific Co., Wash.

? *Amphiodon alosoides* Raf.
= *Hiodon alosoides* Rafinesque.
Jour. Phys., Paris, 421. 1819.
GOLDEYE.

Thwaites, II, 143: "precisely the form and about the size of the well known fish called the *Hickary Shad or old wife.*" Coues (II, 362) identified it as *Hyodon alosoides.*

Discovered and described by Lewis, June 11, 1805, above junction of Marias R. with Missouri. Chouteau Co., Montana.

? *Ictalurus furcatus* Lesueur
= *Pimelodus furcatus* Lesueur
= *Ameirus ponderosus* Bean.
Cuvier & Valenciennes, Hist. Nat. Poiss., 9:136. 1840.
BLUE CATFISH.
See Jordan, Evermann, and Clark *Check List,* 152.

Gass, 35: "Two of our men last night caught nine catfish, that would together weigh three hundred pounds." Coues (I, 88) : "The species is doubtless *Amiurus ponderosus.*"

Taken from Missouri near mouth of Vermillion R., Aug. 25, 1804. Clay Co., S.D. on north, Dixon Co., Nebr., on south.

? *Ictalurus punctatus* (Raf.)
= *Silurus punctatus* Raf.
Amer. Monthly Mag., 359. 1818.
CHANNEL CATFISH.

Thwaites, I, 90: "This evening Guthrege [Goodrich] Cought a *White Catfish* . . . tale much like that of a *Dolfin.*" Coues (I, 54) : "*Ictalurus punctatus.*"

Taken from Missouri at Camp White Catfish, just above mouth of Platte R., July 24, 1804. Mills Co., Iowa, on east, Sarpy Co., Nebr., on west.

? *Mylocheilus lateralis* Agassiz & Pickering. Amer. Jour. Sci. Arts, 231. 1855. COLUMBIA RIVER CHUB. See J. E. & C. *Check List,* 112.

Thwaites, IV, 326: "caught several chubbs with a bone." Coues (III, 970) identified as *Mylochilus caurinus.* See also Burroughs, 336.

Taken from Columbia, April 26, 1806, below mouth of Umatilla River. Benton Co., Wash., on north, Umatilla Co., Oregon, on south.

? *Pantosteus platyrhynchus* (Cope) = *Minomus platyrhynchus* Cope. Proc. Amer. Phil. Soc., 14:134. 1874. MOUNTAIN SUCKER.

Thwaites, V, 266: "One of the men brought me a fish . . . a red streak passed down each side." Coues (III, 1138) identified as *P. jordani,* the accepted name in 1893. See also Burroughs, 264.

Taken from Yellowstone R., July 16, 1806, just east of present-day Livingston, Park Co., Montana.

? *Platichthys stellatus* (Pallas) = *Pleuronectes stellatus* Pallas. Zoog. Rosso.-Asiat., 3:416. 1811. STARRY FLOUNDER.

Thwaites, IV, 163: "The flounder is also an inhabitant of salt water." Identified by Coues (III, 891) as *P. stellatus.*

Referred to by Lewis, Mar. 13, 1806, at Fort Clatsop, Clatsop Co., Oregon.

? *Ptychocheilus oregonensis* (Richardson) = *Cyprinus* (*Leuciscus*) *oregonensis* Richardson. Fauna Bor.-Amer., 3:305. 1836. NORTHERN SQUAWFISH.

Thwaites, IV, 335: "they take their fish which at present are a mullet." Coues (III, 976) identified as "*P. oregonensis* probably."

Encountered by Lewis, Apr. 29, 1806, at mouth of Walla Walla River, Walla Walla Co., Wash.

Salmo clarkii Richardson = *Salar lewisi* Girard. Fauna Bor.-Amer., 3:225. 1836. CUTTHROAT TROUT.

Thwaites, II, 150: "Goodrich had caught half a dozen very fine trout . . . have generally a small dash of red on each side behind the front ventral fins." Coues (II, 367): "The identical fish named *Salar lewisi* by Girard."

Discovered and described by Lewis, June 13, 1805, at Great Falls, Cascade Co., Montana.

Salmo gairdneri Richardson. Fauna Bor.-Amer., 3:221. 1836. STEELHEAD TROUT.

Thwaites, IV, 167: "met with another species [of trout] . . . of a dark colour on the back." Coues (III, 893) det. as "*S. gairdneri,* steelhead salmon trout."

Described by Lewis, Mar. 13, 1806, at Fort Clatsop.

? *Stizostedion canadense* (Smith) = *Lucioperca canadensis* Smith. Griffith's ed. Cuvier's Regne Anim., Fishes, 275. 1836. SAUGER.

Thwaites, II, 142: "fish of two different species, one about 9 inches long of white colour." Coues (II, 362) identified as "a percoid fish, *Stizostedion canadense*."

Pulled from Missouri, June 11, 1805, above mouth of Marias R., Chouteau Co., Montana.

Thaleichthys pacificus (Rich.) = *Salmo* (*Mallotus*) *pacificus* Richardson. Fauna Bor.-Amer., 3:226. 1836. EULACHON; CANDLE FISH.

Thwaites, IV, 102: "a species of small fish which now begin to run, and are taken in great quantities in the Columbia." Coues, II, 807.

Described by Lewis and drawn by Clark, Feb. 24–25, 1806, at Fort Clatsop. See frontispiece, Thwaites, IV, for Clark's drawing.

REPTILES AND AMPHIBIANS

? *Amyda spinifera spinifera* (Lesueur) = *Trionyx spiniferus* Lesueur. Me. Mus. Hist. Nat. Paris, 15:258. 1827. SOFT-SHELLED TURTLE.

Thwaites, V, 307: "cought . . . a Soft Shell turtle." Coues (III, 1159) identified it as *Aspidonectes spinifer.*

Caught by Clark, July 29, 1806, where Tongue River empties into Yellowstone at present-day Miles City, Custer Co., Montana.

Bufo boreas boreas (Baird & Girard) = *B. boreas* Baird & Girard = *B. columbiensis* Cope. Proc. Ac. Nat. Sci. Phila., 6:174. 1852. COLUMBIAN TOAD.

Thwaites, V, 87: "a large species of frog [toad] . . . larger than our bull frog." Coues (III, 1018) identified it as *Bufo columbiensis.*

Observed by Lewis, May 30, 1806, at Camp Chopunnish, Clearwater River, Idaho Co., Idaho.

Crotalus viridis oreganus (Holbrook) = *C. oreganus* Holbrook. N. Amer. Herp., Ed. 1, 4:115. 1840. NORTHERN PACIFIC RATTLER.

Thwaites, IV, 323: "several rattlesnakes killed by the party." Coues (III, 968) said *C. lucifer.*

Killed April 25, 1806, near present-day Roosevelt, Klickitat Co., Wash.

Crotalus viridis viridis Rafinesque = *C. confluentus* Say. Amer. Monthly Mag., Crit. Rev., 4 (1):41. 1818. PRAIRIE RATTLER.

Thwaites, II, 160: "found a large rattlesnake . . . he had 176 scuta on the abdomen and 17 half formed on the tale." Coues (II, 373) identified it as *C. confluentus.*

Described by Lewis, June 15, 1805, at Great Falls, Cascade Co., Montana.

Heterodon nasicus nasicus (Baird & Girard) = *H. nasicus* Baird & Gir. Stansbury's Expl. Surv. Great

Thwaites, II, 264: "I saw a black snake . . . the belly of which was as black as any other

Discovered by Lewis, July 23, 1805, not far from present-day Townsend, Broad-

Salt Lake, 352. 1852.
WESTERN HOG-NOSE SNAKE.

part or as jet itself." Coues (II, 434) referred to it as *H. simus nasicus.*

water Co., Montana.

Hyla regilla Baird & Girard.
Proc. Ac. Nat. Sci. Phila., 6:174.
1852.
PACIFIC TREE FROG.

Thwaites, V, 87: "a smal green tree-frog." Coues (III, 1018) identified as *H. regilla.*

Observed by Lewis, May 30, 1806, at Camp Chopunnish, Idaho Co., Idaho.

Phrynosoma douglassi douglassi (Bell)
= *Agama douglasii* Bell.
Trans. Linn. Soc. London, 16:105. 1833.
PIGMY HORNED TOAD.

Thwaites, V, 80: "a speceis of Lizzard . . . native of these plains . . . I have called them horned Lizzard." Coues, III, 899.

Described by Lewis, May 29, 1806, at Camp Chopunnish, Idaho. The range of this subspecies, according to Stejneger and Barbour, is Oregon and Washington.

Phrynosoma cornutum (Harlan)
= *Agama cornuta* Harlan.
Jour. Ac. Nat. Sci. Phila., 4:299.
1825.
PLAINS HORNED TOAD.
See Schmidt's *Check List*, 133–134.

Thwaites, VII, 300: "a horned Lizzard, a native of the Osage plains."

On May 18, 1804, Lewis sent Jefferson a specimen from St. Louis.

Pituophis sayi sayi (Schlegel)
= *Coluber sayi* Schlegel.
Essai Physion. Serp., Pt. 2, 157.
1837.
BULL SNAKE; SAY'S PINE SNAKE.

Thwaites, VI, 124: "This snake is vulgarly called the cow or bull snake from a bellowing noise." Coues (II, 437) identified it as *Pituophis sayi?.*

Described by Lewis, Aug. 5, 1804, near mouth of Niobrara River. Bon Homme Co., S.D., on north, Knox Co., Nebr., on south.

? *Pseudomys troosti elegans* (Wied)
= *Emys elegans* Wied.
Reise Nord Amer., 1, Pt. 4, 213.
1838.
WATER TERRAPIN.

Thwaites, II, 186: "saw a number of water terripens." Coues (II, 391) identified as "doubtless *Emys elegans* of Maximilian."

Noted by Lewis, June 25, 1805, at Great Falls, Cascade Co., Montana.

Rana pretiosa pretiosa (Baird & Girard)
= *R. pretiosa* Baird & Girard.
Proc. Ac. Nat. Sci. Phila., 6:378.
1853.
WESTERN FROG.

Thwaites, IV, 216: "the frogs are croaking in the swam[p]s." Coues (III, 915) identified as *Rana pretiosa?.* C. V. Piper (Thwaites, V, 87) supplied same determination.

Noted by Lewis, Mar. 29, 1806, near mouth of Lewis's River. Cowlitz or Clark Co., Wash., on north, Columbia Co., Oregon, on south.

? *Sceloporus occidentalis* Baird

Thwaites, IV, 155:

Encountered by Lewis,

& Girard.
Proc. Ac. Nat. Sci. Phila., 6:175.
1852.
WESTERN FENCE LIZARD.

"The reptiles of this country are the rattlesnake garter snake and the common brown Lizzard." Noted also, V, 870. Coues (III, 899) identified as *S. graciosus* or *S. occidentalis.*

April 24, 1806, near present-day Roosevelt, Klickitat Co., Wash.

? *Thamnophis ordinoides vagrans* (Baird & Girard)
= *Eutaenia vagrans* B. & G.
Cat. N. Amer. Rept., Pt. 1, 35.
1853.
WESTERN GARTER SNAKE.

Thwaites, II, 266: "Observed a great number of snakes . . . [one] is much like the garter snake of our country." Coues (II, 437) identified as *Eutaenia vagrans.*

Discovered by Lewis, July 24, 1805, near present-day Townsend, Broadwater Co., Montana.

? *Thamnophis sirtilas concinnus* (Hallowell)
= *Tropidonotus concinnus* Hallowell.
Proc. Ac. Nat. Sci. Phila., 6:182.
1852.
NORTHWESTERN GARTER SNAKE.

Thwaites, IV, 211: "Saw a great number of snakes . . . much the form of the common garter snake of the Atlantic coast." Coues (III, 898) suggested *Eutaenia concinna* or *E. pickeringi.*

Found on Deer Island, Mar. 28, 1806, above Cowlitz River, Cowlitz Co., Wash.

Triturus torosus torosus (Rathke)
= *Triton torosus* Rathke
= *Diemyctylus torosus* Cope.
In Eschscholtz, Zool. Atlas, Pt. 5, 12. 1833.
CALIFORNIA NEWT; WARTY SALAMANDER.

Thwaites, IV, 155–156: "There is a speceis of water lizzard [salamander] of which I saw one only just above the grand rapids of the Columbia." Coues (III, 900): "yet another hitherto unrecognized discovery of Lewis and Clark."

Described by Lewis, March 11, 1806, at Fort Clatsop. Discovered at "grand rapids," namely Cascades.

BIRDS

Aechmophorus occidentalis (Lawrence)
= *Podiceps occidentalis* Lawr.
Baird, Cassin, and Lawrence, Rep. Expl. and Surv. R.R. Pac., 9:894. 1858.
WESTERN GREBE [A.O.U. 1].

Thwaites, IV, 142: "this bird is not more than half the size of the speckled loon . . . dives for security when pursued." Coues (III, 882): "This is the original and an easily recognizable description of this bird."

Described by Lewis, March 7, 1806, at Fort Clatsop.

Anser albifrons frontalis Baird
= *A. frontalis* Baird.
Baird, Cassin, and Lawr., Rep.
Expl. and Surv. R.R. Pac.,
9:762. 1858.
WHITE-FRONTED GOOSE [A.O.U.
171].

Thwaites, IV, 170:
"There is a third spe-
cies of brant in the
neighbourhood of this
place which is about
the size and much the
form of the pided
brant." Coues, III,
884. Burroughs, 197–
198.

Described by Lewis,
March 15, 1806, at
Fort Clatsop. See also,
facing p. 172 of
Thwaites, IV, Clark's
sketch of goose head.

Asyndesmus lewis (Gray)
= *Picus torquatus* Wilson.
Amer. Orn., 3:31. 1811.
LEWIS'S WOODPECKER [A.O.U.
408].

Thwaites, II, 252: "I
saw a black wood-
pecker (or crow) to-
day about the size of
the lark woodpecker
as black as a crow."
Coues, II, 428.

Discovered by Lewis,
July 20, 1805, north of
Helena, Lewis and
Clark Co., Montana.

Aythya collaris (Donovan)
= *Anas collaris* Donovan.
Brit. Birds, 6:147. 1809.
RING-NECKED DUCK [A.O.U. 150].

Thwaites, IV, 210:
"One of the hunters
killed a duck . . .
a size less than
the duckinmallard."
Coues (III, 889) : "L.
and C. are again the
discoverers of a new
species."

Described by Lewis,
March 28, 1806, above
Fort Clatsop.

Bonasa umbellus sabini (Doug-
las)
= *Tetrao Sabini* Douglas.
Trans. Linn. Soc. London, 16,
Pt. 1, 137. 1828.
OREGON RUFFED GROUSE [A.O.U.
300c].

Thwaites, III, 76: "A
brown and yellow spe-
cies [of pheasant] that
a gooddeel resembles
the phesant common
to the Atlantic
States." Also IV, 129.
Coues (III, 872) : "No
question . . . L. and
C. are the discoverers
and first describers of
the Oregon ruffed
grouse."

First noted by Lewis,
Sept. 20, 1805, on.
Lolo Trail. De-
scribed, March 3,
1806, at Fort Clatsop.

? *Branta canadensis hutchinsii*
(Richardson)
= *Anser Hutchinsii* Rich.
Fauna Bor.-Amer., 2:470. 1831.
HUTCHINS'S GOOSE [A.O.U. 172a].

Thwaites, I, 370: "Saw
. . . a small species of
geese." Coues (I, 296)
identified as *Bernicla
hutchinsi*. Burroughs
(195) thought *B. c.
leucopareia* (Brandt)
more likely.

Seen by Lewis, May 5,
1805, above mouth of
Poplar River, Mon-
tana. Roosevelt Co.
on north, McCone
Co. on south.

Branta canadensis leucopareia
(Brandt)
= *Anser leucopareia* Brandt.

Thwaites, IV, 145:
"The small goose of
this country is reather

Described by Lewis,
March 8, 1806, at Fort
Clatsop.

Bull. Sci. Acad. Imp. St. Petersb., 1 (5) :37. 1836.
LESSER CANADA GOOSE [A.O.U. 172d].

less than the brant." Burroughs (195) : "Lewis and Clark may be credited with the discovery of the lesser Canada goose." Coues (III, 885) identified this small goose as *Bernicla hutchinsi.*

Bubo virginianus occidentalis Stone.
Auk, 13 (2) :155. 1896.
MONTANA HORNED OWL [A.O.U. 375j].

Thwaites, I, 308: "One of the party killed a large hooting owl . . . more booted." According to A. C. Bent (*Birds of Prey*, II, 348) : "Probably the first of this subspecies killed by white man."

Discovered by Lewis, April 14, 1805. The explorers camped that night in Mountrail Co., N.D.

? *Bubo virginianus saturatus* Ridgway.
U.S. Geol. Exp. 40th Parallel, 4, Pt. 3, Orr., 572. 1877.
DUSKY HORNED OWL [A.O.U. 375c].

Thwaites, IV, 129: "We also met with the large hooting Owl . . . on the Kooskooskee river." Coues (III, 875) identified as *B. v. saturatus.* Could have been *C. v. lagophonus* or, as Burroughs (209) suggests, *B. v. occidentalis.*

Described by Lewis, March 3, 1806, at Fort Clatsop, but seen, as stated, on the Kooskooskee (Clearwater), in Idaho Co., Idaho.

Canachites canadensis franklinii (Douglas)
= *Tetrao Franklinii* Douglas.
Trans. Linn. Soc. London, 16, Pt. 1, 139. 1829.
FRANKLIN'S GROUSE [A.O.U. 299].

Thwaites, III, 77: "Three species of Phesants . . . [one] with a red stripe above the eye." Also IV, 128–129. Coues (III, 870) : "We clearly recognize another species discovered by Lewis and Clark."

Discovered by Lewis, Sept. 20, 1805, on Lolo Trail, Idaho. Described, March 3, 1806, at Fort Clatsop.

Catoptrophorus semipalmatus inornatus (Brewster)
= *Symphemia semipalmatus inornatus* Brewster.
Auk, 4 (2) :145. 1887.
WESTERN WILLET [A.O.U. 258a].

Thwaites, II, 17–18: "I killed four plover this evening of a different species from any I have yet seen." Coues (I, 304) : "This bird is the semipalmated tattler or willet."

Discovered and fully described by Lewis, May 9, 1805. Expedition camped that night above present-day Fort Peck Dam, Valley Co., Montana.

Centrocercus urophasianus urophasianus (Bonaparte) = *Tetrao urophasianus* Bonap. Zool. Jour., 3 (10) :213. 1827. SAGE GROUSE [A.O.U. 309].

Thwaites, II, 124: "I saw a flock of the mountain cock . . . with a long pointed tail." Coues (I, 350) : "The bird Lewis here mentions is the sage-grouse."

Discovered by Lewis, June 5, 1805, on Marias River, Chouteau Co., Montana.

? *Chordeiles minor hesperis* Grinnell = *C. virginianus hesperis* Grin. Condor, 7 (6) :170. 1905. PACIFIC NIGHTHAWK [A.O.U. 420d].

Thwaites, II, 200: "The large goat sucker lays it's eggs in these open plains." Coues (II, 398) identified as *C. henryi,* though Burroughs (235), because of range, inclines to *hesperis* as the subspecies.

Mentioned by Lewis, June 30, 1805, at Great Falls, Cascade Co., Montana.

Colaptes auratus luteus Bangs. Auk, 15 (2) :177. 1898. NORTHERN FLICKER [A.O.U. 412a].

Thwaites, VI, 187: "The lark woodpecker, with yellow wings, and a black spot on the brest . . . has appeared." Reid and Gannon (19) identify as *C. a. luteus.*

Reported by Lewis, April 11, 1805, at Fort Mandan, McLean Co., N.D.

Corvus brachyrhynchos hesperis Ridgway = *C. americanus hesperis* Ridg. Man. N. Am. Birds, 362. 1887. WESTERN COMMON CROW [A.O.U. 488b].

Thwaites, III, 257: "I observe . . . crows in abundance." Burroughs (248) suggests *C. b. hesperis.*

Reported by Clark, Nov. 29, 1805, at Tongue Point, near present-day Astoria, Oregon.

Corvus caurinus Baird. Baird, Cassin, and Lawrence, Rep. Expl. and Surv., R.R. Pac., 9:559, 569. 1858. NORTHWESTERN CROW [A.O.U. 489].

Thwaites, IV, 129: "The crow is here [at Fort Clatsop] much smaller yet it's note is the same." Coues (III, 874) identified as *Corvus caurinus.*

Described by Lewis, March 3, 1806, at Fort Clatsop.

Corvus corax sinuatus Wagler = *C. sinuatus* "Lichtenst." Wag. Isis von Oken, 22, Heft 7, col. 748. 1829. AMERICAN RAVEN [A.O.U. 486].

Thwaites, IV, 129: "Ravens build their nests in great numbers along the . . . clifts of the Columbia river."

Mentioned by Lewis, March 3, 1806, at Fort Clatsop. Different from subspecies *C. c. principalis* known to L. & C. in the East.

Cyanocitta stelleri annectens (Baird) = [*Cyanura stelleri*] var. *annectens* Baird.

Thwaites, III, 75: "I have observed two birds of a blue colour . . . [one] resembles

Described by Lewis, March 4, 1806, at Fort Clatsop, though he first saw this species

Baird, Brewer, and Ridgway, Hist. N. A. Birds, 2:281. 1874.
BLACK-HEADED JAY [A.O.U. 478c].

the jay bird." IV, 132: "The blue crested Corvus [jays] . . . natives of a piney country invariably." Coues (III, 876) identified mountain form as *C. s. annectens*.

on the Lolo Trail, Sept. 20, 1805.

Dendragapus obscurus richardsonii (Douglas) = *Tetrao Richardsonii* Douglas. Trans. Linn. Soc. London, 16, Pt. 1, 141. 1829.
RICHARDSON'S BLUE GROUSE [A.O.U. 297b].

Thwaites, II, 256: "I also saw two fesants today of a dark brown colour much larger than the phesant of the U'States." Coues (II, 430) identified as *D. o. richardsonii*.

Discovered by Lewis, July 21, 1805, north of Helena, Lewis and Clark Co., Montana.

? *Dendrocopos villosus harrisi* (Audubon) = *Picus Harrisi* Audubon. Birds Amer. (folio), 4:417. 1838.
HARRIS'S WOODPECKER [A.O.U. 393c].

Thwaites, IV, 246: "We saw . . . the small speckled woodpecker with a white back." Coues (III, 930) identified as *Picus villosus harrisi*.

Referred to by Lewis, April 5, 1806, above mouth of Willamette R., Multnomah Co., Oregon.

? *Dendrocopos villosus hyloscopus* (Cabanis & Heine) = *Dryobates hyloscopus* C. & H. Mus. Hein., 4, Th. 2, sig. 9, 69. 1863.
CABANIS'S WOODPECKER [A.O.U. 393d].

Thwaites, V, 136: "Saw the speckled woodpecker." Coues (III, 1044) identified as *Picus villosus hyloscopus*.

Seen by Lewis, June 15, 1806, on Lolo Trail, Idaho Co., Idaho.

Dryocopus pileatus picinus (Bangs) = *Phloeotomus pileatus picinus* Bangs. Proc. New Eng. Zool. Club, 4:79. 1910.
WESTERN PILEATED WOODPECKER [A.O.U. 405c].

Thwaites, IV, 132: "The large woodpecker or log cock . . . [is] the same with those of the Atlantic states." Burroughs (242): "Specimen seen at Fort Clatsop undoubtedly the western subspecies."

Referred to by Lewis, March 4, 1806, at Fort Clatsop, and elsewhere on other dates.

? *Eremophila alpestris leucolaema* Coues. Birds Northwest, 38. 1874.
PRAIRIE HORNED LARK [A.O.U. 474c].

Thwaites, VI, 187: "The Prarie lark, bald Eagle, & the large plover have returned." Reid & Gannon (19) tentatively identified as prairie horned lark or Saskatchewan horned lark.

Noted by Lewis, April 10, 1805, at Fort Mandan, McLean Co., N.D.

Euphagus cyanocephalus
(Wag.)
= *Psarocolius cyanocephalus*
Wagler.
Isis von Oken, 22, Heft 7, col.
758. 1829.
BREWER'S BLACKBIRD [A.O.U.
510].

Thwaites, II, 186:
"The young black-
birds which are al-
most innumerable
. . . just begin to fly."
Coues (II, 391) iden-
tified as Brewer's
blackbird.

Mentioned by Lewis,
June 25, 1805, at
Great Falls, Cascade
Co., Montana.

Fulmarus glacialis rodgersii
(Cassin)
= *Fulmarus Rodgersii* Cassin.
Proc. Acad. Nat. Sci. Phila., 326.
1862.
PACIFIC FULMAR [A.O.U. 86.1].

Thwaites, IV, 141: "A
white gull . . . at the
base of the up[p]er
Chop there is an eli-
vated orning." Coues
(III, 881) identified
as Pacific fulmar.

Described by Lewis,
March 7, 1806, at Fort
Clatsop. Clark made
sketch of head; see
Thwaites, IV, facing
p. 140.

? *Gavia arctica pacifica* (Lawr.)
= *Colymbus pacificus* Lawrence.
Baird, Cassin, and Lawrence,
Rep. Expl. and Surv., R.R.
Pac., 9:887, 889. 1858.
PACIFIC LOON [A.O.U. 10].

Thwaites, IV, 142:
"The Speckled loon
found on every part
of the rivers of this
[Pacific] country."
Coues (III, 881)
identified as "proba-
bly" the Pacific loon,
"which is the com-
monest loon along the
coast of Oregon and
Calif."

Described by Lewis,
March 7, 1806, at Fort
Clatsop.

Gymnorhinus cyanocephalus
Wied.
Reise N. Amer., 2:21. 1841.
PIÑON JAY [A.O.U. 492].

Thwaites, II, 295: "I
also saw . . . a blue
bird about the size of
the common robbin."
Coues (II, 454) iden-
tified as piñon jay,
"here first discovered
and described."

Discovered by Lewis,
Aug. 1, 1805, on Jef-
ferson River, Mon-
tana. Madison Co. on
south, Jefferson Co.
on north.

Lanius ludovicianus excubi-
torides Swainson
= *L. excubitorides* Swainson.
Sw. & Rich. Faun. Bor.-Amer.,
2:115. 1831.
WHITE-RUMPED SHRIKE [A.O.U.
622a].

Thwaites, II, 140: "I
saw a small bird today
. . . about the size of
the blue thrush or
catbird." Coues (II,
361) identified as
white-rumped shrike.

Described by Lewis,
June 10, 1805, at
mouth of Marias
River, Chouteau Co.,
Montana.

? *Larus glaucescens* Neumann.
Naturg. Vögel Deutschlands,
10:351. 1840.
GLAUCOUS-WINGED GULL [A.O.U.
44].

Thwaites, IV, 140: "A
species [of gull] . . .
of a light brown
colour with a whitish
or mealy coloured
back." Coues (III,
881) identified as
"young *Larus glauce-*
scens."

Described by Lewis,
March 7, 1806, at Fort
Clatsop.

? *Larus occidentalis occidentalis* Audubon
= *Larus occidentalis* Audubon.
Orn. Biogr., 5:320. 1839.
WESTERN GULL [A.O.U. 49].

Thwaites, IV, 140: "The large grey gull . . . with a greyish brown back." Coues (III, 881) identified as "young *Larus occidentalis.*"

Described by Lewis, March 7, 1806, at Fort Clatsop.

? *Larus philadelphia* (Ord)
= *Sterna Philadelphia* Ord.
Guthrie's Geog., 2nd Am. ed., 319. 1815.
BONAPARTE'S GULL [A.O.U. 60].

Thwaites, IV, 140: "A small speceis [of gull] . . . white except some black spots about the head." Coues (III, 881) identified as Bonaparte's gull.

Described by Lewis, March 7, 1806, at Fort Clatsop.

Nucifraga columbiana (Wilson)
= *Corvus columbianus* Wilson.
Amer. Orn., III:29. 1811.
CLARK'S NUTCRACKER [A.O.U. 491].

Thwaites, III, 17: "I saw to day [a] Bird of the woodpecker kind." Coues (II, 530): "This is the remarkable bird afterward called Clark's crow."

Discovered by Clark, Aug. 22, 1805, near present town of Tendoy, on Lemhi River, Lemhi Co., Idaho.

Numenius americanus americanus (Bechstein)
= *N. americanus* Bechstein.
Latham, Allg. Uebers. Vögel, 4, Pt. 2, 432. 1812.
LONG-BILLED CURLEW [A.O.U. 264].

Thwaites, II, 180: "Saw . . . the large brown curloo." Coues (II, 388): "The curlew I suppose to be *Numenius longirostris* [now *N. americanus*] which is common in that country." Reid & Gannon (17) agreed with Coues.

Observed by Lewis, June 23, 1805, at Great Falls, Montana; also, Apr. 17, 1805, in western N.D. (see Thwaites, I, 318).

Olor columbianus (Ord)
= *Anas columbianus* Ord.
Guthrie's Geog., 2nd Am. ed., 319. 1815.
WHISTLING SWAN [A.O.U. 180].

Thwaites, IV, 147–148: "The small swan differs only from the larger one in it's size and note . . . it's note . . . begins with a kind of whistleing sound." Coues, III, 885–886; also Burroughs, 199.

Described by Lewis, March 9, 1806, at Fort Clatsop.

Oreortyx pictus pictus (Douglas)
= *Ortyx picta* Douglas.
Trans. Linn. Soc. London, 16, Pt. 1, 143. 1829.
MOUNTAIN QUAIL [A.O.U. 292a].

Thwaites, IV, 252: "Last evening Reubin Field killed a bird of the quail kind." Coues (III, 936): "probably the first de-

Discovered and described by Lewis, Apr. 7, 1806, above mouth of Washougal River. Multnomah Co., Oregon, on south,

scription ever penned of the beautiful mountain quail." Burroughs (221) preferred *O. p. palmeri* Ober.

Clark Co., Wash., on north.

Pedioecetes phasianellus columbianus (Ord)
= *Phasianus columbianus* Ord. Guthrie's Geog., 2nd Am. ed., 317. 1815.
COLUMBIAN SHARP-TAILED GROUSE [A.O.U. 308a].

Thwaites, IV, 121: "The Grouse or Prarie hen is peculiarly the inhabitant of the Great Plains of Columbia." Coues (III, 868): "The account of the bird is excellent; it furnished the original basis of *Phasianus columbianus*."

Described by Lewis, March 1, 1806, at Fort Clatsop, Clatsop Co., Oregon.

Pedioecetes phasianellus campestris Ridgway.
Proc. Biol. Soc. Wash., 93. 1884.
PRAIRIE SHARP-TAILED GROUSE [A.O.U. 308b].

Thwaites, I, 145: "Saw . . . a great number of Grous." Reid & Gannon (17) identify as *P. p. campestris*. Burroughs (211) preferred *P. p. jamesi* Lincoln. L. & C. may well have discovered both subspecies.

Discovered by Lewis and Clark, Sept. 12, 1804, in S.D. Charles Mix Co. on north of Missouri, Gregory Co. on south.

Perisoreus canadensis obscurus Ridgway
= *P. Canadensis* var. *obscurus* Ridgway.
Bull. Essex Inst., 5 (11):194. 1873.
OREGON JAY [A.O.U. 485].

Thwaites, III, 309: "The smaller corvus with the white breast . . . still continue with us." Coues (II, 743) identified as *P. obscurus*. Jackson (298) preferred the subspecies *P. c. capitalis* Ridg. L. & C. very likely discovered both races.

Referred to by Lewis, Jan. 3, 1806, at Fort Clatsop.

? *Phalacrocorax auritus auritus* (Lesson)
= *Carbo auritus* Lesson
= *Phalacrocorax dilophus* (Swain.).
Traite d'Orn., livr. 8, 605. 1831.
DOUBLE-CRESTED CORMORANT [A.O.U. 120].

Thwaites, III, 139: "Here I saw a great number of . . . black Comerants." Coues (II, 650): "Cannot be specified, but were probably *P. dilophus*."

Observed by Lewis and Clark, Oct. 20, 1805, on Columbia below mouth of Umatilla River. Klickitat Co., Wash., on north, Morrow Co., Oregon, on south.

Phalaenoptilus nuttallii nuttallii (Audubon)
= *Caprimulgus nuttallii* Aud.

Thwaites, I, 197: "I cought a whipprwill Small & not com-

Discovered by Lewis and Clark, Oct. 17, 1804, just below

Birds Amer., 7:350. 1844.
NUTTALL'S POOR-WILL [A.O.U. 418].

mon." See also Thwaites, VI, 132 and Coues, I, 171.

mouth of Cannonball River, N.D. Sioux Co. on west, Emmons Co. on east.

Pica pica hudsonia (Sabine) = *Corvus hudsonicus* Sabine. App. Frankl. Jour., 671. 1823. BLACK-BILLED MAGPIE [A.O.U. 475].

Thwaites, I, 151: "Killed . . . a remarkable *Bird* (*Magpy*) of the *Corvus* Species." See also Thwaites, VI, 130–131 and Coues, I, 118.

Discovered Sept. 16, 1804, near site of present-day Chamberlain, S.D. Lyman Co. on west of Missouri, Brule Co. on east.

Piranga ludoviciana (Wilson) = *Tanagra ludoviciana* Wilson. Amer. Orn., 3:27. 1811. WESTERN TANAGER [A.O.U. 607].

Thwaites, V, 111: "We met with a beautiful little bird in this neighbourhood." Coues (III, 1035): "The earliest description of the Louisiana tanager."

Discovered and described by Lewis, June 6, 1806, at Camp Chopunnish on Clearwater River, Idaho.

? *Podiceps grisegena holböllii* Reinhardt = *P. Holböllii* Reinhardt. Videnskab. Medd., 76. 1853. RED-NECKED GREBE [A.O.U. 2].

Thwaites, IV, 152: "The larger speceis [of divers] are about the size of the teal . . . the beak is streight and pointed." Coues (III, 888): "probably the red-necked grebe."

Described by Lewis, March 10, 1806, at Fort Clatsop.

Rhynchophanes mccownii (Lawr.) = *Plectrophanes Mccownii* Lawr. Ann. Lyc. N.Y., 5:122. 1851. McCOWN'S LONGSPUR [A.O.U. 539].

Thwaites, II, 120: "A small bird which in action resembles the lark." Coues (I, 349) identified as *R. mccownii.*

Discovered by Lewis, June 4, 1805, on Marias River, Chouteau Co., Montana.

Selasphorus platycercus platycercus (Swainson) = *Trochilus platycercus* Swain. Phil. Mag., n.s., 1 (6):441. 1827. BROAD-TAILED HUMMINGBIRD [A.O.U. 432].

Thwaites, V, 136: "Found the nest of a humming bird." Coues (III, 1044): "Credit Lewis and Clark with the discovery of this species."

Discovered by Lewis, June 15, 1806, just west of Hungry Creek, on Lolo Trail, Idaho.

Spinus tristris pallidus Mearns. Auk, 7 (3):244. 1890. PALE GOLDFINCH [A.O.U. 529a].

Thwaites, II, 130: "These birds sung most enchantingly; I observed among them the . . . goldfinch." Burroughs (258) identified as *S. t. pallidus.*

Discovered by Lewis, June 8, 1805, on Marias River, Montana.

? *Sterna forsteri* Nuttall. Man. Orn. U.S. and Canada, 2:274. 1834. FORSTER'S TERN [A.O.U. 69].

Thwaites, V, 237: "Saw an unusual flight of white gulls about the size of a pigeon with the top of their heads black." Coues (III, 1133): "most probably *S. forsteri.*"

Seen by Lewis, Aug. 7, 1806, on Missouri just above mouth of Yellowstone River, N.D. Williams Co. on north, McKenzie Co. on south.

Sterna albifrons antillarum (Lesson) = *Sternula Antillarum* Lesson. Descr. Mamm. et Ois., 256. 1847. LEAST TERN [A.O.U. 74].

Thwaites, VI, 124: "I have frequently observed an aquatic bird in the cours of asscending this river." Burroughs (231) identified as *S. a. antillarum.*

Fully described by Lewis, Aug. 5, 1804, on Missouri. Washington Co., Neb., on west, Harrison Co., Iowa, on east.

Sturnella neglecta neglecta Audubon = *S. neglecta* Audubon. Birds Amer., 7:339. 1844. WESTERN MEADOWLARK [A.O.U. 501.1].

Thwaites, II, 180: "There is a kind of larke here that much resembles the bird called the oldfield lark . . . the note differs considerably." Coues (II, 387–388) identified as western meadowlark.

Discovered by Lewis, June 22, 1805, at Great Falls, Cascade Co., Montana.

? *Troglodytes troglodytes pacificus* Baird = *T. hyemalis* var. *pacificus* Baird. Rev. Amer. Birds, sign. 9, 138; sign. 10, 145. 1864. WESTERN WINTER WREN [A.O.U. 722a].

Thwaites, IV, 133: "There are two species of the flycatch, [one] a small redish brown species with a short tail." Coues (III, 876) identified as western winter wren.

Noted by Lewis, March 4, 1806, at Fort Clatsop.

Zenaidura macroura marginella (Woodhouse) = *Ectopistes marginella* Wood. Proc. Acad. Nat. Sci. Phila., 6 (3) :104. 1852. WESTERN MOURNING DOVE [A.O.U. 316a].

Thwaites, V, 176–177: "The dove . . . [is] found in this valley [of the Bitterroot River.]" Lewis reported this common dove elsewhere in the West, and may be credited with its discovery.

Mentioned by Lewis, July 1, 1806, where Lolo Creek empties into Bitterroot River, Missoula Co., Montana.

MAMMALS

Alces alces shirasi Nelson = *A. americanus shirasi* Nel. Proc. Biol. Soc. Wash., 27:72. 1914.

Thwaites, V, 194: "Reubin Fields wounded a moos deer

Noted by Lewis, July 7, 1806, near Lewis and Clark Pass, Lewis

SHIRAS'S MOOSE.

this morning." See also Hall & Kelson's distribution map (II, 1015). Coues (III, 1032): "Here Lewis and Clark lead all the naturalists, as usual, for the American moose . . . had no scientific standing in their day."

and Clark Co., Mont. Ordway (210), on May 10, 1805, reported seeing several near mouth of Milk River, Montana.

Antilocapra americana americana (Ord)
= *Antilope americana* Ord.
Guthrie's Geog., 2nd Am. ed., 2:292, 308. 1815.
PRONGHORN.

Thwaites, I, 147: "Killed a Buck Goat [i.e., pronghorn] of this Countrey." Coues (I, 109): "This animal was new to science when discovered by Lewis and Clark."

Discovered by Lewis and Clark, Sept. 14, 1804, near mouth of Ball Creek, Lyman Co., S.D.

Antilocapra americana oregona V. Bailey.
Proc. Biol. Soc. Wash., 45:45. 1932.
OREGON PRONGHORN.

Thwaites, IV, 287: "The hunters informed me that they saw some Antelopes." See Hall-Kelson distribution map (II, 1023).

Encountered April 16, 1806, on Columbia just below Celilo Falls. Klickitat Co., Wash., on north, Wasco Co., Oregon, on south.

Aplodontia rufa rufa (Raf.)
= *Anisonyx? rufa* Rafinesque.
Amer. Monthly Mag., 2:45. 1817.
MOUNTAIN BEAVER; "SEWELLEL."

Thwaites, IV, 109: "*Sewelel* is the Chinnook and Clatsop name for a small animal found in the timbered country on the coast." Coues (III, 861): ". . . one of the most remarkable animals discovered by Lewis and Clark."

Described by Lewis, Feb. 26, 1806, at Fort Clatsop, "only from the skin and a slight view which some of our hunters have obtained of the living animal."

? *Blarina brevicauda brevicauda* (Say)
= *Sorex brevicauda* Say.
Long's Exped., 1:164. 1823.
SHORT-TAILED SHREW.

Thwaites, I, 281: "1 Tin box containing insects mice &c." The mice may have been shrews. Dr. Barton later commented on the animals "of the genus Sorex" shipped by L. & C. from Fort Mandan to Jefferson. See Jackson, *Letters*, 276.

The "mice" in shipment of natural history specimens which left Fort Mandan on April 7, 1805.

Canis latrans latrans Say.
Long's Exped., 1:168. 1823.
COYOTE.
Hall-Kelson map (II, 845) indicates coyotes met by L. & C. on Pacific coast belonged to subspecies *C. l. umpquensis* Jackson.

Thwaites, I, 155: "Killed a Prarie Wolff . . . barks like a Small Dog." Spanish writers such as Miguel Venegas mentioned it on earlier dates, but L. & C. were first to make it known to contemporary scientists.

Collected first specimen, Sept. 18, 1804, near site of present-day Chamberlain, S.D.

Canis lupus nubilus (Say)
= *C. nubilus* Say.
Long's Exped., 1:169. 1823.
PLAINS GRAY WOLF.

Thwaites, I, 155: "The large Wolves are verry numorous." L. & C. farther west, according to Hall-Kelson map (II, 849), met two other races: *C. l. irremotus* Gold., in Montana, Idaho, and Interior Basin, and *C. l. fuscus* Rich. west of the Cascades.

Observed first, May 30, 1804, near site of present Leavenworth, Kansas, and from there commonly to western limits of its range.

Castor canadensis missouriensis V. Bailey.
Jour. Mamm., I:32. 1919.
MISSOURI BEAVER.

Thwaites, I, 65: "A large Pond containing Beaver." Farther west L. & C., according to Hall-Kelson map (II, 549), met three other races: *C. c. taylori* Davis, *C. c. leucodontus* Gray, and *C. c. idoneus* Jewett & Hall.

First mentioned July 3, 1804, near Iatan, Platte Co., Mo., and from there on frequently, but most abundantly in region of Three Forks, Montana.

Cervus canadensis roosevelti Merriam.
Proc. Biol. Soc. Wash., 11:272. 1898.
ROOSEVELT'S ELK.
Named by C. Hart Merriam in honor of T. Roosevelt.

Thwaites, III, 263: "This is the first Elk we have killed on this side the rockey mounts." Gass (229) reported 131 elk killed by party from Dec. 1, 1805, to March 20, 1806.

L. & C. killed first Roosevelt's elk at mouth of Columbia on Dec. 2, 1805. Exact spot was Tongue Point, in sight of present-day Astoria, Oregon.

Cynomys ludovicianus ludovicianus (Ord)
= *Arctomys ludovicianus* Ord.
Guthrie's Geog., 2nd Am. ed., 2:292, 302. 1815.
BLACK-TAILED PRAIRIE DOG.

Thwaites, I, 141: "Discovered a Village of Small animals that burrow in the grown." Coues (I, 110–111): The prairie dog was "then unknown to science."

First collected by L. & C. Sept. 7, 1805, Boyd Co., Neb.

Dama hemionus hemionus
(Rafinesque)
= *Cervus hemionus* Raf.
Amer. Monthly Mag., 1 (6) :436.
1817.
MULE DEER; BLACK-TAILED DEER.

Thwaites, I, 152:
"Colter Killed . . . a
curious kind of Deer."
Coues (III, 844):
"Yet another discov-
ery of Lewis and
Clark."

Discovered Sept. 17,
1804, below present-
day site of Chamber-
lain, S.D.

Dama hemionus columbianus
(Richardson)
= *Cervus macrotis* var. *col-
umbianus* Richardson.
Fauna Bor.-Amer., 1:257. 1829.
COLUMBIAN BLACK-TAILED DEER.

Thwaites, III, 237:
"The Deer of this
Coast differ materially
from our Common
deer." Coues (II,
715): "This is the
original description
of the Columbian
black-tailed deer."

Discovered by Clark,
Nov. 19, 1805, north
of Cape Disappoint-
ment, Pacific Co.,
Wash.

Dama virginianus macroura
(Rafinesque)
= *Corvus* [*sic*] *macrourus*
Rafinesque.
Amer. Monthly Mag., 1:346.
1817.
WHITE-TAILED DEER.

Thwaites, I, 21: "R.
Fields kill a Deer to
day." According to
Hall-Kelson map (II,
1009), L. & C. met
four subspecies of
white-tailed deer w.
of Mississippi: (1)
D. v. macroura
(Raf.); (2) on High
Plains *D. v. dacoten-
sis* (Gold. & Kell.);
(3) beyond Cont. Di-
vide, *D. v. ochroura*
(Bailey); and (4) on
Pacific Coast, *D. v.
leucura* (Douglas).

L. & C. killed their
first deer, May 19,
1804, just above St.
Charles, Mo. St.
Charles Co. on north,
St. Louis Co. on south.

Enhydra lutris nereis (Mer-
riam)
= *Latax lutris nereis* Merr.
Proc. Biol. Soc. Wash., 17:159.
1904.
SEA OTTER.

Thwaites, III, 237:
"Maney Indians
about one of which
had on a robe made
of 2 sea orters skins."
According to Hall-
Kelson (II, 950) this
subspecies ranges
from Straits of Juan
de Fuca south, while
the range of *E. l.
lutris* (L.) is farther
north.

L. & C. never did see
a live sea otter; appar-
ently first saw furs,
Nov. 20, 1805, while
encamped on Baker's
Bay, north side of Co-
lumbia estuary, Pa-
cific Co., Wash.

Erethizon dorsatum epixanthum
Brandt
= *E. epixanthus* Brandt.
Mem. Acad. Imp. Sci. St.
Petersb., Ser. 6, Sci. Math.

Thwaites, I, 362: "We
saw an unusual num-
ber of Porcupines
from which we de-
termined to call the

Discovered by L. & C.,
May 3, 1805, at mouth
of Porcupine (now
Poplar) River, Mon-
tana. Roosevelt Co.

Phys. et Nat., 3:390. 1835.
YELLOW-HAIRED PORCUPINE.

Eutamias townsendii townsendii
  (Bachman)
= *Tamias townsendii* Bach.
Jour. Acad. Nat. Sci. Phil., 8, Pt.
  1, 68. 1839.
TOWNSEND'S CHIPMUNK.

Felis concolor missoulensis
  Goldman.
Jour. Mamm., 24:229. 1943.
MOUNTAIN LION; PANTHER;
  COUGAR.

Lepus townsendii campanius
  Hollister
= *L. campestris* Bachman.
Jour. Acad. Nat. Sci. Phil.,
  7:349. 1837.
WHITE-TAILED JACK RABBIT.

Lynx rufus fasciatus Raf.
= *L. fasciatus* Rafinesque.
Amer. Monthly Mag., 2 (1): 46.
  1817.
OREGON BOBCAT.

? *Lynx rufus pallescens* Merr.
= *L. fasciatus pallescens* Mer-
  riam.
N. Am. Fauna, 16:104. 1899.

river after that ana-
mal." According to
Hall-Kelson map (II,
782), *E. d. epixan-
thum* ranges from
eastern Montana to
the Pacific.

Thwaites, IV, 107:
"The ground squirrel
is found in every
part of the country."
Coues (III, 859):
"We may presume,
from the locality, that
Tamias townsendi is
the species they act-
ually have in view."

Thwaites, II, 304:
"Reubin Fields killed
a large Panther." *F.
c. missoulensis*, ac-
cording to Hall-Kel-
son map (II, 957), is
found throughout
Montana and Idaho.
F. c. oregonensis Raf.
occurs in western
Wash. and Oregon.

Thwaites, I, 147:
"Shields killed a *Hare*
like the mountain
hare of Europe."
Coues (I, 116): "The
hare is the northern
jackass-rabbit, *Lepus
campestris.*"

Thwaites, IV, 92–93:
"The tyger Cat is
found on the borders
of the plains and in
the woody country
lying along the Pacific
Ocean." Coues (III,
847): "This is quite
distinct from the
Canada lynx."

Thwaites, I, 236: "I
. . . have a Cap
made of the Skin of
the *Louservia* [loup-

on north, Richland
Co. on south.

Alluded to by Lewis,
Feb. 25, 1806, at Fort
Clatsop.

Killed by Fields, Aug.
3, 1805, on Jefferson
River, between Three
Forks and Twin
Bridges, Montana.

Discovered by L. & C.,
Sept. 14, 1804, near
present-day Chamber-
lain, S.D.

Described by Lewis,
Feb. 21, 1806, at Fort
Clatsop.

Lewis and Clark,
April 7, 1805, shipped
"the skin of a Lou-
cirvia" from Fort

NORTHERN BOBCAT.

cervier, or lynx]." See Hall-Kelson map (II, 970) for range of *L. r. pallescens*. See also Burroughs (92).

Mandan to Jefferson (see Thwaites, I, 281).

Marmota flaviventris avara
(Bangs)
= *Arctomys flaviventer avarus* Bangs.
Proc. N. Eng. Zool. Club, 1:68. 1899.
YELLOW-BELLIED MARMOT.

Thwaites, IV, 320: "Saw . . . a Moonax which the natives had tamed." *M. f. avara*, according to Hall-Kelson map (I, 324), occurs in western Idaho and eastern Wash. and Oregon.

Observed by Lewis, April 24, 1806, on north side of Columbia above mouth of John Day River, Klickitat Co., Wash.

Marmota flaviventris nosophora Howell.
Proc. Biol. Soc. Wash., 27:15. 1914.
YELLOW-BELLIED MARMOT.

Thwaites, II, 377: "I have also observed some robes among them of . . . moonox." This subspecies inhabits western Montana and eastern Idaho (see Hall-Kelson, I, 324).

Noted by Lewis, Aug. 20, 1805, among Shoshoni on Lemhi River, Lemhi Co., Idaho.

Mephitis mephitis hudsonica Richardson
= *M. americana* var. *hudsonica* Rich.
Fauna Bor.-Amer., 1:55. 1829.
STRIPED SKUNK.

Thwaites, II, 74: "We saw a Polecat this evening." This race ranges from Great Lakes west across Dakotas and Montana to Idaho. See Hall-Kelson map, II, 935.

Lewis and Clark discovered this subspecies, May 25, 1805, above mouth of Musselshell River, Fergus Co., Montana.

Mephitis mephitis notata
(Howell)
= *Chincha occidentalis notata* Howell.
N. Amer. Fauna, 20:36. 1901.
STRIPED SKUNK.

Thwaites, IV, 118: "Abundant . . . particularly in the neighbourhood of the great falls [Celilo] and narrows." *M. m. notata* occupies a small range in n. Oregon and s. Wash. east of Cascades. See Hall-Kelson map, II, 935.

Lewis alluded to this race, Feb. 28, 1806, while at Fort Clatsop.

Mustela frenata longicauda
Bonaparte
= *M. longicauda* Bonaparte.
Mag. Nat. Hist., 2:38. 1838.
LONG-TAILED WEASEL.

Thwaites, I, 218: "We got a white weasel . . . of an Indian." Coues (I, 191): "This is the *Putorius longicauda* . . . in winter of the color said, in summer brown and yellowish."

Obtained Nov. 9, 1804, at Fort Mandan. On Apr. 7, 1805, L. & C. shipped "a white *weasel*" to Jefferson (see Thwaites, I, 281).

? *Mustela erminea invicta* Hall.
Jour. Mamm., 26:75. 1945.
ERMINE.

Thwaites, II, 378:
The Shoshoni "attach
from one to two hun-
dred and fifty little
roles of Ermin skin
[to their tippets]."
This subspecies, ac-
cording to Hall-Kel-
son (II, 905), occu-
pies w. Montana and
n. Idaho.

Reported by Lewis,
Aug. 20, 1805, while
among Shoshoni on
Lemhi River, Lemhi
Co., Idaho.

Neotoma cinerea cinerea (Ord)
= *Mus cinereus* Ord.
Guthrie's Geog., 2nd Am. ed.,
2:292. 1815.
BUSHY-TAILED WOOD RAT; PACK
RAT.

Thwaites, II, 205: "In
moving some of the
baggage we caught a
large rat." Coues (II,
400): "The Rocky
Mountain pack-rat
. . . then new to sci-
ence."

Discovered by Lewis
and Clark, July 2,
1805, at Great Falls,
Cascade Co., Montana.

Neotoma floridana (Ord)
= *Mus floridana* Ord.
Bull. Soc. Philom., Paris, 181.
1818.
EASTERN WOOD RAT.

Thwaites, I, 37: "Sev-
eral *rats* of Consider-
able Size was Caught
in the woods to day."
According to Hall-
Kelson (II, 284), this
was probably *N. f.
osagensis* Blair.

Discovered May 31,
1804, below mouth of
Osage R., Missouri.
Osage Co. on south,
Callaway Co. on
north.

*Oreamnos americanus ameri-
canus* (Blainville)
= *R[upicapra] americana*
Blainville.
Bull. Soc. Philom., Paris, 80.
1816.
MOUNTAIN GOAT.

Thwaites, III, 30:
"(*Capt. C saw one at
a distance to day.*"
Coues (III, 851):
Lewis and Clark "are
the actual discoverers
and first describers of
this remarkable ani-
mal."

Seen Aug. 24, 1805, in
Lemhi Co., Idaho.
Lewis wrote first de-
scription Feb. 22,
1806, at Fort Clatsop.

Ovis canadensis auduboni
Merriam.
Proc. Biol. Soc. Wash.,
14:31. 1901.
AUDUBON'S MOUNTAIN SHEEP.

Thwaites, I, 343:
"Joseph Fields . . .
saw a big horned ani-
mal." Hall-Kelson
map (II, 1031) shows
this race occupying
the western Dakotas
and a narrow portion
of eastern Montana.

Seen by J. Field,
April 26, 1805, at
mouth of Yellowstone
R., McKenzie Co.,
N.D. *O. c. canadensis*
was the race L. & C.
met farther west.

Phoca vitulina richardii
(Gray)
= *Halicyon richardii* Gray.
Proc. Zool. Soc. London,
28. 1864.
HARBOR SEAL.

Thwaites, III, 150:
"Great numbers of
Sea Otters [seals] in
the river below the
[Celilo] falls."

First seen Oct. 23,
1805, at Narrows of
Columbia, more than
100 miles from Pa-
cific. Identified then
as sea otters, though

L. & C. later admitted mistake. See Thwaites, IV, 99–100.

Procyon lotor hirtus Nelson & Goldman. Jour. Mamm., 11:455. 1930. RACCOON.

Thwaites, I, 48: "We caught a racoon." L. & C. actually traversed ranges of three new subspecies: (1) *P. l. hirtus* from the Mississippi to Montana; (2) *P. l. excelsus* in Idaho and Interior Basin; (3) *P. l. pacificus,* w. of Cascades. See Hall-Kelson map (II, 885).

First encountered June 13, 1804, near Chariton R., Mo. Again on Oct. 21, 1805, on Columbia above John Day R. On Feb. 25, 1806, Lewis wrote: "The Rackoon is found . . . on this coast in considerable quantities."

Scapanus townsendii (Bachman) = *Scalops townsendii* Bachman. Jour. Acad. Nat. Sci. Phila., 8:58. 1839. TOWNSEND'S MOLE.

Thwaites, IV, 113: "The *Mouse* and *Mole* of this neighbourhood are the same as those native animals with us." Coues (III, 864): "The common mole of the Columbia differs not only specifically but also generically from that of the eastern part of the United States."

Referred to by Lewis, Feb. 26, 1806, at Fort Clatsop.

Sciurus griseus griseus Ord = *S. griseus* Ord. Jour. Phys. Chimie, Hist. Nat. Arts, 87:152. 1818. WESTERN GRAY SQUIRREL.

Thwaites, IV, 106: "The large grey squirrel appears to be a native of a narrow tract of country . . . just below the grand falls [Celilo] of Columbia." Coues (III, 854).

Described by Lewis, Feb. 25, 1806, at Fort Clatsop.

Spermophilus columbianus columbianus (Ord) = *Arctomys columbianus* Ord. Guthrie's Geog., 2nd Am. ed., 2:292. 1815. COLUMBIAN GROUND SQUIRREL.

Thwaites, V, 69: "There is a species of Burrowing squirrel common in these plains [along Clearwater]." Coues (III, 856) identified as *S. columbianus.*

Described by Lewis, May 27, 1806, at Camp Chopunnish. In 1853 Audubon and Bachman named this same species *Arctomys lewisii.*

Spermophilus tridecemlineatus pallidus J. A. Allen. Proc. Boston Soc. Nat. Hist., 16:291. 1874.

Thwaites, II, 216: "The men also brought me a living ground sqiurrel . . .

Discovered and described by Lewis, July 8, 1805, at Great Falls, Cascade Co., Mon-

THIRTEEN-LINED GROUND SQUIR-
REL.

with a much larger number of black or dark bro[w]n stripes." Coues (II, 405) : "A find of remarkable interest."

tana.

? *Sylvilagus audubonii baileyi*
(Merriam)
= *Lepus baileyi* Merriam.
Proc. Biol. Soc. Wash., 11:148.
1897.
DESERT COTTONTAIL.

Thwaites, I, 148: "I saw great numbers of Rabits." These could have been *S. floridanus similis* Nelson. Farther west L. & C. must have met with Nuttall's cottontail, *S. nuttallii grangeri*. See Hall-Kelson map (I, 261).

Encountered Sept. 15, 1804, near mouth of White R., S.D.

Tamiasciurus douglasii douglasii (Bachman)
= *Sciurus douglasii* Gray.
Proc. Zool. Soc. London, 88. 1836.
DOUGLAS'S SQUIRREL; CHICKAREE.

Thwaites, IV, 106: "The small brown squirrel is a beautiful little animal." Coues (III, 858) : "It is quite a distinct form, evidently recognized as such by Lewis and Clark."

Described by Lewis, Feb. 25, 1806, at Fort Clatsop.

Tamiasciurus hudsonicus richardsoni (Bachman)
= *Sciurus richardsoni* Bachman.
Proc. Zool. Soc. London, 100.
1839.
RICHARDSON'S RED SQUIRREL.

Thwaites, IV, 107: "The small grey squirrel common to every part of the rocky mountain." Coues (III, 855) : "The question might be raised whether it be *S. richardsoni* or *S. fremonti*." Hall-Kelson map (I, 400) shows range of latter too far south.

Described by Lewis, Feb. 25, 1806, at Fort Clatsop.

Taxidea taxus neglecta
Mearns
= *Taxus americana neglecta*
Mearns.
Bull. A. Mus. Nat. Hist., 3:250. 1891.
WESTERN BADGER.

Thwaites, IV, 110: "The badger, wrote Lewis, "is an inhabitant of the open plains of the Columbia." L. & C. were, therefore, the discoverers of this subspecies. See Hall-Kelson map (II, 927).

Described by Lewis, Feb. 26, 1806, at Fort Clatsop.

? *Thomomys talpoides rufescens* Wied

Thwaites, I, 289: "I have observed . . .

Described by Lewis, April 9, 1805, above

= *T. rufescens* Wied.
Nova Acta Phys.-Med. Acad.
    Caes. Leop.-Car., 19 (Pt. 1):
    378. 1839.
POCKET GOPHER.

the work of an ana-mal [which] resembles that of the common salamander common to the sand hills of the states of South Carolina and Georgia." See Hall-Kelson map (I, 438–439). Range of *T. t. talpoides* too far north.

mouth of Knife River, N.D.

Ursus horribilis horribilis
    Ord
= *Ursus horribilis* Ord.
Guthrie's Geog., 2nd Am. ed.,
    2:291. 1815.
GRIZZLY BEAR.

Thwaites, I, 350: "About 8 A.M. we fell in with two brown or yellow [*white*] bear."

Killed first grizzly, Apr. 29, 1805, just below Big Muddy Creek [Martha's R. of L. & C.], Mont. Roosevelt Co. on north, Richland Co. on south.

Vulpes fulva macroura
    Baird
= *V. macrourus* Baird.
Stansbury Expl. and Surv.
    Val. Gr. Salt Lake, 309.
    1852.
GREAT-TAILED FOX.

Thwaites, IV, 93–94: "The large red fox of the [Columbian] plains . . . [is] the same which we met with on the Missouri." Coues (III, 848): "The 'large red fox of the plains' is certainly that representative of the common red fox which was called *Vulpes macrourus* by Baird."

Referred to by Lewis, Feb. 21, 1806, at Fort Clatsop.

Vulpes velox velox (Say)
= *Canis velox* Say.
Long's Exped., 1:487. 1823.
SWIFT FOX.

Thwaites, II, 213: "There is a remarkable small fox which . . . burrow in the praries something like the small wolf." Coues (II, 404) identified as *Vulpes velox*. According to Hall-Kelson (II, 860), the swift fox may be only subspecifically different from the kit fox, *Vulpes macrotis*.

Discovered by Lewis, July 6, 1805, at Great Falls, Cascade Co., Montana.

Of the 122 species and subspecies listed above, Lewis and Clark discovered 65 west of the Continental Divide and 57 east. Among the early naturalists who described them, George Ord led all others with 10. Rafinesque and John Richardson (English) described seven each, and Thomas Say five.

Appendix C

Locations of Lewis and Clark Journals, Maps, and Related Materials

While investigating aspects of the Lewis and Clark Expedition presented in this study, of necessity I spent countless hours locating material. It occurs to me, therefore, that the following information might be welcomed by future students of the Expedition. The list lays no claim to completeness, but it does include those items which have been most important to me—as well as some not so important. The enumeration is alphabetical according to locations.

Academy of Natural Sciences of Philadelphia

Lewis and Clark Herbarium. More than 200 dried, preserved plant specimens brought back by the explorers.

Alexander Wilson's original sketches of Lewis's woodpecker and Clark's nutcracker.

Letters pertaining to the botany and zoology of the Expedition by Charles J. Maynard, Witmer Stone, and Edward Tuckerman.

American Museum of Natural History, New York

Lewis and Clark medal of the "first grade," with the likeness of Jefferson on the obverse and clasped hands on the reverse. It was discovered in 1899 at the mouth of Potlatch (Colter's) Creek, Idaho, by Lester S. Handsaker of an engineering corps when grading for a railway embankment. It later passed into the hands of Edward D. Adams of New York City who presented it to the American Museum of Natural History. For illustrations and account of discovery see *The Trail of Lewis and Clark* by Olin D. Wheeler (II, 123). In this same work (I, 139) is a description of the three grades of medals carried by Lewis and Clark: "one, the largest and the preferred one, 'a medal with the likeness of the President of the United States'; the second, 'a medal representing some domestic animals'; and third, 'medals with the impression of a farmer sowing grain'." See also Cutright, "Lewis and Clark

Indian Peace Medals," *Bull. Missouri Hist. Soc.,* XXIV, no. 2 (Jan., 1968), 160–167.

American Philosophical Society, Philadelphia

Original manuscript journals of Lewis and Clark. Nine volumes:

Volume 1:

       Codex A—Clark. May 13, 1804—August 14, 1804.

       Codex Aa—Lewis. May 15 and May 20, 1804.

       Codex B—Clark. August 15, 1804—October 3, 1804.

       Codex Ba—Lewis. September 16 and 17, 1804.

       Codex C—Clark. October 4, 1804—April 7, 1805.

Volume 2:

       Codex D—Lewis. April 7, 1805—May 23, 1805.

       Codex E—Lewis. May 24, 1805—July 16, 1805.

       Codex F—Lewis. July 17, 1805—August 22, 1805.

       Codex Fa—Lewis. August 1–4, 1805.

       Codex Fb—Lewis. August 23–26, 1805.

       Codex Fc—Lewis. September 9–10, 1805.

       Codex Fd—Lewis. September 19–22, 1805.

       Codex Fe—Lewis. Weather, etc. April–June, 1805; July, August, September, 1805.

       Codex G—Clark. July 2, 1805—October 10, 1805.

Volume 3:

       Codex H—Clark. October 11, 1805—November 19, 1805.

       Codex I—Clark. November 19, 1805—January 29, 1806.

       Codex Ia—Lewis. November 29, 1805—December 1, 1805.

       Codex J—Lewis. January 1, 1806—March 20, 1806.

       Codex K—Lewis. March 21, 1806—May 23, 1806.

Volume 4:

       Codex L—Lewis. May 24, 1806—August 8, 1806.

       Codex La—Lewis. July 3–15, 1806.

       Codex Lb—Lewis. August 9–12, 1806.

       Codex M—Clark. June 7, 1806—August 14, 1806.

       Codex N—Clark. August 15, 1806—September 24, 1806.

       Codex O—Lewis. Astronomical observations, geographical notes. May 18, 1804—March 30, 1805.

Volume 5:

       Codex P—Clark (also Lewis and another hand). Natural history notes, etc. April 9, 1805—February 17, 1806.

       Codex Q—Clark and Lewis. Miscellaneous notes, natural history. 1804–1806.

Codex R—Clark and Lewis. Miscellaneous notes, natural history. May, 1804—March, 1806.

Codex S—Lewis, letters to Pres. Jefferson: (a) announcing return of Expedition to St. Louis; (b) discovery of the Yellowstone, etc.

Codex T—Single page (unidentified).

Volume 6:

Notebook containing botanical notes, meteorological data, etc.

Lewis's Journal. August 30, 1803—December 12, 1803 (Pittsburgh to St. Louis).

Journal of Sgt. John Ordway.

Clark. Journal (rough draft). January 6–10, 1806.

Clark. Diary.

Nicholas Biddle. Notes on queries. Ca. April, 1810.

Volume 7:

Miscellaneous papers: (a) Estimate of the Western Indians; (b) A List of the Names of the Different Nations and Tribes of the Lake of the Woods.

Volume 8:

Miscellaneous papers: (a) Summary View of Creeks and Rivers; (b) Summary View of Nations.

Volume 9:

Donation Book, containing a list of dried plants collected in the far West by M. Lewis and presented to the American Philosophical Society; also, list of minerals and fossils.

Titian R. Peale's Sketch Book. This includes drawings as follows: (a) Lewis's woodpecker by Charles Willson Peale; (b) mountain quail by Peale; (c) "fisher" by Peale; and (d) horned toad by Peale or Pietro Ancora.

The American Philosophical Society is, of course, the repository for many other items, for example, Jefferson's instructions to André Michaux, and St. Mémin's crayon sketch of the Mandan chief, Big White, with inscription on back which reads: *"Mandan, hommé Le Grand Blanc, venu a Philadelphia accompagné par Messrs. Lewis and Clark."*

Corcoran Gallery of Art, Washington, D.C.

Portraits of Lewis and Clark by artist Charles B. J. F. de St. Mémin.

Filson Club, Louisville, Kentucky

Oil portrait of Clark painted by the Kentucky artist Joseph Bush.

A single horn of a Rocky Mountain goat brought back from the Expedition by Clark. This horn came down in the family of Clark's sister, Fanny, and was left to the Filson Club by one of her descendants.

Historical Society of Pennsylvania, Philadelphia

Charles Willson Peale's "Memorandum of Specimens and Artifacts," a book in which Peale recorded accessions (see pp. 43–45 for Lewis and Clark objects).

Correspondence, such as letters of Lewis to Jefferson dated December 19 and 28, 1803.

Indian speech to Jefferson and the Secretary of War, January 4, 1806.

Joslyn Art Museum, Omaha, Nebraska

Maximilian's journals, papers, and artifacts and over 400 of Bodmer's field sketches and watercolor paintings.

Leonard, Dr. K. O., Garrison, North Dakota

Indian peace medal, three and three-sixteenths inches in diameter, thought to have been one presented by Lewis and Clark to Big White (Sheheke).

Library Company of Philadelphia

History of Louisiana by Antoine Le Page Du Pratz (2nd English ed., 1774). On the fly leaf of this book is an inscription in Lewis's handwriting which reads: "Dr. Benjamin Smith Barton was so obliging as to lend me this copy of Monsr. Du Pratz's history of Louisiana in June 1803. it has been since conveyed by me to the Pacific Ocean through the interior of the Continent of North America on my late tour thither and is now returned to its proprietor by his Freind and Obt. Servt. Meriwether Lewis, Philadelphia, May 9th, 1807."

Library of Congress, Washington, D.C.

Among the many documents important to the Lewis and Clark student are: (a) Thomas Jefferson Papers; (b) Jefferson's signed copy of his January 18, 1804, Message to Congress; (c) Jefferson's instructions to Lewis and Clark (dated June 20, 1803); (d) invoice of articles forwarded from Fort Mandan to the President of the United States; (e) Biddle Family Papers; (f) biographical sketch of Lewis by Jefferson (to Paul Allen, August 18, 1813).

Luna House Historical Society, Lewiston, Idaho

Adze thought to have been given by Lewis and Clark to the Nez Perce chief, Twisted Hair.

Maryhill Museum, Maryhill, Washington

Two Lewis and Clark medals of the "third grade." The obverse shows a man sowing wheat (hence the name "sowing medal") and the reverse the words, "Second Presidency of Geo. Washington MDCCXVI." These medals were presented to Maryhill Museum by Mary Underwood Lane, descendant of a Chinookan Indian chief.

Mercantile Library, St. Louis, Missouri

Original painting of Clark by the artist, Chester Harding.

Missouri Historical Society, St. Louis, Missouri

Field Book of Clark bound in folding elk skin, fastening with a thong and button. On inside of skin cover is a sketch of the floor-plan of Fort Clatsop. The book is inscribed as having been presented at St. Louis in 1843 to J. J. Audubon by D. D. Mitchell, Superintendent of Indian Affairs. It contains courses and distances and first drafts of daily occurrences from September 11 through December 31, 1805.

Clark's journal from April 7 through July 3, 1805. Includes "Draught of the Falls and Portage of the Missouri."

Clark's journal from January 30 through April 3, 1806. Includes sketches showing head flattening, Chinook canoes, Oregon grape leaves, condor head, sage grouse, and "white salmon trout"; also, map of entrance of "Multnomah" River.

Clark's journal from April 14 through June 6, 1806. Includes rough sketch showing Bitterroot River and Traveller's Rest Creek, and another locating Indian villages on Columbia immediately below Celilo Falls.

Clark's journal, with weather records for January and December, 1804, and for January, October, November, and December, 1805; sketches of "Great Rapids of the Columbia," "Long and Short Narrows of the Columbia," "Great Falls of Columbia River," and "A Sketch of the Columbia Rivers and its Waters and the Situation of the Fishing Establishments of the Nations above the Enterance of Lewis's river—given by the Cho-pun-nish, So-kulk and Chim-na-pum Indians." The five journals above were presented to the Missouri Historical Society in 1923 by Julia Clark Voorhis, granddaughter of William Clark.

Notebook containing (a) distances from Fort Mandan to Cape Disappointment; (b) distances on Pacific Coast to N.N.W.; and (c) distances on Pacific Coast to S.S.E.

Names of remarkable places.

Lewis's Account Book.

Lewis's notes on salines and proposed districts.

Numerous other papers and documents, such as: (a) Inquiries Relative to the Indians of Louisiana; (b) Fort Clatsop Orderly Book; (c) Clark's list of seeds brought back by the Expedition; (d) printed prospectus of Lewis and Clark's tour to the Pacific Ocean; (e) Pierre Chouteau Letterbook.

Lewis and Clark Correspondence. Includes, for example, Lewis's letter to his mother from Fort Mandan dated March 31, 1805.

Relics: (a) English telescope used by Lewis on Expedition; (b) Lewis's watch "with double, or hunting, case of silver, made in England in 1796–97"; (c) compass used by Clark; (d) magnet used by Clark.

Portraits: (a) crayon of Lewis by Charles St. Mémin, in original frame of gold leaf with mat of black glass decorated in gilt; (b) full-length portrait of Clark (with cane) by Chester Harding, painted in 1820 by Harding when Clark was fifty. It is thought that the head only was painted by Harding, the remainder by Harding's assistant John J. Douberman; (c) bust-length portraits of Clark and his wife (Julia Hancock) by John Wesley Jarvis.

Monticello (Thomas Jefferson Memorial Foundation), Charlottesville, Virginia

Elk and moose antlers brought back by Lewis and Clark. (Some doubt exists as to whether the moose antlers are legitimate relics of the Expedition, since the journals make no mention of a moose killed at any time.)

Silhouette of Meriwether Lewis. Artist unknown.

Leg bone and jaws of *Mastodon americanus* obtained by Clark at Big Bone Lick, Kentucky. These were obtained and sent to Jefferson after the Expedition had returned.

Museum of Comparative Zoology, Harvard University, Cambridge, Massachusetts

Skin of Lewis's woodpecker *(Asyndesmus lewis)*. This skin, originally in Peale's Museum, came to the Museum of Comparative Zoology from the Boston Museum. According to Witmer Stone, formerly Curator of Birds at the Academy of Natural Sciences of Philadelphia, it is "without much doubt the original specimen [collected by Lewis and Clark], and probably the only one of this historic [zoological] collection that is still extant." (See Thwaites, VI, 121.)

National Archives, Washington, D.C.

This repository includes such important Lewis and Clark papers and documents as: (a) Lewis's list of requirements for outfitting the Expedition; (b) orders from the War Department; (c) supplies from private vendors; (d) summary of purchases; (e) War Department copy of what is probably the earliest Lewis and Clark map; (f) Lewis and Clark speech to the Oto Indians; (g) financial records of the Expedition; (h) correspondence (War Department).

New York Historical Society, New York City

Crayon sketches (each 17 × 22 ins.) by St. Mémin as follows: (1) "Indian of the Iowas of the Missouri"; (2) "Osage Warrior"; (3) "A Delaware Indian"; (4) "Chief of the Little Osages"; (5) "Indian Girl of the Iowas of the Missouri"; (6) "Cachasunghia, Osage Warrior"; (7) "Osage Warrior"; and (8) "Payouska, Chief of the Grand Osages."

Correspondence, including John Ledyard's letters to Jefferson.

Oregon Historical Society, Portland

Lewis and Clark medal, two and one-quarter inches in diameter, with likeness of Jefferson on obverse and clasped hands on reverse.

Lewis's branding iron.

Private George Shannon's "Housewife" (sewing kit).

Iron pot or skillet. Allegedly given to a 15-year-old Multnomah Indian by Lewis and Clark as they descended the Columbia. (This information is from Allan Gibbons, Curator of Collections, Oregon Historical Society.)

Correspondence, including Sgt. John Ordway's letter to parents dated April 8, 1804 (see Jackson, *Letters,* 176).

Peabody Museum of Archaeology and Ethnology, Harvard University, Cambridge, Massachusetts

Ethnological items acquired "from the heirs of Moses Kimball after the fire (1899) at the old Boston Museum": (a) buffalo robe (1805), decorated with quill work; (b) elk antler bow (1805); (c) Cree woman's dress (1804) of leather; (d) Sioux raven bustle (1805) (badge of office); (e) Nootka basket hat (1805) made of cedar bark and bear grass; (f) Sauk otter skin bag (1805 or 1806); (g) Chinook fiber skirt (1805 or 1806). Other objects in the Peabody originated in Peale's collection, some of which are possibly Lewis and Clark's.

Smithsonian Institution, Washington, D.C.

Silhouettes of Indians by Charles Willson Peale. These are of Plains Indians comprising one or another of the delegations sent to visit Jefferson by Lewis and Clark.

Air gun regarded as possibly the one carried by Lewis and Clark on the Expedition. Dr. Roy M. Chatters, Washington State University, an authority on air guns, has written me: "At this point I rather doubt that it was the gun carried on the expedition as some of the parts appear to be similar to those not developed for about 20 years after the expedition ended."

Ethnological objects from Columbia River reputedly obtained by George Catlin from William Clark (see Chap. 22, p. 356).

State Historical Society of Wisconsin, Madison

Sergeant Charles Floyd's journal.

Private Robert Frazer's Prospectus [Proposals for Publishing by Subscription Robert Frazer's Journal from St. Louis in Louisiana to the Pacific Ocean . . .].

Appendix C 455

University of Chicago, Newberry Library

Original journal of Private Joseph Whitehouse, beginning May 14, 1804, and concluding November 6, 1805. "Three distinct notebooks, the largest 6 × 8½ inches in dimensions, which are crudely stitched together within a cover consisting of an irregular scrap of limp hide, possibly elk skin. The third and last book is incomplete, for at least three leaves have been torn therefrom at the end." (See Thwaites, VII, 29n.)

Recently discovered continuation of Whitehouse's journal. Carries the Expedition through the winter of 1805–6 but ends abruptly as the return trip gets under way.

University of Pennsylvania Museum, Philadelphia

Fragments of two Mandan pots returned by Lewis and Clark. Presently on long-term loan to the University Museum from the American Philosophical Society and the Academy of Natural Sciences. One pot consists of a nearly complete rim and neck and about 14 body shards, and the other of an incomplete rim and neck and six fragments.

University of Virginia, Alderman Library, Charlottesville

Papers, including memorandum of Lewis's personal effects, prepared November 23, 1809, following Lewis's death.

Correspondence.

Washington State University, Holland Library, Pullman

Lewis and Clark medal, with likeness of Jefferson on obverse and clasped hands on reverse. Found (1964) in canoe burial at confluence of Palouse River with Snake River, Franklin County, Washington.

Winterthur Museum, Winterthur, Delaware

Water color (7¼ × 6⅞ ins.) of "Osage Warrior" by St. Mémin. This warrior accompanied the first (1804) delegation sent east by Lewis and Clark. (In 1954 Parke-Bernet Galleries of New York City sold five additional St. Mémin water colors of Indians, apparently ones formerly owned by Mrs. Luke Vincent Lockwood. For more about these water colors see Wollon and Kinard, "Augustus J. Foster and 'The Wild Natives of the Woods', 1805–1807," *Wm. and Mary Quart.,* ser. 3, 9 (April, 1952), 191–214. Our efforts to ascertain present whereabouts of these paintings have failed.)

Yale University, Beinecke Library, New Haven, Connecticut

Clark's field notes. Loose sheets between 13 large desk-blotter-size pages. (See *The Field Notes of Captain William Clark 1803–1805,* edited with an Introduction and Notes by Ernest Staples Osgood, Yale University Press, New Haven and London, 1964.)

Maps: (a) 54 maps of the route of the Lewis and Clark Expedition to the Pacific coast and back, 1804–6; and a detailed map by Clark of the continent from the Mississippi Valley to the Pacific and from the junction of the Missouri and Mississippi Rivers and the Gila River to the Great Lakes and Vancouver Island; (b) 55 maps, from 15½ × 9½ to 129 × 73½ cms. Some of the maps were carried on the Expedition by Lewis and Clark, but the majority were drawn by Clark en route. Four groups: (1) maps copied from contemporary Spanish and French maps: Nos. 2–4; (2) seven maps of the Missouri from St. Charles to Mandans. Mr. Aubrey Diller, author of "Maps of the Missouri River before Lewis and Clark," in *Studies and Essays . . . in Honor of George Sarton* (New York, 1946), states his belief that this group is the map by John Evans sent to Lewis and Clark by Jefferson, January 13, 1804, or a copy of it; (3) two maps based on information secured from the Indians during the winter at Fort Mandan; (4) 42 maps of the route followed by the Expedition from Fort Mandan to the Pacific and on the return journey. See *Western Americana Mss. in Yale University Library* compiled by Mary C. Worthington, Yale University Press, New Haven, 1952, pp. 167–171.

Draft of a receipt of compensation to Lewis and Clark. Receipt lists 31 members of the Expedition.

Bibliography

Abel, Annie Heloise. "Trudeau's Description of the Upper Missouri," *Mississippi Valley Historical Review*, 8, June–Sept., 1921.

———, ed. *Tabeau's Narrative of Loisel's Expedition to the Upper Missouri*. University of Oklahoma Press, Norman, 1939.

Abrams, Leroy, and Roxanna S. Ferris. *An Illustrated Flora of the Pacific States*. 4 vols. Stanford University Press, Stanford, Calif., 1923, 1944, 1951, 1960.

Adelman, Seymour. "Equipping the Lewis and Clark Expedition," *Bull. American Philosophical Society*, 1945.

Alden, Roland H., and John D. Ifft. "Early Naturalists in the Far West," *Occasional Papers of the California Academy of Sciences*, No. XX, San Francisco, 1943.

American Ornithologists Union. *American Ornithologists Union Checklist*. 5th ed. New York, 1961.

Appleman, Roy E. "Lewis and Clark: The Route 160 Years After," *Pacific Northwest Quarterly*, 57, no. 1, Jan., 1966.

Audubon, Maria R. *Audubon and His Journals*. With zoological and other notes by Elliott Coues. Vols. I and II. Charles Scribner's Sons, New York, 1897.

Bakeless, John. *Lewis & Clark: Partners in Discovery*. William Morrow & Co., New York, 1947.

———. "Lewis and Clark's Background for Exploration," *Journal of the Washington Academy of Sciences*, 44, Nov., 1954.

———, ed. *The Journals of Lewis and Clark*. New American Library, New York, 1964.

Bancroft, Hubert H. *Native Races of the Pacific States of North America*. 5 vols. Appleton, New York, 1875–76.

Barbour, William R. "The Guns of Lewis and Clark," *Gun Digest,* 18th ed., 1964.

Barnhart, John Hendley. "Brief Sketches of Some Collectors of Specimens in the Barton Herbarium," *Bartonia,* 9, 1926.

Barton, Benjamin Smith. *Elements of Botany: or Outlines of the Natural History of Vegetables.* Philadelphia, 1803.

Beard, J. H. "The Medical Observations and Practice of Lewis and Clark," *Scientific Monthly,* 20, May, 1925.

Bent, Arthur Cleveland. *Life Histories of North American Gallinaceous Birds.* Bulletin 162, Smithsonian Institution, Washington, D.C., 1932.

Bestor, Arthur E., David C. Mearns, and Jonathan Daniels. *Three Presidents and Their Books.* University of Illinois Press, Urbana, 1963.

Betts, Edwin Morris, ed. *Thomas Jefferson's Farm Book.* Princeton University Press, Princeton, N.J., 1953.

————, ed. *Thomas Jefferson's Garden Book. Memoirs,* Vol. 22, American Philosophical Society, Philadelphia, 1944.

Biddle, Nicholas, ed. *History of the Expedition Under the Command of Captains Lewis and Clark, to the Sources of the Missouri, thence Across the Rocky Mountains and down the River Columbia to the Pacific Ocean. Performed During the Years 1804–5–6.* By order of the Government of the United States. Prepared for the press by Paul Allen. 2 vols. Philadelphia, 1814. (A copy of this original 1814 edition, described as in near perfect condition, was sold in 1967 by Parke-Bernet Galleries, New York City, for $35,000.)

Bourlière, François. *The Natural History of Mammals.* Alfred A. Knopf, New York, 1954.

Brackenridge, Henry Marie. *Journal of a Voyage up the Missouri River in 1811* (Vol. VI of *Early Western Travels,* edited by R. G. Thwaites). Arthur H. Clark Co., Cleveland, Ohio, 1904–6.

————. *Views of Louisiana.* Quadrangle Books, Inc., Chicago, 1962.

Bradbury, John. *Travels in the Interior of America* (Vol. V of *Early Western Travels,* edited by R. G. Thwaites). Arthur H. Clark Co., Cleveland, 1904–6.

Brown, Roland W. "Jefferson's Contribution to Paleontology," *Jour. Wash. Acad. Scis.,* 33, no. 9, Sept. 15, 1943.

Burns, Frank L. "Charles W. and Titian R. Peale and the Ornithological Section of the Old Philadelphia Museum," *Wilson Bulletin,* XLIV, no. 1, March, 1932.

————. "Miss Lawson's Recollections of Ornithologists," *The Auk,* 34, July, 1917.

Burpee, Lawrence J., ed. *Journals and Letters of Pierre Gaultier de la Vérendrye.* The Champlain Society, Toronto, 1927.

Burroughs, Raymond Darwin. *The Natural History of the Lewis and Clark Expedition.* Michigan State University Press, East Lansing, 1961.

————. "The Lewis and Clark Expedition's Botanical Discoveries," *Natural History*, LXXV, no. 1, Jan., 1966.

Butterfield, L. H., ed. *Letters of Benjamin Rush*. 2 vols. American Philosophical Society, Philadelphia, 1951.

Cappon, Lester J. "Who is Author of History of the Expedition under the Command of Captains Lewis and Clark (1814)?" *William and Mary Quarterly*, 19, Pt. 2, Apr., 1962.

Catlin, George. *The North American Indians*. 2 vols. Leary, Stuart & Co., Philadelphia, 1913.

Chittenden, H. M. *The American Fur Trade of the Far West*. 2 vols. Academic Reprints, Stanford, Calif., 1954.

Christy, Bayard H. "Alexander Lawson's Bird Engravings," *The Auk*, 43, no. 1, Jan., 1926.

Chuinard, Dr. E. G. "The Medical Aspects of the Lewis and Clark Expedition," Friends of the Library, Oregon State University, Corvallis, 1965.

Cope, Edward Drinker. *The Crocodilians, Lizards, and Snakes of North America*. Report of U.S. National Museum, Washington, 1900.

Corner, George W., ed. *The Autobiography of Benjamin Rush*. Princeton University Press, Princeton, N.J., 1948.

Coues, Elliott. "An Account of the Various Publications Relating to the Travels of Lewis and Clarke [*sic*], with a Commentary on the Zoological Results of the Expedition," *Bull. U.S. Geol. and Geogr. Survey of the Territories*, No. 1, Washington, 1874.

————, ed. *The Expeditions of Zebulon Montgomery Pike*. 3 vols. Philadelphia, 1895.

————, ed. *History of the Expedition Under the Command of Lewis and Clark*. 4 vols. Francis P. Harper, New York, 1893.

————. "Notes on Mr. Thomas Meehan's Paper on the Plants of Lewis and Clarke's Expedition Across the Continent," *Procs. Acad. of Nat. Scis. of Phil.*, 1898.

————, ed. *New Light on the Early History of the Greater Northwest: The Manuscript Journals of Alexander Henry and David Thompson*. 2 vols. Ross & Haines, Inc., Minneapolis, 1965.

———— and J. A. Allen. "Monograph of North American Rodentia," *U.S. Geol. Survey of the Territories*, Washington, 1877.

Criswell, Elijah H. *Lewis and Clark: Linguistic Pioneers*. University of Missouri Studies, 15, no. 2, Columbia, Mo., 1940.

Cutright, Paul Russell. "I gave him barks and saltpeter," *American Heritage*, XV, no. 1, Dec., 1963.

————. "Lewis and Clark and Du Pratz," *Bull. Missouri Hist. Soc.*, XXI, no. 1, Oct., 1964.

————. "Lewis and Clark and Cottonwood," *Bull. Missouri Hist. Soc.*, XXII, no. 1, Oct., 1965.

————. "Jefferson's Instructions to Lewis and Clark," *Bull. Missouri Hist. Soc.,* XXII, no. 3, Apr., 1966.

————. "Meriwether Lewis Prepares for a Trip West," *Bull. Missouri Hist. Soc.,* XXIII, no. 1, Oct., 1966.

————. "Well-travelled Plants of Lewis and Clark," *Frontiers,* 31, no. 3, Feb., 1967.

————. "The Odyssey of the Magpie and the Prairie Dog," *Bull. Missouri Hist. Soc.,* XXIII, no. 3, Apr., 1967.

————. "Lewis and Clark Begin a Journey," *Bull. Missouri Hist. Soc.,* XXIV, no. 1, Oct., 1967.

————. "Lewis and Clark Indian Peace Medals," *Bull. Missouri Hist. Soc.,* XXIV, no. 2, Jan., 1968.

————. "Meriwether Lewis and the Marias River," *Montana, the Magazine of Western History,* XVIII, no. 3, July, 1968.

————. "Meriwether Lewis: Zoologist," *Oregon Hist. Quart.,* LXIX, no. 1, March 1, 1968.

————. "Meriwether Lewis: Botanist," *Oregon Hist. Quart.,* LXIX, no. 2, June 2, 1968.

Denig, Edwin T. "Of the Arickaras," ed. by John C. Ewers, *Bull. Missouri Hist. Soc.,* VI, no. 2, Jan., 1950.

————. "Indian Tribes of the Upper Missouri," ed. by J. N. B. Hewitt, *46th Annual Report* of Bur. Amer. Ethnology, Washington, D.C., 1930.

DeVoto, Bernard. *Across the Wide Missouri.* Houghton Mifflin, Boston, 1947.

————. *The Course of Empire.* Houghton Mifflin, Boston, 1952.

————, ed. *The Journals of Lewis and Clark.* Houghton Mifflin, Boston, 1953.

Dillon, Richard. *Meriwether Lewis.* Coward-McCann, New York, 1965.

Doughty, J. and T. *The Cabinet of Natural History and American Rural Sports.* 2 vols. John Doughty, Philadelphia, 1830–32.

Douglas, David. *Journal Kept by David Douglas During His Travels in North America, 1823–1827.* William Wesly & Sons, London, 1914.

Driggs, Howard R. *The Old West Speaks.* Prentice-Hall (Bonanza Books), Englewood Cliffs, N.J., 1956.

Ewan, Joseph. "Frederick Pursh, 1774–1820, and His Botanical Associates," *Procs. Amer. Phil. Soc.,* 96, 1952.

Ewers, John C. "George Catlin, Painter of Indians and the West," *Ann. Rept.* Smithsonian Inst., Washington, D.C., 1955.

————. "The Indian Trade of the Upper Missouri before Lewis and Clark: An Interpretation," *Bull. Missouri Hist. Soc.,* V, no. 4, July, 1954.

————. *Artists of the Old West.* Doubleday & Co., Garden City, N.Y., 1965.

Faxon, Walter. "Relics of Peale's Museum," *Procs. Museum of Comp. Zoology,* LIX, 1915.

Fernald, M. L. "Some Early Botanists of the American Philosophical Society," *Procs. Amer. Phil. Soc.,* 86, no. 1, Sept., 1943.

Franchère, Gabriel. *Narrative of a Voyage to the Northwest Coast of America* (Vol. VI of *Early Western Travels,* edited by R. G. Thwaites). Arthur H. Clark Co., Cleveland, 1904.

Friis, Herman R. "Cartographic and Geographic Activities of the Lewis and Clark Expedition," *Jour. Wash. Acad. of Scis.,* 44, Nov., 1954.

Gallatin, Albert. *A Synopsis of the Indian Tribes in North America. Trans. Amer. Antiq. Soc. Archaeologica Americana,* 11, Worcester, Mass., 1836.

Garver, Frank Harmon. "Lewis and Clark in Beaverhead County." Reprinted from *The Dillon Examiner,* issue of Dec. 10, 1913. Western Montana College of Education, Dillon, 1964.

Gass, Patrick. *A Journal of the Voyages and Travels of a Corps of Discovery, under the Command of Capt. Lewis and Capt. Clarke of the Army of the United States.* Edited by David McKeehan. Ross and Haines, Minneapolis, 1958.

Gibbs, George. *Tribes of Western Washington and Northwestern Oregon. Contribs. North Amer. Ethnology,* 1, Washington, D.C., 1877.

Gill, Larry. "The Great Portage," *Great Falls Tribune,* Great Falls, Mont., Aug. 15, 1965.

Gilmore, Melvin Randolph. "Uses of Plants by the Indians of the Missouri River Region," *33rd Ann. Rept.* of Bur. Amer. Ethnology, Washington, D.C., 1919.

Godman, John D. *American Natural History.* 3 vols. H. C. Carey & I. Lea, Philadelphia, 1826.

Gray, Ralph. "Following the Trail of Lewis and Clark," *Natl. Geog. Mag.,* CIII, no. 6, June, 1953.

Gregg, Josiah. *Commerce of the Prairies.* Edited by Max L. Moorhead. University of Oklahoma Press, Norman, 1954.

Guthrie, William. *A New Geographical, Historical and Commercial Grammar; and Present State of the Kingdoms of the World.* 2nd Amer. ed. 2 vols. Johnson & Warner, Philadelphia, 1815.

Hall, E. Raymond, and Keith R. Kelson. *The Mammals of North America.* 2 vols. Ronald Press Co., New York, 1959.

Harlan, Richard. *Fauna Americana.* Anthony Finley, Philadelphia, 1825.

Harris, Burton. *John Colter.* Charles Scribner's Sons, New York, 1952.

Harris, Edward. *Up the Missouri with Audubon.* University of Oklahoma Press, Norman, 1951.

Harshberger, John W. *The Botanists of Philadelphia and Their Work.* T. C. Davis & Sons, Philadelphia, 1899.

Hazlitt, Ruth, trans. and ed. "The Journal of Francois Antoine Larocque from the Assiniboine River to the Yellowstone—1805," *Sources of Northwest History,* No. 20, State University of Montana. Reprinted from History Section of *The Frontier, A Magazine of the Northwest,* XIV, nos. 3 and 4; XV, no. 1, 1934.

Harvey, Athelstan George. *Douglas of the Fir: A Biography of David Douglas, Botanist.* Harvard University Press, Cambridge, Mass., 1947.

Hebard, Grace R. *Sacajawea.* Arthur H. Clark Co., Glendale, Calif., 1933.

Hernandez, Francisco. *Nova plantarum, animalium et mineralium Mexicanorum historia.* Rome, 1651.

Hitchcock, C. Leo, Arthur Cronquist, Marion Ownley, and J. W. Thompson. *Vascular Plants of the Pacific Northwest.* Parts 2, 3, 4, and 5. University of Washington Press, Seattle, 1955–64.

Hodge, Frederick Webb. *Handbook of American Indians North of Mexico.* 2 vols. Bull. 30, Smithsonian Inst. Bur. Amer. Ethnology, Washington, D.C., 1907.

Hult, Ruby El. "Guns of the Lewis and Clark Expedition," Wash. State Hist. Soc., Pacific Northwest Historical Pamphlet Number One, 1960.

Irving, Washington. *Astoria, or Anecdotes of an Enterprise Beyond the Rocky Mountains.* G. P. Putnam's Sons, New York, 1849.

Jackson, Donald. "Some Books Carried by Lewis and Clark," *Bull. Missouri Hist. Soc.,* XVI, no. 1, Oct., 1959.

———. "A New Lewis and Clark Map," *Bull. Missouri Hist. Soc.,* XVII, no. 2, Jan., 1961.

———. "The Race to Publish Lewis and Clark," *Penna. Mag. of Hist. and Biog.,* LXXXV, no. 2, Apr., 1961.

———. "The Public Image of Lewis and Clark," *Pacific Northwest Quarterly,* 57, no. 1, Jan., 1966.

———. "Some Advice for the Next Editor of Lewis and Clark," *Bull. Missouri Hist. Soc.,* XXIV, no. 1, Oct., 1967.

———, ed. *Letters of the Lewis and Clark Expedition with Related Documents 1783–1854.* University of Illinois Press, Urbana, 1962.

———, ed. *The Journals of Zebulon Montgomery Pike.* 2 vols. University of Oklahoma Press, Norman, 1966.

Jacob, John G. *The Life and Times of Patrick Gass.* Wellsburg, Va., 1859.

Jaeger, Edmund C. "Does the Poor-will Hibernate?" *Condor,* Jan.-Feb., 1948.

———. "Further Observations on the Hibernation of the Poor-will," *Condor,* 51, 1949.

Jefferson, Thomas. "A Memoir of the Discovery of Certain Bones of a Quadruped of the Clawed Kind in the Western Parts of Virginia," *Trans. Amer. Phil. Soc.,* 4, 1799.

———. *Notes on the State of Virginia.* Lilly and Wait, Boston, 1832.

Jordan, David Starr. *A Guide to the Study of Fishes.* Henry Holt & Co., New York, 1905.

———, and Barton Warren Evermann. *American Food and Game Fishes*

(Nature Library, Vol. V). Doubleday, Page & Co., Garden City, N.Y., 1920.

————, Barton Warren Evermann, and Howard Walton Clark. *Check List of the Fishes and Fishlike Vertebrates of North and Middle America North of the Northern Boundary of Venezuela and Colombia*. Part II, Report U.S. Commissioner of Fisheries for 1928. Washington, D.C., 1930.

Josephy, Alvin M., Jr. *The Nez Perce Indians and the Opening of the Northwest*. Yale University Press, New Haven, Conn., 1965.

Kelly, Howard A. *Some American Medical Botanists*. Southworth Co., Troy, N.Y., 1914.

Koch, Elers. "Lewis and Clark Across the Bitterroot Range," U.S. Dep't. Agriculture, Forest Service, Missoula, Mont., 1962.

Larpenteur, Charles. *Forty Years a Fur Trader*. Lakeside Press, R. R. Donnelley & Sons Co., Chicago, 1933.

Lehmann-Hartleben, Karl. "Thomas Jefferson, Archaeologist," *Amer. Jour. Archaeology*, 47, 1943.

Lewis, Grace. "The First Home of Governor Lewis in Louisiana Territory," *Bull. Missouri Hist. Soc.*, XIV, no. 4, part 1, July, 1958.

Lewis, Capt. Meriwether, and Capt. William Clark. *A Statistical View of the Indian Nations Inhabiting the Territory of Louisiana*. American State Papers, Indian Affairs, No. 113, 9th Cong., 1st Sess., 1806.

Lincoln, A. "Jefferson the Scientist," *Pacific Discovery*, XVII, no. 4, July-Aug., 1964.

————. "Jefferson and the West," *Pacific Discovery*, XVII, no. 1, Jan.-Feb., 1964.

Long, Major Stephen H. *Account of an Expedition from Pittsburgh to the Rocky Mountains*. Compiled by Edwin James. 2 vols. H. C. Carey and I. Lea, Philadelphia, 1823.

Loos, John Louis. "William Clark's Part in the Preparation of the Lewis and Clark Expedition," *Bull. Missouri Hist. Soc.*, July, 1954.

Lucas, Frederic A. "Thomas Jefferson—Paleontologist," *Natural History*, XXVI, 1926.

Luttig, John C. *Journal of a Fur-trading Expedition on the Upper Missouri, 1812–1813*. Edited by Stella M. Drumm. Argosy-Antiquarian Ltd., New York, 1964.

McCracken, Harold. *George Catlin and the Old Frontier*. Dial Press, New York, 1959.

McDermott, John Francis. "William Clark's Museum Once More," *Bull. Missouri Hist. Soc.*, XVI, no. 2, Jan., 1960.

McMahon, Bernard. *The American Gardener's Calendar*. Philadelphia, 1806.

McKelvey, Susan Delano. *Botanical Exploration of the Trans-Mississippi West*. Arnold Arboretum of Harvard University, Boston, 1955.

Malone, Dumas. *Jefferson and His Time.* Vol. 3, *Jefferson and the Ordeal of Liberty.* Little, Brown and Co., Boston, 1962.

Martin, Edwin T. *Thomas Jefferson: Scientist.* Henry Schuman, New York, 1952.

Masson, L. R. *Les Bourgeois de la Compagnie du Nord-Ouest.* 2 vols. L'Imprimerie Générale A. Coté et Co., Quebec, 1889.

Mattes, Merrill J. "On the Trail of Lewis and Clark with Thomas Hart Benton," *Montana, the Magazine of Western History,* XVI, no. 3, July, 1966.

Maximilian, Prince von Wied. *Travels in the Interior of North America, 1832–1834* (Vols. XXII—XXV of *Early Western Travels,* edited by R. G. Thwaites). Arthur H. Clark Co., Cleveland, 1906.

Mease, James. *The Picture of Philadelphia.* B. and T. Kite, Philadelphia, 1811.

Meehan, Thomas. "The Plants of Lewis and Clark's Expedition Across the Continent, 1804–1806," *Procs. Acad. of Nat. Scis. of Philadelphia,* Jan.–March, 1898.

Meisel, Max. *A Bibliography of American Natural History.* Premier Pub. Co., Brooklyn, 1924–26–29.

Miller, Gerrit S., Jr., and Remington Kellogg. *List of North American Recent Mammals.* Bull. 205, U.S. Nat'l. Museum, Smithsonian Institution, Washington, D.C., 1955.

Nasatir, A. P., ed. *Before Lewis and Clark.* 2 vols. St. Louis Historical Documents Foundation, St. Louis, 1952.

Newcombe, C. F., ed. *Menzies' Journal of Vancouver's Voyage.* Archives of British Columbia, Memoir No. V, Victoria, 1923.

Nuttall, Thomas. *The Genera of North American Plants.* 2 vols. Philadelphia, 1818.

Osborn, Henry Fairfield. "Thomas Jefferson as a Paleontologist," *Science,* n.s., LXXXII, Dec. 6, 1935.

Osgood, Ernest Staples, ed. *The Field Notes of Captain William Clark, 1803–1805.* Yale University Press, New Haven, Conn., 1964.

Parker, Rev. Samuel. *Journal of an Exploring Tour Beyond the Rocky Mountains.* Ithaca, N.Y., 1840.

Peake, Ora Brooks. *A History of the United States Indian Factory System, 1795–1822.* Sage Brooks, Denver, 1954.

Pearson, T. Gilbert, ed. *Birds of America.* Garden City Pub. Co., New York, 1944.

Peattie, Donald Culross. *A Natural History of Western Trees.* Houghton Mifflin Co., Boston, 1953.

Peden, William, ed. *Notes on the State of Virginia,* by Thomas Jefferson. University of North Carolina Press, Chapel Hill, 1955.

Peebles, John J. "Rugged Waters: Trails and Campsites of Lewis and Clark in the Salmon River Country," *Idaho Yesterdays,* Summer Issue, 8, no. 2, 1964.

Pennell, Francis W. "Historic Botanical Collections of the American Philosophical Society and the Academy of Natural Sciences of Philadelphia," *Procs. Amer. Phil. Soc.,* 94, 1950.

———. "Travels and Scientific Collections of Thomas Nuttall," *Bartonia,* 18, 1936.

———. "The Elder Barton—His Plant-Collection and the Mystery of His Floras," *Bartonia,* 9, 1926.

———. "Benjamin Smith Barton as a Naturalist," *Procs. Amer. Phil. Soc.,* 86, no. 1, Sept. 25, 1943.

Peterson, Roger Tory. *A Field Guide to Western Birds.* Houghton Mifflin Co., Boston, 1941.

Phelps, Dawson A. "The Tragic Death of Meriwether Lewis," *William and Mary Quarterly,* 3rd ser., XIII, no. 3, 1956.

Phillips, Maurice Earl. "The Academy of Natural Sciences of Philadelphia," *Trans. Amer. Phil. Soc.,* 43, 1953.

Pike, Major Zebulon M. *An Account of Expeditions to the Sources of the Mississippi, and Through the Western Parts of Louisiana, to the Sources of the Arkansas and Pierrejuan Rivers.* C. and A. Conrad & Co., Philadelphia, 1810.

Piper, Charles Vancouver. *Flora of the State of Washington.* Vol. XI, Contribs. U.S. Nat'l. Herbarium, Smithsonian Inst., Washington, D.C., 1906.

Point, Father Nicholas. *Wilderness Kingdom.* Trans. by Joseph P. Donnelly, S.J. Holt, Rinehart and Winston, New York, 1967.

Poole, Edwin A. "Charbono's 'Squar'," *The Pacific Northwesterner,* 8, no. 1, 1964.

Powell, John Wesley. *Indian Linguistic Families of America North of Mexico. Seventh Annual Rep't.* of Bur. Amer. Ethnology, Smithsonian Inst., Washington, D.C., 1891.

Pursh, Frederick. *Flora Americae Septentrionalis.* 2 vols. White, Cochrane & Co., London, 1814.

Quaife, Milo M., ed. *The Journals of Captain Meriwether Lewis and Sergeant John Ordway.* Publications of State Hist. Soc. of Wisconsin, Madison, 1916.

Ray, Verne F. "Lower Chinook Ethnographic Notes," *Univ. of Washington Pubs. in Anthropology,* 7, no. 2, Seattle, May, 1938.

——— *et al.* "Tribal Distribution in Eastern Oregon and Adjacent Regions," *Amer. Anthropologist,* 40, 1938.

———, and Nancy O. Lurie. "The Contributions of Lewis and Clark to Ethnography," *Jour. Wash. Acad. Scis.,* 44, Nov., 1954.

Reid, Russell. "Sakakawea, the Bird Woman," *State Hist. Soc. North Dakota,* Bismarck, 1950.

————, and Clell G. Gannon. "Birds and Mammals Observed by Lewis and Clark in North Dakota," *N. Dak. Hist. Quart.*, 1, July, 1927.

Rhoads, Samuel N. "George Ord," *Cassinia, Procs. Delaware Valley Ornith. Club,* XII, 1908.

————, ed. *A Reprint of the North American Zoology,* by George Ord. Haddonfield, New Jersey, 1894.

Richardson, John. *Fauna Boreali-Americana; or the Zoology of the Northern Parts of British America.* 4 vols. John Murray, London, 1836.

Rudd, Velva E. "Botanical Contributions of the Lewis and Clark Expedition," *Jour. Wash. Acad. Scis.*, 44, Nov., 1954.

Salisbury, Albert and Jane. *Two Captains West.* Superior Pub. Co., Seattle, 1950.

Sargent, Charles Sprague. "The First Account of Some Western Trees," *Garden and Forest,* X, Jan. 20 and Jan. 27, 1897.

Scharf, J. Thomas, and Thompson Westcott. *History of Philadelphia.* 3 vols. L. H. Everts & Co., Philadelphia, 1884.

Schmidt, Karl P. *A Check List of North American Amphibians and Reptiles.* 6th ed. Amer. Soc. Ichthyologists and Herpetologists, University of Chicago Press, Chicago, 1953.

Schmidt-Nielsen, B., *et al.* "Water Conservation in Desert Rodents," *Jour. Cell. and Comp. Physiology,* 32, 1948.

Schorger, A. W. *The Passenger Pigeon.* University of Wisconsin Press, Madison, 1955.

Sellers, Charles Coleman. *Charles Willson Peale.* 2 vols. American Philosophical Society, Philadelphia, 1947.

————. "Peale's Museum," *Trans. Amer. Phil. Soc.,* 43, 1953.

Seton, Ernest Thompson. *The Life Histories of Northern Animals.* 2 vols. Charles Scribner's Sons, New York, 1909.

Setzer, Henry W. "Zoological Contributions of the Lewis and Clark Expedition," *Jour. Wash. Acad. Scis.,* 44, Nov., 1954.

Simpson, George Gaylord. "The Beginnings of Vertebrate Paleontology in North America," *Procs. Amer. Phil. Soc.,* 86, no. 1, Sept. 25, 1843.

Skarsten, M. O. *George Drouillard.* Arthur H. Clark Co., Glendale, Calif., 1964.

Sowerby, E. Millicent, comp. *Catalogue of the Library of Thomas Jefferson.* 5 vols. Library of Congress, Washington, D.C., 1952.

Space, Ralph S. "Lewis and Clark Through Idaho," Tribune Pub. Co., Lewiston, Idaho, 1964.

Spaulding, Kenneth A., ed. *On the Oregon Trail, Robert Stuart's Journal of Discovery.* University of Oklahoma Press, Norman, 1953.

Spier, Leslie, and Edward Sapir. "Wishram Ethnography," *Univ. of Wash. Pubs. in Anthropology,* 3, no. 3, Seattle, 1930.

Stejneger, Leonhard, and Thomas Barbour. *A Check List of North Ameri-

can Amphibians and Reptiles. 4th ed. Harvard University Press, Cambridge, Mass., 1939.

Stetson, Sarah P. "William Hamilton and His 'Woodlands'," *Penna. Mag. of Hist. and Biog.,* 73, 1949.

Stevens, Gov. Isaac I. *Reports of Explorations and Surveys from the Mississippi River to the Pacific Ocean.* Senate Ex. Doc. No. 46, 35th Cong., 2nd Session, 1853–55.

Stucker, Gilbert F. "Whither the Wide Missouri?" *Nat'l. Parks Magazine,* Aug., 1965.

Swan, James G. *The Northwest Coast; or Three Years' Residence in Washington Territory.* Harper & Bros., New York, 1857.

Swanton, John R. *The Indian Tribes of North America.* Bull. 145, Bur. Amer. Ethnology, Smithsonian Inst., Washington, D.C., 1952.

Thwaites, Reuben Gold, ed. *Original Journals of the Lewis and Clark Expedition.* 8 vols. Dodd, Mead & Co., New York, 1904–5.

———, ed. *Early Western Travels.* 32 vols. Arthur H. Clark Co., Cleveland, 1904–6.

———. "William Clark: Soldier, Explorer, Statesman," *Missouri Hist. Soc. Publications,* II, no. 7, Oct., 1906.

———. *Brief History of Rocky Mountain Exploration.* Appleton, N.Y., 1904.

Tomkins, Calvin. "The Lewis and Clark Case," *The New Yorker,* Oct. 29, 1966.

———. *The Lewis and Clark Trail.* Harper & Row, New York, 1965.

Townsend, John K. *Narrative of a Journey Across the Rocky Mountains and a Visit to the Sandwich Islands, Chili, &c.* Henry Perkins, Philadelphia, 1839.

True, Rodney H. "Some Neglected Botanical Results of the Lewis and Clark Expedition," *Procs. Amer. Phil. Society,* 67, 1928.

Vinton, Stallo. *John Colter, Discoverer of Yellowstone.* Edward Eberstadt, New York, 1926.

Webb, Walter Prescott. *The Great Plains.* Ginn & Co., New York, 1931.

Wedel, Waldo R. *Observations on Some Nineteenth-Century Pottery Vessels from the Upper Missouri.* Bull. 164, Bur. Amer. Ethnology, Smithsonian Inst., Washington, D.C., 1957.

West, Helen B. "Meriwether Lewis in Blackfeet Country," U.S. Dep't. Interior, Bur. of Indian Affairs, Blackfeet Agency, Museum of the Plains Indian, Browning, Montana, 1964.

———. "The Lewis and Clark Expedition: Our National Epic," *Montana, the Magazine of Western History,* XVI, no. 3, July, 1966.

Wheat, Carl I. *Mapping the Transmississippi West.* 3 vols. Inst. of Historical Cartography, San Francisco, 1958.

Wheeler, Olin D. *The Trail of Lewis and Clark, 1804–1806.* 2 vols. G. P. Putnam's Sons, New York, 1904.

Will, Drake W. "The Medical and Surgical Practice of the Lewis and Clark Expedition," *Jour. Hist. of Medicine and Allied Sciences,* XIV, no. 3, 1959.

Will, George F., and H. J. Spinden. "The Mandans, a Study of Their Culture, Archaeology and Language," *Papers, Peabody Mus. Archaeology and Ethnology,* III, no. 4, Harvard University, Boston, 1906.

Willoughby, Charles C. "A Few Ethnological Specimens Collected by Lewis and Clark," *American Anthropologist,* n.s., Oct.–Dec., 1905.

Wilson, Alexander. *Birds of America.* 9 vols. Bradford & Inskeep, Philadelphia, 1808–14.

Wilson, Charles Morrow. *Meriwether Lewis of Lewis and Clark.* Thomas Y. Crowell Co., New York, 1934.

Wistar, Caspar. "A Description of the Bones Deposited by the President in the Museum of the Society," *Trans. Amer. Phil. Soc.,* 4, 1799.

Wolff, Eldon G. *Air Guns.* Milwaukee Museum Publications in History, No. 1, 1958.

Wollon, Dorothy, and Margaret Kinard. "Sir Augustus J. Foster and 'The Wild Natives of the Woods'," *William and Mary Quarterly,* 3rd ser., LX, no. 2, Apr., 1952.

Yates, Ted. "Since Lewis and Clark," *The American West,* II, no. 4 (Fall), 1965.

Youmans, W. J. *Pioneers of Science in America.* Appleton, N.Y., 1896.

Young, F. G. "The Higher Significance in the Lewis and Clark Expedition," *Quarterly of the Oregon Hist. Soc.,* VI, no. 1, March, 1905.

Index

I have used the following abbreviations: ANS for the Academy of Natural Sciences of Philadelphia; APS for the American Philosophical Society; L&C for Lewis and Clark; LCE for Lewis and Clark Expedition; ML for Meriwether Lewis; TJ for Thomas Jefferson; and WC for William Clark.